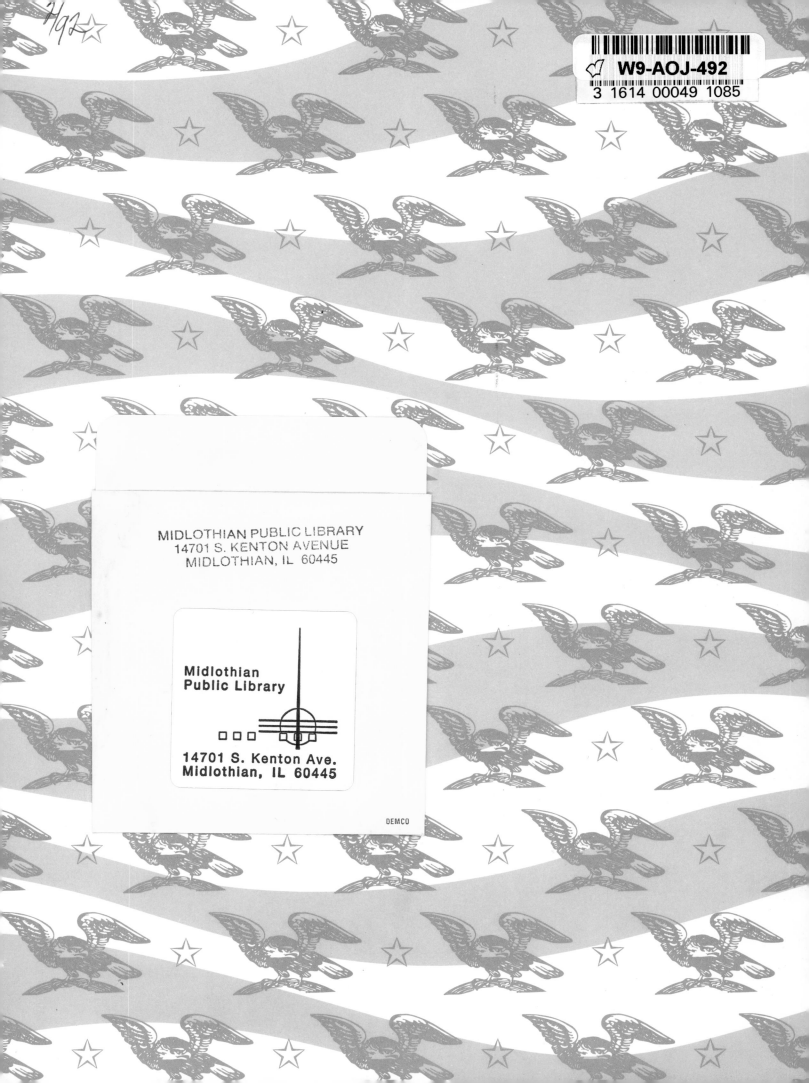

THE
U.S.A.

A CHRONICLE IN PICTURES

THE
U.S.A.
A CHRONICLE IN PICTURES

NEIL WENBORN
With a foreword by Walter Cronkite

SMITHMARK

Title page *Presidents in stone: Washington, Jefferson, Roosevelt and Lincoln commemorated at the Mount Rushmore Memorial, South Dakota.*

Author: Neil Wenborn

Contributors: Lynda F. Zamponi (chronologies) Kay Garcia (Columbus to Independence)

Designer: Christopher Matthews

First published in the United States in 1991 by SMITHMARK Publishers Inc.
112 Madison Avenue, New York, New York 10016

Copyright © 1991 Reed International Books Limited

This edition was first published in Great Britain in 1991 by the Hamlyn Publishing Group Limited, a division of Reed International Books Limited, Michelin House, 81 Fulham Road, London SW3 6RB

SMITHMARK books are available for bulk purchase for sales promotions and premium use. For details write or telephone the Manager of Special Sales, SMITHMARK Publishers Inc., 112 Madison Avenue, New York, New York 10016, (212) 532-6600

ISBN 0 8317 1399 2

Typeset by MS Filmsetting Limited, Frome, Somerset
Produced by Mandarin Offset
Printed and bound in Singapore

Contents

Foreword by Walter Cronkite   *9*

Columbus to Independence by Kay Garcia

The New World: America 1492–1607   *10*

The Growth of English Settlements in North America (1607–1689)   *19*

Growth of the European Colonial Powers (1689–1773)   *30*

Strains on Britain's Empire   *41*

1770s   *50*
Independence
The Revolutionary War

1780s   *56*
The Constitution
President Washington

1790s   *68*
President Adams

1800s   *72*
Louisiana Purchase
Lewis and Clark

1810s   *80*
War with Britain

President Monroe

1820s   *88*
Missouri Compromise
Monroe Doctrine

1830s   *92*

The Age of Jackson
The Alamo
Trail of Tears

1840s   *104*
Mexican War
Gold Rush

1850s   *118*
California Statehood
"Bleeding Kansas"

John Brown

1860s   *128*
Civil War

Death of Lincoln
Reconstruction

1870s   *146*
President Grant

"Wild West"
Ku Klux Klan

1880s   *160*
The Gilded Age
Death of Garfield

1890s   *172*
Populism
Spanish War

1900s   *186*
San Francisco 'quake
Theodore Roosevelt
Progressivism
Trustbusting

1910s   *200*
Mexican Revolution
First World War

1920s   *222*
Prohibition
Gangsterism
Jazz
Wall Street Crash

1930s   *246*
The Great Depression
The New Deal

The Dust Bowl

1940s   *264*
Second World War
Atomic Bomb
Truman Doctrine

1950s   *294*
Korean War

President Eisenhower
McCarthyism

1960s   *314*
Death of Kennedy
Martin Luther King

Space Race

1970s   *346*
End of Vietnam War
Watergate
President Carter

1980s   *366*
President Reagan

Iran–Contra Scandal
AIDS
End of Cold War

1990s   *392*
War in the Gulf

The following abbreviations are used in the chronologies

AAA	Agricultural Adjustment Administration
Adml	Admiral
AFL	American Federation of Labor
Atty Gen.	Attorney General
Brig. Gen.	Brigadier General
Capt.	Captain
CIA	Central Intelligence Agency
CIO	Congress of Industrial Organizations
Comdr	Commander
Commo.	Commodore
E.	East
EPA	Environmental Protection Agency
ERA	Equal Rights Amendment
FCC	Federal Communications Commission
FERA	Federal Emergency Relief Administration
FTC	Federal Trade Commission
Gen.	General
Gov.	Governor
HEW	Department of Health, Education and Welfare
ICC	Interstate Commerce Commission
IWW	Industrial Workers of the World
KKK	Ku Klux Klan
LI	Long Island
Lt	Lieutenant
Maj.	Major
Mt	Mount
N.	North
NATO	North Atlantic Treaty Organization
NRA	National Recovery Administration
NSC	National Security Council
NYC	New York City
OAS	Organization of American States
OPA	Office of Price Administration
OPM	Office of Production Management
PM	Prime Minister
Pres.	President
RAF	Royal Air Force (British)
Rep.	Representative
Riv.	River
S.	South
SEATO	Southeast Asia Treaty Organization
Secy	Secretary
Sen.	Senator
SLA	Symbianese Liberation Army
St	Saint, Street
TVA	Tennessee Valley Authority
UAW	United Auto Workers
UMW	United Mine Workers
UN	United Nations
UNESCO	United Nations Educational, Scientific and Cultural Organization
USAF	United States Air Force
USS	United States Ship
USSR	Union of Soviet Socialist Republics
Vice Pres.	Vice President
W.	West
WPA	Works Progress Administration

State Abbreviations

Ala.	Alabama
Alas.	Alaska
Ariz.	Arizona
Ark.	Arkansas
Calif.	California
Colo.	Colorado
Conn.	Connecticut
Del.	Delaware
Fla.	Florida
Ga.	Georgia
Hawaii	Hawaii
Ida.	Idaho
Ill.	Illinois
Ind.	Indiana
Iowa	Iowa
Kan.	Kansas
Ky.	Kentucky
La.	Louisiana
Me.	Maine
Md.	Maryland
Mass.	Massachusetts
Mich.	Michigan
Minn.	Minnesota
Miss.	Mississippi
Mo.	Missouri
Mont.	Montana
Nebr.	Nebraska
Nev.	Nevada
NH	New Hampshire
NJ	New Jersey
NM	New Mexico
NY	New York
NC	North Carolina
N. Dak	North Dakota
Ohio	Ohio
Okla.	Oklahoma
Ore.	Oregon
Pa.	Pennsylvania
RI	Rhode Island
SC	South Carolina
S. Dak	South Dakota
Tenn.	Tennessee
Tex.	Texas
Utah	Utah
Vt.	Vermont
Va.	Virginia
Wash.	Washington
W. Va.	West Virginia
Wis.	Wisconsin
Wyo.	Wyoming

We hold these truths to be self-evident: that all men are created equal; that they are endowed by their Creator with certain unalienable rights; that among these are life, liberty and the pursuit of happiness.

Declaration of Independence

Foreword

Five hundred years ago, come 1992, Christopher Columbus landed in the new world and became known as the discoverer of America. Then came the settlers, hardy stock seeking freedom and economic opportunity, and willing to risk a terrible struggle and their very lives to find and assure them.

In the five centuries since Columbus' landing, the United States has grown from a sparsely inhabited wilderness into the most powerful nation on the face of the earth; from a subject people, owing allegiance to a foreign crown, to a bastion of the democratic principle.

The story told in the pages of this book is an inspiring one. But it is also a cautionary tale. As with any other glorious enterprise, the path to freedom has known many wrong turns and false trails, and will doubtless know others along its torturous route. The history revealed in these pages pays eloquent testimony to the many noble minds and achievements that have helped to shape the America we know today – from the Founding Fathers, who carved out a Constitution from the threat of anarchy, to the countless men and women who carved out a nation from a wilderness. But it has its darker chapters too – its witness of inequality and oppression, of shattered promises, of civil war. It is a record of both human fallibility and the human spirit's ability and power to transcend adversity.

More, perhaps, than that of any other country, the history of the United States of America reflects the history of Western democracy itself. For all their philosophical pedigree in the works of such writers as Hume, Locke, and Paine, the Declaration of Independence and the Constitution remain genuinely revolutionary documents, whose influence is undiminished even today. We have only to look at the revolutionary movements now sweeping through Eastern Europe, and even through the Soviet Union itself, to see the extent to which emerging democracies still turn to the American constitutional model for inspiration and support. The bold experiments by which America claimed and upheld its independence more than two centuries ago have become the foundation of all our liberties.

If those liberties are to be sustained, if their fruits are to be extended ever more widely to all people, regardless of their race, creed, or gender, if, above all, we are to learn from our mistakes as well as our triumphs, we must know our own history. This book, in helping to bring that history alive, will make it easier for us to do so.

Walter Cronkite

Columbus to Independence

THE NEW WORLD: AMERICA 1492–1607

Land Ahoy!

It was ten o'clock in the evening on October 11, 1492, when Christopher Columbus sighted a land mass he believed to be part of the Orient. He had led 90 men in three ships in relentless pursuit of a new route to the East and the treasure trove of spices there. As he gazed at the coast of Salvador in the Bahamas, Columbus failed to realize that he had found for his Spanish royal patrons a new world. He would die without ever knowing otherwise.

Columbus was not the first European to find this continent – but he was the best documented. Five hundred years earlier in the 9th century a group of exiled Irish found their way to the Eastern shores from their settlement in Iceland. According to legend, St. Brendan the Navigator sailed to America in a hide-bottomed boat with a party of monks.

In the 11th century the legendary Norsemen fearlessly explored the oceans of the world in the quest for knowledge and booty. Ireland, Iceland and Greenland all knew the terror inspired by a Viking sail. The Norsemen eventually found America and landed in Nova Scotia or Newfoundland and attempted to establish a colony called Vinland. Leif, son of the dreaded and infamous Eric the Red, led one of the first raiding parties. Remnants of the Norse settlement remained for several hundred years but news of what the Irish and the Vikings had discovered died with them.

All of 15th-century Europe was ignorant of what lay across the sea to the west. The world had been explored overland for the most part but no one was interested in what lay to the west until 1453 when the city of Constantinople fell to the Moslem Turks. The strategic importance of Constantinople, which is now Istanbul, was crucial since it was the gateway to the East. With the bitter enmity between Moslems and Christians which persisted throughout the centuries, Moslem control of Constantinople effectively meant the end of trade with the East for all the Christian nations of Europe.

In the 15th century spice was as important a commodity as oil is today. It played a vital role in the European economy because much of the food was unwholesome and was highly spiced to hide the rancid taste. The Columbus venture was, in the context of its time, as complex and important as deep sea oil exploration. The risks were very high but so were the rewards, and the man who found an alternative way into the East would achieve great recognition and wealth.

Across the Great Divide

People were traveling, spurred on by the need for food, shelter, and security, 40 thousand years before Columbus. Despite the huge expanse of the Pacific Ocean, Asia and America are separated by only 20 miles of sea at the Bering Strait. This cold and uninviting stretch of water separates the eastern corner of Siberia from the most westerly point in Alaska. This is the route by which the very first settlers arrived in America. They were probably Mongol tribesmen looking for a better hunting area or fleeing their enemies.

As the travelers moved farther south, away from the bleak northern parts of the continent, they found conditions which were ideal for their survival. There was an abundance of wild animals, fish, plants, and fertile land. The continent stretched from the heavily wooded East through the prairies into the mountains and deserts of the West. In the East, blueberries and wild ginger covered the forest floor, the rivers brimmed with fish, and the woods abounded with bears, wolves, beavers, and other wildlife. The vast, high prairies in the center were home to great herds of buffalo, stretching as far as the eye could see. West of the enormous Mississippi Valley lay the majestic Rockies and Cascade mountains with their plunging waterfalls, hot springs, high peaks, and huge ravines.

Christopher Columbus: a questionable sense of direction.

The Native Peoples of North and South America

In the 15th century it is estimated that there were about 500,000 people in North America. The original native peoples of this continent have been known as Indians since the voyage of Columbus because he thought he had found India. Early life among them was nomadic but social structures developed gradually and broad ranges of tribes emerged with different customs and lifestyles. The tribes developed an intimate relationship with the land and all that it supported and they evolved and created their social and economic structures based on the geography of the land. Many of these peoples were hunters, some were farmers, and others were primarily fishermen.

The Iroquois people from the forest regions around Lake Erie and Lake Ontario were farmers, inveterate warriors but a settled people who lived in wooden houses. By contrast the Teton Sioux tribe from the prairie regions never farmed but fed largely off the buffalo herds and followed them around in their endless migrations, living in the more mobile "tipi."

It was in South America, however, where the native American peoples developed the most complex societal structures and civilizations. They were tough and tyrannical rulers who practiced human sacrifice and torture. Between 500 BC and 1500 AD the Incas in Peru, the Maya in Guatemala, and the Aztecs in Mexico established vast empires and built huge stone cities, monuments of which still stand today. The splendor of these civilizations rivaled Rome, Egypt, and Greece.

While the North American tribes did not build magnificent cities, their development was no less sophisticated. They established fine legal, social, and democratic systems. Although communal violence was a major feature of the native American lifestyle, the inter-tribal fighting which has damaged the reputation of these fine peoples was by no means practiced by all tribes. Many of the myths that lie behind the traditional depiction of the American Indian were exaggerations of the white Europeans to justify the wholesale theft, enslavement, disease, murder, and deceit to which the Indians were subjected.

The North American "Indians"

When the first European settlers arrived in North America they were usually given a friendly greeting by the settled tribes. The surprise and unpreparedness of the Indian peoples to deal with the European invaders cannot be underestimated. Despite their sophistication and oneness with the earth, many of the tribes spent their lives naked, knew nothing of the wheel, and had no knowledge of metals. European guns were not only frightening because of their sound but because of the very substances from which they were made. Horses, goats, cattle,

and dogs were all new to America. The native Americans who chose to farm had never had domesticated animals, and horse-drawn carriages with wheels must have been an extraordinary novelty.

The Europeans, however, were at a tremendous disadvantage when dealing with the earth. The Indians had a wealth of infinite knowledge about the fish, plants, and animals of their land; their lives depended on knowing the habits of each and every type of animal and the properties and benefits of all the plants.

There were common features between the different tribes. All of them were skilled at surviving off the land, tracking animals, and manufacturing what they needed. The earliest tribes lived underground or in caves but by the time the Europeans had arrived the peoples had developed the crafts and skills necessary to survive life in the open.

An ancient culture: an Algonquin Indian village.

Wood, animal skin, and bones were their raw materials. The Hopi and Zuni peoples in Arizona and New Mexico were excellent farmers and weavers and constructed some of the earliest houses.

Canoes, bows, and arrows were all made from wood and needed skilled craftsmanship. So did toboggans and snow shoes, both of which were invented by the Indians. Animal skins were used for clothing and footwear while animal bones provided the raw material for tools and weapons. Beaver teeth made excellent knives, for example.

In the nomadic tribes the role of men was generally to hunt and defend the tribe from attack. The women were relied upon to carry out almost everything else. They farmed and carried, manufactured clothing, prepared food, and made weapons. The role of women was essential to the social fabric.

The social structure was essentially communal rather than individualistic. Whole tribes would often sleep in one dwelling and eat the same food. All tribe members would share equally in the proceeds of a successful hunt or raid.

There was a common belief in the immortality of the soul and a widespread belief that the earth was populated by spirits who were either good or evil and had to be appeased. There were regular religious festivals, which featured feasting and dancing, in all the tribes to ward off the evil spirits and invoke the protection of the good. Often there were sacrifices, sometimes human. The details of the religious practices varied from tribe to tribe depending on the region and which spirits were particularly revered. However, all tribes had priests, medicine men, shamans who supposedly had a special relationship with the spirits and could call upon them to help the tribe in times of hardship, sickness, pestilence, and war.

Indians at their meat, one of John White's detailed observations of Indian customs in the 1590s.

Misrepresentation of the Native Americans

All the native American peoples were fiercely territorial. Theirs was a hard life and when they found an area which could sustain them they protected it against all intruders. When they made war it was fierce and unforgiving.

There are few peoples who have been so grossly misrepresented in the history of the world as the native American "Indians." Kindness and courtesy were hallmarks of their welcome to the first explorers. Indeed the whole American tradition of Thanksgiving celebrates the aid and assistance given to the first colonists by the Indians, without whom they would not have survived their first winter in the New World. The Indians only waged war on the Europeans when attempts were made either to enslave them or to steal their land. It is only recently that their slanderous reputation gained in Western novels and cinema has been revised.

Because their customs were alien to the invading Europeans it was easy to depict them as godless, vicious animals. It justified then, as it still does today in some minds, the ruthless and systematic elimination of whole races in the name of progress, expansion, commerce, and profit.

European Colonization of the Americas

Christopher Columbus

Many people believed that Christopher Columbus was mad. It was certainly true that his mathematics were suspect since he thought Japan and China were no more than 2500 miles west of the Canary Islands. Some sailors and navigators in the 15th century still believed the earth was flat, although a spherical earth was taught in all the European universities. Inevitably there were people who told Columbus he would fall off the edge of the world. Columbus had read of the adventures of Marco Polo and was up to date on the latest thinking and theories on the development of the universe but his problem lay in trying to convince others of the feasibility of his great dream.

In concept and logistics it was a massive undertaking for its time and it was expensive. Ships had to be designed, built and provisioned. Columbus simply did not have the money so he sought out sponsorship. His first port of call was the King of Portugal who turned him down flat. His vision of the profits he might make did not diminish over the next eight years while he endured the

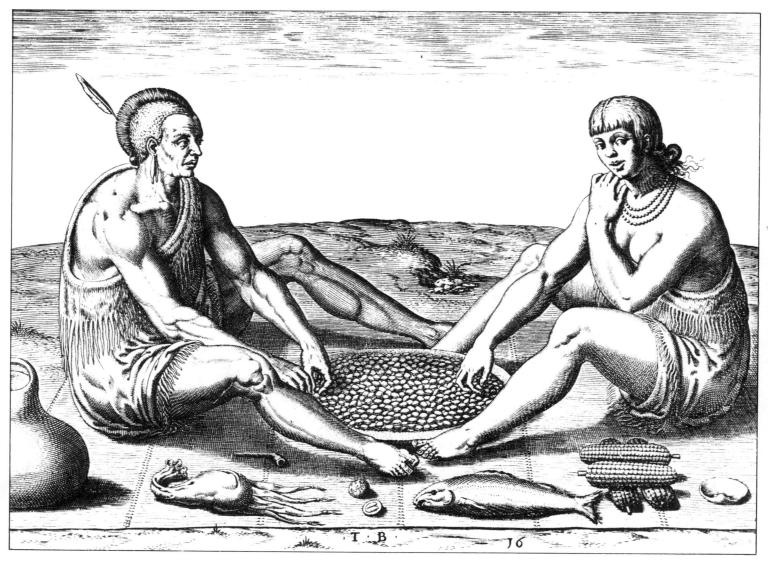

painstaking task of gaining audiences with the kings of France and Spain who proved no more enthusiastic than the King of Portugal. Part of Columbus' financing problem was that he was trying to drive a hard commercial bargain. He required honors and 10 per cent of all treasures found on his expeditions. Finally his breakthrough came with King Ferdinand and Queen Isabella of Spain who reviewed the project and its costs, assessed the risk factor, and decided to back the venture.

It was a time of turmoil and depression in Europe. The authority and power of the Catholic Church were beginning to wane because it was regarded increasingly as greedy and élitist. The Catholic Church and European politics were inextricably linked. The need to spread the faith and thereby support political power was a pressing issue in Catholic Spain. This was the atmosphere in which Columbus had struggled for eight long years to put together his tiny fleet of three caravels and sail off to find a new way to the East.

The *Santa Maria*, the *Pinta* and the *Nina* sailed on the evening of August 2, 1492. As Columbus gazed out over the Atlantic Ocean and headed into the unknown he carried a personal letter of introduction from the King and Queen of Spain to the Emperor of China. While he did not reach the East, he found the Bahamas and his voyage heralded the beginning of many centuries of exploration, discovery and colonization.

In February 1493, Columbus wrote to Luis de Santangel of the beauty and fertility of the lands he had discovered:

... The lands thereof are high, and in it, there are many havens on the sea-coast, incomparable with any others that I know in Christendom, and plenty of rivers so good and great that it is a marvel. The lands thereof are high, and in it are very many ranges of hills, and most lofty mountains incomparably beyond the island of Tenerife, all most beautiful in a thousand shapes, and all accessible, and full of trees of a thousand kinds, so lofty that they seem to reach the sky....

Columbus was pleased that the islands he found were abundantly supplied with natural resources, including gold, pearls, and foodstuffs. But most important, the Bahamas had spices.

A year later, in 1494, Spain and Portugal divided up the new lands. Under the Treaty of Tordesillas Spain took the west and Portugal took the east, including the Bahamas and the valuable spice. Spain, although disappointed at the time, was pleased with the division later when the riches of South America were discovered and began to flow into her coffers.

Columbus sailed back to Spain where he was welcomed as a hero. He had left some of his men on the island of Haiti in a little settlement called Hispaniola. The explorer had no difficulty raising funds for his second expedition and set off six months later with a bigger fleet and with a greater certainty that he would find the Asian mainland. The fleet

A new world: Columbus lands on the island of San Salvador in the Bahamas, 1492.

found its way back to Haiti but discovered that all of the men had been killed by the natives. Their deaths marked the beginning of a pattern which affected relationships between whites and native Indians for many centuries.

In the beginning the Indians welcomed the Europeans and happily exchanged their gold for brass trinkets. Soon the Spaniards wanted the gold for free and began to forcibly remove it. Gold fever spread and prompted expeditions into the countryside accompanied by pillaging. The Indians had no choice but to fight back.

After his initial voyage of discovery Columbus returned to the Bahamas and went to South America many times but his fame dwindled after the first two voyages. It was Vasco de Gama who made his way around the Cape of Good Hope and it was Ferdinand Magellan who introduced sailors to the real route to the East, in 1520-1521, when he and three ships found their way to what is now the Philippines. The vast new continent discovered by Columbus would be named after another adventurer, a trader and navigator from Florence called Amerigo Vespucci.

The Spanish Conquest of Mexico and South America

The stronghold of Hispaniola founded by Columbus was the center of Spanish power in the area for many years to come. It served as a starting point for the exploration and conquest of South America and it was home to adventurers, soldiers, priests, conquistadors, geographers, and cartographers while they undertook expedition after expedition in search of glory and gold.

One of the best known of all the expeditions was led by Hernando Cortes who arrived on the coast of Mexico in 1519 with 11 ships and 550 men. The natives thought he was the legendary saviour Quetzacoatl who would save them from the tyranny of the Aztecs, and Cortes accepted the role, immediately recruiting some of the natives into his army and using others as guides as he waged war on the Aztecs. He captured Montezuma's capital city and finally defeated the Aztecs at Teotihuacan. The discovery here of immense wealth and treasure encouraged the Spanish to explore the whole of South America, using the most barbaric of tactics to conquer the native peoples.

The most famous and horrific stories are of the Spanish atrocities against the South American Incas, Aztecs, and Maya in the lands between Mexico and Peru. The absolute barbarism of the Spanish was fueled by two factors: Spain's pressing need for gold to finance itself in Europe and the perverse evil of the Catholic Church's insistence on converting the natives to Christianity whatever the cost. The stakes were high. Poor adventurers could become millionaires by confiscating the property of pagans who would not bow down to "the one true Lord." Those who would not convert were murdered by the most horrible methods such as slow strangulation or burning at the stake. One king who was being burned at the stake was offered the rite of the baptism one more time so that he would go to heaven. Even as the flames rose about him he refused because he said he feared he

The Mississippi becomes Hernando de Soto's last resting place.

might go there and "meet only Christians."

Many of the clergy who accompanied the soldiers protested vehemently about their behavior. There were numerous reports received by the Vatican and successive popes about the massacre and enslavement of the Indians. Whole towns were slaughtered. In Acoma, New Mexico, 600 people were wiped out by the Spaniards in a day. Indians who survived the massacres were often put to work as slave labor to mine for gold and other precious metals.

There were some genuine attempts to bring the benefits of Europe to the New World. Some new methods of farming and new crops were introduced to the continent. It was a tiny compensation for the wholesale destruction of the native civilizations on a scale comparable to the havoc created centuries earlier in Europe by the Barbarians and the Vandals.

When they first set out from Europe the Spanish and Portuguese explorers had been searching for the Spice Islands of Indonesia. The need for a new trade route to the East motivated Columbus, Vasco de Gama, and Magellan. They eventually found what they had been seeking, but along the way had literally stumbled across a whole continent and had very quickly dominated and exploited it. In about 30 years the Spanish conquered and acquired more land than Rome had taken in 500 years, organized and administered all they conquered, intro-

duced the arts and letters of Europe, and converted millions to their faith. It is not surprising that the biggest influences in South America, Mexico, and some parts of the United States today are Spanish and Portuguese.

The Spanish in North America

The hunger for gold and riches inevitably drove the Spanish north. Rumors and stories of hoarded wealth abounded and they were determined to find it. On Easter Sunday, in 1513, Juan Ponce de Léon landed on the North American mainland at the mouth of the St. John river. He named the area Florida after the Spanish name for Easter Sunday, Pascua Florida. The 53-year-old explorer was in search of a fabled island where there was supposed to be a fountain of eternal youth.

The native peoples of North America had also heard stories and rumors in the 21 years since Columbus' voyage – tales of the cruelty of the white men who came in boats across the sea. Juan Ponce de Léon and his men were quickly ejected by the natives and went back to the Caribbean. Later Léon returned and eventually died after another confrontation with the natives. The conquistadors kept on coming and the Indians, outarmed and outmaneuvered, were often quelled by the ferocity of the Spanish advance.

It is Hernando de Soto who is said to have been the first European to glimpse the banks of the mighty Mississippi in 1540. Ironically, it was one of the last things he saw. The exploration of North America took a much greater toll on the Spaniards. Starvation and disease plagued de Soto's expedition, most of his troops died and he himself was laid to rest in the Mississippi. The survivors took four years to return to what is now called the Tampa Bay area in Florida with nothing to show for their endeavors.

Many explorers were searching for Cibola, the mythical "Seven Cities of Gold." In 1540 Francisco Vasquez de Coronado set out from Mexico with an enormous expedition to find these fabled cities. A Franciscan called Friar Marcos, who had wandered around Texas on a mission from Pope Paul III specifically to check the plausibility of the rumors, claimed to have seen Cibola. What he had seen in his travels through Arizona and Texas was a collection of Zuni towns with no treasures whatsoever. His mistake, or deliberate lie, was enough to convince the Viceroy of Mexico, Don Antonio de Mendoza, to dispatch Coronado on a wild goose chase which led him through Texas and Arizona up to the Gulf of California and Nebraska before abandoning the search and marching all the way back to Mexico City. En route, one of Coronado's officers found the Grand Canyon and this expedition resulted in further rumors of another city of tremendous riches, El Dorado.

Compared to the success and speed of Spanish advances in South America, the attempts to explore, colonize, and convert the continent north of Mexico were disastrous and costly. The conquistadors led by men like Cancello, Guido de las Bazares, Francis de Garay, and Vasquez de Ayllon walked hundreds of miles from Mexico in full armor. They hacked their way through the forests, waded across rivers, struggled across the burning hot plains, and sank in the mosquito-infested swamps. The pitiless and unforgiving nature of the terrain was not offset by any rewards. There was no gold, no jewels, and little to hunt. The natives of Texas and Florida did not immediately open their arms and delight in being converted to Catholicism.

The King of Spain finally did a cost-benefit analysis and declared, on September 23, 1561, that enough was enough. There should be no further trips into Florida. Although the Spanish still laid claim to the land, they did not move into it, thus leaving the way open for the English and French in subsequent centuries.

Division of the Spoils

The French

Spanish repatriation of the loot from expeditions was the trigger for French, Dutch, and English involvement in the New World. Pirates lay in wait for the galleons laden with their cargos of gold and precious stones. Many of these pirates had a semi-official relationship with their own monarchs, who received a share of all booty.

King Francis I of France, a greedy ruler desperately in need of funds to sponsor his war with the Hapsburg Emperor Charles V, decided to ignore the Treaty of Tordesillas, which Portugal and Spain had established in order to divide the New World between themselves, and sent his own pioneers off in the hunt for treasures, the passage to the Orient, and suitable bases from which to attack Spanish galleons, which were carrying approximately 15 million dollars worth of gold per annum. One of the most successful of these raids was on the fleet carrying home the spoils from Cortes' plundering of Mexico. When the Spanish complained about this behavior, Francis replied "Show me the clause in Adam's will by which he divided the world between my brothers of Spain and Portugal."

Spanish investment in the exploration of the Americas had been a drain on the economy and the convoys were not well protected on the high seas as a result. Spain was no longer able to prevent other nations from exploiting the New World.

The first man to explore under the French flag was, ironically, a Spaniard. Giovanni da Verrazano reached the North Carolina coast in 1523 and traveled along it as far as Maine, in his search for the elusive passage to the Orient. He found what was later to become New York and his brother roughly charted Chesapeake Bay under the mistaken notion that it was a strait which would lead them to the East.

Verrazano never found the passage but he did come across native Americans which he reported to his employer, the King of France. His letters give an insight into the minds of the early explorers and touch on common themes, such as the reaction of the Indians to the arrival of white men:

...Many people who were seen coming to the seaside fled at our approach, but occasionally stopping, they looked back upon us with astonishment, and some were at length induced, by various friendly signs, to come to us. These showed the greatest

The Americas as they appeared to 16th-century map-makers.

delight on beholding us, wondering at our dress, countenances and complexion....

Like Columbus, he also remarks upon the beauty and fertility of the countryside:

An outstretched country appears at a little distance rising somewhat above the sandy shore in beautiful fields and broad plains, covered with immense forests of trees, more or less dense, too various in colors, and too delightful and charming to be described....

... It abounds also in animals, as deer, stags, hares, and many other similar, and with a great variety of birds for every kind of pleasant and delightful sport....

From Verrazano's report to the King of France of the Carolina coast, 1523.

The French explorers traveled much farther north than the Spanish and Portuguese and soon reached Canada. It was a Frenchman called Jacques Cartier who revealed the future possibilities for the fur trade on expeditions in 1534 and 1543. He went as far as Montreal and to the St. Lawrence River. Like many before and after him, Cartier became obsessed with the thought of vast and undiscovered riches which could be his for the taking. He was told a story, by an Indian chief, of a huge, glittering city in the north called Saguenay, filled with treasures and spices.

Saguenay was as real as Cibola or El Dorado. The Indians who spun these wonderful tales for the white men could hardly have expected the kinds of response they got. When Francis I of France heard about the glittering city he authorized the gathering of an immense fleet, under the command of Cartier, which set sail in search of this shimmering city of the imagination. The dreams were fruitless. Appropriately, Cartier returned with a ship load of fool's gold and some worthless crystalline stones. On a more practical note, however, his tales of the new land incited some Breton fishermen to sail to the east coast of both the United States and Canada and barter with the Indians over the range of furs they found there.

The fur traders carried on successfully for the next 40 years. Fur was widely used in Europe and Canada proved a useful source of supply, particularly since the animals of the Russian forests had almost been hunted to extinction. The French traded but did not explore until 1603 when Samuel Champlain charted the northern parts of America. He was the first to recognize the real potential for trade and settlement and it was he who established Quebec as the French center of trade in Canada.

But the French did not confine their desires to Canada. As European divisions over religion pitted monarch against monarch, the conflict inevitably spilled over into the outposts of their empires.

Catherine de Medici of France sponsored an explorer called Jean Ribault to found a colony of French Huguenots in Florida on land claimed by the Catholic Spanish King Philip II. Ribault set off in February 1562 with 150 sailors and two ships and arrived

Jacques Cartier, seaman, explorer, and bounty-hunter.

on May 1, to the great relief of the entire crew. Once again, explorers recorded a scene of beauty and plenty. At the mouth of the St. John's River they left a stone column decorated with the French coat of arms and sailed on to claim more of the coast for Huguenot France.

After several months of exploration, Ribault left a group of men in Florida to retain it for France and set sail for home, promising to return in six months. After the six months had expired and there was no sign of Ribault, the camp became anxious and, when stocks of food started to run low, the men panicked. They built a makeshift boat and tried to travel home. Many died on the way and there are even stories of cannibalism on board their raft. Eventually, they were picked up by an English ship and brought back to England. Their stories were perhaps the way that the English heard of the French settlement in the New World.

In the meantime the Spanish had heard about the French "invasion" and a force had been sent to eject the invaders. Finding no one at the French garrison, the Spaniards contented themselves with burning the fort to the ground. The Spanish were protective of the sea routes around Florida in particular because an enemy based there would be able to threaten the galleons returning to Europe with their booty. They were becoming more and more worried about the safety of their possessions in this rich and exciting place.

The next French expedition to Florida, in 1564, established Fort Caroline, which was to be the battlefield of one of the first conflicts between European nations over the sovereignty of the new continent, as its headquarters.

The voyage was led by René de Laudonnière and is recorded by the drawings of Jacques le Moyne de Morgues. They set out from Le Havre and it took the three ships two months to travel to the site of Ribault's landing. There they found the natives not only friendly but generous with gifts. There was certainly no suggestion that the Indians

would do the white men any harm. They were mainly intrigued by the color and complexion of European skin, and their splendid clothes.

The local chief was called Satourioua. Accompanied by about 1000 men in fabulous clothes and jewelry, he came to the site of the proposed French fort. His meeting with Laudonnière was very formal and the Frenchman had to adhere to all the Indian customs. He had to wait for permission to talk to Satourioua and was required to promise friendship so as to gain the help of Satourioua's men in building his fort.

In the early days of foreign involvement in America it was very important to obey local customs because without the blessing of the local chief, intruders were at the mercy of the tribesmen. Only when a secure military base had been built or an alliance had been made with another, more powerful chief, could the Europeans begin to dictate the terms and ignore the local rules. This was exactly what happened in this instance. After the French finished building at Fort Caroline at the mouth of the St. John's River, they refused Satourioua's demand for soldiers to help him wage his war. Instead, they formed an alliance with a neighboring chief against Satourioua. The French continued the white man's penchant for speaking with a forked tongue.

Although they had been so unsuccessful in exploring it, the Spanish still thought of Florida as theirs and were offended by these non-Catholic Frenchmen attempting to claim it as theirs. Action was needed and, in the summer of 1565, Pedro Menéndez de Aviles led a fleet of five Spanish ships to rid Florida of the French troublemakers.

Menéndez did not know that a fleet of French ships bearing Ribault back from France had recently arrived at Fort Caroline. Ribault knew he was about to be attacked and headed to sea to counterattack the Spanish fort, St. Augustine. But Menéndez landed his men away from the French fort and marched them through the forest. The Spaniards had the advantage of surprise over the French and the battle was over in less than an hour. Afterward, more than half the French lay dead and Ribault's force was to suffer even further. The ships which he took to capture St. Augustine had been scattered and destroyed by a storm which blew in overnight. The surviving French troops were washed up on the shore and the Spaniards were able to kill them all at will. Ribault himself was captured and, although he pleaded on behalf of his men, Menéndez was merciless. Ribault and the rest of his forces were killed. On his departure Menéndez nailed a sign onto a tree at Fort Caroline. It read, "I do this, not as to Frenchmen, but as to Lutherans."

The Spanish slaughter of the French is one of the most infamous incidents in the history of the struggle for Florida and demonstrates how bitter were the religious differences in Europe. Accounts include stories of eyes being plucked out and bodies hacked to pieces. Philip of Spain took time to make the details public and when he did the French were furious. Although the

Spanish claimed that the French presence in Florida was an intrusion on foreign territory, the French promised revenge. Two years later Dominique de Courgues, a Spanish-hating Catholic, decided to avenge the massacre of his countrymen. He was as merciless as his notorious predecessor and very few Spaniards survived. His departing note read, "I do this, not as to Spaniards, but as to Traitors, thieves and murderers."

The Spanish were similarly shocked by this behavior but they did not respond this time. This stretch of coastline had seen enough violence and killing. The Spanish retained their base at St. Augustine, which still stands today, the oldest European town in southern America. Yet, the Spanish never devoted as much time, energy and money to developing their interests in southern America as they had in South America. The lure of gold was the strongest incentive and there simply did not seem to be enough in Florida to inspire them to expeditions of the scale of Cortes' in 1519.

The English

In the 15th and early 16th centuries England was a small and poor country surrounded by enemies. Hostile and independent Scotland sat on the northern border, the age-old enemy France lay to the east and the ever troublesome Irish to the west steadfastly refused to accept that they had been conquered. This was not a time for great adventures but things were changing. Spanish gold from the New World was buying English wool and trade was improving.

The English had been thrilled by the sight of the Spanish ships returning with the spoils from the New World. Word was further spread by the survivors of Jean Ribault's first French expedition who had been picked up by English ships. Ribault himself had gone to England in 1563 to escape from the French Catholics and his stories had inspired an interest in these new lands far to the west.

Henry VIII's split from the Roman Catholic Church added strength to a growing English nationalism and made a split with Spain inevitable. A middle class began to develop in England and new markets and products were needed.

The Spanish fortification at St. Augustine, Florida – southern America's oldest European settlement.

The English also believed that going west would reveal a new route to the Orient. Explorers John and Sebastian Cabot, Martin Frobisher, and Henry Hudson had already searched for the North-West Passage, so the English court did have some firsthand accounts of the sea route. More came from some of England's legendary adventurers, including the slave trader Sir John Hawkins. In the 1560s Hawkins began making runs from Plymouth to Africa and then to Spanish America. Slaves were needed in Spanish America because the native Indians were dying rapidly when put to work in the mines.

Queen Elizabeth I (1558–1603) believed that it was her religious and patriotic duty to "singe the king of Spain's beard." This was an open invitation and official sanction to steal the Spanish wealth on the high seas. Those who accepted the invitation were known in England as sea dogs.

Although Sir John Hawkins was welcomed in the Spanish colonies in America because of his good manners and attractive prices, he was set upon by the Spanish fleet off Vera Cruz on one occasion and was roughly handled. His flag captain was 24-year-old Francis Drake. "El Draque" was a name feared by the Spanish thereafter and Drake became their sworn enemy. He raided the Isthmus of Panama and the coastal towns repeatedly. One of the towns he razed was St. Augustine, capital of the Spanish empire in Florida and the South. In 1577 he took off on a memorable voyage around the world which would last three years.

Drake's object was to steal from the Spanish by raiding their lumbering, unprotected galleons far from home. He entered the South Seas through the Strait of Magellan, traveled along the coast of Chile and Peru, terrorized the Spaniards there and found the Spanish treasure ships off Panama. After attacking them and loading up with all the treasure he could carry, Drake traveled north to California. He did not dare return the way he had come for fear of capture by the Spanish. In the spring he sailed across the Pacific in his only remaining ship, *The Pelican*. He arrived back in England after crossing the Indian Ocean and heading up the west coast of Africa.

King Philip of Spain was furious and demanded that Drake be tried for piracy. Queen Elizabeth welcomed him as a hero and knighted him aboard his ship which had been renamed *The Golden Hind*. Elizabeth's actions were a direct challenge to the King of Spain, who gave orders for the assembly of a huge armada to invade England. The Spanish Armada was defeated by English ships in 1588, marking the beginning of the end of Spain's supremacy. Dominance of the high seas by the Royal Navy was the key element in England's rise to power.

Even before the defeat of the Spanish Armada there had been English attempts to establish colonies in America. In 1583 Sir Humphrey Gilbert established a site in what is now St. John's, Newfoundland, but Gilbert and his crew were lost in a storm on their way home. The following year Queen Elizabeth gave permission and encourage-

The search for the Northwest Passage: Henry Hudson's expedition ends in despair as he is set adrift by his crew, June 23, 1611.

ment to Sir Walter Raleigh, a half-brother of Sir Humphrey Gilbert, to build colonies in the New World at his own expense. He spent a fortune on the attempt and failed. Raleigh's ships landed at Roanoke Island, cruised the area for several months and decided it was ripe for settlement. The farming land was good and it was a convenient base from which to attack Spanish ships on their way home across the Atlantic. Raleigh named his land Virginia and sent out a group of colonists. But the first colony failed and a second group was dispatched in 1587, the year before the Spanish Armada. Raleigh became pre-occupied with the war between England and Spain and the colonists were forgotten for three years. Relief ships finally arrived at Roanoke in late 1590 but not one colonist was left. No one ever discovered what happened to the 117 men, women and children of the "Lost Colony."

One of the reasons for the English failure to establish colonies in America was lack of funding. Sir Walter Raleigh lost his fortune in his attempt. There were better profits to be made from attacking the Spanish galleons as was demonstrated by the English pirate, Captain Thomas Cavendish who captured a Manila galleon in 1587. When his ships sailed up the Thames they were decked with damask sails and each of his sailors wore a silk suit and a chain of pure gold.

The early attempts at English colonization came at a time when the whole of England was beginning to burn brightly with new energy. It was the time of Shakespeare and great advances in literature. There was a great desire to start a new England in which all the best of the past would be conserved but where life would have a better quality than anything conceivable in the Europe of the time.

Many of the early colonists, including Sir Humphrey Gilbert, were inspired by Sir Thomas More's book *Utopia*, which had been first printed in 1516. More presented a vision of an ideal colony on an island somewhere in the New World with "air, soft, temperate and gentle; the ground covered with green grass." This place would be full of people "governed by good and wholesome laws," everyone would be honestly employed and no one exploited or overworked. There would be complete religious liberty and, although virtue would be cultivated, this would not mean "sharp and painful virtue." The Utopians would not "banish the pleasure of life."

There was not much pleasure in the lives of common Englishmen of the period. There was large-scale unemployment as farming methods became modernized and life was a welter of misery, insecurity, and corruption. A new life in a New England was a very attractive proposition.

THE GROWTH OF ENGLISH SETTLEMENTS IN NORTH AMERICA (1607–1689)

Jamestown: The First Permanent English Settlement

The turn of the century in 1600 brought a great number of changes to England. The wars with Spain and Scotland ended and three years into the 17th century a new ruler, James I, was on the throne. Just three years into his reign he divided the new land of Virginia between two colonial companies, based in Plymouth and London, under a special charter. When King James I granted these charters he made an important promise and declaration. Everyone who served either company in the English colonies was to retain the rights and privileges of English subjects. These rights, though not always upheld, stemmed back to the 1215 Magna Carta or Great Charter. When King John made excessive financial demands and ignored the English barons' traditional rights, they banded together to draft the Magna Carta which stated that all government should be constitutional, con-

ducted according to law and custom. It limited the King's demands and protected the interests of Church leaders, merchants, and townspeople. It did, however, fall short of representing all the people. It excluded peasants, for example, but it was significant and revolutionary at the beginning of the 13th century.

Fifty years after the Magna Carta, in 1265, Parliament was established as England's legislative body. It was divided in two bodies, the House of Commons and the House of Lords. Whenever English subjects in the 16th and 17th centuries wanted to uphold their rights as citizens, they could look to Parliament. The idea of rights of citizenship would cross the Atlantic and have momentous effect.

King James I granted the London Company, later to be called The Virgina Company of London, the land around Roanoke, where Sir Walter Raleigh had unsuccessfully tried to establish a settlement earlier. At Christmas time in 1606 three small ships headed down the Thames and out into the Atlantic. The London Company's first colonists were on their way. The ships sailed past the Azores, the Canary Islands, and the West Indies before turning north and heading for a site clear of the Spanish in Florida and the French in Canada.

The voyage was expected to have taken two months and the 120 settlers were amply provisioned. But they spent five months at sea and it was not until May of 1607 that Captain Christopher Newport guided the ships *Susan Constant*, *Godspeed*, and *Discovery* into Chesapeake Bay. The extended

time at sea had cost the colonists dearly. On the voyage 16 had died and the 104 survivors were low in provisions and had missed the planting season.

Trouble continued for this expedition. Captain Newport, a somewhat poor leader, had selected a terrible site for the settlement – a low, wooded island in a river they had named after King James. Jamestown, as the site was called, was surrounded by mosquito-infested swamps, key ingredients for dreaded attacks of malaria.

To make matters worse, the men, most of whom were gentlemen with no practical knowledge of survival, did not take time to dig wells but drank from the river itself. Nor did they take time out to build proper shelters, so they were drenched with rain in summer and left freezing in winter. The reasons for Jamestown's inability to thrive were clear. The London Company had unrealistic expectations of the colonists' abilities and lacked informed knowledge of the area. The settlers were expected to hunt for gold where there was none, find the North-West Passage when neither the James nor the Chickahominay rivers led to the Pacific, and to convert the Indians to Christianity. They were told to produce "all the commodities of Europe, Africa and Asia and supplye the wantes of all our decayed trades." It was an impossible order.

On June 15, 1607, Captain Newport set sail for his return to England. Jamestown's

Captain Newport and his colonists go ashore at Jamestown.

first leader was replaced for ineptness, hoarding supplies and removing himself from the hardships endured by his fellow settlers. A new manager was appointed.

The ship's departure must have caused the settlers to ponder on the wisdom of accepting a one-way ticket into the wilderness. With the ship gone they could no longer barter with the sailors for food from the ship's stores and would have to rely entirely on their own resources. From May to September 50 more men died. Sturgeon and sea crabs had kept them going for a time but they, too, were gone. Provisions were seriously depleted and there was a great amount of internal strife and discontent.

The Survival of the Colony

Captain Newport's successor delegated managerial duties to a Captain John Smith. Smith's direction turned the colony from a foundering, unsuccessful gold hunt into a well-tuned communal effort where each person had to pull his own weight. In his own words he "set some to mow, others to bind thatch, some to build houses, others to thatch them," all under the motto "No Work, No Food." But Smith was not an aloof dictator; he worked alongside the others and selflessly saw that they had proper lodgings before seeing to his own needs.

Smith ordered the men to dig wells, clear land, plant corn and other crops, as well as building the much needed houses. He quickly realized that the future of the colony depended on its ability to trade and began to manufacture clapboard from the trees of the surrounding forests. His early attempts at trade brought him into conflict with the Indians but he eventually triumphed in his relationships with them.

In one incident Smith was going down river with six or seven men, hampered by language barriers, in a boat without sails. There were not enough people or supplies. Upon meeting a group of Indians, he tried to engage them in courteous trade and when this failed, he attacked them. In the skirmishes that followed, the Indians lost one of their sacred idols and quickly requested peace in order to retrieve it. Smith seized the opportunity to negotiate an exchange of beads, copper, and hatchets for a boatload of food. The Indians loaded his boat with venison, turkeys, wild fowl, and bread and danced and sang as the colonists departed!

Smith's attempts to keep the colony together were hampered by the scheming of disgruntled factions. More than once there were plots to steal a trading boat and return to England but Smith uncovered each of the plots in time to prevent them from going into action.

After six months the rivers were covered with swans, geese, ducks, and cranes. The colony was abundant with food. Feasts were held daily and the earlier plots to escape were a thing of the past. Nobody wanted to return to England.

The pressure to find the North-West Passage was still present, however, and Captain Smith, smarting from criticism of his failure to discover the head of the Chickahamania

The stuff of legend: the Indian "princess" Pocahontas intervenes to prevent the execution of John Smith by her father, Powhatan.

River, set out on another voyage with a small group of men. He did reach the head of the river but only after further loss of life in a confrontation with the Indians in which Smith himself was wounded in the thigh and taken captive. He and his force had been outnumbered by about 300 hostile natives.

In the six or seven weeks of his captivity Smith's esteem among the Indians grew. A round ivory double compass fascinated onlookers and was regarded as some kind of talisman by the Indians. Another reason for his change of status was a note he wrote to the settlement at Jamestown. The note requested gifts for the Indians and, since it resulted in the promised items, the natives believed that either the paper had a mysterious power of speed or John Smith was in some way divine. Nevertheless, Smith's status among his captors had not improved sufficiently to save his life. He was brought before the Emperor Powhatan at Meronocomoco and his head was placed on two great stones in readiness for his execution by stoning. The Emperor's daughter Pocahontas took pity on him and held his head in her arms. She then laid her own head on top of

Smith's and prevented the execution. Her father relented and arranged for Smith to be escorted back to Jamestown.

Ultimately, the inspirational and unifying force of Captain Smith was lost to the colony in 1609 when he was seriously injured in a gunpowder explosion and decided to go back to England. He never returned to the colony he had saved.

Another Turn for the Worse

Smith's departure was followed by serious food shortages over the next two years. The colonists dubbed 1609 and 1610, "the starving time." They became completely disheartened and eventually decided to travel back to England. In an extraordinary occurrence of good timing, they met a new group of colonists arriving at the mouth of the James River. The new arrivals had boats filled with supplies, so, they turned around and decided to try again.

The new man in charge, Governor Dale, was not impressed with Jamestown in 1611. He wrote to the King expressing concern about the possibility of making a success with "sutch disordered persons, so prophane, so riotous ... besides of sutch diseased and crased bodies." But the marriage of old and new brought renewed hope to Jamestown. The original settlers had learned from their mistakes and helped the new ones to avoid them. The new colonists brought much needed skills in carpentry and other trades but the struggle continued until the colony could begin to trade successfully.

The Seeds of Jamestown's Prosperity

Natives of the Americas introduced European explorers to tobacco in the mid-16th century. Its arrival in England is sometimes attributed to Sir Walter Raleigh and other times to Sir John Hawkins. No matter who was responsible for importing it, tobacco was becoming very popular throughout Europe by the early 1600s.

Although detailed medical knowledge about tobacco's harmful effects did not exist at the time, the introduction of the "noxious weed" was debated in society. Many critics, most notably King James I, believed it contributed to ill health. He called the habit:

a custome lothsome to the eye, hatefull to the nose, harmefull to the braine, dangerous to the lungs, and in the blacke stinking fume thereof, neerest resembling the horrible stigian smoke of the pit that is bottomelesse.

Clearly the king was not a man to mince his words. But despite his opposition and further claims that it dried up a person's brain and wasted the body, the demand grew. Tobacco became Jamestown's source of prosperity and dictated the entire way of life in the new colony.

In 1610 the colonists began to experiment with tobacco production but it was not until farmer John Rolfe brought the West Indian variety grown in Cuba to Jamestown that the colony was able to produce tobacco acceptable to the English palate. Rolfe, incidentally, was later to marry the Princess Pocahontas who had saved Captain John Smith's life.

The first shipment of tobacco was sent to England in 1615. The success of the crop is most evident from the export figures. In 1616, 2500 lbs were shipped. The following year more than 20,000 lbs were exported and that number more than doubled in 1618 to 50,000 lbs. Virginia was now outselling Spain and her colonies who had held the lion's share of the tobacco trade.

The instant success of the tobacco crop determined the growth of the Virginia colony. Although the village concept of living had been brought with the original settlers from England, the tobacco plant ruled supreme. The colonists abandoned communal living and created huge plantations with homes at the center of each. The famous "southern hospitality" was born in Jamestown during this period since, with no newspapers, plantation dwellers were starved of news and human contact. Passersby on land or water were hailed and almost forced to partake of food, drink, and lodgings so that they would pass on tidbits of information to slake the thirst of the plantation owners.

The building of the plantations made it necessary to clear the land of forests. This greatly angered the native Indians and began to sow the seeds of disaster. Indeed,

the success of the tobacco crop halted other developments so that the colony was still importing foodstuffs from England ten years after it had been founded.

A Year of Great Change

By 1619 there were 1000 settlers in Jamestown and farms stretched for 20 miles along the banks of the James River. A year earlier each man who had paid for his passage had been given 50 acres of land. Colonists had begun to own fields and could sell the products they grew there. This put increasing pressure on the availability of land and led to inevitable confrontations with native Indians.

By now craftsmen had been brought in to

A new life: after her dramatic rescue of Captain Smith, Pocahontas was captured by the English, married John Rolfe, and died in England under her baptismal name of Rebecca.

organize factories for the production of glass, wine and silk and, in 1619, a new leader was brought into the London Company. Sir Edwin Sandys, second son of the Archbishop of York, was concerned about the colony's reliance on tobacco because he felt it was detrimental to a sound and politically stable community. He started a five-year plan to launch new industries. It was a grand scheme to introduce vintners from France, lumbermen from the Baltic and

A new lease of life: women join the male settlers at Jamestown.

ironworkers from England but it was to run into difficulties.

Meanwhile other major events were happening in this momentous year. Women, totaling 60 in number, arrived in the colony for the first time and thereby assured the development of family units and a civilizing influence. It was a sign that the colony was coming of age.

The Beginning of Self-government

This was also the year in which democracy took its first halting steps in the New World. Before 1619 the London Company selected people to rule the colony. In 1618 the company authorized the new Governor to summon a representative assembly with the power to make bylaws, subject to the overall approval of the company in London.

This first representative government was called the House of Burgesses. There were 22 members, two from each of the 11 settled districts, who were elected by the votes of every man over the age of 17. The House of Burgesses met for the first time on July 30, 1619, in a Jamestown church. The session lasted six days through appalling midsummer heat and one man actually died during the proceedings. Few laws were passed and

those that were had to be sent to London for approval, but the seeds of self-determination had been sown.

The Seeds of Human Bondage

A Dutch Trading Company brought 20 black African natives to Jamestown in 1619. Although they were brought originally as indentured servants bound for a period of years, this incident was the precursor of the slave trade on North American shores. While some of the Africans served out their indentured time to compensate for the cost of their trip to the colony and then acquired land to work for themselves, they were the exception. In less than 20 years it was slavery in all but name. By the 1660s all pretense was gone and slavery had arrived in name too.

Slavery was not new to the Europeans. They had been raiding Africa and enslaving Blacks for more than a century. Just as slaves had provided the Spanish with necessary, cheap labor for gold mining during the 16th century, a drop in tobacco prices was the economic imperative which established slavery in Virginia. The farmers with the lowest labor costs were in a very competitive position. There were difficulties getting indentured white servants from England and the Royal African Company was ruthlessly efficient at delivering a self-propagating labor force. In addition, human

prejudice contributed to the development of slavery.

Population Growth

The early success of the tobacco trade encouraged many to emigrate to the colony although fatalities during the voyage west were high. Overcrowding on the ships, inadequate facilities, disease, malnutrition, and fatigue took their toll on the immigrants but they still kept coming – so many, in fact, that the colony could barely cope with the overcrowded conditions caused by the influx of 4000 people in just four years.

And despite Sir Edwin Sandys' plan for diversification there were problems. The London Company was having some financial difficulties. The costs of transporting vinters, lumbermen and ironworkers was more expensive than anticipated. Many of the new arrivals immediately dropped the practice of their much needed skills to cash in on the surefire success of tobacco growing. Some did start the ironworks and some did plant the planned vineyards but all too many set about clearing the land for the tobacco crop.

This greatly increased the demand for land and eventually the Indians retaliated. On March 22, 1622, they swept through the undefended plantations, destroying every outlying farmhouse as they went and flattening every settlement outside Jamestown.

The power of advertising: publicity material such as this helped stimulate further immigration to the New World in the early years of the 17th century.

Three hundred men, women, and children were killed. Even John Rolfe who had married the Indian princess was not spared. The advances of three years had been undone in a single night.

The Indian attack on Jamestown provided a good excuse for Sandys' enemies to petition the King. They convinced him that the bankrupt, faction-torn colony had been grossly mismanaged. In 1624 the Virginia Company of London was dissolved legally and the colony became a royal province. The King appointed a Governor with the power of veto and a 12-member council to assist him. The House of Burgesses remained intact.

The colonists did not object. There was less interference from the King than there had been from the Virginia Company of London. Charles I was well aware of how much money he was collecting from the customs duties on Virginia tobacco.

The Colony Retaliates and Continues

The survivors of the 1622 Jamestown massacre exacted revenge on the Indians. One story tells of 250 Indians coming to talk peace. As they raised their cups to drink to harmonious relations all 250 were poisoned.

The last recorded Indian attempt to oust the English settlers from Virginia was in 1644. The Indians failed and nothing could now stop the steamroller effect as the settlers consumed more and more land. Tobacco crops drained the earth of nutrients and, after a few short years of production, left the land worthless. The thirst for land and the dispossession of the Indians continued.

English Colonies in the Northeast

The English colonization of America had two main motivations, profit and religious freedom. King James I believed in the "Divine Right of Kings" and during his reign, from 1603 to 1625, he tried to make and enforce laws without Parliamentary consent. His successor, Charles I, continued the tradition, ruling without Parliament for 11 years, from 1629 to 1640. Freedom of speech and religious freedom were greatly curtailed and this led to a mass exodus to the colonies and later, in 1642, resulted in England's Civil War. The King of England was also the head of the Church of England and all English citizens regardless of their own religious beliefs had to belong to the Church of England and contribute to its support.

There were two prominent groups of religious dissenters in the early 17th century, one known as the Pilgrims or Separatists and the other known as the Puritans. They came from different backgrounds and their aims differed but they were both instrumental in the birth and growth of the Massachusetts colonies and the rest of New England.

The Pilgrims

The Pilgrims were known as Separatists because they did not believe the Church of England could be reformed and simply wanted to break away. In 1608 a group fled from their homes in Nottinghamshire, Lincolnshire, and Yorkshire to the Netherlands. There, first in Amsterdam and then in Leyden, they found the religious tolerance they sought but they resisted integration and fiercely defended their English customs and language. They turned down an offer of passage to the New Netherlands, but the idea of America as the solution to their needs had been planted.

Though most of the Pilgrims were uneducated, a few among them were scholars with connections to a prominent member of the Virginia Company of London. This connection eventually led to their passage on the *Mayflower* in September, 1620. Their sponsor to the New World was the unlikely figure of Sir Edwin Sandys. Sandys was regarded by the Pilgrims as an arch enemy because of his Archbishop father. But Sandys admired the Pilgrim scruples and arranged a land grant and financing. They were to settle considerably north of Jamestown where they could practice their own religion and be responsible to the Government of Virginia in all secular matters.

The *Mayflower* and the *Speedwell* made the first false start from Southampton in early September of 1620. The *Speedwell* was finally abandoned after repeated breakdowns and attempted repairs and the *Mayflower* sailed off alone on September 16, 1620. Although the main motivation for the voyage was religious freedom, the fact is that less than half the 100 passengers were Pilgrims. Thirty-five of the Pilgrims had

journeyed from Leyden in the Netherlands. The rest of the travelers were servants, indentured servants, artisans, cooks, gunners, and a doctor. The reasons for travel must have been as varied as the travelers. One young cooper, John Alden, went on the voyage purely for the adventures it might hold.

The land granted by the London Company to the Pilgrims was a stretch south of the Hudson River. But during the voyage the ship was blown off course and, on November 11, it landed in a harbor off Cape Cod far from the target settlement area and well outside the jurisdiction of the London Company.

Some accounts suggest that the captain would not venture any farther than that, because in his opinion, one part of this new world was no different from another. In any event, the landing posed a problem because the Pilgrims were not where they were supposed to be and were away from the rule of law and order of the Virginia Company. There were discontented and mutinous speeches from some of the non-Pilgrims and this provoked the Separatist leaders to prepare a document which effectively would establish the basis for self-government. According to William Bradford, the ship's chronicler and later Governor, many of the non-Pilgrims had boasted "none had the power of command over them." The colonists had to move quickly to maintain order.

The sails were furled and in the small ship's cabin, the Mayflower Compact was drafted and signed. It was not a plan for government but it was an agreement to obey whatever laws the colonists themselves would pass. After Virginia's House of Burgesses, the Mayflower Compact became the next building block towards self-government in America. It was bolder than the Virginia assembly because it was prepared completely independently of the Crown and the governing company and its creators believed it to be as effective as any patent because they were outside the bounds of the London Company's rule. The belief in its effectiveness was not misplaced as this simple document guided the colonists through the rough period ahead and endured in its own right for many years.

The Pilgrims did not make the mistake of the original Jamestown settlers. They took their time looking for the best location and after more than a month of surveying the coastline they decided on a site on the southwestern shore of what is now Cape Cod Bay. English explorers had been there earlier and called it Plymouth. The site had many advantages including a small but good harbor, a brook of clear fresh water, and a hill which could be defended against attack. It had once been the site of an Indian village and was surrounded by cleared fields. The landing at Plymouth Rock was to become, in later years, symbolic of a new nation's beginnings and schoolchildren would re-enact it for generations to come.

The settlers started to build houses in the cold winter months. It was the harshest winter of their lives. Although very few had died on the long sea voyage most of the

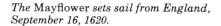

colonists had been weakened by it and were, therefore, prone to scurvy and other diseases. The onslaught of the bitter cold, combined with exposure, quickly began to take its toll. The colony became a sick bay and a mortuary.

During the worst of the winter only six or seven settlers were well at any one time. But according to William Bradford, the leader of the group, those six or seven showed the best side of humanity. They cheerfully toiled at the risk of their own health to tend to the sick. William Brewster and Miles Standish were two names counted among the best of these Samaritans.

The *Mayflower* overwintered at the colony because the settlers had not been able to build enough shelters before an epidemic took hold. The ship was needed as a base. The ship's crew did not carry on in the same exemplary fashion as the Samaritans among the colonists. Many of the crew turned their backs on the sick and infirm because they feared that the colonists were contagious. When the sailors, too, got sick they were very surprised at the generosity and caring they received from the same people they had shunned.

By March of the following year, 1621, only 50 of the 102 passengers who landed were alive. As the harsh winter passed into spring the worst of times was over. The coming of some native American friends also changed the fortunes of settlement.

Help from the Indians

During the winter some Indians had appeared stealthily in the distance and had disappeared just as quietly. In March an Indian called Samoset came and astonished the settlers with his somewhat faltering but nonetheless understandable English. He had learned his English from another Indian named Squanto who was to become a key figure in the survival of this weakened but determined colony.

Squanto had been captured by an English sea captain and trader named Thomas Hunt who took him to Spain and sold him as a slave. But the Pawtucket Indian escaped and found his way to England where he lived for two years before returning to America on a trading ship. He made two more Atlantic crossings, acting as a guide and interpreter for trading missions and when he returned after his final crossing he found his entire tribe had died of an epidemic.

Squanto befriended the Pilgrims and negotiated a peace treaty with the local chief Massasoyt. According to Bradford, he "continued with them and was their interpreter and was a special instrument sent from God for their good beyond their expectation. He directed them how to set their

The birth of New England: John Alden and Mary Chilton lead the Pilgrim Fathers ashore at Plymouth Rock, Massachusetts.

Settlers celebrate the first Thanksgiving with the Indians who have helped them.

corn, where to take fish and to procure other commodities, and guided them to unknown places and never left them till he died.''

With Squanto's help available, not one of the settlers decided to join the *Mayflower* on its trip back to England when it departed on April 5, 1621. In the autumn they were rewarded for their patience and faith as the pumpkin, squash, bean, and Indian corn seeds that Squanto gave them yielded a harvest. Although the plenty would not be constant, their fortunes had turned around. During this period 35 new colonists arrived with no supplies and on the brink of starvation. But the settlers were ever more determined to succeed. When food produce was low they followed the Indian custom of hunting for New England clams at low tide.

The settlers also became exporters for the first time. When the ship that had carried the 35 new settlers departed, it carried clapboard as well as beaver and other skins. The cargo was worth £500, a small fortune in those days.

The First Thanksgiving

By the end of the first year the colony was flourishing and in the autumn of 1621 several days were set aside for recreation and thanksgiving. The guests at the celebration included the newly arrived settlers from England and about 100 local Indians.

The three days of Thanksgiving have been modified and the offerings of water fowl, wild turkey and venison have been scaled down since those early times. But centuries later, on the last Thursday of November, people throughout America of all races and beliefs still gather around a table for a symbolic commemoration of a determined people and their eventual triumph.

New threats required the Plymouth colonists to take yet more survival measures. The Narraganset tribe threatened but could not shatter the now strong colony. By March of 1622 the entire town was enclosed in a strong stockade and the colonists were well versed in emergency procedures. The common mood in the town was cheerful and every family could boast of a garden plot which would make any English person proud.

The colony did not attract many new

people and was later to become part of the bigger Massachusetts Bay Colony in 1691, but it was an important period. The Pilgrims were the first permanent New England settlers. Their landing at Plymouth Rock, their bold Mayflower Compact, and their feast of Thanksgiving have come to symbolize the rights, freedoms, and prosperity of the New World.

The Puritans

The next great influx of people seeking religious freedom were called the Puritans. Like the Pilgrims they had problems with the Church of England and its leader, the King. The Puritans felt that the Church of England was too similar to the Roman Catholic church and wanted further reform. They wanted to "purify" the existing religious establishment and carry reformation to its "rightful" or "logical" conclusion. Within the framework of the Church of England they wanted to straighten out the tenets in accordance with their own interpretation of the Bible. Their faith appealed to the business classes and rising capitalists because it preached the virtues of good business and ranted against the sins of idleness, frivolity, extravagance, and moral corruption.

The reforms introduced by the Puritans were thwarted by the first two Stuart Kings, James I and Charles I. The group was told that it would be ousted if it did not conform to the existing Church of England. Since they could not, they left voluntarily.

Inspired by the Pilgrims' successful colonization and backed by the high finances of their own company, the Puritans began to migrate in 1630 when the first 1000 men, women, and children set sail with John Winthrop. This initial group was already three times larger than the Pilgrim colony, which at that time numbered only 300. There were small fishing and trading post settlements up and down the coastline but the area was very sparsely populated. That would change.

For ten years shipload after shipload would arrive on the Massachusetts shores. At the end of the decade more than 20,000 English settlers were living in the Puritan Massachusetts Bay Colony. Its growth was explosive and, although the Pilgrims had paved the way, it was the Puritans who were largely responsible for the settlement and growth of Northeast America.

The Puritan Charter: The Vital Clause

When the first Puritans sailed in 1630 their destiny was very largely in their own hands. Although Virginia had its own form of self-government with the House of Burgesses, the London Company always had the last word. The Puritans, on the other hand, brought both the charter and the company with them for the first total "hands on" government.

These companies were joint stock trading companies, set up in Europe to engage in overseas trade. They were much like modern corporations, as stockholders invested money and elected a few people to manage the company. The stockholders did not have the benefit of limited liability but they did have exclusive trading privileges. English companies received a monopoly to trade in specific parts of the world and this gave them full control over trading posts and colonies established by them. The Muscovy Company had been trading in Russia since 1555 and the Levant Company had been active in the Near East.

Owning one's own company, as a colony, had distinct advantages. But there was a special clause in the Puritan charter which allowed the formation of self-government. This clause stated that stockholders were not required to meet in a specific place. Since most of the stockholders were those very same Puritans who wanted to leave England, voting in America seemed the pragmatic application of the charter's clause.

John Winthrop, who led the first group of Puritans across the Atlantic in 1630, was a crucial player in the entire plan, and in the Puritan charter's careful wording. He was Governor of the colony and Governor of the Company of Massachusetts Bay in New

The seal of the Massachusetts Bay Company.

England. This had previously been called the New England Company and consisted of a group of backers who obtained their patents originally from the Plymouth Company and who then obtained a Royal Charter for Massachusetts Bay.

By bringing both charter and company with them across the Atlantic the Puritans had assured themselves of as much self-determination as was legally possible at the time. The only person who could interfere in their decision making was the King of England. The King had interfered in the Jamestown colony in 1624 by eliminating the London Company and turning the settlement into a Royal Colony. The Puritans were certainly aware of this when they laid their own plans.

The Crown attempted to put Massachusetts under direct control later in 1686 when James II combined it with New York and New Jersey, thereby abolishing representative government and appointing a colonial governor. But the growing seeds of self-determination were too firmly implanted by then for a temporary setback to stop the forward motion of democracy and freedom from crown rule. John Winthrop and his successors clearly molded the area into their own image of church, state, and general way of life.

The Massachusetts Bay Colony

Life in the Massachusetts Bay Colony was a bizarre combination of democracy and repression. The tenets included the trial by jury concept, the protection of life and property by due process of law, freedom from self-incrimination, and no taxes on those who could not vote. The right to vote was given only to those who were members of the church.

The rulers directed every facet of life, work, play, morals, and worship. No other religions were tolerated in the community and there were strict laws on personal conduct. Petty thieving, drunkenness, and sing-

ing bawdy songs were offenses which would result in a prison sentence. Raillery, any sign of merriment or levity near a church, meant that the offender would be put on public display in the stocks and subjected to ridicule. Adultery was punishable by death.

The Puritans had arrived in Massachusetts very well prepared. The first 1000 passengers on board their 17 ships had ample supplies of food, clothing, and tools. They had, among their number, the skilled carpenters, masons, blacksmiths, shipbuilders, and other tradesmen needed. They began to build their villages north of Plymouth.

Since the sect believed that financial success was a sign of God's approval, it had always attracted wealthy businessmen. Their work ethic made them successful in fur trading and the cod fishing industry. Cod became as important to the Puritan colonies as tobacco was to the Jamestown colony.

The colony was full of paradoxes. After craving religious freedom for themselves, they denied it to others once they had power. But they had no trouble separating business from religion. They sold cod fish to the Roman Catholics because they paid the highest price. They also supplied slave-owning plantations with fish, beef, and vegetables.

The leaders held the community in an iron grip to strict totalitarian control. They restricted all government powers to the company's lawmaking body called the General Court. Only stock or shareholders could belong to the General Court and this excluded all but a small minority of the settlers.

Inevitably demands were made for a share in the government and Winthrop and his colleagues loosened the control somewhat. All Puritan men who were good Church members were given the right to vote and each town was given the right to send representatives to the General Court. Wealth or origin were not the determinants. It was adherence only to the faith prescribed by the Puritans which was considered. Any freeman who met the religious requirements could achieve the very highest post in the congregation.

The rigid class systems upon which society in England was based were already breaking down in the colonies. There were new opportunities for upward mobility. But the rigidity of the laws on worship was suffocating to anyone who wanted freedom either in religion or in daily life.

Repression Gone Rampant

From its very beginning the Massachusetts Bay Colony was dictatorial. The leaders prescribed a rigid and inflexible way of life and set of beliefs. There was no separation of church and state. In Puritan society the state was formed as a "government of Christ in exile." The central core of the Puritan existence as a sect and the reasons for the Puritans immigrating to America was the creation of a life which could reflect Puritan biblical interpretations.

Although they had been dissenters themselves, they would not tolerate any dissen-

sion within their own ranks and dissenters were persecuted. They were hounded to confess and convert, they were put out into exile, and they were put to death. Baptists and Quakers were considered agents of the devil and anyone who was even slightly eccentric could be deemed a witch. Within their own ranks anyone who did not totally agree with the orthodox views of government or religion could be banished.

In 1640, as the Puritan grip on power began to slip, the first sporadic witchcraft executions began. By the end of the century, the witchcraft persecution had become frenzied. Manipulative leaders and hysterical, bigoted neighbors contributed to 20 executions in Salem. There was later evidence that the Puritan leaders staged the trials in a desperate attempt to maintain control over the people.

The ironfisted rule of the Puritans led to the formation of other communities in New England. Areas of Maine, New Hampshire, Connecticut, and Rhode Island were settled in the first half of the 17th century by people who would not conform to the political and religious policies of the Massachusetts Bay Colony.

The Founding of Rhode Island

Of all the early Massachusetts settlers none was more outspoken than Roger Williams. He was a deeply religious young man who arrived in the colony in 1631. He soon became the pastor in a town called Salem later to be famous for its witchcraft trials. Williams believed that it was wrong to take land from the Indians and insisted that the settlers pay them for it. He also preached that political leaders should have no say in religious matters and that individuals had the right to worship God as their consciences dictated. These two concepts which would be cornerstones of the American way – separation of church and state and government by the will of the people – did not please the Puritan leadership. They believed that government's main purpose was to enforce the will of God.

The Puritan leadership decided that Williams was a menace and would have to be sent back to England. But the young man escaped and hid with his friends, the Narragansett Indians. He lived with them for several months and in 1636, along with some old friends, established the village of Providence.

Ann Hutchinson was another who challenged the authority of the Puritan leadership. She was a forceful, courageous member of a prominent family and a devout student of the Bible who was condemned as a heretic and exiled. She, her husband, and a group of supporters founded another settlement in Narragansett Bay.

Roger Williams secured a charter for the colony of Rhode Island in 1644 which stated that the government of Rhode Island rested upon the consent of the governed. The residents were guaranteed the right to worship as they wished and all adult males had a vote. Later, however, there were restrictions on the right to vote. In 1663 it became confined to those who were landowners. But even so, Rhode Island offered more freedom to settlers than anywhere else in New England.

Connecticut, Maine, and New Hampshire

Connecticut, Maine, and New Hampshire were founded as a result of more pioneering initiatives. In 1635, Reverend Thomas Hooker and most of his Newtown Massachusetts (now Cambridge) congregation decided to clear Connecticut's wilderness for themselves. They founded Hartford and were soon surrounded by other neighboring settlements.

Beginning in 1629, settlements were established in what is now Maine and New Hampshire. By the late 1630s, substantial numbers of settlers were moving north. Some of the Massachusetts leavers went even further afield, abandoning several English settlements altogether. Lady Deborah Moody, a wealthy landowner from Salem,

portant rivers and were also in a position to attack English ships north or south of them.

As the Dutch expanded, they ran into the New Englanders to the north and the Virginians and Marylanders to the south. Conflict was inevitable. The English also coveted control of the trade on the Hudson River because it was the source of a very rich fur trade with the Iroquois Indians and so, in 1664, a large English fleet sailed into the Hudson River ready for battle. The Dutch Governor, Peter Stuyvesant, could see immediately that his forces were hopelessly outnumbered and pulled down the Dutch flag without a shot being fired.

Charles II granted this newly acquired vast region to his younger brother, the Duke of York. Consequently, the English colony of New York came into being. The gift included much of the mid-Atlantic area as well as the islands of Nantucket and Martha's Vineyard and all of Maine east of the Kennebec River. Having been the subject of such generosity, the 30-year-old Duke of York parceled out the land lavishly to his friends. He gave New Jersey, a sparsely settled wilderness, to Lord John Berkeley and Sir George Carteret.

Although New Jersey had some Dutch and Swedish colonists and a few small villages of former New Englanders, the region was slow to grow. In 1702, after it had changed hands a number of times, the King claimed it back as a royal colony.

was warned in 1643 to give up her unorthodox religious views. She left with some supporters and received a Dutch patent for a self-governing community on Long Island where she maintained good relations with the Dutch governors and maintained religious freedom for her community.

Colonies on the Mid-Atlantic Coast

Between the northern and southern strongholds, other colonies began to form in the early 17th century. Lord Baltimore was granted a charter by King Charles I to develop a coastal region that was to become Maryland. The promise of profit seemed to have been at or near the forefront of this development. Lord Baltimore hoped to profit from renting land to European colonists but there was a religious motive as

well. He was concerned to find a refuge for persecuted Catholics.

The eight peers who were given the charter to develop North and South Carolina planned to gain by commercially producing semitropical foods and raw materials such as indigo, sugar cane, and tobacco.

In 1664 Charles II reclaimed the New Netherlands which had been Dutch and Swedish settlements since 1614. The center of New Netherlands was New Amsterdam, which is now New York City, on the tip of Manhattan Island. Henry Hudson, an Englishman, had been working for the Dutch East India Company in 1610 when he charted the river that now bears his name. The Dutch moved into the area and, although the colony was slow to grow, the site was of considerable strategic importance. The Dutch controlled trade on im-

Pennsylvania and Delaware

The 1680s added William Penn's Pennsylvania to the list of English colonies. Penn, at the age of 22, had heard a Quaker sermon and had been converted. His membership of the Society of Friends, one of the most disliked religious groups in England at the time, shocked and angered his father. But Penn persisted and his father, an Admiral in the Royal Navy, eventually relented, leaving him a large inheritance which included a debt owed to him by King Charles II.

In 1681, King Charles, who was in serious financial trouble, paid his debt to William by giving him a charter instead of money, making William the proprietor of a huge land grant. Penn realized that successful settlement of the land granted to him was dependent upon access to the sea. In 1682, Penn obtained a second grant which gave him that access. The second parcel of land granted was later to become Delaware.

William Penn called his colony Pennsylvania and the Penn family governed both it and Delaware until the Revolutionary War. Pennsylvania was a "Holy Experiment," according to its founder, and attracted large numbers of settlers. Penn even published pamphlets in English, French, Dutch, and German which invited honest, hardworking

Manhattan: the earliest known view of New Amsterdam, later New York, 1651.

people to settle in his new colony.

Penn promised religious toleration, representative government and cheap land and settlers poured in. Quakers from England, Wales, and Ireland, Scotch-Irish Presbyterians, Swiss and German Protestants, and Jews from all over Europe settled in the new colony. Penn kept his promise and ensured peace with the Indians by buying his land from them. African slaves were brought in but not in large numbers, although slavery was legally recognized.

King James II

By the mid-1680s, the English colonies, north, south and on the mid-Atlantic coast, were well established and growing. Then, in 1685, there was an obstacle to self-determination. The Duke of York became King James II and, in 1686, he began repressive actions. James combined New Jersey, New York, and New England into the Dominion of New England, abolished representative government and appointed a colonial Governor. People on both sides of the Atlantic were extremely unhappy with these policies of absolute rule.

But when the revolt came, it sprang up in England, not in the colonies as had been expected. In 1688, the Glorious Revolution drove James from the throne and a year later England adopted a Bill of Rights which included the right of representative government. The new king and queen, William and Mary of Orange, restored the colonial charters, and the representative assemblies once again regained their power.

Transported Over the Sea

The 17th-century colonists, battling for survival in the wilderness, brought with them a transplanted set of intellectual, spiritual, political, and legal ideals. The rights of citizens and representative government, free speech, free press, trial by jury, and the rule of law were principles ingrained in the English heritage, even if they were more honored in the breach than in the observance. Much that was English in the New World was changed in a subtle way and began to become American. The breaking down of class barriers was one of the major developments.

English visitors voiced shock at the variety of social classes they found among the plantation owners. It was not uncommon for individuals to pay off their passage to the colony by service to a master and then to become a landowner, often a very prosperous one. Since landowners could be elected to the House of Burgesses, the legislative body became a melting pot of classes.

Although class barriers never totally disappeared, the chance to rise in financial gain and status became a cornerstone of the emerging nation's thinking. The ideal of equality was firmly planted.

Daily Life

Even before Jamestown became prosperous the "gentlemen" settlers in the wilderness still wore the inappropriate clothes of their homeland. Some even brought starch to keep their ruffs stiff.

In the South, settlers had to abandon the

King Charles II grants William Penn a charter for Pennsylvania.

village concept in order to build the plantations but they quickly built little villages within the plantations with brick yards, carpenter shops, blacksmiths, spinning and weaving houses, and schools. All colonists, Southerners and even the northern Puritans, began their day according to English custom, with a morning draft of beer or ale.

The English language spoken by the settlers quickly began to change as it absorbed words from various languages. From the local Indians came words such as hickory, squash, canoe, and toboggan. From the Dutch came stoop, waffle, cruller, and cookie. From the French came bureau, gopher, chowder, and prairie. Since the colonists had to attempt to describe a new world, they made up new words, such as bullfrog, eggplant, backlog, snowplow, cold snap, trail, and popcorn.

Heritage

Much of American business ideology is modeled on the hard-work ethic of the Puritans and later constitutions were modeled on their government bodies. Connecticut's 1662 Charter was so comprehensive in terms of clarity of thought and self-determination, that it remained unchanged as the state constitution after the War of Independence. The Puritans also promoted higher education and established Harvard University in 1636.

GROWTH OF THE EUROPEAN COLONIAL EMPIRES (1689–1773)

English Expansion

Growth, conflict and diverging lifestyles characterized the period of American history from 1689 to 1763. Delaware became the 12th colony when it separated from Pennsylvania in 1704 and Georgia became the 13th in 1733. People were flooding to the other colonies and the population grew from approximately 360,000 in 1713 to nearly 1.5 million in 1750. By the 1760s there were about two million English colonists.

Georgia

James Edward Oglethorpe is credited with founding the Georgia colony. Oglethorpe was an associate of Dr. Thomas Bray, an Anglican clergyman and a great English philanthropist who promoted libraries in England, Wales, and the colonies. Oglethorpe was part of a Parliamentary committee assigned to review the state of English jails. One of the glaring problems was the Catch 22 situation of debtors.

Debtors could not be released from jail until they paid their debt, but while confined they had no means of getting the money to redeem themselves. If they were eventually released out of charity, they were usually destitute with no way to support themselves.

Oglethorpe saw the colonies as an answer. The Association of Dr. Bray obtained the Georgia land grant promising 50 acres of free land for each individual released from debtors' prison and sent to the New World. Starting in 1733, for eight years, more than 1800 charity colonists were sent from various nations and more than 1000 arrived on their own.

The trustees did not fully comprehend the nature of the problems they would face. They took a principled stand and banned slaves but many of their colonists found difficulty living on their 50 acres without cheap labor and headed into neighboring South Carolina, which was more prosperous and which did not have the same restriction. The trustees also banned rum, and without quinine or rum, the settlers who stayed were prone to disease in the malarial lowlands and many died. As the population dropped, the trustees were forced to remove the restrictions and, in 1751, granted the colonists an assembly. When their 20-year proprietorship expired they allegedly handed the colony back to the Crown with pleasure!

Other Settlers

In the first 12 colonies expansion occurred with a flood of immigrants. Since Britain was the only colonial power which would accept foreigners, discontented Germans became a valuable population booster to the English controlled areas. They entered primarily via Philadelphia, some settled there and others moved further inland.

Another large group of immigrants was from Ulster in Northern Ireland. These were Protestant Irish, mostly of Scottish descent. The Protestant Scots had moved into Ireland taking up the land of dispossessed Catholics at the same time as the original English settlements were starting in Virginia. The poorer people left for a new life in America rather than face continuing religious conflict in Northern Ireland.

Carving out a living: a groundplan for the town of Savannah, Georgia, in 1734, showing the inhospitable forest which surrounded the site.

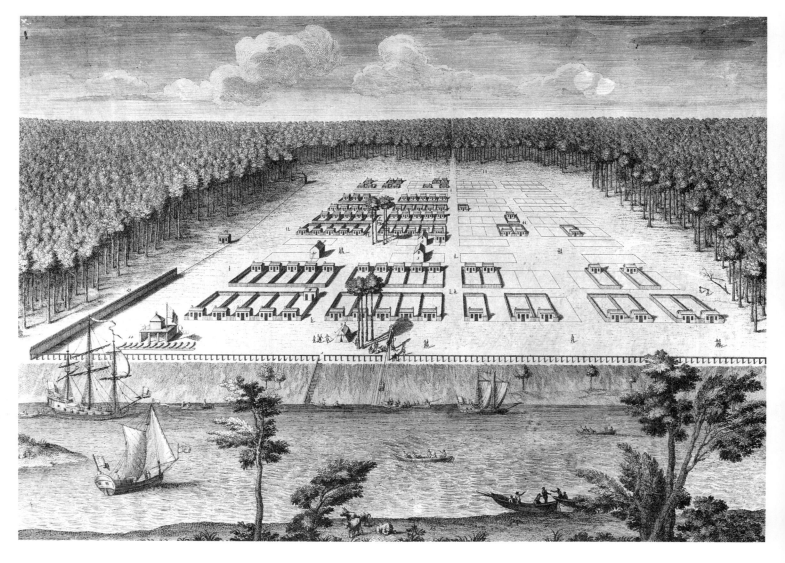

Trade and Commerce

The delicate balance of trade governed the mercantile economic system of the 16th, 17th, and 18th centuries. The basic idea was for a country to export more than it imported and to gain a surplus of national wealth, preferably in the form of gold and precious metals which were universally exchangeable. Each nation in the mercantile system sought an advantage and therefore promoted protectionism, levied duties, created exclusive trading privilege treaties, and passed laws to destroy other nations' commerce. Inevitably this led to international tension and strife.

This was the environment in which the American colonies first entered the arena of world trade. Their success was partly due to their unique and abundant products and partly to the extensive coastline and easy access to the sea. Sometimes the colonies were helped by British Acts of Trade but often succeeded in spite of them.

The British Acts of Trade

The Navigation and Trade Acts were brought into being to help Britain and her possessions survive and be competitive in the world's mercantile economy. In the previous century Dutch shipping supremacy threatened to drive England and other countries from the sea. As a result Britain passed the first of a series of laws addressing this and other obstacles to a favorable balance of trade. The legislation, introduced in 1651, decreed that only British ships could carry goods imported from Africa, Asia, and America into any British empire port. Since the American colonists were British citizens, the Act was a great advantage to American industry, especially to shipbuilding.

American colonists could build, operate and sail their own vessels. By the 1770s, colonial shipyards were building about one third of all merchant ships sailing under the British flag, creating great wealth for many colonial merchants.

From 1660 to 1673, a series of variations on a single Navigation Act gave the colonists both restrictions and advantages. The first, in 1660, allowed certain colonial products, specifically tobacco, cotton, sugar, and indigo, to be shipped *only* to England. Later versions expanded and altered the list. An Act of 1663 added further restrictions. Colonists had to buy most manufactured goods from England and all European goods sent to the colonies had to go via England. The goods would be unloaded and reloaded onto British ships and the authorities could collect duties directly.

This direct control helped protect English manufacturing and could protect the cargo from pirate attack. To compensate for the restrictions the colonies were given some preferential treatment, and to protect the tobacco industry in America, cultivation of tobacco was banned in England.

Throughout the 18th century there were more and more restrictions on how trade could be conducted in the colonies. Often the laws were prompted by the agitation of special interest groups lobbying Parliament. In one such move London's Worshipful Company of Hatters succeeded in promoting a 1732 Act which limited the number of hatters' apprentices allowed in the colonies and which banned the export of colonially-manufactured hats even to other neighboring colonies.

The 1733 Molasses Act came from British West Indies lobbying. The act forced colonists to buy all molasses and sugar from the British West Indies. This was achieved partly by levying large taxes on French, Dutch, and Spanish West Indian products. But the British West Indies could not meet the demand alone and sometimes, despite the high

British protectionism: in 1732 American hatmakers such as this one were forbidden to export their wares to Britain.

taxes on the competition, the British prices were as high or higher than the French, Dutch or Spanish. The angry North American colonists decided to smuggle what they needed. Shipmasters obtained false invoices from Jamaica to cover shipments from the French islands.

In 1750, the English iron industry promoted a law which forbade steel mills and steel tool furnaces in the colonies. Ten years later, North America had a thriving iron industry. The colonists simply ignored the law. Most of the trade laws prior to 1763 were not enforced. The British government adopted a policy of "salutary neglect," amounting to the turning of an official "blind eye."

All 13 colonies depended on British and European goods. In return, Britain and Europe valued the colonial furs, naval supplies such as pitch and tar, tobacco and other products. But the colonies could not rely strictly on the English and European markets. When the duplicated products were made in Britain, they were banned. New trade outlets had to be found.

New England and the middle colonies established new markets which improved their fortunes. They developed a triangular trade route between the West Indies, Africa, and North America. On the first leg came sugar, molasses, gold, and silver came from the West Indies to North America. The colonists produced rum in their distilleries from the West Indian products and the rum, along with iron, was sent on the second leg of the journey to Africa. The third leg was from Africa to the West Indies and the cargo was gold and slaves.

There was also a two-way trade between the Caribbean and America. The colonies sent grain, fish, meat, cloth, soap, house construction materials, and casks in exchange for sugar, molasses, and gold. Grain and flour from the Chesapeake Bay ports to the West Indies rivaled tobacco as the top American export. The city of Baltimore was founded in 1729 principally in order to provide flour mills for Maryland and Pennsylvania wheat.

Currency in the colonies was a problem.

There was a ban on the export of English coins and the colonists tried issuing their own paper money. They attempted to mint their own bullion imported from the West Indies but all their attempts were thwarted by the British. The Spanish Piece of Eight, the forerunner of the silver dollar, was the only coin in free circulation. The colonists ultimately turned to paper promissory notes, or "bills of credit," which would later become the dollar bill.

Colonial Tensions

The continued expansion of the English colonies in America was experiencing a number of obstacles. The push west was curtailed by a formidable barrier – the Appalachian Mountains. The other barrier was a string of French forts along the Ohio valley. Tensions were inevitable.

The French and English colonies were expanding in different ways. The French occupied a larger area but had fewer settlements. They had farms along the St. Lawrence River and a chain of trading posts and forts through the Great Lakes and the upper Mississippi. French interests were still directed primarily toward the lucrative fur trade.

Although Louis XIV (1643–1715) was determined to populate Canada, his own policies were restrictions on the growth of the colony. He did not trust the French Protestant Huguenots and he barred them from going to New France. These disgruntled French people would have quickly boosted the populations of the French colonies. They left France anyway and, for

the most part, moved to England, Germany, and the Netherlands. Some went to America and settled in the English colonies, often becoming quite prominent and influential residents.

One of Louis' positive policies was to give cash grants to settlers who had large families of 10 or more. But another policy was that no one who was not of French nationality could settle in New France. This was a marked contrast to the English policy of open invitation to all Europeans.

The combined policies were not successful in settling New France. In the 1750s, when the English settlements boasted a population of 1.5 million, New France could only tally between 50,000 and 60,000 farmers, fur traders, and hunters.

French Settlements

The English were confined to a narrow coastal strip between the Atlantic and the Appalachians and the coastal rivers did not lead inland. The French, on the other hand, could follow their natural system of rivers and lakes, including the St. Lawrence, the Mississippi, and the Great Lakes, and could use this network of waterways to move deeply into the continental interior.

The positioning of their forts and trading posts also served to block English western expansion. In the early 1700s, the French held two extremely important gateways, New Orleans and Quebec.

The North was the primary area of French

Populating Canada: Quebec in the late 17th century.

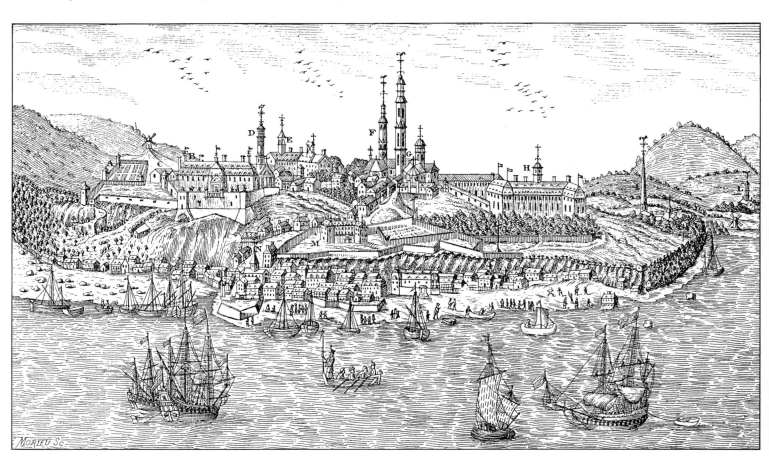

settlement. Colonists had to contend with more frigid winters than the British and had only the St. Lawrence River as a major route to the sea. With 1400 miles of open coastline the English had an easy approach from abroad to deliver supplies and people. Land was not as freely available to the French, and life in Canada was more closely regulated by French royalty. Heavy punishments were doled out for criticizing royalty and holding public meetings.

As tensions mounted between the English and the French, it was the French who appeared to have the advantage in America. The colonists consisted of more soldiers and frontierspeople than the loosely organized English band of merchants and farmers in their fiercely individualistic colonies.

Grand Alliance

In spite of the rise in England's fortunes in the colonies it was her arch enemy France which was the most powerful country in Europe at the end of the 17th and beginning of the 18th centuries. This was the time of Louis XIV, and France was considered to be so powerful that a defensive alliance was formed in 1686 against French expansionism. One of the leaders was William of Orange. The alliance was called the League of Augsburg and involved several German states, the Netherlands and Sweden.

In spite of the League, the French attacked the German regions of the Palatinate in 1688. In 1689, a new expanded alliance – called the Grand Alliance – involving England, Austria and Spain was formed. The League of Augsburg War, or The War of the Grand Alliance, started in Europe in 1689 and continued for nine years. In the colonies it was known as King William's War.

King William's War

French frontier attacks on English colonies seemed to provoke the North American conflict in King William's War. The Massachusetts colony took a bold step when it decided to retaliate by reaching Canada by sea and taking Quebec.

In May 1690, Sir William Phips led an expedition which captured Port Royal without bloodshed. The French Governor surrendered and the people were offered their lives and property if they swore allegiance to William and Mary of England. But Phips' force looted the residents' properties. Phips himself allegedly left with the Governor's silver, wigs, shirts, and garters.

Two months later Phips led a second expedition to Canada. He had some 40 ships and more than 2000 men. Although the numbers must have been impressive enough, the French were undaunted. They had been expecting the attack. Frontenac, the French Governor, had left Montreal a few days early and came to defend Quebec.

Surrounded by an array of French officers at the Chateau Louis, a lone English envoy presented a letter in the name of King William, demanding the surrender of all French forts and castles in Canada.

Frontenac did not acknowledge King Wil-

The Comte de Frontenac who led the French against the English in defense of Quebec.

liam because the French still supported the deposed Catholic English King James II who was still trying to regain the crown. The French wanted an ally against the growing strength of the Grand Alliance. But Louis XIV's hopes of an English counter-revolution and ultimate ally were dashed when James II was defeated at the Battle of the Boyne in Ireland in 1690.

Frontenac declared that he would answer the English demand "... from the mouths of my cannon and with my musketry!" The French repelled every offensive taken by Phips and the battered colonial fleet sailed away after a single week.

On the European continent, and at sea, the war raged on, ending indecisively. On the American continent the war continued with little consequence. After frustrated attempts by Massachusetts to conquer French Canada, Peter Schuyler of New York led another force in 1691. They approached Canada by Lake Champlain. Nothing was really determined and the only major result of the expedition was that many innocent Canadian settlers were killed in the hostilities.

In 1697, the Treaty of Ryswick ended the War of the Grand Alliance in Europe. The pact was signed by France on one side and by England, Spain, and the Netherlands on the other. Almost everything on the European continent which had been captured was returned. The only concession won by the English was a recognition of William and Mary as legitimate King and Queen.

In the colonies the only land victory had been the English capture of Port Royal which was handed back to the French. The Treaty of Ryswick should have ended King William's War in America. However, the war dragged on between French Canada and New England for another two years. The only thing accomplished by the extra two years of bloodshed was a further reduction in the population of the future state of Maine.

Sir William Phips who attempted to conquer French Canada for England in 1690.

The War of the Spanish Succession (1702–1713)

After only three years of peace the frontier struggle erupted again between the English and the French. The reason, on this occasion, was a dispute over who should be the next King of Spain. Three people laid claim to the throne of King Charles II before he died. Louis XIV of France claimed it for his eldest son who was a grandson of Philip IV of Spain; Joseph Ferdinand, the electoral Prince of Bavaria and a great grandson of Philip IV, claimed it; and Leopold I, the Holy Roman Emperor, who had married a daughter of Philip IV, claimed it for the Archduke Charles, his son from a second marriage.

The French, Dutch, and English did not find Archduke Charles acceptable. But England and Holland did not want to see a French-Spanish alliance either. So France and England agreed that Joseph Ferdinand of Bavaria should inherit the throne as soon as the gravely ill Charles II died. But Joseph Ferdinand died before the King of Spain and the King of Spain, on his deathbed in 1700, named Louis XIV's grandson Philip, Duke of Anjou, as his only successor. As soon as Queen Anne ascended to the British throne she declared war on France to contest the issue. Spain, Portugal, Bavaria, and Savoy sided with France while the Netherlands and most of the German states sided with England.

The New England settlers were still determined to win Canada, and during Queen Anne's War, as it was known in the colonies, there was more direct involvement from England and greater attempts to unify the major colonies under one leadership.

A unified front was strongly proposed by Colonel Samuel Vetch of Boston. Originally from Scotland, Vetch, along with many other prominent Boston merchants, was convicted of trading with the enemy in 1706, four years into the war. But his sentence was annulled because the English author-

Queen Anne of Great Britain (1665–1714).

ities were encouraged by and supportive of his military proposals. Vetch was proposing a major expedition against the French.

In March of 1709, a royal circular announced the grand scheme to all the English colonies. The plan involved a fleet from England carrying five regiments of British regular troops who would be backed by militia from Massachusetts and Rhode Island. This fleet would attack Quebec by sea. Montreal would be attacked overland from Albany by a joint force of militia from New York, Connecticut, New Jersey, and Pennsylvania backed up by an auxiliary force of Indians.

Some of the colonies enthusiastically supported the plan. Pennsylvania refused to participate but New Jersey donated £3000. At long last, the necessary militia and money were found and the plan was ready to go into operation. It was to be led by Francis Nicholson who had served as the Governor or Lieutenant Governor of New York, Virginia, and Maryland.

Ultimately, the English sent the troops earmarked for Quebec to Portugal. English naval commanders in the Americas refused to help. Nicholson and Peter Schuyler went to England to try to raise support. Although the massive offensive on Quebec and Montreal was shelved, they did manage to secure backing for a scaled down expedition which was to attack Port Royal in Acadia, which is now Nova Scotia. The English Government contributed a few warships and a regiment of marines.

In 1710, Nicholson commanded the force and led the attack on Port Royal. Samuel Vetch, who had originally suggested the idea, was the force's adjutant general. Port Royal surrendered after a week. Acadia became the British province of Nova Scotia, and Port Royal was renamed Annapolis Royal after Queen Anne.

Following his success, Nicholson returned to England to once again propose an all-out attack on Canada. There had been changes in England and Nicholson received enthusiastic support. This time a British fleet carrying seven regiments of British

troops backed by local militia from New England attacked Quebec and a land force attacked Montreal from Albany. Even the Quakers contributed money, turning a blind eye to its use.

The expedition was a humiliating failure due to a combination of faintheartedness and incompetence among the English military commanders. In August of 1711, the fleet sailed into the bay of the St. Lawrence and promptly ran several ships aground. Hundreds of soldiers were lost. Then, although they still had a superior force, they decided to retreat. The British withdrawal also effectively ruined their plan for the overland attack on Montreal.

The colonists still wanted to fight the Canadians but Britain was withdrawing from the war in Europe and preliminary negotiations were soon underway for the first peace conference, which took place in 1712.

The Treaty of Utrecht (1713)

Instead of a single treaty, Utrecht was actually a series of separate political and commercial treaties between individual nations. France, for example, signed separate political and commercial treaties with England, the Netherlands, Savoy, Portugal, Prussia, and the Holy Roman Empire. England signed a separate treaty with Spain.

A Bourbon dynasty was accepted in Spain but the French-Spanish threat had to be dealt with and Philip V of Spain, Louis XIV's grandson, had to renounce any claims to the French throne.

England emerged from the conflict with increased prestige largely due to her maritime prowess. The acquisition of Port Mahon on the island of Minorca and Gibraltar also strengthened England's position in the Mediterranean.

In the colonies, the French recognized British sovereignty over the Hudson Bay area and Newfoundland. Hudson Bay was particularly significant because of the fur trading company that had been operating there since 1670. The ceding of Nova Scotia to the British was very significant. Louis XIV was very reluctant to hand it over and he retained Cape Breton with its great fortress of Louisbourg, hailed as the "Gibraltar of the New World."

In the West Indies, England acquired St. Kitt's which was formerly St. Christopher's, but France retained the rest of her islands. Under its separate treaty with Spain, England was given exclusive rights to supply African slaves to the Spanish-American colonies for the next 30 years.

While Britain's material gains were small the importance of the outcome of the Treaty of Utrecht was that the French were no longer the invulnerable force they once had been.

A Peaceful Interlude

The years following the 1713 Utrecht Peace gave colonists an opportunity to develop, expand and prosper, although the English-French truce in America was an uneasy one.

The rivalry inevitably continued as the French advanced steadily further inland meeting the traders from New England, New York, Pennsylvania and Virginia moving west to trade with the Indians.

When Louis XIV died, in 1715, France was effectively ruled for a period by Cardinal Feuri, who removed many commercial restrictions, giving a great boost to French trade. The French merchant fleet grew from 300 ships in 1715 to 1800 20 years later.

On the American continent, French and English merchants traded surreptitiously. French merchants got lower priced goods in Albany and New York, while English traders purchased furs from the French and sometimes directly from the "coureurs de bois." The "coureurs de bois," or "runners of the woods," were unlicensed adventurous traders who ventured deep into the forests, stayed with the Indians through the winter and returned laden with furs to the trading centers.

By 1725, the English were turning a profit from the fur trade. Many Albany merchants were buying most of their skins illegally from the French but some were moving west, forging their own alliances with the Indians and obtaining their own merchandise.

In the first half of the 18th century the French and the English had their eyes on the west and on each other. In 1721, the English King was asked to fortify passes and build forts in the Great Lakes area to disrupt the easy flow of French traffic between Quebec and the Mississippi River. The French, in the meantime, were building a string of forts across the continent. Officially, the French were carrying out surveys and built stockades as defenses against the Indians. They were used, among other things, to keep an eye on the English. On New Year's Day in 1743, an expedition from one of these forts sighted the Big Horn range of the Rockies. It was a measure of how far west the exploration had come.

Continued Involvement in European Conflict

The War of Jenkins' Ear (1739–1741)

Captain Robert Jenkins, master of the ship *Rebecca*, was reputed to be a smuggler. He was picked up by the Spanish coastguard and, in a skirmish, had one of his ears cut off. His handling by the Spanish and, in particular, his severed ear offered an excuse to protest to many English people who were jealous and envious of Spain's commerical success. The case was dramatically and emotionally debated in Britain's House of Commons. Things became so heated that the English Prime Minister, Sir Robert Walpole, finally agreed to declare war on Spain.

Most of the battles were naval engagements led by Admiral Edward Vernon. Thousands of English colonists volunteered. Many died of yellow fever. One survivor was George Washington's older brother.

The fur trade: Indians bringing beaver skins to English traders.

On his return he named the family home "Mount Vernon" after the Admiral.

The war ended without any major result after two years of intermittent conflict.

War of the Austrian Succession (1744)

Even while the War of Jenkins' Ear was underway, there was further conflict on the European mainland. Once again, it was over the issue of royal succession. The Holy Roman Emperor, Charles VI, died in 1740 and the battle was on to see who would succeed him. Charles, knowing he had no male heir, had spent over 25 years trying to get all the major powers in Europe to agree that the succession in the Hapsburg line should be via his daughters. Most states agreed and his daughter Maria Theresa was recognized, but Frederick II of Prussia saw Charles' death as an opportunity, and invaded part of Silesia.

King George's War (1744–1748)

This was known in the colonies as King George's War when fighting broke out four years after hostilities had opened in Europe. The protagonists were, once again, England and France. France tried to regain Port Royal, which she had lost in Queen Anne's War but the assault, in 1744, failed. The following year the British fleet successfully attacked and captured the "Gibraltar of the New World," Fort Louisbourg on Cape Breton Island.

The victory was to be short won. King George handed Fort Louisbourg back to the French three years later in exchange for Madras, India. India had been a battleground since 1746 following an invasion by Afghanistan and a great deal of internal strife. Both France and England coveted India in their struggle to gain the colonial upper hand.

The real winner in Europe, after the Treaty of Aix-la-Chapelle in 1748, which ended the War of Austrian Succession, was King Frederick II of Prussia. Although he lost the right to succeed as Holy Roman Emperor, he held onto the territory he had seized in Silesia and Prussia and emerged as the real force to be reckoned with in the disparate Germanic states.

The French and Indian War (1754–1763)

The 1748 peace accord was a mere pause in the struggles on both sides of the Atlantic. Nothing had been settled and bitter rivalry between France and England continued to simmer. There had always been minor skirmishes, border disputes, and commercial harassment but there had not been, until the mid 1750s, a real showdown. As long as the English stayed east of the Appalachians and the French confined themselves to Canada and Louisiana there was unlikely to be a major conflict.

But when the English crossed the Appalachians to expand farther West, and when the French felt a need to connect their holdings in the North and South, the stage was set for an explosion. Center stage was the Ohio Valley. It would host the first all-out confrontation designed to allow only one power to continue with its "natural" progression and to force the other to retreat.

The origins of the war began in 1748 when wealthy Virginians formed the Ohio Company to extend settlements westward. Many members were planters interested in land speculation and the fur trade. The Loyal Company and the Greenbriar Company followed the Ohio Company's lead.

The French moved quickly and sent expeditions down the Ohio River, burying lead plates as territorial markers. For the next three years trouble was barely suppressed as the French and English fought in another contest to see which side could buy the most alliances with the native American Indians. The English were supposed to be the best at this method of securing allegiance, thereby ensuring their spread farther and farther over Indian land.

The French had good relations with the Indians because they did not clear the land and cut down the forests like the English but they could not compete with the lavish English goods. In June of 1752, the French, backed by their allies the Algonquin tribe, attacked the Picawillany village to confiscate English goods for trading with the Indians.

The following year the French started to build a chain of forts connecting Lake Erie

with the Ohio River. Virginia Governor Robert Dinwiddie responded to the building of the first two stockades by sending the young George Washington to demand the peaceful departure of the French. Washington informed the French that the land had been the property of the Crown of Great Britain since 1609, but the demand was ignored.

The Governor decided to build a fort close by the current site of Pittsburg at the fork of the Ohio River. The fort was only half finished when the 100 Virginians building it were confronted by a force of 1000 French soldiers. The Virginians retreated and the French built Fort Dusquesne on the same site.

As tensions rose, the English Board of Trade instructed the Royal Governors to meet with the Six Nations of the Iroquois and to forge an alliance with them. The Iroquois were a powerful confederacy, consisting originally of Five Nations from the New York area: the River Mohawk, lakes Seneca, Cayuga, Onandaga and Oneida. They had been joined by the Sixth Nation of the Tuscaroras from South Carolina in 1700. The Tuscaroras had been driven from their homelands by white settlers.

The meeting called to celebrate this new bond of friendship has become known as the Albany Congress. During the Congress a long time was spent debating colonial union. Benjamin Franklin and William Hutchinson presented the Albany Plan of Union. The plan would give the Union power to build forts, raise armies, equip fleets, and levy taxes and it would give its president the power to declare war, make peace and negotiate treaties among other powers. Unfortunately, the timing was not right because the colonies were still too individualistic. The Albany Plan was not ratified and the unified French were once

Recruitment poster, French and Indian War.

Colonel William Pepperell leads New Englanders at the siege of Louisbourg.

again facing a fragmented array of squabbling colonies.

The French controlled the heartland of America and it was up to the English to break through. George Washington led one of the first attempts. He went to the frontier to build Fort Necessity, a couple of miles from his earlier attempt where the French now had Fort Duquesne. Washington's men were attacked and defeated by a small force of French and Indians on July 4, 1754. The war was on.

In the fall British redcoats arrived under the command of General Edward Braddock. The following year Braddock led his English regulars and a strong Virginian militia against Fort Duquesne. But the attack was repelled and Braddock was killed.

The English launched abortive attacks on the French forts of Niagara and Crown Point. The French even managed to build a new fort at Ticonderoga in order to back up Crown Point at Lake Champlain. In an entire year of fighting, in 1755, there was only one English victory. It was led by an Irishman, William Johnson, who was awarded a baronetcy for winning a battle at Lake George.

The following year, 1756, was no better for the English, who suffered a string of defeats. Fort William Henry on Lake George surrendered to the French; General Montcalm captured the English fort of Oswego on Lake Ontario; and the British fleet failed to stop the French landing 3000 troops in Canada. George Washington and his militia protected the open land of the Shenandoah Valley against the Indians but with great difficulty.

It is perhaps not surprising that the English were not doing very well. The Seven Years War had begun in Europe and Asia in the same year and the French were riding high. They took the island of Minorca in the Mediterranean, Calcutta in India and sided with the Austrians to defeat the Prussian Frederick II.

The Seven Years War

The Seven Years War was a result of the rivalry between Austria and Prussia in Europe and Britain and France in America and India. In the classic European dance of convenience, everyone changed partners. Britain joined Hanover in backing Prussia and France sided with Austria, Russia, Saxony, Sweden, and Spain.

At first the war in America was seen as a secondary theater but when William Pitt became Secretary of State in Britain he changed strategies. Pitt saw the war in America as pivotal. As a result, he subsidized Frederick II and used his navy to control the seas. His military might was concentrated in America.

Pitt made radical and sweeping changes in the military, appointing bold, young leaders. His new strategy began to work. In July 1758, General Jeffrey Amherst, Brigadier General James Wolfe, and Admiral Boscawen recaptured the heavily fortified Louisbourg off the Nova Scotia coast. It was a lengthy struggle but gave the English a good strategic advantage in cutting off French reinforcements and supplies.

A month later, Colonel John Bradstreet of Massachusetts captured Fort Frontenac, a chief French supply depot on Lake Ontario. Bradstreet moved quickly, efficiently and surreptitiously. He took advantage of the natural waterways and used the knowledge of local colonial frontiersmen for speed and secrecy. His force captured or destroyed 76 guns, 10,000 barrels of provisions and a wealth of trade goods.

In the same year, Brigadier General John Forbes, with George Washington leading one of his brigades, marched on Fort Duquesne at the fork of the Ohio River. He took a route different to the one taken by General Braddock three years earlier. In some places he even cut his own road through the Alleghenies.

Forbes' advance reconnaissance parties ran into some opposition, which alerted the French. By the time Forbes arrived with his three split brigades, his enemy had burned down the fort, decamped, and fled. This was the end of a French presence, at this point, on the Ohio. The land was soon to be dominated by a new English fort, Fort Pitt, the predecessor of Pittsburg, Pennsylvania.

Elsewhere, the French were also faring badly. Admiral Edward Hawke won a decisive victory over the French fleet at Quiberon Bay, which effectively prevented the French from sending any reinforcements to Canada. Guadeloupe fell to a combined British naval

Denied the fruits of victory: General James Wolfe, who died at the age of 32 leading the successful attack on Quebec in 1759.

and military expedition, Fort Niagara fell to Sir William Johnson and, finally, in the "campaign of the year", the long sought prize of Quebec fell to General James Wolfe who led almost 5000 men down the St. Lawrence River by boat.

The Quebec plan called for Wolfe to meet General Amherst with his land brigade but Amherst captured both Crown Point and Ticonderoga forts en route and did not make it to Quebec. Wolfe carried on alone and, after a number of preliminary attacks, concentrated his forces on the Plains of Abraham and broke through on September 13, 1759. General Wolfe and his French counterpart General Montcalm both died in the battle. But Wolfe is still revered as a military commander for his leadership, tactics, and strategic prowess.

The following year saw the fall of the other major French jewel in Canada, Montreal. Montreal's surrender to combined armies from Oswego, Ticonderoga, and Quebec marked the end of French colonial power in America.

The war in Europe continued and, in 1762, Spain joined on the French side. Britain captured Havana and Manila from the Spanish, then George III fired William Pitt and opened peace talks with his enemies. He is alleged to have bought his peace by handing over some of the recent British conquests.

There were two peace treaties at the end of the Seven Years War. The Treaty of Hubertusburg settled the German struggle by restoring the pre-war status quo but, nonetheless marked a rise in the influence of Prussia. The Treaty of Paris put an end to the colonial struggles. Britain took all of North America, with the exception of the Louisiana territory, and most of India.

The English guaranteed religious freedom for Catholics in Canada and gave French inhabitants 18 months to sell property and emigrate. They allowed some fishing rights to French subjects and gave the islands of St. Pierre and Miquelon to France to shelter fishing people. Any fortification of

the islands was, however, forbidden.

The Spanish acquired Cuba from the English. In addition, New Orleans and its land mass were given to Spain by France. But the Spanish had to hand over all their territory in America, other than New Orleans, to the British. England handed over Guadeloupe, St. Lucia, Marie Galante, Desirade, and other islands to France. English residents there were given the same rights as French residents in Canada. France gave Grenada, St. Vincent, Dominica, and Tobago to Britain.

Victory was sweet for the British and their colonists in America. But the war debt had to be paid – glory has its price. The price would be very high indeed.

Life In the Colonies

City Life

In the early 18th century life in the colonial cities of Boston, New York, Philadelphia, and Charleston was not very different from that in England. Because there were so few architects in the colonies, the local builders emulated and imitated the English Georgian styles. Churches were often based on the designs of eminent architects such as Sir Christopher Wren.

On the eastern seaboard there was a great deal of profitable trading contact with England and the rest of Europe. The colonists were, therefore, up to date on progress in the Old World. The wealthier families sent their sons to England for general education and also for specific tutoring in medicine at Edinburgh and law at London's Inns of Court. Between 1713 and 1773 thirteen colonists, including the great Benjamin Franklin, received the highest scientific honor of the English speaking world, the fellowship of the Royal Society of London.

The cities in the East varied in size and lifestyle. Philadelphia was the largest at this time with 20,000 inhabitants. New York and Boston were close behind, with Charleston, South Carolina, boasting a population of about 10,000. Baltimore, Maryland, was a small coastal settlement with only a few thousand people. Recreation was frowned upon in Boston but New York was geared for entertainment and enjoyment; one fourth of all New York buildings were beer houses.

Philadelphia was reputed to be the most civilized city and was considered to be most like an English city in the mid-18th century. People spoke like the British and fashioned their homes and clothes similarly. Like the magnificent city of Williamsburg, the streets were planned. William Penn had laid out a board grid of north-south, east-west thoroughfares which were quite different from the winding streets of other towns.

After William Penn, Benjamin Franklin became the next force in molding the city. He had moved from Boston in 1723 and played a major role in Philadelphia's acquisition of paved streets, street lighting, a public library, hospitals for the mentally and physically ill, and police and fire departments. He also played a significant role in

The Little Apple: New York City in 1746.

establishing medical care for the poor and more humane prisons.

Philadelphia was a bustling port. In 1754, more than 470 vessels visited its busy harbor. Glassmaking was a Philadelphia speciality, mainly carried out by skilled German immigrants. In a market house, country men and women sold their butter, cheeses, meat, and vegetables in a tradition that has carried through to today's Reading Market in the city.

Country Life

Most farm communities in New England, New Jersey and Pennsylvania were established close to the coast. Many were actually small villages of populations between 50 and 100 families.

Houses originally had been little more than covered pits but gradually many were built in the full Swedish log cabin style. Later on, improvements included laying wooden flooring, cutting windows, and adding lofts. Eventually, the rough logs were covered with clapboard. Even the original cabins had a huge fireplace for warmth and for cooking. People ate fish from the rivers and lakes, game from the forests, pigeons, wild rabbits, squirrels, vegetables, and poultry. To take advantage of the natural daylight, farmers rose with the dawn and went to bed at sunset. Only the rich could afford candles and oil lamps on a regular basis.

English cloth was available, for those who could afford it, at the local village general store. Other English luxury imports like

tableware and pewter were also available. Other than the store and the church, the village would not have much else to offer in the way of services. Schools and doctors were scarce in the settlements.

People married young and were then likely to move further inland in search of cheap land. When a family was ready to build, the neighbors all joined in to make quick work of the construction. Building houses was the beginning of the American tradition of neighborliness and community spirit.

The most renowned of the farmers were the Pennsylvania Dutch. They were not from Holland, however. The name stems from "Deutsch" or "German" and these farmers were among the many German settlers who entered the American continent via Pennsylvania. Their barns were larger and more intricate than their houses, nestling on the hillsides to protect them from the wind. They also made improvements in the traditional Swedish log cabins and by the mid 1700s most Pennsylvania Dutch houses were built in stone.

African Descendents

Of the two million inhabitants in the colonies, almost a quarter were of African birth or background. Some white colonists were beginning to speak out against the slave trade but others became even more strict for fear of a revolt among the growing black population.

In some places, slaves could not meet together, travel from the Southern plantations, or learn to read or write. Occasional reports of revolts in the West Indies brought more restrictions. In New York more than

30 slaves were executed in 1741 because there was simply a rumor of a revolt in the planning.

Most of the slaves were in the South working on the tobacco, indigo or rice plantations but the black Africans were not confined to laboring in the fields. A South Carolina newspaper listed 28 trades in the 1730s using slave labor. In New England, Blacks were worked as farm laborers, lumberjacks, carpenters, barrelmakers, blacksmiths, millers, fishers, and shipbuilders. In New England the slaves had some rights. Trial by jury was allowed, they could buy property if they had the money, and they could attend church but were segregated.

Not all Blacks in the colonies at this time were slaves. Some were descendents of the original indentured servants. Some were freed for good service, others were freed more cynically, to avoid being provided for in old age. While some black men owned farms and businesses, none were allowed to vote during the 18th century, except for one brief period in North Carolina. Blacks could not serve in the militia in peace time but could be called on in time of war.

Education

The 18th century in the colonies saw the founding of great seats of learning. The first American university had been founded at Harvard in 1636, followed quickly by William and Mary in 1694.

Yale University was incorporated in 1701, opened a year later, and was permanently located in New Haven, Connecticut in 1716.

Princeton University was originally chartered in 1746, opened a year later, and was rechartered in 1748. It was, at that time, called the College of New Jersey and was founded by "New Light" evangelical Presbyterians to train ministers.

Columbia University was an Anglican institution founded in 1754 and originally called King's College.

The University of Pennsylvania was founded in 1740 as a charity school. Benjamin Franklin helped it become an academy in 1751. It received a charter in 1755 and ten years later was the first colonial institution to have a medical school. The college was more free than all others in the colony under ecclesiastical control.

Brown University was chartered in 1764 as Rhode Island College. Founded by Baptists, it opened in 1765 and then moved to Providence in 1770.

Rutgers University was opened in 1766 by

Dutch Reformed Church members and was originally called Queen's College.

Dartmouth College was chartered in 1769 and opened a year later. It was founded by a Yale graduate, Eleazar Wheelock, who was a force in Indian education and raised funds in England to train Indian preachers.

The second medical school in the colony opened at Columbia University in 1767.

By today's standards the colleges were small. The largest student body would have numbered around 200. Most students followed prescribed courses consisting of rhetoric, philosophy, mathematics, and the ancient classics. Modern languages and sciences were becoming more popular.

The multi-talented Benjamin Franklin helped to promote an interest in the natural sciences. His inventions – the Franklin Stove, bifocal eyeglasses, the lightning rod, and an improved glass harmonica – were all reasons for his being honored by the Royal Society in London for his scientific achievements. It was through his dangerous experi-

ment of flying a kite in a thunderstorm that Franklin became credited with having discovered electricity.

Learning and education grew with the spread of libraries and newspapers throughout the colonies. The first theater opened in Williamsburg, Virginia in 1716 and, by the middle of the century, professional English troupes of players were touring the colonies.

Internal Differences

Despite all the threats to the colonies from other forces, there was continual struggle and bickering between the colonies themselves. Border disputes were common. One of these disputes, between Maryland and Pennsylvania, was serious enough to be taken to the English Court of Chancery. Between 1763 and 1767 two of the King's surveyors charted the boundary. Their names were Charles Mason and Jeremiah Dixon. After the Revolutionary War the Mason-Dixon Line was extended to mark

The seeds of future conflict: Black slave labor on a tobacco plantation.

Harvard in 1739.

other state boundaries and it eventually indicated the separation between the slave-holding and free states, or the North-South divide.

The Great Awakening

Although religious control was lessening, even in Puritan New England, not everyone was willing to turn attention from the sacred to the secular. As East-Coast society grew richer, freer and more cosmopolitan, some felt that it had been gained at the expense of the religious and ethical values they were trying to uphold. As a result, a counter movement began against the growing tolerance. It was called the Great Awakening and was a series of religious revivals which swept through the colonies.

As early as 1719, such a revival began in Rariton, New Jersey, in Theodorus Frelinghuysen's Dutch Reformed Church. Most accounts date the beginning of the Great Awakening to 1734, when Yale graduate and minister Jonathan Edwards began to give rousing sermons on the nature of sin.

Presbyterians, Methodists, and Baptists followed suit. Only the Anglicans and the Quakers were immune from the fervor. The Methodist revivalist minister George Whitefield spread the word on a two-year tour in which he danced about the pulpits, made violent gestures, and ranted.

Such extremists were frequently anti-intellectual and some even promoted book-burning. But the movement did spawn at least four universities and contributed to the movement against slavery.

Black Africans were becoming angry about their segregation at church and in at least one case broke away and formed their own church. Although accepted as members in a few isolated churches, the black members were set apart. A Baptist congregation in Virginia provided separate chapels and a Methodist church in Philadelphia kept aside separate rows at the back. Angered by the African pews, the black members withdrew and formed the African Methodist Episcopal Church, in 1787.

Spreading the word: a Methodist preacher in Baltimore.

STRAINS ON BRITAIN'S EMPIRE

Britain was on the crest of a wave in the year 1763. The end of the Seven Years War had expanded and established an empire which stretched completely around the globe and her old rival, France, was no longer a power to be reckoned with.

British people had an extraordinary sense of pride – the sun did not set on the British Empire. Ships, loaded with goods for trade, crammed the harbors. British military and government officials traveled all over the world to bring riches home to the mother country. For many, the future could not have seemed brighter.

But crests are followed by troughs and 1763 was also the beginning of the end. Four major wars had left Britain heavily in debt. The new acquisitions of land and people all over the world added a tremendous burden on the administration and finances of the empire. In addition to the war debts, more money was needed for military defense and government administration.

Paying the British Debts of War

The British set about gathering the necessary money through a series of new taxes. The colonies were expected to contribute substantially toward the upkeep of the Empire. They had, after all, from the British Government's perspective, been established for the purpose of boosting British wealth, prosperity, and trade.

The colonial perspective was different. The colonies felt that if they were to be taxed, they should have representation in the British Parliament. "No Taxation without Representation!" was the common cry of the time.

In America the colonies had produced a number of strong, eloquent leaders who were quite capable of establishing self-governing bodies. Indeed, while Britain was heavily involved in the Seven Years War, much of the government of America had been quietly taken over by the Americans. Each colony had its own assembly. Even as far back as 1754, the Board of Trade had reported that the New York assembly "... have wrested from your Majesty's Governor, the nomination of all offices of government, the custody and direction of the public military stores, the mustering and direction of troops raised for your Majesty's service and in short almost every part of executive Government."

With the flourishing prosperity of the colonies in America it was becoming increasingly difficult for the colonists to see advantages in being involved with the mother country. What was the point of using all their hard work and business acumen to benefit a people and administration 3000 miles away?

An important factor in the developing situation, as the infant colonies grew to adolescence, was the nature of the people in the colonies. Most had left Europe because they were having a hard time or had been ill-treated. There was a deep mistrust of European administration.

Apart from the army and foreign affairs, including trade, most of America was under home rule already. Britain's grip on the colonies began to slip. A series of events and attempts at legislation prepared the ground for a full-scale revolt against Britain and the American War of Independence.

The Royal Proclamation

In the aftermath of the Seven Years War there were difficulties in the areas newly acquired by Britain from the French. An Ottowan Indian chief named Pontiac was deeply concerned that settlers would now cross the Appalachian mountains into his tribe's hunting grounds around Fort Apache and seize control of them for farming. Pontiac was also angry about the high price of trade goods, particularly ammunition. In what became known as Pontiac's Conspiracy he led several tribes on a rampage, sacking nearly all British forts west of Niagara.

The whites were furious and vengefully attacked all things Indian. In Pennsylvania a number of harmless Christian Indians were massacred in a furious retaliation. It was only after the forts had been successfully recaptured with the help of British regular troops that the two sides came to an agreement. Pontiac declared "We shall reject everything that tends to evil, and strive with each other, who shall be of the most service in keeping up that friendship that is

Attack the best form of defense: the Indian chief Pontiac rallies support against the British.

41

so happily established between us."

The problem of what to do with land west of the Appalachians still remained. Suddenly it seemed vulnerable. The fur traders of the area took the side of the Indians in wanting to keep the farmers out.

King George III was a stubborn man and by no means a clever statesman. His government ministers were equally short-sighted. Their response to the problem was the Royal Proclamation of October 7, 1763. It was designed as a method of government for all the territories Britain now controlled. The action did not achieve anything. Britain should have sent good men in to manage the large new areas but instead simply wrote divisions down on a piece of paper.

The Proclamation's most controversial point was to exclude all settlers from the disputed land west of the Proclamation Line, along the Appalachians, until a decision was made on what to do with it. The British hoped this would prevent any more Indian aggression. All of the country from the Mississippi to the Appalachians and from Florida to Quebec was reserved for the Indians. The document read "We do strictly forbid, on pain of our displeasure, all our loving subjects from making purchases or settlements whatever in that region."

But five of the 13 colonies had been given coast to coast land grants and the Royal Proclamation seemed to renege on this. The whites were furious: Britain, in their view, was preventing the natural development of the colonies.

The Proclamation also assigned boundaries to the new lands of Quebec, East Florida, West Florida, and Grenada. Labrador, with its valuable fisheries, was placed under the care of the Government of Newfoundland. Regional governments were to be set up as soon as possible and began in 1764. There was to be an Indian service, under the care of white officials. There was also a licensing and tariff system for traders. The "Plan of 1764" also tried to sort out the maze of conflicting colonial laws. It looked good on paper but was too sweeping to put into practice.

No one was satisfied. The fur traders who had wanted to prevent farming on the land found they were not allowed to go and trap there. The traders who supplied the trappers would also lose out. People who had already bought enormous areas of land in the prohibited zone were extremely angry.

Most of the land had been bought up by private companies. The largest was the Vandalia or Walpole Company, set up by Benjamin Franklin, George Croghan, and Thomas Wharton of Philadelphia. The company had shares which were distributed, often for free, to the most influential British politicians of the day, including the Walpoles themselves, George Grenville (who was to become Prime Minister of Great Britain), and Lord Camden.

The company planned to buy ten million acres of what was to become Ohio for £10,000. They had originally planned to buy one million acres but Franklin, astutely, arranged for the extra nine million as well.

Franklin and his colleagues "greased palms" in an age where bribery was a way of life with politicians. They also mounted the largest advertising campaign since the first settlers were urged to go to the Americas. There were other such plans. Franklin was involved with Sir William Johnson in an ambitious project called Charlotonia which was a proposal to purchase what is now Illinois and Wisconsin. Sir William Johnson had been in charge of Indian affairs on behalf of the British Government in 1755 and had bought as much land from the Indians as he could. John Stuart who had been in charge of the Indian affairs in the South had done the same thing. Richard Henderson was trying to secure Tennessee with his Transylvania project; General Phineas Lyman sought a crown grant for half of Tennessee and Kentucky; and Major Thomas Mant tried to get an area slightly bigger than Michigan to be settled by veterans.

At the end of the Seven Years War there was no shortage of British soldiers in the American colonies. General Amherst estimated that the colonies required a garrison of 5000 regular troops. The British Government sent 10,000. It was a way of making the colonies pay for expensive British armies. Costs of maintaining the colony rose from £70,000 in 1748 to more than £350,000 in 1764. That was when the British began to tax the colonies heavily.

The national debt in Britain was £130 million at the end of the Seven Years War. It had doubled during the war. Landowners in Britain were paying 20 per cent income tax and they wanted all British subjects to pay the same. The colonists argued that they should not be taxed without their own representation in the British Parliament.

The Sugar Act of 1764 ensured a market for sugar produced in the plantations of the British West Indies.

The Sugar Act

The first of the seriously disputed taxes was the Sugar Act, officially known as the Revenue Act of 1764, which was a duty on molasses and sugar imported from outside the British Empire. It was designed not simply to raise money but also as a trade protection measure for the sugar planters in the British West Indies. It was quite upfront about its intentions. The preamble to the Act of Parliament stated: "... a revenue be raised in your ... Majesty's dominions in America for defraying the expenses of defending, protecting and securing the same."

The Sugar Act was a strengthening of the 1733 Molasses Act. Taxes on sugar products were so high after the 1733 Act that there was widespread, open smuggling in America. In order to make smuggling less profitable the British reduced the duty to one sixth of the 1733 figure.

But the British planned to enforce the new Act. The policy of "salutary neglect" was well and truly gone. Naval patrols made spot inspections of ships entering harbors and officials searched warehouses and sometimes even private homes. Customs inspectors had widespread powers and could enter people's homes and businesses at any hour of the day or night. Rewards were offered for informing on neighbors. Many colonial merchants who had smuggled molasses all their lives were put out of business.

The Act also put a tax on expensive European imports to America like silk, wine, and linen; and it restricted the export from America of skins and furs, which could only be sent to England. In an effort to change the drinking habits of the Americans, the Act heavily taxed Madeira wine, which the wealthier colonists were very fond of, at £7 per double hogshead. British port was taxed at only ten shillings a double hogshead.

There was a tentative move to boycott all imports under the new tax laws. The *New York Gazette* of November 22, 1764 stated:

The Young Gentlemen of Yale College have unanimously agreed not to make use of any foreign spiritous liquors.... The Gentlemen of the College cannot be too much commended for setting so laudable an example. This will not only greatly diminish the Expenses of Education, but prove, as may be presumed, very favorable to the Health and Improvement of the Students. At the same Time all Gentlemen of Taste, who visit the College, will think themselves better entertained with a Good Glass of Beer or Cider, offered them on such Principles, than they could be, with the best Punch or Madeira.

The Currency Act

The second of the disputed taxes was the Currency Act. This forbade the issuing of paper money in America and required that taxes must be paid in gold or silver coins. Money had been scarce in the colonies even

Bostonians reading the controversial Stamp Act, 1766.

before Parliament passed the Currency Act. Since 1750, the balance of trade between America and Britain had shifted in Britain's favor and, in addition to shipping goods, the colonists were also sending currency shipments. It posed a real problem for the availability of currency to carry out business and pay taxes.

The Quartering Act

Hot on the heels of the Currency Act came the Quartering Act of 1765 which required the colonies to provide barracks and supplies for any British troops stationed in America.

The Stamp Act

The Sugar, Currency, and Quartering Acts did not raise enough money. Britain then imposed the first international tax on things such as newspapers, legal documents, and cards. The Stamp Act stated that all documents were taxable and in order to prove the taxes had been paid they should be stamped. The Act was expected to raise £60,000 to pay for "defending, protecting and securing the colonies." There was summary justice for offenders. An admiralty court without a jury tried each case.

The lack of any kind of Royal Commission in America to look into colonial taxation was a real problem for government policy on the issue until the War of Independence.

In the House of Commons, the politician and philosopher Edmund Burke described the reading of the Stamp Act as "languid." There was fury in America. The bill hit the professional and merchant classes the hardest. It was also regarded as a tax on reading and writing. Business crashed alarmingly and imports from Britain fell by £300,000 in just three months.

An organization of professional people called "Sons of Liberty" forced officials involved with the tax to resign and burned all stamped paper. The phrase "Sons of Liberty" had been used by Isaac Barré, a young Irish member of the British Parliament, to describe the Americans. He was one of the few to oppose the law in Britain.

A remarkable series of riots swept through the colonies. In Boston, an effigy of the local stamp distributor was hanged by a chanting mob. They then turned on the distributor himself and tore down his shop. Having tasted blood, they set off in search of Chief Justice Hutchinson, later to become Governor Hutchinson, and the royal customs collectors. The crowd looted and burned their houses.

The worst of the violence was in New York. Led by Isaac Sears, a ship's master, a crowd took to the streets on the day the Act was first enforced on November 1, 1765. The angry mob chased Lieutenant Governor Colden through the streets to the safety of a British warship and then went on a rampage. They attacked the fort at the Battery where they burned all the stamped paper and they broke into the Governor's coach house and destroyed his carriages. Then they marched up Broadway to an estate on the Hudson which was leased by an officer of the British garrison. He had, tactlessly, remarked that he would "cram the Stamp Act down the people's throats." They gutted his house, destroyed its contents, drank his liquor and wrecked his garden. The violence had an immediate effect. Officials were afraid to attempt to gather the tax. Business went on as usual without the stamping.

Britain was shocked and surprised by the colonial reaction. The colonies had been allowed a full year to come up with some alternative, acceptable form of taxation but had failed to do so.

The colonies saw the Stamp Tax as something new. In effect it was direct taxation to the British. They were already paying direct taxes to their own assemblies, where they had their own representatives and so they objected strongly to paying any direct taxes to Britain without being represented in the British Parliament. Nine of the 13 states sent representatives to a Stamp Act Congress where the Act was called "a manifest tendency to subvert the rights and liberties of the colonists." The Congress decided that the only direct taxes acceptable to the American colonists would be from their own assemblies and legislatures. However, the British Government was not about to grant representation in the House of Commons to

the Americans.

As the Americans banded together to form nonimportation agreements and ban the import of British goods, British merchant businesses began to be hit hard. Many merchants faced financial ruin and began to demand a repeal of the legislation.

In March, 1766 the British Government, at the instigation of the "great commoner" William Pitt, repealed the Stamp Act. There was widespread rejoicing in the colonies. In New York, the Sons of Liberty erected a huge flagpole, called a Liberty Pole, and gathered around it to pledge themselves to the cause of liberty.

While the Americans were rejoicing at their victory, the British moved fast and within days passed the Declaratory Act which made it clear that the British Parliament had the right of "full power and authority to make laws to bind the colonies and people of America ... in all cases whatsoever." It was a tried and trusted formula. The 1719 Irish Declaration Act had kept Ireland in bondage for years.

Few in the colonies knew about or noticed the passage of the Act. William Pitt and King George III were being praised and honored all over the Eastern seaboard. Ironically, the King and Pitt detested each other and George III had spent a great amount of his time trying to oust Pitt's party, the Whigs, from office. Statues of George III and Pitt were, however, side by side in New York's Battery. On the King's birthday, two steers were roasted and there was a free street party.

The Americans had banded together against Britain in a political contest and had won on this single issue. They began to feel their own power. In reality, the score was three to one in favor of the British.

The Townshend Acts

The debts of the Seven Years War still had to be paid and the costs of maintaining adequate forces throughout the Empire were rising.

The major lesson for the British in the Stamp Act debacle was the willingness of the American assemblies to organize the taxes themselves. But the British Empire did not learn lessons easily.

In 1767, Charles Townshend became the new Prime Minister of Britain. He was remarkably ambitious, and when he was taunted by George Grenville in Parliament that he would not dare tax the American colonies he responded immediately, "I will, I will!"

Townshend's new Government came up with a series of indirect taxes and import duties on items such as lead, glass, and tea. It might have been ideal because the Americans did not seem to have too much of a problem with indirect taxes. But the British made another classic colonial mistake – brutal enforcement. The new taxes were backed up by the Writ of Assistance, or search warrant, which gave customs officials the right to go through any ship and ransack it simply on suspicion. The colonists believed they were vulnerable to all

Charles Townshend, British Prime Minister and instigator of taxes in the American colonies.

kinds of abuse. When the news of the Townshend Acts reached America in the fall of 1767, the colonists reacted strongly to what they saw as an infringement of their rights as British citizens.

In New York, soldiers sent to enforce the Acts were denied quartering in the town. The British Government suspended New York's assembly in retaliation. Samuel Adams of Massachusetts sent a letter to all the other colonies calling for organized resistance. Maryland, Georgia, and South Carolina openly joined Massachusetts. The British immediately suspended their assemblies as well.

The British Secretary of State for the Colonies, the Earl of Hillsborough, said that the Massachusetts letter to the other colonies excited in America "an unjustifiable opposition to the constitutional authority of Parliament." Hillsborough wanted Adams transported to England for trial.

Nonimportation agreements were signed by some colonists. Once more, mobs roamed the streets, assaulting customs officials and attacking British ships. The British regular soldiers were now seen as the enemy and were taunted in the streets because of their red uniforms as "Bloody Back!," "Lobster" and finally the name that stuck, "Redcoat!"

The American assemblies were concerned about the violence. They wanted to stop trouble in the streets without backing down on the issue of taxes.

James Otis wrote in the *Boston Gazette*: "The Tax! The Tax! is undoubtedly at present the matter of grievance; and this I think a great one; But redress is to be fought in a legal and constitutional way."

John Dickinson of Pennsylvania wrote of Britain:

Moderation has been the rule of her conduct. But now, a generous, humane people, that so often has protected the liberty of strangers is inflamed to tear a privilege from her own children, which if executed, must, in their opinion, sink them into slaves: And for what? For a pernicious power, not necessary to her ... but horridly dreadful and detestable to them.

However, Dickinson advised that resistance should be conducted "peaceably-prudently-firmly-jointly." His book *Letters from a farmer in Pennsylvania to the Inhabitants of the British Colonies*, which was serialized in the *Pennsylvania Chronicle and Universal Advertiser*, was an instant success with the colonists. There was no greater work on American political theory until Thomas Paine's *Common Sense* in 1776.

Once again Americans were calling for representation in the British Parliament. Governor Bernard of Massachusetts Bay felt it was the only solution. Massachusetts was regarded as the hotbed of dissent in America. The Puritan ethic of the inhabitants tended to clash with the values of Europe at the time.

Governor Bernard of Massachusetts was becoming increasingly unpopular because of his efforts to send Samuel Adams to England for trial. Eleven members of the Massachusetts council wrote to the Secretary of State for the Colonies, calling for Bernard's removal from office. They accused him of "aiming at exorbitant and uncontrollable power, with a desire to represent things in the worst light, with unmanly dissimulation and with untruth," as well as "want of candour, with indecent, illiberal, and most abusive treatment" of them. Bernard left in 1769 and was replaced by his deputy, Hutchinson.

The Boston Massacre

Although martial law had not been declared, a large force of British soldiers and ships was sent to Boston. The soldiers could only be used with permission of a magistrate but the Bostonians loathed them. The presence of the English soldiers was attacked in newspapers, they were abused on the street, and occasionally there were fistfights.

The tension mounted and every now and then, there would be skirmishes between the soldiers and the Bostonians. Insults, snowballs, and stones were often thrown. But eventually the soldiers' patience snapped. On March 2, 1770, some ropemakers and a band of soldiers had had a more serious brawl than usual. The commander of the British garrison wrote a pained letter of complaint to Governor Hutchinson. But that was just the beginning.

On March 5, there was a cry of "Fire!" It was a false alarm but crowds took to the streets. They were in an ugly mood and started abusing a guard at the customs house and then began to throw stones at him. Some claimed the guard had hit a young boy earlier in the evening. A crowd of about 60, some armed with blunt instruments, moved menacingly on the lone guard, who shouted for help. A Captain Preston led six men, on the double, to assist the guard. The soldiers were quickly surrounded by the mob, chanting "Redcoats! Redcoats! Redcoats!" Someone from the crowd moved forward and prodded one of the soldiers and the soldier fired into the crowd and killed an escaped slave called Crispus Attucks. All the other soldiers fired at close range. No one is sure whether they fired in panic or whether Preston gave the order. Two more people were killed outright, two others were mortally wounded, and another six were injured.

Bostonians reacted immediately as news of the massacre spread. Church bells rang and people streamed into the streets beating drums and banging on pots and pans. Somehow, the excitement died down without further bloodshed. Captain Preston and his men were arrested and held in prison, probably as much for their own protection as to appease the crowds.

The next day, at a town meeting, Samuel

The "Boston Massacre," March 5, 1770.

Adams, whom the British had marked as a troublemaker since he sent his circular letter to the other colonies over the Townshend Acts, demanded the withdrawal of the English regiments from the city. The Governor agreed. The people of Boston also demanded that Preston and his soldiers be put on trial. The Governor agreed to that as well.

The defense attorneys for the soldiers were Josiah Quincy and John Adams, who was to become the second President of the United States. Neither was a lover of the British but they were good lawyers and believed in fair trial. They wanted to make it a test case and they did well for their clients. Two of the soldiers were given light sentences for manslaughter and the rest walked free.

Samuel Adams was a quiet, softspoken man with a slightly quavering voice. He was at his best writing pamphlets and dealing with committees. It was Otis and Joseph Warren, two other members of the Sons of Liberty, who delivered most of the public speeches.

Economic Sanctions

The British merchant traders were, once more, feeling the effects of the American ban on British imports. The nonimportation agreements to protest the Townshend Acts were working. The new Prime Minister of Britain, Lord Frederick North, was deeply concerned at the widening rift in relations and repealed the Townshend Acts in 1770. America breathed a sigh of relief.

There was a constant ebb and flow of measures and countermeasures afterward. King George III said that there must "always be one tax, to keep up the right." In the law which replaced the Townshend Acts there was a small import duty on tea.

In 1772, colonists from Rhode Island decided to attack *The Gaspee*, a ship heading for England carrying taxes for the British exchequer. The ship was destroyed. British authorities rounded up suspects and despite the fact that Rhode Island was a self-governing colony, they transported all the subjects to Britain for trial.

The next move came from Britain. The Government decided to pay the wages of the judges and Governor of Massachusetts, making them answerable to Britain rather than to Massachusetts. Samuel Adams reacted cleverly by setting up the Committee of Correspondence. This was a kind of public relations organization designed to inform the world of events in and around Boston and to influence public opinion. It was so successful that other colonies began similar schemes.

While King George III was especially obstinate about the American colonies, the colonists were just as stubborn in response. When the King insisted on the paltry tax on tea in order to maintain his right to tax the Americans, the colonists promptly stopped drinking and importing tea.

The British East India Company suffered from the drop in sales and was quickly in financial straits. This hurt many members of Parliament who held substantial shares in

the company. As Benjamin Franklin had discovered, such a boycott was the only way that large commercial projects could get the backing they needed at Parliamentary level.

The British East India Company also had a very good relationship with the British Army. The Army had been called out to support the company's commercial problems in the past.

The British Parliament gave the company a loan of public money, under the Tea Act of 1773, to help move the vast stockpiles of tea in their warehouses, and then came up with a law which allowed the company to lower the price of tea to the consumer without loss of profits to the company. Effectively, the company was allowed to cut out the middle men, the British merchants, and sell directly to the colonies. The company and the British Parliament thought the Americans would be glad to get the attractively priced tea.

But, once again, the British misjudged the mood in America. The Americans saw the move as a tea monopoly for the British East

After the tea party: this 1774 cartoon shows Bostonians forcing tea down the throat of a tarred and feathered tax collector.

India Company. Anyone who was involved in importing tea and did not buy from the British East India Company would go out of business because of the subsidized British prices. But what if the British Government granted more monopolies of this kind? What would happen to American trade?

There were riots all along the East Coast. Tea was deliberately stored in damp cellars in Charlestown so that it would rot. New York and Philadelphia blockaded their harbors so that the East India Company vessels could not land. A full ship of tea leaves was set on fire in Annapolis. The last straw came in 1773 when colonists, dressed as Indians, crept on board ships in Boston Harbor and destroyed 342 chests of tea. This was the Boston Tea Party. Many colonists disapproved of the violent actions.

But Governor Tryon of New York wrote to

the Earl of Dartmouth to say that he could not see any way to land the tea except "under the Protection of the Point of the Bayonet and Muzzle of the Cannon, and even then I do not see how the Sales and Consumption could be effected."

The British were now incensed. Destruction of property was a far greater sin than nonpayment of taxes. Throwing away good tea was the absolute, bitter end. The British felt they had been taking a conciliatory role since the Seven Years War in attempting to smooth over any conflicts. The Boston Tea Party was an embarrassment. The Parliament passed the so-called Intolerable Acts to suppress unrest and make an example of Massachusetts. The Port of Boston would be shut down until the price of the dumped tea was paid; town meetings would be stopped and the Massachusetts Charter of 1691 was effectively revoked; a new and powerful military Quartering Act was brought into being; and people suspected of crimes under British law would be transported to London and tried there.

General Thomas Gage was made Governor of Massachusetts and given more soldiers to help him. At the same time the British finally made a firm decision on the lands west of the Appalachian mountains and denied Massachusetts, Connecticut and Virginia their coast-to-coast grants by extending the borders of Quebec as far west as the Mississippi River. The Quebec Act guaranteed the same structure of French law to the old French lands as well as religious freedoms to practicing Roman Catholics.

Raising the minutemen: Paul Revere rides into legend during the night of April 18, 1775.

Moves Towards Independence

The Continental Congress

The First Continental Congress was held in Philadelphia on September 5, 1774. It was not a revolutionary body but was an attempt to organize against the Intolerable Acts. John Adams came from Massachusetts, Thomas Mifflin from Pennsylvania, Stephen Hopkins from Rhode Island, Richard Henry Lee and Patrick Henry from Virginia, and Christopher Gadsden from South Carolina. There were moderates like Peyton Randolph and George Washington of Virginia, John Dickinson of Pennsylvania, and the Rutledges of South Carolina. There was also a smattering of conservatives, especially from New York. All states were represented except Georgia.

The Congress called for a British subject's "rights, liberties and immunities" and for "free and exclusive power of legislation in their own several legislatures." Once more, they brought in the weapon of nonimportation agreements, as well as exportation agreements. They were determined to make a stand. As the business was wound up on the last day's debate, they agreed to meet again in the spring of 1775 if the Intolerable Acts were not withdrawn. Some of the colonists began to talk of defending their rights by force of arms if necessary.

The American War of Independence Begins

There was deep suspicion on both sides. General Gage, the British commander in Boston, used spies to gather information on the rebellious colonists, who were now being called Patriots. His spies quickly discovered that many Patriots were drilling openly on the village greens, cleaning their guns and storing powder and ammunition. They were preparing for battle.

Gage decided that he might be able to prevent problems if he moved quickly. He planned to move on the village of Concord and a number of others where the colonists were storing their ammunition. Gage moved his men out of the heavily defended city at night on April 18, 1775 but the British were being watched also. Two lights shone briefly from the steeple of the Old North Church in Boston. It was a signal to waiting Patriots in Charlestown that the British were on the move. The man who was monitoring the British movements rowed across to Charlestown and, along with his comrades, began a ride into history. His name was Paul Revere. He, William (Billy) Dawes Jr., and Dr. Samuel Prescott rode through the night wakening everyone with a cry of alarm and pounding on farmhouse doors to raise the "minutemen," the Patriots who had pledged to be ready to fight at a minute's notice.

The British troops had rowed across the River Charles and reached Lexington by dawn. They were faced by a gathering of militia on the village green. The commander of the British patrol, Major Pitcairn, ordered the colonists to drop their weapons and leave the green. The colonists began to move off the green but held onto their weapons. Someone fired a shot and the British troops immediately fired a number of rounds without waiting for orders. When the smoke cleared, eight colonists were dead and another ten were wounded.

The British marched on to Concord, cut down a liberty pole, set fire to the court-

house and destroyed some of the colonists' weapons. But when they were confronted by Patriots at Concord's North Bridge, they withdrew and headed back to Boston.

The countryside was swarming with angry colonists by this point. The British were attacked from all sides. The British commander wrote afterwards, "There is not a stone wall or house ... from whence the Rebels did not fire upon us." The battered remains of the British force arrived back in Boston with 73 dead, 174 wounded, and a further 26 missing.

The city was surrounded that night by 16,000 militia and ringed by the bonfires of rebellion. Boston was a stalemate. But in May came the news that the "Green Mountain Boys" of Vermont, led by Ethan Allen, had captured the British forts of Ticonderoga and Crown Point. The powder, shot and cannons from the forts were on their way to Boston to aid the Patriots.

The Second Continental Congress

On May 10, the Second Continental Congress met, as arranged. The situation was hotly debated. Samuel Adams of Massachusetts and Patrick Henry of Virginia argued in favor of declaring independence but the more conservative factions led by Pennsylvania's John Dickinson won. The Congress assured the King that they had not "raised armies with ambitious designs of separating from Great Britain." But the Congress made clear that tyranny would be resisted by force, if necessary, and appointed George Washington of Virginia as Commander in Chief of the Continental Army.

The Battle of Bunker Hill

Before Washington could take control of the Patriot forces besieging Boston, the British, under General Gage, decided to attack the massed colonial militia outside the city. The battle, which has gone down in folklore as the Battle of Bunker Hill, was actually fought on nearby Breed's Hill.

The Battle of Bunker Hill began on June 17, 1775 when Gage attacked the colonists in three bold assaults. The Patriots withdrew when their ammunition was gone. They had lost 450 men. But the cost of victory for the British was very high. Over 1000 Redcoats were dead or wounded on the battlefield.

King George III proclaimed the colonists to be rebels, ordered a tight blockade of Boston and hired 10,000 German mercenaries from Hesse to help in the fight against the Americans.

The Struggle Continues

The Second Continental Congress sought help from several European countries including Spain, France, and the Netherlands. They also tried to enlist the support of the French Canadians but were not successful.

But early in 1776, George Washington managed to take the strategic Dorchester Heights overlooking Boston. The British fleet now lay anchored and vulnerable below him. Realizing their position, the

The first shots of the War of Independence: Patriots and Redcoats clash at Lexington, Massachusetts, April 19, 1775.

British under a new commander, Sir William Howe, abandoned Boston and sailed for Halifax on March 17, 1776 with the entire British garrison and about 1000 civilians who had stayed loyal to the British King.

In another pivotal victory, Patriot leader James Moore defeated an army of 2000 Loyalists. The Loyalists were supposed to have joined with Lord Charles Cornwallis and Sir Henry Clinton at Wilmington and Brunswick in North Carolina. The Patriots knew about the plan and ambushed the Loyalists at Moore's Creek Bridge. They ripped up the planking on the bridge, greased the poles below with soap and tallow, and then lay in wait for the Loyalists. As the weary Loyalist soldiers, who had marched all night, tried to struggle across they were cut down in a storm of fire.

A total of 850 Loyalists were captured along with weapons, wagons, supplies, and a large amount of gold. When Cornwallis, Clinton and a British fleet headed by Sir Peter Parker arrived, they found no Loyalist troops waiting and sailed away again. The plan to keep South Carolina loyal was shattered.

Thomas Paine

Common Sense, a pamphlet by Thomas Paine, was one of the inspirations to the colonists who wanted to declare independence. Published in January 1776, it was an inflammatory document. Paine wrote, in ringing tones, that America had grown into a new and different nation with interests of its own. "... Arms, as the last resource, must decide the contest.... Everything that is right or reasonable pleads for separation. The blood of the slain, the weeping voice of nature cries , *'Tis Time to Part!'* "

The Declaration of Independence

There was a great deal of logical argument to support a declaration of independence. As citizens of an independent nation, captured Patriot soldiers could demand to be treated as prisoners of war and not to be shot as rebels; the Patriot governments could seize the property of all Americans who stayed loyal to the British Crown; and the chance of raising support among the states of Europe for a war of independence was greater.

On June 7, 1776, Richard Henry Lee of Virginia introduced a resolution to the Second Continental Congress declaring the United Colonies to be independent. On June 11, before voting on the motion, the Congress appointed a committee of five to write a formal declaration of independence. The five were Thomas Jefferson, Benjamin Franklin, John Adams, Robert R. Livingston and Roger Sherman. Jefferson was asked by the others to draft the document.

On June 28, the committee presented Jefferson's declaration, with a few changes by Franklin and Adams. But the Congress decided to debate and vote on Lee's motion first. On July 2, the motion was adopted and the United States of America was declared to be independent of Britain.

In June 1776, Congress appointed a committee to draft a declaration formally severing America's links with Great Britain. Thomas Jefferson was delegated to prepare the first draft of the document. (Significantly, one of the changes made to Jefferson's original wording by the committee was the deletion of a clause attacking Britain for its support of the African slave trade, which Jefferson, despite being a slave owner himself, condemned as "an assemblage of horrors".) Congress approved the declaration at Philadelphia on July 4, 1776. The first of the rebels to put his signature to it was the President of the Congress, John Hancock, who wrote his name in bold flourishing strokes, in order, he said that King George could read it without spectacles.

IN CONGRESS, JULY 4, 1776.

The unanimous Declaration of the thirteen united States of America,

When in the Course of human events, it becomes necessary for one people to dissolve the political bands which have connected them with another, and to assume among the powers of the earth, the separate and equal station to which the Laws of Nature and of Nature's God entitle them, a decent respect to the opinions of mankind requires that they should declare the causes which impel them to the separation. — We hold these truths to be self-evident, that all men are created equal, that they are endowed by their Creator with certain unalienable Rights, that among these are Life, Liberty and the pursuit of Happiness. — That to secure these rights, Governments are instituted among Men, deriving their just powers from the consent of the governed, — That whenever any Form of Government becomes destructive of these ends, it is the Right of the People to alter or to abolish it, and to institute new Government, laying its foundation on such principles, and organizing its powers in such form, as to them shall seem most likely to effect their Safety and Happiness. Prudence, indeed, will dictate that Governments long established should not be changed for light and transient causes; and accordingly all experience hath shewn, that mankind are more disposed to suffer, while evils are sufferable, than to right themselves by abolishing the forms to which they are accustomed. But when a long train of abuses and usurpations, pursuing invariably the same Object, evinces a design to reduce them under absolute Despotism, it is their right, it is their duty, to throw off such Government, and to provide new Guards for their future security. — Such has been the patient sufferance of these Colonies; and such is now the necessity which constrains them to alter their former Systems of Government. The history of the present King of Great Britain is a history of repeated injuries and usurpations, all having in direct object the establishment of an absolute Tyranny over these States. To prove this, let Facts be submitted to a candid world. —

He has refused his Assent to Laws, the most wholesome and necessary for the public good. — He has forbidden his Governors to pass Laws of immediate and pressing importance, unless suspended in their operation till his Assent should be obtained; and when so suspended, he has utterly neglected to attend to them. — He has refused to pass other Laws for the accommodation of large districts of people, unless those people would relinquish the right of Representation in the Legislature, a right inestimable to them and formidable to tyrants only. — He has called together legislative bodies at places unusual, uncomfortable, and distant from the depository of their public Records, for the sole purpose of fatiguing them into compliance with his measures. — He has dissolved Representative Houses repeatedly, for opposing with manly firmness his invasions on the rights of the people. — He has refused for a long time, after such dissolutions, to cause others to be elected; whereby the Legislative powers, incapable of Annihilation, have returned to the People at large for their exercise; the State remaining in the mean time exposed to all the dangers of invasion from without, and convulsions within. — He has endeavoured to prevent the population of these States; for that purpose obstructing the Laws for Naturalization of Foreigners; refusing to pass others to encourage their migrations hither, and raising the conditions of new Appropriations of Lands. — He has obstructed the Administration of Justice, by refusing his Assent to Laws for establishing Judiciary powers. — He has made Judges dependent on his Will alone, for the tenure of their offices, and the amount and payment of their salaries. — He has erected a multitude of New Offices, and sent hither swarms of Officers to harrass our people, and eat out their substance. — He has kept among us, in times of peace, Standing Armies without the Consent of our legislatures. — He has affected to render the Military independent of and superior to the Civil power. — He has combined with others to subject us to a jurisdiction foreign to our constitution, and unacknowledged by our laws; giving his Assent to their Acts of pretended Legislation: — For Quartering large bodies of armed troops among us: — For protecting them, by a mock Trial, from punishment for any Murders which they should commit on the Inhabitants of these States: — For cutting off our Trade with all parts of the world: — For imposing Taxes on us without our Consent: — For depriving us in many cases, of the benefits of Trial by Jury: — For transporting us beyond Seas to be tried for pretended offences: — For abolishing the free System of English Laws in a neighbouring Province, establishing therein an Arbitrary government, and enlarging its Boundaries so as to render it at once an example and fit instrument for introducing the same absolute rule into these Colonies: — For taking away our Charters, abolishing our most valuable Laws, and altering fundamentally the Forms of our Governments: — For suspending our own Legislatures, and declaring themselves invested with power to legislate for us in all cases whatsoever. — He has abdicated Government here, by declaring us out of his Protection and waging War against us. — He has plundered our seas, ravaged our Coasts, burnt our towns, and destroyed the lives of our people. — He is at this time transporting large Armies of foreign Mercenaries to compleat the works of death, desolation and tyranny, already begun with circumstances of Cruelty & perfidy scarcely paralleled in the most barbarous ages, and totally unworthy the Head of a civilized nation. — He has constrained our fellow Citizens taken Captive on the high Seas to bear Arms against their country, to become the executioners of their friends and Brethren, or to fall themselves by their Hands. — He has excited domestic insurrections amongst us, and has endeavoured to bring on the inhabitants of our frontiers, the merciless Indian Savages, whose known rule of warfare, is an undistinguished destruction of all ages, sexes and conditions. In every stage of these Oppressions We have Petitioned for Redress in the most humble terms: Our repeated Petitions have been answered only by repeated injury. A Prince, whose character is thus marked by every act which may define a Tyrant, is unfit to be the ruler of a free people. Nor have We been wanting in attentions to our British brethren. We have warned them from time to time of attempts by their legislature to extend an unwarrantable jurisdiction over us. We have reminded them of the circumstances of our emigration and settlement here. We have appealed to their native justice and magnanimity, and we have conjured them by the ties of our common kindred to disavow these usurpations, which, would inevitably interrupt our connections and correspondence. They too have been deaf to the voice of justice and of consanguinity. We must, therefore, acquiesce in the necessity, which denounces our Separation, and hold them, as we hold the rest of mankind, Enemies in War, in Peace Friends. —

We, therefore, the Representatives of the united States of America, in General Congress, Assembled, appealing to the Supreme Judge of the world for the rectitude of our intentions, do, in the Name, and by Authority of the good People of these Colonies, solemnly publish and declare, That these United Colonies are, and of Right ought to be Free and Independent States; that they are Absolved from all Allegiance to the British Crown, and that all political connection between them and the State of Great Britain, is and ought to be totally dissolved; and that as Free and Independent States, they have full Power to levy War, conclude Peace, contract Alliances, establish Commerce, and to do all other Acts and Things which Independent States may of right do. — And for the support of this Declaration, with a firm reliance on the protection of divine Providence, we mutually pledge to each other our Lives, our Fortunes and our sacred Honor.

John Hancock

Button Gwinnett
Lyman Hall
Geo Walton.

Wm Hooper
Joseph Hewes,
John Penn

Edward Rutledge.

Thos Heyward Junr.
Thomas Lynch Junr.
Arthur Middleton

Samuel Chase
Wm Paca
Thos. Stone
Charles Carroll of Carrollton

George Wythe
Richard Henry Lee
Th Jefferson
Benja Harrison
Thos Nelson jr.
Francis Lightfoot Lee
Carter Braxton

Robt morris
Benjamin Rush
Benja Franklin
John Morton
Geo Clymer
Jas. Smith.
Geo. Taylor
James Wilson
Geo. Ross
Caesar Rodney
Geo Read
Tho M:Kean

Wm Floyd
Phil. Livingston
Frans. Lewis
Lewis Morris

Richd Stockton
Jno Witherspoon
Fras. Hopkinson
John Hart
Abra Clark

Josiah Bartlett
Wm Whipple
Saml Adams
John Adams
Robt Treat Paine
Elbridge Gerry
Step Hopkins
William Ellery
Roger Sherman
Sam el Huntington
Wm Williams
Oliver Wolcott
Matthew Thornton

"**Y**ESTERDAY" wrote John Adams to his wife on July 3, 1776, "the greatest question was decided, which ever was debated in America, and a greater perhaps, never was or will be decided among men." The question to which he referred was indeed a momentous one: the previous day the Continental Congress had approved a resolution that the Thirteen Colonies of America should shake off their colonial status and become truly independent of Britain.

Meanwhile, in a boarding house in Philadelphia, the Virginian Thomas Jefferson had been drafting a document which was to become one of the milestones of Western democracy. On July 4, the day after Adams wrote his letter, the Declaration of Independence was accepted by Congress. After years of simmering revolt, and more than 14 months after the fateful shot had been fired

at Lexington, America celebrated its first Independence Day.

The Revolutionary War

The celebrations were to be short-lived. In justifying rebellion against a government which had betrayed its subjects, the fledgling nation was defying the greatest military and economic power in the world. Even as the ink dried on the signatures at the bottom of the Declaration, some 35,000 British troops were converging on New York, where George Washington, with a force little more than half that size, was bracing himself for the attack. By the end of September New York was in the hands of the British army, and by the end of the year Washington's weary and demoralized troops; many of whom had simply drifted

Crowds gather in Philadelphia to celebrate the declaration of American Independence.

home to their farms when the going got tough, had been forced back to the banks of the Delaware at Trenton, New Jersey. Of his 18,000 men only 5000 remained.

But if the outlook appeared bleak for America at the end of Independence year, Great Britain too had military and political problems. For a start, she had to ferry all her troops over 3000 miles of ocean in ships which could take up to ten weeks to make the journey. The officers who were sent to bring the colonies back into the fold were often incompetent and sometimes showed a sneaking sympathy for the rebel cause, and years of European war had left her with no other major power to turn to for support.

Perhaps most significant of all, she faced in America a type of warfare very different from the kind her soldiers were used to. Guerrilla war in the countryside meant that every bush and every tree could conceal an enemy. The only way to stamp out the rebellion altogether would be to occupy the entire inhospitable country – a military task that was to prove beyond even the vast imperial means of Great Britain.

Enter the French

Despite the loss of Philadelphia to the British after the Battle of Brandywine Creek on September 9, 1777, by the end of the year the tide had begun, slowly but surely, to turn in America's favor. News of the rebels' victory over Burgoyne's forces at Saratoga in October spread through Europe like wildfire and finally convinced the French that it was time to translate their covert support for the revolution into an open alliance.

The entry of the French on to the American stage changed the complexion of the war completely. Not only did it bring the rebels new naval and fire power; it also extended the theater of war to the Carib-bean, where prized British possessions were now at risk.

In the short term, though, it simply stiffened Britain's resolve to smash the revolution. By the end of 1778 General Sir Henry Clinton's forces had established a dangerous bridgehead in the South by occupying Savannah, Georgia, and throughout the following year the British concentrated on marshaling loyalist militias from among the Georgians themselves. The royal Governor of the colony returned from London to take up his old post, and December 1779 saw Clinton gathering his forces for a concerted assault on South Carolina, from where he hoped to march North to total victory. Even with French support the rebels seemed powerless to stop him. As the decade closed – the decade in which the seeds were sown of what was to become the most powerful nation in the world – the prospect of "life, liberty and the pursuit of happiness" seemed remote indeed from its three million war-stricken people.

The Liberty Bell was rung in Philadelphia to mark the reading of the Declaration.

1776

JAN 1 Gen. George Washington raises 13-stripe Continental flag before headquarters at Cambridge, Mass.

5 New Hampshire adopts first state constitution

10 *Common Sense* by Thomas Paine published in Philadelphia, Pa

MAR 1 France proposes to Spain secret measures to aid American colonies

3 Silas Deane appointed colonial agent to France

4-5 Americans capture Dorchester Heights, overlooking Boston Harbor

7-17 British, led by Gen. William Howe, leave Boston and join 1000 Loyalists for trip to Nova Scotia

26 South Carolina adopts state constitution

APR 6 Congress orders ports open to all nations except Great Britain

12 North Carolina Provincial Assembly is first to instruct delegates in Congress to support independence of American colonies from Great Britain

MAY 2 French King Louis XVI consigns military aid to American revolutionaries

9-16 Colonial navy occupies Nassau and captures large military arsenal

10 Congress issues resolution authorizing each of 13 colonies to form new provincial government

JUN 7 Virginia delegate to Congress presents resolution calling for independence

11 Congress appoints John Adams, Benjamin Franklin, Thomas Jefferson, Roger R. Livingston and Roger Sherman as committee to compose declaration of independence; Jefferson to prepare draft of document

12 Congress appoints committee headed by John Dickinson, to prepare draft plan of confederation

12 Virginia Convention endorses first state bill of rights as part of Virginia constitution

28 Draft of Declaration of Independence presented to Congress for consideration; revisions made by Adams and Franklin

29 Virginia adopts state constitution

JUL 2 10,000 British soldiers land on Staten Island, NY

2 Congress adopts Virginia resolution calling for independence; New York abstains from vote

2 New Jersey adopts state constitution

2 New Jersey passes first colonial statute granting women's suffrage

4 Declaration of Independence adopted by Continental Congress, signed by John Hancock

6 Declaration of Independence published for first time in *Pennsylvania Evening Post*

12 John Dickinson presents plan for confederation of 13 colonies to Congress

13 *Pennsylvania Evening Post* opposes use of titles of rank by inhabitants of America

AUG 2 Declaration of Independence signed in Philadelphia, Pa, by majority of Congress

10 Adams, Franklin and Jefferson suggest 'E Pluribus Unum' as motto for seal of US

The American Revolution

The revolution which swept through the Thirteen Colonies of America in the 1770s had its roots in the British Government's imposition of swingeing taxes on the American people without allowing them political representation. Resentment was focused on King George III, who was widely seen as the nub of a conspiracy to deprive the colonists of their liberties, and statues of whom were torn down all over America (top left). In 1775 the rebellion in the colonies flared into outright war, as patriotic "minutemen," who had been drilling for some time in towns and villages throughout the country (inset right), clashed with British Redcoats at Lexington, near Concord, in Massachusetts. The following year, after lengthy debate in Congress, America unilaterally declared her independence from Britain. At that time John Adams estimated that only a third of the American people actively supported independence, while a third

were undecided and another third (on whom the British General Sir William Howe drew for loyalist support – below left) actively opposed it. In the ensuing war, however, British atrocities and acts of American bravery such as those at the bloody Battle of Bunker Hill on the Charlestown Peninsula (background), rallied many doubters to the rebels' cause. By the time the British General, Lord Cornwallis, surrendered his army at Yorktown in 1781 (top right), the war had killed and maimed a higher proportion of Americans than any other conflict on American soil except the Civil War, but the Thirteen Colonies had become the independent States of America.

CHA

BOSTON

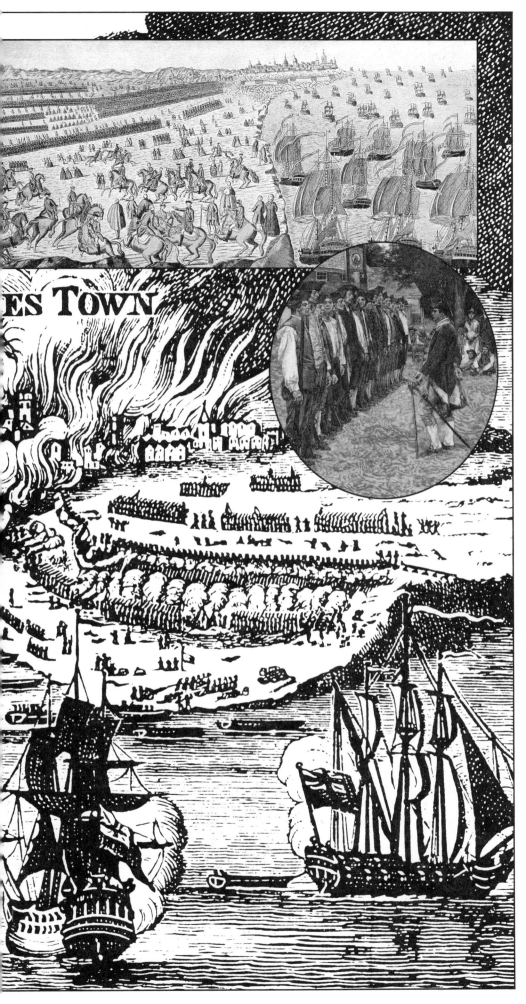

ES TOWN

27-29 In Battle of Long Island, patriots defeated by British under Gen. Howe

SEP Shakers' Society establishes first settlement in United Colonies at Watervliet, NY

6 First submarine attack, by David Bushnell's *Turtle,* launched unsuccessfully against British flagship *Eagle* in New York Bay

9 Congress resolves that words 'United States' replace words 'United Colonies'

11 John Adams, Benjamin Franklin and Edmund Rutledge meet with Adm. Lord Howe in peace conference on Staten Island, NY; Gen. Howe demands revocation of Declaration of Independence

15 British occupy New York City

21 Fire sweeps NYC, destroys nearly 300 buildings

21 Delaware adopts state constitution

26 Congress appoints Benjamin Franklin, Thomas Jefferson and Silas Deane as diplomatic commissioners to negotiate treaties with European nations

28 Pennsylvania adopts state constitution

OCT 9 Spanish missionaries on California coast establish mission San Francisco de Asis

28 In Battle of White Plains, NY, British forces inflict heavy casualties on Gen. Washington's army

NOV 10 First salute to US flag occurs when volley of 11 guns fired by Fort Orange on St Eustatius in Dutch West Indies

11 Maryland adopts state constitution

DEC 5 Phi Beta Kappa Society founded at College of William and Mary

18 North Carolina adopts state constitution

25 Gen. Washington crosses Delaware River for surprise attack on British-Hession garrison at Trenton, NJ

26 In Battle of Trenton, NJ, Washington's forces inflict major defeat upon British

Also this year

★ Philadelphia Friends' Meeting excludes slaveholders

★ John Leacock's political satire *The Fall of British Tyranny, or American Liberty Triumphant* published

1777

JAN 3 Battle of Princeton, NJ, Washington's forces defeat three British regiments

15 Residents of New Hampshire Grants declare independence, and establish 'republic of New Connecticut'

FEB 5 Georgia adopts state constitution

APR 20 New York adopts state constitution

MAY 20 In Treaty of De Witts Corner, Cherokees surrender all territory in South Carolina

JUN 14 Congress adopts Stars and Stripes, displaying 13 stars and 13 stripes, as American flag

17 British Gen. John Burgoyne begins planned invasion of colonies from Canada with 7700 men

JUL 12 'Republic' of New Connecticut renames itself Vermont and adopts constitution mandating manhood suffrage and banning slavery

20 In Treaty of Long Island, NY, Overhill Cherokees cede all of western North Carolina territory east of Blue Ridge Mountains and Nolichucky River

AUG 4 Gen. Horatio Gates replaces Gen. Philip Schyler as commander of Continental Army of the North

16 In Battle of Bennington, Vermont, militiamen, reinforced by Massachusetts troops, defeat British

SEP 9-11 Battle of Brandywine at Chadd's Ford, Pa., Washington's force of 10,500 driven toward Philadelphia by 15,000 British under Howe

19 In First Battle of Saratoga at Bemis Heights, NY, American forces defeat British under Gen. Burgoyne

26 British under Howe occupy Philadelphia, Pa

OCT 7 In Second Battle of Saratoga at Bemis Heights, NY, American forces defeat British

17 British Gen. Burgoyne surrenders entire force to Gates in 'Convention of Saratoga'

NOV San Jose, first secular community in California, established on Guadalupe River

15 Congress endorses Articles of Confederation

Independence Day

The Declaration of Independence, drafted by Thomas Jefferson of Virginia and slightly amended by Benjamin Franklin and John Adams, was adopted by Congress on July 4, 1776 (above). A seminal document in the history of modern democracy, it declared: "We hold these truths to be self-evident, that all men are created equal, that they are endowed by their Creator with certain unalienable Rights, that among these are Life, Liberty and the pursuit of Happiness."

The Stars and Stripes

The American flag, which was to become a potent symbol for the people of the newly-formed republic, was designed by Judge Francis Hopkinson of Philadelphia, a painter, poet, and musician, as well as one of the signatories of the Declaration of Independence. Thirty-seven stars were to be added to the original thirteen over the next two centuries.

Ticonderoga

Ticonderoga, on Lake Champlain, where Ethan Allen's "Green Mountain Boys" seized the British fort on May 10, 1775.

Thomas Paine (1737–1809)

One of the most influential thinkers and writers of the age, Tom Paine electrified American readers with his arguments for independence in the pamphlet *Common Sense*.

16-20 British capture Fort Mifflin and Fort Mercer, gaining complete control of Delaware River region

17 Articles of Confederation submitted to states for ratification

28 John Adams appointed Commissioner to France

DEC 17 France recognizes American independence

23 Conway Cabal, plot to discredit Gen. Washington and replace with Gen. Gates, revealed

1778

FEB 6 Franco-American Treaty of Amity and Commerce and Treaty of Alliance signed in Paris

MAR 19 South Carolina adopts state constitution

MAY 8 Gen. Henry Clinton replaces Gen. Howe as commander of all British forces in American colonies

30 Settlement of Cobleskill, NY, burned by Iroquois Indians instigated by Loyalists

JUN 17 Congress rejects offers of British Peace Commission, insists on independence

18 British evacuate Philadelphia

27-28 In Battle of Monmouth, NJ, Gens. Washington and Clinton fight to a stand-off

JUL 3-4 Force of Loyalists and Indians massacres settlers in Wyoming Valley, northern Pennsylvania

9 British naval force raids and burns Fairfield, Conn.

10 France declares war against Great Britain

AUG 30 American forces withdraw from Rhode Island

SEP 14 Congress appoints Benjamin Franklin as American diplomatic representative to France

NOV 11 Force of Loyalists led by Walter Butler and Indians led by Mohawk Chief Joseph Brant massacres settlers of Cherry Valley, NY

DEC 10 John Jay chosen as president of Continental Congress

29 British capture Savannah, Ga

1779

JAN 29 British capture Augusta, Ga

APR 1-30 North Carolina and Virginia troops attack Chickamauga villages in Tennessee in retaliation for Indian raids on colonial settlements

MAY 10 British capture and burn Portsmouth and Norfolk, Va

JUN 1 British capture Stony Point and Verplanck Point, NY

16 Spain declares war against Great Britain, but makes no alliance with America

JUL 5-11 New York Gov. William Tyron leads Loyalist expedition to raid Connecticut coastal towns

15 American Gen. Anthony Wayne recaptures Stony Point, NY

AUG March against Six Nations: Americans under Gen. John Sullivan destroy Indian villages in Genesee Valley, NY

19 American Maj. Henry Lee drives British from Paulus Hook, last major garrison in New Jersey

29 Americans under Gens. Sullivan and James Clinton defeat Loyalist-Indian force under Maj. John Butler and Mohawk Chief Joseph Brant

SEP Spanish Gov. Galvez of Louisiana captures British gulf coast ports of Baton Rouge, Manhac and Natchez

1-5 Gen. Sullivan heads northwest to destroy 40 Seneca and Cayuga villages in retaliation for Loyalist-inspired attacks on frontier settlers

27 Congress appoints John Adams to negotiate peace with Britain, John Jay named minister to Spain

Also this year

★ First Universalist congregation organized by John Murray of Gloucester, Mass.

The Arts

★ Mercy Otis Warren's play *The Motley Assembly*

THE 1780s were the decade in which American independence came of age. They began with the 13 states still embroiled in a bitter and increasingly destructive war with their former colonial masters and ended with the leading figures of the revolution taking up their places in George Washington's first administration. In the meantime came years of turmoil and uncertainty as America's first attempts at establishing a constitutional framework crumbled towards anarchy under the conflicting interests of her individual states. This was a time of economic collapse, as the true cost of the war and its aftermath manifested itself in an apparently endless spiral of inflation and unemployment.

However, these were also years of expansion and discovery. Before the decade was out, the first major wave of westward migration had carried the pioneering spirit across the Appalachians into the virgin territories ceded by Britain at the end of the war. And perhaps above all, they were the years in which political order was imposed on developing chaos as, under the watchful eyes of the world, some of the foremost political thinkers of the age painstakingly chiseled out the foundation-stone of modern America, the Constitution of the United States.

The Final Stages of the War

The dawn of 1780 saw the American army reduced to a ragged shadow of the force which had driven the British out of Boston in March 1776 and had fought tooth and nail to defend New York against the Redcoats in the weeks after the Declaration of Independence. General Sir Henry Clinton had reestablished British rule over Georgia and was pushing up into South Carolina, releasing slaves and laying waste to the countryside as he went. In May the American army suffered a humiliating blow when the town of Charleston and its 5000-man garrison fell to Clinton's forces after a lengthy siege. Clinton then retired to New York, leaving his fellow general Lord Cornwallis to continue the campaign. It was clear that North Carolina and Virginia – and with them the entire rebel cause – were in jeopardy unless the British advance could be halted.

Congress reacted by sending General Horatio Gates, the victor of Saratoga, to command the American forces in South Carolina. Washington had his doubts about Gates' appointment and these were soon to be proved tragically well-founded. In August 1780, Gates' men were thoroughly routed by Cornwallis at the battle of Camden. The defeat, which left the British confident of a swift victory, was in many ways the darkest hour of the war for the colonists. But dawn was about to break.

In October an army of backwoodsmen descended on British and loyalist forces at King's Mountain on the border of North and South Carolina and wreaked bloody revenge for Camden. As news of the victory spread, American morale rocketed and within a few months Cornwallis' campaign was bogged down under the harassment of

patriotic guerrillas and regular American forces, now commanded by Nathanael Greene. Giving up all hope of recovering the Carolinas, Cornwallis' demoralized army made its way northwards into Virginia and fortified itself at Yorktown on the James Peninsula in Chesapeake Bay. Here Cornwallis became the victim of a magnificent piece of military coordination as the American army, now reinforced by French troops under Count Rochambeau, closed in on the town. At the same time a French naval task force headed by Admiral de Grasse sailed from the Caribbean to block the entrance to Chesapeake Bay. The strategy worked: caught by the American–French pincer movement, Cornwallis had no choice but to surrender, and on October 17, 1781, the 8000 British troops in Yorktown laid down their arms. There could be no doubt about what Yorktown meant. When he heard the news of Cornwallis' capitulation the British Prime Minister, Lord North, said simply "it's all over."

Peace and Land

Unfortunately, the timetable for peace was decided not by armies in America but by the political situation in London. King George III, less clear-sighted than his first minister, persisted in refusing to countenance American independence. He even threatened to abdicate over the issue. It took a change of ministers and another year of war before the British would sit down at the negotiating table with Benjamin Franklin and the other American representatives in Paris.

Under the terms of the Treaty of Paris, which was finally signed on September 3, 1783, Britain officially recognized America's independence and the boundaries of the new nation were defined. Although there would be further territorial disputes as the years went by, the signatories agreed that the United States consisted of all the lands to the east of the Mississippi (with the exception of New Orleans and Florida, which were held by the Spanish) and everything south of the Great Lakes, Quebec and Nova Scotia.

During the 1780s the lines drawn on the map were given real meaning by a wave of emigration from the coastal states. Following in the footsteps of such pioneers as the legendary Daniel Boone, thousands of men, women, and children abandoned the relative security of life to the east of the Appalachians for the hazards and rewards of the largely unknown western territories. In 1788 alone some 18,000 people made their way along the Ohio river to start new homes in the West. By the end of the decade the land between the Appalachians and the Mississippi, which had been the province of a few hundred scattered frontiersmen before Independence, could boast a settler population of more than 100,000.

The Land Ordinance of 1785 and the Northwest Ordinance of 1787 set about establishing the ground rules for the organization of this new territory. In addition to specifying the administrative layout of the townships, the Ordinances laid down the

British peace propaganda cartoon of 1782.

criteria by which new territories could find political representation and, in due course, become states. Once the population of a territory reached 60,000 it could become a fully fledged state with all the same rights as the existing states. The foundations were laid for a westward expansion which was to bring the new states of Kentucky and Tennessee into the Union by the end of the next decade. But the Ordinances had also sown the seeds of a future conflict even more far-reaching than the Revolutionary War. For among the constitutional freedoms guaranteed to the new states was freedom from slavery. It was an issue that was to acquire a deep and tragic significance in the following century.

The State of the Union

For a country exhausted by war, many of whose major towns were still occupied by the British on the eve of signing, the Treaty of Paris was a brilliant diplomatic achievement. It was also to be the starting point for a period of reconstruction and reevaluation almost as traumatic as the war itself.

Since the beginning of the war in 1775 scarcely a single white American family had escaped its grasp: some 200,000 of the colonies' three million people had taken an active part in the conflict and perhaps as many as 20,000 of them had died in it. The population had also declined by some 100,000 loyalists, who had fled the country rather than live under an independent American government.

If the human cost of the hostilities had been high, so had the economic cost. The war left America with a national debt of almost $43 million, the vast majority of which was owed to her own citizens. Old patterns of trade had been disrupted and acres of productive land ravaged. The currency was weak to the point of worthlessness, and as the decade wore on the trade deficit assumed terrifying proportions. Congress, denied powers of taxation by a people long outraged by the high fiscal levies of the British Government, was helpless to intervene.

John Adams, America's first ambassador to England, presented to George III.

The States and the Union

It was not only in the economic sphere that the 1780s were to demonstrate the weakness of central government in the newborn American nation. In many ways the history of this first decade after Independence is the history of the attempt by the American people to forge for themselves a political system within which to live and prosper. It is a history of false starts and violent differences which were to bring the country to the very brink of disaster.

Their involvement in the war had stiffened the resolve of many ordinary people in America to ensure a place for themselves in the decision-making structure of the new country. Most people felt that republicanism was the only form of government for an independent America. Only republicanism seemed to offer government by the people, and for the people and to avoid the risk of despotism in a monarchical system like the one from which the country had just freed itself. But how the balance of power between the central government and the states – between order and liberty, authority and the individual – was to be struck was a question it would take the rest of the decade to answer.

America as it emerged from the Revolutionary War was still a collection of 13 more or less independent states. In a process which began even before the Declaration of Independence, each of the states developed its own constitutional arrangements along broadly republican lines, but these systems varied in detail from state to state. At one end of the spectrum, for example, Pennsylvania drafted a highly democratic constitution. At the other, its neighbor Maryland organized itself on far more conservative principles.

At the national level, on the other hand, government was virtually non-existent at the beginning of the 1780s. For years the American people had smarted under the yoke of a strong régime which demanded loyalty and money from them without offering proper representation in return. Despite the reservations of Washington and others, the last thing the majority of people wanted, now that they had achieved Independence, was a return to powerful centralized government. As a result, the first stab at an independent constitution for the United States – the Articles of Confederation, which were ratified in 1781 – gave Congress the barest minimum of powers over the individual states. Unfortunately, events were yet again to prove Washington's doubts justified.

Local and inter-state rivalries were rife during the decade. Trade disputes and conflicting territorial claims often led to strained relations and even, in the case of one claim disputed by Pennsylvania and Connecticut, to open war. Within the states themselves, opposing interests, which could often be identified with the propertied and the unpropertied classes, struggled for polit-

1780

MAR 1 Pennsylvania enacts antislavery legislation

18 Forty to One Act makes Continental paper money redeemable at 1/40 of face value

MAY 12 American Gen. Lincoln surrenders Charleston, SC, to British under Clinton, worst American defeat

25 Threat of mutiny at Gen. Washington's winter camp near Morristown, NJ, after severe winter and deflation of Continental money

JUN 11 Massachusetts state constitution ratified by popular vote at special convention; bill of rights includes antislavery sentiment

AUG 16 In Battle of Camden, SC, Americans under Gen. Gates severely defeated by British under Gen. Cornwallis

SEP 8 British under Cornwallis begin invasion of NC

23 British Maj. John Andrew captured near Tarrytown, NY, carrying secret plans for Benedict Arnold's surrender of West Point, NY

25 Benedict Arnold escapes to British ship *Vulture*

OCT 7 In Battle of King's Mountain, NC, American frontiersmen capture British-Loyalist force; victory is turning point in war in South

10 Resolution of Congress urges states to cede western lands to Union and pledges that they will be resettled and admitted to Union as states

DEC 20 Great Britain declares war on The Netherlands

Also this year

★ In *Holmes v. Watson*, NJ court declares invalid an act of its legislature; first case of state court declaring a law unconstitutional

★ American Academy of Arts and Sciences organized at Boston, Mass.

1781

JAN 5 Benedict Arnold and British troops plunder and burn Richmond, Va

20 NJ troops mutiny in Pompton

MAR 2 Congress adopts new name, 'The United States in Congress Assembled'

15 In Battle of Guilford Courthouse, NC, British forced to leave North Carolina for Virginia

SPRING Continental money has no value

MAY 9 British surrender of Pensacola completes Spanish conquest of western Florida

JUL 20 Rebellious slaves in Williamsburg, Va, set fire to capitol and other buildings

SEP 5-8 In naval battle off Yorktown, Va, French fleet of De Grasse defeats British fleet

6 Benedict Arnold plunders and burns port of New London, Connecticut

ical supremacy. The issue of paper money in settlement of war debts became a particular bone of contention as time went on. In some cases creditors who refused to accept paper money even received death threats from their debtors.

A weak and bankrupt Congress was powerless to resolve these local difficulties, let alone the problems of the nation as a whole. In 1783 the dissatisfaction of those who wanted to see the strength of national government increased became so intense that a military coup – the so-called Newburgh Conspiracy, which had the backing of such leading figures as the financier Robert Morris, General Horatio Gates, and Alexander Hamilton – was only narrowly averted by Washington's refusal to endorse it. But the flashpoint had merely been delayed.

Forging a Constitution

At the end of 1786 serious trouble erupted in Massachusetts when the grievances of a number of farmers finally boiled over into open rebellion. Led by one Daniel Shays, a former captain in the Continental Army, the mob went on the rampage, forcing court-

Shays' Rebellion, which did more than any other single event to push America down the road to a Federal Constitution.

George Washington's inauguration on the balcony of Fredrick Hall, New York, April 30, 1789.

houses to close, and releasing prisoners. When they attacked the United States arsenal at Springfield in an attempt to arm themselves, the State Governor responded by sending troops to put down the uprising. He appealed to central government for help, but none was forthcoming. Congress had neither funds nor soldiers to send. Its impotence was all too clearly revealed.

Shays' Rebellion sent shock waves through the whole country. It seemed to open up a terrifying vista of lawlessness and anarchy. It also seemed to many of those who had led the revolution to make a mockery of America's claims to effective republican government in the eyes of the world. Federalism soared to the top of the political agenda.

Within three months of the events at Springfield a group of some of the leading political figures from the individual states met in Philadelphia to discuss the future government of the United States. They included such remarkable men as George Washington, Benjamin Franklin, James Madison, Gouverneur Morris, Roger Sherman, and Alexander Hamilton. The 55 members of this Federal Convention, which grew out of a meeting to discuss a commercial dispute between Virginia and Maryland, set as their agenda no less a task than the redrafting of the Articles of Confederation in order to meet what they called "the exigencies of the Union." It soon became clear that this would in effect mean creating a new constitution for the United States.

Two struggles lay ahead. The first took place at the Convention itself, as proponents of different governmental systems presented their plans and argued their cases. For four months the delegates debated the nature of the government under which they wanted themselves and their fellow citizens to live. In the hot and stuffy atmosphere of the Old State House in Philadelphia patience often wore thin and tempers ran high. But all those involved recognized the fundamental importance of the questions they were considering and each deadlock was finally resolved by compromise. By September 17, 1787, the widely different and hotly contested views of this extraordinary gathering of political thinkers and activists had been welded into a document which represents one of the greatest achievements in the history of the democratic process. The Constitution of the United States was ready to be put before the people.

The second struggle took place in the country at large. Before it could be adopted, the new Constitution had to be endorsed by at least nine of the 13 states. Anti-federal feeling still ran high in America, and the complete independence of individual states was an article of faith with many of those who had suffered under British rule. It was not until May 1788 – after months of propaganda, persuasion, and further compromise – that New Hampshire became the ninth state to ratify the Constitution, and not until 1790, after a Bill of Rights had been appended to it in the form of the first 10 Amendments, did all 13 states give it their blessing.

The Constitution which emerged from this long and painful gestation vested the government of the country in three bodies: Congress, the office of President, and the Supreme Court. The first of these, Congress, was divided into two parts: the Senate and the House of Representatives. States would be represented in the House of Representatives in proportion to the size of their populations and in the Senate on an equal footing, with two members each. The Constitution also set the President's term of office at four years.

Provision was made for Congress to amend the Constitution if necessary, a provision which would lead to the appending of 15 clauses, in addition to the 10 Bill of Rights Amendments, over the next 200 years. With these exceptions the Constitution drafted at the Old State House during those four difficult months of 1787 forms the basis on which the United States is governed to this day. The stage was now set for the formation of America's First Federal Government.

Washington's First Administration

"I do solemnly swear that I will faithfully execute the Office of President of the United States, and will, to the best of my ability, preserve, protect, and defend the Constitution of the United States." With these words, spoken from the balcony of Fredrick Hall in New York on April 30, 1789, and repeated by every President since, George Washington, the hero of the Revolutionary War, became the first President of the United States of America.

Before the end of this most formative decade of American history, all the key posts of his first administration had been filled by men tried and found trustworthy in the independence struggle and the troubled years which followed the end of the war. In the Treasury Washington was able to rely on the extraordinary financial acumen of the young Alexander Hamilton. At his disposal as Secretary of State he could call upon the no less remarkable powers of the author of the Declaration of Independence, Thomas Jefferson. Governor Edmund Randolph of Virginia became America's first Attorney General and General Henry Knox, Washington's former chief of artillery, her first Secretary of War.

The difficulties facing the new administration would test the mettle of these men to the limit. Many of the problems left by the war had still to be addressed and many had become even more deeply rooted since the beginning of the decade. But for all the daunting enormity of the task before them, the men who had drafted the Constitution, many of whom were now its first officers, had planted the cornerstone of the political stability essential for that task to be fulfilled. The America which emerged from the 1780s was still a confederation of 13 states with differing views and fiercely independent identities, but the foundations of national consciousness had been firmly laid. What time and the will of the American people would build on them is the story of the next two centuries.

28-OCT 19 Siege of Yorktown, force of 8000 British under Cornwallis surrenders to allied force of 9000 Americans and 7000 French

NOV 5 The Netherlands offers large loan to US

DEC 31 Bank of North America at Philadelphia chartered by Congress

Pueblo de los Angeles founded in California

1782

JAN 1 Loyalist exodus from America begins

FEB 27 British House of Commons votes against continuing war in America

MAR 5 British Parliament enacts legislation empowering English Crown to negotiate peace with US

7 American militiamen massacre 96 Christian Delaware Indians at Gnadenhutten in Ohio territory in retaliation for terrorist raids of other Indian tribes

APR 12 American-British peace talks begin as Benjamin Franklin meets with Richard Oswald

19 The Netherlands recognizes US independence

20 Congress adopts Great Seal of the United States

AUG 7 Washington creates Badge of Military Merit, or Purple Heart

OCT 8 US and The Netherlands sign treaty of commerce and friendship, negotiated by John Adams

NOV 10 In last battle of Revolutionary War, George Rodgers Clark attacks Shawnee village of Chillicothe in Ohio territory in retaliation for Blue Licks attack

30 Paris: Franklin, Jay, Adams, Laurens and British negotiator Oswald sign preliminary peace treaty

DEC 14 British forces evacuate Charleston, SC

15 French object to not being consulted by Americans before signing of preliminary peace pact with Britain

24 French troops leave Boston for France

Also this year

★ Emancipation law enacted by Virginia legislature through efforts of Thomas Jefferson

★ Use of scarlet letter to identify adulterers discontinued in New England

★ Harvard Medical School opens

★ First complete English Bible printed in US published in Philadelphia by Robert Aitken

1783

JAN 20 England signs preliminary articles of peace with France and Spain

FEB 3 Spain recognizes US independence

4 Britain declares end to hostilities in America

5 Sweden recognizes US independence

25 Denmark recognizes US independence

MAR 10 Maj. John Armstrong anonymously circulates address among officers of Washington's main camp at Newburgh, NY

LATE MAR Congress issues funds for payment of Continental Army officers

APR 11 Congress formally proclaims end to Revolutionary War against Great Britain

26 7000 Loyalists set sail from NY for Canada

JUN 5 *Vermont Gazette*, first newspaper in state, begins publication in Bennington

24 Congress relocates to Princeton, NJ following protest of unpaid soldiers in Philadelphia

JUL 2 English order in council closes British West Indies to trade with US

8 Massachusetts Supreme Court proclaims abolition of slavery in the commonwealth

SEP 3 Treaty of Paris signed by Great Britain and US, formally ends Revolutionary War

3 Britain signs peace pact with France and Spain at Versailles, ceding Florida to Spain

The Founding Fathers

Seldom in history have events thrown up so many remarkable men in the same place and at the same time as those who shaped the United States of America during the latter part of the 18th century. Politicians, statesmen, political thinkers, and military strategists, many of the Founding Fathers were also men of enormous learning and of considerable artistic and scientific accomplishments.

George Washington, 1732-1799, (1) who first came to prominence in the 1750s as a young colonel in the last Colonial Wars, was to establish a lasting and unrivaled place in the affections of the American people for the courage and skill with which he guided the new republic through its early years. As commander-in-chief of the rebel forces in the Revolutionary War, Washington played a crucial role in the independence struggle. Unlike many military heroes, however, his skills made the transition to civil authority with resounding success. A prime mover in the drafting of the Federal Constitution, his two terms as the first U.S. President laid a firm foundation for achievements of the next two centuries.

Benjamin Franklin, 1706-1790, (2) began his career as an assistant on his father's newspaper, and quickly established himself as a journalist of great distinction. Active in all the major events on the road to American Independence – from the Albany Plan of Union in 1754 to the Federal Convention of 1787 – Franklin was also one of the foremost scientific minds of the age. The inventor of the lightning conductor, the Franklin stove, the glass harmonica (he was an accomplished musician), and a number of maritime instruments and techniques, he also made a major contribution to the understanding of electricity.

Thomas Jefferson, 1743-1826, (3) the principal author of the Declaration of Independence and the third President of the United States, was also the greatest American architect of his time, as well as an inventor, naturalist, educationalist, and writer on a range of subjects from linguistics to theology.

The young republic was able to call on the diplomatic skills of such men as John Jay, 1745-1829, (4), who was instrumental in negotiating the Peace of Paris in 1783 and went on to become the first Chief Justice of the United States, and John Adams, 1735-1826 (5), a central figure in the independence struggle, the first Vice President of the United States its second President, and father of John Quincy Adams. Other leading lights of the Federal Convention were Gouverneur Morris, 1752-1836, (6), who, with Jay, drafted New York's state constitution at the tender age of 24, and James Madison, 1751-1836, (7), later the country's fourth President.

OCT 7 Virginia House of Burgesses enacts legislation granting freedom to black slaves who served in Continental Army during Revolutionary War

31 New Hampshire convention proclaims constitution, adopted in popular election

NOV 3 Army disbands by congressional order

DEC 23 Washington resigns commission as commander in chief of Continental Army before Congress at Annapolis

1784

JAN 14 Congress ratifies Treaty of Paris

FEB 22 *Empress of China* sails from NY for Canton by way of Cape Horn, beginning US trade with China

MAR 15 Bank of New York organized

JUN 26 Spain closes lower Mississippi River to American navigation

SEP 22 Russians establish first permanent settlement on Kodiak Island at Three Saints Bay

OCT 5 Dutch Reformed Church Synod establishes first theological seminary in America

22 In Second Treaty of Fort Stanwix, Six Nations of Iroquois cede all claims to territory west of Niagara River; Ohio tribes reject pact

NOV St John's College chartered in Annapolis, Md, under Episcopalian auspices

1 Treaty of August with Creek peoples expands Georgia's northern boundary west from Tugaloo to Ocanee River

DEC 24 James Madison publishes his *Remonstrances Against Religious Assessments*, which advocates separation of church and state

24 Methodist Episcopal Church formally organized at Baltimore

Also this year

★Connecticut and Rhode Island adopt laws for gradual emancipation of black slaves

★ First bale of cotton shipped to England

★ Benjamin Franklin invents bifocals

1785

JAN 1 Maine's first newspaper, *Falmouth Gazette and Weekly Advertiser,* published

21 A treaty negotiated at Fort MacIntosh divests Chippewa, Delaware, Ottawa and Wyandot tribes of nearly all land in present-day state of Ohio

27 Georgia charters first state university with no religious ties

FEB 7 Georgia founds Bourbon County in area of present-day states of Alabama and Mississippi; Spanish also claim region

24 John Adams named Minister to England

MAR 28 Virginia and Maryland commissioners attend Mount Vernon conference, draft agreement on navigation of Chesapeake Bay and Potomac River and agree to invite Pennsylvania to join pact

MAY 5 Treaty of Dumpling Creek transfers territory of Cherokee Indians to 'State of Franklin'

8 Land Ordinance of 1785 authorizes sale of minimum lots of 640 acres at $1.00 per acre

JUL 11 Massachusetts Legislature passes resolutions recommending convention to revise Articles of Confederation

SEP 10 US and Prussia sign treaty of commerce

OCT 10 Spain orders Georgia to surrender claim to Bourbon County

NOV 28 Treaty of Hopewell between US commissioners and Cherokees voids Treaty of Dumpling Creek

30 US Minister to Great Britain John Adams demands that Britain relinquish military posts along Great Lakes and in Ohio

THE CONSTITUTION

Facsimile of the first
page of the original
Constitution of the
United States.

"We the people of the United States, in Order to form a more perfect Union, establish Justice, insure domestic Tranquility, provide for the common defence, promote the general Welfare, and secure the Blessings of Liberty to ourselves and our Posterity, do ordain and establish This CONSTITUTION for the United States of America." So begins the document on the basis of which the United States is governed to this day, and which represents a milestone in the history of democratic institutions.

The Constitution of the United States, drafted by a committee of 55 men in the Old State House in Philadelphia during four months of intense debate in 1787, replaced the Articles of Confederation, which gave too little power to central government to guide the new republic through the storms of its early years. The new Constitution was a compromise between states'-rights and Federalist lobbies, but gave the Federal Government a much stronger hand than had the discredited Articles.

The first article of the Constitution defined the powers of the legislative branch of government – the Congress of the United States – and established the basis of election to the House of Representatives and the Senate; the second laid down the rights and duties of the executive branch – the Presidency of the United States; and the third enshrined the constitution and remit of the judicial branch – the Supreme Court – and defined

the crime of treason. The remaining four articles dealt with the rights and duties of the individual states; the mechanism for ratifying the Constitution and for amending it if necessary; and miscellaneous responsibilities of the United States Government and its officers. Before the Constitution was ratified by all the states, a Bill of Rights was appended to it in the form of ten amending clauses, guaranteeing U.S. citizens such basic human rights as freedom of expression, religion, and assembly, and establishing the important (and later controversial) principle that "the powers not delegated to the United States by the Constitution, nor prohibited to it by the States, are reserved to the States respectively, or to the people."

The ship Hamilton *is paraded through the streets of New York City as part of the celebrations on the ratification of the Constitution in 1789.*

The Constitution is presented to George Washington in the Old State House, Philadelphia, on September 17, 1787.

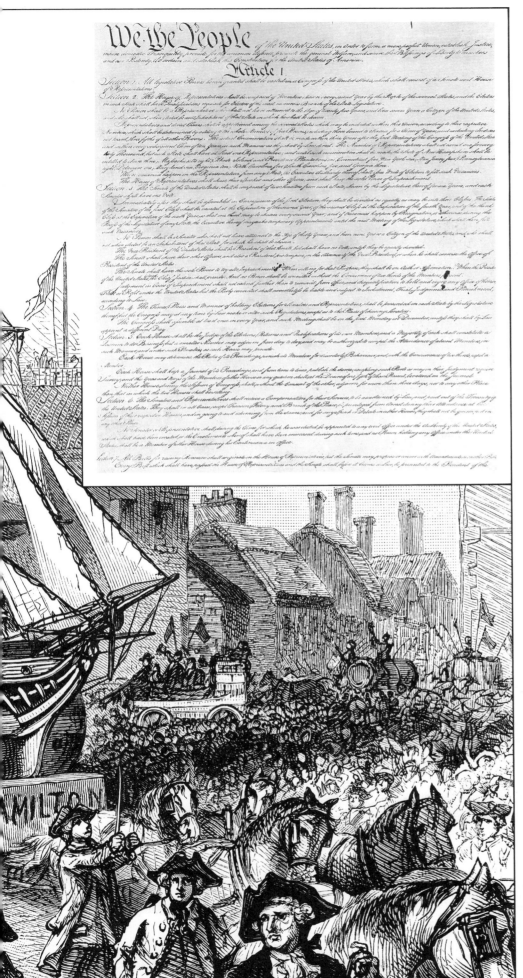

DEC 5 Maryland Legislature accepts proposals of Mount Vernon conference and suggests that Delaware be invited to join pact

Also this year

★ Slavery becomes illegal in New York

★ Primogeniture abolished in Virginia

★ Regular stage routes linking New York City, Boston, Albany and Philadelphia initiated

★ Little River turnpike authorized by state of Virginia

★ Noah Webster's *Sketches of American Policy* published

1786

JAN 21 Virginia Legislature summons all states to convention at Annapolis to consider matters of commerce

FEB 28 British respond negatively to 30 November 1785 demand of US Minister John Adams

JUN 17 Charles River toll bridge between Boston and Charleston opened

28 Thomas Barclay executes anti-piracy treaty with Morocco in exchange for gifts valued at $10,000

JUN-AUG Post-war depression reaches lowest point

AUG 7 Series of proposed amendments to strengthen Articles of Confederation presented to Congress

7 Early federal Indian act establishes two departments, or reservations, for granting licenses for Indian trading and settling

8 Congress adopts coinage system based on Spanish milled dollar

22-25 50 Massachusetts town representatives meet in Hatfield to discuss economic depression

29 Jay-Gardoqui Agreement, to close Mississippi to American navigation for 25 years, rejected by Congress

31 Armed mob prevents session of Northampton, Mass., court in aftermath of Hatfield conference

SEP 11-14 Only Va, Pa, De, NJ and NY attend Annapolis Convention; new convention called in Philadelphia to discuss social and political reforms

20 Armed mob marches on New Hampshire Assembly attempting to force passage of paper money issue

25 In *Trevett v. Weeden*, Rhode Island state court rules that law passed by legislature contrary to state constitution is null and void

26 Bankrupt farmer Daniel Shays leads armed band of insurgents to disrupt state supreme court session in Springfield, Mass.

OCT 16 Congress authorizes establishment of US mint

NOV 30 Insurrection in eastern Massachusetts suppressed with capture of Job Shattuck

Also this year

★ First recorded strike in US called by printers in Philadelphia

★ First consul appointed for US foreign service, Maj. Samuel Shaw of Massachusetts, named consul to China

★ First steamboat in America, built by John Fitch, sails on Delaware River

★ *Pittsburgh Gazette*, first newspaper west of Alleghenies, established by John Scull and Joseph Hall

★ Metcalf Bowler's *Agriculture and Practical Husbandry* published

The Arts

★ Philip Freneau's *Poems*

★ John O'Keefe's play *The Poor Soldier*

1787

JAN 18-19 4400-man Massachusetts militia force assembles to confront rebels led by Daniel Shays in Springfield

26 In Shays' Rebellion, Shays leads 1200 insurgents in unsuccessful attack against federal arsenal at Springfield, Mass.

MAR Massachusetts Legislature offers pardon to most participants in Shays' Rebellion

Revolution in France

Events in Europe were to dominate the American political agenda in the closing years of the 18th century. The French revolution in 1789 was supported by a majority of Americans. Right: the taking of the Bastille, July 14, 1789.

Setting a Seal on Independence

The Great Seal of the United States of America (left) incorporating the bald eagle that was to become the symbol of the emerging nation and the motto "E pluribus unum," signifying unity in diversity.

A Hero's Welcome

Below: George Washington receives a rapturous welcome from crowds lining his route as he enters New York City after the signing of the Treaty of Paris in 1783.

The "Peculiar Institution"

Below: the U.S. Constitution guaranteed that the Federal Government would do nothing to outlaw the slave trade until 1808 at the earliest.

10 Franklin College chartered in Lancaster, Pa, under German Reformed auspices

MAY 25 Constitutional Convention commences in Independence Hall, Philadelphia

JUN 19 Constitutional Convention delegates vote to develop national government proposed in Virginia Plan

JUL 13 Northwest Ordinance establishes government with ultimate statehood in area north of Ohio River, slavery prohibited

16 Roger Sherman presents Connecticut Compromise, advocating proportional representation in lower house of legislature and equal representation in upper house

18 Treaty of Morocco, promising respect for American commerce, ratified by Congress

19-26 Constitutional Convention draws up rough draft of Constitution

AUG 6-10 Debates on draft of Constitution

11 *Kentucky Gazette*, first newspaper in Kentucky published in Lexington

SEP 17 Thirty-nine delegates to Constitutional Convention vote to endorse final form of Constitution, prepared by Governeur Morris

17 Constitutional convention adopts resolution to submit Constitution to Congress

28 Congress votes to submit Constitution to state legislatures for ratification

OCT 27 *The Federalist Papers,* by Alexander Hamilton, James Madison, and John Jay, begin publication in New York's *The Independent Journal*

DEC 7 Delaware becomes first state to ratify Constitution

12 Pennsylvania becomes second state to ratify Constitution

18 New Jersey, becomes 3rd state to ratify Constitution

Also this year

★ William Samuel Johnson appointed president of Columbia College, first noncleric president in any English or American college

★ First secondary school chartered by the regents of the University of the State of New York

1788

JAN 2 Georgia becomes 4th state to ratify Constitution

9 Connecticut becomes 5th state to ratify Constitution

FEB 6 Massachusetts ratifies Constitution, with recommendation of amendment

27-MAR 26 Massachusetts Legislature receives petition from liberated slaves; Massachusetts Assembly considers protest and passes anti-slavery bill

MAR 24 RI rejects Constitution by popular referendum

APR 7 Marietta, at mouth of Muskingum River, settled by Ohio Company of Associates, beginning settlement of Northwest Territory

28 Maryland becomes 7th state to ratify Constitution

MAY 23 South Carolina becomes 8th state to ratify Constitution

JUN 21 New Hampshire becomes 9th state to ratify Constitution, Federal Constitution formally adopted by US

21 New Hampshire convention proposes 12 amendments to Constitution

25 Virginia becomes 10th state to ratify Constitution; proposes bill of rights and 20 alterations

JUL 26 New York becomes 11th state to ratify Constitution; proposes bill of rights

SEP 13 Congress issues detailed directives for choosing of presidential electors, guidelines for choosing the President and date for first session of new Congress

25 Congress presents 12 proposed amendments to Constitution to states

OCT-DEC Plunge in commodity prices halted

NOV 1 Congress under Articles of Confederation adjourns

21 North Carolina becomes 12th state to ratify Constitution

Going West

Ever since the first settlers had established themselves on the Eastern coast of America in the early 17th century, there had been a small but perceptible movement of people toward the West. Driven forward by ever-increasing pressures on land in the East and by the prospect of rich farming and adventure in the West, the frontier – which was to become so formative a part of the American experience – had reached the great barrier of the Appalachians by the time Independence was declared in 1776. A handful of pioneers had already found their way into the trans-Appalachian West before the Revolutionary War, but it was in the 1780s that this trickle began to build up into a tide that would change the face of America over the course of the next century. In 1788 more than 900 boats, bearing more than 18,000 people, together with their belongings and livestock, set off down the Ohio River from Pittsburgh (founded 30 years before by a party which included the legendary trailblazer, Daniel Boone (below)) at the head of a movement that would carry not only the pioneering spirit but also the institution of slavery into what one Cherokee chief prophetically called the "dark and bloody ground" of Kentucky and Tennessee. In the same year, the formation of the Ohio Company of Associates gave significant new impetus to Northwestern migration, especially from New England.

By 1790 there were more than 100,000 Americans living in the largely unexplored territory between the Appalachians and the awe-inspiring Mississippi (opposite, top), many of them in stockaded settlements, eking out a meager living from the stubborn soil, and in constant danger of Indian attacks and natural catastrophes. At a time when, even in the most heavily settled areas of the country, mobility was hampered by appalling roads and rudimentary forms of transport – even the relatively sophisticated stagecoaches (opposite bottom) covering no more than 30 miles a day – these settlers came to represent a strand of rugged self-reliance which would leave an indelible mark on the American people's image of themselves in the coming years.

23 Maryland proposes cession of ten-square-mile land tract on Potomac River to US for federal town and seat of national government

Also this year

★ James Wilkinson conspires with Spanish at New Orleans to separate Ky and Tenn. from Union

★ New Orleans fire destroys most French and Spanish style buildings

1789

JAN 7 First national election for presidential electors

23 Georgetown University, first Catholic college in US, founded by Father John Carroll

FEB 4 Electors cast their ballots

MAR 4 First Congress under Constitution convenes in New York City without quorum

APR 1 House of Representatives achieves quorum and begins operation; Pennsylvania Representative Frederick Augustus Muhlenberg chosen as Speaker of the House

6 Senate achieves quorum

6 Presidential ballots counted, George Washington elected President, John Adams elected Vice President

21 John Adams takes oath of office and is seated as presiding officer of Senate

30 Washington inaugurated in New York City as first President of US, delivers Inaugural Address

MAY 7 First inaugural ball

7 American branch of Church of England reorganized as Protestant Episcopal Church in Philadelphia; *Book of Common Prayer* revised

12 Society of Saint Tammany, Antifederalist fraternal organization, established in NYC

JUN 1 First act of Congress establishes procedure for administering oaths of public office

JUL 4 Congress passes first Tariff Act

14 French Revolution begins with fall of Bastille

20 Tonnage Act levies 50 cents per ton on foreign ships in American ports

27 First executive department, Department of Foreign Affairs, established by Congress

AUG 7 War Department established by Congress

SEP 2 Treasury Department established by Congress

11 Alexander Hamilton named Secretary of the Treasury

12 Henry Knox named Secretary of War

15 Department of Foreign Affairs renamed Department of State

22 Treasury Department established by Congress

24 Federal Judiciary Act provides for Attorney General and begins Federal system of district, circuit and supreme courts

26 Samuel Osgood named Postmaster General, Edmund Randolph named Attorney General, John Jay named Chief Justice of Supreme Court, Thomas Jefferson named Secretary of State

29 US Army established by Congress

29 First Congress under Constitution adjourns

OCT 20 New Jersey becomes first state to ratify Bill of Rights

26 First national Thanksgiving established by congressional resolution and President's proclamation

DEC Virginia cedes land tract on Potomac River, including Alexandria, to Federal Government for federal district and national capital

11 University of North Carolina chartered in Chapel Hill

18 Virginia consents to release counties of Kentucky territory from jurisdiction

21 Georgia Legislature sells 25.4 million acres, mostly claimed by Spain, to three Yazoo land companies for $207,580

Also this year

★ Virginia Capitol built at Richmond from plans by Thomas Jefferson

THE YEARS between Washington's inauguration as the first President of the United States and the start of Thomas Jefferson's election campaign of 1800 saw changes which were to leave a permanent imprint on the American way of life.

At home, it was the decade in which party politics were born, as opinion in Congress divided sharply over Alexander Hamilton's controversial financial policies. Overseas, the French Revolution and the turmoil in Europe which followed it forced America to redefine her international position and provided an additional focus for domestic differences.

Washington's first administration saw the consolidation of federal government in the United States. His second demonstrated on the international stage his capacity for political vision and commonsense statesmanship. When he retired from active public life in 1797, his status as the father of the American nation was already assured. It is an indication of the respect and affection in which Washington was held by the American people that his decision not to run for a third term in office established a principle with almost the same force as a constitutional amendment. His approach to foreign policy, too, was to serve as a pattern for America's international relations for many years to come.

Alexander Hamilton

The economic problems facing America at the beginning of the 1790s were enormous. Few of the scars left by the Revolutionary War had healed. Some, denied the treatment which only effective national government could give, had become festering wounds during the course of the previous decade. In particular, the national debt had risen to a staggering $54 million, the vast majority of it still owed to American citizens. In addition to this, the individual states had run up gigantic war debts of their own.

The man Washington appointed as the first U.S. Secretary of the Treasury at this crucial time was his former lieutenant Alexander Hamilton. It was an inspired choice.

Alexander Hamilton (1757–1804).

The Federal Government faced its first major challenge in the so-called Whiskey Rebellion of 1794. Hamilton's tax on distilleries enraged Western farmers, some of whom refused to pay it and rioted, attacking officials. Washington mobilized some 13,000 men to put down the insurrection. Two ringleaders were convicted of treason but pardoned.

Hamilton was a relatively young man – only in his early thirties when he took office – but he possessed precisely the qualities of imagination, intellect, and determination demanded by the herculean task ahead. He had very clear ideas about the sort of America he wanted to see and the way to go about creating it. Unfortunately for the cause of governmental unity, they were not views shared by all of his Cabinet colleagues.

Hamilton's prime objective was to make America creditworthy again in the eyes of the world. He aimed to pay off the national debt in full, and to create a strong economy based on manufacturing. In the process he also wanted to ensure that the people with the greatest economic power had the greatest interest in preserving the stability and strength of the Federal Government. To this end the Government took over the war debts of the individual states and issued interest-bearing government Bonds against them and the national debts. These bonds were of course bought almost exclusively by people with funds to invest. The financial success of America's Government was now inextricably linked with the financial success of her wealthiest citizens.

Hamilton also levied taxes on certain consumer items, one of which – a tax on the whiskey produced by so many Western farmers as a means of profiting from their surplus grain – was to provoke open rebellion in 1794. However, it was his plans for a central bank on the British model which provided the catalyst for the first major split in the Government's own ranks.

The Birth of Party Politics

For those in the administration who were suspicious of Hamilton's motives, the proposal for a central bank of the United States looked dangerously like an attempt to give the central Government more wide-ranging powers than the Constitution permitted. Already alarmed by what they saw as a transfer of power away from the ordinary people of America, Thomas Jefferson and James Madison opposed the formation of the bank, which they believed would carry the process of centralization one step closer to plutocracy. Washington disagreed and the bank went ahead. But the seeds of party politics had been sown.

By the end of 1791 the label "Republican" had already attached itself to those in Congress who, like Jefferson and Madison, believed in a broadly based decentralized government. Those who took Hamilton's view became known as "Federalists." Ironically, the one thing almost all of those involved had in common was a deep dislike of party politics.

The developing factionalism became more and more polarized as the presidential election of 1792 approached. There was no dispute about who should be President: Washington was unanimously reelected. Controversy centered on the vice presidential candidate, with the Republicans backing George Clinton of New York and the Federalists backing the sitting Vice President, John Adams.

In the event, Adams was successful. But by the time Washington convened his second administration, the arena of American party political conflict had expanded far beyond the shores of the United States itself. Events in Europe had begun to exert a major influence on the pattern of party loyalties at home. In September 1792 France had been declared a republic, and in January 1793 Louis XVI had become the most eminent of the Revolution's victims. In February, the month before Washington took up his second term of office as President, France declared war on Great Britain.

Treaties and Neutrality

France was still America's major European ally. It was French money and French firepower which had helped Washington's army defeat the British during America's own Revolution, and the ideals of the 1789 French Revolution – however tarnished they were now beginning to show themselves in practice – had struck a sympathetic chord in many American hearts. But war was another matter. With the American economy only now beginning to regain its strength after the disastrous damage inflicted by one all-out confrontation with

Britain, Washington was not about to be drawn into a second.

The war in Europe focused party differences at home as no domestic issue had yet done. Jefferson was a great admirer of the French revolutionaries, whose cause he saw as identical with that of the Americans in the 1770s, and many of his Republican followers felt the same way. Hamilton, on the other hand, saw the Revolution as an outbreak of anarchy, a view shared by many other Federalists. Both agreed, though, that war with Britain would be a disaster for the United States.

Washington immediately set about putting America's international affairs in order, bringing to the task his customary diplomatic skill and sensitivity. In April 1793 he declared that the United States would remain strictly neutral in the conflict between France and Great Britain. This not only irritated the French, whose newly appointed chargé d'affaires in America was busily recruiting support for the republic's cause; it also annoyed the British, who soon began attacking shipping bound for French ports in the West Indies and encouraging Indian aggression in the northwest of the country. Washington reacted to the first threat by demanding that France withdraw its chargé d'affaires – though in the event he stayed – and to the second by sending an envoy to London and an army to the Northwest.

Both returned with successes to report, though "Mad Anthony" Wayne's victory over the British-backed Indians at the Battle of Fallen Timbers (after which the Indians were forced to cede, among other territories, most of present-day Ohio) was far more popular at home than John Jay's treaty, which, despite settling a number of financial and territorial disputes to the United States' advantage, was seen as a sell-out because Britain still insisted on the right to make arbitrary searches of American ships at sea, and to restrict American trade with the West Indies.

Finally, in 1795, Washington concluded a treaty with Spain which put to rest a number of disputes which had been rankling for some time. In particular, Spain conceded navigation rights on the Mississippi and the use of New Orleans as a staging post for American goods. The Treaty of San Lorenzo el Real also set the 31° latitude as the line of the southern U.S. border.

The Spanish treaty put the last piece in the complex diplomatic jigsaw of the early 1790s. For the moment the United States was at peace.

Conflict with France

It was not to last. In France the guillotine had claimed the lives of most of the leaders who had been friendly towards the United States, and their place had been taken by the Directory. Relations between the two countries plummeted. With the bizarre XYZ affair, in which French agents representing the foreign minister demanded enormous sums of money from the U.S. before they would begin to negotiate, tension mounted towards open conflict. The American public

and politicians alike were outraged by what they saw as the arrogance of the Directory. American naval forces were strengthened, and for almost two years American and French ships conducted an undeclared war at sea. Known as the Quasi-war, the hostilities were to end only with the overthrow of the Directory by Napoleon Bonaparte in 1800.

Adams and Washington

The 1790s saw two Presidents in office in the United States. In 1796, in a moving farewell address, George Washington took leave of his people, exhorting them to avoid factionalism at home and permanent alliances abroad, and passed the torch of office to his successor, the former Vice President John Adams. In stark contrast to the violence with which power changed hands in France in the years following the Revolution there, the change-over from Washington's second administration to Adams' first was smooth and peaceful. Only a few years earlier, not many Americans, let alone foreigners, would have dared to believe it possible.

Like Washington, John Adams had been one of the leaders of the Revolution. Associated with many of its key moments, his courage and love of his country were universally acclaimed. He was, however, a less easy man to get on with than his former boss and his political judgment was less clearsighted. He also suffered from the personal opposition of Alexander Hamilton, whose increasingly Napoleonic ambitions were no less dangerous outside the Cabinet than within it. Adams' determination in a crisis was not always well-directed, and the anti-Republican Alien and Sedition Acts, which were passed in the closing years of the decade, were seen by many as a dangerous overreaction, threatening the cherished freedoms of the First Amendment.

Washington's reputation, on the other hand, seemed immune to change. It remained as high out of office as it had been when he was President. There could be no neater summary of his unique position in the affections of the American people than that of Henry Lee when he described Washington as "first in war, first in peace, first in the hearts of his countrymen."

As the 18th century drew to a close the stage was set for a period of unprecedented expansion. The election of 1800 was to settle the presidency on Thomas Jefferson – the author of the Declaration of Independence and the man who would preside over changes in the physical, economic, and social fabric of the United States as far-reaching as any that had taken place under his predecessors in office. Like Adams, Jefferson too would become President without any of the bitter upheavals which accompanied the transfer of power in France. It is perhaps the greatest tribute of all to Washington's own exercise of presidential power that the democratic process should have seemed so secure in America only 13 years after the members of the Federal Convention had first put on paper the principles of the U.S. Constitution.

1790s

President Adams

1790

MAR 26 Naturalization Act requires two-year residency for new citizens

APR 17 Death of Benjamin Franklin in Philadelphia

29 Rhode Island 13th state to ratify Constitution

JUL 10 House votes to locate planned national capital on ten-square-mile site along Potomac River

OCT 18 Five-year Indian war begins in Northwest

DEC 21 Samuel Slater begins production in first American cotton mill, in Pawtucket, RI

1791

FEB 25 Washington signs bill chartering Bank of US

3 Whiskey Act sets excise tax on distilled liquors

4 Vermont enters Union as 14th state

APR 26 In Treaty of Holston River, Cherokees cede most of land in upper Tennessee River Valley to US Government in return for promise that rest of lands will not be infringed upon

JUN 12 Slaves revolt in Louisiana

DEC 15 First 10 amendments to Constitution, Bill of Rights, goes into effect when Virginia ratifies it

1792

MAY 17 New York Stock Exchange organized

JUN 1 Kentucky enters Union as 15th (slave) state

DEC 5 George Washington elected for second term

Also this year

★ Republican Party, also known as Democratic-Republican or Antifederalist Party, formed

1793

JAN 23 Accusations of corruption against Alexander Hamilton lead to official inquiry into Treasury

FEB 1 France declares war on Great Britain, Spain and The Netherlands

12 Congress passes Fugitive Slave Act

MAR 22 Pres. Washington issues proclamation of neutrality toward France and England

MAY 9 French government orders seizure of neutral ships carrying supplies to enemy ports

JUN 8 Britain orders seizure of neutral vessels carrying provisions to French ports

JUL 31 Thomas Jefferson resigns as Secretary of State, assumes leadership of antifederalist Democratic Republican Party

OCT 28 Eli Whitney of Mulberry Grove, Ga, files application for patent for the cotton gin

NOV 6 British order calls for seizure of neutral vessels carrying exports from islands of the French West Indies

25 Slaves set series of devastating fires in Albany, NY

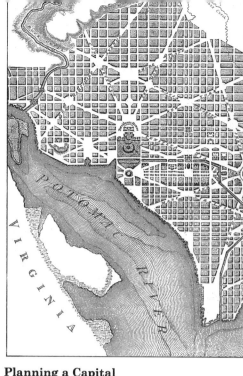

The XYZ Affair

Worsening relations with France during the early days of John Adams' presidency deteriorated still further when an American attempt at conciliation was rudely rebuffed by the French Government – the Directory – in October 1797. Following a spirited statement of American national pride in Congress, the President sent Elbridge Gerry, John Marshall, and C. C. Pinckney to Paris on a diplomatic mission to cool the international temperature. However, Talleyrand, the French Foreign Minister, not only refused to meet the three envoys, but sent three agents of his own to meet them with a series of wholly unacceptable demands. These agents, referred to as X, Y and Z in the report Gerry and his colleagues sent back to the President, insisted on an apology for what they saw as Adams' insult to France in his speech to Congress, together with a huge personal payment for Talleyrand and a $10 million loan for the French Government. The cartoon (above) reflects American outrage at the affair, showing the French Government as a many-headed monster.

Planning a Capital

The new city of Washington D.C. as planned by Major Pierre Charles L'Enfant under the supervision of the man for whom it was named.

Eli Whitney's Cotton Gin

In 1793 Eli Whitney, a Connecticut schoolteacher living in Georgia, invented a machine which was to change the way of life of the Southern states and, in the process, bring America one step closer to Civil War. The cotton gin (right) enabled planters to clean their cotton crops some 300 times faster than was possible by hand, thus vastly increasing the productive potential of the plantation system. The machine quickly became available on a commercial basis and hastened the march of "King Cotton" throughout the South, spreading in its train the divisive institution of Black slavery.

Bank of the United States, Philadelphia

The issue of whether or not the United States should have a central bank divided opinion sharply in the 1790s. The bank was the cornerstone of Alexander Hamilton's plans for the financial regeneration of the republic, but was bitterly opposed by Jeffersonian Republicans. Washington threw his weight behind Hamilton.

MAR 22 Slave trade with foreign nations banned

JUN 5 Neutrality Act prohibits enlistment of US citizens in service of foreign countries and forbids supplying of foreign armed vessels in US ports

JUL Whiskey Rebellion breaks out in Pennsylvania

NOV 19 Jay's Treaty secures promise of British withdrawal from military posts in US territory

Also this year

★ Philadelphia Lancaster Turnpike, first major turnpike in America, completed

1795

JAN 7 In Yazoo Land fraud, corrupt Georgia Legislature sells 35 thousand acres in Yazoo River territory to companies for 1.5 cents per acre

29 Naturalization Act requires five-year residency

31 Alexander Hamilton resigns as Secretary of the Treasury, replaced by Oliver Walcott

19 Secretary of State Edmond Randolph resigns under suspicion of corruption

SEP 5 Treaty of peace and amity with Algiers guarantees tribute to Barbary pirates

OCT 27 Treaty of San Lorenzo with Spain sets US southern boundary at 31st parallel and guarantees right to navigate Mississippi

1796

FEB 15 France announces that Jay's Treaty annuls French treaties with US

MAR 8 In *Hylton v. US*, Supreme Court rules on constitutionality of act of Congress for first time

APR 22 Supreme Court rules that treaties made under Constitution are federal law

MAY 18 Land Act mandates survey of public lands in Northwest Territory, authorizes sales in minimum lots of 640 acres at $2.00 per acre, initiates credit system

JUN 1 Tennessee enters Union as 16th (slave) state

JUL France proclaims that it will capture and search all ships of neutral nations bound for British ports

NOV 4 Treaty with Tripoli seeks end to pirate raids

15 France suspends diplomatic relations with US

DEC 7 John Adams elected President, Thomas Jefferson elected Vice President

1797

AUG 28 US signs treaty with Tunis

OCT 18 XYZ affair opens

1798

JAN 8 11th Amendment of Constitution, forbidding suit against state by citizen of another state ratified

APR 7 Mississippi Territory formed by act of Congress

JUN 6 Abolition of imprisonment of debtors

13 Commerce with France and dependencies suspended

18 Naturalization Act extends required time of residence for citizenship from 5 to 14 years

25 Alien Act authorizes President to deport dangerous or treasonable aliens in time of peace

JUL 6 Alien Enemies Act permits wartime arrest, imprisonment and banishment of any enemy aliens

14 Sedition Act declares any antigovernment activity a high misdemeanor

1799

MAR 29 New York passes gradual emancipation law

DEC 14 Death of George Washington at Mount Vernon

THE FIRST ten years of the 19th century in America were dominated by the beliefs and personality of Thomas Jefferson, who took the oath of office as the third President of the United States on March 4, 1801. A passionate believer in democracy and the rule of reason, his presidency turned out not to be the time of radical upheaval feared by the newly usurped Federalists. Instead, it was a period of remarkable self-confidence and expansion. During Jefferson's first term of office, the size of the United States was doubled at a stroke by the purchase of the vast territory of Louisiana from Napoleon's France. The stream of pioneers heading for the trans-Appalachian West became an unstoppable flood, and the expeditions of such intrepid explorers as Lewis and Clark extended the American people's knowledge of the land they inhabited further than ever in the direction of the Pacific Ocean.

However, the events of Jefferson's second term of office were to put the successes of his first in serious jeopardy. His determined attempt to avoid being drawn into the war now raging in Europe led only to economic stagnation and serious discontent at home. The last years of his presidency were overshadowed by the effects of his ill-judged trade embargo and by splits in the party whose birth and growth he had done so much to foster. Despite all his efforts, when Jefferson stepped down in 1809, the country he bequeathed to his successor, James Madison, was, not for the first time in its brief history, teetering on the brink of all-out war with Great Britain.

"The world's best hope"

Many of the men who had wielded most influence under Washington and Adams regarded the arrival of Thomas Jefferson to the presidency with some trepidation. There were Federalists who saw him as a new Robespierre, and the aristocratically minded Alexander Hamilton, for many years Jefferson's chief political sparring partner, predicted "dangerous innovations" and disorder.

They were wrong. From the very first Jefferson was anxious to promote unity and understanding. His inaugural address set the tone in phrases well worthy of the author of the Declaration of Independence. "We are all Republicans – we are all Federalists," he said. "If there be any amongst us who would wish to dissolve this Union or to change its republican form, let them stand undisturbed as monuments of the safety with which error of opinion may be tolerated where reason is left free to combat it." He committed his administration to a light but sure touch on the reins of power. The Government of the United States was, he said, "the world's best hope."

Jefferson's uncluttered approach to life reflected the idealistic enthusiasm of a nation poised on the threshold of maturity. As the new century dawned, an astonishing two thirds of the rapidly growing population of the United States was less than 26 years old. The country to the west of the Appalachian Mountains was still virtually untamed, and the continent beyond seemed to promise room and resources for endless generations of American men and women. On the banks of the Potomac River land was being cleared and plans drawn up for a new capital city to be named after the greatest of America's founding fathers. If Jefferson's presidency turned out not to be the revolution so many of his enemies had dreaded, it was nonetheless a time of new beginnings in many different areas of American life.

"The noblest work of our whole lives"

Perhaps the most important of all the contributions Jefferson made to the development of the country during his years as President was the Louisiana Purchase.

In 1803, in what has often been called the biggest real estate deal in history, America bought from France the vast territory of Louisiana. Far larger than the present state of that name, the Louisiana territory stretched for some 2000 miles from the banks of the Mississippi in the east to the foothills of the Rocky Mountains in the west. The transaction almost doubled the size of the country and created huge new potential for expansion. The American Minister in Paris who helped negotiate the deal was quick to recognize its historical significance. Describing it as "the noblest work of our whole lives," he said: "From this day the United States take their place among the powers of the first rank."

It came about almost by accident. Until 1800 the territory of Louisiana had belonged to Spain. However, in that year Napoleon Bonaparte bullied the Spanish into an agreement whereby they would hand it over to France as soon as he was able to set up a governor in the crucial port of New Orleans. Rumors of the secret deal soon leaked out in America, raising the ugly specter of a major European power (which Spain hadn't been for years) on her western borders. The fears were justified. Napoleon saw Louisiana as the first giant stepping stone to an American empire for France, and he now set about establishing a military presence there. In 1802 he signed a truce with Great Britain and invaded the island of St. Domingue (now Haiti and the Dominican Republic), from which he hoped to move against the mainland. In the same year the Spanish governor of New Orleans closed the port to American ships.

Western settlers demanded war and threatened to take matters into their own hands if they didn't get it. Jefferson, however, had other plans and immediately sent envoys off to Paris with an offer to buy New Orleans from Napoleon. Negotiations dragged on for some weeks without success. But Napoleon was running out of time. His troops in St. Domingue were being decimated by resistance and disease, and the truce with Britain was looking decidedly shaky. In April 1803, in a shock development, the French Foreign Minister, Talleyrand, suddenly offered to sell, not just the port of New Orleans, but the whole territory of Louisiana. If he hadn't, Jefferson would have allied himself to his old enemy Great Britain in order to keep the French off American soil. As it was, the price was agreed at $12 million and the deal was signed. Jefferson swallowed his doubts about whether the purchase was constitutional: after all, America had gained over 800,000 square miles of territory for only $2 million more than he had been prepared to pay for New Orleans alone. At less than four cents an acre, he was not going to risk Napoleon's having second thoughts, and the deal was approved by the Senate in October 1803.

The biggest real estate deal in history: the U.S. Commissioner, Captain Amos Stoddart, meets Napoleon's delegate during the ceremonies held in St. Louis on March 9, 1804, to mark the official handing over of the Louisiana territory to the United States. The 800,000 square miles of Louisiana cost the U.S. Government less than 4 cents an acre.

John Marshall, Chief Justice of the U.S.

Aaron Burr, arch-conspirator.

"Even to the western ocean"

The Louisiana Purchase gave added impetus to the tide of westward emigration and discovery which had begun to gather pace in the 1790s. Major expeditions were dispatched into the virgin territories and came back with stirring tales to tell. The most famous of these expeditions was the one led by two U.S. army officers, Captain Meriwether Lewis and Lieutenant William Clark. Lewis and Clark, together with some 40 men, set off from St. Louis in May 1804 and sailed along the great Missouri, Snake, and Columbia Rivers to the shore of the Pacific Ocean. (They had, in fact, been beaten to it by traders from New England, who sailed up the coast, but history has awarded them the laurels.) Only one member of the expedition was lost in all its arduous three and a half years. Lewis and Clark built a fort – Fort Clatsop – at the mouth of the Columbia and returned with detailed accounts of their discoveries among the Indians and the northwestern wilderness they were the first Americans to see. But the most important consequence of their journey was that it established an American claim to the lands they explored. The Indians would have cause to regret their winter hospitality.

Midnight Judges and Midnight Intrigue

The elections of 1800–1801 brought the Republicans to power in the Senate and the House of Representatives. Jefferson, himself a Republican, filled his Cabinet with like-minded men. But the third arm of the Government – the Supreme Court – was a different matter. John Adams, Jefferson's predecessor, had spent the last hours of his term of office frantically signing commissions in order to pack the judiciary with Federalist sympathizers.

These so-called "midnight judges" were to prove a major bone of contention during Jefferson's first administration. The new President contested some of the appointments (which included one demented alcoholic!), but in the process made an implacable enemy of the Federalist Chief Justice, John Marshall. This antagonism was to produce two judgments of great significance for the constitutional future of the United States. The first was the establishment of the principle of judicial review, by which the legislative decisions of Congress can be examined and declared unconstitutional by the Supreme Court. The second was a restriction of the definition of treason to the actual performance of treasonable acts against the Government of the United States. This last judgment came about as a result of a bizarre conspiracy by Jefferson's first Vice President, Aaron Burr.

Burr was a colorful and controversial figure even before his election to the vice presidency in 1800. The focus of a short-lived Federalist attempt to hold on to power during the election campaign itself, he became the decade's most famous intriguer. Before the presidential election of 1804, which returned Jefferson to power in a Republican landslide, the President had dropped Burr from the ticket, choosing George Clinton as his vice presidential candidate instead. This stirred Burr's simmering resentment into outright enmity. He let himself be conscripted into an anti-Jeffersonian scheme to create a secessionary northern confederation of states, centered on fiercely Federalist New England. The scheme fell apart, largely because Alexander Hamilton refused to support it. As a result, Burr challenged Hamilton to a duel and shot him dead. It was a sorry end to a sorry saga. It also cut short the career of the man who had been Washington's chief lieutenant in both war and peace and without whose financial genius the United States might have been a very different place today.

But the conspiracy which led to Chief Justice Marshall's judgment was Burr's second attempt at self-aggrandizement. During Jefferson's second term of office, the former Vice President apparently hatched a wild scheme to become Emperor of Mexico after snatching the country from Spain by force of arms. He also planned to set up an independent republic in the newly acquired Louisiana territory. The plan had all the ingredients of a boy's adventure story and crumbled as quickly under the cold touch of reality. Burr was arrested and stood trial. There was no conviction, but Marshall's judgment on what constituted treason became set in stone.

MAR 8 Napoleon Bonaparte receives American peace commissioners respectfully

APR 4 Congress passes first Federal Bankruptcy Act, applying to merchants and traders; Robert Morris released from debtors' prison

24 Library of Congress established by act of Congress

29 In case of American mercantile vessel *Polly*, court accepts principle of 'broken voyage;' American ships may carry goods from the French West Indies to France if goods are landed at American port and duty paid

APR-MAY Congressional party caucuses nominate candidates for President and Vice President: Federalists nominate John Adams for President and Charles Pinckney for Vice President, Democratic-Republicans nominate Thomas Jefferson for President and Aaron Burr for Vice President

MAY 6 Pres. Adams requests resignation of Secretary of War James Mc Henry due to suspicion of conspiracy

7 Northwest Territory divided; western portion becomes Indiana Territory

10 Public Land Act authorizes land sales of 320 acres at $2 per acre on installments over four years

12 President dismisses Secretary of State Timothy Pickering due to suspicion of conspiracy

JUN Federal Government moves from Philadelphia to permanent federal capital of Washington on Potomac River

SEP 30 Treaty of Marfontaine, or Convention of 1800 ends undeclared naval war with France

OCT 1 France acquires Louisiana from Spain in secret Treaty of San Ildefonso

NOV 1 Middlebury College chartered in Middlebury, Vt

DEC 3 Presidential election; ballots not counted until February 11, 1801

FEB 11 Electoral ballots counted for presidential election of 1800 reveals Jefferson-Burr tie

17 Election of Thomas Jefferson as President and Aaron Burr as Vice President decided by House on 36th ballot

27 District of Columbia placed under jurisdiction of Congress

MAR 3 Pres. Adams makes several last-minute appointments of 'midnight judges'

4 Thomas Jefferson inaugurated President, Aaron Burr inaugurated Vice President

14 Yusuf Karamanli of Tripoli declares war on US for insufficient tribute

AUG 6 Presbyterian camp meeting in Cane Ridge, Ky, begins Great Revival of the West

Embargo

Jefferson could have done without the distraction of Burr's hare-brained schemes. He had more pressing matters to attend to. Events in Europe were starting to threaten America's security. Just as the successes of Washington's first administration had been put at risk by deteriorating relations between France and Britain during his second, so now the same thing seemed to be happening to Jefferson. War had broken out in earnest between Great Britain and Napoleon's France in 1803 and would continue well into the next decade. The repercussions for America were to be immense.

The main arena of conflict was the high seas. Britain prohibited neutral ships from trading with ports under Napoleon's control and claimed the right to stop and search them. It also claimed the right to impress back into service with the Royal Navy any British deserters found serving with the American merchant fleet (and since conditions in the British navy were often harsh, there were many such men). At the same time, Napoleon gave notice that France would seize any ships allowing themselves to be searched by the British, and he set about impounding American cargoes to fill his war chest. Caught in the middle, America's hugely profitable foreign trade seemed under serious threat. But the greatest blow was to American pride. Resentment focused on British harassment and impressment, and after the affair of the U.S.S. *Chesapeake*, when an American frigate was fired on and some of its crew impressed by a British gunboat, relations with Britain fell to a new low.

Tempers ran high in the United States, but Jefferson was determined to remain at peace. Quiet diplomacy had prevented America being sucked into war during his first administration. Could it not pay dividends now, too? Instead of declaring war on Britain, the President declared a comprehensive trade embargo. Under the terms of the Embargo Act of 1807, no American ship would be permitted to sail for any foreign port. Many countries were now heavily reliant on American trade and American ships, and Jefferson hoped that his sanctions would quickly bring France and Britain to their senses. Instead they split America down the middle.

Opposition to the embargo mounted as its damaging effects on America's trading position became more and more evident. New Englanders in particular resented the curb on their maritime freedom and the fall-off in orders for shipbuilding. Voices were raised for secession from the Union. The Republican Party itself, a united political force when Jefferson swept the board in the presidential election of 1804–1805, split into warring factions over the issue. Cotton prices fell sharply in the South and many shipping concerns went out of business. The situation could not continue, and just three days before Jefferson left office, the Embargo Act was repealed. But by then the seeds were already sown of a second conflict with Britain on the scale of the Revolutionary War.

Thomas Jefferson

The third President of the United States was one of the most remarkable men of modern times. The principal author of the Declaration of Independence and one of the shaping forces of the new republic, his interests extended far beyond politics. He was an avid geographer, botanist, and naturalist, and took a keen personal interest in the opening up of the Western territories and in the accounts of those who explored them. A slave-owning landowner, he nonetheless examined with unusual lack of prejudice the whole question of the position of Blacks in American society. He was also a committed educationalist and came to regard the University of Virginia, which he founded and designed, as his greatest and most lasting achievement.

Jefferson's influence on the artistic growth and self-confidence of the United States was second only to his influence on its political development. He was one of the most accomplished architects of the age. More than any other man, he was responsible for the introduction of the neo-classical style into America, its reasoned proportions and echoes of past republican glories a fitting expression of the ideals of the new country. His Virginian country estate, Monticello (below), remains one of the pinnacles of American architecture, and he is fittingly commemorated today by the neo-classical Jefferson Memorial in Washington (right).

From his style of dress to his furnishings, everything about Jefferson reflected his deeply-rooted belief in democracy and rationalism. The British ambassador was appalled to be received by the President in slippers, corduroys, and casual jacket, but others were charmed by the dedicated informality with which he substituted written messages for the presidential address to Congress and replaced the great presidential receptions of former years with intimate dinner parties around a circular table. Above all, Jefferson believed that man's nature was perfectible through reason and that America was the country to prove it. Of his Government he wrote "We are acting for all mankind." It was a sense of mission which perfectly expressed the idealism of the young American nation.

1802

JAN 8 Revolutionary War claims of Great Britain against US settled at $2,664,000 by commission, as provided by Jay's Treaty

9 Ohio University chartered in Athens, Ohio

FEB 6 Congress recognizes war with Tripoli and empowers the President to arm American vessels

MAR 27 Treaty of Aliens among France, England, Spain and The Netherlands ends European hostilities

APR 6 Excise duties abolished by Congress

14 Naturalization Act of 1795, requiring five years residency, reinstated

24 Georgia cedes western lands to US, last of original states to do so

30 Enabling Act permits any territory organized under Ordinance of 1787 to become state, refers specifically to Northwest Territory

MAY 3 Washington, DC, incorporated as city by act of Congress, Mayor to be appointed by President

AUG 11 American and Spanish diplomatic representatives sign convention providing for commission to settle claims of inhabitants of both countries against each other

OCT 16 Spanish officials at New Orleans withdraw US right of deposit

NOV 29 Ohio constitution for state government approved by convention

1803

FEB 24 In *Marbury v. Madison*, Supreme Court rules act of Congress null and void when in conflict with Constitution, establishes principle of judicial review

MAR 1 Ohio enters Union as 17th state, first in which slavery is illegal from beginning

APR John James Audubon is first American to tag birds for scientific purposes

19 Spain restores to American traders right of deposit at port of New Orleans

MAY 2 In Louisiana Purchase, France sells Louisiana territory to US for approximately $415 million

JUN 7 Gov. William Henry Harrison signs treaty with nine Indian tribes for cession of Indian lands around Vincennes along Wabash River

20 Meriwether Lewis and William Clark given instructions by Pres. Jefferson for exploratory expedition to West

AUG 31 Lewis and Clark Expedition sets out down Ohio River

OCT 31 American frigate *Philadelphia* captured in Tripoli harbor

NOV 30 Spanish formally complete cession of Louisiana territory to France

DEC 20 Louisiana territory formally transferred by France to US at New Orleans

31 Middlesex Canal links Merrimac River with Boston Harbor

Also this year

★ First tax-supported public library founded in Salisbury, Conn.

1804

FEB 15 New Jersey Legislature passes act for gradual emancipation of slaves

25 Democratic-Republican congressional caucus unanimously nominates Jefferson for second term and George Clinton of New York for Vice President

MAR 26 Land Act of 1804 reduces minimum price for public lands to $41.64 per acre, permits sale of 160-acre tracts and liberalizes credit terms

Napoleon Bonaparte

Both Thomas Jefferson's greatest triumph and his greatest failure as President derived in large part from the ambitions of Napoleon Bonaparte (right, center), who overthrew the French Directory in 1800. It was Napoleon's Caribbean entanglements, and the war looming on the horizon with Great Britain as a result of his plans for European domination, that led him to proffer the sale of the Louisiana territories to the U.S. in 1803. And it was Napoleon's maritime policy, with its seizures of American shipping, which prompted Jefferson's dangerously misguided embargo and provided an ignominious end to one of the greatest presidencies in American history. The turmoil in Europe during the Napoleonic period was largely to determine the U.S. political agenda under Jefferson's successor too.

The Indian Princess

The first decade of the new century saw a revival of interest in the story of the Indian Princess, Pocahontas. Pocahontas, the daughter of the Indian chief, Powhatan, was credited with saving the life of Captain John Smith, a soldier of fortune who sailed to America with the early settlers in the first years of the 17th century. She interposed herself between Smith and her father, who had captured and was about to kill him.

The Tripolitan War

One of the first problems to confront Jefferson as President was that of the Barbary pirates, who had been a threat to international shipping off the North African coast for years, and had taken to demanding extravagant protection money from the United States in return for a safe passage. In May 1801, after America had refused to meet his demands for an increase in these so-called "tributes," the Bashaw of Tripoli declared war on the United States. In the ensuing conflict, which continued until 1805, Commodore Stephen Decatur (right) distinguished himself by his daring naval exploits.

The Textile Industry

The textile industry was highly important to the economy of New England in the first half of the 19th century. Cotton produced by the South was spun and woven for sale both inside and outside the United States in such mills as Samuel Slater's in Rhode Island and Massachusetts (above).

26 Territory of Orleans and District of Louisiana formed by act of Congress

MAY 14 Lewis and Clark Expedition begins ascent of Missouri River

18 Napoleon Bonaparte becomes Emperor of France

JUL 11 Alexander Hamilton shot and killed by Aaron Burr in duel at Weehawken, NJ

AUG 13 Gov. W.H. Harrison purchases land between Wabash and Ohio Rivers in Indiana Territory from Delaware Indians

18 & 27 Indiana Gov. Harrison signs two treaties at Vincennes for cession of Indian lands north of Ohio River and south of tract ceded in treaty of 1803

SEP 25 Twelfth Amendment, providing for election of President and Vice President on separate ballots, ratified

NOV 3 In treaty at St Louis, Sauk and Fox tribes cede five million acres of land to US with right to remain while tract is public land

DEC 5 Thomas Jefferson wins election for second term, George Clinton elected Vice President

1805

JAN 11 Michigan Territory formed by division of Indiana Territory

MAR 2 District of Louisiana becomes Louisiana Territory, with capital at St Louis, by act of Congress

4 Thomas Jefferson inaugurated for second term, George Clinton inaugurated vice president

APR 26-29 American force captures port city of Derna in Tripoli

MAY 25 Strike by Federal Society of Journeymen Cordwainers in Philadelphia suppressed, leaders arrested

26 Lewis and Clark Expedition sights Rocky Mountains

MAY-SEP Aaron Burr tours Mississippi Valley region and meets with Gen. James Wilkinson

JUN 4 Treaty with Tripoli ends war

AUG 9 Lt Zebulon Montgomery Pike leaves St Louis to explore sources of Mississippi River

DEC 9 Ninth Congress convenes with Democratic-Republican majority

1806

FEB 12 Senate issues resolution condemning British naval hostilities against American commercial shipping

APR 18 Nicholson Act, or Nonimportation Act, forbids importation from England of long list of items

MAY 16 British Foreign Minister Charles James Fox proclaims naval blockade of European coast from Brest to Elbe River

30 Former Tennessee Supreme Court Judge Andrew Jackson kills lawyer Charles Dickinson in duel

JUL 15 Lt Zebulon Montgomery Pike begins second expedition, leading party to explore Southwest

SEP 23 Lewis and Clark Expedition returns to St Louis, ending two-year journey

NOV 15 Yale University's *Literary Cabinet*, first college magazine, appears

21 Berlin Decree of Napoleon declares British Isles in state of blockade

27 Pres. Jefferson issues warning to citizens against joining illegal expeditions against Spanish

DEC 31 James Monroe and William Pinkney sign faulty trade treaty with Great Britain

1806-1807 Aaron Burr plots creation of independent state at expense of US, Spain or both

Also this year

★ Congress authorizes construction of Natchez Trace, route following Indian trail, 500 miles from Nashville, Tenn., to Natchez, Miss.

our rout lay along the ridge of a high
course S 20. W. - 18. me usus the snow far

Thursday September 19th 1805.

Set out this morning a little after
continued our rout about the same cou
as S. 20. W. for 6 miles when the ridge te
me to our inexpressable joy discover

Expedition hazards: a canoe turns over after striking a tree.

Lewis and Clark holding council with a group of Indians.

Clark's drawing of a heathcock from his journals.

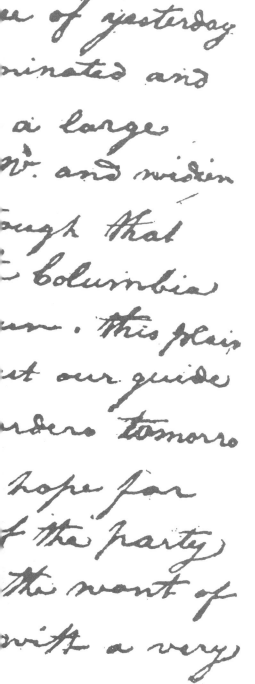

Meriwether Lewis (1774–1809)   *William Clark (1770–1838)*

THE LEWIS AND CLARK EXPEDITION

Less than seven months after the Louisiana Purchase was finalized, one of the most important fact-finding missions in history set out to explore the vast newly-acquired territories between the Mississippi and the Pacific Ocean. The expedition was a personal scheme of President Jefferson's, whose intellectual interest in its findings was further fired by the practical benefit of discovering an overland route to the Pacific and the potential political advantage of establishing an American claim to the Oregon country.

Jefferson chose his private secretary, Meriwether Lewis, and an army lieutenant, William Clark, to head the 42-man expedition, which left St. Louis on May 14, 1804. The group made their way up the Missouri River to the South Fork (in the present-day state of Montana) and on into what is now North Dakota, where they spent the winter with the Mandan Indians. From there, in 1805, they continued in dugout canoes to the Great Divide of the Rocky Mountains, which they successfully crossed. Negotiating the white water of the Snake River, they reached the great Columbia River and followed it to the shores of the Pacific Ocean in November 1805. Here they established Fort Clatsop, where they wintered before returning to St. Louis on September 23, 1806.

Lewis and Clark's notebooks provide a meticulous account of their epic journey, from the cornucopian flora and fauna of the Great Plains to the customs and rituals of the Indian tribes they encountered. Despite the many hazards of the expedition (including the separation of part of the group when a tree on which the leaders had posted directions was gnawed down by a passing beaver!), only one of its members failed to return.

1807

JAN 7 British Order in Council prohibits commercial shipping in coastal waters of France and allies

FEB 19 Aaron Burr arrested in Alabama

MAR 2 Importation of slaves prohibited after January 1, 1808 by act of Congress

JUN 22 USS *Chesapeake* fired upon by British HMS *Leopold*, four alleged deserters removed

JUL 2 Pres. Jefferson issues proclamation calling for all British warships to vacate territorial waters of US

AUG 3 Treason trial of Aaron Burr begins in Richmond, Va, federal circuit court

17-21 Robert Fulton's steamboat *Clermont* makes first round trip on Hudson from New York to Albany

SEP 1 Aaron Burr acquitted of treason

NOV 15 Non-Importation Act becomes effective

DEC 17 Napoleon Bonaparte's Milan Decree further restricts neutral trade

22 Embargo Act prohibits all trade with foreign countries and prohibits all American ships from leaving US for foreign ports

1808

JAN 1 Importation of slaves prohibited after this date, by act of Congress

9 Embargo Act of 1807 supplemented by additional Embargo Act

MAR 12 Congress passes Third Embargo Act

APR 6 John Jacob Astor incorporates American Fur Company

17 Napoleon Bonaparte's Bayonne Decree orders seizure of any US ship entering harbors of France, Italy and Hanseatic League

JUL 12 *The Missouri Gazette* published in St Louis, first newspaper west of the Mississippi

NOV 10 In Osage Treaty, Osage tribe cedes all of its lands in present-day Missouri and Arkansas north of Arkansas River to US

DEC 7 James Madison elected President, George Clinton elected Vice President

1809

JAN 9 Enforcement Act reinforces Embargo Acts

FEB 20 In *US v. Peters, or Olmstead Case*, Supreme Court upholds authority of Federal courts over state laws

MAR 1 Non-Intercourse Act repeals Embargo Acts, reopens all overseas commerce to American shipping, except that of France and Great Britain

1 Congress establishes Territory of Illinois, formed from western portion of Indiana Territory

4 Thomas Jefferson retires to private life at Monticello, near Charlottesville, Va

4 James Madison inaugurated President, George Clinton inaugurated Vice President

APR 19 Pres. Madison issues proclamation reinstituting trade with Great Britain, based upon Erskine Agreement

MAY 22 Eleventh Congress convenes for first session, Federalists have doubled in number in House

30 British Foreign Secretary George Canning rescinds Erskine Agreement

JUN John Stevens' steamboat *Phoenix* makes ocean voyage from New York to Delaware River

JUL 2 Chief of Shawnee tribe, Tecumseh, begins campaign to establish defensive confederacy of tribes to resist westward progress of American settlers

AUG 9 Pres. reinstates Non-Intercourse Act after repudiation of Erskine Agreement by Great Britain

THE COUNTRY whose presidency Thomas Jefferson handed on to his former Secretary of State, James Madison, in 1809 was almost twice the size of the one he had inherited from John Adams eight years earlier. With territorial expansion had come an expansion in national self-confidence and a boom in trade which placed the United States among the world's foremost exporting nations. But all this seemed threatened by the time Madison took the oath of office. What the depredations of the British and French navies had been unable to do on the high seas, Jefferson's own policy had achieved at home. His trade embargo had cut a swathe through America's trading revenues – which up until then had actually continued to boom despite British and French hostility – and had sown division and dissatisfaction throughout the country. Three days before Madison took up residence in the newly completed White House, the embargo had been repealed and replaced with what seemed to be a less controversial piece of legislation, the Non-Intercourse Act. Under this act, trade with Britain and France was banned, on the understanding that it would be resumed with either country if they stopped attacking American shipping at sea.

But America was already slipping downhill into war. An influential group of hawks in Congress reflected the feeling of many Americans in the South and West that the country was being humiliated by the European powers. For many it was time to establish once and for all that the United States was an independent republic, not to be pushed around by her former colonial masters. To them the war with Britain, which broke out in 1812 and lasted until 1815, seemed just like a second war of independence.

The war and its aftermath dominated American thinking during this turbulent decade. It was a war which many, both in America and elsewhere, saw as unnecessary and which had just as catastrophic an effect on American trade as had Jefferson's embargo. Furthermore, the treaty which ended it did little more than restore the status quo that had existed on the eve of the hostilities, with even the deeply resented British right of impressment still intact. But it also resulted in a great upsurge of national pride. The achievements of the Revolutionary War had been consolidated. America had established its right to exist in the eyes of the world. The century was to see another long and bloody conflict on American soil, the first rumblings of which could be heard, distantly, as the decade ended. But it would be a hundred years before the United States would again be drawn into a conflict between European powers.

Prelude to War

At the top of James Madison's agenda when he took office was the question of America's relations with the major European powers. The embargo was gone, swept off the statute book by a tide of public unrest, but restrictions on trade with France and Britain remained, and both powers continued to harass American vessels and insult American pride. Madison entered into negotiations with Britain in order to find a peaceful solution to what was becoming an increasingly dangerous problem. On the one hand, he wanted to continue Jefferson's policy of economic sanctions in a modified form, on the other, he had to contend with the ever more belligerent nationalism of a body of Southern and Western politicians. Led by the redoubtable Henry Clay, they became known as the "War Hawks" and lost no opportunity to advance their belief in the need for a military solution to America's difficulties. Madison had neither Jefferson's diplomatic sense nor his qualities of leadership to bring to the crisis, and, as the months went by, he found himself led by events he was less and less able to control.

The negotiations with Britain fell apart when the British Foreign Secretary, George Canning, intransigently refused to withdraw the Orders in Council under which Britain was searching and seizing American ships. In 1810 Congress reopened American trade with all powers, but let Britain and France know that if either of them stopped attacking American ships, she would resume non-intercourse with the other. Napoleon saw his opportunity to align America with the French cause and announced that French seizures of American ships were now at an end. It wasn't in fact true, but Madison, trapped between warring factions at home, wanted to believe it and proceeded to cut off all trade with the British Empire.

Tensions were further increased by apparent British support of the Northwestern Indian tribes in their attacks on American settlers. These years were a time of Indian revival. Two charismatic leaders – Tecumseh and his twin brother, a priest-figure known as "The Prophet" – had arisen among the Shawnees and were canvassing support from the Southern Creeks and Cherokees for a grand confederation of Indians to defend their tribal hunting grounds against the ever advancing white man. After the Battle of Tippecanoe on the Wabash River, where the Indians were routed by Governor William H. Harrison of the Indiana Territory (a future President of the United States), relations with Britain reached a new low. The voices of the Hawks rose louder than ever. Henry Clay and his supporters urged war and the invasion of Canada. Congress voted increases in military spending. With reelection in the offing, Madison issued an ultimatum to Britain to withdraw the Orders in Council, but Canning still held firm. The question of war or peace was put before Congress. It voted for war.

The Shawnee chief, Tecumseh (right), whose attempt to revive Indian fortunes by allying himself with the British led to his death at the Battle of the Thames (below) on October 5, 1813.

Opposition to the war was strongest in the New England states, where a secret meeting of anti-Madison Federalists at Hartford, Connecticut, in 1814 was seen as treasonable by loyalists.

Mr. Madison's War

America's second war with Great Britain happened because news traveled so slowly at the beginning of the 19th century. If communications had been quicker, Congress would have known that, only days before war was declared in June 1812, Britain had withdrawn the hated Orders in Council. A similar irony hangs over the end of the war. The Americans' greatest victory, Andrew Jackson's famous defense of New Orleans, occurred in the closing hours of the hostilities, after a peace treaty had already been signed between Britain and America in Ghent. One can only wonder how different the course of American history might have been if the telegraph had been invented in 1812.

The years of war were a testing time for the United States. Despite the military build-up of recent months, she could call on very few regular troops, and the size of her navy was no match for that of the greatest maritime nation in the world. Worse still, there was much opposition to the war at home. The vote in Congress produced only a moderate majority in favor of war, and most of New England, seeing a threat to its trading supremacy, remained solidly opposed to it throughout. They refused to fund a conflict which they dismissed contemptuously as "Mr. Madison's war." (When Madison was reelected in 1812, only Vermont among the New England states supported him.) Some would not allow their militias to serve outside the state boundaries, and on at least one occasion local militiamen watched as their fellow Americans were massacred rather than cross the state line to help. Others continued to trade with the enemy throughout the war. Tempers ran high as delegates from some of the Northern states even set up a special convention at Hartford, Connecticut to discuss ways in which they could safeguard their interests under the Constitution, and there was much talk of treason.

For the hastily gathered American forces, the war at first went badly on land and somewhat better at sea. The invasion of Canada, for which the War Hawks had been clamoring for so long, was launched and beaten off in a series of defeats which left Detroit in the hands of the enemy. Meanwhile, U.S. frigates were holding their own against British warships off the coast, with the U.S.S. *Constitution* living up to her vaunted nickname of "Old Ironsides." However, both defeat and victory were to be short-lived. By the end of 1813 the war had turned in America's favor on land, with the magnificent victory of Captain Perry over the British on Lake Erie, the subsequent recovery of Detroit, and the defeat of Tecumseh's Indians at the Battle of the Thames. But the entire eastern coast was blockaded by the British navy, placing a stranglehold on American commerce and proving the fears of the New Englanders for their livelihood only too well justified.

Enter "Old Hickory"

1814 was a trying year for the United States. Having driven Napoleon into exile in Europe, Britain was now free to concentrate on her American war and launched a major invasion plan, attacking Washington and New Orleans from the sea and New York from Canada. By August Washington had fallen to Major General Robert Ross, whose 4000 Redcoats set fire to a number of buildings, including the White House, the President himself making an ignominious last-minute escape to avoid capture. However, the expedition foundered at its next port of call, Baltimore, where the defending American forces fought off the British attack with a determination that provided the inspiration for Francis Scott Key's "The Star-Spangled Banner."

The planned attack on New York fared equally badly. General Sir George Prevost led a force of some 10,000 men down from the Canadian border to Lake Champlain. There he awaited the arrival of a British naval

One result of the siege of Baltimore.

1810s

War with Britain

President Monroe

1810

MAR 23 Napoleon's Rambouillet Decree orders confiscation and sale of all US ships in French ports

MAY 1 Macon's Bill No. 2 repeals Non-Intercourse Act and guarantees restoration of non-intercourse with either France or Britain if one or the other revokes offensive decrees before March 3, 1811

JUL 12 Journeymen Cordwainers trial begins in NYC; cordwainers accused and convicted of illegal conspiracy for strike action intended to raise wages

AUG 5 Napoleon instructs French Foreign Minister Duc de Cadone to inform US that France will revoke Berlin and Milan decrees after November 1 if US will declare non-intercourse against Great Britain

5 Napoleon's Trianon Decree orders seizure of all US ships in French ports

SEP 26 American settlers living in western portion of Spanish West Florida seize fort at Baton Rouge, declare region between New Orleans and Pearl River to be Republic of West Florida and seek annexation to US

OCT 27 Pres. Madison proclaims US annexation of West Florida to Territory of Orleans

NOV 2 Pres. Madison reinstates trade with France and proclaims non-intercourse with Britain, effective February 2, 1811

1811

JAN Four hundred slaves rebel in Louisiana and march on New Orleans

15 Congress adopts secret resolution authorizing conditional annexation of East Florida

FEB 2 Russian settlers land at Bodega Bay, above San Francisco, to establish Fort Ross

MAR 4 Bank of the US dissolved

APR 12 Colonists sponsored by John Jacob Astor establish first permanent American settlement in the Pacific Northwest

SEP 11 First inland steamboat, *New Orleans*, sets sail from Pittsburgh, Pa, down Ohio River to New Orleans

NOV 20 Construction of Cumberland Road, main route for colonization of Far West, begins

DEC 16 Major earthquake centered on New Madrid, Mo., changes topography of 30,000-square mile area

1812

MAR 3 First foreign aid act authorizes $50,000 for Venezuelan victims of earthquake

APR Indians raid frontier settlements in Northwest region

force to support his assault on the American garrison at Plattsburg. It never came. The American Captain, Thomas Macdonough, engaged the much stronger British fleet on the lake and defeated it in a hard-fought battle, which was to prove the turning point of the whole war. Prevost was left with no choice but to head back to Canada.

That only left the New Orleans prong of the invasion force, and in December 1814 Sir Edward Pakenham arrived in the Gulf of Mexico with another 10,000 men. But by this time American forces in the South were under the command of one of the most extraordinary characters to be forged in the cauldron of the war.

Andrew Jackson was a Tennessee Senator and plantation owner, who had emerged as a leading figure in the campaigns against the Creek Indians in the early months of 1814. A stern and forthright disciplinarian, Jackson led the 2500-strong militia force which had roundly defeated the Upper Creeks at the decisive Battle of Horseshoe Bend on the Tallapoosa River in March. (After the battle, the Indians had been forced to sign away vast tracts of their land in the South – land which was to become the heart of the cotton belt in Alabama and Georgia.) Jackson then pressed on down into Florida to mop up another British–Indian rising before occupying Pensacola and Mobile. His exploits earned him the respect of his men (who dubbed him "tough as old hickory"), the rank of Major General, and the command of American forces in the South and West.

It was Jackson and his men with whom Pakenham had to deal at New Orleans. In the early days of 1815, the Redcoats attacked Jackson's defenses, but were beaten back with appalling casualties. It was all over in about 20 minutes. The British lost more than 2000 men, including Pakenham himself. Of Jackson's men, only 13 lay dead.

The "era of good feelings"

A peace agreement had already been signed by American and British negotiators in Ghent by the time Jackson became "the Hero of New Orleans." The treaty, news of which reached America shortly after Pakenham's defeat, was ratified by Congress on St. Valentine's Day 1815. It laid the basis for establishing an agreed border between Canada and the United States, but left open most of the other questions which had been the immediate cause of the war.

Strangely enough, this didn't seem to matter much to either side. The important thing was that the war itself was over. In the United States, there was a sense of euphoria quite beyond what her military showing or the Treaty of Ghent warranted. Above all else, there was a strong sense of pride that America had taken up arms successfully for the second time against the most powerful empire on earth, and had demonstrated that she could defend her people, her rights, and her independence. The war laid the groundwork for a period of more harmonious relations between Britain and America. By the end of the decade the Great Lakes had been demilitarized, and not even Jackson's ad-

venturist hanging of two British subjects during a punitive raid against Indians in Florida in 1818 led to a resumption of hostilities. Britain and the United States have not been to war with one another again from that day to this.

The effect of the end of the war on American politics was electrifying. Where there had been division, there was a sudden outbreak of unity. The tide of nationalism rose irresistibly, and the one-time Jeffersonian, James Madison, inaugurated a program of reforms which outdid even the arch-Federalist Alexander Hamilton's measures under Washington's first administration. The Bank of the United States, which had caused such controversy in the 1780s and had been quietly allowed to die under Madison's first Republican administration, was now raised from the grave. Military spending was increased, and the one plank of Hamilton's program which had not been implemented under Washington – a system of protectionist tariffs – now sailed through Congress.

The climate of American politics had changed. This was only too obvious in the 1816 election, in which Madison's Secretary of State, James Monroe, stood for president. Monroe had been a supporter of the war and had attracted his share of New England anger. But the closing months of Madison's second term of office eclipsed all previous differences. In 1816 Monroe was elected in a landslide victory. The voters spoke of "an era of good feelings." Like "the New Deal" more than a century later, it was a phrase which captured the imagination of the American people. A new age seemed about to begin.

Darkening Skies

During the disruption of the export trade which had resulted from Jefferson's embargo and the ensuing war, American industry had taken its first significant step

James Monroe, America's fifth President.

towards manufacturing. (Madison's tariffs were partly designed to protect these new industries against the "dumping" of cheap British goods on the American market.) The march of "King Cotton" began in earnest with the wider availability of Eli Whitney's epoch-making cotton gin, which enabled planters to process their crops 300 times more quickly than had been possible before mechanization. An intensive program of road and canal building began to open up America's internal communications with unprecedented speed. And the country expanded again with the acquisition from Spain for $5 million of the much disputed Florida territory and her claim to the Oregon country in the North.

With the expansion came easy credit, as frontier farmers bought land in the expectation of later profits. The credit boom, and the proliferation of paper money issued by the so-called "wild-cat" banks of the West, helped to create one of the two dark clouds which loomed over the close of the decade. In 1819 the new central bank took belated steps to curtail credit by requiring the wildcat banks to redeem their issues of paper money from their reserves. Panic swept the country. Banks closed, factories went into bankruptcy, and land and commodity prices plummeted. It seemed as if the era of good feelings had overstretched itself as each region looked to its own survival. With the crash of 1819, the pendulum began to swing back towards sectionalism.

The other storm cloud also gathered as a result of the rapid westward expansion. During the decade, five new states were admitted to the Union: Louisiana in 1812, Indiana in 1816, Mississippi in 1817, Illinois in 1818, and Alabama in 1819. But it was with the application of Missouri in 1819 that trouble erupted. Missouri was a slaveholding state, and its admission would have disrupted the delicate balance between free and slave states that had so far been maintained in Congress. Controversy arose when the House proposed an amendment to Missouri's constitution, prohibiting the further introduction of slaves. It was an issue over which feelings ran dangerously high. The slavery question rocketed to the top of the political agenda. In the short term, the so-called Missouri debate was resolved by a compromise whereby Maine – which had formerly been part of Massachusetts – was simultaneously admitted to the Union as a free state, and a northern limit (the 36° 30′ parallel) was set for the creation of future slave states. The more far-sighted of America's political leaders knew, however, that this was not a permanent solution. The problem could not be shelved indefinitely, and its implications were frightening. Jefferson, now an old man, wrote that "this momentous question" woke him "like a firebell in the night," and John Quincy Adams, the son of the second President of the United States and soon to be President himself, confided ominously to his diary that he regarded the Missouri question as "a title page to a great, tragic volume." It was a volume which would only be fully opened 40 years later.

One of Washington Irving's most enduring creations, Rip Van Winkle (above), awoke to literary fame in 1819. Irving's *Sketch Book*, published that year, included not only the tale of Rip Van Winkle, but also the famous "Legend of Sleepy Hollow," and confirmed the success of its author's earlier work, *Diedrich Knickerbocker's History of New York* (1809).

Emma Willard

The decade saw the first stirrings of a movement toward wider educational opportunities for American citizens, with the beginnings of the public school system. This movement was reflected in the first campaigns for greater educational equality for women in the United States. Prime among early advocates of women's rights was Emma Willard (left) who founded America's first college for women, the Waterford Academy, in Waterford, New York, in 1819. The struggle for equality was to be a long and often bitter one. Only 100 years later, in August 1919, would American women receive the vote.

4 Ninety-day embargo placed on all vessels in US harbors

20 Death of Vice President George Clinton

30 Territory of New Orleans enters Union as Louisiana, slave state

MAY 14 Spanish West Florida added to Mississippi Territory by Congress

JUN 1 War of 1812 begins

4 Missouri Territory established

16 British proclaim suspension of orders in council affecting neutral shipping, effective June 23

19 Pres. Madison officially proclaims US to be in state of war with Great Britain

23 Great Britain revokes orders in council affecting neutral shipping, unaware of US declaration of war

JUL 17 US port of Michilimackinac surrenders to British; incident encourages Indians to ally with British

AUG 16 American Gen. William Hull surrenders Detroit to British

29 British PM Lord Castlereagh rejects US peace proposals

SEP 30 British Adm. Sir John Borlase Warren, from Halifax, offers armistice to US Government

DEC 2 James Madison wins election for second term, Elbridge Terry elected Vice President

29 University of Maryland chartered in Baltimore, Md

1813

MAR 4 James Madison inaugurated for second term, Elbridge Terry inaugurated Vice President

APR 27 Americans raid York (present-day Toronto), capital of Upper Canada, and set fire to government buildings

MAY 26 British raid and bombard coastal settlements along southern Atlantic Coast

AUG 30 Creek War begins as Mississippi Valley Creek Indians attack Fort Mims and massacre hundreds

SEP 10 In Battle of Lake Erie, American fleet defeats British

18 British evacuate Detroit, Mich.

OCT 5 In Battle of the Thames, north of Lake Erie, Americans defeat British and Indian forces

NOV 4 PM Lord Castlereagh offers negotiation for end to war

4 Pres. Madison accepts British offer of negotiation

DEC 17 Embargo law forbids trade with British

29-30 British burn Buffalo, NY, and Black Rock Navy Yard

30 British schooner *Bramble* arrives at Annapolis, Md, under flag of truce, bearing British peace dispatches

1814

JAN 25 Congress modifies war embargo due to Nantucket Island, Mass., famine

MAR 27 In Battle of Horseshoe Bend, Ala., Gen. Andrew Jackson defeats Creek and Cherokee Indians, ending war

APR 6 Napoleon Bonaparte overthrown

14 Embargo Act and Non-importation Act repealed by Congress

25 British extend war embargo to New England

JUL 22 In Treaty of Crenville, tribes of Delaware, Miami, Seneca, Shawnee and Wyandot Indians make peace with US and are required to declare war on British

25 In Battle of Lundy's Lane, near Niagara Falls, most violent battle of War of 1812, Americans withdraw to Fort Erie

AUG 8 US peace commissioners meet British commissioners at Ghent in The Netherlands

9 In Treaty of Fort Jackson, some of Creek peoples cede 20 million acres to US

The War of 1812

America's second war of independence was a controversial affair. Encouraged by Henry Clay and his so-called "War Hawks," Madison allowed himself to be maneuvered toward confrontation with Britain by Napoleon, but from the very first there was considerable opposition to the war at home, especially in New England. What began as a grandiose attempt to end British infringement of American freedom at sea, conquer Canada, and crush militant Indian resistance to white expansionism quickly became a struggle for survival as Great

Britain once more turned her imperial might against her ill-prepared former colonies. In 1814 the nation's capital itself fell to the Redcoats, the President fleeing into the hills of Virginia as General Ross' soldiers set the city ablaze.

If the peace treaty which concluded the war actually left matters pretty much as they stood on the eve of the hostilities, it nonetheless made a massive difference to the national mood. Widely seen (at least in retrospect) as a triumph by the American people, the war made the reputations of a number of its partici-

pants, including two future presidents. Andrew Jackson's defensive victory at the Battle of New Orleans (background) set him firmly on the road to the White House, even though its military significance was nil, the peace treaty having already been agreed by the time it took place. And William Harrison's rout of Tecumseh's confederacy at the Battle of the Thames confirmed the reputation he had already gained as a scourge of the Indians by his 1811 victory at Tippecanoe.

American frontiersmen give George III a sticky time.

Washington in flames during British bombardment and occupation of August 1814.

"Old Ironsides" battles it out with HMS Guerriere.

24-25 British force invades Washington, DC; US Army and government officials flee to Virginia; British burn Capitol, White House and other government buildings

SEP 14 Words of 'Star Spangled Banner' written by Francis Scott Key during bombardment of Fort McHenry before Baltimore

NOV 5 American troops evacuate and blow up Fort Erie, abandon plan to invade Canada

7 Gen. Jackson captures Pensacola as part of plan to invade Spanish Florida

DEC 24 Treaty of Ghent signed with Great Britain, ends War of 1812

Also this year

★ Boston textile manufacturer Francis Cabot Lowell builds first American plant to manufacture cloth from raw cotton by power machinery in Waltham, Mass.

1815

JAN 5 New England Federalists disband

FEB 6 Inventor John Stevens granted first American railroad charter, in NJ

14 Treaty of Ghent ratified by Senate; Pres. Madison declares end of war

MAR 3 Congress authorizes hostilities against the Dey of Algiers for protection of US commerce

3 Policy of trade reciprocity with all nations authorized by Congress

JUN 30 Stephen Decatur signs treaty with Dey of Algiers, ending war against Algeria and Barbary Coast pirates; Dey agrees to cease hostilities against American shipping, free prisoners and end tribute demands

JUL 3 Representatives of US and Great Britain sign commercial convention, nullifying discriminatory duties and permitting US to trade with British East Indies

26 Decatur exacts treaty from Tunis in North Africa guaranteeing end of interference with American commercial shipping in Mediterranean, end of tribute demands and compensation for vessels

JUL-SEP Treaties of Portage des Sioux, signed by three US peace commissioners with 2000 Indians, open territory below Lake Michigan for settlement

AUG 5 Decatur exacts treaty from Tripoli

1816

MAR 14 Congress passes bill to establish second Bank of the US

20 In *Martin v Hunter's Lessee*, Supreme Court rules that 1789 Judiciary Act constitutionally supports right of Supreme Court to review decisions by state courts

APR 27 Treaty of 1816 maintains protective duties of War of 1812

JUN 11 Gas Light Company of Baltimore, Md, established to provide street lighting

JUL 9 Cherokees cede lands in northern Maine to US

27 US government expedition destroys Fort Apalachicola, refuge for runaway slaves and hostile Indians, in Spanish East Florida

DEC 4 Democratic-Republican James Monroe elected President, Daniel D. Tompkins elected Vice President

11 Indiana admitted to Union as 19th state, slavery forbidden

13 The Provident Institution for Savings, in Boston, Mass., chartered as first savings bank in US

28 American Colonization Society founded in Washington DC, to resettle freed blacks in Africa

Also this year

★ 'The year in which there was no summer' in New England

★ George E. Clymer introduces hand-printing press

Tippecanoe

The battle that made a president: General William H. Harrison's men rout Tenskwatawa (the Prophet)'s Indians at Tippecanoe Creek, Indiana, on November 7, 1811.

The Creek War

Left: the War of 1812 marked the end of the Creek Indians' influence in the Mississippi Territory. Drafted, albeit reluctantly, into Tecumseh's great Indian confederation, the Upper Creeks felt the full force of Andrew Jackson's punitive prowess after they attacked Fort Mims on the Alabama River. Jackson emerged from relative obscurity in Tennessee to command a ruthless campaign against the Creeks in the early months of 1814. On March 27, he crushed them at the decisive battle of Horseshoe Bend on the Tallapoosa River, and forced their leaders to sign away some two-thirds of the future state of Alabama.

Thar She Blows!

Right: the American whaling industry continued to grow during this period, and would later provide the background for Melville's masterpiece, *Moby-Dick*.

1817

JAN 7 Second Bank of the US opens in Philadelphia

MAR 3 Alabama Territory formed from eastern part of Mississippi Territory

4 James Monroe inaugurated President, Daniel D. Tompkins inaugurated Vice President

15 New York State Legislature authorizes construction of Erie Canal

APR 28-29 Rush-Bagot Agreement between US and Great Britain limits number of naval vessels on Great Lakes and other inland waterways

JUL 27 Ohio Indians cede four million acres of their remaining lands in northwestern Ohio to US

AUG 28 *Philanthropist*, abolitionist newspaper, begins publication in Mt Pleasant, Ohio

NOV 20 First Seminole War (1817-18) begins with settlers' attack on Florida Indians

DEC 10 Mississippi enters Union as 20th (slave) state

Also this year

★ University of Michigan founded at Detroit, Mich.

★ Law school established at Harvard

1818

JAN Transatlantic ship crossings on regular monthly basis initiated between US and Great Britain

APR 4 Congress adopts US flag with 13 alternate red and white stripes and white star on blue for each state

MAY 24 Gen. Jackson seizes Spanish post of Pensacola, Fla, ending First Seminole War

JUN 20 Connecticut State Legislature rescinds property requirement for voting

OCT 5 Connecticut state constitution adopted by popular vote

19 Chickasaws cede to US all of their lands between Mississippi River and northern part of Tennessee River

20 Convention of 1818 between US and Great Britain establishes 49th parallel as common boundary from Lake of the Woods to continental divide, leaves Oregon boundary question unsettled for 10 years, allows American citizens to fish in waters off Newfoundland and Labrador and renews convention of 1815

DEC 3 Illinois enters Union as 21st (free) state

Also this year

★ Cumberland Road opened from Cumberland on Potomac River to Wheeling on Ohio River

1819

FEB 2 In *Dartmouth College v. Woodward*, Supreme Court rules that private corporate charter is a contract, therefore it cannot be revised or broken by a state

22 In Adams-Onis Treaty, Spain cedes East Florida to US and renounces claims to West Florida; US renounces claims to Texas and assumes debts owed to Spain by US citizens; and boundary between US and Spanish territories is defined

Mar 2 Congress passes first legislation regulating immigration, requiring ships' captains to provide descriptive lists of passengers brought on each voyage

2 Arkansas County of Missouri Territory reorganized as Arkansas Territory

6 In *McCulloch v Maryland*, Supreme Court denies right of states to tax agencies of national government

DEC 14 Alabama enters Union as 22nd (slave) state

Also this year

★ Financial panic due to banking expansion, land speculation and business readjustments strikes US and results in collapse of state banks and foreclosure of western property by Bank of the US

★ University of Virginia at Charlottesville founded by Thomas Jefferson

The Arts

★ Washington Irving's *Sketchbook*

THE 1820s began inauspiciously with the immediate after-effects of the great financial panic of 1819 and the deep ill-feeling left by the Missouri debate. After the cosmetic compromise of 1820, Missouri was officially admitted to the Union as a slave state in 1821, but the wounds left by the controversy continued to fester under the surface. The irreconcilable differences between the North and the South over the question of slavery had emerged into the light with terrifying distinctness and, as time would tell, the specter thus raised could not be laid to rest by such half-measures, however well-intentioned they might be.

In international affairs, on the other hand, the decade marked a new and hopeful beginning. The United States was at peace and feeling a new confidence in its position in the world. In 1823 President James Monroe laid down the principles which would govern American foreign policy for the rest of the century and beyond, and which established the basis for relations with the old colonial powers of Europe.

In other ways, these were directionless years. John Quincy Adams, who was elected President in 1824, aroused bitter opposition in Congress, and his term of office made little lasting impression on the nation. Throughout there hovered in the background the still commanding presence of Andrew Jackson, the "Hero of New Orleans," whose bid for the presidency in 1824 had been thwarted by Adams' maneuverings. In the 1828 election, however, he swept into the White House to begin what was widely seen as a new epoch in American life. Later historians have named it "the Age of Jackson." But as "Old Hickory's" eager supporters clambered over the plush White House furnishings in their muddy boots on his inauguration day in 1829, there were many contemporary observers who saw in it instead the beginning of the rule of "King Mob."

The State of the Nation

By the beginning of the decade, the American nation had come a long way since the difficult days of the Independence struggle. Political institutions regarded as radical experiments when they were introduced had stood the test of time and proved themselves against foreign intervention. The country had expanded from 13 states to 22, and had acquired enormous new territories, many of which had yet to be explored and settled. Its population had grown to nearly ten million – two-and-a-half times larger than it had been only 30 years before – of whom almost a fifth were Black, the great majority of them slaves in the Southern states. A vast tide of westward emigration had swelled the population of the trans-Appalachian territories over the preceding decades and was continuing unabated, creating, in the fiercely independent figure of the frontier farmer, the basis of a new political force. But in the process, traditional Indian hunting grounds were being steadily and systematically eroded as more and more tribes were driven westward to make room for white settlers.

During the 1820s, the resentment this caused was heightened by forced resettlement, which would claim thousands of Indian lives and Indian acres over the coming decades.

The foundations of American manufacturing had been laid during the years of the second war with Britain, and although it would be a long time before America could match the industrial muscle of the European powers, a process of urbanization and industrialization had begun which would have far-reaching effects on the American way of life. In the meantime, the land-hungry march of "King Cotton" continued in the Southern states, supplying the European textile industry with its raw materials and entrenching the divisive institution of slavery ever more deeply in the workings of the American economy. Expansion had brought new land, new people, and new confidence. But it had also brought new problems, the dangers of which were only just beginning to be glimpsed as the 1820s began.

The Monroe Doctrine

Changes in South America were much on the minds of the American administration in the years following the end of the war of 1812. Many former colonies there had shaken off the chains of colonial government and become independent republics, and the United States was watching their progress with interest. So were the European powers, though from a very different perspective. The Franco–Spanish axis was eager to reestablish power over former Spanish colonies in Latin America and Britain was eager to stop them. In 1823, in a move which took Monroe and his Secretary of State, John Quincy Adams, by surprise, the British asked America for help in doing so. The President, after taking advice from many quarters, turned them down. His reasons for doing so were enshrined in his address to Congress in December 1823. Largely ignored at the time, they were later to be revived under the name of the Monroe Doctrine.

The principles Monroe laid down in his speech were to be the guiding lights of American foreign policy for many years to come and are still an important element in it today. He proclaimed that the American continent was no longer to be seen as the subject for future European colonization; that any attempt by the European powers to extend their political systems to the Americas would be seen as an act of aggression; that America would not interfere in the affairs of any existing European colonies; and that she would keep out of all European wars over European matters. It was no less than a recognition that in future the guardianship of what Monroe tellingly described as "this hemisphere" lay not with the Old World but with the New. Monroe's words may have seemed more vision than substance in the 1820s, but the role he and Adams foresaw was one America would expand into in reality as the century progressed.

John Quincy Adams

The son of the second President of the United States himself became President in 1825. "Reserved, cold, austere and forbidding" was his own description of his bearing, and it was true enough to bring him few friends during his term of office. Things went badly for him from the start. The first ballot gave Andrew Jackson more electoral votes than any of the other candidates (who included Adams; Henry Clay, the leading "War Hawk" of the previous decade; and John C. Calhoun, Adams' future Vice President), but not enough for an overall majority. Adams and Clay then struck a secret deal, whereby Clay gave the support of his states to Adams in return for the promise of the post of Secretary of State in Adams' administration. The deal gave Adams victory in the second ballot. Legal though it was, it outraged Jackson's supporters, who demonstrated their resentment by blocking Adams' every move in Congress. The resulting polarization of the Adams–Clay faction on the one side and the Jackson–Calhoun faction on the other fed the roots of what was to become the Republican–Democrat divide. For the moment, though, it produced only deadlock and frustration. When Adams left the White House in 1829 – embroiled in a dispute about the so-called Tariff of Abominations, a measure which revived memories of the hated British taxes of the 1760s – he was a bitter and disappointed man.

The "Hero of New Orleans"

There could hardly be two temperaments more different than Adams' and that of the man who succeeded him as President. Andrew Jackson of Tennessee had won his spurs on the frontier and made his reputation in the field of battle. During the war of 1812, his exploits had aroused the greatest patriotic fervor, but many doubted whether his qualities were equally suited to the highest office in the land. Among them were those who remembered how his raid on Florida in 1818 had shaken the newly signed peace to its foundations. Their minds would hardly have been set at rest by the unprecedented scenes which attended his inauguration in Washington in 1829. A mob of farmers, frontiersmen, well-wishers, and hangers-on celebrated noisily in the White House itself, damaging carpets and furniture and clambering through windows to get at the punch. For those whose image of the presidency was based on the Virginian tradition of Washington and Jefferson, this self-styled champion of the common man came as a culture-shock of the first order. The values of the new West had come to the White House. They were to leave an indelible mark on the life of the nation.

"Jackson is to be President, and you will be HANGED."

1820s

Missouri Compromise

Monroe Doctrine

1820

FEB 3 Illinois Sen. Jesse B. Thomas proposes Missouri Compromise, permitting admission of Maine as free state and admission of Missouri as slave state and prohibiting slavery in western territory of Louisiana Purchase north of 36° 30′

MAR 15 Maine admitted to Union as 23rd (free) state

DEC 6 James Monroe and Daniel D. Tompkins win election for second terms

1821

JAN 17 New Spain gives Moses Austin Texas land grant for settlement of 300 American families

FEB 24 Mexico declares independence from Spain

MAR 5 James Monroe and Daniel Tompkins inaugurated for second terms

JUN 1 Waterford Academy for Young Ladies, first women's collegiate level school in America, founded by Emma Willard in Waterford, NY

JUL 1 Gov. Andrew Jackson receives Florida territory from Spanish

AUG 10 Missouri enters Union as 24th (slave) state

SEP 4 Czar Alexander I of Russia claims American Pacific coast north of 51st parallel and closes surrounding waters to foreign commercial shipping

Also this year
★ American Colonization Society founds Republic of Liberia in West Africa for freed US slaves

1822

MAR 30 Florida Territory organized, combining East and West Florida

JUL 24 US diplomatic note protests Russian claim to American Pacific coast and threatens possibility of war if claim is put into effect

SEP 3 Fox and Sauk tribes sign treaty with US permitting them to live in Wisconsin Territory and ceding Illinois to Federal Government

NOV In Congress of Vienna, Holy Alliance of Austria, France, Prussia and Russia agree to support Spain's attempt to recover former New World colonies

1823

JUL 17 US informs Russia that American continents are no longer subjects for new European colonies

OCT 9 In Polignac Agreement between Great Britain and France, France renounces intentions of helping Spain regain former colonies in America

DEC 2 Monroe Doctrine announced by the President

John Quincy Adams (1767–1848)

The son of John Adams – one of the leading lights of the 1776 Revolution and the second President of the United States – John Quincy Adams (left) himself became President in 1825. Sadly for him, the glorious associations of the Adams name were not enough to overcome either his austere personal demeanor or the bitter opposition of his Jacksonian opponents in Congress, which between them contrived to make his presidency a catalogue of political misjudgments and blocked initiatives. Following his defeat by Jackson in the presidential election of 1828, Adams took up a seat in the House of Representatives, where he continued to exercise a powerful influence on American life right up to his death, not least by his opposition to slave-owning interests.

The Erie Canal

Completed in 1825 after eight years' work, the Erie Canal (below) linked Lake Erie with the Hudson River and opened up the Great Lakes area to trade with New York. By 1854 it was carrying merchandise to an annual value of some $94 million, stimulating the phenomenal growth of cities such as Cleveland, Chicago, and Detroit.

The Last of the Mohicans

The 1820s saw the publication of James Fenimore Cooper's distinctively American trilogy of novels, *Leatherstocking Tales*, including perhaps his most famous work, *The Last of the Mohicans* (above), which in 1826 reintroduced to the reading public the character of Natty Bumppo, hero of its predecessor in the series, *The Pioneers* (1823).

Changes in South America

The years between 1815 and 1822 saw a remarkable series of changes in South America, as independence movements, largely inspired by the nationalist leader Simon Bolivar (right), swept away the imperial power of the Old World in country after country. This upsurge of republicanism was watched with excited interest by the United States – one of only two independent states in the New World in 1815 – which, seeing its own struggle for independence reflected in South American events, lent support to the rebels and promptly recognized the emerging independent governments. By 1822 only Belize, Bolivia, and the Guianas remained under colonial control in South America. It was the U.S. administration's fear that France and Spain would mount a joint offensive to regain the former colonies which prompted the formulation of the Monroe Doctrine in December 1823.

in annual message to Congress, any attempt by Europeans to colonize Americas or interfere in internal affairs of Western Hemisphere will not be tolerated by US and US will not interfere in European affairs

1824

APR 17 Treaty concluded in which Russia accepts 54°40' as southern limit of US west coast expansion; treaty also removes commercial shipping ban

DEC 1 Presidential election; no candidate receives electoral majority

1825

FEB 9 John Quincy Adams elected President in House
12 In Treaty of Indian Springs, tribal leaders cede all lands in Georgia to US and promise to migrate west by September 1, 1826; treaty rejected by most Creeks
21 Amherst College chartered in Amherst, Mass.

MAR 4 John Quincy Adams inaugurated President, John C. Calhoun inaugurated Vice President
24 Mexican state of Texas-Coahuila opens to American settlers

OCT 26 Erie Canal, connecting New York City with Great Lakes, completed

The Arts
★ Henry Wadsworth Longfellow's poems 'Autumnal Nightfall,' 'Woods in Winter,' 'The Angler's Song' and others published in *United States Literary Gazette*

1826

JAN 24 Treaty of Washington abrogates Treaty of Indian Springs (1825); Georgia Creek Indians cede smaller area to US and agree to evacuate lands by January 1, 1827

MAR 1 Lafayette College chartered in Easton, Pa

JUL 4 Deaths of former Presidents John Adams and Thomas Jefferson on 50th anniversary of Declaration of Independence

Also this year
★ Pennsylvania law makes kidnapping a felony, thereby nullifying Fugitive Slave Act of 1793

1827

FEB 28 Baltimore and Ohio Railroad chartered by state of Maryland

NOV 15 Creek Indians sign second treaty, ceding remainder of their western Georgia lands to US

Also this year
★ First Mardi Gras celebration in New Orleans initiated by American students

1828

JAN 24 Indiana University chartered in Bloomington as Indiana College
APR 21 Noah Webster's *American Dictionary of the English Language* published
MAY 19 'Tariff of Abominations' passes Congress and is signed by Pres. Adams, thwarting plans to discredit Pres. Adams by bill's defeat
DEC 3 Andrew Jackson elected President, John C. Calhoun elected Vice President

1829

MAR 7 Andrew Jackson inaugurated President, John Calhoun inaugurated Vice President
7 Enthusiastic Jackson supporters overwhelm White House reception
DEC Texas declared exempt from Mexican anti-slavery decree of September 15 by Mexican Pres. Guerrero

THE "Age of Jackson" had begun. Andrew Jackson himself would remain in the White House only until 1837 – which was one term longer than he had originally intended – but his influence was to be felt in American life until the Civil War and beyond. During these years there was an upsurge of democratic feeling in the United States. Jackson was no enlightened intellectual in the Jefferson mold, but he was a self-reliant fighter who knew the rigors of frontier life at first hand, and his supporters saw in him the victory of the common man. They argued for the removal of "artificial distinctions" between people and the extension of equality of opportunity to all – or at least to all white American men. That said, Jackson himself was no blind supporter of the states'-rights lobby, as events would shortly prove in the most dramatic fashion, and his exercise of the office of President was more autocratic than that of any of his predecessors. But he seemed to represent a new stage in the growth of individualism and national self-determination that had begun before the Declaration of Independence.

Jackson was no stranger to controversy, and feelings ran high on more than one occasion during his presidency. There were outcries against his style of leadership, his enemies dubbing him "King Andrew." There were crises within the Administration, such as the bizarre affair of Mrs. Eaton, which led to the rise of Martin Van Buren, and there were crises within the Union, such as the so-called Nullification Controversy, which was perhaps the greatest threat to the survival of the republic since its foundation some 60 years earlier. The decade also saw Jackson pursuing a determined feud against the Bank of the United States, which he called

Jackson's presidency marked the beginning of the end for the great Southeastern Indian tribes. This cartoon catalogues the injustices inflicted on the Cherokees, whose forced resettlement in 1838 led to thousands of deaths.

"The Monster." His success in bringing it to its knees was won only at the cost of economic collapse, and Martin Van Buren was left to pick up the pieces.

In other ways too the decade represented a time of deepening divisions in American life. Foreign relations – both with Great Britain and with the new-born republic of Mexico – were strained by developments in Canada and Texas during Van Buren's presidency, and domestic tensions, especially over the slavery issue, continued to grow. In the West, the territorial ambitions of settlers in Texas gave to American folk-lore the stubborn heroism of the Alamo. In the South, conservative plantation owners dug themselves in against the rising tide of anti-slavery sentiment in the North. And, along the frontier, the forced resettlement of those Indian tribes who had not already given up the struggle moved into top gear, resulting in thousands of deaths and a legacy of bitterness which has not been expunged to this day.

Mrs. Eaton

The first crisis of Jackson's presidency was at first sight a purely local matter, which suddenly exploded into the political arena from the dinner-tables of fashionable Washington. Jackson's Secretary of War, John H. Eaton, had married the daughter of a Washington inn-keeper after a prolonged affair, most of which had been conducted during her husband's absence overseas. Washington society, led by the wife of the Vice President, John Calhoun, refused to recognize the unfortunate Mrs. Eaton, whose personal life immediately became public property. The whole affair might have been confined to the world of gossip, but for Martin Van Buren, the Secretary of State, who seems to have used it skilfully to his own political advantage. Whether or not at Van Buren's instigation, the Vice President's enemies used the Eaton scandal to drive a wedge between Calhoun and Jack-

son, who had championed Mrs. Eaton throughout. After it was brought to the President's attention that Calhoun had censured him in no uncertain terms for his controversial raid on Florida in 1818, Calhoun's days of influence at the White House were numbered, and Martin Van Buren's rise to power, which saw him elected President as Jackson's successor in 1835, had begun.

The Nullification Crisis

The next crisis Jackson had to face was far more serious than the Eaton affair. The Nullification Crisis, which broke in 1832, opened old wounds in the battle between states' rights and the rights of the Union. What began as a squabble about the sale of public lands blew up into a major constitutional issue which brought the United States to the very brink of civil war.

The crisis had its roots in the previous decade, when Congress had passed a highly political Tariff Act which soon became known as the Tariff of Abominations. South Carolina considered itself particularly ill-served by this piece of legislation, and in the quarrel which followed, Calhoun had written a paper propounding his theory of nullification. The gist of Calhoun's argument was that the U.S. Constitution was a compact between the states and that individual states should therefore be the ultimate arbiters of whether what Congress did was constitutional. This meant that a state could "nullify" an act of Congress and could appeal to other states for support. If it didn't get their support, it could secede from the Union.

The whole argument revived in 1830 when a famous debate took place in Congress between Senator Hayne of South Carolina and the charismatic Daniel Webster of Massachusetts. Hayne put forward Calhoun's view of the Constitution, to be answered by Webster in a long and powerful speech, ending with the famous words: "Liberty *and* Union, now and forever, one and inseparable." Jackson lost no time in making it clear that his sympathies lay with Webster. The opposing views represented a disaster waiting to happen. The new Tariff Act of 1832 provided the opportunity.

The protectionist measures in the 1832 Act benefited Northern manufacturers more than Southern cotton growers, and South Carolina was as implacably opposed to them as it had been to those in the Tariff of Abominations. The state legislature declared the act null and void, refused to collect duties, and began to gather an army of volunteers to resist coercion by the National Government. Jackson moved swiftly and decisively at this moment of crisis. He announced that resistance to the Union by armed force was treason and threatened to send 50,000 men against South Carolina if it proceeded further down the road to secession. In words that recalled his exercise of discipline in the field of battle, he even talked of hanging Calhoun.

In the long run bloodshed was avoided. Calhoun resigned the vice presidency

Andrew Jackson in old age.

and entered into an unlikely partnership with Henry Clay, the author of the hated Tariff Act, to get the legislation changed. At the same time Jackson was tempering his public militarism with private diplomacy, and a compromise was reached whereby South Carolina could back off without losing too much face. All those involved breathed a sigh of relief. Jackson had passed the first major test of his presidential mettle with flying colors.

The Alamo and After

Texas in the 1830s was still a province of the newly established republic of Mexico. The Mexicans had encouraged settlers to cross the border from the United States, but in 1830 they evidently realized that things had gone too far. By 1835 there were some 20,000 Americans in Texas, outnumbering the Mexicans four to one, and it was clear that, unless steps were taken to prevent it, the great land-hungry nation on its eastern borders would soon swallow the province whole.

In 1836, angered by what they saw as Mexican high-handedness, the American settlers ousted the Mexicans from their garrison at San Antonio and declared Texas an independent republic. The ruler of Mexico, General Antonio López de Santa Anna, immediately set off at the head of an army of 3000 men to put down the rebellion. A mere 180 Americans held the Mexican forces at bay in a small frontier mission house known as "the Alamo." The siege continued for ten days, with Santa Anna's army receiving heavy losses. Finally, though, superior numbers won the day, and the entire American garrison was wiped out, the wounded being slaughtered after the victory. Among the dead were the legendary backwoodsman, Davy Crockett, and Jim Bowie of Bowie-knife fame.

Santa Anna dealt equally bloodily with the other remaining Texan garrison at Goliad before pressing on to the San Jacinto River. Here he met a Texan force of 750 men under General Sam Houston. Despite being heavily outnumbered, Houston's men, whose battle cry was "Remember the Alamo!," routed the Mexican army and captured its leader. Texan independence was assured. The republic drafted a constitution based on that of the United States – with the significant difference that it explicitly legalized slavery – and elected Houston its first President. It then applied to the United States for annexation.

However, admission to the Union was slow in coming. Texas was a slave territory, and Northern Congressmen were anxious to avoid disturbing the delicate political balance established between slave and free states by the Missouri Compromise. President Jackson was busily engaged in ensuring the succession of Martin Van Buren at the time and was eager to steer clear of the slavery issue in an election year. Not until the very last day of his term of office – March 3, 1837 – did he officially recognize the new republic. It would be another eight years before Texas was annexed to the United States.

"Little Van"

Martin Van Buren – "Little Van" to his detractors – was destined to spend his term of office in Andrew Jackson's shadow. By no means an insignificant politician, he nonetheless got a bad press both during his presidency and thereafter. In part, this was the result of the economic crisis which engulfed the United States after the great financial panic of 1837, but it was also due to his reticence on the Texas issue and his refusal to be drawn into war with Great Britain over the *Caroline* incident, in which a band of Canadians set fire to the American ship of that name near Niagara Falls, killing an American seaman in the process. Americans had been assisting Canadian rebels, and the *Caroline* was clearly destroyed under orders from Britain, but Van Buren succeeded in cooling tempers on all sides, and further conflict between America and her former colonial masters was avoided, much to the disappointment of the hawks.

1830s

The Age of Jackson

The Alamo

Trail of Tears

1830

APR 6 Joseph Smith organizes *Church of Latter-Day Saints* (Mormons) at Fayette, NY

6 Colonization law of Mexico forbids further colonization in Texas territories by US citizens and prohibits importation of black slaves

10-JUL 16 Jedediah Strong Smith and William Sublette lead first covered wagon train from Missouri River to the Rockies

MAY 7 Treaty of commerce and navigation signed with Ottoman Empire

28 Indian Removal Act, for removal of Indians to lands west of the Mississippi, signed by Pres. Jackson

29 Preemption Act offers settlers who have cultivated public land during previous 12 months up to 160 acres of land at $1.25 per acre

JUL 15 Sioux, Sauk, Fox and other Indian tribes sign treaty at Prairie du Chien, Wn, ceding to US most of present-day states of Iowa, Missouri and Minnesota

AUG 28 Peter Cooper's *Tom Thumb,* first American-built locomotive, runs from Baltimore to Endicott's Mills on Baltimore and Ohio Railroad

SEP Anti-Masonic Party, first major third party in history of US politics, holds first national convention in Philadelphia

15 Choctaw Indians, in treaty at Dancing Rabbit Creek, cede nearly 8 million acres of their land east of Mississippi to US in exchange for land in present-day state of Oklahoma

16 Oliver Wendell Holmes writes poem 'Old Ironsides' for *Boston Daily Advertiser*

Also this year

★ Failure of revolution in Germany results in new wave of German immigration

1831

JAN 1 *The Liberator*, abolitionist newspaper edited by William Lloyd Garrison, begins publication in Boston

15 *Best Friend,* first American-built locomotive in service, makes passenger run on South Carolina railroad from Charleston to Hamburg

MAR 18 In *Cherokee Nation v. Georgia*, Supreme Court denies right of Cherokee tribe, considered 'domestic dependent,' to sue in Federal courts

APR 5 Commercial treaty concluded with Mexico

7 Resignation of Secretary of War John Eaton from Pres. Jackson's cabinet starts cabinet break-up

18 New York University chartered as University of the City of New York

One Jacksonian legacy Van Buren could have done without: The great financial depression of 1837–1840.

The Anti-slavery Movement

The 1830s saw the beginning of the first concerted anti-slavery movement in the United States. The depth of feeling on the slavery issue had shown itself with terrifying clarity during the Missouri Debate of 1819–1820, and politicians of all persuasions were reticent about reopening it if it could be avoided. Nevertheless it was clearly not an issue that would go away of its own accord. On the contrary, the hardening of attitudes which had taken place after the Missouri Compromise had rendered it more intractable than ever. Jackson saw its shadow in the Nullification Crisis, saying prophetically that the next pretext for secession "will be the Negro, or slavery question." It also played its part in determining the attitude of the United States towards the

The war of words: An early issue of the controversial anti-slavery paper The Liberator, *first published in 1831.*

Texan question, which was to assume dangerous proportions over the coming decade.

1831 saw the first issue of the anti-slavery paper, *The Liberator*, published in Boston by William Lloyd Garrison, which demanded freedom and the vote for all American Blacks. A number of anti-slavery societies sprang up in the North during the years that followed, and by 1836 there were more than 500 of them. Perhaps the most influential of these was the American Anti-slavery Society, founded in 1833 under the auspices of the fiercely courageous campaigner, Theodore D. Weld. Such views could still be dangerous for those who held them, especially after the rebellion of Nat Turner, a slave from Southampton, Virginia, in which a number of whites were killed. Campaigners were often attacked, even in the North, and at least one editor of an anti-slavery newspaper was lynched.

While many politicians in the North were eager to avoid antagonizing the South over the slavery issue, many in the South were taking steps to suppress anti-slavery views. There were those who saw this as a threat to wider liberties than those of the negro, and by the middle of the decade the son of the Chief Justice was able to say, "We commen-

ced the present struggle to obtain the freedom of the slave; we are compelled to continue it to preserve our own." In 1839, in an extraordinary legal case, a significant blow for liberty was struck by none other than the former President, John Quincy Adams, when he defended the *Amistad* mutineers, a group of slaves who had killed the crew of the slave-ship that was bringing them to America. Arguing for the natural right to freedom of all mankind, Adams succeeded in persuading the Supreme Court to set the mutineers free and return them to Africa. The decision was all the more remarkable because the Supreme Court at the time had more Southerners than Northerners among its members.

Going West

Throughout the decade the western migration continued. The first caravan of covered wagons found its way from Missouri to the foot of the Rockies in 1830, and in 1831 Nathaniel J. Wyeth, a young businessman from Massachusetts, established the Oregon Trail from Independence, Missouri, along the valley of the Platte River, through the South Pass, and along the valley of the Snake River to the Columbia River. It was a route many were to follow over the coming years, encouraged by a government eager to extend American settlement ever further westward.

Meanwhile the Indians were going westward too. But whereas the white western tide was a voluntary one, moved by the spirit of adventure and exploration, the red one was a sorry affair of harassment, broken promises, and thousands of deaths. The policy of forced resettlement had been drawn up by no less a democrat than Thomas Jefferson, but it was left to Andrew Jackson to put it into practice. During the 1830s the four great southeastern tribes – the Choctaws, the Creeks, the Chickasaws and the Cherokees – were systematically driven out of their tribal homelands. The last to surrender were the Cherokees, whose removal to the Indian Territory (now Oklahoma) in 1838 led to the deaths of a quarter of the entire nation. In Cherokee history it became known as the "Trail of Tears."

MAY 26 Wesleyan University chartered in Middlestown, Conn.

JUL 4 Treaty to settle spoilation claims from Napoleonic Wars concluded with France

4 Dr Samuel Francis Smith's song *America*, written to tune *'God Save the King'*, first sung at Worcester, Mass

AUG 10 Term 'Old Glory,' denoting US flag, first used by William Driver of Salem, Mass.

21 Nat Turner leads violent slave insurrection in Southampton, Va. results in stringent laws in South

SEP 26 Anti-Masonic Party holds first national nominating convention with platform and delegates from 13 states; nominates William Wirt of Maryland for President and Amos Ellmaker of Pennsylvania for Vice President

30-OCT 7 Free trade convention meets in Philadelphia to send message to Congress

OCT 26 Protective tariff convention opens in New York

DEC 12 John Quincy Adams presents in House 15 petitions from Pennsylvania calling for abolition of slavery in District of Columbia

1832

MAR 3 In *Worcester v. Georgia*, Supreme Court declares that Federal Government has jurisdiction over Indians and their territories within a state

27 Creek Indians sign treaty ceding their territory east of the Mississippi to US

APR 6 - AUG 2 Black Hawk War begins in northern Illinois and Southern Wisconsin when Sauks under Black Hawk recross the Mississippi and take village, hoping to regain ceded land

7 Gettysburg College in Gettysburg, Pa, chartered as Pennsylvania College under Lutheran auspices

MAY 9 In Treaty of Payne's Landing, fifteen Seminole chiefs cede lands in Florida to US and agree to move west of Mississippi River

16 Treaty of peace and commerce with Chile signed at Santiago

21-22 Democratic Party, formerly Democratic-Republican Party, holds its first national convention in Baltimore; nominates Andrew Jackson for second term and Martin Van Buren for Vice President

JUN Cholera appears in New York City

10 Pres. Jackson vetoes bill to recharter Bank of the US

13 Exploring party led by Henry Schoolcraft finds source of Mississippi River at Lake Itasca, Minnesota

17 Tariff Act of 1832 maintains protective system; high duties remain on textiles and iron

SEP 21 Sauk and Fox tribes sign treaty requiring them to stay on lands west of Mississippi River

OCT 17 Chickasaws cede to US their remaining lands east of Mississippi River

NOV 24 South Carolina Convention passes ordinance which nullifies Tariff Acts of 1828 and 1832

26 First streetcar, *John Mason*, put into operation by New York and Harlem Railroad in NYC

DEC 5 Andrew Jackson wins election for second term, Martin Van Buren elected Vice President

18 Treaty of commerce with Russia signed at St Petersburg

Also this year

★ Oregon Trail becomes main route for settlers of Oregon county

★ First clipper ship, *Ann McLim*, built in Baltimore

1833

FEB 5 University of Delaware chartered as Newark College in Newark, Del., under Presbyterian auspices

12 Henry Clay introduces compromise tariff bill

Nat Turner's Revolt

In August 1831 an event occured in Southampton County, Virginia, which sent shock waves through the Southern states and helped stiffen the resolve of the plantation classes to defend the "peculiar institution" of slavery against any attempt by the Federal Government to interfere with it. A religiously motivated Black slave, Nat Turner, organized an uprising in which a number of slaves went on the rampage, killing some 57 whites. The revolt, which was quickly put down, led to the revenge killings of many Blacks, and Nat Turner (seen here being captured) was hanged for his part in it.

Chief Black Hawk

The Sauk and Fox tribes, under their chief, Black Hawk (left), had been driven out of their tribal lands in Illinois in 1831 by the relentless encroachment of white settlers, but returned the following year in a desperate attempt to escape the famine that faced them in Missouri Territory. They were driven back by the Illinois militia, and many, including women and children, were massacred when they made yet another attempt to recross the Mississippi at Bad Axe. The rollcall of those involved, directly or indirectly, contains some of the most eminent names in American history. The policy of resettlement, enacted by Jackson, was first suggested by Thomas Jefferson; the man placed in charge of the captured Black Hawk was Jefferson Davis; and one of the companies of Illinois militia was commanded by the young Abraham Lincoln.

The Lone Star Republic

Among the countries to shake off the yoke of Spanish imperialism during the 1820s was the Republic of Mexico. The independent régimes which governed the republic in its early days adopted a somewhat ambiguous policy toward the U.S., at first encouraging a massive growth in the numbers of American immigrants into the province of Texas, and then, when Americans outnumbered Mexicans there, clamping down on it and outlawing the slavery that the settlers had brought with them. By the 1830s the advent of a new breed of settler, typified by the frontier toughness of Sam Houston (center right) and the "coonskin Congressman," Davy Crockett (right), had introduced a less governable element into the relatively orderly jurisdiction of Stephen Fuller Austin (far right), and the new men viewed the Mexican change of heart as a calculated insult. In 1836, on the slightest of legal pretexts, they declared Texas an independent republic and ran up the lone star flag over the frontier garrison known as the Alamo.

The Mexican response was swift and bloody. President Santa Anna descended on the Alamo at the head of a sizeable army and, after a bitter 10-day siege, made martyrs of Crockett and his tiny band of co-defenders by slaughtering them to a man (below). It was left to the redoubtable Houston to avenge the Alamo bloodshed in a surprise attack near the site of the present-day city named after him. The vastly larger Mexican army was scattered, the victory no doubt helping to secure for Houston the first presidency of the independent Republic of Texas. Statehood had to await the convenience of the American domestic agenda, but the events of 1836 were to be the prelude to a long drama of troubled relations with the United States' southern neighbor.

16 In *Barron v. Baltimore*, Supreme Court rules that actions of state governments are not subject to Bill of Rights

MAR 2 Pres. Jackson signs 'Force Bill' and Compromise Tariff Bill, averting confrontation with nullification

4 Andrew Jackson inaugurated President for second term, Martin Van Buren inaugurated Vice President

20 Commercial treaty with Siam signed at Bangkok

APR 1-3 Group of Americans living in Texas territory hold convention at San Felipe de Austin and vote to separate Texas from Mexico

JUN 1 Pres. Jackson reorganizes cabinet when it fails to agree over removal of government deposits in Bank of the US

SEP 10 Pres. Jackson announces to cabinet that on October 1 government will no longer use Bank of the US for its deposits; some members refuse to agree with plan

21 Commercial treaty with Sultan of Muscat signed

23 Secretary of the Treasury William G. Duane replaced by Roger B. Taney when he refuses to order removal of deposits from Bank of the United States

26 New Secretary of the Treasury Roger B. Taney orders first removal of government funds from Bank of the US, to be transferred to 23 other states, or 'pet' banks

NOV 13 Shower of shooting stars seen in most parts of North America

DEC 6 American Anti-Slavery Society organized in Philadelphia

26 Henry Clay introduces two resolutions in Senate, censuring Secretary of the Treasury Taney and Pres. Jackson for removal of deposits from Bank of the US

1833-37 Wild speculation in land, canals, roads, banks, buildings and cotton

Also this year

★ Massachusetts becomes last state to separate church and state, with disestablishment of Congregational Church

★ Peterboro, NH, establishes first tax-supported library under state law

★ Oberlin, first coeducational college opens in Oberlin, Ohio; admits Blacks

★ Haverford College, first Quaker college in US, founded in Haverford, Pa

★ Elijah P. Lovejoy establishes anti-slavery newspaper, *Observer*, in St. Louis

★ John Greenleaf Whittier's abolition tract *Justice and Expediency* published

1834

JAN 3 Stephen F. Austin goes to Mexico City to present resolution regarding separation of Texas from Mexico; Mexican government arrests Austin

29 Pres. Jackson orders Secretary of War Louis Cass to dispatch troops to quell riots of workmen along Chesapeake and Ohio Canal; first use of Federal troops in labor dispute

FEB 15 Van Ness Convention, in Madrid, settles claims between US and Spain

MAR 28 Senate adopts Clay's resolution of December 26, 1833, censuring Pres. Jackson and the Treasury for removal of deposits from Bank of the United States

APR 14 'Whig' formally adopted as name of new US political party comprised of anti-Jackson forces

JUN 15 Fur trader N.G. Wyeth establishes first settlement in Idaho at Fort Hall on Snake River

28 Second Coinage Act changes ratio of silver to gold from 15 to 1 to 16 to 1, undervalues silver and drives it from circulation

30 Department of Indian Affairs established by Congress to administer Indian territory west of Mississippi River

JUL 4 Meeting of black/white anti-slavery society at Chatham Street Chapel in New York disrupted by pro-slavery mob; anti-abolition rioting continues until July 12 with destruction of houses and churches

OCT Pro-slavery riot in Philadelphia, approximately 40 houses of blacks destroyed

The Hudson River School

A distinctly American school of painting developed after 1825 in the work of the so-called Hudson River School of artists. Characterized by their Romantic treatment of landscape, the Hudson River School, led by Thomas Cole (1801–1848), an emigré Englishman, and Asher B. Durand (1796–1886), an engraver turned painter, drew their chief inspiration from the natural scenery of America. Cole returned to America in 1832 after a three-year stay in Europe and set up his studio in New York. His *Pioneer Home in the Woods* (right) is typical of the work of the School.

Streetcars

An early New York streetcar of the 1830s. By the end of the decade steam-driven streetcars were already appearing alongside horsedrawn ones.

Daniel Webster

Known as "Black Dan," Webster was one of the most influential voices in Congress from the 1830s to his death in 1852. An inspirational speaker, his "Liberty and Union" speech during the nullification controversy of 1830 achieved overnight fame.

Henry Clay

The president America never had, Henry Clay (1777–1852) nonetheless exercised enormous influence on American affairs in the first half of the 19th century. The young "War Hawk" of 1812, he became the "Great Pacificator" of the Missouri and 1850 Compromises.

"The Monster"

Jackson's effective abolition of the Bank of the U.S., which he called "the Monster," precipitated a flood of less sound paper money and helped cause the panic of 1837.

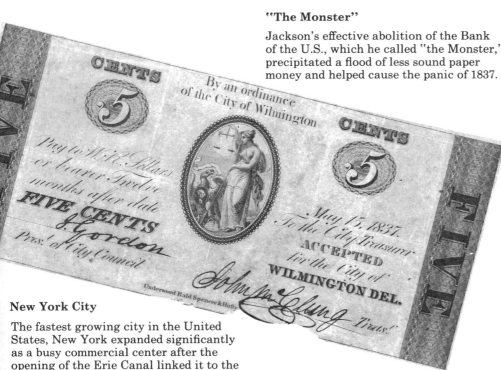

New York City

The fastest growing city in the United States, New York expanded significantly as a busy commercial center after the opening of the Erie Canal linked it to the Northwest. The picture shows the harbor from Brooklyn Heights in 1836.

---

28 US Government demands that Seminole Indians leave Florida, as required by Treaty of Payne's Landing (1832)

NOV 1 Railroad running from Philadelphia to Trenton, NJ, completed

DEC 2 Pres. Jackson, in annual message to Congress, suggests reprisals on French property as response to France's reneging on spoliation agreement

Also this year

★ Steamboat service between Buffalo and Chicago begins on weekly basis

★ National Trades Union of all crafts formed by General Trades Union of New York

1835

JAN 30 Attempt to assassinate Pres. Jackson by Richard Lawrence, later judged insane

MAR 3 US mints established in New Orleans, Charlotte, NC, and Dahlohega, Ga by act of Congress

APR 25 France appropriates funds for US spoliation claims, on condition that Pres. Jackson apologize for, or explain 1834 call for reprisals; Jackson refuses

JUN 30 William B. Travis leads group of Texas settlers to seize Mexican fort at Anahuac

JUL 6 Mob in Charleston, SC, burns impounded abolitionist literature in local post office

8 Liberty Bell cracks while tolling death of Chief Justice John Marshall

AUG 10 Noyes Academy in Canaan, NH, burned to ground to protest enrollment of 14 black students

OCT 21 Pro-slavery mob prevents English abolitionist George Thompson from speaking before Female Anti-Slavery Society in Boston; mob seizes William Lloyd Garrison and drags him through the streets

21 People meeting in Utica, NY, to organize anti-slavery society attacked by mob

NOV Second Seminole War begins when Indians in Florida resist relocation; lasts until August 14, 1843

DEC 15 President of Mexico, Santa Anna, declares unified constitution for all territories of Mexico; Texas settlers announce intention to secede

29 In Treaty of New Echota, Cherokee Indians of Georgia cede all their lands east of Mississippi River for $5 million plus land in the Indian Territory

Wheat crop failure in western areas causes severe economic crisis in region

Also this year

★ Strikes declared illegal by New York court in *The People v. Fisher*, resulting from Geneva strike of August 1, 1833

★ Benjamin Silliman, in series of lectures on geology before Boston Society of Natural History, expresses doubts of biblical theory of creation

★ Telegraph invented by Samuel F.B. Morse

★ Alexis de Tocqueville's *Democracy in America* published in Brussels

1836

JAN James Birney edits first issue of anti-slavery newspaper *Philanthropist* in Philadelphia

11 Abolitionists petition Congress to abolish slavery in District of Columbia; Calhoun refuses to accept petitions and calls them 'foul slander' of the South

15 Pres. Jackson again calls for reprisals against France for failure to pay on US spoliation claim

27 Great Britain offers mediation in settling spoliation claims issue between France and US

FEB 15 Bank of the United States receives new charter in Pennsylvania as Bank of the United States of Pennsylvania

23 Mexican Pres. Santa Anna leads 3000 men in siege on the Alamo

MAR 2 Texas settlers adopt declaration of independence from Mexico and draw up constitution

The *Caroline* Incident

Relations between America and Great Britain deteriorated sharply in the wake of a rebellion against colonial rule in Canada, which erupted in 1837. Interests in the United States supplied the rebel leader, William L. Mackenzie, with men and supplies, some of which were ferried across the border fom New York via the Hudson River in an American steamer called the *Caroline*. On December 29, 1837, Canadian loyalists set fire to the ship while it was moored above Niagara Falls, precipitating calls for war with Britain. The rebellion itself fizzled out without developing into the revolution many Americans hoped to see, but the ramifications of the *Caroline* affair continued to be felt into the 1840s, when one of the Canadians involved was arrested on a murder charge arising from the incident. Only Van Buren's, and later Tyler's, skilful diplomacy averted war.

Congressman Adams

John Quincy Adams' political career was by no means over when he failed to secure reelection to the presidency in 1828. Seen here propounding the right of petition in Congress, he also successfully defended the rights of a group of mutinous slaves in the celebrated *Amistad* case of 1839.

The Colt Revolver

The gun that won the West: The Colt revolver (below), patented in 1835 by Colonel Samuel Colt, enabled its users to fire up to six shots in quick succession without having to reload. The trigger rotated the chamber automatically.

Nathaniel Hawthorne (1894–1864)

Nathaniel Hawthorne, author of *The Blithedale Romance*, *The Scarlet Letter*, and *House of the Seven Gables*.

6 Santa Anna, leading Mexicans, captures the Alamo at San Antonio and massacres garrison

11 Senate begins practice of hearing and rejecting abolitionist petitions

17 Texas adopts constitution which legalizes slavery

APR 20 Territory of Wisconsin established in Western part of Michigan Territory by Congress

21 In Battle of San Jacinto, Texans under Gen. Sam Houston defeat Mexicans and capture Santa Anna

MAY 26 'Gag rule' preventing discussion of abolition petitions, passed by House

JUN 15 Arkansas enters Union as 25th (slave) state

23 Deposit Act, or Surplus Revenue Act, provides for at least one bank in each state to hold public deposits and for distribution among states of Treasury surplus above $5 million

JUL 1 Senate adopts resolution of June 18 recognizing independence of Texas

7 House adopts resolution of June 18

SEP 1 Wagon train of missionaries and their wives led by Dr Marcus Whitman through the South Pass reaches Walla Walla at Columbia and Snake Rivers; first women to cross Rockies

OCT 22 Samuel Houston sworn in as president of the Republic of Texas

NOV 12 Phrase 'the almighty dollar' coined by Washington Irving in story 'The Creole Village' appearing in *The Knickerbocker Magazine*

DEC 7 Democrat Martin Van Buren elected President; no vice presidential candidate receives majority

10 Emory University receives charter as Emory College in Oxford, Ga, under Methodist auspices

Also this year

★ Abolition movement grows; more than 500 societies active in North

★ Meeting of Ohio Anti-Slavery Society ends in violence incited by ruffians hired by town's 'respectable' citizens

★ Ernestine L. Rose circulates feminist petition requesting married woman's right to hold property, to New York Legislature

The Arts

★ Oliver Wendell Holmes' collection *Poems*, including 'Ballad of the Ousterman,' 'My Aunt,' and 'The Last Leaf'

The Greatest Show on Earth

The 1830s saw a sudden growth in the popularity of circuses in the United States, including the one presented by Phineas T. Barnum.

1837

JAN 26 Michigan enters Union as 26th (free) state

FEB 12 Mob of unemployed workers demonstrate against high rents and high prices of food and fuel by ransacking flour warehouses in New York

14 In *Charles River Bridge v. Warren Bridge*, Supreme Court rules against monopoly of transportation routes by one bridge company

MAR Price of cotton falls by nearly one half on New Orleans market

3 Lone Star Republic of Texas recognized by Pres. Jackson on his last day in office

4 Martin Van Buren inaugurated as President, Richard M. Johnson inaugurated Vice President

10 Panic of 1837 begins with suspension of specie payments by New York banks; banks in Baltimore, Philadelphia and Boston follow, 618 banks fail in 1837, and depression continues for seven years

18 University of Michigan chartered in Ann Arbor

APR 20 Massachusetts Senate creates first state board of education

JUN 10 Connecticut passes first general incorporation law in US

AUG 4 Republic of Texas petitions US for annexation

25 US denies annexation request by Republic of Texas

OCT 12 Congress authorizes use of treasury notes, not to exceed $10 million, to improve financial situation

NOV 7 Elijah P. Lovejoy, publisher of abolitionist newspaper, killed by mob in Alton, Ill.

8 Mt. Holyoke Seminary, founded by Mary Lyon, opens

DEC 4 Second session of 25th Congress convenes;

MISSISSIPPI STEAMBOATS

The years before the outbreak of the Civil War in America saw the heyday of the Mississippi steamboat trade. Providing America not only with a commercial lifeline to the Gulf of Mexico, but also with one of its most enduring traditional images, the giant boats, with their galleried tiers, distinctive paddle-housings, and elaborate wrought-ironwork, plied the river's treacherous waters, together with numerous smaller craft, through the very heart of the South.

The steamboat culture was a distinct and hardy one. Its most celebrated son, Samuel Langhorne Clemens, who took his literary *nom de plume*, Mark Twain, from the call of the depth-sounders on the great river, described in his travelogue, *Life on the Mississippi*, a world which largely disappeared after the trauma of the Civil War – a world in

which every boy in every village along the Mississippi yearned to become a river pilot, and every levee was crowded with goods waiting to be loaded onto the waiting ranks of steamboats. The steamboatman was a breed apart, irreverent, self-reliant, and inured to the dangers of a life in which exploding boilers, on-board fires, and the threat of drowning were his everyday companions. In this world, as Twain tells us from his own colorful experiences on the Mississippi as a young man, the pilot was king, taking his orders, not from the steamboat captain, but from the vicissitudes of the everchanging river itself.

Center: Steamboat travel advertisements, 1840.

Below: Loading cotton on the Mississippi.

THE MAIN SALOON

ING ROOM | PROMENADE DECK

Above: Steamboat interiors.

Above: A steamboat race on the Mississippi.

Representative William Slade of Vermont presents anti-slavery petitions, Southern representatives threaten to promote amendment to protect slavery or recommend dissolving Union

29 In *Caroline* Affair, on US shore of Niagara River near Buffalo, Canadian authorities seize and burn US steamboat *Caroline*, leased to Canadian insurrectionists, and kill one American; results in anti-British sentiment

Also this year

★ Horace Mann becomes first secretary of new Massachusetts Board of Education

1838

JAN 3-12 John C. Calhoun responds to abolitionist efforts to abolish slavery in District of Columbia by introducing pro-slavery resolutions into Senate; Senate resolves that slavery should not be interfered with, but refuses to automatically approve annexations that might expand nation's slave territory

5 Pres. Van Buren reacts to destruction of American steamship *Caroline* by urging neutrality in Canadian civil war, warning Americans not to assist Canadian rebels

FEB 15 Representative, John Quincy Adams defies 'gag rule' and introduces 350 petitions against slavery into House; all laid on table

MAY 17 Pro-slavery mob burns Pennsylvania Hall in Philadelphia, site of anti-slavery meetings

21 Congress rescinds Pres. Jackson's Specie Circular of July 11, 1836

29 Group of Americans sympathetic to Canadian rebels burn Canadian steamship *Sir Robert Peel*

JUN 12 Iowa Territory established from Wisconsin Territory

OCT Federal troops remove 14,000 Cherokees remaining in Georgia and force them to travel westward on 'Trail of Tears'

12 Texas Republic formally withdraws offer of annexation to US

21 Pres. Van Buren issues second neutrality proclamations directed toward Canada and orders swift reprisals against Americans violating neutrality proclamation

DEC 11 'Atherton gag,' resolution of Charles A. Atherton of New Hampshire, to prohibit discussion of slavery in House adopted by House

Also this year

★ Underground Railroad organized by abolitionists to provide escape route to North for black slaves

★ Specie payment resumed by most banks

1839

JAN 7 First silver-mining company in US, Washington Mining Company, chartered in North Carolina

FEB 11 University of Missouri chartered as University of the State of Missouri, in Columbia

12 In Aroostook War, Canadians arrest US land agent Rufus McIntire, Maine and New Brunswick mobilize militia; Gen. Winfield Scott arranges truce; and US and Britain agree to refer dispute to boundary commission

APR 11 Treaty with Mexico provides for arbitration of claims made by US citizens

25 France and Texas sign commercial treaty; France becomes first European nation to recognize Texas' independence

NOV 13 Abolitionists hold convention at Warsaw, NY, and form Liberty Party

Also this year

★ Mississippi becomes first state to allow women right to control their own property

★ Charles Goodyear discovers method for vulcanizing rubber

★ Samuel F.B. Morse brings process of photography to US from Paris

★ Joseph Smith moves Mormon community to establish Nauvoo, Ill.

NO SINGLE figure dominated the 1840s as Andrew Jackson had dominated the 1830s, but the new decade continued to see enormous changes in American life. The country's territory almost doubled with the acquisition of the Mexican lands of Texas, New Mexico, and California, and the establishment of the American claim to the Oregon country – an expansion greater even than that represented by President Jefferson's purchase of Louisiana from Napoleon at the beginning of the century. At the same time, new communication networks, including the first real flush of railroad building, opened the country up as never before, bringing with it new relationships, new social patterns, and a new style of politics. The words "Manifest Destiny" gripped the imagination of the American people.

However, this latest expansion – which brought the borders of the United States almost to their present positions – was not achieved without trauma. It was born out of the turbulence of the Mexican War, a conflict which divided opinion in America even more sharply than the war of 1812 and left scars which would take many years to heal. More turbulence followed in its wake. No sooner had California passed from Mexican to American ownership than the first rumor of a gold strike there reached the eastern seaboard. The rush which ensued led to a 14-fold increase in the population of California in the space of a single year and enabled it to apply for statehood. As the decade ended, the Californian application went before Congress. With it went the whole question of slavery. The problem all politicians had been trying to avoid for years had resurfaced more bitterly than ever.

Hard Cider and Log Cabins

The election of 1840 left no-one in any doubt that America was in the grip of a new type of politics. Gone were the aristocratic campaigns of the first John Adams and Thomas Jefferson. In their place had come professional organizers, mass rallies, smear campaigns, and rowdy political ballads. Everyone knew who the candidates were, but few people knew what they stood for. Issues and argument had been supplanted by gimmicks and emotion.

American politics were firmly entrenched in a two-party system. The previous Republican–Federalist divide had been replaced by a division into Democrats (the Jacksonians) and Whigs (the former National Republicans, led by Henry Clay and taking their name from the British party which had opposed George III during the American Revolution). In 1840 the Democratic camp declared for the sitting President, Martin Van Buren. The Whigs passed over their leading light, Clay, and put up as presidential candidate the ageing William H. Harrison, whose chief claim to fame was his victory over Tecumseh's Indian confederation at the Battle of Tippecanoe some 30 years earlier. The vice presidential choice was an odd one. Something of an afterthought in the Whigs' planning (as in

their campaign slogan "Tippecanoe and Tyler too!"), John Tyler was a Democrat and an advocate of states' rights. The Whigs seemed not to mind at the time. Within a year they would have cause to mind a great deal.

The Whigs chanted "Van, Van is a used-up man!" and accused Van Buren of living in the lap of luxury while the ordinary American suffered poverty and neglect. The Democrats responded by taunting that Harrison would be quite content with a log cabin and enough hard cider to drink. The Whigs were delighted and immediately made log cabins and hard cider their election theme. Cider barrels became a feature of broadsheets and rallies, and Whig campaign offices were designed to look like log cabins. Whether Harrison liked this image is open to question. The American electorate certainly did. Harrison and Tyler carried 19 of the 26 states.

Tyler Alone

General William Henry Harrison may once have been up to the rigors of the log cabin life. Now even his inauguration proved too much for him. He caught a chill while making the longest inaugural address in American history and died after just one month in office. "Tyler too" was now President all on his own – the first Vice President to take office without election. The Whigs were appalled. Henry Clay, who had seen himself as Harrison's *eminence grise*, gave up all hope of putting into effect the federal "American System" he had been dreaming of for the last 30 years and resigned his seat in the Senate. He was quickly followed by all the Whigs in the Cabinet, though the redoubtable Daniel Webster stayed on long enough to negotiate a treaty with Britain that finally clarified the American–Canadian border and did away with some of the bad feelings left by the *Caroline* incident. The Whig victory had turned to ashes.

The Lone Star State

The biggest problem on Tyler's plate was Texas. Following its declaration of independence and victory over Santa Anna's Mexicans in 1836, the new republic had applied to the United States for annexation to the Union as a slave state. Annexation would have meant war with Mexico and the reemergence of the slavery question, and few Americans wanted to face either. The Texans had been waiting ever since.

In February 1844 the accidental explosion of a cannon (ironically called "Peacemaker") on board the U.S.S. *Princeton* while she was cruising on the Potomac killed Tyler's Secretary of State, Abel P. Upshur, and allowed the President to replace him with John C. Calhoun, who was known to be strongly in favor of annexation. Calhoun stepped up the pace of negotiations with Texas, not least because the British were eager to keep the new republic outside the Union, and he soon came to an agreement whereby Texas would be annexed not as a state but as a territory. Sam Houston's battle to become a part of the Union seemed to be over at last, but the Senate, anxious to avoid war with Mexico, rejected the agreement.

It was, however, only a temporary setback. Texas became a major issue in the election campaign of 1844, which was won by the pro-annexation Democratic candidate, James K. Polk. Narrow though the victory was, Tyler claimed it as a mandate for annexation and pushed the treaty through Congress before he left office. One of Polk's first actions as President was to sign the act that admitted the Lone Star Republic to the Union on the terms negotiated by Calhoun. These terms included the acceptance of slavery below the latitude agreed in the Missouri Compromise. Since this line ran across the northern tip of the

Election songsheet: "The log cabin march and quick step."

On February 28, 1844, President Tyler and members of his Cabinet were sailing down the Potomac on the U.S.S. Princeton *when one of* its 12-inch guns exploded, killing the Secretary of State, Abel P. Upshur, and the Secretary of the Navy, George E. Badger.

republic, Texas was to all intents and purposes a slave territory.

As far as the Mexican Government was concerned, though, Texas was still theirs. Independence had been hard enough to swallow. Annexation brought a storm of protest. For the moment war was avoided, but it was an uneasy peace. Before Polk had been a year in office it would be shattered completely.

War with Mexico

It was not only on the Mexican front that foreign relations were strained. At the same time that he was signing Texas into the United States, Polk was also issuing a ringing challenge to Great Britain over the much-disputed Oregon territory. "Fifty-four forty or fight!" became the rallying cry of those who, like the new President, claimed Oregon for the United States right up to the border of Alaska on the 54° 40′ latitude. Polk invoked the almost forgotten Monroe Doctrine, Anglo–American relations became very tense, and there was a flurry of diplomatic activity. Eventually, a compromise was reached at the 49th parallel – which is probably what Polk wanted all along – and the last remaining serious territorial dispute with Britain was laid to rest. Polk then turned his attention to Mexico.

If Texas was the immediate cause of the war with Mexico, the prizes which Polk foresaw from victory were the vast territories of New Mexico and California. In the closing months of 1845, he sent an ambassador to the Mexican Government to press the U.S. claim that Texas extended to the Rio Grande in the west – a claim which, for Mexico, only added insult to injury. When the Mexican Government refused to discuss it, Polk provocatively ordered General Zachary Taylor to advance to the Rio Grande with 2000 men. Not surprisingly, the

Mexicans responded by attacking the U.S. troops. A few men were killed, Polk declared that Mexico had shed American blood on American soil, and by May 1846 the two countries were officially at war. The following month an American fifth column under the young explorer John C. Frémont raised the Stars and Stripes over California, and an army of less than 2000 men under Colonel Kearny invaded New Mexico from Kansas, sweeping a much larger Mexican force out of Santa Fe without a fight.

With New Mexico in American hands and Kearny heading for California to finish Frémont's work there, Polk – possibly fearing that Zachary Taylor's successes were raising his political stock too high at home – despatched half of Taylor's men to join an invasion force under General Winfield Scott, who was planning to land at Vera Cruz and take Mexico City itself. As a result, it was a sadly depleted band of 5000 men who met the full onslaught of the 20,000 strong Mexican army at Buena Vista in February 1847. But despite the vast difference in numbers, Taylor and his men held firm and the Mexicans, under Santa Anna of Alamo notoriety, were beaten back. If Polk had intended to ruin Taylor's political chances, he had gone about it the wrong way. Buena Vista was to sweep Taylor into the White House the following year. It also brought to public notice the name of one of his regimental commanders, his son-in-law, Colonel Jefferson Davis.

The remnants of Santa Anna's army turned south to block Scott's march on the capital, but were outflanked at the strategic fortified pass of Cerro Gordo in an action planned by one Colonel Robert E. Lee and executed by, among others, a Lieutenant Ulysses S. Grant. In September 1847 U.S. troops entered Mexico City, and in February 1848 the defeated Mexican Government signed the Treaty of Guadalupe

JAN 8 Gag rule prohibiting discussion of slavery again adopted by House

13 Fire aboard steamboat *Lexington* leaves 140 dead

MAR 31 Ten-hour work day for federal employees in public works established by executive order of the President

APR 1 Liberty Party holds first national convention in Albany, NY and confirms 1839 nomination of James G. Birney of New York for President and nominates Thomas Earle of Pennsylvania for Vice President

MAY 5 Democratic National Convention nominates Van Buren for second term and leaves nomination of vice presidential candidate to states

JUN 20 Samuel F.B. Morse receives patent for telegraph

JUL 4 Independent Treasury Act allowing government exclusive responsibility over its funds and providing for government depositories, becomes law

NOV 13 Republic of Texas signs commercial treaty with Great Britain, which recognizes independence of Texas

DEC 2 Six-month 'Log Cabin and Cider' campaign ends as Whigs win presidential election; William Henry Harrison elected President, John Tyler elected Vice President

Also this year

★ Worldwide Anti-Slavery Convention held in London; American women delegates not permitted to take delegates' seats, women walk out in protest; leads Lucretia Mott, Elizabeth Cady Stanton and others to organize women's rights conferences

The Arts

★ Edgar Allan Poe's collection of short stories *Tales of the Grotesque and Arabesque*

★ Transcendentalists publish journal, *The Dial*, in Boston; Margaret Fuller editor

MAR 7 Whig William Henry Harrison inaugurated President, John Tyler inaugurated Vice President

APR 4 Pres. Harrison dies of pneumonia; Vice Pres. John Tyler becomes first American to succeed to the presidency

JUN First covered wagon train to California departs from Sapling Grove in northeastern Kansas

AUG Caravan of 48 wagons travels over Oregon Trail, Humboldt River and Sierra Nevada Mountains and reaches Sacramento, Ca

13 Independent Treasury Act repealed

Zachary Taylor (1784–1850), whose Mexican War exploits led him to the White House. A soldier rather than a politician, he seems not to have voted in his life.

Hidalgo. In return for $15 million – half what Polk had offered for New Mexico and California before the war began – the United States acquired not only those two territories but also the title to Texas as far west as the Rio Grande.

If it was a humiliating defeat for Mexico, it was also a highly controversial victory for America. Throughout the war many American voices had been raised against the hostilities, some even hoping publicly for the defeat of the U.S. troops. Now the peace treaty was only narrowly passed by a deeply divided Senate. It was not only that many saw the U.S. action as unwarranted aggression (and as late as 1916, Woodrow Wilson still claimed to feel it on his conscience); it was also that the slavery issue now loomed more starkly than ever. The Missouri controversy was fresh in many American minds. Then the admission of one

new state had led to outrage and talk of civil war. The territories now ceded by Mexico would make the best part of seven new states. A reopening of the Missouri wounds seemed inevitable. It happened even more quickly than many expected.

Gold!

The dust had hardly settled on the treaty negotiations with Mexico when the first rumors leaked out of the Sacramento Valley that gold had been found at Sutter's Mill. The news traveled like wildfire, and within months the whole of the eastern United States was alight with it. What happened next is one of the most remarkable episodes in American history.

Lured by the prospect of unheard-of wealth, thousands of Americans from all walks of life headed west, to be joined by like-minded adventurers from all over the world. Abandoning city offices and familiar farmsteads, they risked the perils of the wilderness and the high seas to stake their claim in the distant gold fields. Some died *en route*, succumbing to disease, drought, or

shipwreck on the hazardous journey to the Pacific coast. But most arrived safely, only to find conditions of hardship and internecine greed that must have left many looking wistfully towards the lives they had left behind.

After the initial successes, the pickings turned out to be far more meager than rumors had led the "forty-niners" and their kind to expect. Few fortunes were made by the gold rush and many lives were ruined. But more terrible still was the political cost. The population of California rocketed to an amazing 90,000 by the end of the decade. Most of the increase took place in the single year 1849 and most as a result of emigration from the free states. Not only did this enable California to skip the territorial stage of its development and apply for statehood immediately; it also meant that the constitution the Californians presented to Congress for approval in December 1849 outlawed slavery in the new state.

It was a baptism of fire for the new President, the victor of Buena Vista, Zachary Taylor. Politically inexperienced and apparently politically apathetic, Taylor had hoped to avoid such dangerous waters, and the 1848 election campaign had steered clear of the slavery question along with most other contentious issues. As the new decade began, though, those waters were looking stormier than at any time for 30 years. As in 1819–1820, the battle lines were drawn up over slavery as a result of the admission of a new state to the Union. Again the crisis would be averted by compromise, and again it would prove only to have been delayed. But this time when it broke it would bring with it the full horror of civil war.

Ideals and Communities

America in the 1840s was still in many ways a blank sheet of paper waiting to be written on. The upsurge of popular democracy which was the hallmark of the Age of Jackson created many new movements, each seeking to inscribe its ideals in the social history of the United States. As the great essayist, philosopher, and poet, Ralph Waldo Emerson, wrote of this period, "the ancient manners were giving way."

American literature was already a sturdy plant, which would flower during the next decade in the masterpieces of Herman Melville, Nathaniel Hawthorne, and Walt Whitman. One of its sources of inspiration was the transcendentalism of Emerson and his circle, with their firm belief in the divine potential of the individual human being. It was a belief which informed the thinking of many of the period's leading writers and intellectuals, including Bronson Alcott, James Russell Lowell, Henry Wadsworth Longfellow, and Henry David Thoreau.

Transcendentalism and its associated beliefs were also the spur to some of the many experiments in communal living that swept America during these years, such as Brook Farm at West Roxbury in Massachusetts. This village, which Hawthorne described in his *Blithedale Romance*, was abandoned in 1847, but while it lasted its experiments in minimum regulation, social justice, and educational methods, were highly influential.

Other communities were thrown up by a rising tide of labor reform which also led to the introduction of the ten-hour working day by the Federal Government in 1840 and the recognition by Chief Justice Shaw in 1842 of workers' rights to form trade unions and to strike. The utopian community of New Harmony, Indiana – Robert Owen's experiment in cooperative working and collective ownership of property – may have been short-lived, but the ideals which inspired it were alive and well, as can be seen from his organization in 1845 of a grandly named "world convention to emancipate the human race from ignorance, poverty, division, sin, misery."

Others again derived their impetus from religious movements. Evangelism was seldom far from the surface during the early part of the 19th century, and often expressed itself in the founding of new communities, shut off from the evil influence of the outside world. For example, by 1840 the Shakers – despite their belief in celibacy – had grown to a sect of some 6000 people. Famous for their ecstatic shaking dances during worship and for the beautifully proportioned houses and furniture they crafted during their quieter moments, these disciples of the messianic English emigrée Mary Ann Lee continued to live apart from the world throughout the 19th century and can still claim a few followers today.

Ralph Waldo Emerson (1803–1882), author, poet, and leader of the transcendentalist school of philosophy.

The Mormons

The most famous of all these religious communities, as well as the most enduring and the most influential, was the Church of Latter-day Saints, more commonly known as the Mormons. In 1840 their founder, Joseph Smith of Vermont, published the seminal *Book of Mormon*, which embodied the teachings he claimed had been revealed to him by an angel of the Lord. Fleeing from persecution with his rapidly growing band of followers, Smith founded a community at Nauvoo in Illinois, which had become the fastest growing city in the state by 1844 when Smith himself was murdered by a lynch-mob in nearby Carthage.

Under his successor Brigham Young, the Mormons abandoned Nauvoo in 1846 and undertook an exodus of biblical proportions across the Great Plains – an area declared uninhabitable by a Government survey not so long before. In July 1847 they reached the Great Salt Lake in what was then still Mexican territory. Here Young established a community of some 5000 people to practise the Mormon religion outside the jurisdiction of the United States, only to find that the defeat of Mexico in the Mexican War brought them within it again. With the accession of Utah to territorial status in 1850, however, the Mormons' remarkable efficiency in community-building was recognized by Congress in the appointment of Young himself as Governor. The Mormon influence continues in Utah to this day.

Transport and Cities

Less idealistic in its inspiration, but more significant for the future development of the United States, was the vast increase in the growth of American cities during the decade. The grandiose plans for federal road and canal building, which formed part of Henry Clay's "American System," may have been thwarted by the death of President Harrison, but a transport revolution was taking place all the same. The great age of railway building was yet to arrive, but already by the end of the 1840s there were some 9000 miles of track, most of it concentrated in the Northeast. In addition, miles of roads and canals were constructed at state expense, opening up new trade routes, fueling the expansion of previously insignificant communities, and confirming the importance of established ones. More people moved into cities, or were born in them, in the 1840s than emigrated to the West during the same period. By the end of the decade, Cleveland had grown from a tiny village to a major lake port, and Cincinnati had become an important trading post, with a population of more than 100,000. Chicago, a settlement of 200 people in the mid-1830s, was growing fast and by the end of the next decade would almost have caught up with Cincinnati. Typical of the established towns during these years of expansion, New York saw its population rise from just over 300,000 at the beginning of the 1840s to more than half a million people by the end. In the next ten years it would almost double in size.

19 System of uniform bankruptcy law begins throughout US

The Arts

★ Ralph Waldo Emerson's first series of *Essays*

★ Edgar Allan Poe becomes associate editor of *Graham's Magazine,* founded in Philadelphia

1842

MAR 1 *Prigg v. Commonwealth of Pennsylvania,* Supreme Court rules that Pennsylvania law forbidding seizure of fugitive slaves is unconstitutional, however, enforcement of fugitive slave laws is federal responsibility

3 Massachusetts act requires minimum of education for all children and no longer than 10 hours per day in factory labor for children under 12

7 Ohio Wesleyan University chartered in Delaware, Ohio, under Methodist auspices

21-23 Abolutionist Representative Joshua R. Giddings introduces antislavery resolutions in House; House censures; Giddings resigns seat

30 Congress adopts highly protective Tariff Act of 1842, which raises rates to those of Tariff of 1832

30 Dr. Crawford Lang of Georgia becomes first to use ether as anaesthetic in surgical operation

31 Henry Clay resigns from Senate, after 40 years in public service, to plan Whig campaign for election of 1844

APR 18 Opponents of Rhode Island government declare their own right to vote, based on their own constitution, hold their own election and elect Thomas W. Dorr Governor; Rhode Island run under dual government

MAY Col. John C. Frémont, heads four-year expedition to explore Rocky Mountains in southern Wyoming

SPRING RI General Assembly calls out state militia to remove rebel government; followers of Thomas W. Door unsuccessfully attempt to seize RI state arsenal, flee state, then return

JUN 25 Reapportionment Act dictates that members of Congress, after March 3, will be elected according to districts, equal in number to each state in quota of representatives

AUG 9 Webster-Ashburton Treaty between US and Great Britain signed, defining boundary between Maine and Canada and settling boundary disputes between Atlantic Ocean and Rocky Mountains

SEP 11 Group of Mexican soldiers invade Texas Republic and capture San Antonio

DEC 30 Pres. Tyler, acting on advice of Daniel Webster, in message to Congress, states that US would not approve of attempts by any power to take control of Hawaiian Islands

Also this year

★ In *Commonwealth v. Hunt* Chief Justice Samuel Shaw of Massachusetts rules that a trade union is a lawful organization which is not responsible for illegal acts of individuals and that strike in closed shop is legal

★ Phineas T. Barnum opens American Museum in New York to the public

1843

JAN Dorothea Lynde Dix addresses Massachusetts Legislature on harsh treatment of the insane and publishes 'Memorial to the Legislature of Massachusetts'

APR Rhode Island adopts new constitution with more liberal suffrage

MAY 8 Daniel Webster resigns as Secretary of State

The Mexican War

The controversial war with Mexico between 1846 and 1848 led to the greatest territorial expansion of the United States since Thomas Jefferson's purchase of the Louisiana territory from France in 1804. However, whereas Jefferson's acquisition had been a commercial transaction, President Polk's was widely seen as an act of naked aggression against an independent country already outraged by the annexation of the province of Texas. If the Louisiana Purchase was constitutionally questionable, the acquisition of the vast territories of California, New Mexico, and the far west of Texas was nothing less than "Manifest Destiny" through a gun barrel.

The war, which left an enduring legacy of Mexican bitterness towards the United States, also made the names of several of its commanding officers. Zachary Taylor would never have become President without his victory over Santa Anna's forces at Buena Vista, a battle which also worked wonders for the reputation of Taylor's son-in-law, Jefferson Davis. The campaign which led to the taking of Mexico City in October the same year provided common memories for a couple of its participants, Robert E. Lee and Ulysses S. Grant, who, 18 troubled years later on, would meet again under less glorious circumstances at Appomattox Court House, Virginia.

Above: "Young Hickory:" James Knox Polk, 11th President of the United States.

Center: General Antonio López de Santa Anna, President of Mexico, for whom the war was a costly retribution for the Alamo.

Below: General Winfield Scott enters Mexico City, October 1848.

Right: U.S. troops storm the hilltop fortress of Chapultepec, September 1847.

22 One thousand Easterners leave Independence, Mo, to settle in Oregon territory; beginning of large migration westward

29 John C. Frémont leaves Kansas City, Mo, on second expedition, to explore Rocky Mountains, Snake and Columbia River valleys and California's central San Joaquin Valley

JUL 5 Oregon settlers meeting at Champoeg adopt constitution for provisional government based on laws of Iowa

12 Joseph Smith, Leader of Mormon Church, announces that divine revelation sanctioned practice of polygamy

AUG 14 Second Seminole War ends; Seminoles nearly exterminated

23 Mexican President Santa Anna warns US that American annexation of Texas will be considered tantamount to declaration of war against Mexico

30-31 Liberty Party National Convention in Buffalo, NY, nominates James G. Birney of Michigan for President and Thomas Morris of Ohio for Vice President

Also this year

★ US sends diplomatic agent George Brown to Hawaiian Islands as commissioner and refuses to join Great Britain and France in supporting Hawaiian independence

★ Vermont State Assembly blocks execution of Fugitive Slave Act of 1793

★ North American Phalanx, most important Fourierist community, established in Red Bank, NJ

The Arts

★ John Greenleaf Whittier's *Of My Home*, including 'Casandra Southwick' and 'The Merrimack'

1844

JAN 15 University of Notre Dame chartered in South Bond, Ind., under Roman Catholic auspices

FEB 23 University of Mississippi chartered in Oxford, Miss.

APR 12 Texas Annexation Treaty signed

27 Martin Van Buren and Henry Clay publish letters opposing annexation of Texas, resulting in loss of support for both

MAY 1 Whig National Convention in Baltimore unanimously nominates Henry Clay for President and Theodore Freling Wuyson of New Jersey for Vice President

6-8 Violent clash between native-born American Protestants and immigrant Catholics in Philadelphia

25 Gasoline engine patented by Stuart Perry

27-29 Democratic National Convention at Baltimore nominates James K. Polk of Tennessee for President on eighth ballot and George M. Dallas of Pennsylvania for Vice President

27 Tyler Democrats meet at Baltimore and nominate John Tyler for President

JUN 27 Joseph Smith, leader of Mormons, killed by mob in Nauvoo, Ill.; succeeded by Brigham Young

JUL 3 Caleb Cushing negotiates Treaty of Wanghia between US and China; provides for full trading privileges to American merchants on treaty pacts

AUG 13 Newly ratified constitution in New Jersey allows only white male citizens to vote

20 Pres. Tyler withdraws from presidential campaign

SEP 19 Marquette iron range discovered at head of Lake Superior

DEC 7 James K. Polk elected President, Whig Henry Clay elected Vice President

Also this year

★ Baptist Church splits on slavery question into Northern and Southern conventions

★ Amos Bronson Alcott founds utopian community of Fruitlands, near Harvard, Mass.

★ Albert Brisbane's cooperative, socialized community Alphadelphia Phalanx established in Kalamazoo County, Mich.

EXODUS

Driven out of Nauvoo, Illinois, after the lynching of their founding father, Joseph Smith, the Mormons, led by Smith's charismatic successor, Brigham Young (right), fled persecution by crossing the "Great American Desert" to the edge of the Great Salt Lake, where they founded the independent state of Deseret in 1847.

Left: Several thousand Mormons made the trek across the Great Plains in covered wagons. The journey, which took over a year, was designed to remove the Mormons from U.S. jurisdiction, but events overtook the Latter-Day Saints in the form of the Mexican War.

Below: The modest beginnings of the settlement that was to become Salt Lake City.

Inset, right: Brigham Young *en famille*: The persecution of the Mormons focused particularly on their practice of polygamy, which Joseph Smith had proclaimed to be sanctioned by the biblical text, "And in that day seven women shall take hold of one man." Smith himself went many better than this and took 27 wives, five of whom Brigham Young inherited on his death.

1845

JAN 23 Uniform election day for presidential elections established by Congress

FEB 1 Baylor University chartered by Republic of Texas in Independence, Tex., under Baptist auspices

28 House and Senate adopt joint resolution for annexation of Texas

MAR 3 Florida enters Union as 27th (slave) state

3 Postal Act reduces postage rates to five cents per half ounce for 300 miles and grants subsidies to steamships which carry mail

4 James K. Polk inaugurated as 11th President, George M. Dallas inaugurated Vice President

6 Mexican minister at Washington, General Almonte, protests annexation of Texas and demands passports

MAY 28 Pres. Polk sends detachment of US army, led by Gen. Zachary Taylor to southwestern border of Texas to guard state against Mexican 'invasion'

JUN 15 Secretary of State James Buchanan guarantees US protection if Texas consents to annexation terms

JUL Phrase 'Manifest Destiny' appears in *The United States Magazine and Democratic Review*

7 Texans in convention at San Felipe de Austin accept terms of annexation

AUG Unrest over old Dutch and English leases causes problems in Albany, NY; Delaware County placed under martial law

27 Texans in convention at San Felipe de Austin frame state constitution

OCT 17 Thomas O. Larkin appointed US consul in Monterey by Pres. Polk and instructed to encourage Californians to favor annexation and to block foreign powers' attempts to secure California

NOV 10 John Slidell commissioned by Pres. Polk to negotiate settlement with Mexico for Texas, New Mexico and California

DEC 16 Mexican general leads military takeover of government

20 John Slidell officially informed by Mexican government that he will not be received as Minister Plenipotentiary

29 Texas enters Union as 28th state

1845-1847 Potato famines in Ireland lead to great increase in Irish migration to US

Also this year

★ Methodist Episcopal Church splits on slavery question into Northern and Southern conferences

★ Industrial Congress of the United States organized in NYC

★ NYC fireman Alexander J. Cartwright devises rules for baseball and organizes first baseball club, The Knickerbockers

★ Margaret Fuller's *Woman in the Nineteenth Century* published

The Arts

★ Edgar Allan Poe's *Tales,* including 'The Fall of the House of Usher,' and 'Murders in the Rue Morgue' and *The Raven and Other Poems*

1846

FEB 5 Bucknell University chartered in Lewisburg, Pa as University of Lewisburg under Baptist auspices

10 Mormon migration westward from Nauvoo, Ill, begins; organized and led by Brigham Young

19 Texas formally installs state government at Austin

MAR 26 Colgate University chartered in Hamilton, NY, as Madison University under Baptist auspices

28 Gen. Zachary Taylor leads troops onto left bank of Rio Grande, recognized as Mexican territory, and begins building fort opposite Matamoros

APR 10 Fordham University chartered in Bronx, NY, as St. John's College under Catholic auspices

Famine in Ireland

Between 1845 and 1849 Ireland was gripped by a great famine as potato blight devastated the country's staple crop. Perhaps as many as a million people died of hunger. Another 1.5 million, driven by desperate poverty or by eviction by their landlords in Ireland, found their way to the shores of the United States in the years between the famine and the beginning of the Civil War, helping to make the Irish one of the largest, and in due course one of the most influential, minority groups in America.

The "Pathfinder"

John Charles Frémont (above inset) gained the sobriquet "Pathfinder" as a result of his Far Western expeditions in the 1840s. Funded by his father-in-law, Senator Thomas Hart Benson, he headed the team who planted the Stars and Stripes on a summit of the Rockies (above) and was a central figure in the opening up of California before the Mexican War. His exploits in the West helped win him the Republican presidential nomination in 1856.

Edgar Allan Poe (1809–1849)

The haunted life of the great Southern writer, Edgar Allan Poe, ended prematurely in Baltimore in 1849. Poe's poetry and stories had an enormous influence on European literature.

Samuel F. B. Morse . . .

Had Morse (right) invented the electric telegraph 30 years earlier, he might have prevented the War of 1812. As it was, his epoch-making invention changed the face of communication in America in the 1840s and 1850s. The first message sent over the line – "What hath God wrought!" – might also have been the response of the directors of Pony Express, which the telegraph rendered obsolete.

. . . and his Brainchild

Opening up a continent: The first telegraph lines go up in America. By the Civil War there were more than 50,000 miles of wire across the U.S.

12 Mexican general, Pedro de Ampudia, orders Gen. Taylor to retire beyond Nueces River

13 Pennsylvania Railroad chartered

24 Small Mexican cavalry unit inflicts minor casualities on US troops blockading Mexican town

25 Pres. Polk begins war message to Congress, based on unpaid claims to US nationals and rejection of Slidell

27 Pres. Polk signs Congressional resolution to terminate Oregon Treaty of 1827 with Great Britain

MAY 3 Mexican forces attack Fort Texas, constructed by troops under Gen. Taylor

8 Gen. Taylor defeats Mexicans at Palo Alto

9 In Battle of Resaca de la Palma, Gen. Taylor drives Mexicans across Rio Grande

13 Congress declares state of war exists between US and Mexico by act of Mexico, authorizes recruitment of 50,000 soldiers and $10 million to fight war

18 US forces led by Gen. Taylor cross Rio Grande and occupy Matamoras

MAY-JUN Pres. Polk orders blockades of Mexican ports located on the Pacific Ocean and Gulf of Mexico

JUN 3 Col. Stephen Kearny instructed to occupy Santa Fe, NM, and California

14 Bear Flag Revolt, Republic of California proclaimed at Sonoma by California settlers

17 James Russell Lowell publishes first of 'Bigelow Papers' in *Boston Courier* to voice opposition to Mexican war

19 First match baseball game in US played in NJ; New Yorks beat Knickerbockers, 23-1

26 Great Britain repeals Corn Laws, increasing American exports

JUL 7 Commodore John Sloat lands in Monterey, hoists American flag and claims possession of California for US

AUG 6 Independent Treasury Act readopted by Congress

6 State government for Wisconsin authorized by Congress

8 Pres. Polk asks Congress to appropriate $2 million to purchase territory from Mexico

8 Wilmot Proviso, Pennyslvania Representative David Wilmot introduces amendment to appropriation bill, excluding slavery from territory acquired from Mexico

10 Smithsonian Institution chartered

13 Commodore David Stockton and Capt. John Frémont capture Los Angeles

15 First newspaper in California, *Californian,* begins publication in Monterey

15 Col. Kearny reaches Las Vegas and announces annexation of New Mexico by US

17 Commodore Stockton declares that US has annexed California, will establish himself as governor

18 Col. Kearny occupies Santa Fe, later organizes temporary government for New Mexico

SEP 10 Elias Howe patents sewing machine

20-24 Gen. Taylor battles for four days in Monterrey, Mexico, and occupies city

22 Mexican Californians led by Jose Maria Flores revolt against US, conquer San Diego and Los Angeles and later gain control of all of California south of San Luis Obispo, Flores acts as governor

DEC 12 Treaty signed with New Granada, now Bogota, Colombia, guarantees US transit rights over Isthmus of Panama and guarantees New Granada sovereignty

28 Iowa enters Union as 29th (free) state

1847

JAN 10 American Gen. Kearney captures Los Angeles, hostilities in California end

13 Remaining Mexican forces in California sign Treaty of Cahuenga with Capt. Frémont

FEB 16 University of Louisiana established as state institution in New Orleans

22-23 In Battle of Buena Vista, US forces under Gen. Taylor defeat Mexicans under Gen. Santa Anna

25 State University of Iowa chartered in Iowa City

The "Bear Flag" Revolt

Even before the Mexican War brought it within the ambit of the United States and the discovery of gold there launched its meteoric rise to statehood, California had attracted its share of American settlers. In 1846, under the leadership of William Ide, these pioneering adventurers declared the Mexican province an independent republic and ran up the so-called Bear Flag (left) over Sonoma. The ubiquitous John Frémont was nominated as the republic's first president. On July 11, however, less than a month after the original declaration and two months after Polk declared war on Mexico, the Bear Flag was hauled down and the Stars and Stripes was hoisted in its place.

Irving *et al*

Fanciful though it is, this composite painting, set in Sunnyside, Washington Irving's home in Tarrytown, New York, illustrates the remarkable richness of literary talent active in America at this time. Irving himself sits center right, with Ralph Waldo Emerson seated behind him to his left. To Emerson's left, in Napoleonic pose, sits James Fenimore Cooper, creator of the *Leatherstocking Tales*. Second from the left of the picture stands Oliver Wendell Holmes, gazing abstractedly skyward, while Nathaniel Hawthorne, looking altogether more earthbound, leans against a pillar nearby. Henry Wadsworth Longfellow, the author of *The Song of Hiawatha*, supports himself on the back of a chair in the foreground, carrying his hat and gloves.

The New York Theater Riots

A series of major riots in New York City in the 1840s, 1850s, and 1860s testified to the underlying volatility in American society in the years leading up to the outbreak of the Civil War. In 1849 an unlikely flashpoint was provided by the visit of an English actor, William Charles Macready, to the Astor Place Opera House, New York (left), where he was playing Macbeth. Macready, whose diary recorded his impressions of American life, was seen as an arch-rival to the home-grown thespian, Edwin Forrest, who was also performing in New York at the time. In a curious and destructive upsurge of national feeling, crowds went on the rampage through the streets of the city, chanting anti-British slogans. The military were called out to deal with the crisis, and the ensuring action left many dead and injured.

Clay for President!

The 1844 election represented Henry Clay's third attempt to become President of the United States. If the campaign was dominated by the question of the annexation of Texas, on which Clay changed his stance in mid-election, thus precipitating his final failure to reach the White House, protectionism was still a live issue, as this political demonstration in New York shows. (Clay had been closely associated with the 1832 Tariff Act.)

Fighting "the Demon Rum"

The temperance movement, already highly active in the heavy-drinking 1820s and 1830s, became a much more radical crusade during the 1840s, with total prohibition as its goal. Despite the cosy conventionality of the above propaganda print, "The Fruits of Temperance," the temperance movement was in fact one of the main training grounds for the women's rights campaigners of the second half of the 19th century.

28 American Col. Alexander Doniphan defeats army at Sacramento

MAR 9 US forces under Gen. Winfield Scott land near Vera Cruz, most powerful fortress in Western Hemisphere, in first large-scale amphibian operation in US history

29 US forces under Gen. Winfield occupy Vera Cruz

MAY 1 Smithsonian Institution formally dedicated in Washington, DC

7 American Medical Association organized in Philadelphia, Pa

JUN 6 Peace negotiations with Mexico initiated through British minister Charles Bankhead

JUL 1 First official US postage stamp issued by Post Office Department in five-cent and ten-cent denominations

24 Brigham Young and party of 143 reach valley of the Great Salt Lake

AUG 27 Peace negotiations between US and Mexico end in failure

SEP Native American Party meets in Philadelphia and nominates Gen. Zachary Taylor of Louisiana for President and Henry Dearborn of Massachusetts for Vice President

7 Armistice between US and Mexico ends

11 Stephen Foster's 'Susanna' performed for first time at concert in Eagle Saloon, Pittsburgh, Pa

14 Gen. Scott enters Mexico City

OCT Abolitionist Liberty Party holds convention in New York and nominates John P. Hale of New Hampshire for President and Leicester King of Ohio for Vice President

DEC 6 Abraham Lincoln of Illinois takes seat in house in 30th Congress

Also this year

★ Great migration from the Netherlands to Midwestern state begins

★ New Hampshire passes first state 10-hour work day law

★ Vermont passes state law guaranteeing to wife full ownership of real estate held by her at time of marriage or gained by gift or bequest afterward, however, husband's consent necessary to transfer ownership

1848

JAN 24 Gold discovered in American River near Sutter's Fort in California by James Marshall, results in gold rush of 1849

FEB 2 US signs Treaty of Guadalupe Hidalgo, ending war with Mexico, US receives 500,000 square miles that include future states of California, Nevada, Utah, most of New Mexico and Arizona and parts of Wyoming and Colorado, upon payment of $15 million, Mexico also cedes Texas with boundary at Rio Grande

MAR Senate ratifies Treaty of Guadalupe Hidalgo, Pres. Polk receives appropriation bill to pay Mexico, without Wilmot Proviso

10 Villanova University chartered in Villanova, Pa

MAY 22-26 Democratic National Convention meets in Baltimore and nominates Gen. Lewis Cass of Michigan for President and Gen. William O. Butler of Kentucky for Vice President

29 Wisconsin joins Union as 30th (free) state

JUN 7-9 Whig National Convention meets at Philadelphia and nominates Gen. Zachary Taylor for President and Millard Fillmore of New York for Vice President

JUL 4 Cornerstone of Washington Monument laid

19-20 First American women's convention at Seneco Falls NY, called by Lucretia Mott and Elizabeth Cady Stanton

26 University of Wisconsin chartered in Madison, Wis.

AUG 9 Anti-slavery Free Soil Party nominates Martin Van Buren for President and Charles Francis Adams of Massachusetts for Vice President

14 Pres. Polk signs bill organizing Oregon Territory without slavery

THE GOLD RUSH

In the closing months of the 1840s America was gripped by a kind of national madness, following reports of the discovery of gold in California. The discovery was made by one James W. Marshall at Sutter's Mill in the Sacramento Valley, and launched a blind rush from the Eastern states in an attempt to share in the reportedly fantastic fortunes being hewn and panned from the soil and rivers of the West. The cheery print (near left) of an independent gold hunter on his way to California belies the hardship suffered by many of the forty-niners, and those who followed in their footsteps, as they made their way through the arid, inhospitable wastes of the Great Plains, or across the isthmus of Panama, to the Pacific Coast. Others eschewed the overland route to brave the no less perilous conditions of the sea passage round Cape Horn, often in barely seaworthy vessels. The prospectors came, not only from every part of the United States, but from all over the world. In particular thousands of Australians arrived in California during the Gold Rush years.

If the hazards of the journey failed to deter the gold hunters, the backbreaking work and primitive conditions with which they found themselves confronted at their destination soon took their toll of the less hardy. Life in the gold fields was lawless and violent, and not infrequently short. Nor did the vast wealth of the early rumors materialize for the majority of hopeful prospectors.

Far left: Sutter's Mill in the Sacramento Valley.

Inset left: The man who started it all, James W. Marshall.

Right: Shipping advertisements cashing in on gold fever often failed to reflect the dangerous realities of the sea passage to the Pacific coast.

Below left: Back-breaking labor for little reward: the everyday experience of miners in the West.

Below: An underground working.

FOR CALIFORNIA AND THE GOLD REGION DIRECT!

The Magnificent, Fast Sailing and favorite packet Ship,

JOSEPHINE,
BURTHEN 400 TONS, CAPT.

10th November Next.

RODNEY FRENCH,
No. 103 North Water Street, Rodman's Wharf.

NOV 1 First medical school for women, Boston Female Medical School, opens with enrollment of 12

7 Zachary Taylor elected President, Millard Fillmore elected Vice President

DEC 22 Southern congressmen hold caucus on slavery question

Also this year

★ Failure of revolution in Germany starts great German migration to U.S

★ Swedish migration into Mississippi Valley begins

★ Pres. Polk proposes purchase of Cuba from Spain for $100 million

★ Vermont legislature resolves that slavery should be prohibited in territories and abolished in the District of Columbia

★ New York State grants property rights to women equal to those of men

★ Socialist community at Oneida, NY, founded by Perfectionists under John Humphrey Noyes

★ Associated Press organized by group of NYC journalists

★ Telegraph communication between New York and Chicago established

1849

JAN Amelia Bloomer, temperance and women's rights advocate, begins publishing *The Lily*

FEB 7 *Passenger Cases,* Supreme Court denies right of New York and Massachusetts to charge tax on each entering alien

12 San Franciscans meet to establish temporary government for region

28 Ship, *California,* arrives at San Francisco with first gold seekers from the East

MAR 3 Home Department (Department of the Interior) established by Congress

3 Minnesota Territory established, slavery prohibited

3 Coinage of gold dollar and double eagle authorized by Congress

5 Zachary Taylor inaugurated 12th President, Millard Fillmore inaugurated Vice President

10 Missouri legislature declares that 'the right to prohibit slavery in any territory belongs exclusively to the people thereof'

10 Astor Place Opera House riot leaves 22 dead, 36 injured

MAY 17 Fire in St. Louis, Missouri, destroys over 400 buildings and 27 steamships

AUG 11 Pres. Taylor forbids Americans from making filibustering trips into Cuba

SEP 1 - OCT 13 California constitutional convention meets at Monterey and drafts constitution prohibiting slavery

OCT British naval vessel seizes Tigre Island off west coast of Isthmus of Panama

NOV 13 California constitution ratified by popular vote

22 Austin College chartered in Huntsville, Tex., under Presbyterian auspices

DEC 20 US signs Treaty of amity, commerce and navigation with the Hawaiian Islands

Also this year

★ Cholera epidemic begins in South

★ Pacific Railroad chartered in Missouri, planned to link St. Louis and Kansas City

★ Mail stagecoach line opened between Independence, MO., and Sante Fe

★ Elizabeth Blackwell receives medical degree from Geneva College, Geneva, NY, first American female physician

★ Safety pin patented by Walter Hunt of NYC

★ Spiritualism founded by Margaret and Kate Fox in Rochester, NY

★ Henry David Thoreau's essay *Civil Disobedience* published

THE 1850s were the last decade of peace before American society was engulfed in the tragedy of the Civil War. Those who believed that the Union must be preserved at all costs fought tooth and nail to get the 1850 Compromise through Congress and continued to fight to sustain it during the increasingly difficult years that followed. But there was no holding the slavery question down for good. Every new territorial development in the West seemed to raise it again, and each time it became more difficult to lay it to rest. For most political leaders, the best policy still seemed to be to keep it as quiet as possible and hope that it would go away. In 1854, however, a group of men determined not to avoid the issue any longer met to form a new political party. Borrowing the old Jeffersonian name, they called it the Republican Party and dedicated themselves to halting the extension of slavery beyond those states in which it already existed. Within a few years, the new party was destined to change the face of American political life.

For all the increasingly bloody lawlessness in the troubled new territories of Kansas and Nebraska, for all the inexorable polarization of opinion between the free North and the slave-owning South, the 1850s were nonetheless a decade of remarkable prosperity in the United States. Overseas, American trade grew enormously and important new markets were opened up in the Far East. At home, thousands of Americans continued to act out their "Manifest Destiny" and head for the new and beautiful territories of the Far West. Railway building spread like wildfire across the wide open spaces of the continent, and the manufacturing sector burgeoned, fueling the spectacular growth of the major cities. A new and distinctive self-confidence expressed itself in a dawning golden age of American literature.

At the same time, a chapter was ending in the history of the nation. By the end of the decade, the second generation of great American statesmen – Andrew Jackson, Henry Clay, John Calhoun, Daniel Webster, John Quincy Adams – were all dead and a new generation had taken their place. Among them, as the fateful election of 1860 approached, was a lawyer and former Congressman from Illinois who, for good and ill, would make perhaps a greater mark on American life than any of the great men who preceded him. He was the Republican candidate, Abraham Lincoln.

The Compromise of 1850

The closing years of the 1840s had brought the slavery issue to the surface with greater bitterness than at any time since the Missouri debate of 1819. This time the catalyst was the acquisition by the United States of the territories ceded by Mexico at the end of the Mexican War, and in particular the application of California to join the Union as a free state, thus disturbing the delicate political balance of free state and slave state representation in Congress. Even before the end of the war, a senator by the name of David Wilmot had proposed a resolution banning slavery in all the new territories, and the South could see the principles of the Missouri Compromise (which technically applied only to the lands of the Louisiana Purchase) being swept away on a tide of abolitionism. The Union faced a severe test indeed as the new decade began.

Henry Clay – the one-time leader of the Western "War Hawks," now turned "Great Pacificator" – rose to the challenge with a series of compromise proposals, designed to satisfy both North and South. California would be admitted as a free state, territorial governments would be organized in Utah and New Mexico without reference to the slavery question, harsher laws would be passed to ensure the return of fugitive slaves to their owners, and the domestic slave trade would be abolished in the District of Columbia. As a final sop to Southern opinion, the Texan debt would be taken over by the Federal Government. Like many a proposed compromise, Clay's suggestions satisfied neither side, but despite the ravages of the tuberculosis which would shortly kill him, he argued them in Congress for two whole days. It was a battle of old men. Calhoun, himself a dying man, opposed Clay's plans (even suggesting a constitutional amendment to allow for two Presidents, one elected by the South and one by the North), and Webster, elderly now but still a fiery orator, made his last great speech in support of the Union. But it was left to the younger generation – and notably Stephen A. Douglas of Illinois, known as "The Little Giant" for his diminutive stature and gritty determination – to carry the day for Clay's compromise solution. Once again America breathed a sigh of relief. Both North and South hoped that this time the Compromise would prove a permanent solution. For the time being, few dared countenance the alternative.

The Kansas–Nebraska Act

Within a few years, the uneasy truce established by the 1850 Compromise deteriorated into what was effectively a civil war in the new territory of Kansas. Douglas, one of the chief architects of the Compromise, was also the prime mover in the events that led to its breakdown.

The immediate cause of the controversy was the jockeying for position by different sectional interests over the route of the projected trans-continental railway. Douglas favored the Central Pacific route across the Great Plains, not least because it would run through land in which he had political and financial interests. In 1854 he put a bill before Congress to organize the Great Plains into new territories – Kansas and Nebraska – split along the 40th parallel. In so doing, the Little Giant blundered into a minefield of North–South antagonism. Under the terms of the bill the people of the new territories would be free to decide whether to permit slavery there or not, and both sides were quick to see that this so-called "popular sovereignty" doctrine overrode the limits placed on the extension of slavery by the Missouri Compromise of 1820. The stage was set for a long and bitter battle on the floor of Congress.

Stephen Douglas was nothing if not tenacious, and the Kansas–Nebraska Bill eventually passed. But many Northerners saw it as a victory for the South and determined to do everything within their power to hinder the further extension of slavery in the West. The provision of the 1850 Compromise requiring free states to cooperate in returning runaway slaves to their owners, which was already extremely unpopular in the North, now became virtually unworkable, and a clandestine liberation network, the so-called Underground Railway, was soon helping some 1000 slaves a year to freedom under the "conductorship" of such courageous black escapees as Harriet Tubman.

San Francisco celebrates the admission of California into the Union.

Prelude to civil war: Violence breaks out among delegates to a peace convention in Kansas in the wake of the Kansas-Nebraska Act.

Most significant of all, a new political grouping of anti-slavery men from the existing parties came together to form a new party, the Republican Party, at Jackson, Michigan in 1854. The Republicans drew their support not only from disaffected Northwestern Whigs but also from Democrats opposed to the Kansas–Nebraska Act and from the smaller anti-slavery parties such as the Free-soilers. They made a significant showing in the state elections of 1854 and an even stronger one in the presidential election of 1856. A mere seven years after their formation, they were to put a President in the White House and precipitate the greatest tragedy in American history.

"Bleeding Kansas"

One of the main consequences of the Kansas–Nebraska Act was to shift the theater of the slave battle westward into the new territories. The arithmetic of "popular sovereignty" meant that both sides sought strength in numbers. No sooner had the first Northern settlers begun to move into Kansas (with rifles prominent in their baggage) than organized gangs of so-called "border ruffians" crossed the border from Missouri to establish their own foothold in the virgin territory. Pro-slavery settlements were founded right alongside free ones, and congressional elections were marked by violence, intimidation, and ballot-rigging. Raids and reprisals became the familiar pattern of everyday life, and Kansas quickly collapsed into a tragic spiral of lawlessness and bloodshed.

In one of the worst of the many incidents which earned the territory the epithet of "Bleeding Kansas" during these years, a mob of Missourians sacked and burned the free-state town of Lawrence in 1856 in retaliation for the murder of a pro-slavery man there. In the subsequent anti-slavery reprisals, the name of John Brown achieved notoriety for the first time. Brown, a fanatical abolitionist, sought to avenge the attack on Lawrence by murdering five pro-

slavery men in the middle of the night in a raid on a settlement at Pottawatomie Creek. Three years later, he was captured while leading an attack on the U.S. armory at Harper's Ferry in Virginia as part of a campaign to restore freedom to the Southern slaves by force of arms. Brown was hanged, his mortal remains entering popular mythology in the song "John Brown's body lies a-moldering in the grave,/But his soul goes marching on." Brown was variously hailed as a hero or a madman. It is a sign of how high feelings were running at this time that even so clear-sighted a man as Ralph Waldo Emerson could compare him to Christ.

The Harper's Ferry raid came as the bitter climax to a period of ever-increasing polarization into pro- and anti-slavery factions in America. The unrest extended far beyond Kansas, where a pro-slavery constitution drafted in 1857 was overwhelmingly rejected in favor of a free one by referendum in 1858. Violence even erupted onto the floor of the Senate itself. When Preston Brooks, a representative from South Carolina, beat a Northern abolitionist senator senseless with a gold-handled cane, he was feted throughout the South and showered with replica canes as a mark of respect. Controversy raged too over the Dred Scott case, in which Chief Justice Taney (the man Jackson had promoted to get rid of the central bank for him) declared the Missouri Compromise unconstitutional, thus giving the pro-slavery cause a substantial fillip. The North–South divide was all too ominously evident in the voting patterns at the 1856 presidential election. In this highly charged atmosphere, John Brown's antics convinced many in the South that they would have to leave the Union if the Republican Party ever came to power. The time for compromises was fast running out.

JAN 2 First US commercial treaty with El Salvador ratified

29 In Compromise of 1850, Sen. Henry Clay introduces series of eight resolutions to deal with slavery issue

MAR 7 Sen. Daniel Webster of Massachusetts delivers famous speech in support of Clay compromise

APR 19 Clayton-Bulwer Treaty, signed by US and Great Britain, provides that projected canal across Central America will be neutral, neither government will attempt to control any part of Central America and both will protect area

MAY 4 Fire strikes town of San Francisco

25 New Mexico convention forms state government, sets boundaries of state, bans slavery and applies for statehood

JUL 9 Pres. Zachary Taylor dies of cholera; Vice Pres. Millard Fillmore assumes office

25 Gold discovered on Rogue River in Oregon

SEP 9 California enters Union as 31st (free) state

9 Territories of New Mexico, Utah and Texas organized without restriction on slavery

18 Fugitive Slave Act of 1850 reinforces Act of 1793

20 Slave trade abolished in District of Columbia

20 First federal land grant for railroad construction made to Illinois, Mississippi and Alabama for railroad from Chicago to Mobile

OCT 21 Chicago City Council refuses to enforce Fugitive Slave Act

23-24 First national women's rights convention held in Worcester, Mass., attended by delegates from nine states

DEC 3 Brougham's Lyceum theater opens in NYC

13-14 Georgia state convention votes to stay in Union but threatens secession if Compromise of 1850 is not observed by North

Also this year

★ Cholera epidemic strikes Midwest

★ Steerage fares for immigrants to US drop to $10 but conditions are atrocious

★ *Harper's Monthly Magazine* begins publication in NYC

The Arts

★ Nathaniel Hawthorne's novel *The Scarlet Letter*

★ Emanuel Leutze's painting *Washington Crossing the Delaware*

His soul goes marching on: John Brown mounts the scaffold, December 1859, after being condemned to death for his raid on Harper's Ferry.

Enter Lincoln

There emerged onto the political scene in the late 1850s one of the most remarkable men ever to hold high office in the United States. Abraham Lincoln, the son of a poor frontier family, had served one undistinguished term as a Congressman in the 1840s before returning to the relative obscurity of small-town life in Illinois. A tall, shambling figure with awkward manners and a distracted air, he came to prominence in a series of extraordinary debates with the Little Giant, Stephen Douglas, during the 1858 campaign for election to the Senate as the representative for Illinois. Douglas won the senatorship, but the debates – which focused on the moral aspects of the slavery question – gave Lincoln's reputation a huge boost in Republican circles. They also represented yet another stage in the polarization of American politics, conducted as they were in the shadow of Lincoln's memorable keynote address: "A house divided against itself cannot stand" he said. "I believe this government cannot endure permanently half slave and half free. I do not expect the Union to be dissolved – I do not expect the house to fall – but I do expect it will cease to be divided. It will become all one thing or all the other." His words were to prove all too prophetic over the coming years.

An Expanding Nation

Despite the dark clouds looming on the horizon, America continued to expand and prosper during the 1850s. An explosion of railway building added more than 20,000 miles of track to the fledgling network of 1850, linking the Great Lakes and the western side of the Mississippi to the crucial trading ports of the eastern seaboard. During the same period, thousands of miles of telegraph wire effected a revolution in coast-to-coast communications.

As America's internal communications expanded, so her population burgeoned. The 1850s saw an incredible leap from 23 million to more than 31 million people. The majority of the increase was accounted for by American births, but the decade also saw a staggering rise in immigration to the United States in the wake of natural and political disturbances in Europe, such as the Irish famine of 1845–1846 and the abortive German revolution of 1848. Between 1840 and 1860, 4.2 million people emigrated to the United States – six times the number who had arrived on American shores in the previous 20 years. Within the country, the westward and cityward trends of previous years continued to gather pace, one fueled by new agricultural inventions such as the McCormick reaper and the steel plow and the other by the growth of the manufacturing industries. The population of Texas tripled during the 1850s, and the population of California more than quadrupled from 93,000 to 380,000, even after the excitement of the gold rush had died down. By the end of the decade, a fifth of all Americans lived in the cities.

Foreign trade also boomed during the decade. It was Americans who opened up the Japanese market for the first time in history during the 1850s, and trade with Japan's giant neighbor China continued to flourish. American clippers, such as the revolutionary *Flying Cloud*, launched in Boston in 1851, slashed journey times from continent to continent and became the envy of the maritime world.

A Golden Age of Literature

The 1850s also saw the first great flowering of a distinctively American literature. In the course of this single extraordinary decade were published Nathaniel Hawthorne's greatest works, *The Scarlet Letter* and *The House of the Seven Gables*; Herman Melville's epic novel *Moby-Dick*; Walt Whitman's *Leaves of Grass*; and Henry Wadsworth Longfellow's *The Song of Hiawatha* and *The Courtship of Miles Standish*. Ralph Waldo Emerson's *Representative Men* appeared in 1850, and Henry David Thoreau's masterpiece, *Walden,* in 1854. In 1857 James Russell Lowell founded the influential *Atlantic Monthly*, and Oliver Wendell Holmes' *The Autocrat of the Breakfast Table* appeared the following year.

But no great literature exists in a vacuum, and the tensions as well as the strengths of American society are evident in this remarkable outpouring of talent. It is no coincidence that one of the best-selling works of the decade that was to serve as the overture to the American Civil War was Harriet Beecher Stowe's searing fictional indictment of slavery in the South, *Uncle Tom's Cabin*.

Gold fever abates, but western emigration continues: A family camp on the plains on their way to a new life.

The Song of Hiawatha

Throughout the 19th century, injustices perpetrated against America's Indian population co-existed with a popular romantic cult of Indian life. Henry Wadsworth Longfellow published his verse epic, *The Song of Hiawatha*, in 1855.

Exit Calhoun

The stern countenance of John C. Calhoun, who died in 1850. With Henry Clay and Daniel Webster, he had dominated American political life since John Quincy Adams' presidency.

"I contain multitudes"

One of the towering figures of American literature, Walt Whitman (1819–1892) (above) published his first major work, *Leaves of Grass*, a collection of poems, in 1855. His long flexible lines were to have an enormous impact on the development of modern verse.

JAN 28 Northwestern University chartered in Evanston, Ill. as North Western University under Methodist auspices

FEB 15 Shadrach, fugitive slave, rescued from Boston jail by mob of Blacks challenging new Fugitive Slave Law

MAY 3 San Francisco fire destroys 2500 buildings, causing $12 million damage

15 Erie Railroad, connecting New York with Great Lakes, opens

JUN 5 *Uncle Tom's Cabin* by Harriet Beecher Stowe, begins to appear as serial in *National Era,* antislavery paper published in Washington, DC

9 Vigilantes organized by leading citizens of San Francisco in response to increase in crime rate

JUL 23 In Treaty of Traverse des Sioux, Sioux Indians cede all their lands in Iowa and most of their land in Minnesota to US

AUG 12 Isaac Merritt Singer receives patent for practical sewing machine

DEC 24 Fire in Library of Congress destroys two thirds of collection

The Arts

★ Nathaniel Hawthorne's novel *The House of Seven Gables*

★ Herman Melville's novel *Moby Dick*

1852

FEB 20 First train from East reaches Chicago by way of Michigan Southern Railway

MAR 13 First appearance of Uncle Sam in New York weekly comic *Diogenes, His Lantern*

APR 6 Word 'telegram' first used in *Albany Evening Journal*

21 Tufts College chartered in Medford, Mass., under Universalist auspices

NOV 2 Democrat Franklin Pierce elected President, William R. King elected Vice President

21 Duke University chartered as Normal College in Randolph Country NC, under Methodist auspices

NOV-DEC American or Nativist Party, or 'Know-Nothing' Party attracts more supporters

Also this year

★ First compulsory school attendance law in US passed by Massachusetts

★ Prohibition laws adopted by Massachusetts, Vermont and Louisiana

★ Pennsylvania Railroad between Philadelphia and Pittsburgh completed

1853

FEB Women's Suffrage magazine *Una,* published by Paulina Wright Davis and edited by Caroline H. Dall, issued in Washington, DC

12 Illinois Wesleyan University chartered in Bloomington, Ill., under Methodist auspices

MAR 2 Territory of Washington formed after separation from Oregon Territory

4 Franklin Pierce inaugurated President, William R. King inaugurated Vice President

31 Louisiana State University chartered as Louisiana State Seminary of Learning and Military Academy in Alexandria, La

APR 18 Death of Vice Pres. William R. King

JUL 8 Commodore Perry arrives in Yedo Bay, Japan, to negotiate treaty of friendship and trade

14 Crystal Palace Exhibition of the Industry of All Nations opens in NYC

The Singer Sewing Machine

Every home should have one: Isaac Singer's original mechanical sewing machine (right), patented in 1851. Despite later refinements, the design is still recognizably that of its successors today.

Birth of the G.O.P.

A new force in American politics, the Republican Party, was born in this modest schoolhouse (below) in 1854.

New York World Fair

This "crystal palace" (above), modeled on the one at the British Great Exhibition of 1851, formed the focus of the New York World Fair in 1853.

"Hairy barbarians"

America played a leading role in the opening up of Japan to trade with the outside world. In 1853 Commodore Matthew Perry led an expedition to Tokyo and secured a favorable trade agreement with the Shogun of Kanagawa. This Japanese print (above) depicts a column of U.S. Marines.

Uncle Tom's Cabin

Yet one more indicator of the temporary nature of the 1850 Compromise in shelving the "Negro question" in the United States was the controversy aroused by the publication in

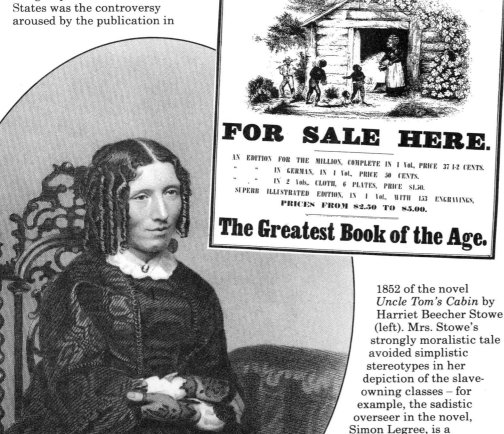

135,000 SETS, 270,000 VOLUMES SOLD.

UNCLE TOM'S CABIN

FOR SALE HERE.

AN EDITION FOR THE MILLION, COMPLETE IN 1 Vol., PRICE 37 1-2 CENTS.
" " IN GERMAN, IN 1 Vol., PRICE 50 CENTS.
" " IN 2 Vols., CLOTH, 6 PLATES, PRICE $1.50.
SUPERB ILLUSTRATED EDITION, IN 1 Vol., WITH 153 ENGRAVINGS,
PRICES FROM $2.50 TO $5.00.

The Greatest Book of the Age.

1852 of the novel *Uncle Tom's Cabin* by Harriet Beecher Stowe (left). Mrs. Stowe's strongly moralistic tale avoided simplistic stereotypes in her depiction of the slave-owning classes – for example, the sadistic overseer in the novel, Simon Legree, is a Northerner – but the book served to generate outrage both in the North, where it became an unprecedented bestseller, and in the South, where it was seen as yet another assault on the perceived rights of the slavocracy.

The Dred Scott Case

In 1857, in a controversial and far-reaching decision, the Supreme Court effectively ruled the Missouri Compromise of 1820 unconstitutional and took the country one step closer to Civil War. Dred Scott (left), a Black slave in Missouri who had visited the North with his master, sued for freedom on the grounds that he had temporarily been a resident of free states. Chief Justice Taney ruled that, as a slave, Scott was not a citizen of the U.S., but rather the property of a citizen, which Congress had no power to take away, wherever he may have lived.

DEC 30 Gasden Purchase, Mexico cedes to US tract of land along present-day southern border of Arizona and New Mexico for $15 million; ideal for railroad route to Pacific Ocean

Also this year

★ Mrs. Amos Bronson Alcott and 73 other women present suffrage petition to Massachusetts Constitutional Convention

★ Baltimore and Ohio Railroad reaches Wheeling on Ohio River

★ New York Central Railroad formed by merger of 10 lines between Albany and Buffalo

1854

JAN 18 American filibuster William Walker proclaims new republic of Sonora, containing Mexican states Sonora and Baja California and establishes himself as president; later tried in US for violation of neutrality

FEB 28 Anti-slavery opponents of Kansas-Nebraska bill meet at Ripon, Wn, and recommend forming Republican Party

MAR 31 Treaty of Kanagawa signed by Commodore Perry with Japan, opens 2 ports for trade with US ships

MAY 6 Transatlantic Cable Communication Company headed by Cyrus W. Field granted charter and 50-year monopoly

26 Kansas-Nebraska Act creates two new territories in which slavery issue will be decided by popular sovereignty

26 Anti-slavery mob attacks Federal court house in Boston in unsuccessful attempt to rescue accused fugitive slave Anthony Burns

31 Pres. Pierce issues statement against filibustering invasions of Cuba

JUN 5 Reciprocity Treaty between US and Britain settles disputes over fishing rights between US and Canada and allows a duty-free entry of certain commodities

JUL 15 First newspaper in Kansas, *Kansas Weekly Herald,* begins publication

19 Wisconsin Supreme Court releases a Mr Booth, convicted of rescuing runaway slave, and declares Fugitive Slave Act unconstitutional

OCT 18 Ostend Manifesto, drafted by US ministers Buchanan, Mason and Soule in Ostend, Belgium, declares that US intends to acquire Cuba from Spain and will resort to force if Spain refuses to cooperate

NOV 29 G.W. Whitfield elected congressional representative from Kansas when 1600 armed ruffians cross border from Missouri to vote for pro-slavery candidate

DEC 30 First US oil corporation, Pennsylvania Rock Oil Co., established in New Haven, Conn. by George H. Bissell and Jonathan J. Eveleth

1854-1858 War for 'Bleeding Kansas'

The Arts

★ Henry David Thoreau's series of essays *Walden*

1855

JAN 25 Iowa Wesleyan College chartered as Iowa Wesleyan University in Mt Pleasant, Iowa, under Methodist auspices

FEB 17 Construction of telegraph line from Mississippi River to the Pacific authorized by Congress

24 Act creating first US Court of Claims signed by the President

MAR 3 Ostend Manifesto published in US; receives such a negative public reaction that Secretary of State William I. Marcy refuses to support it

30 Kansas' first territorial legislature elected by armed pro-slavery 'Border Ruffians' from Missouri; Territorial Governor allows fraudulent election to stand

JUL 2 Pro-slavery Kansas Legislature adopts strict pro-slavery laws and expels anti-slavery legislators

31 Andrew Reeder removed from governorship of Kansas Territory by Pres. Pierce

LET MY PEOPLE GO

During the 1850s, gathering moral and political outrage in the North and elsewhere against the "peculiar institution" of slavery was matched by ever more aggressive defense of the slave system by those in the Southern states whose way of life depended on it, and who saw abolitionism as a direct assault on states' and individual property rights. Historians differ in their view as to whether slavery could have remained a viable system of labor in the longer term, but there is no doubt that the institution itself was by now inseparably bound up with the still largely agricultural economy of the South (below right). Slaves, bought and sold in markets such as the one at Charleston in South Carolina (bottom), had no rights as citizens and, while many slave-owners were no doubt kindly and responsible, others were prepared to use to the full

their draconian powers of punishment and authority over their unpaid labor force. As hundreds of slaves continued to escape to the free states with the help of the clandestine support system known as the Underground Railway (whose most famous "conductor" was the redoubtable Harriet Tubman (right)), Southerners were outraged by the North's failure to enforce the provisions of the Fugitive Slave Act that had formed part of the 1850 Compromise. Abolitionist presses operated in continual danger of attacks such as the one launched against the offices of an anti-slavery newspaper in Alton, Illinois (below left), and by the end of the decade it was clear that what Jackson had called the "Negro question" had reached an impasse to which all solutions other than open conflict seemed to have failed.

Selling a mother from her child.

Chained slaves working in the fields.

Hunting a runaway slave with guns and dogs.

"They can't take care of themselves."

SEP 3 William Walker, backed by Accessory Transit Company, exploits Nicaraguan civil war and declares himself dictator; remains for two years

5 Anti-slavery settlers in Kansas hold convention at Big Springs, repudiate fraudulently elected territorial legislature and request admission to Union as free state

OCT 1 J.W. Whitfield reelected Congressional Representative for Kansas Territory by Border Ruffians from Missouri

9 Anti-slavery supporters independently elect former Governor Andrew Reeder as Congressional Representative for Kansas Territory

OCT 23-NOV 12 Topeka Constitution, establishing Governor and legislature and outlawing slavery in Kansas, adopted by free-soil Kansans

NOV 26-DEC 7 In Wakarusa War, 1500 Border Ruffians camped on Wakarusa River plan to attack anti-slavery town of Laurence in Kansas Territory but withdraw after discovering that town is defended

15 Free-soil Kansans approve Topeka constitution and law barring Blacks from Kansas

Also this year

★ Approximately 400,000 immigrants arrive in New York City

★ New York State Immigration Commission leases Castle Garden, at bottom of Manhattan Island, for reception of immigrants

★ Prohibition laws adopted by New York, New Hampshire, Delaware, Iowa, Michigan and Nebraska

★ Mrs. Carl Schurz, pupil of Friedrich Froebel in Germany, establishes first American kindergarten

★ *Daily News* established in NYC

The Arts

★ Henry Wadsworth Longfellow's poem *The Song of Hiawatha*

★ Walt Whitman's book of poetry *Leaves of Grass*

1856

JAN 15 Free-soil Kansans elect their own governor and legislature

FEB 11 Pres. Pierce issues proclamation against both Border Ruffians and free-state men seeking unlawful control in Kansas Territory

MAR 4 Anti-slavery government in Topeka, Kansas, petitions Congress for admission to the Union

MAY 21 Armed pro-slavery force attacks Laurence, Ks, station on underground railroad and kills one person

22 South Carolina Representative Preston S. Brooks attacks Massachusetts Sen. Charles Sumner as he sits at his desk in Senate chamber

24 Anti-slavery force led by John Brown retaliates by killing five pro-slavery Kansans along Pottawotamic Creek

JUL 4 Federal troops from Fort Leavenworth, Ks, dispense Free-state legislature in Topeka

AUG 18 Annexation by US of any small Guano island unclaimed by another government authorized by Congress

SEP 15 Gov. Geary uses Federal troops to stop armed Missourians marching on Kansas

NOV 4 Democrat James Buchanan elected President, John C. Breckinridge elected Vice President

Also this year

★ Western Union Telegraph Company established

1857

MAR 4 James Buchanan inaugurated President, John C. Breckinridge inaugurated Vice President

6 In *Scott v. Sandford,* Supreme Court rules that slave Scott cannot bring suit in Federal court; results in protest from Northerners and Republicans

AUG 24 Panic of 1857 begins with failure of NY branch of Ohio Life Insurance and Trust Company

SEP 11 Mountain Meadow Massacre, 120 California-bound migrants killed by Indians aroused by Mormon

THE AGE OF THE RAILROADS

Few developments made so profound an impact on the American way of life as the coming of the great railroads. In a country of vast distances and widely separated settlements, they acted as a unifying force, sustaining the networks of commerce and communication essential to the life of an expanding nation. At the same time, the great railroad companies became among the most powerful and profitable interests in the country, bending local legislatures to their will, and making and unmaking towns, areas, and reputations at the stroke of a pen.

The 1850s saw an enormous expansion in these networks, which had been cautiously extending themselves in the North and Southeast of the country since the first track was laid in 1830. Between 1850 and

Construction work on one of America's early railroads.

The railroad route to California.

Early sleeping cars.

1860 the length of track in the United States more than tripled to a staggering 30,000 miles, the most important lines being run by the Baltimore and Ohio (the first American railroad company), the Erie, the New York Central, and the Pennsylvania. In 1869 railroad history was made by the completion of America's first transcontinental line, when the Union Pacific and Central Pacific Railroads met at Promontory Point, Utah, and by the end of the century the United States had a greater railway network than the whole of Europe, with some 200,000 miles of track in operation. As one observer was moved to comment, the American people took to railroad building "as if it were the cradle in which they were born."

America's first steam locomotive, 1828.

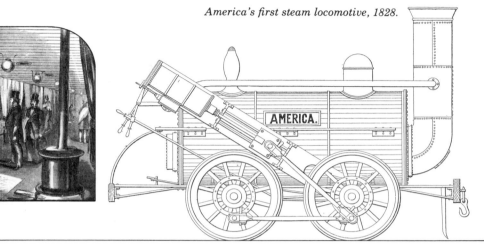

Crowds turn out to greet the arrival in Jamestown of the first Atlantic and Great Western train from New York.

fanatic John D. Lee, angered by Pres. Buchanan's order to remove Brigham Young from governorship of Utah

OCT Exhibition of Pre-Raphaelite paintings organized in NYC

OCT 5 Free State legislature elected in Kansas Territory

19-NOV 8 At Lecompton Constitutional Convention, pro-slavery forces contrive hitch to guarantee legalization of slavery in Kansas

DEC 21 Pro-slavery Lecompton Constitution adopted in Kansas Territory; Free State Party members refuse to vote

Also this year

★ Failure of 4932 businesses

★ Cooper Union founded in NYC by Peter Cooper

★ *Atlantic Monthly* founded in Boston, James Russell Lowell editor

★ *Harper's Weekly* founded, George William Curtis editor

1858

MAY 11 Minnesota enters Union as 32nd (free) state

JUN 16 Abraham Lincoln, in accepting Republican Party nomination for Senator from Illinois, asserts 'I believe this government cannot endure permanently half slave and half free'

18 US and China sign treaty of peace, friendship and commerce

JUL 29 Treaty with Japan completed by Townsend Harris; becomes basis of Japan's trade relations with foreign powers for rest of century

AUG 5 First transatlantic cable completed

AUTUMN Gold discovered on Cherry Creek in Kansas Territory, 90 miles from Pike's Peak

OCT 9 Overland Mail stage completes first trips connecting West and East coasts, reaching St Louis from San Francisco after 23 days and 4 hours

Also this year

★ Financial panic continues; 4222 businesses fail

★ Religious Revival of 1858, fueled by financial panic, sweeps country

1859

FEB 14 Oregon enters Union as 33rd (free) state

MAR 7 In *Alabama v. Booth,* Supreme Court declares Fugitive Slave Act of 1850 constitutional

APR 4 Song 'Dixie', written by Dan D. Emmett for Bryant's Minstrels, first publicly sung in Mechanics Hall, New York

23 First newspaper in Colorado, *Rocky Mountain News,* begins publication in Auraria

MAY 12 Southern Commercial Convention, meeting in Vicksburg, Miss., adopts resolution that all laws, state and Federal, prohibiting African slave trade should be repealed

JUN First major US silver deposit discovered in Camstock Lode, Nevada

AUG 27 Edwin L. Drake strikes oil while drilling near Titusville, Pa, beginning modern oil industry

OCT 16-18 Radical abolitionist John Brown and 21 others seize Federal arsenal at Harper's Ferry

DEC 2 Radical abolitionist John Brown hanged in public square of Charleston, Va

Also this year

★ Great Atlantic and Pacific Tea Company founded in general store on Vesey Street, NY

★ Massachusetts Institute of Technology established at Cambridge, Mass.

★ South Dakota's first newspaper *The Democrat,* published at Sioux Falls

The Arts

★ Henry David Thoreau's 'A Plea for Captain John Brown'

The Civil War

THE 1860s were the most traumatic period in the whole of American history as the nation that had led the world in democracy was plunged into an internecine conflict which would leave some 600,000 Americans dead and a bitter legacy of hatred, debt, and destruction. Most people knew, at the beginning of this tragic decade, that a showdown was inevitable, but not even the most pessimistic could have foreseen the horrors which civil war would bring or the staggering cost in human lives, money, and goodwill that would haunt the American people long after the fighting was over and the troubled years of reconstruction had begun.

The Formation of the Confederacy

Despite the attempts of the lame duck President James Buchanan to find a way of saving the Union, it was clear that the election of Abraham Lincoln in November 1860 had split the country into two opposed camps along North-South lines. Within a month of the election result, South Carolina declared its secession from the United States in ringing terms, and by the beginning of February 1861 it had been joined by Mississippi, Alabama, Florida, Georgia, Louisiana, and Texas. On February 4 the rebel states formed the Confederate States

Jefferson Davis, the first and only President of the Confederate States of America.

Abraham Lincoln, the 16th President photographed in 1860 by Mathew Brady.

of America and elected Jefferson Davis of Mississippi as President. The new Confederacy then drew up a constitution based on that of the United States, with the significant difference that it built in legal safeguards for slavery and strongly defended the rights of individual states against the central government.

The First Shot

The outbreak of hostilities was not long delayed. Lincoln's inaugural address called for calm and reconciliation, but events had already developed a momentum of their own. In particular, the new President had to face the thorny question of reprovisioning Fort Sumter in Charleston harbor, a Union fort in Confederate territory whose supplies would shortly run out. The Confederacy had made it clear that any attempt at resupply would be regarded as an act of war, and for some time Lincoln hesitated. If he provoked the flashpoint, would it drive into the arms of the Confederacy the crucial Upper Southern states which had so far held out against secession? Or would it bring them to his side in the battle to save the Union? Finally, in early April 1861, he decided to send in the resupply vessels. The Confederacy responded with an artillery barrage against the fort. The first shots of the Civil War had been fired.

North and South

Fort Sumter resulted in an immediate hardening of positions. Throughout the North a tide of Unionist fervor swept thousands of men to the recruiting offices in response to Lincoln's call for 75,000 volunteers. Davis' call for 100,000 men met with a similar response. But most significant of all, Lincoln's gamble drove the Upper South into the Confederate camp. Within two days of his call to arms, Virginia, outraged by what it saw as an attempt at coercion, voted

to secede from the Union (although some western counties refused to do so, soon to become the new state of West Virginia) and provided the Confederacy with a new capital, Richmond, little more than 100 miles from Washington. Arkansas, Tennessee, and North Carolina followed. Delaware remained staunchly Unionist, but it was touch and go whether Maryland, Missouri, and Kentucky would follow suit. In the end all stayed with the Union cause, but the secessions of April and May had nonetheless almost doubled the size of the Confederacy in its first four months of life.

The battle lines were now drawn up. On the face of it, the odds looked firmly stacked in the North's favor. The Union had some 22 million people, as against the Confederacy's nine million (more than a third of whom

Charleston high society watches as Fort Sumter is bombarded by Confederate guns.

were slaves). The North also had the best of the nation's industry and infrastructure, and the vast majority of its wealth. But the South had the stronger military tradition and in Robert E. Lee, who after much soul-searching resigned his commission in the United States Army to take command of the Confederate forces in Virginia, a general of immense experience and stature. Davis also believed that Great Britain would soon come to the aid of the Confederacy because of her dependence on Southern cotton, but Britain had in fact been stockpiling for some time and simply switched to other markets to ensure her supply. (Despite representations from both sides and some very tense moments, neither Britain nor any other European power threw its weight into the scales of the American struggle.) As the two armies gathered in the month following Fort Sumter, both sides hoped for a swift and decisive victory.

The First Battle of Bull Run

In July 1861, buoyed up by the success of an early campaign to drive the Confederates out of what later became West Virginia, Lincoln sent off an army of 30,000 men in an attempt to take Richmond and defeat the Confederacy at a single stroke. There was a gala atmosphere as the army marched, accompanied by well-wishers and press reporters. The festivities quickly melted away, however, when after about 30 miles the Unionists met a Confederate force of 22,000 men under General P. G. T. Beauregard at Bull Run Creek. Battle was joined, the Confederates, hard pressed for a while, were reinforced by troops from the Shenandoah valley, and the Union army turned on its heel and ran. The first major engagement of the war saw the Army of the Potomac routed and straggling back to Washington in humiliating disarray. The South had stood firm – it was at Bull Run that Lee's lieutenant, Thomas Jackson, earned the sobriquet "Stonewall" – and all hope of a swift end to the war evaporated.

Admired even by his enemies: Robert E. Lee, commander of the Confederate forces.

Above: "Stonewall" Jackson: his heroism helped determine the outcome of the Battle of Bull Run.

Below: The first battle of the Civil War: Union forces are routed at Bull Run Creek, Virginia.

1860s

Civil War

Death of Lincoln

Reconstruction

1860

FEB 15 Wheaton College chartered as Illinois Institute in Wheaton, Ill., under Methodist auspices

MAR 19 Elizabeth Cady Stanton addresses New York State Legislature on women's suffrage

APR 3 Pony Express mail service begins between St Joseph, Missouri, and Sacramento, Ca

23-MAY 3 Delegates from eight Southern states leave Democratic National Convention after dispute over platform; convention adjourns without making nominations

10 Tariff Bill passes House, opening era of protectionism

14 US receives first Japanese diplomat to visit foreign state

JUL-OCT Presidential campaign overwhelmed by slavery and sectionalism issues

NOV 6 Republican Abraham Lincoln elected President, Hannibal Hamlin elected Vice President

DEC 20 South Carolina holds state convention at Charleston and secedes from the Union

27 South Carolina state troops seize Fort Moultrie and Castle Pinckney

28-29 South Carolina delegation visits Washington and demands that President remove all Federal troops from Charleston

30 South Carolina state militia seizes Federal arsenal at Charleston

31 Pres. Buchanan replies to South Carolina commissioners that he cannot remove Federal troops from Charleston

1861

JAN 3 Georgia state troops seize Fort Pulaski

9 Mississippi state convention votes to secede from the Union

9 Unarmed Federal supply ship *Star of the West* fired on by South Carolina state battery at Charleston harbor

10 Florida secedes from the Union

11 Alabama secedes from the Union

18 Vassar Female College founded by Matthew Vassar

19 Georgia secedes from the Union

26 Louisiana secedes from the Union

29 Kansas admitted to Union as 34th (free) state

FEB 4 Delegates of seceding states meet to form Confederate States of America

9 Confederate Provisional Congress elects Jefferson Davis President and declares that laws of US

An uneasy relationship: Abraham Lincoln wonders what McClellan is waiting for.

"I can't spare this man; he fights:" Lincoln's verdict on Ulysses S. Grant (above) proved justified. His strategic genius revived the Union's fortunes.

"All quiet along the Potomac"

After the Battle of Bull Run, Lincoln put the young and somewhat vainglorious George B. McClellan in charge of the Army of the Potomac, with the task of building it into an effective fighting force. McClellan worked wonders with the training and morale of his men, but showed an almost incredible reluctance to make any move against the enemy. Believing, quite wrongly, that he was greatly outnumbered by the Confederate army, he kept his men in Washington until even Lincoln was heard to mutter that if McClellan didn't want to use them, he wouldn't mind borrowing them himself. For the rest of 1861 and the early months of 1862, the Army of the Potomac remained in its quarters.

Enter Grant

By the beginning of 1862 the Union, which had had only 16,000 men under arms at the outbreak of hostilities, could boast an army of no less than 600,000 as against the Confederacy's 250,000. While all remained quiet along the Potomac, part of this army was seeing action along the Tennessee, Cumberland, and Mississippi rivers. In February 1862 Union troops captured the strategic Confederate strongholds of Fort Henry and Fort Donelson, thus making possible a deeper penetration of Confederate territory via the waters of the Tennessee and the Mississippi. The man who commanded this operation was Ulysses S. Grant, a distinguished veteran of the Mexican War, where he had served with Robert E. Lee. Since the heady days of the Mexico City campaign, however, Grant had fallen on hard times, and the beginning of the Civil War saw him working in his father's leather goods store in Galena, Illinois. The Tennessee campaign of 1862 was to be the beginning of a glorious road which led him not only to high command and victory in war, but eventually to the White House itself.

"The father of waters:" The Mississippi saw some of the fiercest fighting of the war, as Union forces battled to wrest the vast natural supply line from Confederate control.

A Pyrrhic victory: Grant defends Shiloh at the cost of 13,000 of his men.

The Battle of Shiloh

Following his successes at Fort Henry and Fort Donelson, Grant advanced on the important railroad juntion at Corinth, a large Union force under General Buell marching south from their capture of Nashville to join him in the assault. However on 6 April, at Shiloh, just north of Corinth, Grant's army was ambushed by Confederate forces under General Johnston and suffered losses of some 13,000 men. Only when Buell arrived with reinforcements was the Confederate attack beaten off, Johnston himself being killed in the action, together with 11,000 of his troops. The Battle of Shiloh slowed the Union advance in the West to a virtual standstill, although Grant went on to take Corinth and occupied Memphis on the banks of the Mississippi in June. Shortly after Shiloh, a naval force under Captain Farragut captured the crucial port of New Orleans, the plan having been for Grant and Farragut to converge on the Confederate stronghold at Vicksburg further up the river. For the time being, though, this maneuver proved impossible to execute.

The revolving gun turret of the U.S.S. Monitor, *which took part in the first "battle of the ironclads," Hampton Roads, 1862.*

Constitution are not inconsistent with Confederate Constitution and will remain in force

18 Jefferson Davis inaugurated President of the Confederacy; 'Dixie' played at ceremonies

22 President Lincoln travels by secret train to Washington; warned in Baltimore of assassination plot

23 Texas secedes from Union

MAR 2 Territories of Nevada and Dakota divided from Territory of Utah

4 Abraham Lincoln inaugurated President, Hannibal Hamlin inaugurated Vice President

4 Confederate flag of Stars and Bars adopted

11 Confederate Congress adopts Constitution of Confederacy, declaring states' rights and protecting slavery

APR 11 South Carolina demands surrender of federal garrison at Fort Sumter

12 Civil War begins when South Carolina forces under Gen P.G.T. Beauregard open fire on Fort Sumter

13 Federal garrison at Fort Sumter, South Carolina, surrenders due to lack of supplies

15 Pres. Lincoln declares state of 'insurrection' and calls for 75,000 volunteers for three months service

17 Virginia secedes from Union

19 First casualities of Civil War occur when troops of Massachusetts 6th Regiment, en route to Washington, DC, are stoned by secessionist mob in Baltimore

19 Blockade of Confederate ports ordered by Pres. Lincoln

19-20 Norfolk Navy Yard destroyed and evacuated by Union forces

MAY 6 Arkansas secedes from Union

20 North Carolina secedes from Union

21 Richmond, Va, designated capital of Confederacy

JUN 8 Tennessee secedes from Union; 11th and final state to do so

27 Central Pacific Railroad incorporated in California

JUL 2 Pres. Lincoln authorizes suspension of privilege of habeas corpus in certain cases

21 In first battle of Bull Run, near Manassas, Va, Union forces routed by Confederates

22 Resolutions in US Congress state that war is being fought 'to preserve the Union' and not to abolish slavery

AUG 5 Congress passes first income tax law as war finance measure

30 Union Gen. John C. Frémont institutes martial law in Missouri and declares slaves of secessionists freed; Lincoln countermands on September 2

SEP 13 First naval engagement of war occurs when Union Lt J.H. Russel raids Southern navy yard in Pensacola, Fla., and burns Confederate privateer Judah

OCT 21 In Battle of Ball's Bluff, Va, Union forces defeated; approximately 1900 Northern soldiers killed

DEC South Carolina planters near coast burn year's cotton crop to prevent seizure by Union troops

Also this year

★Telegraph connection from New York to San Francisco completed

1862

FEB Julia Ward Howe's 'Battle Hymn of the Republic' appears in *Atlantic Monthly*

6 Gen. Ulysses S. Grant and Commodore A.H. Foote initiate campaign against Southern strongholds in Mississippi valley, capturing Fort Henry on Tennessee River

8 Roanoke Island, NC, captured by Union forces under Gen. Ambrose E. Burnside

16 Confederate Fort Donelson, near Nashville, Tenn., surrenders to Gen. Grant after four days' siege

22 Confederate Constitution and presidency declared 'permanent,' no longer 'provisional'

MAR 6-8 In Battle of Pea Ridge, Ark., Confederate army of 16,000 attacks and is defeated by Union Army of 10,500

APR 6-7 In Battle of Shiloh at Pittsburg Landing, Tenn., Confederates under Gen. A.S. Johnston attack

The Peninsula Campaign

In April 1862, a full year after the war had started, McClellan finally felt ready to lead his army out of Washington in another attempt to take the Confederate capital at Richmond. His plan was to ferry his army down the Potomac and into Chesapeake Bay before marching up the Yorktown Peninsula towards Richmond, and by May his 100,000-strong force had the outskirts of the city in their sights. Here his paranoid belief in the superior numbers of his opponents – though he actually faced an army only half the size of his own – led him to advance far more cautiously than was necessary, and gave Lee the chance to mount a daring defense strategy. Sending the trusty "Stonewall" Jackson up the Shenandoah valley to threaten Washington, Lee ensured that Lincoln would be unable to provide McClellan with the reinforcements he was so anxiously demanding from the troops left behind to defend the capital. He then advanced against McClellan's positions, and over a period of a week drove him back down the peninsula, inflicting and sustaining enormous losses. The battles of the so-called "Seven Days" left McClellan's men still in a strong position and the General asked Lincoln for reinforcements in order to make another attempt on Richmond, this time via

Petersburg, the route Grant would later use with such success. But Lincoln had lost faith in him. Instead he ordered McClellan to withdraw and reinforce the Washington army in an attack on Richmond from the north. The Peninsula Campaign was over.

Above: The Army of the Potomac encamped at Cumberland Landing, Virginia.

Below: The bloodiest day of the war: McClellan defeats Lee at the Battle of Sharpsburg on Antietam Creek, September 17, 1862.

The Second Battle of Bull Run

The army Lincoln now sent south from Washington under General Pope met Confederate forces under Lee and Jackson in August on the same battlefield at Bull Run that had seen the Union army's defeat the previous summer. By attacking before McClellan's army had time to join up with Pope's, Lee ensured that the result was just as humiliating for the Unionists this time. Pope led his men back to Washington, where he was relieved of his command.

Sharpsburg and Fredericksburg

With the Union now on the defensive, Lee pressed home his advantage by crossing the Potomac into Maryland. But McClellan had come across a leaked copy of his plans and went to meet him, with a force almost twice the size of the Confederates', at Sharpsburg on Antietam Creek on September 17. It was the bloodiest day's fighting of the entire war. Lee lost around 11,000 men and McClellan even more. The Confederates were forced to retreat, but it was a victory won at too high a cost to do much for Union morale. Lincoln replaced the discredited McClellan with General Burnside, and the Army of the Potomac headed south again in December, only to meet defeat at the hands of Lee at the battle of Fredericksburg, which left another 12,000 Union soldiers dead. On the eastern front 1862 ended as it had begun, with stalemate.

"Henceforward and forever free"

If nothing else, the campaigns of 1862 had subtly changed the nature of the war. Lincoln had been waiting for a conspicuous Union victory in order to enact his Preliminary Emancipation Proclamation, which declared that all slaves in the rebellious territories would be free from January 1, 1863. Sharpsburg, inglorious though it was, was victory enough for Lincoln to make his announcement. From then on the war,

Unknown soldiers: Some of the more than 23,000 dead who fell on the battlefield at Sharpsburg (Antietam).

which Lincoln had previously insisted was a war to preserve the Union, took on something of the character of a crusade against slavery. It may not have made much difference on the battlefield, but it certainly affected the way in which the war was seen by liberals overseas.

Carnage at Fredericksburg: The scene at Marye's Heights after the Union attempt to take Lee's fortified position on the hill.

Union Army under Gen. Grant; 100,000 soldiers engaged, heavy losses on both sides

25 Union Adm. Farragut occupies New Orleans

MAY 5 Army of the Potomac captures Williamsburg, Va

15 Department of Agriculture established by Congress

20 Pres. Lincoln signs Homestead Act, granting up to 160 acres at $1.25 per acre to five-year settlers

JUN 19 Slavery abolished in federal territories by act of Congress

26-JUL 2 In Seven Days' Battle, Confederate Gen. Lee drives Union Army of the Potomac under Gen. McClellan off peninsula, away from Richmond; ends Union Army's Peninsular Campaign

JUL First Black troops organized in Union's First Carolina Regiment

1 Congress enacts antipolygamy legislation directed toward Mormons

1 Pacific Railway Act authorizes construction of first transcontinental railroad, Union Pacific – Central Pacific

30 Cincinnati paper coins term 'Copperhead' to denote Southern sympathizers

AUG 18 Sioux uprising , led by Chief Little Crow, begins in Minnesota

30 In Second Battle of Bull Run, near Manassas, Va, Union forces defeated by Confederates

SEP 15 Confederates under Gen. Jackson capture Harper's Ferry, Md

17 In Battle of Antietam, Md, Gen. Lee's first invasion of North prevented by Union troops under Gen. McClellan; bloodiest one-day battle of the war

22 Pres. Lincoln's preliminary Emancipation Proclamation approved by Cabinet

OCT 23 Pres. Lincoln's Emancipation Proclamation published in Northern newspapers

NOV 4 Gatling gun patented by Richard Gordon Gatling

DEC 13 In Battle of Fredericksville, Va, over 12,000 Union soldiers under Gen. Burnside killed by Confederates under Gen. Lee

31-JAN 2 In Battle of Murfreesboro, or Stove's River, Tenn., Union and Confederate forces fight to a draw; Union advance toward Chattanooga temporarily halted

Also this year

★ John D. Rockefeller, age 23, invests $4000 in oil refining business

★ University of Maine established as State College of Agriculture and the Mechanic Arts at Orono

1863

JAN 1 Emancipation Proclamation formally takes effect but actually frees no slaves at this time since it applies only to areas not under Union control

30 Gen. Grant begins Vicksburg Campaign to open Mississippi to Union

FEB 24 Territory of Arizona formed from Territory of New Mexico

25 National banking system established by Congress

MAR 3 Territory of Idaho formed from territories of Washington, Utah, Dakota and Nebraska

3 First national Conscription Act demands registration of men aged 20 to 45; exemption allowed by substitution of payment of $300

3 National Academy of Sciences chartered by Congress

APR 13 Continuous-roll printing press patented by William Bullock of Pittsburgh, Pa

MAY Gold discovered in Alder Gulch (Montana); Virginia City develops over night

1-4 In Battle of Chancellorsville, Va, Confederates under Gen. Lee defeat Union Army of the Potomac under Gen. Hooker; major Southern victory, although Gen. 'Stonewall' Jackson is mortally wounded

17 Union Gens. Sherman and McPherson defeat Confederates under Gen. Johnston and occupy Jackson, Miss.

JUN 20 West Virginia enters Union as 35th state, with constitution mandating gradual emancipation of slaves

Gettysburg and Vicksburg

After the stalemate of 1862, events moved fast in the early months of 1863. The Army of the Potomac issued forth from its base again, this time under General "Fighting Joe" Hooker, only to suffer a second bloody defeat near Fredericksburg at the Battle of Chancellorsville. Despite the loss of "Stonewall" Jackson, shot by mistake by a Confederate sniper, Lee's success at Chancellorsville encouraged him to invade Pennsylvania in June. Here he ran into a Union army under General George Meade near the small market town of Gettysburg. Three days of fierce fighting ensued, during which Lee lost more than a third of his entire force of 70,000 men. On July 4 he led his defeated men back to the Potomac.

The very same day, in the western theater, the delayed plan to take the Confederate port of Vicksburg by a two-pronged assault under Farragut and Grant came to fruition. The so-called "Confederate Gibraltar" surrendered to Grant's six-week siege, giving Lincoln the best Independence Day possible. With the fall of Fort Hudson five days later, the Mississippi, a vital Confederate supply route, was now entirely in Union hands. "The Father of Waters," said Lincoln, "goes again unvexed to the sea." It was the beginning of the end for the Confederacy.

The Lieutenant General

Following Vicksburg, Grant was put in charge of the Union forces in the West and soon distinguished himself again by relieving the Confederate siege of Chattanooga, confirming the town – a crucial nerve center of the Confederacy – as a Union possession and driving the Confederate forces under General Bragg back to Atlanta. In March 1864 Grant was given the post of Lieutenant General, which had not been held by anyone since George Washington, and overall command of all the Union armies. Union morale was high as Grant led the Army of the Potomac into Virginia for what he hoped would be the final assault on Richmond. The campaign was to prove one of the costliest of the war for the Union forces. Lee's men engaged Grant's in the densely wooded Wilderness area near Chancellorsville and inflicted heavy casualties. However, rather than retreating to Washington as his predecessors had done, Grant steadfastly continued south towards the Confederate capital. Over the next five weeks Lee harried his army at every opportunity. In bloody engagements at Spotsylvania Court House, North Anna, and Cold Harbor (where Grant lost 7000 men in half an hour in what he later said was the only action of the war he regretted ordering) the Union army lost an astonishing 50,000 men. But throughout the campaign, which saw Grant besieging Petersburg, south of Richmond, by June, the Confederate forces had been on the defensive. In the meantime William Tecumseh Sherman had been busy in the West.

Right: Battle of Chancellorsville, May 1863.

Left: The turning point: Union forces under General Meade force Lee's army to retreat with heavy casualties at Gettysburg, July 3, 1863.

Right: The beginning of the end for the Confederates: Union soldiers take up their positions for the nine-month siege of Petersburg, June 1864.

Below: The three-day Battle of Chattanooga, November 1863, won, after bitter fighting, by the Union forces.

JUL 1-3 In Battle of Gettysburg, Pa, Confederate Army defeated by superior numbers and strong defensive positions of Union Army; South suffers nearly 28,000 casualties to Union's 23,000; turning point of war

4 In Siege of Vicksburg, Miss., 29,000 Confederate troops surrender with city to Union Gen. Grant; Union gains control of the Mississippi; Confederacy splits north to south

8 Port Hudson, Mississippi, last major Confederate stronghold on Mississippi River, surrenders to Union forces after six-week siege

13-16 Antidraft riots in New York City; 1000 killed or wounded

SEP 9 Confederate Army evacuates vital rail center of Chattanooga, Tenn.; Union forces occupy city

OCT 3 Pres. Lincoln proclaims last Thursday in November as Thanksgiving Day

19 Pres. Lincoln delivers Gettysburg Address at dedication of military cemetery on Gettysburg battlefield

23-25 In Battle of Chattanooga, Tenn., Union Armies under Gen. Grant systematically capture Confederate positions and drive Gen. Bragg's army away from city, ending siege

DEC 3 Confederate forces withdraw from Knoxville, Tenn.

8 Pres. Lincoln issues Proclamation of Amnesty and Reconstruction, offering pardon to Confederates who take loyalty oath

Also this year

★ Desertions among armies of both sides average approximately 10 percent

★ Cornelius Vanderbilt secures control of New York and Harlem Railroad

★ Tweed Ring begins in New York City with appointment of William M. Tweed as Street Commissioner

★ Free delivery of mail begins in largest cities

★ University of Massachusetts founded as Massachusetts Agricultural College at Amherst, Mass.

★ *Daily Telegram,* first newspaper in Wyoming, published at Fort Bridges

1864

JAN 19 Arkansas adopts new antislavery constitution

FEB 20 In Battle of Olustee, Union attempts to capture Florida fail

APR 12 In Fort Pillow massacre, Black Union troops massacred after fort's surrender

MAY 5-6 In First Battle of the Wilderness, near Chancellorsville, Va, armies of Grant and Lee engage in inconclusive two-day conflict

8-12 In Battle around Spotsylvania, Va, armies of Grant and Lee engage in five days of inconclusive fighting

26 Territory of Montana formed from part of Territory of Idaho

JUN 3 In Battle of Cold Harbor, Va, Gen. Lee wins last victory over Union forces

27 In Battle of Kenesaw Mountain, Union Gen. Sherman's forces defeated

JUL 2 Northern Pacific Railroad chartered by Congress

2-13 Confederate forces under Gen. Jubal A. Early raid Maryland, heading for Washington, DC

4 Immigration Act permits immigration of contract labor

30 Union forces under Gen. Burnside explode mine beneath Confederate fort at Petersburg, Va, and suffer 4000 casualties

AUG 5-23 In Battle of Mobile Bay, Ala., Federal Adm. David Farragut leads flagship into Mobile Bay and captures port, closing it to Southern blockade runners

SEP 1 Atlanta evacuated by Confederate Gen. Hood and occupied by Union Gen. Sherman; much of city burned

OCT 19 In Battle of Cedar Creek, Va, Union forces under Gen. Sheridan force Confederates under Gen. Early to withdraw from Shenandoah Valley

The March to the Sea

After the fall of Chattanooga, General Sherman led an army of 100,000 men eastward into Georgia in what became the least resisted and most destructive campaign of the war. Starting in May 1864, he had taken Atlanta by September and proceeded to cut through the heart of Georgia, destroying everything in his path, until he reached the coast at Savannah in December. The city surrendered on Christmas Day, shortly after Union forces under George Thomas destroyed a Confederate force of 50,000 men near Nashville. It was a welcome Christmas present for Lincoln to add to his reelection to the presidency the previous month – itself a remarkable achievement, not only because his prospects had looked exceedingly dim at times during the election campaign, but also because such a campaign was being held at all during an all-out civil war. In February 1865 Sherman's devastating triumphal march reached the South Carolina state capital, Columbia, which he razed to the ground. By March he was in North Carolina and apparently unstoppable. It seemed only a matter of time before he would meet up with Grant within striking distance of Richmond.

Above: The materials of war: Union soldiers guarding cannon and ammunition at City Point, Virginia, in 1864 – one of Mathew Brady's many telling war photographs.

Below: Civilians hurry to evacuate the Confederate capital, Richmond, as Grant's bombardment begins. Jefferson Davis escaped the day before Union troops entered the city.

Above: William Tecumseh Sherman, whose "march to the sea" cut a trail of devastation through the heartland of the Confederacy, leaving cities and countryside in ruins.

Below: Destroying the infrastructure of the South: Sherman's troops tear up railroad tracks at Atlanta, Georgia, before burning the city, November 1864.

Above: The ruins of Richmond after the Union assault. Such scenes, repeated throughout the South, show the enormity of the task of reconstruction.

31 Nevada enters Union as 36th state

NOV 8 Abraham Lincoln wins election for second term, Andrew Johnson elected Vice President

16 Gen. Sherman with Union army of 62,000 begins march across Georgia to Savannah and the sea, leaving Atlanta in flames and destroying everything in path

25 Confederate attempt to burn NYC fails; 12 fires set by arsonists at hotels, theaters and docks extinguished

29 Federal troops under Col. G.M. Chivington massacre Cheyennes in Sand Creek, Col., ending year of uprising

DEC 22 Gen. Sherman occupies Savannah and completes march eastward to the sea, bisecting South horizontally

Also this year

★ 'In God We Trust' first appears on two-cent piece

★ Confederate desertions increase to over 50 percent by end of year

★ First successful US advertising agency started by George Presbury Rowell

★ University of Kansas established at Lawrence, Kan.

★ North Dakota's first newspaper *Frontier Scout,* started at Fort Union

★ First newspaper in Montana Territory *Montana Post,* begins publication

1865

JAN 9 Pro-Union convention in Tennessee adopts antislavery amendments to state constitution

16 Union Gen. Sherman begins campaign of destruction north through Carolinas

FEB 1 US Congress proposes 13th Amendment, prohibiting slavery

3 Pres. Lincoln meets in peace conference with Confederate Vice Pres. Stephens and others, on board Union transport River Queen off Hampton Roads

17 Columbia, SC, occupied by Gen. Sherman, burns; unclear who starts blaze

22 Union forces capture last open Confederate port, in Wilmington, NC

MAR 2 Pres. Lincoln rejects request for negotiations made by Gen. Lee; demands surrender before negotiation

3 Freedmen's Bureau established by Congress to aid former slaves

4 Abraham Lincoln inaugurated for second term, Andrew Johnson inaugurated Vice President

13 Confederate Pres. Davis signs bill allowing slaves to enlist in army, enlisted slaves to be freed

27-28 Pres. Lincoln meets Gens. Grant and Sherman; deplores further bloodshed and urges offering of generous surrender terms to Confederacy

APR 1 In Battle of Five Forks, Va, Gen. Sheridan repulses Confederate assault at strategic crossroads outside Petersburg; last important battle of war

2 Gen. Lee withdraws Confederate army from Petersburg ending six-month siege, and advises Pres. Davis to move Confederate government out of Richmond

3 Union troops enter Petersburg and Richmond

5 Pres. Lincoln arrives in Richmond and tours city

7 Federal Gen. Grant formally requests surrender of Confederate Gen. Lee; Lee asks Grant for terms

8 Confederate Gen. Lee surrenders to Gen. Grant at Appomattox Court House, Va

11 Pres. Lincoln, in last public address, urges reconstruction in spirit of generous conciliation

13 Gen. Sherman captures Raleigh, NC, ending march

14 Pres. Lincoln shot by John Wilkes Booth at Ford's Theater in Washington, DC; Secretary Seward stabbed by co-conspirator

15 Pres. Lincoln dies at age of 56; Vice Pres. Andrew Johnson sworn in as President three hours later

18 Confederate Gen. J.E. Johnston surrenders to Gen. Sherman in North Carolina

26 Assassin John Wilkes Booth cornered, in pain and mortally wounded, near Bowling Green, Va

27 Worst ship disaster in US history occurs when steamer *Sultana* explodes on the Mississippi; 1700 die, most of them Union soldiers returning from Southern prisons

Surrender at Appomattox

The Confederate cause seemed lost by the beginning of 1865. In an act of terrible irony, Jefferson Davis even had to arm the slaves in order to sustain the war effort. In April, after a siege of more than nine months, Lee's army was forced to surrender Petersburg to Grant's superior numbers. Richmond could now no longer be defended, and Davis evacuated it. The next day the Union troops moved in, soon to be followed by Lincoln himself, speaking words of reconciliation.

On April 9, Lee, no longer able to continue the war, met Grant at Appomattox Court House to discuss the terms of surrender. In a moving scene, the two former colleagues recalled happier times together before Lee put his signature to the generous terms Grant offered him. Lee's men were disbanded and allowed to go back to their farms. The American Civil War was officially over.

Lee graciously acknowledged the generosity of Grant's surrender terms as the two generals met at Appomattox Court House. The Confederate officers were allowed to keep their small-arms, the men their horses "for the spring plowing." Grant silenced his men's cheers as Lee rode away.

Black Regiments

In the early days of the war, Congress forbade even free Blacks to sign up, but after the Emancipation Proclamation, more than 180,000 Blacks were to serve in the Union armies. Black regiments such as the 107th Colored Infantry (above) and the 54th Massachusetts Infantry distinguished themselves in the field of action, despite Confederate orders that all black officers were to be put to death on capture. Some 66,000 Blacks died in the fighting.

The Assassination of Lincoln

In the few weeks before all the fighting was brought to an end, there were to be many more casualties. The most eminent of them was the President himself. Five days after the meeting at Appomattox, Abraham Lincoln was shot in the head by John Wilkes Booth, a Southern sympathizer, while watching a play at a Washington theater. With his death there passed from the political scene the only man who might have been able to conduct the Union safely through the painful period of reconstruction which now lay ahead. Lincoln's assassination left America without a leader of stature at the very moment when she needed one most.

Lincoln's assassination, and the simultaneous knife attack on Secretary of State Seward, led to a massive manhunt for the murderer and his presumed accomplices. John Wilkes Booth, a young actor, who shouted "The South is revenged" after shooting Lincoln, was himself shot in Virginia two weeks later.

29 Commercial restrictions removed from most parts of South, except Texas, by order of Pres. Johnson

MAY 2 Pres. Johnson offers $100,000 reward for capture of Jefferson Davis, charged with complicity in assassination of Pres. Lincoln

4 Confederate Gen. Richard Taylor surrenders to Union Gen. Edward R.S. Canby, ending all resistance east of Mississippi

5 First railroad train robbery occurs at dawn at North Bend, Ohio, when Ohio and Mississippi Railroad train is derailed by gang

10 Jefferson Davis captured at Irwinville, Ga, and imprisoned in Fortress Monroe

13 Gen. Kirby Smith surrenders Confederate forces west of the Mississippi, ending all organized resistance

29 Pres. Johnson puts 'Restoration' plan into effect, issuing proclamation of amnesty to those participating in rebellion, specifying categories of persons who must apply for pardon and naming provisional Governor of North Carolina to help reorganize and prepare state for reentry into Congress

JUN 2 Last naval act of war occurs at Galveston, Tex., as Confederates surrender last seaport

6 Missouri ratifies new state constitution and is readmitted to Union

6 Pres. Johnson offers amnesty to Confederate prisoners of war who will take oath of allegiance

13 Pres. Johnson names provisional governors for Alabama, Florida, Georgia, Mississippi, South Carolina and Texas

JUL 1 All Southern ports opened to foreign trade by executive order

SEP 5 South Carolina repeals ordinance of secession

NOV 18 Mark Twain (Samuel Langhorne Clemens) becomes famous when 'Jim Smiley and His Jumping Frog' is printed in *New York Saturday Press*

24 Mississippi establishes Black Codes, for inhibiting lives of Black inhabitants of South

DEC 1 Writ of habeas corpus restored by presidential decree

2 Alabama becomes 27th state to ratify 13th Amendment

4 Thirty-ninth Congress convenes; delegates from reconstructed former Confederate states denied recognition and seats

4 House votes to establish Joint Committee on Reconstruction, called Committee of Fifteen, with nine Republican representatives and six Democratic Senators

12 Senate agrees to Joint Committee on Reconstruction

16 Secretary of State Seward informs Napoleon III that his plans for Mexico will damage relations between France and US

18 Thirteenth Amendment, abolishing slavery in US, ratified by 27 states; formally declared in effect by Secretary of State Seward

24 Ku Klux Klan formed in Tennessee by Thomas M. Jones and others

1865-1873 Epidemics of smallpox, typhus and yellow fever occur in New York, Philadelphia, Boston, Baltimore, Washington, New Orleans and Memphis

Also this year

★ Clara Barton conducts government sponsored search for missing soldiers of Civil War

★ Congress authorizes free delivery of mail in all cities with populations of 50,000 or more

★ John D. Rockefeller and Samuel Andrews form oil refining company at Cleveland, Ohio

★ Natural gas sold for first time in US by Freedonia Gas Light and Water Works Company, Freedonia, NY

★ John Batterson Stetson opens one-man hat factory in Philadelphia, Pa

★ Yale School of Fine Arts, first department of fine arts in US college, opens at Yale University

★ Cornell University founded at Ithaca, NY

★ University of Kentucky established as Agricultural and Mechanical College of Kentucky University in Lexington, Ky

★ Purdue University chartered as Indiana Agricultural College in West Lafayette, Ind.

The Arts

★ Walt Whitman's poetry collection *Drum Taps*

Reconstruction

THE CIVIL WAR left America exhausted, bitter, and divided. More than half a million people had died at the hands of their fellow Americans. Thousands more were left permanently scarred in mind and body. The economic cost of the war will never be known for sure, but historians have estimated that it may have cost the two governments as much as $20 billion – five times the entire expenditure of the Federal Government up to that time.

The war had been fought to preserve the Union and it had done so, at least on paper. But the wounds went very deep. Resentment was rife in both North and South, but it was especially strong in the secessionist states, whose economies had been wrecked by the conflict. The South had been the main theater of war, and military operations – including Sherman's scorched earth policy, which had cut a swathe of destruction some 75 miles wide through the heart of the former Confederacy – had wreaked havoc throughout the countryside. Plantations had been devastated, livestock and crops destroyed or impounded, railroads broken up, and towns razed. Many of the major cities in the South lay in ruins and civil order had broken down almost completely. As one Southern governor said, "The desolations of war are beyond description."

Most paralyzing of all to the Southern way of life was the freeing of the slaves that had followed the end of the fighting. With emancipation the entire basis of the plantation system was removed at a stroke. Some three million Blacks simply walked off the estates and headed into the countryside or the towns. Although no longer slaves, they

were to find themselves still the victims of poverty, disease, and naked racial prejudice, as they sought to acquire for themselves the status and education denied to them so long by Southern laws. The problem of the freedman was to loom over the years of Reconstruction, as the American people began the long and painful task of re-establishing normal life amid the ravages of war.

Above: Freedmen: A group of Black Americans taste freedom for the first time among the ruins of war-ravaged Richmond.

Below: Emancipation removed the very foundation of the South's rural economy. Scenes like these were common as more than a third of the Confederate states' population – the newly-freed Blacks – left the plantations. Tens of thousands died of disease or hunger.

Andrew Johnson

With the assassination of Lincoln only days after Appomattox, his Vice President, Andrew Johnson, assumed the office of President. Johnson was a Democrat from Tennessee, and had been the only senator from a secessionist state to remain at his post in Washington in 1861. There was no doubt about his devotion to the Union, but his political skills were far inferior to Lincoln's. His term of office was marked by confusing changes of political direction, and disfigured by outbursts which were at best tactless and at worst disastrous. The new President faced a monumental task which would have tested to the limit the qualities of a far greater man. Unfortunately, at this crucial moment in American history, Johnson's own character added yet another obstacle to those which had already been strewn in the path of Reconstruction.

Right: "To bind up the nation's wounds:" President Andrew Johnson contemplates the enormity of the task left him by Lincoln's death.

Frederick Douglass (1817–95)

The freed Blacks did not want for inspirational leaders in the early years of Reconstruction. Perhaps the most famous of them was Frederick Douglass (left) who had escaped to the North from slavery in Maryland in 1838 to become an ardent advocate of abolition. A powerful speaker and writer, Douglass was the author of *Narrative of the Life of Frederick Douglass* and *My Bondage and My Freedom*. In 1869 he became the first president of the National Convention of Colored Men, an organization campaigning for Black suffrage.

1866

FEB 12 Secretary of State Seward demands of Napoleon III that time limit be set for French evacuation of Mexico

12 First formal observance of Lincoln's birthday held in Capitol

22 Pres. Johnson, speaking from steps of White House, violently denounces Joint Committee on Reconstruction; statement erodes his support in Congress

MAR 2 Joint Committee on Reconstruction's resolution dictates that Confederate states will not be seated in Congress until admitted by authority of Congress

APR 1 Western Union absorbs US Telegraph Company and becomes first complete monopoly serving all parts of the country with uniform rates

2 Pres. Johnson declares end to state of insurrection in Alabama, Arkansas, Florida, Georgia, Louisiana, Mississippi, North Carolina, South Carolina, Tennessee and Virginia

9 Congress passes Civil Rights Bill of 1866, intended to protect freedmen over Pres. Johnson's veto

JUN 16 Congress proposes 14th Amendment to provide constitutional definitions of civil rights

JUL 1 Congress imposes 10 percent tax on all State bank notes to tax them out of existence

19 Tennessee is first state to ratify 14th Amendment

24 Tennessee restored as state of the Union

27 Atlantic cable between US and Great Britain completed by Cyrus W. Field and Peter Cooper

30 Race riot in New Orleans results from effort to introduce Black male suffrage; approximately 200 casualities

AUG 20 Pres. Johnson proclaims end to insurrection in Texas and declares that peace, order and tranquility exist throughout US

20 National Labor Congress convenes in Baltimore and forms National Labor Union

NOV Congressional elections place anti-Johnson majorities in both Houses, large enough to override any veto of the Pres.

DEC 21 Sioux Indians, defending traditional hunting grounds, defeat US troops under Col. William Judd Fetterman at Fort Kearny on Bozeman gold trail in Montana Territory

Also this year
★ Postwar depression begins
★ First oil pipe line in US runs from Pithole, Pa, to railroad connection five miles distant
★ Jesse James forms band of brigands in West
★ American Society for the Prevention of Cruelty to Animals chartered in New York by Henry Bergh

1867

JAN 8 Suffrage granted to Blacks in Washington, DC, by bill passed over Pres. Johnson's veto

21 Suffrage granted to all males over 21 in all US territories

MAR 1 Nebraska enters Union as 37th state

2 First Reconstruction Act, passed by Congress over Pres. Johnson's veto, imposes martial law on Southern states, which are to be divided into five districts, and provides for restoration of civil government as soon as states are restored into Union and pass 14th Amendment

2 Tenure of Office Act denies President power to remove officials who have been appointed by and with consent of Senate

2 Command of the Army Act provides that all military orders from President must be issued through General of the Army

2 Department of Education established by Congress

4 Fortieth Congress convenes in March instead of in December to keep watch over the President

APR 5 Voting rights of Blacks denied in Alexandria, Va; 1000 Black votes rejected

Radicals and Moderates

The question which dominated Government thinking in the months after the end of the war was how to deal with the defeated South, and in particular what to do to help the newly freed Blacks. Two factions emerged within the Republican party in answer to this question.

On the one hand were the Radical Republicans, who believed at the outset that they had the support of the President, and who called for strong measures against the South, including the debarment of secessionist politicians from Federal office and the grant of lands to the Blacks. On the other were the Moderate Republicans who also believed in the protection of Black civil rights by constitutional amendment, but wanted a less punitive approach to Southern Reconstruction. Johnson talked tough but acted gentle. Pursuing his own policy while Congress was out of session, he offered a presidential pardon to almost everyone in the South who had taken part in the war, appointed civil governors, and instructed the Southern states to draw up new constitutions and ratify the Thirteenth Amendment outlawing slavery. Most did. But most also introduced so-called "Black codes," which in many cases amounted to a virtual reimposition of slave status.

When Congress reconvened in December 1865, it was furious. Congressmen hammered out a compromise between Radical and Moderate views in bills which, among other measures, proposed to extend the life of the Freedmen's Bureau, an important Government help agency for Blacks, and to reduce (by the Fourteenth Amendment) the Congressional representation of states which denied Blacks the vote. Johnson seems to have had a brainstorm at this point and denounced the prime movers in the compromise, Thaddeus Stevens and Charles Sumner (the Senator who had been beaten unconscious at his desk during the "Bleeding Kansas" years), even accusing them of trying to get him killed. He vetoed the bills and told the South not to ratify the Fourteenth Amendment. The months went by, and after the crucial Congressional elections of 1866, it became clear that the President was seriously out of step with the views of the Republican Party and the people.

The Reconstruction of the South

In March 1867 Congress passed the First Reconstruction Act over the presidential veto. The Act removed Johnson's civil governors in the South and placed the 10 states which had refused to ratify the Fourteenth Amendment under the interim military governorship of five major-generals. Local officials were removed and replaced by Northerners (the so-called "carpetbaggers"), sympathetic Southerners (the so-called "scalawags"), or Blacks. Electoral and administrative systems were thoroughly reorganized and new (and generally more democratic) state constitutions were drawn up. By the end of 1868, new state governments had been set up in all but Mississippi,

Texas, and Virginia; elected representatives had taken up their places in Congress; and the army was withdrawn. The three remaining states followed in 1870. All ratified the Fourteenth and Fifteenth Amendments, the latter guaranteeing universal manhood suffrage throughout the United States. However, many of the new governments exhibited the corruption that was becoming an ugly feature of post-war political life; and harassment of Blacks continued throughout the South, often accompanied by violence and murder, as organizations such as the Ku Klux Klan (founded in 1865) propagated their doctrine of white supremacy with the rope and the whip.

A satirical cartoon showing the carpetbagger blind to the sack of faults on his back.

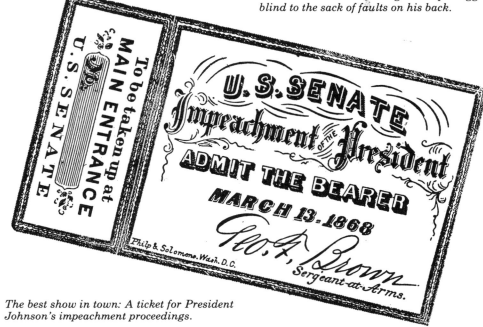

The best show in town: A ticket for President Johnson's impeachment proceedings.

The Impeachment of President Johnson

On the same day that Congress passed the First Reconstruction Act, it also passed an act forbidding the President to dismiss any of his officials, including Cabinet members, without the permission of Congress. By so doing the Radicals hoped to establish the supreme authority of Congress over the other two branches of the Federal Government, and President Johnson was quick to rise to the challenge. He dismissed his Secretary of War, the Lincoln appointee Edwin M. Stanton, who duly refused to go, barricading himself in his office for good measure. Congress then began impeachment proceedings against the President.

The charges against Johnson fell far short of the "high crimes and misdemeanors" required for impeachment under the Constitution. The main crime of which he was accused was, in fact, "reconstructing the rebel states according to his own will." Despite the evident unconstitutionality of the proceedings, it was a close-run thing. In the end Johnson was acquitted by a single vote. The Radicals' attempt to give teeth to their reinterpretation of the Constitution had failed, but Johnson's term of office was already at an end.

President Grant

The Republican nominee and winner of the 1868 presidential election was none other than the Union war hero, Ulysses S. Grant. Already entering folk myth for his exploits in battle, Grant was in reality a disastrous choice for the highest office in the land. He had no political experience – indeed had shown little previous interest in politics at all – and was a dangerously poor judge of character. His qualities of leadership failed to make the transition from military to civilian life, and his pursuit of Radical Reconstruction policies in the South showed a vigor often more suited to the battlefield than to the politics of peace. Despite his personal honesty, Grant's two terms of office were marked by increasing scandal and corruption. For Grant himself, his tenancy of the White House was to prove an inglorious end to a glorious military career. For the American people, it was another troubled episode in the attempt to rebuild a country whose war wounds, as the 1860s drew to a close, had hardly begun to heal.

Elizabeth Cady Stanton (1815–1902)

The 1860s saw an important milestone on the long and arduous road toward equal rights for women in the United States. In 1869 the indefatigable campaigner Elizabeth Cady Stanton (left), together with Susan B. Anthony, formed the National Woman Suffrage Association (NWSA), and in the same year Wyoming became the first territory to extend voting rights to women. It was Stanton who organized the first national Women's Rights Convention with Lucretia Mott at Seneca Falls, New York, 1848, and who played a crucial part in drafting the convention's "Declaration of Sentiments," a document that effectively set the feminist agenda for the next 70 years. Braving the indifference, ridicule, and outright abuse that has confronted them ever since, the reformers committed themselves to overthrowing the "absolute tyranny" of men's rule over women by demanding the right to vote and equal opportunities in property ownership, employment, and education.

16 Free public school system in State of New York established by legislature

23 Second Reconstruction Act passed by Congress over presidential veto

30 US purchases Alaska from Russia for $7.2 million through treaty negotiated by Secretary of State Seward

MAY 14 New York enacts first tenement house law

JUL 19 Third Reconstruction Act passed by Congress over presidential veto

AUG 5 Pres. Johnson requests resignation of Secretary of War Stanton; Stanton refuses to resign

12 Pres. Johnson orders suspension of Secretary Stanton and names Gen. U.S. Grant Secretary of War

28 Midway Islands in the Pacific annexed by US

NOV 25 Judiciary Committee of House proposes impeachment of Pres. Johnson for 'high crimes and misdemeanors'

DEC 2 Charles Dickens gives first reading in a theater in New York City

4 National Grange of the Patrons of Husbandry founded by Oliver Hudson Kelley

7 House rejects resolution that Pres. Johnson be impeached, due to lack of specific act of high misdemeanor

Also this year

★ Credit Mobilier scandal; company formed by Union Pacific directors sells shares at par to Congressmen to ward off investigation

★ First elevated railroad in America begins operation in NYC

★ Pacific Mail Steamship Company opens regular line between San Francisco and Hong Kong

★ Cigarettes first appear in US

★ Howard University chartered as Howard Theological Seminary in Washington, DC; first predominantly Black college to offer complete facilities

★ Johns Hopkins University chartered at Baltimore

★ University of Illinois founded as Illinois Industrial University at Urbana, Ill.

The Arts

★ Steinway and Chickering, American-made pianos, receive first prizes at Paris Exposition

1868

JAN 13 Senate refuses to concur with Pres. Johnson's suspension of Secretary of War Stanton

14 Gen. Grant surrenders office of Secretary of War back to Stanton

FEB 21 Pres. Johnson again dismisses Secretary of War Stanton and appoints Gen. Lorenzo Thomas

22 Spokesman of House Reconstruction Committee, Thaddeus Stevens, drafts formal resolution of impeachment against Pres. Johnson

24 House adopts resolution that Pres. Johnson be impeached for 'high crimes and misdemeanors'

MAR 11 Fourth Reconstruction Act passed

13 Impeachment trial of Pres. Johnson formally begins

16 Vote taken on 11th article of impeachment in trial of Pres. Johnson, 35-19, one less than required for conviction

23 University of California chartered in Berkeley, Calif.

APR Treaty of Fort Laramie ends First Sioux War

MAY 30 Decoration Day celebrated nationally for first time

JUN 22 Akansas readmitted to representation in Congress

25 Alabama, Florida, Georgia, Louisiana, North Carolina and South Carolina readmitted to representation in Congress

25 Eight-hour day for government employees made law by act of Congress

JUL 15 Pres. Benito Guarez returns to Mexico to restore republican government after five-year guerilla war against Napoleon III

The Grange

Growing agrarian discontent found a focus in 1867 with the formation of the Patrons of Husbandry, popularly known as "the Grange." Founded by a Government official to help farmers to weather the agricultural recession of the 1860s, the Grange began life as a social institution, but rapidly developed a political dimension. It enabled farmers to combine to exert influence on local government and to set up co-operative and self-help ventures. By the mid-1870s it could claim more than half a million members and was to prove the seedbed of the later Farmers' Alliances and the highly influential Populist movement of the 1890s.

Driving in the Golden Spike

Railroad history was made on May 10, 1869, when the Central Pacific and the Union Pacific lines linked up at Promontory Point, Utah, completing America's first transcontinental railroad.

The Capitol

1863 saw the completion of another great American symbol, the Capitol Dome in Washington, D.C.

144

Wall Street

The Civil War brought unprecedented prosperity to the North: Wall Street in 1866, looking west toward Trinity Church on Broadway.

"Seward's Folly"?

In March 1867 President Johnson's Secretary of State, William Seward, agreed to buy the province of Alaska from Russia for $7.2 million. The bargain, which cost less, acre for acre, than the Louisiana Purchase, was nonetheless widely criticized in the United States. The cartoon above shows Brother Jonathan taking delivery of Alaska from the Russian iceman while Seward waits in the basement hatch. Within a few years America would come to recognize that "Seward's Folly" was really a highly profitable piece of wisdom.

25 Territory of Wyoming created from parts of Dakota, Idaho and Utah

28 Fourteenth Amendment adopted

SEP Georgia legislature expels black members; military rule reimposed on state and readmission to Congress postponed until state adopts 14th Amendment

OCT Cuba begins 10-year war against Spain

21 Severe earthquake strikes San Francisco causing over $3 million in damage

NOV 3 Republican Ulysses S. Grant elected President, Schuyler Calfax elected Vice President

DEC 3 Trial of Confederate Pres. Jefferson Davis begins in Richmond, Va

25 Pres. Johnson proclaims general amnesty for all who participated in The Rebellion

Also this year

★ First office building to have elevator installed is Equitable Life Assurance Society in NYC

★ Philip D. Armour begins meat packing in Chicago

★ University of Minnesota chartered at Minneapolis

The Arts

★ Louisa May Alcott's book *Little Women*

1869

JAN 12 Blacks form National Convention of Colored Men and name Frederick Douglass president

19 American Equal Rights Association meets in Washington, DC, marking beginning of organized women's movements; Susan Brownell Anthony elected president

23 First state bureau of labor in US organized in Massachusetts

FEB 15 University of Nebraska chartered

24 Tariff Act enacted by Congress to protect US manufacturers

27 Fifteenth Amendment proposed by Congress to guarantee that right to vote will not be denied or abridged on basis of race, color or previous condition of servitude

MAR 4 Ulysses S. Grant inaugurated President, Francis P. Blair inaugurated Vice President

15 Cincinnati Red Stockings becomes first professional baseball team

15 Woman suffrage amendment to Constitution proposed in joint resolution in Congress

APR 10 Judiciary Act amended by Congress to raise number of judges on Supreme Court from seven to nine

10 Board of Indian Commissioners created by act of Congress

10 First transcontinental railroad in US links Union Pacific from east with Central Pacific from west at Promontory Point, Utah

15 National Woman Suffrage Association formed, Elizabeth Cady Stanton elected president

JUL 13 Riots against Chinese laborers occur in San Francisco

SEP 1 Prohibition Party organized by National Temperance Convention in Chicago

24 Black Friday, day of financial panic on Wall Street caused by manipulation of gold market by Jay Gould and James Fisk

NOV 6 First intercollegiate football game played by Princeton and Rutgers at New Brunswick, NJ

DEC 6 Colored National Labor Convention, first national black labor group in America, meets in Washington, DC

10 Wyoming Territory grants full suffrage to women

Also this year

★ Jay Cooke and Company appointed financial agent for North Pacific Railroad

★ Henry J. Heinz and L.C. Noble establish food-packing company at Sharpsburg, Pa

★ Noble Order of the Knights of Labor organized in Philadelphia by tailor Uriah S. Stephens

★ American Museum of Natural History founded in New York City

THE 1870s were in many ways an uninspiring decade in American life. The Civil War had left its mark not only on the landscape and economy of the South, but also on the minds of millions of Americans, bequeathing a legacy of division and distrust which successive governments seemed powerless to erase. Radical Reconstruction had served to keep open the wounds of war in the former Confederacy, and the bitterness it inspired outlasted the policy itself, which was effectively laid to rest after the controversial election of Rutherford B. Hayes to the presidency in 1877. The gradual return of the Southern states to "home rule" during the course of the decade was also a return to many of the values of the old white slavocracy. Hundreds of thousands of Black Americans had tasted freedom and its fruits for the first time, but it was a bitter-sweet taste. Despite widening access to education and political representation, the cause of Black civil rights met discrimination, violence, and indifference at every turn, and the role of the free Black was destined to remain that of the second-class citizen, not only in the South, but throughout the United States, for many years to come.

The decade was also marked by a sorry decline in public morality. Scandal after scandal rocked the Grant administration, as graft and corruption were exposed at the highest levels of society. Movements for reform stalled under the opposition of powerful vested interests, and public confidence in the integrity of government and the commercial sector was badly shaken. Political leaders of stature were in scarce supply,

and the political process itself was riven by factionalism. Sectional interests supplanted broader issues in an undignified scramble for office and influence.

At the same time, a fundamental shift was taking place in the power structure of the United States. If the nation's political masters were showing themselves unimaginative and directionless, its business leaders were emerging as men of vision and energy. The 1870s were to see an unprecedented concentration of industrial and commercial power in the hands of a relatively small proportion of the population. The irresistible spread of the great railroads and the "pooling" of commercial enterprises – a movement which was to lead, in the following decade, to the formation of the great "trusts" – was already creating corporations of enormous size and influence under such remarkable magnates as Andrew Carnegie and John D. Rockefeller. The age of big business had begun.

While the railroad companies were opening up the heartland of the nation with vast new networks of track and commercial power, another new breed of American was making his presence felt along the great cattle trails of the Great Plains. The 1870s and 1880s were the heyday of the cowboy, who, in these few brief years, established a hold on the popular imagination that still has not lost its glamor more than a century later.

Scandal

Despite serving one of the least distinguished first terms of any U.S. President, Ulysses S. Grant was reelected on the Republican ticket in 1872 – partly because of his administration's recent success in settling, by a combination of saber rattling and negotiation, outstanding claims against Great Britain for damage done to American shipping by British-built Confederate ships during the Civil War.

Grant's second term of office was racked by scandal. In revelation after revelation, senior Government officials were shown to be implicated in, or at least turning a blind eye to, corruption on a massive scale. Time after time, Grant himself failed unequivocally to condemn the abuses or their perpetrators. In 1872, the Union Pacific or Credit Mobilier scandal exposed corrupt profiteering in the railroad industry and linked the offending directors to a number of high-ranking Government men, including the Vice President, Schuyler Colfax. The following year, immense ill-feeling was generated by the so-called "Salary Grab," in which Congressmen voted themselves a 50 per cent pay rise (and incidentally also doubled the President's salary), the increase to be paid retroactively to cover the preceding two years! 1875 saw the exposure of the St Louis Whiskey Ring, which had cheated the Government out of millions of dollars of taxes on distilled liquor with the connivance of Grant's own private secretary, General Orville E. Babcock, who was saved from prosecution by the intervention of the President. As if this were not enough, the next

year brought further evidence of spectacular high-level fraud when Grant's Secretary of War, William W. Belknap, was impeached for selling traderships to Indian posts, with the result that supplies bound for those posts were syphoned off by corrupt agents. Belknap resigned to avoid the impeachment proceedings, and Grant accepted his resignation "with great regret." He expressed regret, too, at the forced resignation of the Collector of the New York Customs House after the latter was shown to have been involved in corruption, and he did little to prevent other senior officials from using their positions to amass huge personal fortunes. He also signally failed to carry through the much-needed civil service reforms initiated by the Civil Service Commission of 1871. The Commission itself was allowed to disappear almost without trace in 1875, and it would take the shock of a second presidential assassination to bring it back to life.

Such greed for money and power riddled many other areas of American life during these sorry years. Many of the Reconstruction governments in the South were guilty of corruption, and in a number of states throughout the Union railroad companies had established a position of influence which gave them virtual control over the legislature. The scale of criminal activity was truly breathtaking. In New York City alone, the notorious Tweed Ring, headed by William Tweed, defrauded the city treasury of at least $100 million. Still further battered by the great financial panic of 1873 and the ensuing five-year depression, public confidence sank to an all-time low.

His skills failed to make the transition from war to peace: President Ulysses S. Grant, one of America's greatest military commanders but one of her worst presidents.

Fraud on the grand scale: Thomas Nast's 1872 cartoon depicts the corrupt Tammany "Boss," William Marcy Tweed.

The Ku Klux Klan, a white supremacist organization, here caricatured by Nast, first came to prominence in the Southern states in the years after emancipation of the slaves.

1870

JAN National Woman Suffrage Association holds convention in Washington, DC; Elizabeth Cady Stanton makes plea for woman suffrage before joint committee of Congress

2 Construction of Brooklyn Bridge begins

4 Telegraph operators' strike spreads throughout country

10 Standard Oil Company incorporated in Cleveland, Ohio, by Rockefellers

15 First political cartoon to use donkey as symbol for Democratic Party appears in *Harper's Weekly*

26 Virginia readmitted to representation in Congress

FEB 9 US Weather Bureau established by Congress

12 Utah Territory grants full suffrage to women

23 Mississippi readmitted to representation in Congress

25 Sen. Hiram R. Revels, first Black in Congress, takes seat

MAR 30 Texas readmitted to representation in Congress

30 Fifteenth Amendment adopted

MAY 25-27 Fenians, anti-British Irish group, continue ineffectual raids across Canadian border

31 Ku Klux Klan Act of 1870 or Enforcement Act, adopted to enforce 15th Amendment

JUN 13 Pres. Grant announces that US will maintain strict non-intervention in Cuban rebellion

15 Pres. Grant forces resignation of Attorney General Ebenezar R. Hoar in attempt to get votes for annexation of Dominican Republic; Amos. T. Akerman of Georgia replaces Hoar

22 Department of Justice, supervised by Attorney General, established by Congress

30 Senate rejects Hamilton Fish's treaty of annexation of Dominican Republic

JUL 8 Senate consents to signing of US-Great Britain Treaty for suppression of African slave trade

14 Internal Revenue and Tariff Act of 1870 eliminates excise taxes and makes slight changes in tariff duties to satisfy protectionists

24 First railroad car from Pacific coast reaches New York City

AUG 1 Women vote for first time in election in Utah Territory

4 Democrats regain control of North Carolina Legislature, ending era of carpetbag Republicans

SEP 20 *New York Times* publishes first editorial attacking Tweed rule in New York City

"His Fraudulency"?

The presidential election of 1876 did nothing to restore public morale. In fact, it provided further evidence of corrupt practice and presented the American people with an unprecedented constitutional difficulty.

Both the major political parties had chosen candidates with clean records. The Republican, Rutherford B. Hayes of Ohio, had an unsullied reputation for honesty, and the Democratic nominee, Samuel J. Tilden of New York, had played a leading role in smashing the Tweed Ring. Unfortunately, the election was less spotless than the candidates. Three Southern states put in two sets of electoral votes each, one counted by a Republican and the other by a Democratic election board, and Oregon's votes were also in dispute. The result of the entire election depended on which sets of votes were counted, a question on which the Constitution gave no definitive guidance. After much discussion, accusation, counter-accusation, and negotiation, a compromise was finally reached in March 1877, a mere two days before the as yet unelected President was due to be inaugurated. Hayes was elected in return for concessions to the Democratic South, including the virtual ending of Radical Reconstruction. But the whole business left a nasty taste in the mouth. Many Tilden supporters felt that their man had been cheated of his rightful place in the White House, and referred to Hayes as "his Fraudulency." Yet again the nation seemed to be denied the healing balm of consensus just when it needed it most.

Civil Rights

The end of Reconstruction in the Southern states marked a watershed in the short history of the movement for Black civil rights in America. With Hayes' withdrawal of Federal troops from the few states in which they were still garrisoned, the South largely returned to the white conservative rule of so-called "Redeemer" governments, who soon set about reversing, or at least stalling, much of the progressive state legislation of the preceding years. Especially (but by no means exclusively) in the South, Blacks found themselves effectively excluded from real political or social influence – a process facilitated by a series of Supreme Court decisions severely limiting Federal enforcement of the Fourteenth Amendment. The civil rights legislation of the early 1870s – including the Enforcement Acts of 1870 and 1871, the Ku Klux Klan Act, and the Civil Rights Act of 1875 – had been somewhat half-heartedly applied even under Grant. With the end of Reconstruction under President Hayes, they lost many of their remaining teeth. It would be many years before the Government again took up the cause of its Black citizens where the electoral compromise of 1877 had left it.

Big Business

The 1870s saw the beginning of a trend in American life which was to establish both a new power bloc at home and a position of unprecedented industrial eminence for the United States on the international stage. It was also a trend which caused concern among many observers, who feared the passing of power from the people and their elected representatives into the hands of the burgeoning commercial conglomerates. The new divisions opening up in American society as big business grew ever bigger found their most ominous expression in the bitter violence of the Great Strike of 1877.

Some of the most famous names in American corporate history first came to public notice during this decade. In 1870 a young entrepreneur from Cleveland, one John D. Rockefeller, incorporated the Standard Oil Company of Ohio, which, bolstered by some questionable deals with the railroads, was to give him a virtual monopoly on the oil pipelines of the eastern United States by the end of the decade. The Panic on Wall Street of 1873 cleared the decks of competition for the rising House of Morgan and its American head, the wily financier John Pierpoint Morgan. In 1875 the first Bessemer converters were installed in Andrew Carnegie's giant J. Edgar Thomson steel works, a milestone on the road to revolution in the American steel industry. And throughout the decade the boards of the mammoth railroad corporations continued to develop the business and financial management techniques which are now the basis of commercial enterprises the world over.

Cowboys and Indians

The decade also saw the beginning of the end of the frontier, as more and more Americans took the trail westward into the Great Plains. Discoveries of rich mineral resources, the long arm of the railroads, and perhaps above all the general availability, for the first time, of barbed wire and windmills – one making it infinitely cheaper to enclose large areas of land and the other facilitating the drawing of water for irrigation – fueled a population movement which would attain unprecedented dimensions over the next 20 years.

One striking feature of this great movement of peoples was the rise of the cattleman. During the 1870s and 1880s, thousands of cowboys – one in four of them Black – took to the arduous but highly profitable life of the open range, and in so doing created a legend that was to become a staple of the movie industry and popular fiction in the next century. Millions of head of cattle were driven in huge herds along the trails from Texas northward into the High Plains of Colorado and Wyoming, taking with them a new frontier culture which, though not per-

Many were killed when rioting erupted in Pittsburgh, Baltimore, Buffalo, Chicago, San Francisco, and other major cities following a 10 per cent cut in railwaymen's wages in 1877. Here the Sixth Maryland Regiment fires on strikers in Baltimore.

haps as glamorous as the popular image would suggest, was just as independent and often just as lawless. It was a culture which helped to decimate both the main native populations of the Great Plains prior to its arrival: the Indians and the buffalo which formed the basis of the Indian way of life.

Throughout the decade the Plains saw ugly clashes between Indians and settlers as the great tribes – Sioux, Crows, Cheyennes, Arapahoes, Comanches, and Kiowas – fought to resist the ever more determined incursions of the white man. Matters came

to a head in 1876 when gold-miners moved into the Sioux reservation in the Black Hills, South Dakota. The campaign that followed witnessed the massacre of General George Custer and his 264 men at the Little Big Horn, and the bloody defeat of the Sioux. The story was the same in the Mountains, the tribal home of the Nez Percés, the Apaches, and the Utes. The Indians who did not resist the white settlers were driven out of their lands. Those who did suffered military retribution and forced resettlement. For the tribes who had hunted on the Plains for generations before the first Americans arrived, the centennial celebrations of American Independence in 1876 must have seemed a hollow mockery. As for the buffalo from whom they derived their livelihood, within 20 years less than 1000 would remain unslaughtered. A century earlier there had been 60 million.

The Chicago Fire

Hundreds died and thousands were made homeless by a major fire which swept through Chicago in October 1871. Large areas of the city were left in ruins by the conflagration, which followed an exceptionally dry summer. The damage was estimated as running into hundreds of millions of dollars.

Grand Central Station

The picture, from *Harper's Weekly*, shows Grand Central Station, New York, in February 1872, shortly after construction work was completed at the junction of Fourth Avenue and 42nd Street. The imposing building was demolished to make way for the present station in 1910.

OCT 3 Secretary of the Interior Jacob D. Cox pressured to resign by Congress loyal to 'robber barons'

DEC North Carolina Gov. William Woods Holden becomes first state governor to be impeached

5 Forty-first Congress convenes with every state represented

Also this year

★ J.H. Rainey of South Carolina becomes first Black member of House

★ First boardwalk in America completed at Atlantic City, NJ

★ First comprehensive graduate program of studies initiated at Yale and Harvard

★ Loyola University chartered as Ignatius College in Chicago, Ill.

★ Ohio State University chartered as Ohio Agricultural and Mechanical College at Columbus, Ohio Stevens Institute of Technology established at Hoboken, NJ

★ Syracuse University established at Syracuse, NY

★ Wellesley College founded as Wellesley Female Seminary

The Arts

★ Corcoran Art Gallery, Washington, DC, incorporated

★ Metropolitan Museum of Art, NY, incorporated

★ Museum of Fine Arts, Boston, incorporated

1871

FEB 21 Territorial government provided for District of Columbia

28 Supplementary Enforcement Act provides for federal supervision of elections in any city with population over 20,000

MAR 3 Civil Service Commission established by the President

3 Indian Appropriation Act makes Indians national wards and nullifies treaties

27 University of Arkansas founded as Arkansas Industrial University at Fayetteville, Ark.

APR 7 Illinois Railroad Act creates railroad and warehouse commission with power to fix maximum rates and prohibit discrimination

20 Ku Klux Klan Act of 1871 authorizes President to suspend writ of habeas corpus and to enforce 14th Amendment by use of Federal troops

MAY US naval vessels destroy five Korean forts in effort to secure favorable treaty with Korea

8 Treaty of Washington between US and Great Britain provides for joint commission to settle fishing and boundary disputes, arbitration of Alabama claims and arbitration of San Juan Island maritime boundary dispute by German emperor

JUL 8 William 'Boss' Tweed exposed in series of articles published in *New York Times*

12 Riot between Irish Catholics and Irish Protestants in NYC leaves 52 dead

SEP 4 Citizen commission to investigate Tammany Hall formed at Cooper Institute, NYC

OCT 2 Mormon leader Brigham Young arrested for practicing polygamy

8 Chicago fire destroys city, kills 250

8 Fire destroys Peshtigo, Wis., kills 600

24 Race riot in Los Angeles, Calif.; 15 Chinese laborers lynched

27 William 'Boss' Tweed arrested for taking at least $100 million in fraudulent contracts, kickbacks, false vouchers and other corrupt practices

Also this year

★ Jay Gould contributes to bail Thomas Nast's cartoons in *New York Times* and *Harper's Weekly* show Tweed Ring in NYC

The Arts

★ James McNeill Whistler's painting *Arrangement in Grey and Black (Whistler's Mother)*

The Panic of 1873

In September 1873 the United States was swept by a major financial panic following the collapse of the influential banking firm of Jay Cooke and Company. The New York Stock Exchange closed down for several days after stock prices, driven to unstable heights by months of intense speculative activity, fell abruptly. Banks, railroads, and hundreds of smaller companies went into bankruptcy as the panic spread, triggering a depression that was to last for several years. Left: The San Francisco Stock Exchange, September 1873.

The New South

Business confidence was slow to return to the war-ravaged Southern states during the Reconstruction years. Despite the growth, in the 1870s and after, of new industries such as iron and steel, and of new cities with them, the Southern economy remained mainly agricultural, with large areas laid out to cotton. Below: Loading cotton on the levee at New Orleans.

Yellowstone National Park

In 1872 Congress inaugurated America's first National Park, Yellowstone, 2.2 million acres of spectacular scenery in Idaho, Montana, and Wyoming.

Playing the Market

"Jubilee Jim" Fisk, one of the most notorious speculators of the age, here caricatured as the Barnum of Wall St.

The New West

Attractive credit terms and new farming techniques encouraged new settlement. Nebraska, virtually virgin territory in the 1860s, began to be settled after 1870.

1872

FEB 2 Date of congressional elections set by act of Congress as first Tuesday after first Monday in November, effective 1876

17 Senate rejects treaty with Samoan Islands giving US exclusive coaling station at Pago Pago and role of 'protector' of Samoa

22 National Labor Convention nominates David Davis of Illinois for President and Joel Parker of New Jersey for Vice President

22 Prohibition Party nominates James Black of Pennsylvania for President

MAR 1 Yellowstone Park established by act of Congress

APR 10 Arbor Day inaugurated in Nebraska

MAY 1 Liberal Republicans nominate Horace Greeley for President and B. Gratz Brown for Vice President

22 Amnesty Act removes restrictions from most of those excluded from elective office by 14th Amendment

23 Workingmen's National Convention nominates Ulysses S. Grant for second term

JUN 5-6 Republican National Convention nominates Ulysses S. Grant for second term and Henry Wilson for Vice President

6 Tariff Act makes 10 percent reduction in duties on all major imported items

10 Freedmen's Bureau discontinued by Congress

JUL 9 Democratic National Convention nominates Horace Greeley for President and Gov. Benjamin Gratz Brown of Missouri for Vice President

SEP 4 New York *Sun* begins exposure of Credit Mobilier scandal

17 US awarded $15.5 million on *Alabama* claims under Treaty of Washington

OCT 21 San Juan Islands awarded to US by German Emperor William I under Treaty of Washington

NOV Susan B. Anthony, Vice-President-at-large of National Woman Suffrage Association, casts vote for President and is arrested and fined $100

5 Ulysses S. Grant wins election for second term, Henry Wilson elected Vice President

9 Fire in Boston rages for three days, killing 13 and destroying $7 million in property on 65 acres

29 Death of editor of New York *Tribune* Horace Greeley

Also this year

★ Jehovah's Witnesses organized as Russellites by Charles Taze Russell

★ Montgomery Ward and Company, first mail order house, opens in Chicago

★ University of Oregon at Eugene and Portland established

The Arts

★ Oliver Wendell Holmes' *The Poet of the Breakfast Table*

★ Mark Twain's book *Roughing It*

★ English photographer Edweard Muybridge conducts early experiments in photographing moving objects in project sponsored by US government

1873

FEB 12 Coinage Act of 1873, or 'Crime of 1873', drops silver dollar, except special coin for use in Orient, from list of coins

18 House Committee investigating Credit Mobilier Scandal finds Massachusetts Representative Oakes Ames guilty of bribery and recommends expulsion, but House merely censures

MAR 3 'Salary Grab' Act increases salaries of Congress by 50 percent and doubles salaries of President and Justices of Supreme Court

3 Coal Lands Act offers public coalbearing lands for $10 to $20 per acre

7 Ulysses S. Grant inaugurated for second term, Henry Wilson inaugurated Vice President

Woman Suffrage

The ratification of the Fourteenth and Fifteenth Amendments, extending the franchise to Black men, served as a further spur to the women's movement in America. In 1870 Wyoming became the first territory to give women the vote on equal terms with men, and in 1871 the suffragist Victoria Woodhull presented a petition to the Judiciary Committee of the House of Representatives, making a case for universal female suffrage (right). Her arguments were rejected by the Congressmen.

Gold in the Black Hills

The discovery of gold in the Black Hills area of Dakota Territory led to an influx of prospectors in the 1870s. It also resulted in escalating tension between white settlers and Sioux Indians, on whose land the gold was found.

The Republican Elephant

The Republican elephant made its first appearance in this Nast cartoon of 1874, prompted by rumors that President Grant would stand for a third term. Despite its unflattering connotations, it was quickly embraced as the symbol of the G.O.P.

John D. Rockefeller

The 1870s were the decade in which John D. Rockefeller established himself as undisputed king of the American oil industry. His Standard Oil Company was formed in 1870 when he was just 31. By 1879, when he consolidated the Standard Oil Trust, he had succeeded in crushing almost all competition.

Mary Baker Eddy

In 1875 Mary Baker Eddy (1821–1910) (above), of Lynn, Massachusetts, laid down the principles of Christian Science, including her belief in spiritual healing, in her book *Science and Health with Key to the Scriptures*. In 1879 she founded a new church in accordance with them.

APR 14 In *Slaughter Houses* cases, Supreme Court declares that 14th Amendment does not give federal jurisdiction over all civil rights

AUG Farmers of West, uprooted by debt due to grasshopper plagues and droughts, move into factory cities

SEP 8 New York Warehouse and Security Company fails, casting gloom over business world

18 Brokerage firm Jay Cooke and Company overinvolved in finance of Northern Pacific, fails, precipitating country into five-year depression

18 Thirty-seven banks and brokerage houses close

20 New York Stock Exchange closes for ten days

20 Secretary of the Treasury releases $26 million in legal tender

30 New York Stock Exchange reopens

OCT 19 First code of football rules drafted by representatives of Yale, Princeton, Columbia and Rutgers universities

31 Filibustering ship *Virginian*, fraudulently flying US flag and carrying men and munitions to insurgents in Cuba, captured by Spanish gunboat; 53 passengers and crew, including eight Americans, executed

Also this year

★ Panic of 1873: 5000 business fail in first year

★ Silver discovered in Nevada in Great Bonanza mine

★ Grasshopper plagues devastate West

★ Cornelius Vanderbilt leases Lake Shore and Michigan Southern Railroad, completing railroad control from New York to Chicago

★ William 'Boss' Tweed found guilty and sentenced to 12 years in prison with fine of $12,000; released after one year

★ Cable car, invented by Andrew S. Hallidie, first used in San Francisco

★ Bethlehem Steel Works established in Pennsylvania

1874

JAN 20 'Salary Grab' Act of 1873 repealed, with exception of increases for President and Supreme Court Justices

MAR 11 Potter Law, Granger legislation in Wisconsin, regulates railroad freight rates within state

23 Granger legislation in Iowa regulates rail freight rates within state

APR 15 Pres. Grant recognizes Republican Elisha Baxter as Governor of Arkansas

MAY 8 Massachusetts adopts first 10-hour work day for women

16 Williamsburg Dam in Massachusetts breaks and floods Mill River Valley, causing millions of dollars worth of property damage and 100 deaths

JUL Chautagua Movement begun by Lewis Miller and John H. Vincent

4 First steel arch bridge, built across Mississippi River and St Louis

SEP 17 White League of New Orleans, in revolt against state government, suppressed by Federal troops

NOV 4 Democratic majorities return to House

7 First cartoon featuring elephant to symbolize Republican Party appears in *Harper's Weekly*

18-20 Delegates from 17 states meet in Cleveland, Ohio, to form Women's Christian Temperance Union

DEC 7 Seventy-five blacks killed in attack on Vicksburg, Miss., courthouse

Also this year

★ Greenback Party organized in Indianapolis

★ Social Democratic Workingmen's Party organized in New York

★ Potato bug reaches Atlantic coast states

★ Osteopathy developed by Dr Andrew T. Still

★ University of Nevada established at Elke, Nev.

The Arts

★ Mark Twain and Charles Dudley Warner's novel *The Gilded Age*

The Centennial Exposition

America celebrated her first 100 years of independence in grand style in the summer of 1876 by mounting a massive exhibition in Philadelphia. Millions of visitors from all over the world flocked to the specially erected halls, in which were displayed many examples of American creativity in the arts and the practical sciences. One of the centerpieces of the exhibition was the giant Corliss steam engine, housed in the popular Machinery Hall, which was ceremonially started by President Grant and the visiting Emperor of Brazil (above).

Alexander Graham Bell

Perhaps the greatest single attraction at the Centennial Exposition was the booth occupied by Alexander Graham Bell (seen, right, in a photograph taken that year).

Bell had taken the opportunity of the exhibition to demonstrate a new and revolutionary device, the telephone, which he had invented in Boston in March 1876.

Andrew Carnegie

Preeminent among the industrial magnates who emerged during the 1870s was Andrew Carnegie (1835–1919) (left), who was soon to dominate the iron and steel industry not only in America but worldwide. The son of a poor Scottish immigrant, Carnegie amassed a personal fortune of some $450 million, three quarters of which he gave away after his retirement in 1901.

Thomas Edison

The 1870s also saw the emergence of perhaps the most prolific inventor of all time, Thomas Alva Edison (1847–1931). It was his patenting in 1878 of the phonograph (bottom, with Edison himself, and top), a recording device which prefigured the gramophone, that rocketed him to fame, but he had been inventing since 1868. In 1874 his quadruplex telegraph effectively doubled the capacity of the telegraph wire, and in 1877 his carbon telephone transmitter opened up commercial possibilities for Bell's new invention. On October 21, 1879, he demonstrated his carbon filament lamp (middle), ushering in a new era of cheap mass illumination. Edison founded the world's first industrial research laboratory at Menlo Park, New Jersey, which was soon turning out an astonishing 400 patents a year.

1875

JAN 14 Specie Resumption Act passed

30 Hawaiian Reciprocity Treaty declares that no Hawaiian territory can be acquired by 3rd power

MAR 1 Civil Rights Act guarantees equal rights in public places and prohibits exclusion from jury duty

3 Tariff Act of 1875 raises rates 10 percent

30 In *Minor v. Happersett*, Supreme Court declares that 14th Amendment does not deprive state of right to establish suffrage requirements

MAY 1 Whiskey Ring scandal surfaces

3 US becomes member of Universal Postal Union

JUL Dwight Lyman Moody begins evangelistic revival meetings in East

SEP 1 Murder conviction leads to breakup of terrorist secret society 'Molly Maguires'

OCT Second Sioux War erupts

NOV 17 Theosophical Society of America founded in NYC by Helena Petrovna Blavatsky

DEC 4 William 'Boss' Tweed escapes from prison and flees to Cuba

15 Resolution against presidential third terms approved by House

25 Chicago *Daily News* founded

Also this year

★ Luther Burbank sets up plant nursery in California and develops new strains of plant through crossbreeding

★ Football uniforms first worn at match between Harvard and Tufts

1876

JAN 1 Philadelphia Mummer's parade organized in celebration of American centennial

FEB Secretary of War William W. Belknap charged with offering contractor control over trading posts at Fort Sill in Indiana Territory

MAR Ogalala Indians defeat Gen. Crook at Rosebud Creek

2 Impeachment proceedings against Secretary of War Belknap recommended by House

7 Alexander Graham Bell patents telephone

27 In *United States v. Cruickshank*, Supreme Court declares that 14th Amendment does not protect Blacks from actions of individuals infringing on their rights

APR 2 National league baseball plays first official game; Boston beats Philadelphia 6-5

MAY 7 Prohibition Party National Convention nominates Gen. Green Clay Smith of Kentucky for President and Gideon T. Stewart of Ohio for Vice President

18 Greenback Party National Convention nominates Peter Cooper of New York for President and Samuel F. Cary of Ohio for Vice President

JUN 6 US branch of Masonic Order, Imperial Council of the Ancient Arabic Order of Nobels of the Mystic Shrine, organized by Dr Walter Fleming

14-16 Republican National Convention nominates Rutherford B. Hayes of Ohio for President and William A. Wheeler of New York for Vice President

25 In Battle of Little Big Horn in Montana, Gen. Custer and Seventh Cavalry slaughtered by Sioux Indians, led by Chief Gall, Crazy Horse and Chief Two Moons

25 Bill to issue unlimited coinage of silver introduced in House by Richard P. Bland of Missouri

27-29 Democratic National Convention nominates Samuel J. Tilden of New York for President and Thomas H. Hendricks of Indiana for Vice President

AUG 1 Colorado enters Union as 38th state

SEP Sitting Bull escapes to Canada

NOV 7 Samuel J. Tilden wins majority of popular votes but dispute over fraudulent election practices and electoral votes leaves final decision with Congress

23 William 'Boss' Tweed sent back to New York by Spanish authorities

THE WILD WEST

The 1870s saw the first concerted opening up of the vast and largely unsettled territory between the Midwestern states and the Pacific, as the frontier began to move out across the inhospitable wilderness of the Great Plains. Three different and often conflicting cultures drove this remarkable movement of people, the last phase of that westward expansion that had characterized American society since the earliest days. They were the farmers, the miners, and the cowboys.

The harsh soil and low rainfall of the Great Plains, together with the cost of enclosing large areas of land, had long acted as a barrier to wide-scale settlement. In the 1870s, however, the commercial availability of the steel plow, the windmill, and, above all, barbed wire, led many families to brave the hard and lonely challenge of farming on the Plains. At the same time, the mining frontier drew hundreds of thousands of settlers to the West in the years after the discovery of gold in Colorado and Nevada in the 1850s and 1860s. New mining towns, such as the notorious communities of Lead and

Far left: Home on the range: a cowboy roping a steer.

Middle left: Contemplating a life of crime: the young Jesse James.

Left: "Wild Bill" Hickok, shot dead in Deadwood while playing poker in 1876.

Below: Deadwood, Dakota Territory, in 1876.

DEC 12 First prohibition amendment proposed by Henry W. Blair of New Hampshire

29 *Pacific Express* plunges into gorge at Ashtabula, Ohio, killing 84

Also this year

★ Dewey Decimal System of library classification originated by Melvil Dewey

★ Charles Sanders Peirce invents pragmatism

★ Thomas A. Edison invents mimeograph

★ NYC's Central Park completed

★ *Harvard Lampoon*, first undergraduate humor magazine in US, begins publication

1877

JAN 2 Carpetbag government ends in Florida with inauguration of Democrat George F. Drew as Governor

29 Electoral Commission Bill passed by Congress to decide outcome of disputed presidential election of 1876

MAR 1 In *Peek v. Chicago and Northwestern Railroad Company*, Supreme Court declares for Grange Movement, declaring that state has power to regulate intrastate and interstate traffic originating within its boundaries

1 In *Munn v. Illinois*, Supreme Court declares for Grange Movement, declaring that state has power to regulate warehouse and intrastate railroad rates

2 Senate President announces election of Rutherford B. Hayes as President and William A. Wheeler as Vice President

5 Rutherford B. Hayes inaugurated President, William A. Wheeler inaugurated Vice President

APR Four eastern railroads, New York Central, Erie, Pennsylvania and Baltimore and Ohio, call off rate war; agree to fix rates among themselves and cut wages by 10 percent

10 South Carolina turns Democrat when Federal troops withdraw by order of the President

24 Last Federal troops policing South withdrawn from New Orleans; carpetbag rule ends

JUN Nez Percé battle U.S. Army in Idaho; Chief Joseph defeated by Col. Nelson Miles in attempt to reach Canada; tribe forced on to malarial Oklahoma reservation

1 Society of American Artists founded by sculptor Augustus Saint-Gaudens and fellow artists

14 First Flag Day commemorates 100th anniversary of US flag

JUL 14 Great strike of 1877 begins as workers walk out on Baltimore and Ohio Railroad

16 Violence erupts during strike on Baltimore and Ohio at Martinsburg, W. Va; Secretary of War sends Federal troops to break up strike

20 Nine strikers killed and seven wounded in Baltimore when State militia fire at crowd to prevent them from reaching railway station

21 Pennsylvania militia attacks strike supporters in Pittsburgh; riot ensues

26 Unorganized strike gathering in Chicago attacked by police and cavalry; 19 die

31 By this date, 40,000 coalminers are on strike in Scranton, Pa; action results in 10 percent raise and strike spreads through most coal-producing states

NOV 23 American Halifax Fisheries Commission gives Great Britain $5.5 million for North Atlantic privileges under Treaty of Washington

DEC 15 Thomas A. Edison files patent for phonograph

26 Workingmen's Party reorganized as Socialist Labor Party at convention in Newark, NJ

Also this year

★ Silver rush to Leadville, Colo., begins

★ Charles Elmer Hires introduces root beer

157

Deadwood in Dakota, sprang up, often in a matter of days, in the wake of each new discovery. Life in these towns was frequently lawless and violent, with heavy drinking, gambling, whoring, and street fighting only too commonplace. Finally, the culture of the cowboy transformed life on the Plains during the short but colorful heyday of the Cattle Kingdom, as vast herds of cattle were driven northwards along the great trails from Texas and New Mexico to the railroad terminals of Missouri and Kansas or the Union Pacific.

Clashes between cowboys, farmers, and miners were frequent and often bloody during these years. But the main losers from the settlement of the New West were the Indian tribes of the Great Plains, whose traditional way of life was all but destroyed by the Colt revolver, the annihilation of the buffalo, and the advent of diseases brought by the white man.

Far right: Contrary to the popular image, one in four cowboys was Black. Perhaps the most famous of them was Nat Love, better known as "Deadwood Dick," here photographed in the 1870s.

Near right: As many murders as years: Billy the Kid (William H. Bonney), one of the Wild West's most notorious outlaws, shot dead in 1881 at the age of 21.

Below: The cowboy. gained a remarkable hold over the American popular imagination, as this Frederick Remington picture, "A Dash for the Timber," and countless books and movies testify.

The opening of the New West spelt the end of the Indian way of life. The sorry history of white relations with native Americans was summed up by President Hayes in 1877 when he spoke of "broken promises and acts of injustice." For example, it was the invasion by miners of territory promised to the Sioux in perpetuity that sparked off the notorious "battle" of Little Big Horn, in which General Custer and his 264 men were wiped out by Indians under Sitting Bull and Crazy Horse in June 1876. Above: A delegation of Dakota Oglala Indians in Washington.

1878

JAN 1 Knights of Labor established as national organization

10 Women's Suffrage Amendment introduced into Congress by Sen. A.A. Sargent

14 In *Hall v. Cuir*, Supreme Court finds that railroads need not provide equal accomodations to all passengers regardless of race

17 Congress ratifies treaty of friendship and commerce with Samoa

28 First telephone exchange opens at New Haven, Conn.

FEB 28 Bland-Allison Act provides for limited silver coinage

MAY Massive epidemic of yellow fever sweeps through South, claiming 14,000 lives by winter

JUN 11 Permanent constitution for District of Columbia provided by act of Congress

JUL 15 Edison Electric Light Company established in New York City by Thomas A. Edison

27 'Western' George L. Leslie commits $3 million burglary of Manhattan Institute for Savings

AUG 21 American Bar Association formed at Saratoga, NY

DEC In Dull Knife Campaign in Wyoming Territory, Northern Cheyennes escape from malaria-ridden reservation in Oklahoma; they fight off capture for months, but eventually are forced to surrender to US Army and are returned to reservation

9 Joseph Pulitzer purchases St Louis *Dispatch* for $2500

Also this year

★ Post-Civil War deflation of currency reaches lowest point

★ Geologist Alexander Winchell dismissed from Methodist Vanderbilt University in Nashville, Tenn., for contradicting biblical chronology

★ George Eastman of Rochester, NY, begins manufacture of photographic dry plate

★ Joseph Pulitzer merges St Louis *Dispatch* with John A. Dillon's *Post*, creating St Louis *Post-Dispatch*

1879

JAN 1 Resumption of specie payments by US government

FEB 15 Women lawyers gain right to practice law before Supreme Court by act of Congress

MAR 3 US Geological Survey created within Department of the Interior

MAY 4 California adopts new constitution which forbids employment of Chinese laborers

8 George B. Selden files first patent application for gasoline-driven automobile

JUN Large black exodus from South to Kansas

SEP Uprising of Ute Indians in Colorado; entire Ute nation forced into reservation

OCT 19-21 Thomas A. Edison perfects carbon filament lamp in laboratory at Menlo Park, NJ

Also this year

★ F.W. Woolworth opens five-and-ten-cent store in Utica, NY

★ Arc lamp system of street lighting installed in Cleveland and San Francisco by Charles F. Brush

★ First intercity telephone system established between Boston and Lowell, Mass.

★ Lincoln County (New Mexico) cattle war with William Bonney, alias 'Billy the Kid,' ended by Federal troops

★ Prof. C.H. Troy forced to resign from Southern Baptist Seminary, Louisville, Ky, for espousing scientific interpretation of Bible

★ Radcliffe College, Cambridge, Mass., established as adjunct to Harvard University

★ Madison Square Garden opens in NYC

★ Henry George's *Progress and Poverty*, published

CO-OPTING the words of the great novelist Mark Twain, historians have referred to the period of American life which followed the end of Reconstruction in 1877 as "the Gilded Age," and it is a description which captures both the vast increase in the wealth of the nation during these years and the superficiality of many of the ways in which that wealth was expressed, especially by the great industrial magnates.

It was an age of contrasts. In political life, America returned to an evenly balanced two-party system, in which power seemed the only important issue and where there was little difference in policies between Republicans and Democrats. The White House was occupied by a succession of somewhat bland Presidents – Hayes, Garfield, Arthur, Cleveland, Harrison – who left little mark on the life of the nation. At the same time, Congress was dominated by powerful figures such as Thomas B. Reed and James G. Blaine, whose influence was nonetheless exercised mainly in their own or their party interests.

But while the ship of state drifted largely rudderless through the unfamiliar seas of post-bellum American life, the ship of industry continued to forge ahead, steered by captains with a ruthlessly clear sense of direction, and stoked by the dynamism of the American people themselves. The United States was busy turning itself into the greatest industrial power on earth. Here too, though, all was not plain sailing. Industrial growth was opening up its own disturbing gulfs – between the buzzing commercial North and the still war-ravaged,

agricultural South; between the great trusts and the small farmsteads of the West; between Black and white; and perhaps above all, between the fabulously rich and the desperately poor.

Many observers of the national scene in the last third of the 19th century bore witness to an underlying malaise in American society, a sense that something had been lost of the ideals on which that society had been founded. America was at peace – indeed, there was no foreign policy to speak of during most of the 1880s – and the trauma of the Civil War was behind her. There was a golden opportunity to shape the nation anew, to adapt the body politic to the new challenges of a new age. While politicians squabbled and big business mushroomed towards monopoly, there were many who felt that the chance to mold the future was being squandered.

The Assassination of Garfield

The decade opened inauspiciously indeed. The election of 1880 went by a whisker to the Republican "dark horse" candidate, General James A. Garfield of Ohio – a man not altogether untainted by the scandals of the second Grant administration – with Chester A. Arthur as his Vice President. What sort of President Garfield might have been we shall never know. For if the national vote was pretty evenly divided between Republican and Democrat, factionalism was dangerously rife within the Republican Party itself, with so-called "Stalwarts" and "Halfbreeds" battling it out for supremacy in the ranks. On July 2, 1881, a mere four months after taking office, Garfield was shot in the back at Washington railway station by Charles J. Guiteau, a disappointed officeseeker (one among hundreds who crowded into the White House lobby during these years). As Garfield lay fatally wounded,

Guiteau is said to have boasted "I am a Stalwart, and Arthur is President now."

Cleaning up

"Chet" Arthur actually became President only in September 1881 when his unfortunate predecessor finally gave up the struggle for life. If Guiteau and his like had hoped for an easy ride under the new administration, they were in for a rude awakening. Arthur – as shocked as the general public by what Garfield's assassination said about the state of the so-called "spoils" system – immediately launched a major campaign to clean up the civil service. The Pendleton Act of 1883 revived the Civil Service Commission which Grant had allowed to die on the vine, and Arthur's support gave it the teeth to do its job. The initiative was the first significant step on the road to creating a professional civil service in America, with appointments to office dependent, not on personal influence or political allegiance, but on individual merit determined by open examinations.

Blaine v. Cleveland

The presidential election of 1884 was a noholds-barred affair. The Republican Party split, with the so-called "Mugwumps," or Liberal Republicans, throwing their weight behind the already weighty Democratic nominee, Governor Grover Cleveland of New York. The Republican candidate was that perennial (and perennially disappointed) aspirant to the highest office in the land, James G. Blaine. The campaign itself was even more raucous and dirty than the ones that brought Jackson and Harrison to the White House. The candidates' private lives became public property, with Cleveland's supporters making great play of Blaine's dubious financial dealings and Blaine's

America's second presidential assassination: Charles Guiteau is apprehended after shooting President Garfield in the back in Washington on July 2, 1881. The President died on 19 September.

replying with the accusation that Cleveland had fathered an illegitimate child. Chants of "Blaine! Blaine! James G. Blaine!/The continental liar from the state of Maine!" were countered, with equal delicacy, by shouts of "Ma! Ma! Where's my pa?" from the Blaine faction. The voting was as close as the policies. Whether because the electorate regarded extra-marital sex as less reprehensible than corruption, or because Blaine lost the Irish-American vote by some tactless anti-Catholicism, Cleveland found himself the victor, but the swing from the voting patterns of the previous election was the smallest in American history.

Grover Cleveland

Grover Cleveland – later to become the only U.S. President to be reelected for a non-consecutive second term – was a well-meaning if somewhat inflexible man. Like his predecessors, Hayes and Arthur, he made an honest showing in office, but left few, if any, political monuments. He continued Arthur's clean-up of the civil service and, as the first Democratic President since the end of the Civil War, orchestrated the reintroduction of Southerners to positions of responsibility in the Cabinet and the Supreme Court, opening in the process almost as many wounds as he healed. He also expended much effort on an ultimately unsuccessful attempt to reduce the level of tariffs, which he claimed benefited only the very small proportion of workers who yet worked in the manufacturing industries. Perhaps the greatest achievement of his first term, though, was one for which he could take little personal credit, the Interstate Commerce Act of 1887. The Act, the result of public pressure for control of the ever more powerful railroads, was the first piece of legislation in American history to bring a major national industry under the regulation of the Federal Government.

"A billion dollar country"

The 1888 election returned a Republican administration under the presidency of Benjamin Harrison, the grandson of President Harrison of "Tippecanoe and Tyler too" fame. Following the lead given by "Chet" Arthur earlier in the decade, Congress voted a major program of naval expenditure and also boosted service pensions to astonishing levels. As a result, the 51st Congress, which convened in December 1889, was to spend a staggering $1 billion. When upbraided for extravagance, the Speaker of the House of Representatives, the autocratic Tom Reed, replied that the United States was now "a billion dollar country."

He was right. The America of the 1880s was a vastly richer, vastly more populous country than the America which had emerged from the cauldron of the Civil War. In this one decade alone, the value of her industrial output had risen from just over $5 billion to just over $9 billion, and national wealth as a whole was valued at $65 billion by 1890. Perhaps most significant of all for the future development of the United States,

Mark Twain (Samuel Langhorne Clemens).

by the end of the 1880s the population had more than doubled since the eve of the Civil War, from 31 million to almost 63 million people.

"The Gilded Age"?

Given the speed and intensity of that development, it is perhaps not surprising that cracks were beginning to appear in the social fabric. Public unease with the power of the giant corporations triggered the first legislative moves against the trusts at the end of 1889, and the first rumblings of agrarian discontent were also audible to those who had ears to hear. Furthermore, the bitterness of the 1877 railroad strike still simmered below the industrial growth of the 1880s and in 1886 100,000 workers were involved in a national strike demanding an eight-hour working day.

The "Negro Question," no longer in the political foreground since the Compromise of 1877, had by no means been answered; harassment and routine exclusion from the political process had become familiar features of life for Afro-Americans, especially in the South, and even such exciting expressions of Black culture as the birth of ragtime music in the 1880s bore witness to the failure of American society to assimilate its former slaves.

The tensions are also evident in the development of American literature during these years. The optimism of William Dean Howells – the so-called "dean of American letters" – was already tinged with the doubts which would eventually lead him to despair of American civilization. And in the works of Mark Twain – who published his masterpiece, *Huckleberry Finn*, in 1884 – mischievous mockery of his fellow Americans was gradually darkening into the bitterness of *The Mysterious Stranger* and *The Man that Corrupted Hadleyburg*. For the man who named an epoch, as for many of those who lived through it with him, the gold of the Gilded Age went only surface deep.

1880

MAR 1 In *Strauder v. West Virginia*, Supreme Court finds it unconstitutional to exclude Blacks from jury duty

8 Pres. Hayes declares any canal across Isthmus of Panama under US control

APR Wabash, Ind., becomes first town to be completely lit by electricity

JUN 2-8 Republican National Convention nominates James A. Garfield of Ohio for President and Chester A. Arthur for Vice President

9 National Convention of Greenback Labor Party nominates James B. Weavor of Iowa for President and B.J. Chambers of Texas for Vice President

17 Prohibition Party nominates Neal Dow of Maine for President and A.M. Thompson of Ohio for Vice President

22-24 Democratic National Convention nominates Gen. Winfield S. Hancock of Pennsylvania for President and William E. English of Indiana for Vice President

OCT 4 University of Southern California founded at Los Angeles, Calif.

NOV 2 James A. Garfield elected President, Chester A. Arthur elected Vice President

8 French actress Sarah Bernhardt makes American debut at Booth's Theater in NYC

17 Chinese Exclusion Treaty signed by US and China, permits US to restrict immigration of Chinese laborers

Also this year

★ Capt. David L. Payne leads first of light 'boomers' raids from Kansas into Oklahoma territory to illegally seize lands

★ Major gold strike in Alaska leads to development of Juneau

★ George Eastman patents successful roll film for cameras

★ Bryn Mawr College for women chartered in Bryn Mawr, Pa

1881

JAN 19 Western Union Telegraph Company established by financiers Jay Gould and William, H. Vanderbilt, consolidating Western Union, American Union and Atlantic and Pacific companies

FEB 19 Kansas is first state to prohibit sale of liquor

MAR *The Story of a Great Monopoly* by Henry Demarest Lloyd, aimed at Standard Oil Company, published

3 Central registration agency for protection of trademarks authorized by Congress

The Metropolitan Museum of Art

The Gilded Age saw the foundation of a number of public libraries, museums, and art galleries in the United States, including the famous Metropolitan Museum of Art in New York, the Marquand Gallery of which is shown left.

Labor Day

Vast changes were taking place in the American way of work during these years. From a predominantly agricultural economy at the outbreak of the Civil War, the United States was busy transforming itself into a fully-fledged manufacturing power, with machinery and factory processes replacing manual labor and artisanship across a wide range of industries. Strikes and unrest were one symptom of change. A more celebratory manifestation of the growing strength of labor was the massive crowd which turned out in New York's Union Square for the first ever Labor Day parade in 1882 (below).

John Singer Sargent

1884 was a turning point in the career of the prolific American portrait painter John Singer Sargent (1856–1925) (above). The scandal which erupted over his portrait *Madame X* (actually Madame Gautreau, the controversial New Orleans socialite) when it was exhibited at the Paris Salon that year led Sargent to move to London.

George Eastman

The art of photography was made accessible to a mass market when George Eastman (1854–1932) (right), the inventor of roll film, launched his new and easily operated camera, the Kodak, in 1888.

Anti-Chinese Feeling

The 1849 goldrush and the need for labor on the transcontinental railroad had brought thousands of Chinese to the U.S.. By the 1880s they had become the object of intense suspicion, discrimination, and violence, especially in California, the state with the largest Chinese community, and in 1882 Congress passed a law suspending further Chinese immigration for 10 years. The cartoon shows a Chinese being chased out of San Francisco by the new American steam washer.

4 James A. Garfield inaugurated President, Chester A. Arthur inaugurated Vice President

MAY 21 American Red Cross organized by Clara Barton

JUL 2 Pres. Garfield shot in Washington DC, railroad station by Charles J. Guiteau, disgruntled office seeker

4 Tuskegee Normal and Industrial Institute founded by Booker T. Washington in Alabama

SEP 19 Pres. James A. Garfield dies

20 Chester A. Arthur inaugurated President

NOV 17 Federation of Organized Trades and Labor Unions of the United States formed by Samuel Gompers

29 Secretary of State Blaine launches Pan-American movement, inviting Latin American nations to meet in Washington in 1882

DEC 1 Secretary of State Blaine declares Hawaiian Islands part of American system, within bounds of Monroe Doctrine

1 Southern Pacific Railroad completed between New Orleans and the Pacific

1881-1900 23,800 strikes and lockouts occur in US

Also this year

★ Migration of Russian Jews to US begins

★ Gov. of Missouri offers reward for capture of Frank and Jesse James

★ Star Route Frauds, involving Sen. Stephen W. Dorsey of Arkansas and Post Office Department exposed

★ First central electric power plant in world built on Pearl St, NYC

★ University of Connecticut established as Storrs Agricultural College at Storrs, Conn.

★ Wharton School of Finance and Economy founded within University of Pennsylvania

★ Helen Hunt Jackson's *A Century of Dishonor* published

The Arts

★ Henry James' novels *Portrait of a Lady* and *Washington Square*

★ John Singer Sargent's paintings *Vernon Lee* and *Portrait of a Lady*

★ Mary Cassatt exhibits paintings in Paris

★ Walt Whitman's *Leaves of Grass* withdrawn from publication

1882

JAN 2 Standard Oil Trust organized by John D. Rockefeller

MAR Floods along Mississippi River leave 85,000 homeless

16 Geneva Convention of 1864 for care of wounded war personnel ratified by Senate

22 Edmunds Act prohibits polygamists from voting or holding public office

31 Pension for widows of Presidents Polk, Tyler and Garfield voted by Congress; sets precedent

MAY 6 Chinese Exclusion Act, prohibiting Chinese immigration for 10 years, passed by Congress over President's veto

JUN Severe strikes hit iron and steel industry

JUL 26 US announces acceptance of provisions of Geneva Convention of 1864

AUG 3 Immigration bill bars paupers, convicts and the insane and taxes all immigrants 50-cents

SEP 4 Edison's Pearl Street electricity station begins to supply New York

5 First Labor Day parade held in New York

Also this year

★ University of South Dakota opens at Vermillion

★ New York *Morning Journal* founded by Albert Pulitzer

The Trusts

The decade was marked by a substantial growth in the power of the great industrial combinations or "trusts," and a consequent rise in the volume of public demands for government action to control them. Investigations into the structure and methods of the Standard Oil Company and the sugar and beef trusts revealed the extent to which such interests were able to exercise a stranglehold over commerce in their respective sectors, regardless of the public interest. Both major parties included a commitment to anti-trust measures in their election platforms in 1888, and in 1890 Congress passed the Sherman Anti-trust Act, which outlawed all forms of combination in restraint of trade. For many years, however, the new legislation was to be used mainly to control the activities of trade unions.

Big business swallows up railroad freight while unemployed workers look on.

1889 Nast cartoon depicts the smothering of the liberties of the people by the trusts.

The "Colossus of Roads:" W. H. Vanderbilt.

Haves...

The showiness of wealth in the Gilded Age, and its vast distance from the lives of the ordinary people of America, is nowhere better exemplified than in the massive "stately homes" the big business tycoons were building for themselves during these years. The picture shows the luxurious picture gallery at the Vanderbilts' newly completed mansion, on New York's fashionable Fifth Avenue, in 1883.

...and Have Nots

Meanwhile, on New York's Lower East Side, and in similar slums throughout the nation, hundreds of thousands of people were living in conditions of appalling squalor, without work, welfare, or hope.

The journalist Jacob Riis' photographic record, *How the Other Half Lives*, shocked many when it was published in 1889. Here an old woman sits smoking and beading in a tenement room.

1883

JAN 16 Pendleton Civil Service Reform Act provides for competitive examinations for Federal positions

FEB 15 Flooding on Ohio River devastes Cincinnati

MAR 26 William K. Vanderbilt hosts most expensive fancy dress ball ever given

MAY 9 New York *World* purchased by Joseph Pulitzer from Jay Gould

24 Brooklyn Bridge between Manhattan Island and Brooklyn opened

SEP 8 Northern Pacific Railroad completed

OCT 15 Civil Rights Acts of 1875 found unconstitutional by Supreme Court

NOV 18 System of standard time adopted by railroads of US and Canada

DEC 4 Sons of the American Revolution organized in New York

Also this year

★ Ferdinand de Lesseps begins construction of Panama Canal for French company

★ John J. Montgomery makes earliest recorded heavier-than-air glider flight near Otay, Calif.

The Arts

★ Mark Twain's book *Life on the Mississippi*

★ Benjamin Franklin Keith opens first of 400 vaudeville theaters in Boston

1884

FEB 9 Tornado kills 700 people in South

14 Ohio River flooding devastates Cincinnati

MAR 4 Iowa adopts state prohibition

3-9 Riots occur in Cincinnati over lax administration of justice; 75 killed, 135 wounded

12 Mississippi Industrial Institute and College, first state-supported women's college, chartered at Columbus, Miss.

APR Hocking Valley coal miners strike over wages and working conditions

MAY 17 Anti-Monopoly Party nominates Union Gen. Benjamin F. Butler of Massachusetts for President

28 Greenback Party nominates Union Gen. Benjamin F. Butler for President

SUMMER Mulligan letters incriminating James G. Blaine reprinted in *Harpers Weekly*

JUN 3-6 Republican National Convention nominates James G. Blaine for President and Gen. John A. Logan of Illinois for Vice President

6 'Mugwumps' reform wing of Republican Party bolt following Blaine's nomination

16 Mugwumps convene in New York and agree to support Democratic candidate if liberal

27 US Bureau of Labor in Department of Interior established by Congress

JUL 8-11 Democratic National Convention nominates Gov. Grover Cleveland of New York for President and Thomas A. Hendricks for Vice President

23 Prohibition Party National Convention nominates John P. St John of Kansas for President and William Daniel of Maryland for Vice President

30 Labor Party National Convention supports Democratic Party slate

AUG 5 Cornerstone of pedestal of Statue of Liberty laid at Bedloe's Island in New York harbor

OCT International Prime Meridian Conference meets in Washington, DC, and chooses Greenwich England as prime meridian for world

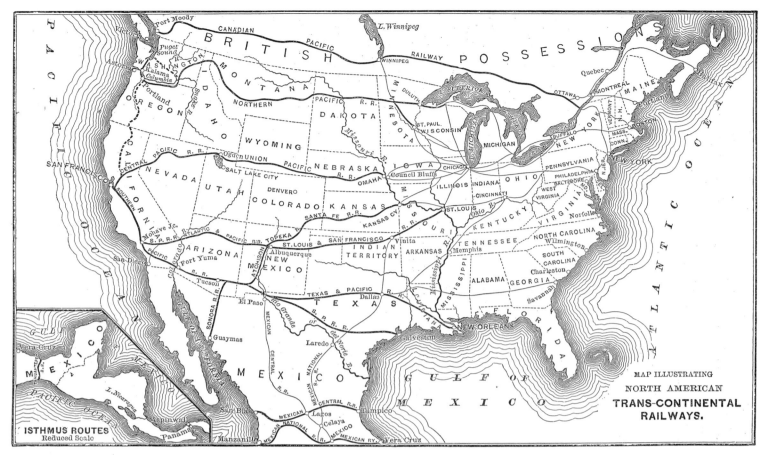

Transcontinental Railroads

The spread of the railroads – this 1883 map shows the network of transcontinental lines – brought both prosperity and demands for Federal regulation.

Brooklyn Bridge

The first traffic flows over Brooklyn Bridge (below), then the world's longest, after its ceremonial opening in May 1883.

All Classes, Ages and Sexes

DRINK

Coca-Cola

The Satisfactory Beverage

It satisfies the thirst and pleases the palate. Relieves the fatigue that comes from over-work, over-shopping or over-play. Puts vim and go into tired brains and bodies.

Cooling-Refreshing-Delicious, Thirst-Quenching

Guaranteed under the Pure Food and Drugs Act, June 30, 1906. Serial No. 3324

5c. Everywhere

The Real Thing

The 1880s saw the birth of an American institution, as J. S. Pemberton began selling a new tonic drink called Coca-Cola in Atlanta, Georgia.

Grover Cleveland

Determined, honest, corpulent, and unpopular: Grover Cleveland (1837–1908), the only man to have had two non-consecutive terms as President of the United States.

The Johnstown Flood

In May 1889 the nation was shocked by news of one of the worst natural disasters ever to hit the United States. Following particularly heavy rain, the town of Johnstown in Pennsylvania became the victim of a massive flood which left some 2000 people dead and many others homeless. The deluge, which reduced Johnstown to ruins, occurred when a dam burst above the town, allowing one of the country's largest reservoirs to empty itself. The picture shows the scene of devastation at Johnstown's Cambria Ironworks after the floodwaters abated.

NOV 4 Grover Cleveland elected President, Thomas A. Henricks elected Vice President

8 McClure's Syndicate, first newspaper syndicate in US, launched by Samuel Sidney McClure

Also this year

★ Cottonseed Trust formed

★ Steel skeleton construction used for first time by William Le Baron Jenne in 10-story Home Insurance Building in Chicago; first skyscraper

★ Tulane University established by Louisiana Legislature

★ John Fiske's *Excursions of an Evolutionist* and *The Destiny of Man in the Light of His Origin* published

The Arts

★ Sarah Orne Jewett's novel *A Country Doctor*

★ Mark Twain's book *Huckleberry Finn*

1885

FEB 21 Washington Monument dedicated in Washington, DC

25 Fencing in of public lands in West prohibited by act of Congress

26 Contract Labor Act prohibits importation of immigrant labor in return for passage to US

MAR 4 Grover Cleveland inaugurated President, Thomas A. Hendricks inaugurated Vice President

13 Pres. Cleveland warns settlers to stay off Indian lands in Oklahoma

JUL 1 Fisheries reciprocity with Canada under 1871 Treaty of Washington terminated by US

AUG 17 Pres. Cleveland orders removal of all illegal fences from western public lands

NOV 25 Vice Pres. Thomas A. Hendricks dies; not replaced

Also this year

★ Linseed oil trust formed

★ Henry Hobson Richardson designs Marshall Field Building, Chicago

★ Henry Ward Beecher's *Evolution and Religion* published

The Arts

★ Ragtime pianist and composer Scott Joplin arrives in St Louis

1886

JAN 1 First Tournament of Roses held in Pasadena, Calif.

19 Presidential Succession Act, provides for succession through Cabinet, in order, in event of death of President and Vice President

FEB 7 Anti-Chinese riots occur in Seattle, Washington; 400 driven from homes; troops called to restore order

14 First trainload of oranges leaves California for East

6 Knights of Labor strike against Jay Gould's Missouri-Pacific railroad system begins; 9000 participate

MAY 1 40,000-60,000 people participate in strikes and demonstrations throughout country in demand for eight-hour day

3 Six people killed by police during McCormick Reaper Manufacturing Company strike

4 Haymarket Square Riot in Chicago; 7 police killed and 60 wounded when bomb explodes during labor rally; anarchists blamed

10 In *Santa Clara County v. Southern Pacific Railroad*, Supreme Court rules that a corporation is a person under 14th Amendment

JUN 19 Trial of eight Haymarket anarchists begins

29 Incorporation of trade unions approved by Congress

30 Division of Forestry approved by Congress

AUG 20 *Haymarket case:* August Spies, Albert Parsons, Adolph Fisher and George Engel sentenced to death; Samuel Fielden and Michael Schwab given life sentences; Oscar Neebe sentenced to 15 years; Louis Lingg hangs himself

Taming the Wilderness

The availability of more sophisticated agricultural equipment helped farmers to work a living from the soil of the West. Above: Harvesting in Oregon, about 1880.

Geronimo

One of the last focuses of Indian resistance, the Apache leader Geronimo (right) surrendered in Arizona in September 1886.

The Oklahoma Land Rush

In 1880 there were, according to official figures, no white settlers at all in the present state of Oklahoma (then part of Indian Territory). By the end of the decade some 259,000 people were living there. One of the main reasons for this spectacular growth was the Federal purchase of three million acres of Indian land for white settlement in 1889. Homesteaders gathered on Cherokee Strip at noon on 22 April, a gun was fired, and they galloped off to stake their claims (above). By nightfall almost two million acres had been claimed.

Desire for Streetcars

The 1880s saw an increase in the popularity of the streetcar as a means of transportation in America's fast-growing cities, especially after electrification. The photograph shows streetcars at the Western terminus of the California Railroad Company in San Francisco in 1883.

The Haymarket Riot

In May 1886 a national strike for an eight-hour day was organized by the Knights of Labor organization. It gained much public sympathy until a bomb was thrown at police during a labor demonstration in Haymarket Square, Chicago, causing deaths and injuries. Seven anarchists were convicted for the bomb attack, but the incident had the effect of discrediting the labor campaign itself.

SEP 4 Geronimo, Apache chief, surrenders to Gen. Nelson A. Miles in Arizona; sent to reservation in Florida

OCT 12 Flood along Texas Gulf kills 250

25 In *Wabash, St Louis and Pacific Railway Company v. Illinois*, Supreme Court rules that state cannot regulate even that portion of interstate commerce that takes place within its borders

28 Statue of Liberty, centennial gift from France, dedicated by Pres. Cleveland

DEC 8 American Federation of Labor organized from Federation of Trades and Labor Unions by Samuel Gompers and Adolph Strasser in Columbus, Ohio

Also this year

★ Peak year of strikes in 19th century; number of workers out is 610,000; property damage amounts to $33,580,000

★ Process for extracting aluminium from ore invented by Charles M. Hall

★ Alternating current system of electricity for commercial purposes introduced by George Westinghouse

The Arts

★ Frances Hodgson Burnett's story 'Little Lord Fauntleroy'

1887

JAN 20 Pearl Harbor, an island of Oahu, leased as naval station by US from Hawaii

FEB 3 Electoral Count Act makes each state responsible for own electoral returns, unless irregular

4 Interstate Commerce Act provides for interstate Commerce Commission to see that rates are just and 'reasonable'

8 Dawes Severality Act attempts to replace Indian reservation system by parceling out tracts of land to individual Indians

23 Importation of opium from China prohibited by act of Congress

MAR 2 Hatch Act provides funds for agricultural experimental stations in most states

3 Tenure of Office Act of 1867 repealed by Congress

AUG 10 Train wreck at Chatsworth, Ill., kills 100 and injures hundreds

SEP 5 Labor Day first observed as legal holiday in New York State

15-18 Hundredth anniversary of formation of Constitution celebrated in Philadelphia

Also this year

★ Free delivery of mail provided in communities of 10,000 and over

★ Territory of Cimarron proclaimed by settlers in No Mans Land, Okla.; not recognized by Congress

★ Sugar, lead, cordage, wire nails and plate glass trusts formed

★ Clark University established at Worcester, Mass.

The Arts

★ Eugene Field's poetry collection *Culture's Garden*, including 'Little Boy Blue' and 'Dutch Lullaby'

1888

FEB Secret ballot introduced in US at municipal election in Louisville, Ky

15 Bayard-Chamberlain Treaty ends new fishing dispute between US and Canada; not ratified by Senate but followed anyway

MAR 12 Great Blizzard of 1888 strikes Atlantic Seaboard centering on NYC, 36-hour snow storm causes $25 million in damage and kills 400 people

MAY 31 Prohibition Party National Convention nominates Clinton B. Fisk of New Jersey for President and John A. Brooks of Missouri for Vice President

JUN 4 Electrocution replaces hanging as method of execution in New York State, effective January 1, 1889

THE STATUE OF LIBERTY

"I lift my lamp beside the golden door." So runs the last line of the poem inscribed at the base of the great statue, called by its creator *Liberty Enlightening the Nations*, but better known today as the Statue of Liberty, which was erected on Bedloe's Island in New York harbor between 1885 and 1886.

The statue was the brainchild of the Alsatian sculptor Frederic Auguste Bartholdi and was a gift from the French Government in token of friendship to the United States. Bartholdi had been working on the 150-foot high monument for more than a decade – the massive torch, held by a disembodied forearm, had been on show at the Centennial Exposition in Philadelphia in 1876 – in collaboration, for part of that time, with the famous engineer Gustave Eiffel, who provided the metal framework for the statue. Only in 1886, however, was *Liberty Enlightening the Nations* finally ready to be shipped from France to New York for installation in its new and permanent home. The stylized figure of a robed woman holding aloft the flame of liberty was designed to be reassembled from some 350 different parts for ease of transportation. The grand opening, which excited a great deal of interest throughout the United States, took place on 28 October, 1886.

Below: The inauguration of the statue.

Right: Minister Levi P. Morton drives the first rivet into the statue's pedestal.

Far right: The Statue of Liberty being presented to the U.S. ambassador in Paris.

Inset: The gigantic torch, with its viewing gallery.

13 Department of Labor without Cabinet status established by Congress

JUL 13 Secretary of State Thomas F. Bayard invites Latin American nations to Inter-American conference

29 Yellow fever epidemic breaks out in Jacksonville, Fla; 4500 cases reported, 400 die

OCT 1 Congress forbids return to US of Chinese laborers who have left country

NOV 6 Republican Benjamin Harrison elected President, Levi P. Morton elected Vice President; Cleveland receives higher popular vote

Also this year

★ George Eastman introduces Kodak, roll film camera

★ Nikola Tesla invents alternating current motor

★ Lick Observatory completed at Mt Hamilton, Calif.

★ National Geographic Society founded in Washington

1889

JAN 19 Robert E. Lee's birthday becomes legal holiday in Georgia

28 Transit workers strike ties up New York City

30 University of Idaho chartered at Moscow, Idaho

FEB 2 *Munsey's Weekly* first published

19 Department of Agriculture raised to Cabinet status by act of Congress

20 Maritime Canal Company of Nicaragua incorporated by Congress for construction and management of canal across country; under US control without financial responsibility

22 Omnibus Bill signed by Pres. Cleveland for admission of North Dakota, South Dakota, Montana and Washington to statehood

MAR 2 First antitrust law passed by Kansas Legislature

4 Benjamin Harrison inaugurated President, Levi P. Morton inaugurated Vice President

15 Seven American, German and British warships in Samoan harbor struck by hurricane during period of critical international impasse; all destroyed except British *Calliope*

APR 22 'Oklahoma Land Rush:' land formally ceded to Indians opened to white settlers by government decree; 50,000 people rush in to claim lots

MAY 9 New Jersey amends its corporate laws to allow chartering of holding companies

31 Johnstown flood kills approximately 2000 when dam holding Conemaugh Lake breaks

JUN 14 Samoan treaty signed by US, Great Britain and Germany establishes tripartite protectorate to oversee Samoa

JUL 8 *Wall Street Journal* first published by firm of Dow Jones and Company at 15 Wall Street, NYC

AUG 6 Sioux Indian reservation of 11 million acres in South Dakota ceded to US

OCT 2 First International Conference of American States meets in Washington, DC, and establishes International Bureau of American Republics (Pan-American Union)

NOV 2 North Dakota enters Union as 39th state

2 South Dakota enters Union as 40th state

8 Montana enters Union as 41st state

11 Washington enters Union as 42nd state

17 Elizabeth Cochrane, known as Nelly Bly, journalist for New York *World*, starts trip around the world to challenge fictitious Jules Verne and 80-day voyage; her record is 72 days, 6 hours, 11 minutes

Also this year

★ First movie film developed by Thomas A. Edison on base devised by George Eastman

★ Singer Manufacturing Company of Elizabeth, NJ, markets first electric sewing machine known in US

★ 'Safety' bicycle introduced, with low wheels of equal size

★ James G. Hill organizes Great Northern Railroad, to link Great Lakes with the Pacific Tower Building erected in NYC

THE 1890s were a turning point in the history of America. The latent tensions of the age of industrialization surfaced in an agrarian revolt which found its political voice in the birth of the Populist party. The financial panic of 1893 and the resulting depression focused the simmering dissatisfaction of many American workers and led to the ugliest labor disputes yet seen in the United States. Conflicting views of how the financial malaise should be cured led to splits in the Democratic Party and the beginning of a lengthy period of Republican ascendancy after William McKinley's victory in the crucial presidential election of 1896.

At the same time, the decade witnessed a sharp reversal in the status of Afro-Americans as many Southern states put into effect a system of racial segregation and effective disfranchisement more thorough-going than any that had been seen since the end of the Civil War. Despite the fact that these policies ran counter to the principles enshrined in the civil rights amendments of the Reconstruction period, they nonetheless received the tacit support of the Supreme Court.

These were also years in which, after a long period of relative isolation, foreign affairs intruded once again on the consciousness of the American people. Disputes with Chile, Hawaii, Britain, and, most dramatically, Spain led to strained relations and, in the case of the confrontation with Spain over Cuban independence, to all-out war. They also led to the beginnings of an American empire, a development seen by many in the United States as a disavowal of the principles on which the republic had been founded. As the Western frontier was finally declared "closed," a new frontier of influence was opening overseas. The closing years of the 19th century saw America emerging onto the international stage as a world power of the first rank. But they were also to see the explosion onto the domestic political scene of a bitter debate about the morality of American imperialism.

"Tramps and millionaires"

The gap between rich and poor continued to widen during the early 1890s. Public pressure led to the passing of the Sherman Antitrust Act in 1890, aimed at regulating the power of the industrial monopolies. But the giant corporations continued to find ways of combining to enhance their strength and their profits, and public resentment continued to fester. By the middle of the decade, one observer of the American economic scene estimated that more than half of the nation's wealth was owned by just one per cent of the population.

Two events helped to bring discontent to a head. The drought of 1886 precipitated an agricultural depression that led to the bankruptcy of thousands of farmers and the financial panic of 1893 set off an economic depression more paralyzing than any since the 1870s.

The so-called "Farmers' Revolt" had been bubbling away under the surface of American political life for years. With commodity prices falling and more and more farmers finding themselves unable to repay their debts, various organizations had been formed to give voice to the grievances of the agricultural community. The Granger movement of the 1860s had given way to the Farmers' Alliance in the 1870s and 1880s, and in 1892 members of the Alliance formed a political party, the People's Party, or Populists, to represent their views at the national level. At their convention in Omaha that year, the Populists drew up a political manifesto which went far beyond the basic demand for agrarian reform and included a commitment to the free coinage of silver (a perennial cause of controversy during these years), the nationalization of the railroad, telegraph, and telephone systems, and controls on immigration into the United States. At the same time, it painted a grim picture of American life, speaking of "a nation brought to the verge of moral, political, and material ruin" and lamenting the creation of "two great classes – tramps and millionaires."

The Populists fielded presidential and vice presidential candidates – both former Civil War generals, one for the Union and one for the Confederate cause – in the presidential election of 1892. Although the real battle was still between the two major parties, with the Democrat Grover Cleveland snatching a second term of office from Benjamin Harrison, the Populists made a better showing at their first election than any new party since the birth of the Republican Party some 30 years before. It was no longer possible to ignore the agrarian depression which had led to half the population of West Kansas abandoning their homes in the previous five years and caused thousands upon thousands of mortgage foreclosures throughout the South and West during the same period.

The great depression, which began within a few weeks of Grover Cleveland's return to the White House, created distress and misery on an even wider scale. Major railroad companies, including the Philadelphia and Reading, the Erie, the Northern Pacific, and the Union Pacific, went bankrupt, dragging banks, farms, and private individuals after them. In 1893 alone, 500 banks closed their doors and 16,000 farmers went bankrupt. By 1895 there were some 3 million people out of work throughout the country. While politicians argued over the relative merits of the gold standard and the silver standard, and the President struggled to reduce the tariff introduced by the McKinley Tariff Act of 1890, the United States was engulfed in a wave of unprecedented labor unrest.

1890 had already seen more strikes than any previous year of the whole century, and a bitter strike at the Carnegie Homestead Steel Works had led to bloody confrontations between striking workers and private security men during the 1892 election campaign itself. In 1894 some 500 unemployed workers from Massillon, Ohio, marched to Washington under the leadership of Carl Browne and Jacob Coxey, to lodge a petition with the President. In a move which won him the undying hatred of many workers, Cleveland sent a corps of baton-wielding police to meet them, and many arrests were made. Later the same year, workers at the Pullman Palace Car Company, outraged by a series of wage cuts, went on strike and organized a boycott of railroads using Pullman coaches. Again the President responded with force. Ignoring the protestations of the State Governor, he sent some 2000 Federal troops into Illinois to break the strike, and a dozen strikers were shot in the resulting violence. Cleveland's first term of office had been undistinguished. His second seemed to many people to be taking the United States to the brink of anarchy.

The Election of 1896

The presidential election of 1896 showed the extent of the damage done to the Democratic cause by Cleveland's misguided inflexibility. The campaign pitted the Republican William McKinley against the charismatic young Democrat William Jennings Bryan of Nebraska, who also received the Populist nomination for his stance on agrarian issues and his passionate support of the free silver cause. Despite a tireless campaign, during which some five million people are estimated to have heard him speak in person, Bryan was defeated. Behind the scenes, the shipping and mining magnate Marcus Alonzo Hanna put his considerable fundraising skills at the service of the Republican Party, in a campaign which helped lay the groundwork for today's electioneering techniques. McKinley won a clear majority (the first for a Republican candidate since Ulysses S. Grant in 1868) and began a period of Republican ascendancy which was to last well into the next century. The election also marked the effective demise of the Populist party as a significant force in American politics.

The man whose time never came: William Jennings Bryan (1860–1925), Populist and three times presidential candidate.

1890s

Black Civil Rights

The 1890s saw an all-out assault on the rights of the Afro-American community in the Southern states. A series of laws were enacted to limit the involvement of Blacks in public life and to impose a régime of segregation which extended from public transport to the education system. Many states introduced literacy qualifications for voters and passed other discriminatory ordinances, the net effect of which was to disfranchise almost all Southern Blacks, and a large number of poor whites into the bargain. Instead of upholding the rights of American citizens under the Thirteenth, Fourteenth, and Fifteenth Amendments, however, the Supreme Court effectively sanctioned their oppression. In two highly significant test cases, Plessy v. Ferguson in 1896 and Williams v. Mississippi in 1898, the Court turned its back on millions of Black Americans, not only giving its blessing to segregation on a "separate but equal" basis, but also upholding the right of individual states to disfranchise their electors by placing qualifications on the right to vote. As the 20th century began, the position of

Labor unrest was rife in the 1890s. Above, Pinkerton detectives, hired to break the strike at the Carnegie Homestead steel works, surrender after strikers attack them. In the end, the strikers themselves were defeated.

American Blacks, especially in the South, was worse than it had been at any time since their emancipation more than 30 years earlier.

International Relations

In the last decade of the century, foreign affairs returned to the political agenda with a vengeance. No sooner had Secretary of State James G. Blaine picked up the threads of the Pan-American Conference proposed by Cleveland during his first term of office than an ugly dispute with Chile in 1891 threatened to unmake the newly-laid foundations of what was to become the Pan-American Union. War between the two countries was narrowly avoided after the United States allowed itself to become involved in a Chilean civil war, but the whole

1890

JAN 25 United Mine Workers formed by Knights of Labor and AFL at Columbus, Ohio

FEB 10 Eleven million acres of Sioux Indian territory in South Dakota opened for settlement

18 National American Women's Suffrage Association formed by American and National women's suffrage groups

MAR 27 In *Chicago, Milwaukee, and St Paul Railroad v. Minnesota*, Supreme Court rules that state cannot set fee so as to deny 'reasonable profit'

APR 28 In *Zeisy v. Harding*, Supreme Court rules unconstitutional state prohibition of sale of package liquor from other states

MAY Bank of America, Philadelphia, fails; causes other failures

2 Oklahoma Territory established by Congress

30 Cornerstone of Washington Memorial Arch in NYC designed by Stanford White, laid

JUN 29 Federal Elections Bill, or Force Bill, sponsored by Henry Cabot Lodge to guarantee black male suffrage in South

JUL 2 Sherman Antitrust Law, introduced into Senate by John Sherman of Ohio, passes

3 Idaho enters Union as 43rd State

10 Wyoming enters Union as first state to have women's suffrage

14 Sherman Silver Purchase Act requires government purchase of 4.5 million ounces of silver each month and issue of paper notes against it

AUG 8 New York Central and Hudson River Railroad strike called by Knights of Labor

8 Original Package Act supports state's right to subject merchandising of goods from another state to its own laws

30 Inspection by Department of Agriculture of pork to be exported provided by act of Congress

SEP 25 Yosemite National Park created by act of Congress

29 Forfeiture of unused land grants to railroads provided by act of Congress

OCT 1 McKinley Tariff Act raises tariffs to highest level ever; includes provision for reciprocity agreements

6 Mormon Church discontinues sanctioning of polygamy

NOV 1 Mississippi adopts new constitution requiring ability to read and understand US Constitution as prerequisite to vote

4 Democratic landslide in congressional elections for House give Democrats 235-88 majority

4 Democrat Benjamin R. Tillman elected Governor of South Carolina; Southern Alliance wins victory over Bourbon Democracy

29 First Army-Navy football game played at West Point, NY; Navy 24, Army 0

Emancipation? The poverty of this Black family bears witness to the all-out assault on Black civil rights that took place in the South during the 1890s.

affair did a lot of damage to Latin American relations. At the same time, a dispute with Great Britain over seal fishing rights in the Bering Sea also threatened to turn ugly, but a resort to arbitration finally hammered out a peaceful solution in February 1892.

However, another quarrel with Britain during the second half of the 1890s brought the two countries close to war. In 1895 America waded into a border dispute between Britain and Venezuela, brandishing an interpretation of the Monroe Doctrine which might well have surprised Monroe himself. When Britain sent troops to the disputed area, Secretary of State Richard Olney responded with a note to the British Prime Minister, Lord Salisbury, warning the Europeans not to interfere and proclaiming: "Today the United States is practically sovereign on this continent, and its fiat is law upon the subjects to which it confines its interposition." It was a direct challenge to Britain, and led to many calls for war throughout the United States. Ultimately however, wiser counsels prevailed,

not least because Britain had her hands full in South Africa at the time, and this dispute, too, was referred to arbitration in 1899.

Meanwhile, in 1893, the United States had become embroiled in a revolutionary uprising against the autocratic rule of Queen Liliuokalani in Hawaii. This messy affair, in which representatives of the substantial American interests in Hawaii orchestrated the overthrow of "Queen Lil" with the help of American marines, led to President Harrison's recommending the annexation of the island group to the U.S. Cleveland, who succeeded to the presidency before Congress had time to act on this recommendation, tried to reverse his predecessor's policy, but eventually gave up, leaving the rebel government in Honolulu to its own devices. Hawaii was finally annexed to the United States in 1898. But by that time America had become involved in an international confrontation which was to have far more significant consequences, not only for the nation itself, but for the whole world.

"A splendid little war"

In 1895 there was an uprising against Spanish rule in the island of Cuba. America had long regarded Cuba as part of her backyard, and the Government followed events there

very closely indeed as Spain sent the notorious Captain-General Weyler to put down the rebellion. Within months, the American press was full of accounts of Weyler's atrocities against the Cuban people, and public opinion began to clamor for the United States to support their independence struggle.

McKinley, newly elected to the presidency, held out for peace, but events would soon overtake him. On February 15, 1898, 260 American sailors were killed when the U.S.S. *Maine* hit a mine in Havana harbor. Many people held the Spanish responsible for the explosion. War fever swept the country. Congress immediately voted $50 million dollars for "emergency" defenses, and McKinley drafted a request for authority to intervene militarily in the Cuban situation. Spain backed down as far as she could, but that wasn't as far as granting independence to her island colony. The verdict of history is that war with Spain could still have been avoided if McKinley had stuck to his original intentions, but the verdict at the time was that Spain should withdraw from Cuba and recognize her independence; if not, America would step in. Congress issued the challenge in April. Spain's response was a declaration of war against the United States.

The fighting itself was short and sharp. Within days of the opening of hostilities, an American task force under Commodore Dewey descended on the Spanish colony of the Philippines and destroyed the Spanish fleet anchored in Manila harbor. By the end of May, an American squadron under Admiral Sampson had blockaded a second Spanish fleet in Santiago harbor on Cuba itself. In June, an American force (little more than a tenth the size of the 200,000-strong Spanish troop presence on the island) landed in Cuba, meeting no resistance. This army included such luminaries as the Confederate veteran, Joe Wheeler, and the former Assistant Secretary of the Navy, Theodore Roosevelt, but it was ill-equipped for a long action – the famous cavalry unit, the Rough Riders, had even left its horses behind in Florida! – and might well have been defeated if Spain had been better organized. But in July, the Spanish fleet decided to make a break for it and was destroyed as it sailed out of Santiago. The entire Spanish army in Cuba then surrendered and sued for peace. A preliminary treaty was signed in August, but before the news filtered out to America's other fighting units the Spanish island of Puerto Rico had also surrendered, and U.S. troops, accompanied by Filipino insurrectionists under Emilio Aguinaldo, had occupied Manila.

The last vestiges of Spain's imperial pride had crumbled, but America's empire was just beginning. John Hay, who had been appointed Secretary of State in 1898, wrote to Theodore Roosevelt, who would soon become President, that it had been "a splendid little war."

Theodore Roosevelt poses with his "Rough Riders" after taking San Juan Hill, Cuba, 1898.

"The taste of Empire"

The war against Spain, and the Treaty of Paris, which officially ended it in February 1899, brought America new problems as well as new possessions and new status. Under the terms of the treaty, Spain recognized Cuban independence, but she also ceded to the United States her former colonies of Puerto Rico, Guam, and, most significantly of all, the Philippines, for which America paid a nominal $20 million.

The price, however, included one fully-fledged rebellion. Aguinaldo's insurgents, having just torn down the Spanish flag, were not about to see it replaced with the Stars and Stripes, however high-mindedly McKinley might proclaim himself to be taking up the white man's burden. America now found itself fighting to put down an independence struggle in the Philippines, only months after fighting to prevent the Spanish from doing precisely that in Cuba. The ghastly irony of the situation was not lost on the American people. The country was split down the middle over America's new-found imperial status, with what the *Washington Post* described as "the taste of Empire" proving sweet to some and bitter as gall to others. Whether empire was compatible with the principles of the Declaration of Independence became the burning issue of the day. The imperial question would dominate the forthcoming presidential election, and would continue to hover over the achievements of the early years of the new century. But the reality of empire was already indisputable. The nation which had grown from the 13 rebellious colonies of the 18th century was entering the 20th century as a colonial power herself. It was a development which would have a profound effect on the rest of the world.

DEC 15 Sitting Bull, chief of Sioux Indians, killed in skirmish with US soldiers along Grand River in South Dakota

29 In Battle at Wounded Knee Creek, South Dakota, Sioux uprising against government agencies crushed by US troops

Also this year

★ 23,000 children employed in factories of 13 Southern states

★ Pyramiding of wealth leads to estimates that 1 percent of the people possess more wealth than the rest of the people combined

★ Two-step dance becomes fashionable

★ Daughters of the American Revolution founded

★ Louis H. Sullivan's Wainwright Building erected in St Louis

★ William James' *Principles of Psychology* published

1891

JAN American Sugar Refining Company, incorporated under NJ laws, takes over entire sugar trust

MAR 3 Circuit Court of Appeals established by Congress

3 Office of Superintendent of Immigration created by Congress

3 Forest Reserve Act authorizes withdrawal of public lands for national forest reserve

14 Mob in New Orleans lynches 11 Sicilian immigrants indicted for murder of Irish chief of police

APR 7 Eight-hour day law passed in Nebraska

4 Edwin Booth appears for last time in *Hamlet* at Brooklyn Academy of Music, NY

MAY 5 Carnegie Hall, NYC, opens with Tchaikovsky program conducted by composer himself

AUG 24 Thomas A. Edison patents Kinetoscope, motion picture camera

SEP 22 Nine hundred thousand acres of Sauk, Fox and Potawatomic Indian lands in Oklahoma opened for settlement by presidential proclamation

OCT 16 Mob in Valparaiso, Chile attacks American sailors from USS *Baltimore*; results in threat of war

NOV 3 William McKinly elected Governor of Ohio

DEC 29 Thomas A. Edison patents radio device for wireless telegraphy

Also this year

★ Whitcome L. Judson patents zipper

★ University of Chicago created with funds from John D. Rockefeller, Sr

★ Twenty-storey Masonic temple built in Chicago; highest building in US

★ Basketball invented by YMCA instructor James Naismith, in Springfield, Mass.

1892

JAN 1 Ellis Island in New York Bay replaces Castle Garden as immigration receiving station

MAR Standard Oil Trust dissolved by Supreme Court

APR 1 Strike called in Coeur D'Alene silver mines in Idaho

19 First American gas-powered automobile perfected by Charles and Frank Duryea in Springfield, Mass.

19 Three million acres of Cheyenne and Arappaho Indian lands in Oklahoma opened for settlement by presidential proclamation

MAY 5 Geary Chinese Exclusion Act requires registration of Chinese residents of US and extends existing laws for 10 years

JUN 3 Confederate President Jefferson Davis' birthday observed as official holiday in Florida

4 James G. Blaine resigns as Secretary of State

7-10 Republican Party National Convention nominates Benjamin Harrison for re-election and Whitelaw Reid of New York for Vice President

Wounded Knee

Dignified with the name of the Battle of Wounded Knee, the massacre of some 200 Dakota Sioux Indians, including women and children, by the U.S. Seventh Cavalry on December 29, 1890, marked the end of a crucial phase in Indian resistance. Prompted by the death during an attempted arrest of Chief Sitting Bull (seen, left, with "Buffalo" Bill Cody), Wounded Knee saw the death of the great Sioux chief Big Foot. Above: collecting the corpses.

Emily Dickinson

Emily Dickinson (1830–1886) (seen here in an 1848 daguerrotype) achieved posthumous fame with the publication of a collection of her poems in 1890.

"Queen Lil"

The redoubtable Queen Liliuokalani (1838–1917), who acceded to the throne of Hawaii in 1891, was destined to be her country's last monarch. American business interests in the islands, whose economy had long been almost entirely dependent on exports to the United States, became increasingly determined to annex Hawaii to the Union during the early part of the decade, and in 1893 the Queen was deposed in a coup backed by U.S. marines. President Harrison willingly presented a treaty of annexation to Congress, but Cleveland, who took over as President before it could be passed, concluded that the rebel government had come to power unlawfully. His attempts to negotiate a solution failed miserably, and Hawaii was annexed in 1898.

The World Columbian Exposition

Chicago became the scene of an opulent world fair in 1893 to celebrate the 400th anniversary of the discovery of America by Columbus. Thousands of visitors flocked to the windy city to visit the attractions of the World Columbian Exposition, including a huge artificial lake circled by neo-classical buildings (above).

21-23 Democratic National Convention nominates Grover Cleveland of New York for President and Adlai Ewing Stevenson of Illinois for Vice President

29-JUL 1 Prohibition Party National Convention nominates John Bidwell of California for President and James B. Cranfill of Texas for Vice President

JUL 1 Strike called against Andrew Carnegie's Homestead Mill, Pennsylvania, by Amalgamated Association of Iron and Steel Workers

4 First national convention of People's or Populist Party in Omaha, Nebr.

6 Clash between 5000 Homestead Steel workers and 300 Pinkerton detectives; 20 killed, hundreds wounded

9 Seven thousand Pennsylvania state troopers ordered to Homestead Works by Gov. Pattison

23 Congress bans sale of alcohol on Indian lands

23 Federal troops sent to Coeur d'Alene mines, Idaho, to force strikers back to work

AUG 28 Socialist Labor Party nominates Simon Wing of Massachusetts for President and Charles H. Matchet of New York for Vice President

OCT 5 Dalton gang nearly wiped out during robbery at Coffeyville, Kan.

15 One million eight hundred thousand acres of Crow Indian reservation opened to settlers

NOV 8 Grover Cleveland elected President, Adlai Stevenson elected Vice President

14 Workers end strike at Homestead Mill with no gain

Also this year

★ Lizzie Borden murder trial

★ General Electric Company formed by merger of Edison General Electric Company with Thomas-Houston Electric Company

1893

JAN 17 Revolution in Hawaii, engineered by US ambassador John L. Stevens and Sanford B. Dole, deposes Queen Liliuokalani

FEB 1 Construction of Black Maria film studio completed at Edison laboratories in West Orange, NJ

1 John L. Stevens declares provisional government of Hawaii a US protectorate and raises US flag over government buildings in Honolulu

15 Hawaiian annexation treaty submitted to Senate

20 Philadelphia and Reading Railroads relinquished to receivers with debts of over $125 million

MAR 1 Diplomatic Appropriation Act creates rank of ambassador

4 Grover Cleveland inaugurated for second term, Adlai Stevenson inaugurated Vice President

9 Hawaiian Annexation Treaty withdrawn from Senate by Pres. Cleveland

10 Fire in Boston kills many and causes $5 million in damage

APR 13 Commander J.H. Blount orders US troops out of Hawaii

15 Issue of gold certificates suspended by US Treasury

MAY 1-OCT 30 World's Columbian Exposition, in Chicago, commemorates 400th anniversary of 'discovery' of America

MAY 5 Securities fall dramatically on New York Stock Exchange

JUN 14 Flag Day observed in Philadelphia

20 American Railway Union formed by Eugene V. Debs

26 Gov. John P. Altgeld of Illinois pardons three of convicted anarchists imprisoned after Haymarket Square riot

27 New York stock market crashes; begins four years of depression

JUL 17 Pres. Cleveland sends J.H. Blount to investigate cause of Hawaiian revolution

AUG 1 National Bimetallic League formed in Chicago to fight for silver

13 Fire in Minneapolis causes $2 million in property damage and leaves 1500 homeless

Electricity

Many great advances in electrical technology – and especially those made by the indefatigable Thomas Edison in the 1870s – had found practical applications on a national scale by the 1890s. The possibilities for cheap large-scale illumination opened up by Edison's carbon filament lamp, first demonstrated in October 1879, had been quickly exploited by Edison himself, whose Pearl Street central power station in New York City (above) went operational in 1882. At the same time, Edison's quadruplex telegraph (1874) effectively doubled the capacity of telegraph wires by enabling two messages to be sent simultaneously in each direction along a single wire. By 1890 the Western Union Telegraph Company, America's leading electrical enterprise, was sending some 50 million messages a year along its 600,000 miles of wire and employed 600 operatives in its main operating room in New York (left). In 1892 a milestone was reached in the history of the American electricity industry when the Edison General Electric Company and George Westinghouse's Thomson-Houston Electric merged, under the tutelary spirit of J. P. Morgan, to form a new company called General Electric. As Joseph Wetzler, the editor of *Electrical Engineer*, wrote in 1891, "electricity is destined to ... bring forth changes in the social order which are even now hardly imagined."

Sweatshop Labor

The gap between rich and poor continued to widen during the 1890s. This photograph shows the sweatshop conditions in a pantmaker's workshop in the Lower East Side of New York City in 1891.

Bicycles and Automobiles

The decade saw a huge increase in the popularity of the bicycle as a mode of transport in America. At the same time, though, a new and far more revolutionary invention was making its first appearance in the United States. In 1892–1893 both Henry Ford of Detroit (below) and the Duryea Brothers of Springfield, Massachusetts, took to the road in their first "horseless carriages," soon to become known as automobiles.

24 Cyclone rips through Savannah, Ga, and Charleston, SC, killing 1000 people and causing severe damage

SEP 16 Cherokee strip between Kansas and Oklahoma opened to settlement

OCT 2 Cyclone kills 200 along Gulf Coast of Louisiana

NOV 1 Sherman Silver Purchase Act repealed

7 Women's suffrage adopted in Colorado

Also this year

★ Financial panic; 74 railroads fall into receivership, 600 banks close, 15,000 commercial houses collapse

★ Mormon Temple dedicated at Salt Lake City Utah; took 40 years to build; cost approximately $12 million

★ American University chartered in Washington, DC, under Methodist auspices

The Arts

★ Mary Cassatt's mural *Modern Women*

★ World premier of Antonin Dvorak's *New World Symphony* in NYC

1894

JAN 8 Fire at site of Chicago's Columbia Exposition destroys virtually all buildings

17 US Treasury offers $50 million bond issue to replenish gold reserve

30 Lexow Committee appointed by NY Senate to investigate NYC scandals, particularly in police department

FEB 8 Enforcement Act of 1871 repealed

MAR 17 Chinese Exclusion Treaty signed; China agrees to exclusion of Chinese laborers from US

APR 5 Riot of striking miners at Connellsville, Pa, leaves 11 dead

20 One hundred thirty six thousand coal miners strike at Columbia, Ohio

30 Coxey's Army of 400 marches from Ohio to Washington to protest unemployment

MAY 11 Strike called at Pullman Palace Car Company to protest wage reduction

31 Senate unanimously agrees that Hawaii should keep its own government and that interference will be considered hostile to US

JUN 21 Democratic Silver Convention held in Omaha, Nebr.; William Jennings Bryan leads convention to free silver coinage plank

26 General railroad strike called by American Railway Union to support Pullman strike

JUL 2 President Eugene V. Debs ordered by federal injunction not to interfere with interstate commerce and postal service

3 US troops sent to Chicago to enforce injuction

4 Republic of Hawaii proclaimed

6 Two strikers killed and several injured when fired upon by US troops in Kensington, Ill.

10 Eugene V. Debs indicted by Federal Grand Jury for failing to comply with injunction

AUG 3 Pullman strike broken

8 Hawaiian Republic officially recognized by US

18 Bureau of Immigration established by Congress

27 Wilson Gormon Tariff Act, including first graduated income tax law, passed without Pres. Cleveland's signature

SEP 1 Fire kills 500 people in Hinckley, Minn.

4 Garment workers' strike called by 12,000 tailors in NYC to protest sweatshops and piecework

NOV 13 US Treasury offers second $50 million bond issue of year

22 US and Japan sign commercial treaty in Washington

DEC 14 Eugene V. Debs sentenced to six months in prison

Also this year

★ Year of widespread labor unrest; 750,000 workers go on strike Southern Railroad Company organized by J.P. Morgan

The Railroads

The power of the railroad tycoons continued to grow in the last years of the 19th century despite the first Government-backed moves to contain their enormous influence. Such feats of engineering as the Dale Creek Bridge (seen above with a two-engined train crossing it) and the Niagara Falls Bridge between the United States and Canada (completed in 1897) carried the network still further afield, while sumptuous interiors such as the one shown in the inset brought something of the splendors of the Gilded Age to the business of travel, at least for those who could afford to take advantage of them.

The Closing of the Frontier?

The heyday of the Wild West may have ended, and the frontier been declared closed by the historian Frederick J. Turner in 1893, but the influence of the pioneering spirit continued to shape the life of hundreds of communities such as Dawson City near the Klondike goldfields.

Henry James

One of the greatest novelists of the age, Henry James (1843–1916) (above) lived for much of his life in Europe, finally becoming a naturalized British citizen in 1915. Many of his most powerful works, however, deal in part with the contrast between American and European society, both of which he viewed with critical detachment. The 1890s saw the publication of his novels *The Tragic Muse* (1890), *The Spoils of Poynton* and *What Maisie Knew* (both 1897), and *The Awkward Age* (1899) and his ghost story *The Turn of the Screw* (1898).

William Randolph Hearst

William Randolph Hearst, the heir to a mining fortune, bought the New York *Journal* in 1896, triggering a vicious circulation war with his arch-rival Joseph Pulitzer, editor of the New York *World*. Journalistic standards fell to new levels of sensationalism, especially in the two papers' treatment of the Spanish War.

JAN 21 In *United States v. E.C. Knight*, Supreme Court declares Sherman Antitrust Act applicable only to monopolies in interstate trade

FEB 8 Federal gold purchase of $62 million made by Treasury from banking houses of J.P. Morgan and August Belmont

27 Insurrection against Spanish rule in Cuba

MAR 18 Two hundred Black settlers depart for Liberia

20 In *Pollock v. Farmers' Loan and Trust Company*, Supreme Court declares income tax clause of Wilson-Gorman Tariff Act of 1894 unconstitutional

JUN 12 Pres. Cleveland calls for cooperation of citizens against giving aid to Cuban insurgents

JUL 4 'America the Beautiful' by Katherine Lee Bates published in *Congregationalist*

AUG 31 First professional football game played in Latrobe, Pa

NOV 5 George B. Selden patents gasoline-driven automobile

DEC 21 Venezuelan Boundary Commission authorized by Congress at request of President

Also this year

★ Hydro-electric generators put into operation at Niagara Falls, NY, by Westinghouse Electric Company

★ Tammany government in New York overthrown

1896

JAN 4 Utah enters Union as 45th state

6 Federal bond issue offered to public

FEB 10 Cuban revolt ruthlessly suppressed by Spanish Gen. Valeriano Weyler

MAR 20 US marines land at Corinto, Nicaragua, to protect US citizens at outbreak of revolution

APR 6 Congress favors granting belligerent status to Cuban revolutionaries and offers arbitration to Spain

6 First modern Olympic Games begin in Athens, Greece; US wins 9 of 12 events

23 First public showing of moving picture presented at Koster and Bial's Music Hall in NYC

MAY 6 Samuel P. Langley flies model airplane 300 feet, in first successful demonstration of flight

18 In *Plessy v. Ferguson*, Supreme Court declares Jim Crow Car Law of Louisiana constitutional; 'separate but equal doctrine'

22 Spain declines US offer of mediation in Cuba

27 Tornado kills 400, injures 120 and leaves 5000 homeless in St Louis, Mo. and East St Louis, Ill.

JUN 4 Henry Ford completes first Ford automobile

16 Republican National Convention nominates William McKinley of Ohio for President and Garret A. Hobart of New Jersey for Vice President

JUL 7-11 Democratic National Convention nominates William Jennings Bryan of Nebraska for President and Arthur Sewall of Maine for Vice President

22-24 National Silver Republic Convention nominates William J. Bryan for President and Arthur Sewall for Vice President

22 Populist Party National Convention nominates William J. Bryan for President and Thomas Watson for Vice President

AUG 12 Gold found in Klondike Creek near Alaska

NOV 3 William McKinley elected President, Garret A. Hobart elected Vice President

3 Idaho grants women's suffrage as amendment to state constitution

Also this year

★ First comic strip of 'The Yellow Kid' appears in New York *World*, inspires term 'yellow journalism'

The Arts

★ Sarah Orne Jewett's novel *The Country of the Pointed Firs*

The Philippine–American War

The end of the Spanish War left the United States embroiled in an ugly conflict with nationalist insurgents in the Philippines. The rebel leader Emilio Aguinaldo's guerrilla forces had fought alongside U.S. troops in the war against Spain to rid themselves of one imperial power. Now they turned against the new imperialism of the United States. The ensuing war was to drag on until 1902.

Above: An 1899 cartoon shows Uncle Sam bogged down in the quagmire of Philippine insurgency.

Left: The fighting in the Philippines claimed some 1000 U.S. and tens of thousands of Filipino lives.

Watching the News

Spreading the news in the pre-television age: crowds gather outside the Tribune Building in New York's Newspaper Row to see the latest news of events in the Spanish War chalked up on giant blackboards.

The United Mine-Workers of America

Prominent in the labor unrest of the 1890s was the United Mine-Workers of America, which became a formidable organization under the leadership of John Mitchell after 1898.

Calamity Jane

One of the most colorful characters of the Wild West, Martha Jane Cannary (1852–1903) (above), better known to history as "Calamity" Jane, served as nurse and Indian scout as well as hell-raiser. The photograph shows her in 1895.

The March King

In 1892 the American composer John Phillip Sousa (1854–1932) (above) organized a military band with which he toured extensively throughout the world, playing his own well-known marches and works by other composers. He also wrote operettas.

JAN 11 Olney-Pauncefort Convention, signed by US and Great Britain, provides for arbitration of territorial disputes between the two

FEB 2 Fire destroys Pennsylvania State Capital at Harrisburg

MAR 4 William McKinley inaugurated President, Garrett A. Hobart inaugurated Vice President

JUN 16 Treaty of Annexation signed by Secretary of State John Sherman and Hawaiian Government

19 Japan makes formal protest against annexation of Hawaii by US

JUL 2 Coal miners' strike in Pennsylvania, Ohio and West Virginia puts 75,000 people out of work

7 Dingley Tariff Bill raises tariffs to highest level yet

14 First shipment of Klondike gold, $750,000 arrives in San Francisco aboard *Excelsior*

SEP 11 Twenty striking miners killed when deputy sheriffs fire on them in Hazleton and Latimer, Pa

14 Hawaiian Republic ratifies annexation treaty

OCT 6 Moderate Premier Sagasta inaugurated in Madrid; soon recalls Gen. Weyler from Cuba

1898

FEB 9 Spanish Minister to US, Señor de Lame, forced to resign when embarrassing letter is published in Hearst's NY *Journal*

15 US battleship *Maine* explodes in Havana harbor

25 Assistant Secretary of the Navy Theodore Roosevelt secretly instructs Commodore George Dewey to be prepared to attack Spanish fleet in the Philippines

MAR 9 Congress appropriates $50 million 'for national defense and each and every purpose connected therewith'

27 US Minister to Spain demands armistice with Cuban rebels, revocation of order to place civilians in camps, US arbitration for peaceful settlement and Cuban relief

28 In *United States v. Wong Kim Ark.*, Supreme Court finds that US citizenship is without respect to race or color

APR 9 Gov. General of Cuba offers rebels armistice

19 Congress in joint resolution on Cuba, recognizes Cuban independence, demands that Spain evacuate island and authorizes President to use force if Spanish fail to comply

21 Spain severs diplomatic relations with US

22 Volunteer Army Act authorizes organization of First Volunteer Cavalry, or 'Rough Riders'

22 Blockade of Cuban ports by US Navy

22 US gunboat *Nashville* captures Spain's *Buena Ventura*

24 Spanish-American War begins when Spain declares war on US

25 War with Spain formally declared by Congress, as of April 21

MAY 1 In Battle of Manila Bay, Asiatic squadron of Commo. George Dewey destroys large Spanish fleet

12 San Juan, Puerto Rico, bombarded by US vessels

12 Louisiana adopts new constitution, allowing disfranchisement of Black citizens under property and literacy tests

JUN 1 Erdman Arbitration Act makes government mediation in railroad disputes legal and blacklists of union laborers illegal

10 Six hundred and forty-seven US Marines land at Guantanamo Bay, Cuba

13 War Revenue Act authorizes bond issue of $200 million, plus excise duties, taxes on tea, tobacco, liquor and legacies

15 Annexation of Hawaii approved in joint resolution adopted by House and Senate

20 Spanish island of Guam in the Pacific captured by Capt. Henry Glass

22 US forces land at Daiquiri, 15 miles from Santiago

24 In Battle of Las Guasimas, US troops under Gen. Joseph Wheeler and Cols. Leonard Wood and Theodore Roosevelt win first land battle of the war

Huddled Masses

The years between 1880 and 1910 saw a significant change in both the scale and nature of the immigration that had played so crucial a role in the development of American society ever since the first colonists arrived on the shores of the New World. Not only did immigration soar to an astonishing total of 18 million people during these 30 years; but also a far higher proportion of those people came from Southern and Eastern Europe than ever before, bringing with them an unprecedentedly broad mix of languages, religions, and cultures. The great majority of the "new" immigrants – Austrians, Hungarians, Poles, Italians, Russian Jews – settled in the cities, often creating distinctive ethnic neighborhoods as the Irish and the Chinese had done earlier in the century. An unprecedented opportunity for the cultural enrichment of the United States, the new immigration also posed enormous problems of assimilation and integration which have not been fully solved even today.

Below: Ellis Island, New York – the first glimpse of a new world for many immigrants to the U.S.

Top left: An immigrant family look towards the Statue of Liberty from Ellis Island.

Bottom left: New arrivals under the shelter of the Stars and Stripes in the Registration Room at Ellis Island.

Top right: Emigrés huddle together on the deck of the S.S. Westernland, *1890.*

Bottom right: Stepping toward a new life – waiting for the ferry from Ellis Island to New York.

JUL 1 US troops suffer heavy casualties in capture of El Caney and San Juan Heights

1 In Battle of San Juan Hill, US suffers heavy losses

3 In Naval Battle of Santiago, Adm. Cervera's Spanish fleet destroyed by US ships while attempting to leave Santiago Harbor

4 US flag raised on vacant Wake Island by US troops en route to the Philippines

7 Annexation of Hawaii Treaty signed by Pres. McKinley

8 Isla Grande, near Manila, occupied by US forces under Adm. Dewey

10 US troops under Gen. Shafter invade Santiago

17 Santiago surrenders, Gen. Shafter takes 24,000 prisoners

25 Puerto Rico invaded by US forces

26 Spain seeks peace terms through French ambassador

30 Pres. McKinley outlines peace terms to Spain: Cuba to be granted independence, Puerto Rico and an island in the Ladrones to be ceded to US and Manila to be occupied by US, pending peace negotiations

AUG 12 Peace protocol with Spain signed

13 Manila surrenders to Gen. Wesley Merritt and Adm. Dewey

OCT 1 Peace negotiations with Spain begin in Paris

NOV 12 Strikers' riot at Virden, Ill., leaves 13 dead and 25 wounded

DEC 10 Treaty of Paris signed by US and Spain formally ends war; Spain abandons claim to Cuba, cedes the Philippines for $420 million and cedes Puerto Rico and Guam as indemnity

Also this year

★ Competition between William Randolph Hearst's New York *Journal* and Joseph Pulitzer's New York *World* in exploitation of Cuban affair fuels war with Spain

1899

FEB 4 Philippine revolt under Emilio Aguinaldo in Manila; lasts for several days

14 Congress approves use of voting machines for federal elections at discretion of individual states

MAR 2 Congress authorizes addition of 65,000 men to Army and requests 35,000 volunteers to suppress rebellion in Philippines

APR 27 Tornado kills 70 and injures over 100 in northern Missouri

28 Peace terms requested by Filipinos; request rejected by Gen. E.S. Otis

MAY 18 First Hague Peace Conference opens; Permanent Court of International Arbitration established

JUL 1 Gideons organized by commercial travelers belonging to Christian Commercial Men's Association of America

19 Secretary of War Russel A. Algen resigns under criticism for Spanish-American War

SEP 6 Secretary of State John Hay requests that countries having commerce, treaties and long-term leases with China maintain 'open door' policy

NOV 21 Vice Pres. Garret A. Hobart dies

24 US control of central Luzon in the Philippines reported to Washington, DC

DEC 2 Samoan Partition Treaty, signed by US, Germany and Great Britain, partitions Samoan Islands between US and Germany

4 In *Addyston Pipe and Steel Co. v. United States*, Supreme Court declares that agreement between corporations to remove competition is violation of Antitrust Law

Also this year

★ United Fruit Company organized

★ Thorstein Veblin's *The Theory of the Leisure Class* published

The Arts

★ Scott Joplin's song 'Maple Leaf Rag'

THE UNITED STATES of America entered the 20th century as a world power of the first rank. The War with Spain had brought her some significant overseas possessions, and with the assassination of William McKinley in 1901 she gained in Theodore Roosevelt a President determined to establish his country's presence as a major force on the international stage. Roosevelt's own presence towers over the formative years of the 20th century, and America's foreign policy during this time reflects his energetic and idiosyncratic personality, whether in the "big stick" of his dealings with Britain, Germany, and Colombia, or the "soft speaking" which brought him the Nobel Peace Prize in 1906.

At home, the first decade of the new century was a time of ferment as the growing progressive movement, spurred on by the investigative journalism of the so-called "muckrakers," sought to tackle the abuses of power and privilege which were increasingly seen to riddle American public life. It was a movement which found its most influential supporter in Roosevelt himself, but throughout the country, at state and municipal level, vigorous local reformers set about the task of weeding out corruption and remolding the machinery of power. These were the years in which the Federal Government not only took its first significant stand against the great corporations in the United States, but also recognized the role it had to play in conserving the nation's vital natural resources. But they were also years in which the division between progressivism and conservatism within the Republican Party began to widen into an unbridgeable gulf – a gulf through which the Democrats would, in the following decade, sail back into power on the trade winds of the New Freedom.

America on the Threshold of the 20th Century

During the course of the 19th century the United States had changed almost beyond recognition. From a federation of 16 states and some five million people, by 1900 she had grown to a nation of 76 million people, and only the states of Oklahoma, New Mexico, Arizona, Alaska, and Hawaii remained to be added to the Union. In addition to her home population, she could boast an overseas empire of nine million people, the majority of them in the newly (and controversially) acquired Philippines. She was also in the grip of what has been described as the largest voluntary movement of people in recorded history: between 1865 and 1940 a staggering total of 33 million immigrants found their way to the shores of the United States. The first decade of the new century saw the high water mark of this extraordinary flood, with more than one million people entering the country every year from 1905 to 1907, especially from the countries of southern and eastern Europe.

But for all its lure as a land of opportunity, America was a divided nation too. The last years of the 19th century had witnessed industrial disputes of unprecedented bitterness, and the first years of the 20th would see the growth, not only of labor organizations such as Samuel Gompers' American Federation of Labor, but also of a fully-fledged socialist movement in the United States. In many areas of life, the power of big business still threatened to undermine the democratic foundations of the U.S. Constitution, and the gap between rich and poor remained conspicuously wide. Racially, too, the country was more divided than at any time since the emancipation of the slaves, with most Afro-Americans living segregated from their white fellow citizens and effectively disfranchised by a conspiracy of state regulations, Federal apathy, and naked intimidation (more than 1000 Blacks were lynched during the first decade of the 20th century alone). Meanwhile, the Black civil rights movement itself was split, with more militant voices beginning to be raised against the moderate reformism of Booker T. Washington and his supporters. The plight of the native Indian population of America was no less dire. Systematically robbed and cheated of their tribal lands and crowded onto remote reservations, their numbers had dwindled to little more than 200,000 by the beginning of the century.

The Problems of Empire

American foreign affairs during these years were dominated by the aftermath of the War with Spain. Under the terms of the Treaty of Paris, the United States had acquired a number of overseas possessions, including Puerto Rico and the Philippines. She had also established an ongoing interest in the future of Cuba, under the terms of an amendment to the Cuban Constitution which gave her the right to intervene in order to maintain an effective independent government in the island. (The Cubans were deemed capable of self-government by 1902 and American troops duly withdrew. When the internal situation deteriorated in 1905, however, America promptly exercised her right to intervene and established a military governorship on the island, only withdrawing again in 1909.)

In 1900 many Americans must have questioned whether the spoils of empire were worth the pain. Not only had the United States inherited a substantial rebellion in the Philippines – a rebellion which was only crushed in 1902 after a long and ugly guerrilla war – there was also an influential body of opinion at home which claimed that imperialism and republicanism were fundamentally incompatible. Rule over colonial subjects brought about unprecedented constitutional difficulties. For example, if the Constitution followed the flag, should every citizen of the Philippines have the right to vote in the United States? And if not, what was the difference between the position of a Filipino under American rule in 1902 and that of an American under British rule in 1775?

In other words, could a democratic republic really expect duties of allegiance from its overseas dependents without giving them full rights of citizenship in return? For the time being, in both Puerto Rico and the Philippines, the answer seemed to be "Yes." The Foraker Act of 1900 gave Puerto Rico a kind of intermediate status between that of a state and that of a territory; while in the Philippines, although military rule and absolute presidential dictatorship had given way to an elected assembly by 1907, ultimate sovereignty remained with Congress, and the islands had to wait until 1946 to achieve full independence.

Theodore Roosevelt

When Theodore Roosevelt was elected Vice President for McKinley's second term of office in 1900, the Republican boss Mark Hanna is reputed to have complained that now only one life stood between "this madman" and the White House. In 1901 that life was cut cruelly short when McKinley became the third U.S. President to die at the hands of an assassin, shot by a Polish-born anarchist at the Pan-American Exposition in Buffalo, New York, on September 6.

At 43, Roosevelt was the youngest man to become President of the United States. However, despite his relative youth, he already had a colorful and varied career behind him. The son of wealthy parents, he had spent time as a rancher in North Dakota after graduating from Harvard, and had served on the Civil Service Commission and as president of the Police Board of New York City before being appointed Assistant Secretary of the Navy by President McKinley. Resigning from this post to join the famous Rough Riders in their Cuban campaign, he returned from the war, covered in glory, to become the Governor of New York. A man of wide-ranging interests and enormous energy, he was to become the personification of the new progressive spirit of early 20th-century America.

Progressivism personified: Theodore Roosevelt (1858–1919), 21st President.

1900

FEB 6 Theodore Roosevelt announces that he will not accept nomination for the vice presidency

MAR *The Smart Set*, literary monthly, first published by William D'Alton Mann

5 Hall of Fame founded in NYC

6 Social Democratic Party National Convention nominates Eugene V. Debs for President and Job Harrison of California for Vice President

14 Gold Standard Act establishes gold dollar of 25.8 grains, nine tenths fine, and puts all forms of US money on parity with it

24 New Carnegie Steel Company incorporated in New Jersey

APR 12 Forakee Act makes Puerto Rico unconsolidated territory of US

30 Hawaii granted territorial status by act of Congress

30 Railroad engineer John Luther 'Casey' Jones dies at throttle of crashing *Cannonball* express

MAY Boxer rebellion breaks out in China

1 Mine explosion at Scofield, Utah, leaves over 200 dead

10 Populist Party National Convention nominates William J. Bryan for President and Charles A. Toun of Massachusetts for Vice President; splinter group holds separate convention

14 In *Knowlton v. Moore*, Supreme Court declares inheritance tax constitutional

14 Carrie Nation leads women through Kansas to damage and destroy saloons and liquor-selling establishments

JUN 2-8 Socialist Labor Party Convention

19-21 Republican National Convention nominates William McKinley for second term and Theodore Roosevelt of New York for Vice President

20 US and other foreign legations besieged in British embassy in Peking, China, by Boxers

27-28 Prohibition Party National Convention

JUL 4-6 Democratic National Convention nominates William J. Bryan for President and Adlai E. Stevenson of Illinois for Vice President

Leon Czolgosz, a Polish-born anarchist, shoots President McKinley.

Muckrakers and Progressives

Progressivism was more a trend of thought than an organized movement. Progressive ideas found expression at every level of American life, from the cities to the White House, and although those who saw themselves as progressives disagreed on many points of detail, they all had in common the desire to reform American social, political, and economic institutions to meet the challenges of a new and radically different age.

During the opening years of the new century, progressivism was given a healthy push in the right direction by the activities of the so-called "muckrakers," a group of journalists and writers who dedicated themselves to uncovering abuses and corruption wherever they found them. Investigative exposés such as Lincoln Steffens' *Shame of the Cities* articles in the influential *McClure's Magazine*, Ida M. Tarbell's *History of the Standard Oil Company*, and David Graham Phillip's *The Treason of the Senate* aroused public outrage and increased the volume of demands for reform. Books such

as Upton Sinclair's *The Jungle*, which exposed appalling conditions in the meat trade, also contributed to the growing national restlessness for change.

In the cities, such tireless reformers as Samuel M. Jones of Toledo, Ohio, and Tom L. Johnson of Cleveland, Ohio, mounted campaigns to root out corruption and undue influence in municipal life, while at state level such independent spirits as Robert M. LaFollette of Wisconsin and William S. U'Ren of Oregon set about curbing the power of the party "bosses" and introducing direct primaries for the election of U.S. senators. Votes for women became another important plank of many progressive platforms, as did the cause of labor reform. After years of malaise, America seemed finally to be getting to grips with the myriad problems spawned by her industrial success.

Trustbusting and Conservation

Roosevelt, a man of peculiarly sensitive political antennae, rode the wave of progressivism so sure-footedly as to appear to be leading the movement at national level. In the process he succeeded in antagonizing conservatives in his own party and elsewhere by what were seen as his attacks on

Conditions in the meat trade, exposed by Upton Sinclair's influential novel The Jungle, *were one of many targets of the muckrakers in the early years of the new century. Here workmen cut and dress beef at a meat-packing plant in Chicago.*

big business and by his forward-looking defense of the country's fast-dwindling natural resources.

Public fears about the excessive influence of the big corporations had been given added impetus by J. Pierpoint Morgan's creation of the giant U.S. Steel Corporation from Andrew Carnegie's company and a number of other iron and steel concerns in 1901. Such fears had been around for a long time, and legislation had already been passed to answer them. The Sherman Act of 1890, for example, had been designed to curtail monopolies by placing legal limits on restraint of trade, but in practice it had mainly been used to break strikes and boycotts by organized labor. Not until Roosevelt did the Federal Government make a concerted attempt to control the great magnates and their companies.

In 1902, the year after he took office, the new President moved against the Northern Securities Company, a giant holding company organized by J.P. Morgan and the railway tycoons James J. Hill and Edward H. Harriman, on the grounds that it would monopolize the entire Northwestern transport system. The action succeeded and Roosevelt found himself both praised and reviled as a "trustbuster." Other such actions followed, including those against the Beef Trust, the Standard Oil Company, and the American Tobacco Company, and his second term of office also saw moves to give real teeth to the Interstate Commerce Act of 1887 which sought to regulate freight charges on the railroads. In labor affairs, too, Roosevelt showed himself to be no conservative in the Grover Cleveland mold. He supervised the establishment of a new Department of Commerce and Labor, and his intervention in the potentially disastrous United Mine Workers' strike of 1902 was sensitive and even-handed.

One of the most important progressive legacies of Roosevelt's years in the White House was a program of conservation measures designed to safeguard U.S. land and resources against the depredations of agriculture and industry. In Jefferson's day the continent had seemed almost boundless, inexhaustible in its productive potential. But a century of unprecedented growth had demonstrated that its resources were far from infinite, and that regulation and planning were essential if the needs of future generations of Americans were to be successfully met. The new President used existing legislation to withdraw hundreds of millions of acres from public sale for the protection of forestland, and launched a major program for the construction of dams, waterways, and irrigation projects. It was a foresightful policy which pitted the interests of the nation as a whole against the vested interests of particular groups. The enthusiastic response to Roosevelt's call for a Conservation Conference in 1908 showed the extent to which it had captured the imagination of the American people.

The Big Stick

Roosevelt's famous proverb – "Speak softly and carry a big stick" – did indeed seem to be the guiding principle of America's foreign policy during the years in which he occupied the White House. In his first term, the big stick was perhaps more evident than the soft talking, but in his second, after the electorate had returned him with the biggest popular majority given to any U.S. president up to that time, a more emollient note crept into his pronouncements about America's role on the world stage. The United States had shown that it could flex its muscles. Now it showed that it could act the part of peacemaker too.

Great Britain, Germany, and, most dramatically, Colombia, felt the big stick of Roosevelt's diplomacy in the opening years of the century. The new President felt strong enough to bully the British Government into a favorable settlement of the long-running Alaskan border dispute, and to threaten the use of force against Kaiser Wilhelm II when Germany attacked Venezuelan coastal fortifications during a quarrel over debt repayments in 1903. Another debt default, this time in the Dominican Republic, prompted the so-called Roosevelt Corollary to the Monroe Doctrine in 1904, in which Roosevelt announced that Monroe's much-quoted dictum actually forbade any

European use of force in the hemisphere and that the United States had sole right to intervene when countries in that hemisphere failed to live up to their financial responsibilities. The fact that there was no European outcry at this extraordinary extension of American jurisdiction indicated how clearly the Old World now recognized the need to remain on good terms with her giant New World neighbor.

Perhaps the most controversial application of the big stick came with America's intervention in the affairs of the Colombian province of Panama in 1903. Since the end of the War with Spain, negotiations had been taking place on a number of fronts towards the building of a canal in Central America to join the Pacific and Atlantic Oceans. Roosevelt's favored route for the canal ran across the isthmus of Panama, but when the Colombian Government proved obstructive to his attempts to lease the land for it, the U.S. lent its tacit support – backed up by a strategically placed warship – to a Panamanian revolution. As Roosevelt later put it, "I took the Canal Zone and let Congress debate." Work on the canal itself began in 1907, and the first ship sailed along it at the beginning of 1914. The big stick had beaten out one of the major trade routes of the modern world.

Speaking More Softly

The Russo-Japanese War of 1904–1905 gave Roosevelt the opportunity to prove his credentials as a mediator. The war resulted from Japan's attempt to prevent Russia from establishing a hold over Korea and Manchuria, which were the objects of its own imperial ambitions. Japan achieved military domination and bankruptcy at more or less the same time, and called on the United States to intervene to negotiate a solution. Roosevelt responded with a demand that Japan recognize America's Open Door policy in China, and, with that precondition accepted, convened a Russo-Japanese peace conference at Portsmouth, New Hampshire. America's involvement not only won Roosevelt himself the Nobel Peace Prize but also began a period of wary mutual respect between Japan and the United States. For example, the President was quick to avert the danger of deteriorating relations when California passed state laws imposing educational segregation on the children of Oriental immigrants. But he was also eager to show that America was no soft touch. In 1908, in a spectacular flourish of military strength, he sent the U.S. Navy on a 46,000-mile trip around the world. What might have been seen as a wantonly provocative gesture was received cordially by the Japanese when the fleet turned up in Tokyo Bay, and helped lay the foundations for an important agreement between the two countries.

Roosevelt had another chance to exercise his mediatory skills in the Moroccan crisis, which brought Europe to the verge of war in 1905. When France refused to accede to German demands for an international conference to arbitrate on Morocco, where French expansion appeared to threaten

One product of the "big stick": The massive Gatun locks under construction during the building of the Panama Canal.

German interests, the Kaiser appealed to America to support the German case. Roosevelt reluctantly did so, and the French were forced to come to the negotiating table at Algeciras in Spain. The negotiations, at which the U.S. was present, failed to halt French expansion in Morocco, and aroused controversy at home, where many felt that Roosevelt was involving himself unnecessarily in purely European affairs. It was an involvement that was to be tragically heightened in the course of the next decade: in the perspective of history, the Moroccan crisis can be seen as a clear step on the road to the First World War.

William Howard Taft

Theodore Roosevelt's prestige on leaving office was such that, like Andrew Jackson before him, he was able to name his own successor for his party's nomination. The man he chose – before setting off for Africa on a big game-hunting tour – was the former Secretary of War, William Howard Taft. A hugely corpulent and good-natured man, Taft's training as a lawyer had imbued him with a caution altogether alien to the Roosevelt way of doing things, and the joys of success in the 1908 presidential election were soon to evaporate in the intense heat of Republican party strife which characterized his presidency. Within months of his inauguration the new President was embroiled in a bitter Congressional battle over the revision of the Dingley Tariff Act of 1897. His stock with the progressives in the Re-

publican Party – now becoming known, ominously, as "insurgents" – was further damaged by his apparent failure to commit his administration to a continuation of Roosevelt's conservation policies, and by the end of the decade he found himself presiding over a fully-fledged split in the party ranks, with the insurgents casting him as the friend of the conservative Old Guard. With Roosevelt watching from a distance as his work seemed about to be unraveled, the stage was already arranging itself for the bitter factional conflicts of the next decade.

William Howard Taft (1857–1930) – facing a split in the ranks of the G.O.P.

AUG 14 US, British, French and Japanese troops rescue legations in Peking

SEP Dr Walter Reed of US Army medical Corps, researching source of yellow fever in Cuba, discovers that it is transmitted by mosquitoes; disease eradicated from Cuba by 1901

8 Hurricane kills 6000 at Galveston, Tex.

OCT 15 Symphony Hall in Boston opens

NOV 3 First automobile show opens in Madison Square Garden, NYC

6 William McKinley wins election for second term, Theodore Roosevelt of New York elected Vice President

DEC 26 State Department negotiations for purchase of Virgin Islands (Danish West Indies) completed

Also this year

★ Wilbur and Orville Wright build first full-scale glider

★ Eastman Kodak introduces Brownie Box Camera

★ First quantity production automobile factory established by Olds Company in Detroit, Mich.

★ International Ladies' Garment Workers Union established

The Arts

★ Jack London's story collection *The Son of the Wolf*

★ L. Frank Baum's book *The Wonderful Wizard of Oz*

★ Theodore Dreiser's novel *Sister Carrie*

★ Albert Pinkham Ryder's painting *Toilers on the Sea*

1901

JAN 10 Spindletop claim near Beaumont, Tex. brings in oil

FEB 2 US Army Dental Corps established by Congress

2 Army Nurse Corps organized as branch of US Army

21 Cuba adopts constitution patterned after US Constitution

25 US Steel Corporation, formed by John Pierpont Morgan, incorporated in New Jersey

MAR 2 Army Appropriations Act, which includes Platt Amendment establishing protectorate over Cuba and Spooner Amendment establishing temporary civil government in Philippines, passed

3 National Bureau of Standards established by Congress

4 William McKinley inaugurated for second term, Theodore Roosevelt inaugurated Vice President

13 Death of 23rd President of US Benjamin Harrison

23 Philippine guerilla leader Emilio Aguinaldo captured by US forces in Luzon

APR 19 Philippine rebellion ends by proclamation

MAY 3 Fire in Jacksonville, Fla, leaves 10,000 homeless

9 Wall Street panic caused by conflict between Hill-Morgan group and Harriman, Kuhn, Loeb and Company over control of Great Northern and Northern Pacific railroad lines

27 Insular Cases involve applicability of US customs laws to Puerto Rico

JUL 4 William H. Taft becomes Civil Governor of Philippines

25 Free trade between Puerto Rico and US proclaimed by Pres. McKinley

SEP 6 Pres. McKinley shot by anarchist Leon Czolgosz while attending reception for Pan-American Exhibition in Buffalo

7 Boxer indemnity agreement pays US $25 million

14 Pres. McKinley dies; Theodore Roosevelt becomes President

OCT 16 Pres. Roosevelt entertains Booker T. Washington at White House; results in violence against Blacks in South

NOV 13 Northern Securities Company incorporated in New Jersey; monopolizes railroads between Great Lakes and Pacific Coast

18 Hay-Pauncefort Treaty with Great Britain authorizes US to build, operate and fortify canal across Central American Isthmus

The San Francisco Earthquake

One of the worst natural disasters ever to strike the United States engulfed the West Coast in the early hours of the morning of April 18, 1906, when a series of earthquakes devastated the city of San Francisco and its surrounding area. The catastrophe, which resulted from unusual seismic activity along the San Andreas fault, destroyed some 3000 acres in the heart of San Francisco itself. Highways were buckled by the tremors, entire blocks of buildings collapsed like cards, and water, gas, and electricity lines were severed.

Still further damage was caused by the ensuing fire, which raged out of control for three days, sweeping through the city's business and industrial districts and reducing whole areas to a mass of tangled, smoking ruins. With rescue operations hampered by the flames, and with parks and high ground crowded with terrified refugees, the city was placed under martial law, looters being shot in the streets. It is estimated that as many as 1000 people may have lost their lives in the disaster and many thousands more were made homeless. In addition to the cost in human misery, the material damage caused by the earthquake has been assessed at more than $200 million.

Below: The aftermath: shocked citizens wander among the shattered streets of San Francisco.

Below inset: This proclamation issued by the Mayor of San Francisco imposes a curfew and threatens anyone found looting with death.

Top: A temporary business establishment in front of the monument set up by the Native Sons of the Golden West on the present site of Golden Gate Park, S.F.

Middle left: Survivors survey the scene of devastation from high ground overlooking the city.

Middle right: The shape of things to come: a steel framed structure, incomplete at the time of the disaster, survives the earthquake intact.

Bottom: Putting a brave face on it: life goes on among the ruins.

PROCLAMATION
BY THE MAYOR

The Federal Troops, the members of the Regular Police Force and all Special Police Officers have been authorized by me to KILL any and all persons found engaged in Looting or in the Commission of Any Other Crime.

I have directed all the Gas and Electric Lighting Co.'s not to turn on Gas or Electricity until I order them to do so. You may therefore expect the city to remain in darkness for an indefinite time.

I request all citizens to remain at home from darkness until daylight every night until order is restored.

I WARN all Citizens of the danger of fire from Damaged or Destroyed Chimneys, Broken or Leaking Gas Pipes or Fixtures, or any like cause.

E. E. SCHMITZ, Mayor

Dated, April 18, 1906.

28 Alabama adopts new constitution, disenfranchising Blacks through literacy and property tests and 'grandfather' clause

DEC 3 Pres. Roosevelt in first annual message to Congress recommends regulation of trusts and corporations

The Arts

★ Frank Norris' novel *The Octopus*

★ Upton Sinclair's novel *Springtime and Harvest*

★ Porter Steele's song 'High Society'

★ *New York in a Blizzard*, panoramic film by Edison Studio

1902

JAN 1 First Tournament of Roses Association football game held at Pasadena, Calif.

18 Isthmian Commission recommends to the President adoption of Panama rather than Nicaragua route

24 Treaty with Denmark signed for purchase of Virgin Islands (Danish West Indies); Danish parliament rejects

FEB Discovery of hookworm in South announced by Dr Charles Wardell Stiles

MAR 6 Bureau of the Census created by Congress

10 Attorney General initiates suit against Northern Securities Company under Sherman Antitrust Act

MAY 12 Coal miners' strike idles 140,000 after UMW President John Mitchell's suggestion of arbitration refused by mine operators

20 US withdraws from Cuba; first President installed

JUN 2 Oregon adopts constitutional amendment providing for initiative and referendum

17 Newland Reclamation Act authorizes construction of irrigation dams across West

28 Isthmian Canal Act authorizes the President to negotiate to purchase rights from France for canal construction

JUL 1 Philippine Government Act authorizes commission to govern islands and declares inhabitants to be citizens of archipelago

AUG 11 Oliver Wendell Holmes named Associate Justice of Supreme Court

12 International Harvest Company incorporated in New Jersey

19 Pres. Roosevelt begins speaking tour of New England and Midwest

SEP 15 US and Mexico become first countries to use Permanent Court of Arbitration at the Hague, to settle back payment of interest

OCT 21 UMW President John Mitchell declares end of coal strike

Also this year

★ Maryland adopts first workmen's compensation law

★ Rhodes Scholarships for study at Oxford established by will of Cecil Rhodes

★ Carnegie Institution of Washington founded

★ Flatiron Building, designed by Daniel Burnham, completed in New York

★ *McClure's* begins publication of Ida M. Tarbell's *History of the Standard Oil Company* and Lincoln Steffens' articles on municipal corruption

★ Helen Keller's *The Story of My Life* published

The Arts

★ George Barr McCuthean's novel *Brewster's Millions*

★ Henry James' novel *The Wings of the Dove*

★ Jack London's novel *A Daughter of the Snows*

★ Owen Wister's novel *The Virginian*

Keeping the Door Open   In 1900 America's so-called Open Door policy in China was threatened by the upsurge of anti-foreign feeling known as the Boxer Rebellion. A number of foreigners were besieged by the Boxers in the British Legation in Peking, until they were relieved in August by an international force of some 19,000 troops, 5000 of them American. Above: U.S. troops march into the Temple of Agriculture, Peking.

A Flying Start   On December 17, 1903, Kitty Hawk, North Carolina, entered history as the scene of man's first successful flight in a heavier-than-air machine. The feat was achieved by the brothers Orville and Wilbur Wright of Dayton, Ohio, in a 605lb plane called "Flyer" (above). The brothers made four flights, the first, by Orville, lasting 12 seconds and covering 120 feet, and the fourth, by Wilbur, lasting 59 seconds and covering 852 feet.

The Pan-American Exposition

Pan-Americanism was high on the political agenda in the early years of the new century. However, the Pan-American Exposition, held at Buffalo, New York, in 1901, is now chiefly remembered as the scene of President McKinley's assassination.

J. P. Morgan (1837–1913)

The most powerful financier in the United States, John Pierpoint Morgan was seen by many as the living symbol of American capitalism. In 1901 his House of Morgan played a central role in the creation of the giant U.S. Steel Corporation.

An Untidy Desk . . .

A New York stockbroker, apparently besieged by bric-à-brac, examines tickertape in his office.

JAN 22 Hay-Herran Treaty, signed with Colombia, provides for 100-year lease on 10-mile-wide strip across Isthmus of Panama for construction of canal

24 Joint Commission established by Great Britain and US to report on Alaskan boundary dispute

FEB 11 Expedition Act gives priority to antitrust cases

14 Department of Commerce and Labor established by Congress

14 General Staff of the Army established by Congress

19 Elkins Act curbs railroad rebates

23 In *Champion v. Ames*, Supreme Court declares that federal police power supersedes state police power

MAR 22 Anthracite Coal Commission recommends shorter hours, 10 percent wage increase and 'open shop'

MAY 23 Wisconsin is first state to adopt direct primary elections

JUL 4 First Pacific communications cable opened between San Francisco and Manila

OCT 1-13 First baseball World Series; Boston Red Sox defeat Pittsburgh Pirates

20 Alaskan Boundary Commission reports in favor of US

NOV 2 Pres. Roosevelt orders US Navy to prevent Colombia from landing troops in Panamanian province, to guarantee success of Panamanian Revolution

3 Revolt of Panama against Colombia occurs at 6 p.m.; US Navy prevents Colombians from reaching Panama

4 Panamanian independence declared

6 Secretary Hay recognizes new Panamanian government

18 Hay-Buneau-Varilla treaty, signed with Panama, gives US rights to 10-mile-wide strip of land

DEC 17 Orville and Wilbur Wright make first four successful airplane flights, at Kitty Hawk, NC

30 Fire at Iroquois Theater in Chicago kills 588; leads to new theater codes

Also this year

★ Pelican Island near east coast of Florida becomes first federal wildlife refuge

★ Ford Motor Company formed by Henry Ford

★ National Women's Trade Union League organized

★ University of Puerto Rico at Rio Pedras, PR, chartered

The Arts

★ Jack London's novel *The Call of the Wild*

★ Kate Douglas Wiggin's novel *Rebecca of Sunnybrook Farm*

★ Victor Herbert's operetta *Babes in Toyland*

★ Max Aaronson in the film *The Great Train Robbery*

★ First film exchange in US established by Harry and Herbert Miles

1904

JAN 4 In *Gonzales v. Williams*, Supreme Court rules that Puerto Ricans are not aliens and may not be refused admission to continental US

7-8 Fire in Baltimore, Md, destroys 2600 buildings

FEB 10 Russo-Japanese War begins

11 Morton Street Tunnel links New York and New Jersey

MAR 14 In *Northern Securities Company v. US*, Supreme Court finds that the company violates Sherman Antitrust Act and orders its dissolution

MAY 5 Socialist National Convention nominates Eugene v. Debs of Indiana for President and Benjamin Hanford of New York for Vice President

14 First Olympic Games held in US open as part of St Louis Exposition in Missouri

23 North European steamship companies cut steerage rates to $10 to entice immigrants

JUN 21-23 Republican National Convention nominates Theodore Roosevelt for President and Charles W. Fairbanks of Indiana for Vice President

29-30 Prohibition Party National Convention

The Ford Motor Company

A turning point in the short history of the motor car was reached in the United States in 1903 with the formation of the Ford Motor Company. The same year, Henry Ford produced his first Model A, which was capable of 30 m.p.h. The Model T, nicknamed the "Tin Lizzie," followed in 1908, at a price of $850. Ford's factories pioneered the assembly line as a production technique, which soon enabled cars to be manufactured at prices within reach of the average pocket.

Left: The joys of motoring: this advertisement from England testifies to the international success of Ford's vehicles.

Below: Model Ts lined up outside a Ford sales office in Topeka, Kansas.

Bottom: A new freedom for the leisured classes: an auto picnic in the Hudson highlands, 1905.

Ford
THE UNIVERSAL CAR
SELLING AGENTS EVERYWHERE.

£135 COMPLETE.
AT WORKS MANCHESTER.

"ALL THE WORLD LOVES A — FORD — EVEN THE MOON BEAMS —"

Good Time Girls

The original Ziegfeld Follies wield tambourines and canes in one of the most popular numbers from their famous stage act.

Madam Butterfly

1906 saw the New York première of Giacomo Puccini's opera *Madam Butterfly*. A tragic love story, it was an enormous success. Fêted in the United States, Puccini returned in triumph in 1910 for the première of *The Girl of the Golden West*.

Cutting a Record

By the beginning of the century the phonograph, invented by Edison as a dictating machine in 1877, was widely used for recording music. The picture shows a band recording around 1900.

JUL 2-8 Socialist Labor Party National Convention

4-5 Populist Party National Convention

6-9 Democratic National Convention nominates Alton B. Parker for President and Henry G. Davis of West Virginia for Vice President

25 Strike of 25,000 textile workers for higher wages begins in Fall River, Mass.

OCT 19 American Tobacco Company formed

27 First part of NYC subway opened

NOV 8 Theodore Roosevelt elected President, Charles W. Fairbanks elected Vice President

DEC 6 Roosevelt Corollary to Monroe Doctrine, specifying that US may exercise 'international police power,' articulated for first time by the President, in annual message to Congress

10 Bethlehem Steel Corporation founded in New Jersey

Also this year

★ National Child Labor Committee formed to promote child labor laws

★ First automobile speed law passed in New York

★ William C. Gorgas begins study of ways to eliminate yellow fever in Panama, to enable construction of canal

★ Lincoln Steffens' *Shame of the Cities* published

The Arts

★ O. Henry's collection of stories *Cabbages and Kings*

★ Guzon Borglum's sculpture *Mares of Diomedes*

★ American Academy of Arts and Letters founded

1905

JAN 20 Protocol signed with Dominican Republic for supervision of its national and international debts

30 In *Swift and Co v. US* Supreme Court declares beef trust illegal

FEB 20 State compulsory vaccination laws ruled constitutional by Supreme Court

23 First Rotary Club founded at Chicago by Paul Percy Harris

MAR Theodore Roosevelt inaugurated for first elective term, Charles W. Fairbanks inaugurated Vice President

APR 17 In *Lochner v. New York*, Supreme Court declares unconstitutional state law limiting maximum working hours for bakers on ground that it violates right of contract

JUN Industrial Workers of the World, militant union, organized in Chicago

8 Pres. Roosevelt invites Japan and Russia to Portsmouth, NH, to negotiate end to war

JUL-OCT Severe yellow fever epidemic in New Orleans; brought under control by federal antimosquito campaign

JUL 29 Taft-Katswia Memorandum: Secretary of War William H. Taft, with President's approval, negotiates secret agreement with Japan to stay out of Philippines in exchange for Korea

AUG 9 Peace conference between Russia and Japan opens at Portsmouth, NH

SEP 5 Treaty of Portsmouth signed by Russia and Japan, ending Russo-Japanese War; Japan is given protection over Korea and receives South Manchurian Railway and southern Liaotung Peninsular; Russia receives Economic compensation

SEP 6-DEC 30 Series of 57 public hearings conducted by New York State investigating committee, headed by Charles Evans Hughes, to expose insurance company scandals

NOV 8 Electric lamps installed in railroad train for first time on Chicago and North Western's Overland Limited, running from Chicago to California

Also this year

★ *Everybody's* publishes Charles E. Russell's articles on Beef Trust and Thomas W. Lawson's 'Frenzied Finance'

★ *McClure's* begins publication of 'The Railroads on Trial' by Ray Stannard Baker

The Arts

★ Edith Wharton's novel *The House of Mirth*

Oil!

The 1900s were a significant decade in the history of the American oil industry. In January 1901 prospectors struck oil at the Spindletop well near Beaumont in Texas (above), confirming hopes that there might be significant reserves to be found there, and heralding a dramatic change in the nature of the state's economy.

Booker T. Washington

In 1901 Booker T. Washington (1856–1915) (right) became the first Black leader to dine at the White House, at the invitation of President Roosevelt. Washington, the founder of Tuskegee Institute in Alabama and author of the autobiographical *Up From Slavery* (1901), was a firm believer in racial equality through education and economic independence. The Southern press denounced his White House visit as "a crime equal to treason."

Upton Sinclair

The prolific novelist Upton Sinclair (1878–1968) (left) was closely associated with the muckrakers, and is particularly remembered for his book *The Jungle* (1906), which was directly influential in the passage of the Meat Inspection Act and the Food and Drug Act.

Get Out of That!

The name of Harry Houdini (1874–1926) has become virtually synonymous with the art of escapology. Born Ernst Weiss, Houdini thrilled audiences during these years with his remarkable feats, including particularly spectacular escapes from chains and handcuffs inside a water-filled milk churn. The photograph shows him about to plunge into the Charles River, Boston, in chains in a 1906 stunt.

Edith Wharton

The young writer Edith Wharton (1862–1937) published her novel, *The House of Mirth*, in 1905. The book was the first of a series exploring the complexities of American society and culture.

Chinatown

Regarded with suspicion and hostility by many Americans, Chinese immigrants tended to live in separate districts such as the famous Chinatown area of San Francisco (below).

MAR 17 Term 'muckraker,' taken from passage in John Bunyon's *Pilgrim's Progress* first applied to authors of exposés by Pres. Roosevelt in address to Gridiron Club, Washington, DC

APR 7 Announcement of successful transatlantic wireless transmission, from New York to Ireland

18 San Francisco devastated by worst earthquake in US history; 500,000 people homeless, over 500 dead

28 New York State passes complete legislative program to reform life insurance business

MAY 7 Alaska granted delegate to House of Representatives

21 US and Mexico establish agreement providing for equitable distribution of waters of Rio Grande for irrigation

JUN 4 Reynolds and Neill report reveals shocking conditions in meat-packing houses

29 Hepburn Act extends jurisdiction of Interstate Commerce Commission by giving it power to regulate rates charged by railroads, pipelines and terminals

30 Meat Inspection Act passed by Congress; legislation is result of Upton Sinclair's novel *The Jungle*

30 Food and Drug Act prohibits sale of adulturated food and drugs and requires honest statement of content on labels

AUG 23 Cuban Pres. Tomàs Estrade Palma requests US intervention in quelling rebellion

SEP 22 One of worst race riots in US history leaves 21 dead in Atlanta, Ga; city placed under martial law

29 US assumes military control of Cuba under Platt Amendment; Secretary of War William H. Taft heads provisional government

OCT 11 San Francisco Board of Education orders segregation of Japanese, Chinese and Korean children in separate school

NOV 8 Theodore Roosevelt becomes first US president to journey abroad when he travels aboard battleship *Louisiana* to Panama to inspect canal

Also this year

★ Lee De Forest invents triode tube, initiating development of radio

★ Heárst's International News Service organized

★ Devil's Tower, Wyo., designated first national monument by Pres. Roosevelt

The Arts

★ Upton Sinclair's novel *The Jungle*

★ George M. Cohan's musical *Forty-Five Minutes from Broadway*

1907

JAN 26 Corporate campaign contributions prohibited by act of Congress

FEB 8 Treaty with Dominican Republic provides for collection of customs by US agent with purpose of satisfying foreign and domestic creditors

20 Immigration Act of 1907 provides for exclusion of 'undesirable' clients

26 General Appropriations Act increases salaries of Cabinet members and Vice President to $12,000 and salaries of senators and representatives to $7,500

MAR 14 Japanese laborers excluded from immigrating to continental US by presidential order

14 Inland Waterways Commission appointed by the President

21 US Marines land in Honduras to protect life and property

JUN 15-OCT 15 Second Hague Peace Conference, attended by 46 nations, forbids war as method of collection of debts

SKYSCRAPERS

American architecture in the 19th century was dominated by the neo-classical tradition established by Jefferson at Monticello and perpetuated by architects such as Richard Morris Hunt, whose graceful buildings formed the centerpiece of the Columbian Exposition at Chicago in 1893. As the century drew to a close, however, a new and more directly functional style began to make itself felt alongside the domes and Vitruvian porticos, sowing the seeds of what is still seen by many people as the most distinctively American contribution to modern architecture.

Despite the fact that the elevator – that essential prerequisite of high-rise building – had been invented in 1854, it was only with the development of high-quality steels that real multi-story building became possible. The fundamental principle of the skyscraper is that the core of the building is provided by a metal frame, capable not only of supporting the external structure but also of giving the flexibility essential to the survival of all tall structures. By this definition, the first true skyscraper is the 10-story Home Life Insurance Building in Chicago, built around a steel and wrought-iron skeleton by the architect William Jenny in 1885. Jenny's work and that of his fellow Chicago architect Louis Sullivan, together with further improvements in the steel-making process, made possible the construction of far taller buildings by the first decade of the 20th century. In 1908, for example, the architect Ernest Flagg set a new record in New York with the 47-story Singer Building, which rose to an unprecedented height of 612 feet. Five years later that record was broken with the opening, again in New York, of the 57-story Woolworth Building, an unlikely amalgam of modern construction techniques and Gothic fantasy which, at 792 feet, was then the tallest building in the world.

Only in the 1920s and 1930s – perhaps the golden age of the skyscraper – did architects begin to dispense with the trappings of an older style in designing their towering new buildings. The Chrysler Building, with its distinctive art deco hood, and the uncompromising modernism of the 102-story Empire State Building, designed by the firm of Shreve, Lamb, and Harmon and opened to much acclaim in 1931, infused the skyscraper with a recognizably contemporary idiom.

Left: A construction worker demonstrates his head for heights during the building of the Empire State Building.

Far right: The Chrysler Building, New York.

Middle right: The Flat-Iron Building, New York.

Right: The king of the skyscrapers, the 1250-foot Empire State Building.

OCT 1 Bank panic begins depression of 1907-08

NOV 16 Oklahoma enters Union as 46th state

DEC 6 Coalmine explosion in Monongah, W. Va kills 361

16 Great White Fleet of 16 US battleships begins cruise around the world

The Arts

★ Florenz Ziegfeld's revue *Ziegfeld Follies*

★ First public showing of color motion picture with sound held in Cleveland, Ohio

1908

FEB 12 First round-the-world automobile race begins in NYC

APR 2-3 Populist Party National Convention

30 Prohibition approved by 267 Massachusetts towns and cities

MAY 10 Socialist Party National Convention

10 First formal observances of Mother's Day held in Grafton and Philadelphia, Pa

28 Child labor bill enacted in District of Columbia

30 Aldrich-Vreeland Act allows banks to issue notes backed by commercial paper and banks of state and local governments

JUN 16-20 Republican National Convention nominates William H. Taft for President and James S. Sherman of New York for Vice President

JUL 4 Socialist Labor Party National Convention

7-10 Democratic National Convention nominates William J. Bryan for President and John W. Kern for Vice President

15 Prohibition Party National Convention

27 Independence Party National Convention

AUG 14 Race riots erupt in Springfield, Ill.; martial law declared

OCT 1 Henry Ford introduces Model T.

NOV 3 William H. Taft elected President, James S. Sherman elected Vice President

The Arts

★ John Fox, Jr's novel *The Trail of the Lonesome Pine*

★ Robert Henri forms Ash Can School of painters

1909

MAR 4 William H. Taft, inaugurated President, James S. Sherman inaugurated Vice President

23 Smithsonian Institution sponsors Theodore Roosevelt's hunting expedition to Africa

APR 6 Robert E. Perry reaches North Pole

MAY 22 Some 700,000 acres of federal land in Washington, Montana and Idaho opened to settlers by the President

JUN 1 NAACP formed by W.E.B. DuBois

28 Second military occupation of Cuba by US troops ends

JUL 12 Sixteenth Amendment, authorizing income tax, proposed by Congress

27 Orville Wright makes new flight duration record of 1 hour, 1 minute and 40 seconds

AUG 2 Lincoln penny issued by Philadelphia Mint

SEP 27 Pres. Taft sets aside 3 million acres of public lands in West for conservation purposes

NOV 13 Explosion at St Paul mine in Cherry, Ill., kills 259 miners

DEC 31 Manhattan Bridge opened

The Arts

★ Gertrude Stein's collection of stories *Three Lives*

★ Winsor McCay's animated film *Gertie the Dinosaur*

★ W.C. Hardy's song 'Mr Crump' or 'Memphis Blues'

THE SECOND decade of the 20th century was to prove one of the most momentous in human history. When it began, the world was still largely divided between the empires of the great Old World powers. By the time it ended, Europe had been plunged into the bloodbath of the greatest war yet experienced, from which she emerged financially crippled and burdened with the loss, not only of the flower of her young men, but also of her faith in the established certainties of pre-war life. Of the major European powers, only Britain came out of the war with her empire more or less intact. Meanwhile, the United States had entered for the first time onto the European military stage, bearing along with her armies the reality of unprecedented economic strength and the vision of a new world order.

At home, too, it was a time of radical change for the United States. With the Republican Party split into bitterly warring camps, the sorry debacle of Taft's last years in the White House gave way to the reforming Democratic administration of President Wilson. The tide of progressivism diverged into the two streams of Roosevelt's New Nationalism and Wilson's New Freedom, only to come together again in the second great wave of Democratic reforms in 1916. By the beginning of his second term of office, Wilson could claim to have implemented not only the Democratic platform on which he was elected in 1912, but also the Progressive platform on which Roosevelt had stood against him!

In foreign affairs, Taft's ill-fated "dollar diplomacy" yielded to the no more successful "missionary diplomacy" of Wilson and his Secretary of State William J. Bryan, under which the United States soon found itself entangled not only in Nicaragua, the Dominican Republic, and Haiti, but also, still more disastrously, in the chaos of the Mexican Revolution. By the second half of the decade, though, the focus of American foreign policy had shifted inexorably towards Europe, where the unprecedented slaughter of the First World War had begun. The question of U.S. neutrality, and how long it could last, dominated the political agenda. American intervention, when it finally came, proved decisive in the military struggle. But the battle for the peace was just beginning. The decade ended with the United States still technically at war with Germany, and with Wilson's vision of a League of Nations in which America would play a central role in the preservation of world peace – a vision for which he had already fought long and hard at the negotiating table in Paris – slowly succumbing to the stranglehold of opposing factions in Congress.

The Election of 1912

It was William Howard Taft's misfortune to preside over a thoroughgoing split in the ranks of the Republican Party – a split which he had neither the personal nor the political skills to heal. Roosevelt had chosen him to carry on the good work of progressivism, but, as much through ineptitude as by

design, Taft had allowed himself to become identified with the Republican Old Guard, and the Congressional elections of 1910 indicated the extent of the revolt against him within the party. When Roosevelt himself returned from his triumphal tour of Europe the same year, he brought with him an updated program of progressive reform, which he was soon propagating under the title of the New Nationalism, and which made him the natural focus of progressive interests in the Republican Party. In 1912 he threw his hat into the ring for the presidential nomination, but found himself runner-up to Taft after a hard-fought struggle at the Republican convention. Undeterred, he stood instead on the newly-created Progressive Party ticket, thus splitting the Republican vote down the middle. Meanwhile, an equally intense battle had been fought for the Democratic nomination, a battle from which the former college professor and Governor of New Jersey, Woodrow Wilson, emerged triumphant.

Despite Taft's nomination as the official Republican Party candidate, the election itself was never anything but a contest between Wilson and Roosevelt. Wilson's platform was a progressive one, with some of the same aims as Roosevelt's. But there were cruicial differences too, especially in the respective candidates' view of big business (which Roosevelt seemed more prepared to regard as inevitable now than he had been when he was President) and the role of the Federal Government in welfare provision (which Wilson, true to Democratic tradition, saw as relatively small). Wilson called his program the "New Freedom."

The election gave Wilson the chance to put that program into practice. Although he received only a minority of the popular vote, he was swept into the White House with more electoral votes than any previous President. The Democratic Party had returned from the political wilderness.

Woodrow Wilson (1856–1924) – visions of a world "made safe for democracy."

The New Freedom

Wilson lost no time in making his mark on the American political scene. Acting more like a Prime Minister than any previous occupant of the White House, he gave a clear personal lead to his party in Congress, even breaking the tradition of more than a century by appearing before Congress in person to urge his own legislative program.

The three main planks of that program were in place by the end of 1914. The Underwood-Simmons Tariff Act of 1913 did all that Taft had so conspicuously failed to do (and more) by lowering tariffs across the board, putting a number of important items on the free list, and introducing a tax on incomes. The Federal Reserve Act of 1913, prompted partly by the effects of the financial panic of 1907, laid the foundations of today's banking and currency system. And in 1914 the Federal Trade Commission Act greatly strengthened the anti-trust legislation of 1890 by placing new limits on combinations in restraint of trade and making it clear that trade unions, against whom that legislation had been used so often in the past, did not in themselves constitute a restraint of trade. In securing the passage of all these acts Wilson demonstrated the extent of his control, over both Congress and public opinion, not least through his remarkable skills as an orator.

It is one of the ironies of the history of progressivism in America that by the time Wilson stood for reelection in 1916 subtle changes in his view of the New Freedom had brought him very close to the New Nationalism of his political arch-enemy Theodore Roosevelt. Convinced by his experience of office that the Federal Government had to play a larger role in the reform process than he had originally intended, he found himself supporting legislation he had vetoed only a couple of years before – including a system of rural credits and, in a significant departure from the Democratic legislative tradition, a Federal act to control child labor in the states.

Wilson and the Mexican Revolution

Wilson and his Secretary of State, the three-time presidential candidate William J. Bryan, introduced a new high-mindedness into American foreign policy which earned their actions during these years the designation "missionary diplomacy." The reversal of Taft's "dollar diplomacy" in China; the setting in motion of a system of self-government for the Philippines; and, perhaps most startling of all, the compensation paid out to Colombia for the Roosevelt administration's part in the Panamanian Revolution, all bore witness to this new and distinctively Wilsonian tone. The new policy expressed itself most clearly in Wilson's profound belief that it was the duty of the United States to help foster democracy and human rights throughout the hemisphere.

But the idealism of the new diplomacy was soon to run aground on the sandbanks of reality. In the interest of democracy,

The Mexican rebel leader Pancho Villa on the march during the Mexican Civil War.

1910s

Mexican Revolution

First World War

1910

FEB 6 Boy Scouts of America formed by William D. Boyce

MAR 17 House Committee on Rules restructured to reduce power of Speaker

17 Camp Fire Girls organized

26 Amendment to Immigration Act of 1907 excludes criminals, paupers, anarchists and diseased persons from US

APR 18 Suffragists present petition of 500,000 names to Congress

MAY 16 Bureau of Mines established

JUN 18 Mann-Elkins Act increases power of Interstate Commerce Commission over railroads and extends jurisdiction to include telephone and telegraph companies

19 Father's Day celebrated for first time in Spokane, Wash.

25 Mann Act, or 'white slave traffic act,' prohibits interstate transportation of women for 'immoral purposes'

25 Postal Savings Bank system established by Congress

25 Publicity Act requires representatives to report campaign contributions

AUG 31 Theodore Roosevelt delivers New Nationalism speech advocating Square Deal policy, in Osawatomie, Kans.

NOV Mexican Revolution breaks out

8 Democrats take control of Congress for first time since 1894

8 Washington state adopts women's suffrage by constitutional amendment

14 First naval aircraft launching from deck of US warship

Also this year
★ Reed College established at Portland, Ore.
★ Frederick W. Taylor's pamphlets *A Piece Rate System* and *Shop Management*
The Arts
★ Ezra Pound's book of essays *The Spirit of Romance*
★ George M. Cohan's play *Get-Rich-Quick Wallingford*

1911

JAN 21 National Progressive Republican League formed in Washington, DC, by Sen. Robert La Follette

FEB Electric automotive self-starter demonstrated by General Motors

MAR 7 US orders 20,000 troops to Mexican border

MAY 1 In *US v. Grimaud*, Supreme Court rules that forest reserves are under jurisdiction of Federal Government

Wilson's Government installed American military régimes in Nicaragua, the Dominican Republic, and Haiti, none of which ended up helping the cause of freedom. Most damaging of all, the new President became embroiled in a revolution in Mexico that brought the United States to the very brink of war.

The recent history of Mexico had been bloody and confused. In 1911 a middle-class revolution under Francisco Madero had overthrown the country's military dictatorship, only to be overthrown in its turn by a counter-revolution of the landed classes led by Victoriano Huerta, who had Madero assassinated. Huerta's presidency was promptly recognized by the governments of the major European powers, but Wilson, knowing that the new régime had only limited support in Mexico, staunchly resisted pressure from the substantial American business interests there to accord it U.S. recognition. Instead he offered to mediate between Huerta and the supporters of Madero, now regrouped under the revolutionary leadership of Venustiano Carranza. Huerta refused, and Wilson began supplying arms to Carranza, whom he saw as the champion of the people. In April 1914 he sent American marines to take the crucial Mexican port of Veracruz, and Huerta fled the country a few months later. Carranza assumed power, only to find himself the object of yet another revolution, this time led by one of his own generals, Francisco "Pancho" Villa. Wilson now unaccountably switched his support to Villa, then, finding he had backed a loser, went back to Carranza again.

A long and bloody civil war ensued. Pancho Villa, pursuing a guerrilla campaign against Carranza and the Americans alike, brought further American military intervention in 1916 after a raid into New Mexico. The presence of U.S. troops on Mexican soil only served to anger Carranza, and the specter of all-out war loomed large. It was a situation Wilson dared not let develop. In 1917, with Villa finally subdued, he officially recognized Carranza's government. War had been avoided, but Wilson's diplomacy, for all its good intentions, had left a legacy of ill will towards the U.S. in many parts of Latin America.

The War in Europe

The President's diplomatic skills faced their severest test in the European arena. In June 1914, at Sarajevo in the Austro-Hungarian province of Bosnia, the fateful shot had been fired which set in motion the well-oiled machinery of war in Europe. By September the pattern of warfare which was to claim millions of lives over the next four years was already set, as the opposing armies of the British-French-Russian Allies and the German-Austro-Hungarian Central Powers dug themselves into the trenches of the Western Front.

America's immediate reaction to the outbreak of war was to proclaim itself neutral. But neutrality was easier to declare than to sustain. The United States had strong trading links with the European powers involved, links which Wilson was determined to keep open, but the British naval blockade made it a great deal more difficult for America to trade with the Central Powers than with the Allies, who also succeeded in raising far larger war loans in the U.S. financial markets. But if strains were placed on American neutrality by the British blockade (and the early years of the war saw a stream of protests by Washington against British violation of neutral shipping rights), they were nothing compared with the strain on American-German relations when Germany began to patrol international waters with her newest weapon, the submarine.

Wilson strove to sustain an even course, but in 1915 an event occurred which put this policy in serious jeopardy. In the early afternoon of May 7, the German submarine *U20* sank the British passenger ship *Lusitania* off the coast of Ireland with the loss of almost 1,200 lives, including those of 124 American citizens. The attack, which vio-

---

The event that took America to the verge of war: a German U-boat sinks the Lusitania.

lated the principles of international law, produced an immediate outcry at home. American public opinion was outraged and many voices called for war. Wilson sent a strongly worded note to Germany, threatening to break off diplomatic relations if such an attack were repeated. The crisis passed, but Bryan, who had favored a more pacific approach, resigned over Wilson's response, and was replaced by the pro-Ally Robert Lansing.

Peace Moves and Preparedness

After the *Lusitania* sinking, Wilson stepped up his pressure on the belligerents in Europe to reach a peaceful settlement. He entered into discussions with the British Government, in which he proposed American mediation to help achieve a "peace without victory," and hinted at the possibility of American intervention on the Allied side to help secure it. He also developed his vision of a post-war League of Nations dedicated to the preservation of world peace. At the same time, he launched a massive program of military and naval expansion at home – the so-called "preparedness" campaign – which laid the groundwork for the mobilization he still hoped to be able to avoid. In 1916 Wilson was reelected for a second term on the slogan "he kept us out of war," but as peace moves stalled in London, and German attacks on unarmed shipping continued, the prospect of American involvement loomed closer.

War Declared

The crunch came in the early months of 1917. At the beginning of February, Germany announced the beginning of a campaign of unrestricted submarine warfare and Wilson broke off diplomatic relations. Later the same month, the British intelligence service showed him a telegram from the German Foreign Minister, Alfred Zimmermann, to the German Minister in Mexico, proposing an alliance with Mexico in the event of America's entering the war, and offering her in return the restitution of the

"lost territories" of New Mexico, Texas, and Arizona. In March, Wilson received news of the republican revolution in Russia, which deposed Tsar Nicholas II and seemed to lend substance to the view that the Allies stood for democracy against the absolutism of the Central Powers. Despite the resistance of a small group in the Senate, Wilson proceeded to arm American merchant ships, and on April 2 he appeared before a joint session of Congress to ask for the authority to declare war on the German Empire. In a moving address, he spelled out the overriding aim of American intervention as the establishment of freedom and world peace. "The world," he said, "must be made safe for democracy." On April 6, 1917, Congress gave him the authority he sought. The United States was at war with Germany.

America at War

The mobilization of America in the First World War was one of the most remarkable episodes in the nation's history. The Federal Government commandeered all industries which were deemed essential to the war effort and took over the administration of the country's railroad and communications systems. A Council for National Defense delegated the day-to-day running of the economic infrastructure to a series of Government agencies such as Bernard Baruch's War Industries Board and Herbert Hoover's Food Administration. At the same time, a Committee on Public Information under George Creel set about mobilizing public opinion against Germany with a zeal whose effects would outlast the war itself, with ugly consequences. Legislation was passed to silence opposition to the war at home, the Espionage Act of 1917 and the Sedition Act of 1918 providing the Government with draconian powers of imprisonment, arrest, and deportation.

Meanwhile, the military effort was moving into top gear. American warships convoyed Allied and American vessels across the Atlantic, and the first American Expeditionary Force ever to set foot on European soil arrived in France by the fall of 1917. Within 18 months of declaring war, America had mobilized an army of more than four million men, two million of whom had been sent to France.

The American military intervention was to prove decisive. When the Russian Government, now in the hands of the Bolsheviks, negotiated a separate peace with Germany at Brest-Litovsk in the closing months of 1917, hundreds of thousands of German troops were redeployed from the Eastern to the Western Front. The plight of the Allies looked grave indeed by the spring of 1918, when the German army began its first Marne offensive. America responded by pouring some 1·75 million troops into France between March and October 1918. The moment of truth came on July 15, when the German army began the offensive known as the Second Battle of the Marne. A quarter of a million U.S. troops played a crucial part in beating off the German assault at Château-Thierry, and by July 18 the

"Not room for both:" the San Francisco Chronicle *lampoons the struggle which dominated Wilson's last years as President.*

last great German drive of the war had been defeated. As the German Chancellor later put it, "The history of the world was played out in three days." By October 1918 the final Allied offensive had driven Germany to sue for peace, and an armistice was declared in November.

The Battle for the Peace

President Wilson played a central part in the peace conference which began in Paris in January 1919. A year earlier he had laid out what he saw as the basis for the peace in his famous Fourteen Points. In particular, he saw the post-war order as resting on the foundation of a League of Nations, at which the United States would have a permanent seat. Wilson soon discovered, however, that the leaders of the victorious powers, Britain's David Lloyd George, France's Georges Clemenceau, and Italy's Vittorio Orlando, were in no mood for his brand of practical idealism. Exhausted and embittered by four years of war, they wanted a settlement which would punish Germany severely for her aggression and would ensure that she was too weak ever to threaten war again. While many of the people of Europe hailed Wilson as a kind of savior from the New World, the President battled it out with the Allied leaders at the conference table. The Treaty of Versailles, which emerged from months of argument and compromise in June 1919, was a far more punitive document than Wilson wanted, but preserved more of the spirit of the Fourteen Points than would have been possible without him. Above all, it retained the provision for a League of Nations.

Now Wilson found he had to fight his battles all over again in Washington. The Congressional elections of 1918 had returned Republican majorities in both houses, and they were determined to give the Treaty a rough ride. In the feverish xenophobic atmosphere of post-war America, many were opposed to an arrangement which would permanently entangle the United States in the web of European politics. Led by Henry Cabot Lodge, the chairman of the Senate Foreign Relations Committee, they insisted on amendments to the League of Nations covenant which would, in Wilson's view, have undone his work completely. With neither side prepared to compromise, a bitter battle ensued, during the course of which Wilson suffered a massive stroke that left him partially paralyzed. The decade closed with the Treaty still unratified. Not until 1921 would America conclude a separate peace with Germany. President Wilson's dream of a permanent American seat at the League of Nations was never to be fulfilled.

15 In *Standard Oil Company of NJ et al v. US*, Supreme Court finds Standard Oil Company in 'unreasonable' restraint of trade

29 In *US v. American Tobacco Company*, Supreme Court orders reorganization of company on grounds that it violates Sherman Antitrust Act

AUG 22 Arizona statehood vetoed by Pres. Taft because state constitution permits recall of judges

SEP 17-NOV 5 First transcontinental flight made by Calbraith P. Rodgers, from Sheepshead Bay, NY, to Pasadena, Calif., in 82 hours, 4 min.

OCT 10 California adopts women's suffrage

16 National Conference of Progressive Republicans nominates Sen. Robert La Folette of Wisconsin for President

NOV 10 Carnegie Corporation of New York established

DEC 21 Treaty of Commerce with Russia (1832) abrogated by joint resolution of Congress to protest Russia's refusal to honor US passports held by Jews and others

The Arts

★ Irving Berlin's song 'Alexander's Ragtime Band'

1912

JAN 6 New Mexico enters Union as 47th state

12 Textile workers' under IWW strike against sweatshop conditions in Lawrence, Mass.

FEB 14 Arizona enters Union as 48th state

MAR 12 Girl Guides, later Girl Scouts, formed by Juliet Low

APR 15 British liner *Titanic* strikes iceberg off coast of Newfoundland and sinks on maiden voyage

MAY 17 Socialist Party National Convention nominates Eugene V. Debs for President and Emil Seidel of Wisconsin for Vice President

30 Death of aviator Wilbur Wright

JUN 5 Marines land in Cuba to protect US interests

18-22 Republican National Convention nominates Willilam Howard Taft and James S. Sherman for second terms

19 Eight-hour work day extended to all under federal contract

25-JUL 2 Democratic National Convention nominates Gov. Woodrow Wilson of New Jersey for President and Thomas R. Marshall of Indiana for Vice President

JUL 10-12 Prohibition Party National Convention

AUG 5 Progressive (Bull Moose) Party nominates Theodore Roosevelt for President and Hiram Johnson of California for Vice President

24 Parcel post system authorized by Congress

OCT 4 Theodore Roosevelt shot by fanatic during campaign tour

NOV 5 Woodrow Wilson elected President by landslide, Thomas R. Marshall elected Vice President

Also this year

★ Massachusetts becomes first state to adopt minimum wage for women and children

★ Prof. Elmer V. McCollum of Yale University discovers vitamins A and B

The Arts

★ Mary Austin's novel *A Woman of Genius*

★ Theodore Dreiser's novel *The Financier*

1913

FEB 17 International Exhibition of Modern Art, known as Armory Show, begins

25 Sixteenth Amendment permits graduated income tax

MAR 1 Webb-Kenyon Interstate Liquor Act passed over President's veto; forbids shipping of liquor into states where its sale is illegal

The War in Europe

Right: Uncle Sam expects every man to do his duty: First World War recruitment poster.

Below: Within 18 months of the declaration of war America had mobilized some four million men, half of whom had been sent to France. The picture shows a mobile recruiting station in downtown New York.

Below right: Conditions on the Western Front were appalling. In the early months of the war the opposing forces had dug themselves into trenches, defining what was to be the pattern of the fighting for the remainder of the conflict. Trench warfare meant that territorial gains were slow and costly, with wave after wave of young men being cut down by enemy machine gun fire as they went "over the top" into the mud and craters of no man's land. Here American troops go into action at Boudaville in March 1918 during the last major German offensive of the war.

Far right: American men and military hardware were decisive in the success of the war effort in France after Russia's conclusion of a separate peace with Germany allowed thousands of German troops to be redeployed from the Eastern Front. Here members of the 313 Field Artillery polish shells for a nighttime offensive at Nixeville in the Meuse region of France in the final months of the war.

I WANT YOU FOR U.S. ARMY

NEAREST RECRUITING STATION

4 Woodrow Wilson inaugurated President, Thomas R. Marshall inaugurated Vice President

4 Department of Commerce and Labor separated into two departments, each with Cabinet status

11 Pres. Wilson refuses to recognize Huerta government of Mexico

APR 8 Pres. Wilson appears before Congress to deliver message on tariff revision; first President to appear in person since John Adams

19 Webb Alien Land - Holding Bill excludes Japanese from owning land in California

MAY 2 New Republic of China recognized by the President

31 Seventeenth Amendment provides for popular election of senators

SUMMER Henry Ford creates automobile assembly line for production of Model T

AUG 26 Keokuk Dam, (world's largest dam) opened across Mississippi River

27 Pres. Wilson announces 'watchful waiting' policy toward Mexico

OCT Floods in southern Texas cause $50 million in damage and 500 deaths

3 Underwood-Simmons Tariff Act lowers tariffs on 958 articles

10 Pres. Wilson presses button to set off explosion of Gamoa Dike, opening Panama Canal

DEC 10 Elihu Root wins 1912 Nobel Peace Prize for his work as Secretary of War

23 Owen-Glass Federal Reserve Act creates Federal Reserve Board

Also this year

★ About 150,000 garment workers successfully strike for reduced hours, union recognition and wage increase

★ Woolworth Building in NYC completed

The Arts

★ Willa Cather's novel *O Pioneers*

★ Dancing couple Vernon and Irene Castle make debut in musical *The Sunshine Girl*

1914

JAN 27 Panama Canal Zone receives permanent civil government by executive order of the President

FEB 13 American Society of Composers, Authors and Publishers organized in NYC

APR 9 Several US Marines land at Tampico, Mexico, for supplies and are arrested and detained

19 Pres. Wilson requests and receives from Congress authorization to use armed force in Mexico to deal with Pres. Huerta

21 US Marines occupy Veracruz, Mexico

22 Mexico severs diplomatic relations with US

25 Pres. Wilson accepts offer of Argentina, Brazil and Chile to mediate dispute with Mexico

MAY 7 Mother's Day, to be celebrated on second Sunday of May, established by Congress

JUN 28 Archduke Franz Ferdinand of Austria assassinated

JUL 15 Mexican Pres. Huerta forced to resign

28 Austria-Hungary declares war on Serbia

31 NY Stock Exchange closes to avoid panic caused by war

AUG 1 Germany declares war on Russia

3 Germany declares war on France

4 Great Britain declares war on Germany

4 German troops invade Belgium

5 US declares neutrality in European wars and offers mediation to belligerents

5 Bryan-Chamorro Treaty with Nicaragua gives US right to build canal, plus 99-year lease on islands and naval base for $3 million

6 Austria-Hungary declares war on Russia

6 US ships $5 million in gold to Europe to aid stranded Americans

10 George Sylvester Viereck begins publication of pro-German weekly newspaper, *The Fatherland*

The Home Front

Right: Two-thirds of the total cost of the war was financed by loans raised from the general public by the sale of Liberty Bonds.

Opposite top: "It is not an army that we must shape and train for war," said Wilson. "It is a nation." So began an economic mobilization on an unprecedented scale. Under the direction of Bernard Baruch, the War Industries Board left no stone unturned to support the war effort: here Girl Guides collect peach seeds for their oil.

Opposite middle: One of the most significant effects of the war effort on the home front was to draft a million women into the workforce for the first time. The expectations of equal employment opportunities so raised were not to be fulfilled after demobilization.

Opposite bottom: German suspects are rounded up in New York, 1917.

Below: American involvement in the war was far from universally popular in the U.S., where many criticized it for lining the pockets of the rich. As the war went on, however, expressions of dissent were ruthlessly suppressed. Eugene Debs, the Socialist leader, was sentenced to 20 years in prison for preaching pacifism, and one film director was even jailed for producing a film about the spirit of the 1776 revolution on the grounds that it stirred up anti-British feeling.

Our Daddy is fighting at the Front for You—
Back him up— Buy a
United States Gov't Bond of the
2nd LIBERTY LOAN
of 1917

WAR WHAT FOR?
FOR PROFITS
OF COURSE!

ON MAY 1

15 Panama Canal opened to shipping

23 Japan declares war on Germany

SEP 2 Bureau of War Risk Insurance established by Treasury Department

5 Wireless stations for transatlantic communication provided for Navy by the President

26 Federal Trade Commission established

OCT 15 Clayton Antitrust Act exempts unions from antitrust laws

22 Revenue Act imposes income tax on earnings over $3000

NOV 2 Great Britain declares North Sea a military area

23 US forces withdrawn from Veracruz

The Arts

★ Robert Frost's collection of poems *North of Boston*

★ Vachel Lindsay's *The Congo and Other Poems*

★ Edgar Lee Masters' first collection of poems published in *Reedy's Mirror*

★ Edgar Rice Burroughs' story *Tarzan of the Apes*

★ Studio Club established in NYC; leads to formation of Whitney Museum

1915

JAN 25 Long distance telephone service between New York and San Francisco inaugurated

26 Rocky Mountain National Park established by Congress

28 Bill to require literacy test for immigrants vetoed by Pres. Wilson

28 US Coast Guard established by Congress

28 US vessel *William C. Frye*, carrying wheat for Britain, torpedoed in South Atlantic by German navy

30 Col. Edward M. House sails to Europe on *Lusitania* to mediate peace settlement

FEB 7 Germany proclaims war zone around British Isles

10 US protests German proclamation of war zone around British Isles

23 Divorce bill requiring six months' residence signed into law in Nevada

MAR 11 Britain declares blockade of German ports

30 US protests British blockade of German ports as interfering with neutral trade

APR 4 Germany protests to US concerning blockade

30 Naval Petroleum Reserve No. 3 created from 9481 acres in Teapot Dome

MAY 1 German Embassy publishes in New York newspapers warning to people traveling in war zone

1 US tanker *Gulflight* sunk by German submarine

7 British passenger ship *Lusitania* sunk without warning by German submarine; 1198 drowned, including 124 Americans

13 First *Lusitania* note, protesting attack and demanding reparations, sent to Germany

24 Pan-American Financial Conference begins in Wash., DC

JUN 8 Secy of State William J. Bryon resigns, unwilling to sign second *Lusitania* note

9 Second *Lusitania* note demands end to attacks on unarmed passenger and merchant vessels

17 League to Enforce Peace organized at Independence Hall in Philadelphia

JUL 2 Erich Muenter, Cornell University German instructor, explodes bomb in US Senate reception room

3 J.P. Morgan shot by Erich Muenter at Glen Cove, LI, for representing British Government in war contract negotiations

15 Evidence of German espionage in US revealed when Secret Service agent acquires portfolio belonging to Dr Heinrich F. Albert, head of German propaganda in US

21 Third *Lusitania* note warns that any future violation of US rights will be deemed 'deliberately unfriendly'

21 'Grandfather clause' in constitutions of Oklahoma and Maryland declared unconstitutional by Supreme Court

The Aftermath

Both on the home front and internationally the aftermath of the war was bitter and divisive. Demobilization was handled far less efficiently than mobilization had been, with the result that millions of veterans were simply dumped back on the job market without any plans for reintegration. Euphoria and victory parades soon gave way to the stark realities of unemployment, soaring inflation, and a sudden upsurge of violent racism and anti-Communism. Meanwhile, President Wilson struggled to moderate the demands of the other Allied leaders for a peace treaty that would bring Germany to its knees, and to argue the case, both in Paris and in Congress, for a League of Nations, with the U.S. as a permanent member.

Left: The 165th Infantry march in victorious procession down Fifth Avenue in New York.

Bottom: Out-of-work men jostle for position at an unemployment office in Los Angeles, 1919.

Below: The "Big Four" take time off from the peace negotiations in Paris. From left to right: David Lloyd George of Great Britain, Vittorio Orlando of Italy, Georges Clemenceau of France, and President Wilson.

25 American vessel *Leelanaw*, carrying flax, sunk off coast of Scotland by German submarine

27 Direct wireless communication completed between US and Japan

28 US Marines land in Haiti to quell revolution; begins 19 year occupation

AUG 5 Latin-American Conference opens in Washington, DC; Argentina, Brazil, Bolivia, Chile, Guatemala, Uruguay and US meet to consider ways of ending chaos in Mexico

10 Plattsburg, NY, military training camp for civilians established by Gen. Leonard Wood

SEP 16 Haiti becomes protectorate of US

OCT 15 US bankers arrange $500 million loan to British and French governments

19 US recognizes Gen. Venustiano Carranza as President of Mexico

21 First transatlantic radio telephone communication made from Arlington, Va, to Eiffel Tower in Paris

NOV 7 Italian liner *Ancora*, carrying 27 American passengers, sunk without warning by Austrian submarine

14 Death of Booker T. Washington

25 Ku Klux Klan revived in Atlanta, Ga, by Col. William J. Simmons

30 Explosion at DuPont munitions plant in Wilmington, Del.; sabotage suspected

DEC 1 President requests standing army of 142,000 and reserve of 400,000

27 Iron and Steel Workers in East Youngstown, Ohio, strike successfully for eight-hour day and other concessions

Also this year

★ Automobile owners offer rides for a 'jitney,' or nickel; origin of taxicab

★ Margaret Sanger arrested on obscenity charges directed toward her book *Family Limitation*, pioneer work on birth control

The Arts

★ Edgar Lee Masters' *Spoon River Anthology*

★ Theodore Dreiser's novel *The Genius*

★ D. W. Griffith's film *The Birth of a Nation*

1916

JAN 7 Germany notifies State Department that it will abide by strict international rules of maritime warfare

10 Mexican Gen. Francisco 'Pancho' Villa forces 18 American mining engineers off train and shoots them

24 In *Brushaber v. Union Pacific Railroad Company*, Supreme Court upholds constitutionality of federal income tax

MAR 9 Pancho Villa leads 1500 soldiers in attack on New Mexico, killing 17 Americans; US troops pursue

24 French vessel *Sussex* sunk by German submarine, killing three Americans

APR 13 Secy of State Lansing warns Germany that US will sever diplomatic relations unless attacks on passenger liners are discontinued

23 Socialist Labor Party National Convention nominates Arthur E. Reimer of Massachusetts for President and Caleb Harrison of Illinois for Vice President

MAY US Marines land in Santo Domingo to quell disorder; begins eight-year occupation

4 German note pledges not to attack any merchant vessel without warning unless ship tries to escape and Britain fails to observe international law regarding blockade

9 President orders mobilization along Mexican border

JUN 3 National Defense Act increases standing army to 175,000 and National Guard to 450,000

7 Progressive Party National Convention nominates Theodore Roosevelt for president; Roosevelt declines nomination

10 Republican Party National Convention nominates Charles Evans Hughes of New York for President and Charles Fairbanks of Indiana for Vice President

Frank Lloyd Wright

One of the greatest architects of the 20th century, Frank Lloyd Wright (1869–1959) first came to prominence in the 1900s and 1910s with his innovative designs for office and residential accommodation in New York and the Midwest. A disciple of the modernist Chicago architect Louis Sullivan, Wright believed that the form of a building should be determined by its function, and that manmade and natural architecture should work in harmony with one another. These principles are embodied in the Robie House in Chicago (above), which, with its distinctive horizontal lines and elegantly counterpointed building materials, typifies the work of his so-called "prairie" period.

Rien Ne Va Plus

The moral reformism which led to the enactment of prohibition legislation in 1919 also expressed itself in campaigns against other forms of addiction, such as petty gambling. Here Government agents vent their spleen against slot machines in Chicago.

The Indianapolis 500

1911 saw the launching of what was to become one of the most prestigious fixtures of the sporting year as the contestants lined up at the starting blocks for the first ever Indianapolis 500 race. The event was held on the newly completed Brickyard track in the Indianapolis suburb of Speedway, and was won by Ray Harroun, a retired driver, who notched up an average speed of more than 74 m.p.h. in the Marmon Wasp he had built for the occasion. The 2½ mile track, constructed from 3.2 million individual bricks, was soon to enter motor racing legend, and within two years was attracting the sort of international competition that has characterized the race ever since. Today the Brickyard can claim to be the world's oldest surviving race track and the "Indy" 500 the world's largest one-day sporting event.

D. W. Griffith (1875–1948)

A controversial milestone in the history of the movie industry was reached in 1915 with the release of David Wark Griffith's historical epic, *The Birth of a Nation*. Set against the colorful background of the Civil War and the Reconstruction period, and dramatizing events from the Southern perspective, the film was criticized in many quarters for inciting racial hatred. However, its effect on the movie-going public and on other film-directors was electric. Effectively marking the beginning of the American tradition of movie spectaculars, *The Birth of a Nation* employed a number of innovative cinematic techniques which have since become the staple of the motion picture industry, including the close-up, the fade-out, and the flashback. In 1919, Griffith joined forces with movie stars Charlie Chaplin, Douglas Fairbanks, and Mary Pickford to form United Artists.

Child Labor

The decade saw the passage of important child labor legislation, including the 1916 Child Labor Act, which forbade interstate trade in products from factories employing children. Ruled unconstitutional in 1918, it was replaced with a new act in 1919.

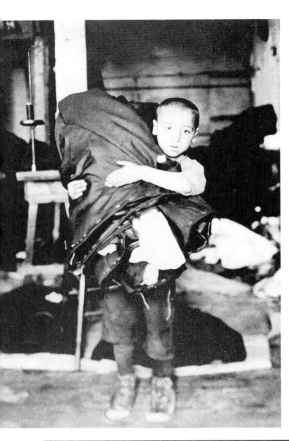

Halley's Comet

In 1910 the reappearance of Halley's Comet, visible once every 75 years, caused enormous excitement throughout the U.S. Predictions of cosmic disaster turned out to be unfounded, but those of Mark Twain – who was born in 1835 and had told the world "I came in with Halley's Comet . . . and I expect to go out with it" – proved entirely accurate.

The *Titanic*

New York crowds stand shocked after learning of the sinking of the *Titanic* on her maiden voyage in April 1912. The liner – the largest in the world – was said to be unsinkable, but went down with the loss of more than 1500 lives after hitting an iceberg in the North Atlantic.

14-16 Democratic National Convention nominates Woodrow Wilson and Thomas R. Marshall for second terms

21 US troops attacked at Carrizal, Mexico; 18 Americans killed or wounded

JUL 17 Federal Farm Loan Act establishes land bank system for maintenance and improvement loans to farmers

21 Prohibition Party National Convention

22 Bombing during San Francisco Preparedness Day parade kills 20 and wounds 40

28 US and Mexico agree to submit dispute to arbitration

AUG 16 Canada and US sign treaty to protect migratory birds in North America

25 National Park Service established by Congress

29 Pres. Wilson urges immediate legislation for eight-hour day to prevent threatened railroad strike scheduled for September 4

SEP 1 Keating-Owen Act bars from interstate commerce any item produced by child labor

3 Adamson Eight-Hour Act provides for eight-hour day and time and a half for overtime on railroads

7 Workmen's Compensation Act brings 500,000 Federal employees under system

OCT 16 First birth control clinic opened by Margaret Sanger, Fania Mindell and Ethel Burne in Brooklyn, NY

NOV 7 Woodrow Wilson and Thomas R. Marshall win election for second terms

7 Jeanette Rankin of Montana becomes first woman elected to House

Also this year

★ Submachine gun, or 'Tommy' gun, invented by Brig. Gen. John Taliafeno Thompson

★ National Research Council organized by National Academy of Sciences

The Arts

★ Carl Sandburg's *Chicago Poems*

★ D.W. Griffith's film *Intolerance*

From Little Acorns...

The modest shopfront of an F. W. Woolworth "5 & 10" store in Montpelier, Vermont, in 1910. Woolworth, a farmer's son from Watertown, New York, went on to become the head of a multi-million dollar retail empire.

Black Civil Rights

Black community leaders march down Fifth Avenue, New York, demanding equal rights. The First World War, in which many Black Americans gave their lives, marked a turning point in the development of Black consciousness in the U.S.

1917

JAN 17 Virgin Islands purchased by US from Denmark for $25 million

22 'Peace without victory' speech by Pres. Wilson before Senate outlines plan for league of peace

31 Germany announces unrestricted submarine warfare

FEB 3 American steamship *Housatonic* sunk by German submarine without warning

3 US severs diplomatic relations with Germany

5 Immigration Act provides for literacy test and bars Asiatic laborers other than Japanese

19 US troops stationed along Mexican border recalled

23 Smith-Hughes Act provides matching funds to states for trade and agricultural schools and creates Federal Board for Vocational Education

24 Pres. Wilson receives Zimmermann note from British; coded message from German Foreign Minister Alfred Zimmermann to German ambassador in Mexico suggesting German alliance with Mexico

26 Pres. Wilson asks Congress for legislation authorizing arming of merchant ships

MAR 2 Jones Act makes Puerto Rico part of US

5 Woodrow Wilson and Thomas R. Marshall inaugurated for second terms

12 President authorizes arming of merchant ships

12 American merchant ship *Algonquin* sunk without warning

15 News of Russian Revolution reaches Washington

15 Czar Nicholas II of Russia abdicates

18 American ships *City of Memphis*, *Vigilante* and *Illinois* sunk without warning

21 American ship *Healdton* sunk without warning

22 US recognizes Kerenski government of Russia

APR 2 Pres. Wilson asks Congress to declare war on Germany

6 US declares war on Germany

213

The Mexican Revolution

Widely seen as the acid test of President Wilson's so-called missionary diplomacy, American involvement in the Mexican Revolution soon became a nightmare for the new administration. Founded on a determination not to acknowledge any government which did not have the support of the Mexican people, Wilson's policy became bogged down in Mexico's volatile internal politics, and his vacillation between support for the Constitutionalist leader Venustiano Carranza and Carranza's flamboyant rebel general, "Pancho" Villa, did irreparable damage to American relations with both. Shocked by the casualties on both sides when he ordered U.S. troops to take Veracruz in support of Carranza in 1914, Wilson attempted to avoid further military entanglements, only to be out-maneuvered by Villa, who lured General Pershing onto Mexican soil in 1916 after a border raid at Columbus.

Above: American troops march into Mexico near Columbus, New Mexico, in 1916.

Below left: Mexican guerrilla fighters hitch a ride.

Below right: U.S. marines raise the Stars and Stripes over Veracruz, 1914.

Occupation of Haiti

American marines at the gates of the presidential palace in Port-au-Prince, Haiti, where Wilson intervened to end factional fighting and install a puppet government in 1915.

The Russian Revolution

The Bolshevik Revolution of Octover 1917 was to have far-reaching consequences for U.S. relations with Russia. Below, Lenin addresses a crowd in Moscow while Trotsky looks on.

14 Committee on Public Information created by executive order to control censorship of news and propaganda releases

MAY 18 Selective Service Act authorizes registration and draft of all men aged 21 to 30

JUN 4 First Pulitzer Prizes awarded by Columbia School of Journalism

24 American Expeditionary Force lands in France

JUL 4 First US flight training field opens at Rontoul, Ill.

24 Congress appropriates $640 million for military aviation

AUG 10 Herbert Hoover put in charge of food program established by Lever Food and Fuel Act

28 Ten suffragette pickets arrested in front of White House

OCT 16 Four suffragettes sentenced to six months in prison

18 Eighteenth Amendment, outlawing manufacture, sale or transportation of alcoholic liquors, passed by Congress and submitted to states for ratification

27 Twenty thousand women march in suffrage parade in New York

NOV 3 First engagement involving US forces in Europe occurs near Rhine - Maine Canal in France when German forces attack American infantrymen training in frontline trenches

6 Women's suffrage made law in New York State by constitutional amendment

6 Bolsheviks overthrow Kerenski government of Russia

10 Forty-one suffragette pickets arrested in front of White House

DEC 7 US declares war on Austria-Hungary

Also this year

★ University of Alaska founded as Alaska Agricultural College and School of Mines at College, Alaska

The Arts

★ Sinclair Lewis' novel *The Innocents*

★ Upton Sinclair's novel *King Coal*

1918

JAN 7 In *Arver v. US*, Supreme Court upholds constitutionality of Selective Service Act

8 Pres. Wilson announces his 'Fourteen Points' for peace in the world in address to Congress

8 First issue of *Stars and Stripes*, Army newspaper, published

26 Food Administrator Herbert Hoover calls for one meatless day, two wheatless days and two porkless days each week

FEB 25 Pres. Wilson authorizes construction of Muscle Shoals Dam on Tennessee River

MAR 3 Russia signs peace treaty with Germany

7 US Army's Distinguished Service Medal authorized by the President

21 German army begins final offensive on Western front

MAY 16 Sedition Act provides penalties for hindering war effort

28 US First Division helps French win Battle of Cantigny, first US military success

JUN 3 In *Hammer v. Dagenhart*, Supreme Court rules Federal Child Labor Law of 1916 unconstitutional due to violation of states' rights

6-25 Marine Brigade of US Second Division captures Bouresche and Belleau Wood after two-week battle with 9,500 casualties

17 In Second Battle of the Marne, in France, Allies halt German four-month drive

JUL 18-AUG 6 Aisne-Marne offensive launched by over 250,000 Americans with French units

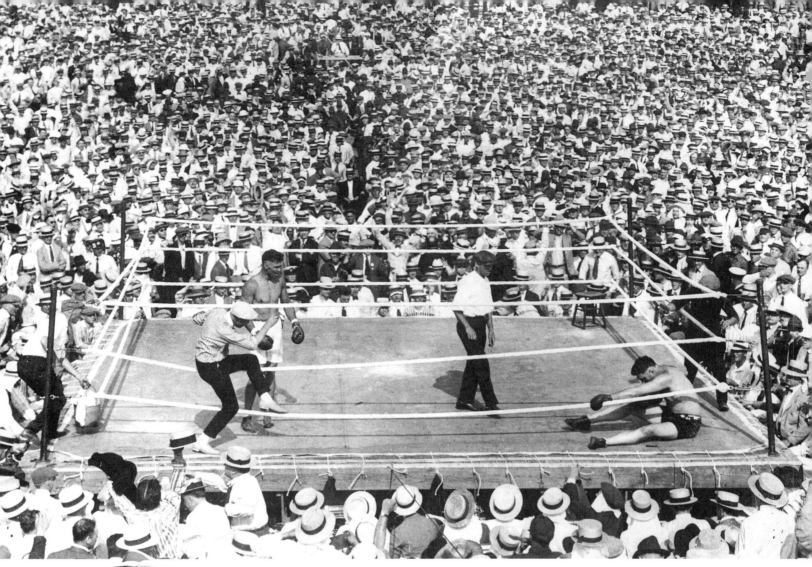

Dempsey *v.* Willard

Jack Dempsey fought his way dramatically into the annals of 20th-century boxing when he defeated Jess Willard in Toledo, Ohio, on Independence Day 1919 to gain the World Heavyweight Title. Before a record crowd of more than 40,000 people, the 24-year-old Dempsey knocked Willard down seven times in the first round alone and after three rounds the fight was stopped.

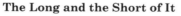

The Long and the Short of It

Vaudeville acts, such as the duo Drane and Alexander (left), were immensely popular in America during the early years of the century.

Enter Tarzan

1914 witnessed the birth of one of the most enduring heroes of modern popular fiction, with the publication of *Tarzan of the Apes* by Edgar Rice Burroughs (1875–1950) (right). Set in the jungles of Africa, Burroughs' novel tells the story of a baby who is brought up by apes after his parents are killed. The book was followed by a number of sequels.

Ragtime

The years around 1910 were the golden age of ragtime in the United States. From its roots in the traditional dance and band music of the American South, ragtime developed into a distinctive musical style, associated particularly with piano compositions, under the direction of such masters of the form as the so-called "Father of Ragtime," Scott Joplin (1868–1917), and W. C. Handy. Ragtime is characterized by syncopated rhythms superimposed on a steady march-like bass. Joplin's *Maple Leaf Rag* (1899) was perhaps the most popular of all ragtime compositions in its own day, though he is now better known for his two-step *The Entertainer* (1902), used in the film *The Sting*.

Below left: The title page of Irving Berlin's Alexander's Ragtime Band *(1911).*

Below right: Sheet music of Scott Joplin's piano score The Entertainer.

Below: W. C. Handy puts some finishing touches to his St. Louis Blues.

AUG Ten thousand Americans join Japan in armed occupation of Vladivostok and some of Siberia

SEP 12-14 US forces take strategic German salient at St Mihiel, capturing 15,000

14 Eugene V. Debs, four-time Socialist candidate for President, sentenced to 10 years' imprisonment for violating Espionage Act of 1917

26-NOV 11 In Battle of Meuse-Argonne, 1.2 million US troops and 135,000 French soldiers attack German position and cut German supply line

OCT Influenza epidemic increases death rate in Boston, New York and Philadelphia by 100%

5 Prince Max of Baden, newly appointed German Chancellor, begins peace overture to Pres. Wilson

NOV 4 Austria-Hungary surrenders

7 False armistice celebrated in US

9 Kaiser Wilhelm II of Germany abdicates

11 Germany signs armistice treaty

The Arts

★ Willa Cather's novel *My Antonia*

★ Booth Tarkington's novel *The Magnificent Ambersons*

1919

JAN 6 Death of 26th President of US Theodore Roosevelt

18 Peace Conference begins in Paris

29 Eighteenth Amendment ratified

FEB Navy Distinguished Service Medal established by Congress

14 Pres. Wilson presents League of Nations Covenant to Paris Peace Conference

MAR 10 In *Schenk v. US*, Supreme Court upholds constitutionality of Espionage Act

15 American Legion formed in Paris

JUN 5 Nineteenth Amendment for women's suffrage passed by Congress and sent to states for ratification

28 Treaty of Versailles signed at Peace Conference in Paris

JUL 1 Daily air mail service established between New York and Chicago

4 Jack Dempsey wins world heavyweight boxing championship

10 Treaty of Versailles and League of Nations Covenant sent by Pres. Wilson to Senate for ratification

14 Embargo on trade with Germany lifted

AUG 31 Communist Labor Party formed in Chicago, Ill.

SEP 3 Pres. Wilson begins public speaking tour in support of Treaty of Versailles and League of Nations Covenant

9 Boston police go on strike

25 Pres. Wilson suffers stroke in Colorado

OCT 28 Volstead Act, or National Prohibition Act, passed by Congress over President's veto; effective January 1920

NOV 19 Treaty of Versailles fails to achieve ratification in Senate

Also this year

★ Father Divine, charismatic Black evangelist, captures public's attention

★ Institute for International Education established under Carnegie Endowment for International Peace

★ H.L. Mencken's *The American Language* published

★ John Reed's *Ten Days That Shook the World* published

The Arts

★ Sherwood Anderson's book *Winesburg, Ohio*

★ James Bronch Cabell's novel *Jurgen, A Comedy of Justice*

RED SOX, WHITE SOX, BLACK SOX

During the first two decades of the 20th century baseball confirmed its standing as the national game of the United States with a surge in popularity that made the World Series – first played in 1903 – one of the most eagerly awaited events in the American sporting calendar. The creation of the World Series also confirmed the dominance of the sport by the two great associations, the National League (founded in 1876 and including the Atlanta Braves, the Chicago Cubs, the New York Mets, and the San Francisco Giants) and the American League (founded in 1900 and including the Boston Red Sox, the California Angels, the Cleveland Indians, the New York

Yankees, and the Texas Rangers). Between 1910 and 1919, the World Series was dominated by the Boston Red Sox (who won in 1912, 1915–1916, and 1918) and the Philadelphia Athletics (1910–1911, 1913). More sensational than the game itself, however, was the so-called "Black Sox" scandal which erupted after the Cincinnati Reds won the 1919 Series. Allegations that a number of Chicago White Sox players, including the legendary "Shoeless" Joe Jackson, had taken part in a conspiracy to lose the Series to the Cincinnati Reds in return for enormous bribes, led to the creation of the post of Baseball Commissioner to police the sport.

This page: Top: Amos Strunck of the Philadelphia Athletics, out at the plate during the 1914 Series.

Bottom left: Ty Cobb, the Detroit Tigers' star outfielder, 1910.

Bottom middle: Christy Mathewson of the New York Giants, pitching his way toward the Hall of Fame.

Bottom right: Joe Tinker of the Chicago Cubs.

Facing page: Top left: Two of the game's greatest: Babe Ruth (left), once a Red Sox pitcher, hit his way into the record books for the New York Yankees; and Lou Gehrig, who held the league record of 2130 consecutive appearances.

Top right: Jim Thorpe demonstrates his prowess with the bat.

Bottom: Ty Cobb does it again.

Votes for Women

"The right of citizens of the United States to vote shall not be denied or abridged by the United States or by any State on account of sex." With these words the goal of almost a century's campaigning by American women was enshrined in the Nineteenth Amendment to the U.S. Constitution, ratified by Congress in 1919 and brought into effect the following year. Women now had the constitutional right to vote.

The long struggle, which had its symbolic birth at the Seneca Falls conference in 1848, moved into top gear in the first two decades of the new century, with women taking leading roles not only in the suffrage movement, but also in other Progressive reform campaigns such as the temperance movement, the child labor reform movement, and the highly controversial birth control movement. Taking up the mantle of the veteran campaigners Elizabeth Cady Stanton and Susan B. Anthony, Carrie Chapman Catt and Dr. Anna Howard Shaw, both Presidents of the National American Woman Suffrage Association (NAWSA), lobbied determinedly for women's rights. In 1916 President Wilson included a commitment to woman suffrage in his reelection platform, and appeared in 1918 before the Senate in person to press for approval of the Nineteenth Amendment.

Above right: Women's suffrage march in Washington, 1913.

Above right: Society women suffragists.

Above inset: Jeanette Rankin of Montana, the first woman to be elected to Congress.

Right: The pioneering spirit: frontier states were the first to give women the vote.

Below: The birth control campaigner Margaret Sanger, who founded the American Birth Control League in 1917.

THE 1920s were a time of rapid change and unparalleled industrial growth in America. The war was over, the nation returning to "normalcy." Government control of the economy gave way to the *laissez faire* Republican administrations of Warren Harding, Calvin Coolidge, and Herbert Hoover, and big business grew ever bigger. Such new manifestations of the spirit of progress as the motor car and the movie theater made far-reaching changes in the fabric of American society, as, more ominously, did the new Federal enforcement of prohibition and the gangsterism it helped to encourage. But in spite of such darker developments, and the shadow of an agricultural depression which lasted throughout the decade, these were years of great self-confidence for the majority of the American people, and when President Hoover took the oath of office in 1929, he was able to look forward with glowing conviction to a future in which poverty would be swept from the face of the nation. Within a few months of his inauguration that dream was rudely shattered by the trauma of the Wall Street Crash.

In world affairs, President Wilson's interventionist idealism, which had done so much to shape the Treaty of Versailles, was replaced by a new spirit of isolationism as America recoiled from the European entanglements which had cost her so many lives and so much disruption. The commitment to peace remained, but the Republican administrations of the 1920s were no longer prepared to police that peace outside the hemisphere. As a result, the two greatest foreign policy achievements of the decade – the Washington Arms Conference and the Kellogg-Briand Pact – were to prove all too hollow when their good intentions were subjected to the mounting international strains of the 1930s.

So these, then, were the undercurrents below the surface of a decade whose most enduring images are those of the "flappers," the Charleston, and the decadent, frantic world of *The Great Gatsby*. As the 1920s drew to a close, that world had already been chilled by the first cold blast of the Great Depression. In the following decade, the inexorable march of events in Europe would signal the end, not only of the Jazz Age and its fragile prosperity, but of a whole era of human history.

Taking off the Harness

The most pressing problem facing the Federal Government at the beginning of the new decade was the problem of demobilization. Not only did four million Americans have to be reassimilated into civilian life; an entire economy had to be returned from Government control to private hands. Nor was the post-war atmosphere in America particularly conducive to the kind of rational planning required to effect such changes smoothly and efficiently. In the wake of the armistice, the United States was swept by a wave of anti-foreign, anti-Black, and anti-Communist hysteria, which saw the number of lynchings, riots, strikes, and

political arrests rocket during 1919–1920. The decade began with a massive police operation throughout the country in the course of which some 6000 suspected Communists were arrested and more than 500 of them deported. It seemed that the harsher emotions of war, encouraged by the Government's own propaganda campaigns, were more easily aroused than laid to rest.

Fortunately, this fevered interlude passed as suddenly as it began, and the administration was free to get down to the serious business of social reconstruction. Remarkably, by the beginning of 1920 all the soldiers who had gone to Europe had returned home, with the exception of a small force in Coblenz. The boards which had been charged with the running of the country's economy were disbanded; the Esch-Cummins Transportation Act returned the railways to private ownership, while greatly strengthening the powers of the Interstate Commerce Commission; and the Merchant Marine Act did likewise for the country's merchant fleet. At the same time, two new Amendments to the Constitution came into force, both of which would have profound effects on American society. One was the Eighteenth Amendment, which banned the sale, purchase, import, or export of alcoholic beverages in the United States (the accompanying Volstead Act even defined such beverages as any with more than 0·5 per cent alcohol content). The other was the Nineteenth Amendment, which gave women the right to vote. The presidential election of 1920 was thus the first in which American women were able to make their voices heard at the polls.

The Ohio Gang

The 1920 election brought the Republican Senator Warren G. Harding of Ohio to the White House in the greatest landslide victory since James Monroe's exactly 100 years before. But Harding's tenure of the highest office in the land was to prove no second "era of good feelings." Rather, it was to go down in history as the most corrupt administration since that of President Grant in the 1870s.

Harding, an undistinguished compromise candidate, who had even had to withdraw from the presidential primaries at one point due to complete lack of support, seems to have been an honest enough man himself, although his tendency to spend as much time playing poker and golf as he spent on affairs of state augured ill for his declared aim of returning the country to "normalcy." The main problem, as he soon began to realize himself, was the friends he appointed to senior positions in his administration. Worry about rumors of corruption among the so-called "Ohio Gang" may or may not have contributed to Harding's early death from a stroke on August 2, 1923; but either way it spared him the revelations of scandalous malpractice which broke shortly after his successor, the Vice President, Calvin Coolidge, was sworn in as President in the early hours of the following morning at his farmhouse in Vermont.

"Normalcy" and scandal: President Harding raises echoes of the Grant administration.

The scale of corruption was breathtaking. Harding's crony and campaign manager, the Attorney-General, Harry M. Daugherty, was removed from office after he refused to give evidence to a Congressional committee investigating charges that the Department of Justice had sold pardons and senior judicial positions. Colonel Charles R. Forbes, Director of the Veterans' Office, ended up in a Federal penitentiary after defrauding his department of millions of dollars, as did Colonel Thomas W. Miller, the Alien Property Custodian, for taking enormous bribes. Perhaps most spectacular of all, the Secretary of the Interior, Albert B. Fall, was found to have conspired with two of the country's leading oil magnates to give them control of the Government's lucrative naval oil reserves at Elk Hills in California and Teapot Dome in Wyoming, in return for substantial personal "loans." Fall, too, went to jail.

A Genius for Inactivity

Calvin Coolidge was reelected to the presidency in 1924. Famous for his taciturnity, his puritanism, and what Walter Lippmann called his "genius for inactivity," he had the dubious distinction of being the only U.S. President to veto more bills than he signed during his time in the White House. In accordance with his stated belief that "the business of America is business," he pursued a policy of *laissez faire* capitalism which resisted calls from the increasingly powerful farm lobby for the Government to support depressed farm prices, and from those, such as Senator George W. Norris, who objected to the sale to private business interests of the hydroelectric power plants at Muscle Shoals, Alabama. It was a policy which helped contribute towards the enormous concentration of commercial power in a few corporate hands during the 1920s. (In the mining and manufacturing sectors alone, some 6000 companies disap-

A genius for inactivity? President Calvin Coolidge contemplates his next utterance.

peared through mergers in the course of the decade.) If Coolidge was inactive, it was an inactivity directed to very clear ends.

The Wider World

After the trauma of the First World War, the majority of the American people favored isolationism. However, despite the failure of Congress to ratify the Treaty of Versailles, America did send unofficial representatives to the League of Nations during the 1920s and also played a leading part in two major international peace conferences. The first, the Washington Arms Conference, held under the auspices of President Harding in November 1921, resulted in a whole network of agreements between the major powers, and succeeded in slowing the incipient naval race between Britain, Japan, and the United States. It also produced agreements on the conduct of modern warfare and the power balance in the Far East, and wrote the Open Door policy into international treaties. The second, the so-called Kellogg-Briand Pact, signed in Paris in 1928, committed the great powers to renouncing war as a means of settling international disputes. Exemplary as statements of high ideals, both the Washington treaties and the Pact were nonetheless riddled with holes, not least in that they provided no mechanism for compelling the signatories to act in accordance with their provisions. This impotence was to be only too clearly revealed in the events of the coming decade.

In Latin America, Coolidge was responsible for the withdrawal of the troops Wilson had sent into the Dominican Republic and Nicaragua, although the latter country was almost immediately reoccupied when civil war broke out. In Mexico, war was once again narrowly averted, this time as a result of the patient diplomacy of Coolidge's former Secretary of War, Henry L. Stimson, after the Mexican Government threatened to nationalize the vast American mining

and mineral interests in the country in line with a previously unimplemented clause in its constitution.

An Era of Prosperity

Herbert Hoover, a world-famous mining engineer and former head of Wilson's Food Administration during the troubled days of the War, swept to victory in the presidential election of 1928 on a tide of national prosperity. In his acceptance speech he proclaimed: "We in America today are nearer to the final triumph over poverty than ever before in the history of any land. We have not yet reached the goal, but, given a chance to go forward with the policies of the last eight years, we shall soon, with the help of God, be in sight of the day when poverty will be banished from this nation."

His faith must have seemed amply justified to the majority of the American people. The nation was living through a period of unprecedented industrial growth. Total national wealth had almost doubled since the outbreak of the First World War, and the average American's income was some 10 per cent higher than it had been at the beginning of the decade. The United States, and particularly New York, had emerged as the world's chief financial center, and the dollar had toppled the pound as the world's leading exchange currency. Vast new industries, such as the electrical and automobile industries, had grown from virtually nothing at the beginning of the century, and their output was radically affecting the ways in which people conducted their daily lives. Henry Ford, in many ways the symbol of America's commercial success during these years, celebrated the production of his ten millionth motor car in 1924, and by the end of the decade the automobile industry was producing some five million vehicles a year. By the same time, more than 100 airlines, spurred on perhaps by the highly publicized

The President of prosperity, soon to be the President of Depression: Herbert Hoover.

1920

JAN 1 Red raids on private homes and labor headquarters in 33 cities, authorized by Atty Gen. A. Mitchell Palmer, result in 4000 arrests, mostly of Russians

16 Prohibition Amendment goes into effect at midnight

18 NY State public school teachers made subject to dismissal for active membership in Communist Party

28 Esch-Cummins Transportation Act creates Railroad Labor Board to supervise railroad regulation

APR 1 Five members of New York Legislature expelled for being members of Socialist Party

MAY 5 Nicola Sacco and Bartolomeo Vanzetti arrested on charges of robbery and murder of shoe factory paymaster in Braintree, Mass.; part of Red hysteria

5-10 Socialist Labor Party National Convention nominates William Wesley Cox of Missouri for President and August Gillhaus of New York for Vice President

8-14 Socialist Party National Convention nominates Eugene V. Debs of Indiana, serving ten-year prison sentence, for President and Seymour Stedman of Ohio for Vice President

JUN 4 Army Reorganization Act establishes peacetime army of 300,000 men

5 Merchant Marine Act continues wartime Shipping Board with authority to sell wartime fleet to private owners and operate unsold vessels

10 Federal Power Commission created by Congress

10 Water Power Act passed by Congress

8-12 Republican National Convention nominates Warren G. Harding of Ohio for President and Gov. Calvin Coolidge of Massachusetts for Vice President

28-JUL 5 Democratic National Convention nominates Gov. James M. Cox of Ohio for President and Franklin D. Roosevelt of New York for Vice President

JUL 13-16 Farmer-Labor Party meets in first national convention and nominates Parley P. Christensen of Utah for President and Max S. Hayes of Ohio for Vice President

21-22 Prohibition Party National Convention nominates Aaron S. Watkins of Ohio for President and David L. Calvin of New York for Vice President

AUG 26 Nineteenth Amendment, granting women suffrage, enacted

The wheels of industry: the Ford Motor Company led the way in introducing modern assembly line production methods to America.

feats of such flying aces as the "Lone Eagle," Charles A. Lindbergh, were plying their novel trade over the United States, covering some 50,000 miles of airspace. Only the persistence of the agricultural depression, which had begun in 1920, seemed to cloud an otherwise shining horizon. But disaster was waiting in the wings.

The Wall Street Crash

For 18 months before that fateful day in October 1929, the bull market on the Stock Exchange had seemed unstoppable. Some major industrial stocks had more than doubled as speculators rushed to the market in ever-increasing numbers in pursuit of quick and sizeable profits. At times more than five million shares were traded each day. Vast funds were moved out of less profitable sectors as investors plowed their money into the stock market. European funds also flooded into the United States, and banks lent some $8 billion to brokers trading shares on the New York Stock Exchange. Soon after his election, President Hoover made attempts to control the market by refusing to lend money to banks that financed speculation, but values continued to escalate, reaching an all-time high on September 3, 1929, when over eight million shares were traded in a single day.

In the same month prices began to fluctuate for the first time, but experts and Government statements assured the public that there was no cause for alarm. They were wrong. On October 24 the bottom dropped out of the market. Panic broke out on Wall Street as prices fell an average of 18 points.

Tickertape machines failed to keep up with the pace of trading as investors scrambled to sell before prices fell still further. More than 12 million transactions were recorded on October 24 alone, and a consortium of banks acted swiftly to contain the situation. But it was only a temporary delay. Share prices soon resumed their relentless fall, plummeting by an unprecedented average of 40 points on October 29. With the value of some leading stocks slashed by over two-thirds, and a staggering $26 billion wiped off the face of the market in the first month of the Crash alone, hundreds of thousands of Americans had seen their entire life savings wiped out in a mere matter of days. It was the first terrible trumpet blast of the Great Depression.

A New Renaissance

Against the background of the prosperity which was to be so abruptly shattered by the Wall Street Crash, America experienced a rebirth of literary excellence unparalleled since the golden age of the 1850s. F. Scott Fitzgerald published the novels which would come to characterize the age for millions of readers: *This Side of Paradise* in 1920, *The Beautiful and Damned* in 1922 and *The Great Gatsby* in 1925. The decade also witnessed the publication of Ernest Hemingway's first novel, *The Sun Also Rises* (1926), which was followed in 1929 by *A Farewell to Arms*. William Faulkner published the first of his famous novels of a declining South, *The Sound and the Fury*, in 1929, and in the same year wrote *As I Lay Dying* while working on the night shift at his local power station. Thomas Wolfe's masterpiece, *Look Homeward, Angel*, also appeared in 1929, and the novels of Sinclair Lewis took the reading public by storm after the publication of his first work, *Main*

Street, an indictment of the narrowness of the small-town perspective on life, in 1920. In the theater, the work of Eugene O'Neill established a distinctively American drama, with the appearance of plays such as *Beyond the Horizon* (1920), *Emperor Jones* (1920), *Desire Under the Elms* (1924), and *Strange Interlude* (1929).

Meanwhile, a new art form, the moving picture, was sweeping the country. By the end of the decade there were some 23,000 movie theaters in the United States, and such screen heroes as Douglas Fairbanks and Rudolph Valentino had acquired almost legendary status with their enraptured audiences. The 1920s saw such classics of the silent screen as Charlie Chaplin's *The Kid* (1921) and *The Gold Rush* (1925), Buster Keaton's *Go West* (1926), and, at the epic end of the spectrum, Cecil B. de Mille's *The Ten Commandments* (1924). In 1927 the film industry moved into a new age with the production of the first "talkie," *The Jazz Singer*, starring Al Jolson, and the following year saw another motion picture milestone with the appearance of Mickey Mouse in Walt Disney's first successful sound movie, *Steamboat Willie*.

In music, too, America was undergoing a new renaissance, as a whole new form – jazz – gave its name to the age. To the disapproval of an older generation and the wild enthusiasm of the young, the innovative sounds of jazzmen such as Jelly Roll Morton, King Oliver, Duke Ellington, and Louis "Satchmo" Armstrong spread the word from the backstreets of New Orleans and Chicago to the rest of the Western world. At the same time, that giant of modern popular music, George Gershwin, was carving out a reputation with musicals such as *Lady Be Good* and such staples of the modern concert repertoire as *Rhapsody in Blue*, both of which were first performed in 1924.

Gangsters

Prohibition helped to create a thriving underworld in America's major cities, with bootleg and racketeering gangs battling it out on the streets. In 1929 one of the most notorious gangland leaders, Al Capone (top), consolidated his hold over the illicit alcohol trade in Chicago in perhaps the grisliest murder of America's gangster years. On the morning of February 14, Capone mobsters disguised as policemen raided a Chicago garage from which the city's rival O'Banion Gang was operating. Under George Bugs Moran, they had been hijacking bootleg whiskey from consignments earmarked for Capone. Seven members of the gang were lined up against the wall and shot dead in what became known as the St. Valentine's Day Massacre (above).

SEP 7 Transcontinental airmail established between New York and San Francisco

NOV 2 Warren G. Harding elected President, Calvin Coolidge elected Vice President

2 First regular broadcasting service initiated by station KDKA in East Pittsburgh, Pa

DEC 10 Woodrow Wilson receives Nobel Peace Prize

Also this year

★ National Leage of Women Voters organized

★ American Farm Bureau Federation formed

The Arts

★ Carl Sandburg's book of poetry *Smoke and Steel*

★ F. Scott Fitzgerald's novel *This Side of Paradise*

★ Sinclair Lewis' novel *Main Street*

★ Edith Wharton's novel *The Age of Innocence*

★ Eugene O'Neill's plays *Beyond the Horizon* and *The Emperor Jones*

1921

JAN 4 War Finance Corporation revived over President's veto

MAR 4 Warren G. Harding inaugurated President, Calvin Coolidge inaugurated Vice President

25 Russia's request to resume trade rejected

APR 2 Prof. Albert Einstein arrives in New York to give lecture on his new theory of relativity at Columbia University

MAY Bipartisan Farm Bloc formed in Congress

19 Emergency Quota Act restricts immigration for any nationality to three percent of number of nationality already in US

27 Emergency Tariff Act increases duties on farm products and other goods

31 Secy of the Navy Edwin Denby transfers naval oil reserves at Elks Hills, Calif., and Teapot Dome, Wyo., to Department of the Interior

JUN 3 Flood of Arkansas Riv. destroys Pueblo, Colo.

10 Budget and Accounting Act establishes Bureau of the Budget and Manual Accounting Office

20 Alice Robertson of Oklahoma becomes first woman to preside over House

25 Samuel Gompers elected President of American Federation of Labor for 40th time

30 William Howard Taft appointed Chief Justice of Supreme Court

JUL 1 Railroad Labor Board authorizes 12 percent cut in wages

2 War with Germany declared at an end by joint resolution of Congress

AUG Ku Klux Klan directs violence toward Blacks and whites in South

16 Labor Department estimates 5,735,000 unemployed

25 Peace treaty with Germany signed at Berlin

SEP 26 Pres. Hoover presides over national conference on unemployment

OCT 5 First World Service radio broadcast

NOV 2 American Birth Control League formed by Margaret Sanger's National Birth Control League and Mary Ware Dennett's Voluntary Parenthood League

12-FEB 6 Washington Armament Conference attended by England, France, Italy and Japan; Russia not invited

11 Unknown Soldier buried at Arlington National Cemetery

The Silent Screen

The 1920s were the last great decade of the silent movie. The enormous popularity of motion pictures created a new pantheon of movie heroes and heroines, with stars such as Rudolph Valentino and Douglas Fairbanks gaining mass followings for their romantic and swashbuckling adventures. So intertwined had the worlds of film and real life become that Valentino's early death in 1926, just five years after *The Sheik* rocketed him to unprecedented cinematic fame as Hollywood's premier heartthrob, occasioned an outbreak of something approaching national hysteria.

The decade saw the release of a number of films which have gained themselves a place, for better or worse, in the annals of cinematic history. 1923 brought James Cruze's classic western *The Covered Wagon* and Cecil B. de Mille's sub-Biblical extravaganza *The Ten Commandments*, soon to be followed by his life of Jesus, *King of Kings*, with its unlikely subtitle "Harness My Zebras, Gift of the Nubian King." Two years later the director King Vidor entered the record books with his enormously popular "epic of the American doughboy," *The Big Parade*, which became the most commercially successful silent film ever. The following year, 1926, saw Ramon Novarro chariot-racing his way to stardom in perhaps the most extravagant of all the silent epics, Fred Niblo's *Ben Hur*.

Far right: Rudolph Valentino smolders at Gloria Swanson in Paramount's Beyond the Rocks, *1922.*

Right: Louise Brooks, one of Hollywood's leading ladies.

Below: Douglas Fairbanks, fresh from his success in The Thief of Baghdad, *swashbuckles again in* Don Q Son of Zorro, *1925.*

Below right: Hollywood's first sex symbol, Clara Bow, the "It Girl."

DEC 13 Pacific treaty signed at Washington Conference by England, France, Italy and Japan

23 Prison sentences of Eugene V. Debs and 23 others convicted under Espionage Act of 1917 commuted by Pres. Harding

Also this year

★ 800,000 immigrants arrive in US

★ Fifty-one percent of population live in cities and towns of 2500 or over

★ Nearly 20,000 businesses fail

★ Severe unemployment and wage cuts from 10 to 25 percent widespread

★ *Reader's Digest* founded

The Arts

★ John Das Passos' novel *Three Soldiers*

★ Booth Tarkington's novel *Alice Adams*

★ Imported copies of James Joyce's novel *Ulysses* confiscated by US Post Office

1922

FEB 6 Nine-Power Treaty signed at Washington Conference to respect territorial integrity of China; formal endorsement of Open Door policy

6 Five-Power Naval Treaty signed by US, Britain, Japan, France and Italy provides for 10-year moratorium on building large vessels

9 World War Foreign Debt Commission established by Congress to settle Allied loans

18 Copper-Volstead Act exempts agricultural cooperatives from antitrust law restrictions

27 Nineteenth Amendment, providing women's suffrage, unanimously declared constitutional by Supreme Court

APR Teapot Dome scandal: Int. Secy Albert B. Fall secretly leases naval oil reserve district to Mammoth Oil Company and subsequently leases second reserve to Edward L. Doheny through an illegal procedure; congressional investigation follows

MAY 26 Federal Narcotics Control Board established

30 Lincoln Memorial dedicated in Washington, DC

JUN 14 Warren G. Harding becomes first President to be heard over radio in broadcast of dedication of Francis Scott Key Memorial in Baltimore

AUG 28 First commercial broadcast by WEAF in NYC

SEP 22 Cable Act specifies that an American woman who marries an alien will not lose her citizenship and a woman marrying an American will not automatically become US citizen

OCT 3 Rebecca L. Felton appointed by Governor of Georgia to seat vacated by death of Sen. Thomas E. Watson; first female senator

DEC 4 Second Central American Conference meets in Washington, DC; US retains right under Roosevelt Corollary to intercede at will in South American affairs

Also this year

★ First successful use of Technicolor film process made by Herbert T. Kalmus

★ Evangelical Church formed by merger of United Evangelical Church and Evangelical Association

The Arts

★ T. S. Eliot's poem 'The Waste Land'

★ F. Scott Fitzgerald's novels *Tales of the Jazz Age* and *The Beautiful and Damned*

★ Sinclair Lewis' novel *Babbitt*

★ Louis Armstrong joins King Oliver's Creole Jazz Band in Chicago as cornetist

1923

JAN 10 US occupation troops stationed in Germany withdrawn

MAR 4 Credit Act adopted to give relief to farmers

2 Senate begins investigation of Veterans' Bureau

5 First old age pension grants enacted in Montana and Nevada

Meanwhile, at the comic end of the movie spectrum, the 1920s saw some of the greatest silent masterpieces. Charlie Chaplin's inimitable mixture of pathos and high slapstick delighted millions in *The Kid* (1921) and *The Gold Rush* (1925), while Buster Keaton's deadpan artistry and daring stunts made him a star with films such as *The Navigator* (1924) and *Go West* (1925). Often regarded as the third member of this classic comic triumvirate, Harold Lloyd perfected his downbeat bespectacled persona in a series of movies which featured some breath-takingly risky stuntmanship. The long-running partnership of Stan Laurel and Oliver Hardy, whose transition to talkies was to be more successful than that of many of their contemporaries, also produced some of its best work during these years.

Left inset: High level clowning for Harold Lloyd in Safety Last *(1923). This famous sequence was shot on an artificial structure atop an existing skyscraper.*

Left: Buster Keaton in The Navigator.

Below: A product of the Hal Roach studios, Laurel and Hardy became one of the most popular double acts of all time, continuing to make films together into the 1940s.

Right: Charlie Chaplin and Jackie Coogan on the wrong side of the law in The Kid.

13 Lee De Forest demonstrates sound motion picture process called Phonofilm

APR 9 In *Adkins v. Children's Hospital*, Supreme Court rules minimum wage law for women and children in District of Columbia is unconstitutional

MAY 4 NY State Prohibition Act repealed by NY State Assembly

JUN 20 Pres. Harding begins tour of the West and Alaska

AUG 2 Pres. Harding dies in San Francisco

3 Calvin Coolidge sworn in as President by his father, a notary public, in Plymouth, Vt

13 US Steel Corporation institutes eight-hour day

SEP 15 Oklahoma placed under martial law by Gov. J.C. Walton due to terrorist activities of Ku Klux Klan

OCT 25 Teapot Dome oil scandal returns to public attention as Senate subcommittee investigation begins

NOV 13 Robert A. Millikan receives Nobel Prize in Physics for isolation of electron

DEC 6 First broadcast of official presidential address

Also this year

★ *Time* magazine begins publication

The Arts

★ E.E. Cummings' first volume of poetry *Tulips and Chimneys*

★ Ernest Hemingway's *Three Stories and Ten Poems*

1924

FEB 3 Death of 28th President of US Woodrow Wilson

MAY 11-13 Socialist Labor Party National Convention nominates Frank T. Johns of Oregon for President and Verne L. Reynolds of Maryland for Vice President

26 Immigration Act lowers quota to two percent of number of nationality already in US and totally excludes Japanese

JUN 5 Prohibition Party National Convention nominates Herman P. Faris of Missouri for President and Marie C. Brehm of California for Vice President

12 Republican National Convention nominates Calvin Coolidge for President and Charles G. Dawes of Illinois for Vice President

19 Farmer-Labor Progressive Party National Convention

JUL 4 Conference for Progressive Political Action nominates Sen. Robert La Follette of Wisconsin for President and Charles W. Bryan of Nebraska for Vice President

10 Worker's Party (Communist) nominates William L. Foster of Illinois for President and Benjamin Gitlow of New York for Vice President; same candidates on Farmer-Labor Progressive Party ticket

AUG 30 Dawes Plan for reorganization of German debt payments and stabilization of its currency formally accepted by Allies and Germany

NOV 4 Calvin Coolidge elected President, Charles G. Dawes elected Vice President

30 Radio Corporation of America demonstrates technique of sending photographs by transatlantic wireless telegraphy, from London to NYC

DEC 13 Death of AFL President Samuel Gompers

27 Treaty with the Dominican Republic supersedes treaty of 1907; ends US military government

The Arts

★ Herman Melville's novel *Billy Budd, Foretopman*

★ O'Neill's plays *All God's Chillun Got Wings* and *Desire Under the Elms*

★ George Gershwin's symphonic work *Rhapsody in Blue*

★ *Saturday Review of Literature* begins publication

★ *American Mercury*, H.L. Mencken editor, begins publication

THE JAZZ AGE

The movement in popular culture with which the 1920s are most closely associated and which served to give a name to the age itself, was the emergence of jazz. Drawing its vitality from the same roots in Black music that had fed the flowering of ragtime in the first two decades of the 20th century, jazz was born in the Deep South, and particularly in the red-light backstreets of New Orleans, around the turn of the century, but rapidly spread throughout the United States via Chicago and New York during the 1920s. Many of its earliest and greatest exponents were Black musicians highly skilled in the art of improvisation which to this day forms the basis of the jazz form – men such as the trombonist King Oliver, leader of the "Creole Jazz Band," and the mercurial pianist Jelly Roll Morton, leader of the "Red Hot Peppers" and creator of such classic numbers as *Black Bottom Stomp* and *Dead Man Blues*. One of the most influential bands to come out of New

Orleans, though, was the all-white "Original Dixieland Band," who were recording as early as 1916 and did much to popularize jazz among non-Blacks.

With the new music came new fashions and new lifestyles, much to the distaste of many members of the older generation. Particularly shocking to conservative sensibilities were the diaphonous high hem-lines, bobbed hair, and uninhibited dances of the so-called "flappers," which were widely seen as symptoms of a decline in national morals among the young.

Far right: Sowing the seeds of jazz: a Black banjo player around 1902.

Right: A flapper shocks her elders.

Below: King Oliver (kneeling) with his "Creole Jazz Band," 1920. Louis Armstrong stands behind him, with trumpet.

Below right: One of the greatest blues singers: Ma Rainey with her "Georgia Jazz Band," 1925.

1925

JAN 5 Nellie Taylor Ross of Wyoming becomes first female governor in US

FEB 21 *The New Yorker*, edited by Harold Ross, begins publication

MAR 4 Calvin Coolidge inaugurated for first elective term, Charles G. Dawes inaugurated Vice President

5 John T. Scopes arrested for teaching Darwin's theory of evolution in public school system of Dayton, Tenn.

JUL 10-21 In Scopes 'monkey' trial, teacher John T. Scopes, defended by Clarence Darrow and Dudley Field Malone and opposed by fundamentalist William Jennings Bryant, loses verdict and fined $100

AUG 3 US Marines leave Nicaragua after 13-year occupation

8 Ku Klux Klan holds massive political demonstration in Washington, DC; 40,000 march down Pennsylvania Avenue

OCT Peak of Florida land boom

Also this year
★ Al Capone begins six years of gang warfare
★ John Simon Guggenheim Foundation established

The Arts
★ Ezra Pound's volume of poetry *Draft of XVI Cantos*
★ Theodore Dreiser's novel *An American Tragedy*
★ F. Scott Fitzgerald's novel *The Great Gatsby*
★ George S. Kaufman and Irving Berlin's musical comedy *The Coconuts*, starring the Marx Brothers
★ The musical comedy *No, No, Nanette*

1926

JAN 27 Resolution permitting US to join World Court of International Justice adopted by Senate

FEB 26 Revenue Act reduces income taxes, surtaxes and others and abolishes many nuisance taxes

APR 29 Debt funding agreement with France cancels 60 percent of French war debt and provides for repayment of $4 billion over 62 years at 1.6 percent interest

MAY 10 US Marines land in Nicaragua to quell revolt

18 Evangelist Aimee Semple McPherson disappears; later turns up in Mexico

20 Air Commerce Act gives Department of Commerce control over licensing of aircraft and pilots

JUL 2 Army Air Corps established by Congress

AUG 6 Gertrude Ederle, 19, of NYC becomes first woman to swim English Channel

SEP 18 Hurricane sweeps Florida and Gulf states, killing 372, injuring 6000 and leaving 18,000 homeless

23 James Joseph 'Gene' Tunney defeats heavyweight boxing champion Jack Dempsey

25 Eight-hour day and five-day week introduced in Ford Motor Company plants

OCT Lightning triggers ammunition depot explosion at Lake Denmark, NJ, killing 31 and causing $93 million in damage

26 Supreme Court rules that President has power to remove executive officers from positions

Also this year
★ Bootleg trade estimated at $3.6 billion for year
★ Sarah Lawrence College established as Sarah Lawrence College for Women in Bronxville, NY
★ Book-of-the-Month Club organized
★ Carl Sandburg's biography *Abraham Lincoln, The Prairie Years*, first two of six volumes, published

The Arts
★ Langston Hughes' volume of poetry *The Weary Blues*
★ Ernest Hemingway's novel *The Sun Also Rises*
★ John Barrymore in the film *Don Juan*, featuring phonographic sound

"Satchmo"

Louis Armstrong (1900–1971) (right), exported his trumpet-playing style from New Orleans to Chicago, where he played with the "Creole Jazz Band" before leading his own group, the "Hot Five."

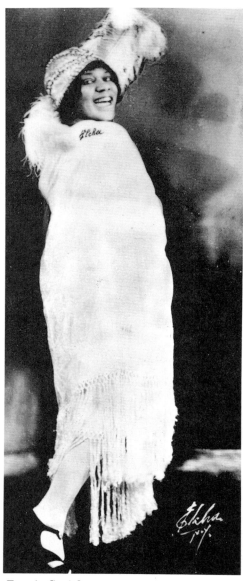

Bessie Smith

Blues, a form with its origins deep within the Black experience of oppression, was one of the strongest strands of the jazz movement. One of the foremost exponents· was the great Black singer Bessie Smith (1894–1937) (above), known to her fans as the "Empress of the Blues," who made her first recordings in New York City in the early 1920s.

"You Ain't Heard Nothing Yet"

With these words Al Jolson, one of America's top entertainers, launched a new age of sound cinema in the first ever "talkie," *The Jazz Singer*, in 1927. Despite the skepticism of many established stars of the silent screen, the movie marked the end of the great age of the silents, as well as confirming the musical reputation of Jolson himself.

George Gershwin

One of the first composers to merge jazz and classical musical traditions, George Gershwin (1898–1937) (above) wrote numerous popular songs as well as the musical *Lady Be Good* and the piano concerto *Rhapsody in Blue* in the 1920s.

The Charleston

One of the quintessential symbols of the Jazz Age, the craze for this frantic and revealing dance, named after the town of its birth, swept the United States in the middle 1920s. Much criticized by members of the establishment, it was avidly embraced by young couples such as the one demonstrating it, somewhat clinically, in the photograph above.

Martha Graham

One of the most influential dancers and choreographers of the 20th century, Pittsburgh-born Martha Graham (left) first appeared on the American stage in 1920 and made her independent debut in 1926 at the age of 31. Known particularly for her interpretations of primitive or myth-ological subjects, Graham formed her own touring dance group in 1929.

Keeping America Dry

The 1920s were the decade of prohibition in America. In 1919 Congress passed the Volstead Act over President Wilson's veto, thus enacting the Eighteenth Amendment and outlawing the liquor trade throughout the country.

It soon became apparent, however, that prohibition was far easier to proclaim than to enforce. Illicit stills and large-scale liquor smuggling soon proliferated, and speakeasies – illegal drinking venues – sprang up behind closed doors throughout the nation. Worse still, the whole liquor business quickly fell under the control of organized crime syndicates such as Al Capone's. Against this clandestine network, often supplied from ships off America's vast and virtually unpoliceable coastline, the Federal Prohibition Bureau was able to muster only some 3000 prohibition enforcement agents, and – despite the remarkable efforts of such colorful "rum ferrets" as Izzy Einstein and Moe Smith, who became

legendary for their ingenuity in locating and closing down speakeasies and between them confiscated some five million bottles of illegal alcohol in the years 1920 to 1925 – the Bureau itself was forced to concede that barely 5 per cent of smuggled liquor was being prevented from entering the country. In 1933 the Twenty-first Amendment repealed the Eighteenth Amendment and prohibition came to an inglorious end.

Left: A Federal prohibition agent closes down a speakeasy.

Below: An agent destroys barrels of beer.

Opposite top: Policemen contemplate one of the largest illegal stills discovered in Washington, D.C.

Opposite middle: A lucky find: prohibition agents confiscate 3000 bags of illicit liquor aboard a coal steamer in New York Harbor.

Opposite bottom: Opening time: drinking to the end of prohibition, 1933.

1927

JAN 7 Commercial transatlantic telephone service opened between New York and London

FEB 18 US and Canada establish diplomatic relations independent of Great Britain

23 Federal Radio Commission established by Congress

APR Mississippi Riv. flood waters cover 4 million acres, causing property loss of $300 million

7 First successful demonstration of television in NYC by Walter S. Gifford, president of A T & T, showing Secy of Commerce Herbert Hoover in Washington office

MAY 20-21 Charles A. Lindbergh makes non-stop solo flight in *Spirit of St Louis* from New York to Paris in 33 and a half hours

JUL 29 Electric respirator, or iron lung, installed at Bellevue Hospital, New York

AUG 2 Pres. Coolidge declines renomination

2 International Peace Bridge, linking US and Canada at Buffalo, dedicated

23 Nicola Sacco and Bartolomeo Vanzetti executed in Massachusetts for 1920 killing of factory guard

SEP 29 Five-minute tornado strikes St Louis, killing 87, injuring 1500 and causing $50 million damage

NOV 13 Holland Tunnel, first underwater motor vehicle tunnel in US, links Manhattan and NJ

Also this year

★ Mechanical cotton picker invented by John D. Rust

★ George Herman 'Babe' Ruth hits 60 home runs

★ First Golden Gloves amateur boxing matches

★ Mount Rushmore, S. Dak., dedicated

The Arts

★ Sinclair Lewis' novel *Elmer Gantry*

★ Oscar Hammerstein II and Jerome Kern's musical *Show Boat*

★ Aaron Copeland's *Concerto for Piano and Orchestra*

★ Al Jolson in the film *The Jazz Singer*, first 'talkie'

★ Academy of Motion Pictures Arts and Sciences formed

1928

JAN 16 Sixth International Conference of American States opened in Havana by Pres. Coolidge

MAY 27 Amelia Earhart takes off from Boston to become first woman to fly across the Atlantic

JUN 12-15 Republican National Convention nominates Herbert Hoover of California for President and Charles Curtis of Kansas for Vice President

26-29 Democratic National Convention nominates Gov. Alfred E. Smith of New York for President and Joseph T. Robinson of Arkansas for Vice President

JUL 11 Farmer-Labor Party National Convention

12 Prohibition Party National Convention

30 First color motion pictures in US exhibited by George Eastman at Rochester, NY

AUG 25 Byrd Antarctic Expedition leaves New York

27 Kellogg-Briand Pact, for outlawing war and settling international controversies by arbitration, signed by US and 15 nations in Paris

NOV 6 Herbert Hoover elected President, Charles Curtis elected Vice President

6 First animated electric sign in US mounted by *New York Times* around top of Times Building in Times Square, NYC, used to report presidential election returns

19 Pres. elect Hoover leaves for goodwill tour of South America

26 International Conference on Economic Statistics of the League of Nations opens in Geneva

Conquering the Skies

The 1920s were a pivotal decade in the history of American aviation. In particular, there occurred in 1927 an event which captured the imagination of the American people as no other event in the saga of man's conquest of the air had ever captured it. At 7.51 a.m. on May 20 that year, a 25-year-old Minnesotan flying ace by the name of Charles A. Lindbergh took off from Curtiss Field, Long Island, in a silver Ryan monoplane called *The Spirit of St. Louis*. His aim was to fly non-stop across the Atlantic to Paris, France, a feat which had not yet been accomplished by a solo pilot, although it had been performed many times by crews, both in planes and in dirigibles. 3610 miles and 33 hours 29 minutes later, *The Spirit of St. Louis* touched down at Le Bourget airfield on the outskirts of Paris, where Lindbergh was greeted by cheering crowds of well-wishers. Not only did his feat earn him the sobriquet "The Lone Eagle" and $25,000 in

prize money; he also received an adulatory hero's welcome on his return to the United States. His enterprise, which administered a significant boost to the U.S. aviation industry, was soon emulated by other pilots, including Clarence Chamberlain, Charles A. Levine, and Amelia Earhart, who became the first woman to fly solo across the Atlantic in 1928. For Lindbergh himself fame was to prove a mixed blessing. Five years later triumph turned to tragedy when his baby son was kidnapped and murdered.

Above: The Spirit of St. Louis *over Paris.*

Above inset: Following in Lindbergh's slipstream: Amelia Earhart, the first woman to fly the Atlantic single-handed.

Opposite top: An unlikely hero: shy, gangling, and aloof, "The Lone Eagle" poses in front of his plane.

Opposite below: New York honors Lindbergh with a ticker-tape parade, June 13, 1927.

DEC 10 Pan-American Conference on Conciliation and Arbitration in Washington, DC

21 Boulder Dam Project Act commits government to participation in production of hydroelectric power

The Arts

★ Stephen Vincent Benét's poem *John Brown's Body*

★ George Gershwin's composition *An American in Paris*

★ Walt Disney's *Mickey Mouse* in the cartoon *Plane Crazy*, first cartoon released by Walt Disney Productions

★ Ash Can School of painting, in NYC's Greenwich Village

1929

JAN 15 Kellogg-Briand Pact ratified by Senate

FEB 2 Federal Reserve Board forbids member banks to make loans for stock speculation on margin

13 Cruiser Act authorizes construction of 19 new cruisers and 1 aircraft carrier; US embarks on naval race

14 In St Valentine's Day Massacre, six Chicago gangsters are lined up against wall and shot to death by rival gang

MAR 4 Herbert Hoover inaugurated President, Charles Curtis inaugurated Vice President

APR 15 Birth Control Clinical Research Center, established in NYC by Margaret Sanger, raided by police acting on complaint by Daughters of the American Revolution

MAY 20 Pres. Hoover appoints National Commission on Law Observance and Enforcement to study effects of Prohibition on US

27 In *US v. Schwimmer*, Supreme Court upholds refusal of citizenship to Rosika Schwimmer, pacifist from Hungary

JUN 15 Agricultural Marketing Act establishes Federal Farm Board for promoting sale of commodities through farmers' cooperatives and stablization corporations

JUL 1 Immigration Act of 1924 goes into effect, delayed from original date, July 1, 1927

AUG Steel and automobile production begins to decline

SEP Common stock price index peaks at 216, climax of three-year bull market

Sixty percent of US citizens have annual incomes of less than $2000 – just enough to supply family with basic necessities

24 Lt Gen. James Doolittle makes first 'blind' airplane flight, at Mitchell Field, NY

OCT 4-9 British PM Ramsay McDonald comes to Washington, DC, to discuss naval parity with Pres. Hoover

23 Panic develops in NY Stock Exchange

24 Black Thursday: NY Stock Exchange collapses; 13 million shares sold

29 Black Tuesday: worst day in history of NY Stock Exchange; 16 million shares sold at declining prices

NOV 13 By this date, $30 billion in capital values have been wiped out in NY Stock Exchange

21 Pres. Hoover holds confidential conferences with representatives of big business and trade unions

29 Lt Comdr. Richard E. Byrd makes first airplane flight over South Pole

DEC 3 Pres. Hoover in annual message to Congress declares that business confidence has been reestablished

Also this year

★ First 'garden community' initiated in Radburn, NJ

★ Trailer, invented by Glen H. Curtis, displayed in NY by Hudson Company

The Arts

★ Dashiell Hammett's detective novels *Red Harvest* and *The Dain Curse*

★ Ernest Hemingway's novel *A Farewell to Arms*

★ Thomas Wolfe's novel *Look Homeward Angel*

★ Georgia O'Keefe's painting *Black Flowers and Blue Larkspur*

★ First Academy Awards presented by Academy of Motion Picture Arts and Sciences

"The lost generation"

The great flowering of literary activity which took place in the United States during the 1920s was underlaid by a deep-rooted sense of disillusionment, both with American society and its values and, by extension, with mankind as a whole. In fiction, this manifested itself most acutely in the novels of F. Scott Fitzgerald, John Dos Passos, Ernest Hemingway, and Sinclair Lewis, and in William Faulkner's first novels set in the fictional Yoknapatawpha County of the Deep South. The work of that great triumvirate of American women writers, Willa Cather, Ellen Glasgow, and Edith Wharton, embodies a similar distrust and critique of American social mores.

The same spirit informs the work of such very different poets as the expatriate T. S. Eliot, whose enormously influential poem *The Waste Land* appeared in 1922; Robinson Jeffers, whose long poetic career, with its deeply pessimistic view of human nature, began in earnest with the publication of *Tamar and Other Poems* in 1924; and Edna St. Vincent Millay, whose *A Few Figs From Thistles* achieved great popularity in 1920. In the latter collection, as in the poems and short stories of Dorothy Parker, which began to appear in the 1920s, disillusionment seems to topple over into a flippant cynicism highly characteristic of the age.

A fundamentally tragic view of the human condition is to be found, too, in the plays of Eugene O'Neill, whose prolific output during the 1920s confirmed him as one of the greatest dramatists ever to emerge in the United States.

F. Scott Fitzgerald (1896–1940), seen above with his wife, Zelda, and daughter, Scottie, in self-consciously jazzy pose, was in many ways the embodiment of the spirit of the 1920s. It was he who dubbed them "The Jazz Age," and whose novels and short stories capture most tellingly the sense of malaise beneath the often glittering surface of the period. His masterpiece, The Great Gatsby (1925) tells the story of a high-living socialite whose wealth and outward success hide unfulfilled desires which eventually lead to tragedy. Fitzgerald's own life was haunted by alcoholism and his wife's nervous collapse.

Ezra Pound (1885–1972) was born in Idaho but lived most of his life in France and Italy where he exercised a powerful influence on the development of modern poetry. A leader of the Imagist school, his voluminous Cantos, begun in 1919, occupied him for the majority of his working life.

T. S. Eliot *(1888–1965). Like Pound, who helped bring him to public attention, Eliot was born in America but lived for most of his life in Europe. His five-part poem* The Waste Land, *its desolate world view expressed through a fusion of contemporary urban imagery and classical and pre-classical myth, was widely seen as a new departure when it was published in 1922.*

William Faulkner *(1897–1962) began his literary career in 1926 with the novel* Soldier's Pay. *His most characteristic works, however, are his series of tragic novels set in the declining South of his own upbringing, beginning with* Sartoris *and* The Sound and the Fury, *both published in 1929. His fiction is structurally highly innovative, and often employs multiple narrative perspectives.*

Thoedore Dreiser *(1871–1945) established his uncompromisingly realist approach to the contradictions and failures of American society in his first novel, the controversial* Sister Carrie, *in 1900. In 1925 he published* An American Tragedy, *a flawed but forceful novel, based on a New York murder.*

Dorothy Parker *(1893–1967). Known as much for her waspish epigrams as for her literary output, Parker published her first volumes of poetry,* Enough Rope *and* Sunset Gun, *in 1926 and 1928 respectively. She also wrote short stories and was a newspaper correspondent and literary critic.*

Robert Frost *(1874–1963). In 1923 Frost won a Pulitzer Prize for his third book of poems,* New Hampshire, *a collection which demonstrates his characteristic qualities of formal and emotional concision. The themes of Frost's poetry draw profoundly on the life and scenery of his beloved New England.*

Rural Poverty

The problem of rural poverty received less attention than the plight of urban slum dwellers, but was often just as dire. Above: Inside a Negro cabin in the Deep South, 1920.

Aimee Semple McPherson

One of the best known women of her time, the evangelist Aimee Semple McPherson, extravagant founder of Los Angeles' Angelus Temple, fell from grace after her mysterious disappearance in 1926 was attributed not, as she claimed, to a bizarre kidnapping, but to a romantic liaison.

Marcus Garvey

The Jamaican-born Black nationalist leader Marcus Garvey (left) exerted a profound influence on Black thought in the 1920s through his United Negro Improvement Association (UNIA) and his newspaper *Negro World*. Preaching Black pride and self-help, he also encouraged a "back-to-Africa" movement. He was deported in 1923.

Raymond Loewy

Illustrator and designer Raymond Loewy produced this *Vogue* ad for Saks Fifth Avenue in 1927.

Another servant in the house

Western Electric
VACUUM SWEEPER
WITH THE MOTOR DRIVEN BRUSH

Advert of The Western Electric Company Limited. — Ask your Dealer for particulars.

Aids to Living

Labor-saving domestic devices heralded a lifestyle revolution, despite the incongruously classical flavor of this ad for a new Western Electric vacuum cleaner.

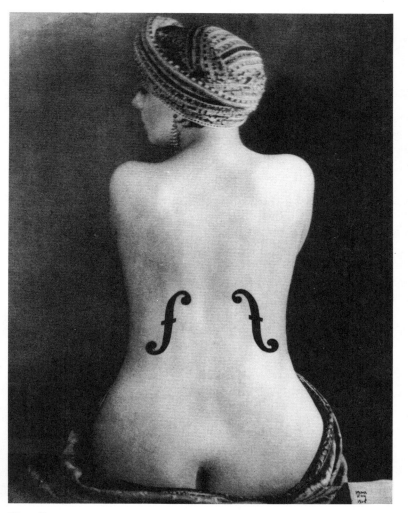

Man Ray

The 1920s saw the development of the surrealist movement in the arts, which found expression in the paintings of Dali and de Chirico and in the work of the innovative photographer Man Ray, one of whose most familiar images, the visual pun shown above, has not lost its capacity to disturb.

First *New Yorker*

The first issue of a new magazine, the *New Yorker*, edited by Harold Ross and specializing in sophisticated contemporary comment, appeared in 1925.

The Big Apple

The bright lights of America's largest and most bustling city are atmospherically captured in this night-time view of Times Square, New York, photographed in 1926.

The Ku Klux Klan

The early 1920s saw spectacular growth in the membership of the Ku Klux Klan, a ritualistic secret society dedicated to white supremacy, anti-Roman Catholicism, and anti-semitism. The Klan, which took its name and structure from those of a white supremacist organization of the 1860s, was founded in Georgia in 1915 by "Colonel" William J. Simmons, an ex-minister, who styled himself Imperial Wizard of the Invisible Empire. From its origins in the Southern states, it quickly became a powerful force in Oklahoma, Oregon, Ohio, and by 1923, under the leadership of Simmons' successor, Hiram Wesley Evans, a Dallas dentist, it claimed to have more than a million members throughout the United States. The picture shows new members being initiated.

The Scopes Case

In 1925 John Scopes (sitting fourth from right above), a young teacher from Dayton, Tennessee, was taken to court for breaking state laws banning the teaching of evolution in schools. Defended by the famous lawyer Clarence Darrow (far left), Scopes lost the case but supporters of creationism, including the aged William Jennings Bryan, were widely discredited by their performance under questioning.

Helen Wills Moody

The U.S. tennis star Helen Wills Moody (above) won her first Wimbledon ladies' singles title in 1927. Her record eight Wimbledon wins remained unbeaten until 1990 when Martina Navratilova took her ninth Wimbledon title.

Isolationism

With the retrospective unpopularity of America's involvement in the First World War, isolationism became a guiding force in her inter-war diplomacy. Some voices, however, such as these two anti-isolationist demonstrators', were raised in favor of a more internationalist outlook.

The Wall Street Crash

America had had her share of stock market panics and financial depressions in the past, but none had so profound an impact on the way of life of the average American citizen as the crash on the New York Stock Exchange on October 24, 1929, and the Great Depression of which it proved to the harbinger.

Near right: The *Philadelphia Inquirer* put a brave face on the Crash in its morning edition of October 25, 1929, noting, with what proved to be pathetically misplaced optimism, that "reassuring statements of America's most powerful banking interests came to the support of a collapsing stock market today and arrested what might otherwise have been the greatest financial debacle in the country's history."

Middle right: Anxious customers from Wall Street brokerage houses scan their newspapers for the latest news of the Crash.

Far right: Not all those who gathered outside the New York Stock Exchange on October 24 came out of panic. Newspapers reported "a holiday mood" on Wall Street as crowds of ordinary citizens congregated on the sidewalks in the hope of seeing "a world series of finance enacted before their eyes."

Below: Milling crowds bring traffic to a halt in Wall Street as news spreads of the stock market collapse.

Below right: Countless fortunes, as well as the life savings of many ordinary people, were wiped out virtually overnight by the financial collapse. Here a businessman seeks to recoup some of his losses by selling his automobile.

Inquirer

ALL DISPLAY CLASSIFIE
FOR SUNDAY'S EDITION
Must Be in The Inquirer Offic
BY 10 O'CLOCK TONIGH

Copyright, 1929, by
The Philadelphia Inquirer Co.

WEATHER—Cloudy   a b c d e f g   TWO CEN

STOCK VALUES CRASH
IN RECORD STAMPEDE
BANKERS HALT ROU

CURIOUS JAM
WALL STREET TO
SEE THE 'SHOW'

Huge Crowd Throngs "Money Lane" Seeking Thrill in Battle of Bulls and Bears

Butcher, Baker and Candle-
stick Maker Rush to View
"World Series" of Fi-

BUSINESS OF NATION

Stock Slump Fails to Dim Tax Cut Hope

WASHINGTON, Oct. 24 (A. P.).—The view that the recent slumps in the stock market will not affect the administration's tax-reduction programme is held by Treasury officials.

The officials regard the slumps as being more in paper profits than in actual values and believe the action was in the nature of a readjustment of the market and that stock prices generally still were above those paid by people who bought them at ordinary stages some time ago.

UPSWING END
WILD SELLING
12,894,650 D

N. Y. Exchange S
Most Violent Drop
Prices Since 19
Ticker Hours Late

Market Rallies as Morg
and Other Financial Gro

ABOVE all else, the 1930s in America were the decade of the Great Depression. In the years which followed the Wall Street Crash of 1929, the United States was plunged into an economic slump of unparalleled severity. Farms, businesses, and financial institutions collapsed into bankruptcy, and unemployment spiraled to unprecedented levels, bringing hunger and hopelessness to millions of Americans. To the relentless march of economic forces was added the natural catastrophe of the Dust Bowl, as drought reduced the breadbasket states to a vast arid desert and drove countless families westward in search of food and shelter.

The crisis confronted the nation's leaders with political and social problems on a scale unseen since the dark days of the Civil War. President Hoover, elected to office on the back of the prosperity of the 1920s, seemed unable to rise to the new and radically different economic challenges of the 1930s, and in 1932 the American people voted in huge numbers for the man who promised them a "new deal," the dynamic Democratic candidate, Franklin D. Roosevelt. The next five years saw that New Deal taking shape, as Congress enacted a far-reaching program of legislation designed to lift America out of depression and return her to prosperity. It was to be a long slow haul. By the end of the decade the United States had weathered the worst of the economic storms, but, despite Roosevelt's inspirational leadership and a vast public spending program, full recovery remained elusive.

The decade also saw the gathering of storm clouds of a different kind, as events in Europe and the Far East threatened to engulf the world in another conflict on the scale of the "war to end war." While America developed her "Good Neighbor" policy in the Western Hemisphere, the forces of authoritarianism were consolidating their hold over the politics of continental Europe. Once again, the United States was to find her isolationist neutrality under pressure from events far beyond her shores, as Britain and France finally abandoned their policy of appeasement in the face of Hitler's ever more blatant expansionism. By the end of the decade, Europe was once more at war. Ironically, that war would give the American economy the boost that Roosevelt's New Deal had failed to administer. But it would also open a new era in world affairs – the era of the superpowers – in which the United States would bind itself more intimately to the security of Europe than ever before.

Brother, Can You Spare a Dime?

Despite the optimism of some contemporary commentators, it became clear within a few months of the catastrophic October 1929 fall in prices on the New York Stock Exchange that the Wall Street Crash was no isolated phenomenon, but the overture to an economic depression of terrifying proportions. Between 1929 and 1933 the national income of the United States fell by more than a half, from almost $88 billion to just

over $40 billion, and foreign trade declined by two thirds. More than 100,000 businesses failed, and some 5000 banks closed their doors. The farming community, which had not even shared in the general prosperity of the 1920s, now found itself sorely pressed: agricultural income declined from around $12 billion to just over $5 billion. Unemployment, already running at two to four million in 1930, rose to seven million the following year, and by 1933 had soared to an estimated 14 million.

Behind these bald figures lay the stark human tragedy of the depression years. At least a third of the American people are estimated to have suffered directly from the effects of unemployment. Thousands upon thousands lined up for soup and bread in the streets of the major cities, until the failure of public funds denied them even that relief. Jobless people, some of them once wealthy businessmen, set up stalls selling apples at the roadsides, and shanty towns of cardboard, wood, and corrugated iron – bitterly

From the Western farmer to the Wall Street stockbroker and the industrial magnate, the Great Depression left its mark in every walk of American life.

known as "Hoovervilles" – sprang up on the outskirts of towns throughout the United States. In some cities, such as Cleveland, half of the workforce were without jobs. In other places, the situation was even worse: in Toledo, Ohio, for example, unemployment reached a staggering 80 per cent. Even at the end of the decade, a single vacancy could attract thousands of hopeful applicants. The United States had known hard times in the past, but never before had hunger and despair stalked so many people in so many walks of life.

Enter Roosevelt

Hidebound in his economic orthodoxy, President Herbert Hoover was widely seen as unequal to the tasks demanded of him at this crucial moment in the nation's history. Not least because of his action in sending troops to disperse the so-called Bonus Expeditionary Force – a group of First World War veterans who marched to Washington in 1932 seeking immediate payment of their bonuses – the result of the presidential election of 1932 represented a massive vote of no confidence in Hoover's administration. Instead, a majority of the electorate turned to the charismatic Franklin Delano

1930s

The Great Depression

The New Deal

The Dust Bowl

1930

JAN Young Plan to supercede Dawes Plan, for reduced schedule of payments of German reparations

2 Pres. Hoover meets with Congressional leaders to discuss development of public works program

21-APR 22 London Naval Conference

FEB 3 Charles Evans Hughes appointed Chief Justice of Supreme Court

10 Major Chicago bootlegging operation shut down; 158 people from 31 organizations arrested

MAR 30 Pluto discovered and named at Lowell Observatory, Flagstaff, Ariz.

31 Public Buildings Act provides for $230 million for construction of public buildings

APR 4 Congress authorizes $300 million for federal aid to states for road construction

22 London Naval Treaty signed by US, Great Britain and Japan

MAY 4 Petition signed by 1028 economists protesting Hawley-Smoot Tariff Bill made public

11 Adler Planetarium, first planetarium in US, opens in Chicago

24 *Literary Digest* poll shows that majority favors repeal of 18th Amendment

JUN 17 Hawley-Smoot Tariff Act signed by Pres. Hoover; raises duties and sets off economic warfare

JUL 3 Veterans Administration established by Congress

AUG 11 American Lutheran Church formed at Toledo, Ohio

SEP 3 First electric passenger train tested by Thomas A. Edison on Lackawanna Railroad between Hoboken and Montclair, NJ

9 Immigration of virtually all foreign laborers prohibited by State Department

OCT Committee for Unemployment Relief appointed by the President

NOV 4 Democrats gain control of House

DEC 11 Bank of the United States, NYC, with 60 branches and 400,000 depositors, closes

The Arts

★ William Faulkner's novel *As I Lay Dying*

★ Dashiell Hammett's novel *The Maltese Falcon*

★ John Dos Passos' novel *The 42nd Parallel*

★ Grant Wood's painting *American Gothic*

★ James Joyce's novel *Ulysses,* seized by customs officials on grounds that it is 'obscene'

Roosevelt who had pledged himself, in his acceptance speech to the Democratic convention in Chicago, to "a new deal for the American people."

Roosevelt, a distant cousin (and also nephew-in-law) of Theodore Roosevelt, was born of wealthy parents in 1882. A former Assistant Secretary of the Navy, Roosevelt had been the Democratic vice-presidential candidate in 1920, and had become the Governor of New York in 1928. Handsome, dynamic, and an excellent public speaker, he had proved his personal courage and determination in his battle against the polio which had partly paralyzed him in 1921. If his platform was actually very similar to Hoover's own, his style was altogether different. He visited many parts of the country in a confident, energetic campaign, and people clearly liked what they saw. Roosevelt won 23 million popular votes to Hoover's 16 million, and 472 electoral votes to Hoover's 59. In his inaugural address, the new President proclaimed his faith that "this great nation will endure as it has endured, will revive and prosper." "The only thing we have to fear," he said, "is fear itself." But even as he spoke, the Depression was moving into a new and more pernicious phase. Over the preceding days, investors had been withdrawing their funds from the banks in panic. By noon on inauguration day – March 4, 1933 – almost all the nation's banks had closed their doors. It was time to translate oratory into action.

Franklin D. Roosevelt preparing to address the American people by radio in one of his famous "fireside chats."

The First New Deal

That action was not slow in coming. Within days of taking office, Roosevelt put in motion the machinery for achieving what he hoped would be the economic recovery of the United States. During its first session in 1933 – the so-called "Hundred Days" – Congress enacted more significant pieces of legislation than in any other comparable period in American history. One emergency act after another helped lay the foundations of that remarkable peacetime mobilization of the American economy known as the First New Deal, with far-reaching effects on a public whose confidence had been badly shaken by the events of the previous three years.

Roosevelt's New Deal – which was drawn up in close consultation with a "Brain Trust" of academics and other advisers – aimed to put the country's financial and industrial system back in order, to provide relief for those who were hardest hit by the Depression, and to create jobs through an intensive program of public works. An Emergency Banking Act enabled the Secretary of the Treasury to investigate the standing of the nation's banks, most of which were able to open their doors again within

The massive Norris Dam on the Clinch River in Tennessee was the first dam to be built by the TVA.

months. The United States was taken off the domestic gold standard, and later, in 1934, the Securities and Exchange Commission was set up to regulate the securities industry and provide a system of investor protection.

The Agricultural Adjustment Act sought to equalize agricultural and manufacturing sector prices by setting limits on production, effectively subsidizing farmers to destroy a proportion of their crops and livestock, and acts were also passed to help indebted farmers avoid foreclosure of their mortgages. In the industrial and commercial field, the National Industrial Recovery Act, described by the President as "probably ... the most important and far-reaching legislation ever enacted by the American Congress," set up the National Recovery Administration (NRA) under Hugh S. Johnson. The NRA encouraged employers to draw up codes of practice for fair competition, abolished child labor, and set minimum wage levels, and thousands of businesses were soon displaying its famous blue eagle symbol, with the words "We do our part."

The Civilian Conservation Corps was created to provide jobs for out-of-work youths, while also taking forward Theodore Roosevelt's conservation program with such ambitious projects as the planting of a 100-mile wide barrier of trees from Texas to Canada to reduce the erosion of land by the wind. Another major conservation initiative which helped create jobs for the jobless was the Tennessee Valley Authority (TVA), set up in 1933 in order to plan for what Roosevelt called "the proper use, conservation, and deployment of the natural resources of the Tennessee River drainage basin ... for the general social and economic welfare of the nation." The TVA was to provide 20 new dams, 650 miles of navigable waterways, and a number of reforestation programs, making the Tennessee the most thoroughly controlled river system in the world. Temporary jobs were also provided for some four million unemployed people by the Civil Works Administration, run by the indefatigable Harry L. Hopkins, while around $4 billion was spent under the Federal Emergency Relief Act to help those in need.

The Second New Deal

Following the Congressional elections of 1934, Roosevelt's New Deal policy moved into its second phase, which was marked by a stronger emphasis on the provision of welfare. The spearhead of the Second New Deal was the Emergency Relief Appropriation Act of 1935, which set up the Works Progress Administration (WPA) under the

An oasis of hope in a barren landscape: a field office of Harry Hopkins' Works Progress Administration.

able leadership of Harry Hopkins. By the end of the year the WPA had created 2.7 million jobs, and had set in motion a major program of public works, ranging from road-building to hospital construction; by the end of its eight-year life, it had provided work for some eight million people who might otherwise have been unemployed.

In July 1935 Congress passed the National Labor Relations Act, which for the first time required employers to recognize employees' collective bargaining rights; and in August the Social Security Act laid the foundations for a national system of welfare provision, introducing pension payments, unemployment benefits, and financial help for the disabled and the needy.

The Dust Bowl

As if the economic conditions of the 1930s were not bad enough, the decade also saw a series of droughts and storms which devastated the Midwestern states, doing enormous damage to crops and livestock, and bringing untold misery to thousands of farming families. Fields which should have held ripening corn were reduced to arid plains by a fatal combination of scorching weather and dust-storms. Millions of tons of topsoil were scoured off by the wind in the worst affected states. Farmers in North and South Dakota, Nebraska, Kansas, Oklahoma, Minnesota, Iowa, Missouri, Montana, Wyoming, Colorado, Texas, and New Mexico saw their livelihoods destroyed, and thousands of refugees made their way westward to California and elsewhere in a pathetic search for jobs and security.

The Election of 1936

As presidential campaigning got underway in 1936, Roosevelt's New Deal came under fire from the Supreme Court, which, in ruling the National Industrial Recovery Act unconstitutional on grounds that also brought into question the constitutionality of other pieces of New Deal legislation, dealt a severe blow to the whole recovery program. But there was already enough evidence of recovery in the country at large for Roosevelt to be returned to office in an almost unprecedented landslide. When the votes were counted, he was found to have won every state except Vermont and Maine, and every city of more than 100,000 people except two, and to have gained 523 electoral votes to his opponent's eight.

Roosevelt lost no time in going into battle against the Supreme Court, proposing a thoroughgoing system of reform designed mainly to give him more support in the judiciary. However, this attempt at coercion only aroused suspicion and, when the Court itself effectively reversed its earlier decisions regarding the constitutionality of parts of the New Deal, it was quietly abandoned. A brief recession in 1937 was worrying enough for a number of potential opponents to back the final stages of the New Deal program, and by the end of the decade it was already clear that, for all its limitations, that program had effected far-reaching changes in American society as well as going some way towards easing the appalling misery of the Great Depression itself.

The Road to War

Meanwhile, events in Europe and the Far East had been developing in new and disturbing directions. The 1930s saw authoritarian, militarist governments in power in Germany, Italy, and Japan, and bore eloquent testimony to the impotence of the League of Nations in the face of determined aggression. The League looked on helplessly as Japan invaded Manchuria in 1931, as Mussolini invaded Abyssinia in 1936, and as German- and Russian-backed factions battled it out in the Spanish Civil War (1936–1939). In 1936 Adolf Hitler, who had taken Germany out of the League when he became Chancellor in 1933, reoccupied the Rhineland, effectively tearing up the demilitarization clauses of the Treaty of Versailles, and in 1938 he annexed Austria to the German Reich in another blatant violation of the Treaty. Britain and France, anxious to avoid war at almost any cost, continued to pursue their policy of appeasement, handing the German-speaking Sudetenland region of Czechoslovakia to Hitler at the 1938 Munich Peace Conference in exchange for a promise of no further aggression, only to see the German army devour the rest of the country the following year. With Hitler's invasion of Poland in September 1939, Britain was finally forced to act. On September 3, after Hitler had failed to respond to an ultimatum that he withdraw his troops from Poland immediately, the British Government declared war on Germany.

The majority of Americans watched these developments with concern, but also with the firm intention of remaining uninvolved. Memories of the First World War were still raw, and had, if anything, become more bitter with the passage of time. Many people felt that America had been lured into that war by financial and business interests, and were determined not to repeat the experience. The Neutrality Act of May 1937 accordingly sought to avoid a replay of the circumstances which had led to American involvement. It prohibited the sale of arms or the making of loans to belligerent governments and insisted that they ship any goods bought in the U.S. in their own vessels. Even when Japanese planes bombed a U.S. gunboat in the Yangtze River in December 1937, American public opinion cried, not for retribution, but for withdrawal of U.S. troops from China. With the outbreak of war in 1939, Roosevelt succeeded in persuading Congress to lift the embargo provisions of the 1937 Neutrality Act in order to supply the Allies, but many voices were raised in opposition. As the war carried on, that reluctance would gradually shift towards a determination that Germany's seemingly unstoppable advances should be halted. But it would take the cataclysmic events of 1941 to fire that determination with anger, and bring America openly into the war.

1931

JAN 7 President's Emergency Committee for Unemployment Relief reports 4 to 5 million unemployed

FEB 24 Procedures for adoption of 18th Amendment ruled valid by Supreme Court

MAR 3 Muscle Shoals Bill, calling for Federal Government to take over operation of hydroelectric facilities constructed during World War I at Muscle Shoals section of Tennessee Riv., vetoed by the President

3 'The Star-Spangled Banner' designated national anthem by Congress

25 Arrest of 'The Scottsboro Boys' in Alabama; charged with and convicted of raping white woman; conviction later overturned by Supreme Court

MAY 1 Empire State Building in NYC dedicated

JUN 20 Pres. Hoover proposes one-year moratorium on all intergovernmental debts and reparations, in effect by July

23 Wiley Post and Harold Gatty begin first around-the-world flight from NY in plane *Winnie May*

JUL 22 Many Kansas counties grant moratorium on taxes to assist farmers with problems caused by bumper crop of wheat and declining prices

SEP 18 Japan marches into Manchuria, violating Kellogg-Briand Pact of 1928

21 Great Britain abandons gold standard

SEP-OCT 827 US banks close; many Americans hoard gold

OCT 5 Hugh Herndon and Clyde Pangborn make first non-stop flight across Pacific Ocean, from Japan to Washington

16 Council of League of Nations invites US to send representative to discussion of Japan's invasion of Manchuria

17 Gangster Al Capone found guilty of income tax evasion in Federal Court in Chicago; sentenced to 11 years in prison and $50,000 fine

18 Death of inventor Thomas Alva Edison

24 George Washington Bridge, linking Manhattan with New Jersey, opened

25 Pres. Hoover and French Premier Laval issue joint statement of agreement to continue gold standard

DEC 7 Hunger marchers turned away from White House when they try to present petition for employment at minimum wage

8 Pres. Hoover, in annual message to Congress, requests emergency reconstruction finance corporation and public works administration

Also this year
★ Harold C. Urey of Columbia University announces discovery of deuterium, heavy isotope of hydrogen

The Arts
★ E.E. Cummings' collection of poetry *ViVa*
★ Pearl S. Buck's novel *The Good Earth*
★ Eugene O'Neill's play *Morning Becomes Electra*

1932

JAN 7 Secy of State Stimson sends notes to Japan and China stating that US will not recognize any territory acquired in violation of Kellogg-Briand Peace Pact

22 Reconstruction Finance Corporation authorized to aid in financing agriculture and industry to stimulate economy

FEB 2 World Disarmament Conference, sponsored by League of Nations, opens in Geneva; US sends representatives

27 Glass-Steagal Banking Act authorizes expansion of credit and release of some government gold to business by Federal Reserve

MAR 1 Charles A. Lindbergh, Jr, child of Col. Charles and Ann Morrow Lindbergh, kidnapped from family's home in Hopewell, NJ

3 Twentieth Amendment, providing for convening Congress on January 3 and for beginnning presidential term on January 20 submitted to states for ratification

The Great Depression

Despite hopes that the Wall Street Crash was a temporary interruption of the prosperity America had known in the 1920s, it soon became apparent that the nation was in the grip of a Depression of unparalleled severity. These are the human faces of that Depression.

Right: The apple seller in the streets of America's major cities became one of the most familiar symbols of the Depression years. Many of those reduced to scraping a living from makeshift fruit stalls had once been successful businessmen.

Insets: With unemployment soaring to an unprecedented 14 million by 1933, and levels in the worst-hit cities reaching 80 per cent, the breadline and the soup kitchen became everyday realities for hundreds of thousands of Americans. Despite the coordinating activities of Hoover's Committee for Unemployment Relief, in the absence of any general system of unemployment insurance the burden of welfare relief fell on local communities and private charities, whose resources were all too quickly depleted.

Background: This extraordinary photograph was taken not in the shanties of the Third World but in New York's Central Park in the early 1930s. Makeshift communities like these, thrown together from scraps of cardboard, wood, and corrugated iron, could be found on the outskirts and, as here, even in the center, of many of America's cities during the Depression, as jobless and workless people gathered in the search for work and shelter. Such shanty-towns were almost universally known as "Hoovervilles," a ubiquitous reminder of the bitterness with which the President's failure to alleviate the crisis was regarded by its many victims.

23 Norris-La Guardia Anti-Injunction Act prohibits use of injunctions in labor disputes

APR-MAY 2 Socialist Labor Party Convention

MAY 20 Amelia Earhart becomes first woman to make solo transatlantic flight from Newfoundland to Ireland; 2026 miles in 13.5 hours

22-24 Socialist Party Convention

28 Communist Party Convention

29 'Bonus Army,' group of 17,000 veterans seeking cash payments for veterans' bonus certificates, begins to arrive in Washington, DC

JUN 14-16 Republican National Convention nominates Herbert Hoover and Charles Curtis for second terms

16-JUL 9 At Lausanne Conference, European governments agree to cancellation of German reparations if cancellation of their World War I debts to US can be arranged

17 Postman Bonus Bill for veterans rejected by Senate; most of Bonus Army leaves Washington DC; 2000 remain

27-JUL 2 Democratic National Convention nominates Franklin D. Roosevelt for President and John Nance Garner for Vice President

JUL 2 Term 'new deal' introduced by FDR in speech accepting Democratic nomination for President

5-7 Prohibition Party Convention

21 Relief and Reconstruction Act signed by the President

22 Federal Home Loan Bank Act to boost home construction adopted by Congress

28 US Army troops under Gen. Douglas MacArthur drive last of Bonus Army out of Washington, DC

AUG 26 Controller of the Currency declares moratorium on foreclosures of first mortgages

FALL Bennington College for women opens in Bennington, Vt

OCT 2 Lytton Commission of League of Nations names Japan as aggressor in invasion of Manchuria

NOV 7 In *Powell v. Alabama*, Supreme Court grants retrial for 'Scottsboro Boys' due to inadequate representation

8 Franklin D. Roosevelt elected President, John Nance Garner elected Vice President

11 Tomb of the Unknown Soldier dedicated in Arlington National Cemetary

Also this year

★ Worst year of depression cripples economy: 13 million unemployed; wages drop to 60 percent less than in 1929, business losses hit $6 billion, agricultural prices drop, industrial production drops to 50 percent of 1929 capacity, banks close

★ First Polaroid glass created by Edwin H. Land

★ James Chadwick discovers neutron

★ Vitamin C isolated and identified by Dr C.C. King

★ Technocracy, management of society by technical experts, becomes popular idea

The Arts

★ Erskine Caldwell's novel *Tobacco Road*

★ Philip Barry's play *The Animal Kingdom*

★ Ferde Grofé's composition *Grand Canyon Suite*

1933

FEB 6 Twentieth Amendment, to eliminate 'lame-duck' Congress and presidential administrations, adopted

15 Pres. Roosevelt escapes assassin's bullet

20 Congress votes to submit 21st Amendment for repeal of Prohibition to states for ratification

24 Japanese delegation to League of Nations walks out of assembly after voting to reject Lytton Commission's report accusing Japan of aggression in Manchuria

25 First US aircraft carrier, *Ranger*, launched at Newport News, Va

MAR 4 Franklin D. Roosevelt inaugurated President, John Nance Garner inaugurated Vice President

4 Frances Perkins becomes first woman Cabinet member when she is named Secretary of Labor

The Dust Bowl

The economic recession of the 1930s was compounded by the natural disaster of the Dust Bowl, as a succession of droughts and storms ravaged the states on which America depended for her agricultural needs. Thousands of farming families, whose lot had always been relatively hard, saw their livelihoods destroyed by a relentless alliance of economic and climatic forces.

Far right: The slightest wind can scour off topsoil parched by months without rain. In the 1930s the arid farmlands of the Midwestern and Southern states were swept by storms of extraordinary severity, raising impenetrable dust clouds and devastating millions of acres of once productive land. This storm in the Texas Panhandle was estimated to have reached windspeeds of 90 m.p.h.

Near right: Forced off their farms by mortgage foreclosures and the prospect of starvation, some 70,000 agricultural refugees fled the worst affected states and made their way to the cities or to the West, contributing to the wretched human flotsam of the "Hoovervilles." Known as "Okies," since Oklahoma was particularly badly hit, many of these migrant workers ended up in California, like this family, photographed in Nipomo in March 1936.

Bottom left: A Wisconsin family pray for rain to fall on their parching farmlands in 1934. Meteorologists, however, were predicting that the abnormal drought conditions could persist for two or three years.

Bottom right: Three farmgirls don gasmasks for protection against dust.

Background: Agricultural machinery rusts, half buried in dust dunes, on an abandoned farmstead in the Guyman area of Oklahoma. Scenes such as this were repeated across the length and breadth of the Dust Bowl states.

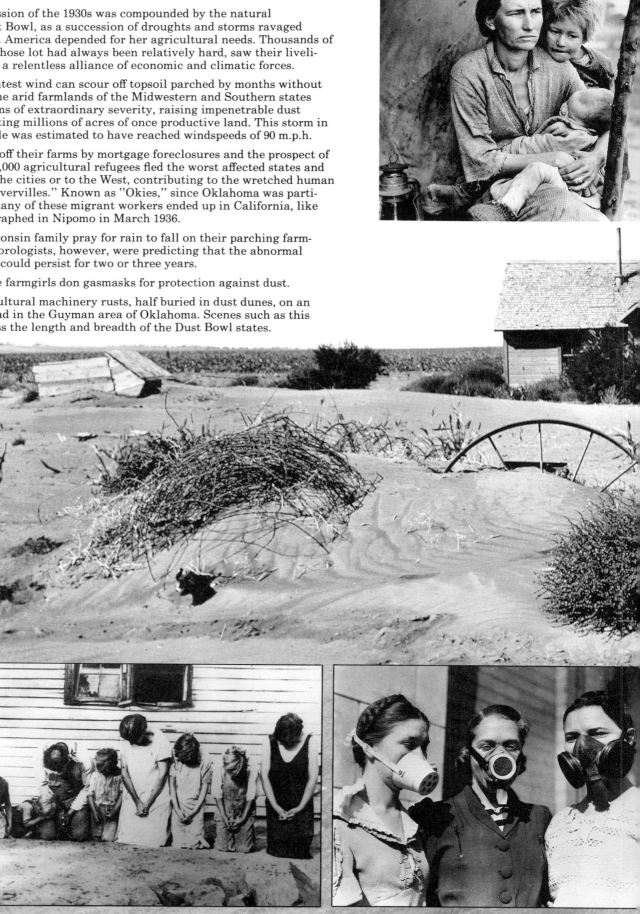

5 Pres. Roosevelt declares nation-wide four-day 'bank holiday' and embargo on exportation of gold, silver and currency

9-JUN 16 Roosevelt's 'Hundred Days:' Congress meets in special session called by the President and enacts principle policies of New Deal

9 Emergency Banking Act gives the President control over all banking transactions and foreign exchange and allows banks to reopen as soon as determined solvent

10-13 Over 1000 banks reopen

22 Beer and Wine Revenue Act legalizes beer and wine with alcoholic content of 3.2 percent and puts tax on both

31 Reforestation Relief Act establishes Civilian Conservation Corps to create jobs

APR 19 US abandons gold standard by presidential proclamation

MAY 12 Federal Emergency Relief Act authorizes immediate grants to states for relief projects

12 Agricultural Adjustment Act for immediate relief to farmers signed by the President

18 Tennessee Valley Authority established to construct dams and power plants along Tennessee Valley

27 Federal Securities Act requires registration and approval of all issues of stocks and bonds

JUN 6 US Employment Service created to cooperate with states

12-JUL 27 London Economic Conference; US disagrees with other nations on issue of currency stabilization

13 Home Owners Refinancing Act creates Home Owners Loan Corporation

16 National Industrial Recovery Act establishes Public Works Administration and National Recovery Administration

16 Banking Act of 1933 establishes Federal Bank Deposit Insurance Corporation

AUG 1 Blue Eagle of NRA first appears in store and factory windows

5 National Labor Board empowered to enforce right of collective bargaining

OCT 10 Treaty of Non-Aggression and Conciliation signed at Rio de Janeiro by nations of Western Hemisphere

13 AFL votes to boycott all German-made products as protest against Nazi treatment of organized labor

14 Germany withdraws from Disarmament Conference in Geneva and announces that it will resign from League of Nations in two years

17 Albert Einstein arrives in US to settle in Princeton, NJ

NOV 7 Fiorello LaGuardia elected fusion-reform mayor of NYC ending 16 years of Tammany control

8 Civil Works Administration established to provide jobs for 4 million unemployed over winter

16 Pres. Roosevelt announces resumption of diplomatic relations with USSR

DEC 5 Twenty-first Amendment ends Prohibition

28 Pres. Roosevelt gives speech in Washington, DC, in which he states: 'The definite policy of the United States from now on is one opposed to armed intervention.'

Also this year

★ *Newsweek* magazine begins publication

The Arts

★ Gertrude Stein's book *The Autobiography of Alice B. Toklas*

★ Aaron Copeland's composition *Short Symphony*

★ Katherine Hepburn in the film *Little Women*

★ The Marx Brothers in the film *Duck Soup*

1934

JAN 4 Pres. Roosevelt asks Congress for $10.5 billion to continue recovery programs

30 Gold Reserve Act passed to give Federal Government control over fluctuations in value of dollar

FEB 2 Export-Import Bank of Washington established

15 Civil Works Emergency Relief Act provides funds for FERA

GOING TO THE MOVIES

In stark contrast to the human misery of the Depression years, and providing some small measure of relief from it, the motion picture industry in the United States entered something of a golden age in the 1930s, with such movie classics as Josef von Sternberg's *The Blue Angel* (which first shot Marlene Dietrich to stardom in 1930) and David Selznick's epic, *Gone with the Wind* (1939). At the beginning of the decade there were estimated to be some 23,000 movie theaters throughout the United States, catering to a weekly audience of some 80 to 100 million people.

Above left: Fred Astaire and Ginger Rogers danced their way into the hearts of millions in *Top Hat* in 1935. Irving Berlin's song "Cheek to Cheek" became an overnight hit.

Above right: Wanting to be alone: the incomparable Greta Garbo.

Right: The most famous film ever made: Clark Gable and Vivien Leigh in the three-hour movie adaptation of Margaret Mitchell's bestselling 1936 novel, *Gone with the Wind*, packed in the audiences for its highly romanticized version of life and love in the Old South.

Opposite top: Audiences fainted with horror as King Kong showed Fay Wray the New York skyline in the 1933 classic.

Opposite middle: The Marx Brothers demonstrating their inimitable brand of anarchic surrealist humor in *Duck Soup*.

Opposite bottom: The most influential Western ever made: John Wayne lends a lady a helping hand in John Ford's *Stagecoach*, 1939.

MAR 15 Henry Ford restores $5-per-day minimum wage to most workers

24 Tydings-McDuffie Act grants independence to the Philippine Islands; independence not proclaimed until July 4, 1946

APR 13 Congress passes act prohibiting loans to any government in default on payments to US

MAY 10-11 Severe dust storm blows some 300 million tons of topsoil from Texas, Oklahoma, Arkansas, Kansas and Colorado into Atlantic Ocean; result of improper plowing

18 Six crime control bills passed by Congress

18 'Lindbergh' Act authorizes death penalty in cases of kidnapping that involve crossing state lines

23 Nylon first produced by Dr Wallace H. Carothers, research chemist at Du Pont laboratories

29 US and Cuba sign treaty releasing Cuba from status as US protectorate under Platt Amendment

SUMMER Strikes occur throughout the country

JUN 6 Securities and Exchange Commission established to regulate exchanges and transactions involving all securities; Joseph Kennedy appointed chairman

7 Corporate Bankruptcy Act simplifies reorganization process

12 Farm Mortgage Foreclosure Act helps farmers to recover property owned before foreclosure

12 Reciprocal Trade Agreement Act authorizes the President, for next three years, to negotiate trade agreements with other nations without consent of Senate

15 National Guard Act makes National Guard part of US Army in time of war or during national emergency

19 Federal Communications Commission established to regulate radio, telephone and telegraph communication

19 Silver Purchase Act authorizes the President to nationalize silver and increase silver holdings

28 Federal Housing Administration established by Congress

JUL 16 Country's first general strike called in San Francisco

22 John Dillinger, Public Enemy No. 1, shot and killed by FBI in Chicago

AUG 6 Last of US Marines leave Haiti, ending 19-year occupation

9 Pres. Roosevelt nationalizes silver

NOV 6 First unicameral state legislature adopted by Nebraska

DEC 3 In *Hamilton v. Regents of the University of California*, Supreme Court upholds right of land grant colleges to require military training

29 Japan denounces Washington Naval Treaty of 1922 and London Naval Treaty of 1930 withdrawal and to take effect December 1936

Also this year

★ 'Oakies' and 'Arkies' migrate to California to escape Dust Bowl

The Arts

★ F. Scott Fitzgerald's novel *Tender Is the Night*

★ Dashiell Hammett's novel *The Thin Man*

★ James Hilton's novel *Goodbye Mr Chips*

★ Catholic Legion of Decency begins censorship of motion pictures

1935

JAN 29 US participation in World Court rejected by Senate

APR 8 Emergency Relief Appropriation Act authorizes $5 billion for work relief and to increase employment through projects

27 Soil Conservation Service established by Congress

MAY 1 Resettlement Administration established to support farm families

6 Works Progress Administration established under Emergency Relief Appropriation Act

Crime and Crime-busting

The mean streets of Depression America witnessed an upsurge of criminal activity during the 1930s.

Left: The young J. Edgar Hoover whose methods were often the subject of controversy, was to dominate the American law enforcement scene for half a century as Director of the Federal Bureau of Investigation (FBI).

Below left and middle: The notorious duo Bonnie Parker and Clyde Barrow, whose armed bank robberies prompted a massive manhunt, ended their four year partnership in crime in a hail of police bullets in Louisiana in May 1934.

Below right: Public enemy number one, John Dillinger poses jauntily with his Colt 38 and a submachine gun. Wanted in several states for murder and armed robbery, Dillinger was infamous for his narrow escapes from justice. His luck ran out in July 1934, however, when Hoover's FBI "G-men" shot him dead outside a cinema in Chicago.

The Lindbergh Baby Case

Tragedy struck the family of Charles Lindbergh (1902–1974), who made the headlines with his "Lone Eagle" flight from New York to Paris in 1927, when his 20-month-old son, Charles Junior, was kidnapped from his home in Hopewell, New Jersey, on March 1, 1932. Despite the payment of a $50,000 ransom, and a nationwide police manhunt, the baby was found murdered in a nearby wood two months later. Bruno Hauptmann, a German illegal immigrant, was arrested in New York in 1934 and charged with the crime. Hauptmann, seen below at his trial (center), was found guilty and sentenced to death. He was executed by electric chair in 1936.

WANTED

INFORMATION AS TO THE WHEREABOUTS OF

CHAS. A. LINDBERGH, Jr.
OF HOPEWELL, N. J.

SON OF COL. CHAS. A. LINDBERGH
World-Famous Aviator

This child was kidnaped from his home in Hopewell, N. J., between 8 and 10 p. m. on Tuesday, March 1, 1932.

DESCRIPTION:

Age, 20 months
Weight, 27 to 30 lbs.
Height, 29 inches

Hair, blond, curly
Eyes, dark blue
Complexion, light
Deep dimple in center of chin
Dressed in one-piece coverall night suit

ADDRESS ALL COMMUNICATIONS TO
COL. H. N. SCHWARZKOPF, TRENTON, N. J., or
COL. CHAS. A. LINDBERGH, HOPEWELL, N. J.

ALL COMMUNICATIONS WILL BE TREATED IN CONFIDENCE

March 11, 1932
COL. H. NORMAN SCHWARZKOPF
Supt. New Jersey State Police, Trenton, N. J.

The Scottsboro Case

Controversy erupted in 1931 over the conviction of nine Black youths for the alleged rape of two white girls in Tennessee. After widespread protests (above), the youths, eight of whom were sentenced to death, appealed to the Supreme Court, which overturned the convictions in two separate decisions in 1932 and 1935.

---

11 Rural Electrification Administration established to bring electricity to areas not served by private utility companies

27 National Recovery Administration declared unconstitutional by Supreme Court

JUN 10 Alcoholics Anonymous organized in NYC

JUL 5 National Labor Relations Act supports right of collective bargaining

29 Thomas E. Dewey appointed special prosecutor in drive against crime in New York State

AUG 14 Social Security Act signed by the President

16 Death of humorist Will Rogers

26 Public Utilities Act requires public utilities to register with Securities and Exchange Commission

30 Revenue Act adjusts taxes to prevent concentration of wealth

31 Neutrality Act forbids shipment of arms and munitions to belligerents once president has declared state of war and authorizes president to prohibit travel by American citizens on belligerent ships

SEP 8 Sen. Huey Long of Louisiana assassinated in Baton Rouge

OCT 5 Pres. Roosevelt announces state of war between Ethiopia and Italy and declares provisions of Neutrality Act to be in effect

OCT 10 George Gershwin's opera *Porgy and Bess* opens at Alvin Theater in NYC

NOV 9 UMW President John L. Lewis becomes chairman of newly formed Committee for Industrial Organizations

15 Commonwealth of Philippines inaugurates first president, Manuel Quezon of Malina

DEC 9 Second London Naval Conference opens; Japan denied request to maintain parity with US and Great Britain, leaves conference

The Arts

★ Thomas Wolfe's novel *Of Time and the River*

1936

JAN 6 Agricultural Adjustment Act declared unconstitutional by Supreme Court

FEB 29 Second Neutrality Act extends act of 1935 to May 1, 1937 and amends it to prohibit loans or credits to belligerents

MAR 2 Treaty with Panama ends US protectorate and enlarges Panama's authority in Canal Zone

2 Soil Conservation and Domestic Allotment Act replaces Agricultural Adjustment Act

25 New London Naval Treaty signed by US, Great Britain and France

APR 25-28 Socialist Labor Party Convention

MAY 9 Ethiopia occupied by Italian Army

9 German dirigible *Hindenburg* arrives in Lakehurst, NJ, completing first scheduled transatlantic dirigible flight

JUN 9-12 Republican National Convention nominates Gov. Alfred M. London of Kansas for President and Col. Frank Knox of Illinois for Vice President

19 Rep. William Lemke, Republican of N. Dak., announces his presidential candidacy on Union Party ticket

22 Virgin Islands granted right to elect own legislature

23-27 Democratic National Convention nominates Franklin D. Roosevelt and John Nance Garner for second terms

26 US Maritime Commission established to develop and regulate Merchant Marine

The *Hindenburg* Tragedy

Thirty-three people died when the giant German airship the *Hindenburg* exploded and burst into flames as it was coming into land at Lakehurst, New Jersey, on May 6, 1937, at the end of a flight from Frankfurt-am-Main.

First Helicopter

The first vertical take-off helicopter was successfully flown on September 14, 1939, at Hartford, Connecticut. At the controls of the revolutionary single-rotary blade VS-300 was the machine's designer, Igor Sikorsky (above).

Howard Hughes

On July 14, 1938, Howard Hughes (above) and four companions landed at New York in their plane the *New York World Fair* after a record-breaking round-the-world flight (3 days 19 hours).

Aaron Copland

The American composer Aaron Copland (above) won great acclaim in 1938 for his ballet score *Billy the Kid.*

Gertrude Stein

Gertrude Stein (1874–1946) (right), the influential American writer, with her secretary and companion, Alice B. Toklas, in New York, October 1934.

Jesse Owens

To the discomfiture of Hitler and his Aryan theories, the Black American athlete Jesse Owens (below) won four gold medals at the 1936 Berlin Olympics.

AUG 5-16 Summer Olympics in Berlin Germany: US wins 20 gold medals; American Jesse Owens wins four gold medals in field and track

NOV 3 Franklin D. Roosevelt and John Nance Garner win election for second terms

DEC 30 Sit-down strike by United Auto Workers begins at General Motors plant in Flint, Mich.

The Arts

★ Margaret Mitchell's novel *Gone With the Wind*

★ John Dos Passos' novel *The Big Money*

★ George S. Kaufman and Moss Hart's play *You Can't Take It With You*

★ Charlie Chaplin in the film *Modern Times*

★ Living Theater begins under Federal Theater Project of WPA

1937

JAN 6 Congress passes resolution prohibiting shipment of munitions to belligerents fighting civil war in Spain

20 Franklin D. Roosevelt and John Nance Garner inaugurated for second term

MAR 1 Supreme Court Retirement Act grants full pay to retiring Justices over 70

1 Reciprocal Trade Agreement Act extends Trade Agreement Act of 1934 to June 1940

1 US Steel Corporation recognizes United Steel Workers

18 Worst school fire in US history kills 294 in New London, Tex.

29 In *West Coast Hotel v. Parrish*, Supreme Court reverses earlier decisions and upholds minimum wages for women

APR 12 National Labor Relations Act of 1935 upheld by Supreme Court

MAY 1 Third Neutrality Act extends neutrality legislation of 1935-36 prohibits sale of securities of belligerent nations in US and use of American ships for carrying arms into belligerent zones and permits sale to belligerents of certain commodities on 'cash and carry' basis

6 German dirigible *Hindenberg* explodes at Lakehurst, NJ, killing 36

6 First coast-to-coast radio program conducted by Herbert Morrison, reporting *Hindenberg* disaster

24 Social Security Act of 1935 upheld by Supreme Court

27 Golden Gate Bridge in San Francisco dedicated

JUN 22 Joe Louis becomes world heavyweight boxing champion

JUL 2 Aviator Amelia Earhart vanishes over Pacific Ocean during around-the-world flight

SEP 2 US Housing Authority created to remedy housing shortage by providing loans to states

14 US ships prohibited from carrying arms to China and Japan by executive order

DEC 11 Italy withdraws from League of Nations

12 US gunboat *Panay* bombed and sunk by Japanese planes in Yangtze River, China

14 Japan apologizes for bombing incident, agrees to pay indemnity and promises no more incidents

Also this year

★ Sharp decline in economic output, after four years of recovery

★ Wave of industrial sit-down strikes

★ Lincoln Tunnel built between Manhattan and NJ

★ National Cancer Institute established

The Arts

★ John Steinbeck's novel *Of Mice and Men*

★ Clifford Odets' play *Golden Boy*

★ Arturo Toscanini becomes conductor of NBC Symphony Orchestra

Ernest Hemingway

Ernest Hemingway (1899–1961), whose novel *To Have and Have Not* was published in 1938, strikes a typically robust pose in Sun Valley, Idaho.

The Golden Gate Bridge

Pedestrians swarm over the Golden Gate Bridge, San Francisco – then the world's longest suspension bridge – after its opening on May 27, 1937.

John Steinbeck

The American author John Steinbeck (1902–1968), painted by Sjernstrom in 1939 the year his most famous novel, *The Grapes of Wrath*, was published.

1938

JAN 28 Pres. Roosevelt submits to Congress request for military expansion, particularly for Navy

FEB 16 Second Agricultural Adjustment Act provides for stabilization of agricultural prices and farmers' incomes

MAR Stock market recession reaches lowest point

13 Hitler declares that Austria has been 'united' with Germany

18 Mexico nationalizes all foreign-owned oil properties

30 Tornado in Midwest kills 36 and causes widespread destruction

31 Former President Herbert Hoover advises US to avoid alliances with European countries lining up against Fascist states

APR 12 First law to require medical tests for marriage license applicants passed in New York State

MAY 17 Naval Expansion Act authorizes expenditure of more than $1 billion for ships, cruisers and carriers over 10-year period

26 House Committee to Investigate Un-American Activities formed

JUN 23 Civil Aeronautics Authority established to regulate air traffic

24 Food, Drug and Cosmetic Act requires detailed disclosure of ingredients on labels

25 Fair Labor Standards Act sets minimum wage at 40 cents per hour and maximum work week at 44 hours

JUL 14 Howard Hughes sets new record flying around the world in 3 days, 19 hours, 14.28 minutes

17 Aviator Douglas 'Wrong Way' Corrigan, unable to obtain flight exit permit for Europe, lands in Dublin, Ireland, and claims he was headed for California

SEP 21 Hurricane strikes Atlantic Coast, devasting New England; 700 die, 2 billion trees downed

26 Pres. Roosevelt sends personal message to governments of Great Britain, France, Germany and Czechoslovakia, urging peaceful settlement to Sudetenland crisis

30 In Munich Agreement, Britain and France allow Germany to take over Sudetenland in Czechoslovakia

OCT 30 Orson Welles broadcasts radio play 'Invasion from Mars,' inspiring widespread panic

NOV 14 US ambassador to Germany recalled for 'report and consultation'

18 German ambassador to US recalled

DEC 6 Former British Foreign Minister Anthony Eden delivers radio address in NYC and warns Americans that all democracies are being threatened by expanding fascist powers

24 Declaration of Lima signed at Eighth International American Conference; reaffirms principle of mutual consultation

Also this year

★ Albert Einstein and Leopold Infeld's *The Evolution of Physics* published

The Arts

★ Thorton Wilder's play *Our Town*

★ Walt Disney's film *Snow White and the Seven Dwarfs*

1939

JAN 12 Two-year defense program costing $535 million recommended by Pres. Roosevelt

30 In *Tennessee Electric Power Company v. Tennessee Valley Authority,* Supreme Court upholds constitutionality of TVA's competition with private companies

FEB 13 Justice Louis Brandeis retires from Supreme Court

27 In *National Labor Relations Board v. Fansteel Metallurgical Corporation,* Supreme Court finds sit-down strike unconstitutional

MAR 14 German army invades Czechoslovakia

APR 1 US recognizes government of Gen. Francisco Franco at end of Spanish civil war

All That Jazz

The popularity of jazz continued unabated during the 1930s, with venues like Harlem's famous Cotton Club attracting such major names as Cab Calloway and Bill Robinson, as well as that pillar of the jazz establishment, Edward Kennedy "Duke" Ellington (1899–1974) (above) and his 11-piece band. Meanwhile, the great Billie Holliday (1915–1959) (top inset), whose renderings of such blues classics as *Strange Fruit* were infused with her personal experience of tragedy, bore witness to the darker side of the jazz world with her chaotic personal life and her drug addiction.

Is It a Bird...?

One of the most enduring creations of the 20th century was launched in the summer of 1939, when the first ever Superman Comic introduced its hero to the American public. The tale of a well-nigh indestructible man concealed in the body of an otherwise unremarkable citizen evidently struck a chord in many minds.

War of the Worlds?

A young actor shot to fame in 1938 with a radio broadcast which has entered the folklore of broadcasting. Orson Welles (1915–1985), photographed above during his controversial virtuoso performance, was reporting a Martian invasion of New Jersey as part of a dramatization of H. G. Wells' novel, *The War of the Worlds*. His account of the aliens' arrival was convincing enough to cause panic among thousands of Americans.

The Power of Advertising

America began to develop all the characteristics of a modern consumer society during the inter-war years, as sophisticated advertising campaigns – some of them, such as this striking poster from the 1930s, featuring slogans that are still familiar today – drew on current trends in the mainstream arts to bring new products to the attention of the mass market.

Hitler and Mussolini

Throughout the 1930s, the dark specter of Fascism was consolidating its hold over Europe. Benito Mussolini had established himself as Duce in Italy, and in 1933 the Nazi leader Adolf Hitler, seen here with the Italian dictator, had become Chancellor of Germany. Hitler lost no time in using his government's almost limitless powers not only to silence all political opposition but also to put in train a program of mass persecution against the Jews. Capitalizing on the German people's sense of outrage at the punitive provisions of the Treaty of Versailles, he also launched a campaign of *Lebensraum*, or living space, which led to the annexation to the German Reich of the Saar, the Rhineland, Austria, the Sudetenland, and Czechoslovakia between 1935 and 1938. Only when Hitler invaded Poland in September 1939 did Britain and France abandon their policy of appeasement and declare war on Germany.

7 Italian army invades Albania

14 Pres. Roosevelt writes to Hitler and Mussolini and asks for 10-year guarantee of peace for Europe and Middle East in return for US cooperation in talks on world trade and armaments; receives no reply

30 New York World's Fair, 'The World of Tommorow,' opens

30 Television first publicly broadcast from Empire State Building, New York

MAY 10 Methodist Church reunited after 109 years; 8 million members

16 Food stamp plan to distribute food to the needy tested in Rochester, NY

JUN 7-12 King George VI and Queen Elizabeth of Great Britain visit Washington

28 Transatlantic passenger air service begins when Pan American Airways' *Dixie Clipper* leaves Port Washington, Long Island, for Lisbon, Portugal, with 22 passengers aboard

JUL 14 Pres. Roosevelt sends special message to Congress to ask for repeal of arms embargo

AUG 2 Hatch Act restricts federal employees from participating in political campaigns; result of campaigning of WPA workers during 1938 election

23 German-Russian non-agression pact signed in Moscow

SEP 1 World War II begins as Germany invades Poland without declaration of war

3 Great Britain and France declare war on Germany

3 Pres. Roosevelt, in fireside chat, declares US neutral

3 British passenger ship *Athena* torpedoed by German submarine off the Hebrides Islands; 28 Americans die

4 Secy of State Cordell Hull restricts travel by Americans to Europe to 'imperative necessity'

5 US proclaims neutrality in war in Europe

8 Pres. Roosevelt declares limited national emergency

17 USSR invades Poland

28 Partition of Poland by Germany and USSR

OCT 2 Secretary of State Hull announces that US does not recognize partition of Poland by Germany and USSR and will maintain diplomatic relations with Polish government in exile in Paris

2-3 Declaration of Panama issued by Inter-American Conference meeting in Panama City; establishes safety zone in seas of Western Hemisphere

11 AFL adopts resolution opposing US involvement in European war and boycotting German, Russian and Japanese goods

18 Pres. Roosevelt issues proclamation closing US ports and offshore waters to submarines of belligerents

25 Nylon stockings go on sale in US

NOV 4 Neutrality Act of 1939 allows sale of arms to belligerents on cash-and-carry basis

30 USSR invades Finland

DEC 5 Former President Herbert Hoover organizes US drive for Finnish relief

10 Congress grants Finland $10 million credit for agricultural supplies

Also this year

★ Edwin H. Armstrong develops frequency modulation (FM), new method of radio transmission and reception

★ Rh factor in human blood discovered by Dr Philip Levine and Dr Rufus Stetson

★ Frank Lloyd Wright's Johnson Wax Company building constructed at Racine, Wis.

★ William Albig's *Public Opinion* published

The Arts

★ John Steinbeck's novel *The Grapes of Wrath*

★ William Saroyan's play *The Time of Your Life*

★ Frank Capra's film *Mr Smith Goes to Washington*

★ Bette Davis in the film *Dark Victory*

★ Judy Garland in the film *The Wizard of Oz*

★ Vivienne Leigh and Clark Gable in the film *Gone With the Wind*

THE 1940s wrought more momentous changes in the political map of the world than perhaps any other decade in history. Europe, North Africa, and the Far East were engulfed in a war more cataclysmic than any the world had seen before, a war from which Europe emerged in physical and financial ruins. The Japanese attack on Pearl Harbor in 1941 catapulted America out of the isolation which had guided her foreign policy since the end of the First World War, and, by the end of the decade, into the position of undisputed leader of the post-war Western power bloc, the North Atlantic Treaty Organization (NATO). Just as the First World War had given painful birth to the League of Nations, so the Second helped create the United Nations. But whereas President Wilson had failed to persuade the American people to give the United States a permanent seat in the League, President Roosevelt and his successor, Harry Truman, bound the destiny of America inextricably to that of Europe.

The need for an organization to preserve world peace was more urgent than ever before. Within months of the end of the hostilities, the battle lines of the Cold War began to harden, as what Winston Churchill called an "iron curtain" fell across Europe, dividing the United States and her allies from the newly acquired empire of the Soviet Union. But most momentous of all

was the fact that the war had unleashed upon the world a new and terrible force, capable of destruction on an enormous scale. The dropping of the first atomic bomb on Hiroshima in 1945 had brought the Pacific War to an abrupt end and had shifted the balance of military power conclusively in favor of the United States. It had also changed the face of world politics irrevocably. The wheels of the nuclear arms race had been put in motion, and with them the development of a weapons system which, for the first time in history, would give mankind the power to destroy itself. From that moment forward, international affairs would be conducted under the shadow of the Bomb. The nuclear age had begun.

The Arsenal of Democracy

In 1940, despite the unease of many Americans who believed that he was taking the country closer and closer towards war, Franklin D. Roosevelt was reelected for an unheard-of third term as President. Meanwhile, the eerie inactivity of the so-called "phony war" in Europe had been swept aside by the explosion of Hitler's *Blitzkrieg*, which saw, in a matter of a few weeks, the fall to Germany of Denmark, Norway, Holland, Belgium, Luxembourg, and France. With the British evacuation of Dunkirk, which left Great Britain facing the might of

Hitler's armies alone, the debate between non-interventionists and internationalists in America entered a new and more intense phase. A Selective Service Act was passed in 1940 to strengthen U.S. forces against the possibility of involvement in the war, and under the Lend-Lease Act the following year America became, in Roosevelt's words, "the great arsenal of democracy" by agreeing to provide equipment and supplies to the beleaguered Allies on whatever basis the President believed would promote the defense of the United States. At the same time, U.S. ships began to convoy British vessels across the Atlantic, and, when German U-boat fire led to the loss of American lives, Roosevelt armed American merchantmen and licensed them to shoot at German submarines. In August 1941, he met the British Prime Minister, Winston Churchill, on the U.S.S. *Augusta* off Newfoundland to sign the Atlantic Charter, an agreement about the shape of the post-war world which owed a great deal to President Wilson's famous Fourteen Points. By this time, the United States was as fully committed to the Allied cause as was possible without actually declaring war on Germany. Events in the Pacific would soon bring her openly into the conflict.

Blitzkrieg: German troops advance through Europe at lightning speed, summer 1940.

1940s

Above: Britain stands alone. Prime Minister Winston Churchill contemplates the future among the ruins of the British parliament buildings, bombed by German planes in May 1941.

Right: A newspaper seller proclaims the beginning of the second war in Europe in a quarter of a century.

Below: A column of Britain's 200,000-strong Expeditionary Force marches toward the front line in France. Within weeks most would be evacauted via Dunkirk.

1940

JAN 3 Pres. Roosevelt submits to Congress budget of $1.8 billion for national defense measures

26 US-Japan trade treaty of 1911 expires; US refuses to renew its terms

FEB 17 Undersecretary of State Sumner Welles travels to Europe to inspect conditions

MAR 18 Italy joins Axis

APR 9 German troops invade Denmark and Norway

20 First electron microscope publicly tested at Radio Corporation of America laboratory in Camden, NJ

29 Pres. Roosevelt asks Mussolini to promote peace in Europe

MAY 10 British PM Neville Chamberlain resigns; replaced by Winston Churchill

10 Germany invades Holland, Belgium and Luxembourg

15 PM Churchill sends first telegram requesting American aid and participation in the war to Pres. Roosevelt

15 First successful helicopter flight in US

16 Pres. Roosevelt asks Congress for greater appropriation for defense in order to increase production of aircraft to 50,000 planes per year

25 Office for Emergency Management established by the President

28 National Defense Advisory Commission appointed by the President

JUN 3 US War Department agrees to sell Britain surplus of obsolete arms, munitions and aircraft

10 Italy declares war on Britain and France

10 Pres. Roosevelt delivers speech at University of Virginia in which he declares that US policy is changing from neutrality to 'non- belligerency'

11 Congress passes Naval Supply Act

13 Congress passes Military Supply Act

14 German army enters Paris

15 National Defense Research Committee established by the President

16 Pétain takes over in France

16 Pittman Resolution authorizes sale of armaments to republics of Western Hemisphere

16 US notifies Germany and Italy that it will not recognize transfer of title from one non-American power to another of any region in Western Hemisphere

17 Russians take over Latvia, Estonia and Lithuania

20 Henry L. Stimson named Secretary of War, Frank Knox named Secretary of the Navy

22 French make peace with Germany

Pearl Harbor

Ever since the Japanese invasion of Manchuria in 1931 (which has been seen by many historians as the true start of the Second World War), Japan had been pursuing an aggressively expansionist policy in the Far East. In 1940 she occupied Northern Indochina, and joined the Axis Alliance with Germany and Italy later the same year. America responded by placing an embargo on essential Japanese supplies in 1941, and negotiations between the two countries stalled over Japan's refusal to meet demands that she withdraw her troops from China.

On December 7, 1941, while talks were still taking place between the two governments, a massive Japanese task force launched an all-out attack on Pearl Harbor and other American bases in the Hawaiian Islands. Despite the fact that intelligence information had suggested that such an attack was imminent, the effects were devastating. Nineteen ships and 120 planes were lost, and more than 2400 men were killed. At the same time, Japanese planes attacked Guam, Midway, Hong Kong, the Malay Peninsula and also the Philippines, where they inflicted serious damage on American aircraft in Manila.

The response in America was immediate and unequivocal. Within two days of the attacks, Congress had given Roosevelt authority to declare war on Japan. Germany and Italy, true to the Axis pact, then declared war on the United States, and on December 11 the United States reciprocated with a declaration of war on Germany and Italy. The last vestiges of American isolationism had been swept away.

Right: Clouds of acrid smoke engulf the U.S.S. West Virginia and the U.S.S. Tennessee during the Japanese attack on Pearl Harbor, December 7, 1941. Both ships were destroyed.

Opposite below: The scene on the deck of the U.S.S. Oklahoma, one of the 19 ships sunk in the Pearl Harbor raid, after the tangled wreckage was recovered from the bed of the harbor.

Below: Japanese planning for the attack on Pearl Harbor and other U.S. bases in the Pacific had been long and meticulous. Intelligence officials had reported detailed Japanese mapping of the Hawaiian area and had forewarned of Japanese fleet movements in the days preceding the raid. This aerial photograph of the base at Pearl Harbor was taken from a Japanese plane as it closed in for the attack.

Mobilizing America

For the second time in less than a quarter of a century, America found herself gearing up for war. The mobilization was breathtaking in scale. The Selective Service authorities registered some 31 million Americans for the armed forces, of whom 15 million had served by the end of the war. The economy was harnessed to the war effort in a massive production program overseen by the War Production Board and, from 1943 onwards, the Office of War Mobilization, with the former Supreme Court Justice, James F. Byrnes, playing the role Bernard Baruch had played during the First World War.

The declaration of war marked the beginning of the real economic recovery that Roosevelt's New Deal had never fully succeeded in bringing about. America's seven million unemployed were almost immediately drafted into this astonishing surge of activity. The aircraft industry alone increased the number of people it employed from just under 50,000 in 1939 to more than 2.1 million in 1944. U.S. military production lines manufactured a staggering 275,000 aircraft, 75,000 tanks, and 650,000 artillery-pieces during the course of the War. By 1942, merchant ships, which had taken 105 days to build at the beginning of the decade, were being turned out in less than a week. At the same time, new military technology was developed to meet the sophisticated needs of modern warfare, including one weapon which was to change the nature of that warfare forever. Between 1941 and 1945 the Federal Government spent a total of around $321 billion on the war effort – twice the total of all Federal expenditure from 1789 to 1941 – and by the beginning of 1944 the industrial output of the United States was twice that of all the Axis powers combined.

Right: Some $100 billion towards the war effort was raised by the issue of U.S. Government liberty bonds.

Below: Mobilization of military production: workers assemble howitzers at General Electric's plant in Erie, Pennsylvania.

As in the First World War women played an important part in the industrial mobilization.

Newly-built B-24 bombers lined up at Ford's Willow Run plant in Detroit.

24-28 Republican National Convention nominates Wendell L. Willkie for President and Sen. Charles McNary of Oregon for Vice President

28 Congress passes Alien Registration Act

JUL 2 Export Control Act authorizes President to stop or restrict export of any material considered vital to US defense

2 First German daylight bombing raid on London

5 Vichy Government severs relations with Britain

9 RAF begins night bombing raids on Germany

10 Pres. Roosevelt submits request to Congress calling for $4.8 billion for defense

15-19 Democratic National Convention nominates Roosevelt for 3rd term and Henry A. Wallace of Iowa for Vice President

20 Congress appropriates $4 billion for a two-ocean navy

30 Declaration of Havana unanimously approved by 21 republics of Pan-American Union

AUG 18 US and Canada create Joint Board of Defense

23 Blitz on London begins

27 Congress authorizes introduction of National Guard into federal service

SEP 3 US gives 50 obsolete destroyers to Britain in exchange for 99-year leases on naval and air bases in Newfoundland and the West Indies

16 Selective Service Act requires men aged 21 to 35 years to register for military training

22 Japan enters Indo-China

25 Pres. Roosevelt announces embargo on export of scrap steel and iron outside Western Hemisphere

27 German-Italian-Japanese 10-year military-economic alliance signed in Berlin

OCT 16 First day for selective service registration

24 Forty-hour work week goes into effect

29 Secretary of War Stimson draws first draft numbers

NOV 5 Roosevelt wins election for 3rd term, Henry A. Wallace elected Vice President

21 John L. Lewis resigns as head of CIO

DEC 20 Office of Production Management established by the President

21 Germany accuses US of 'moral aggression' by providing aid to Great Britain

29 Pres. Roosevelt publicly stresses Axis threat and proclaims US must be 'arsenal of democracy'

The Arts

★ Ernest Hemingway's novel *For Whom the Bell Tolls*

★ Thomas Wolfe's novel *You Can't Go Home Again*

★ Richard Wright's novel *Native Son*

★ Martha Graham's dance *Letter to the World*

★ Charlie Chaplin's film *The Great Dictator*

★ Walt Disney's film *Fantasia*

1941

JAN 6 Pres. Roosevelt sends Lend-Lease Bill to Congress

8 Pres. Roosevelt submits to Congress budget of $10.8 billion for defense

20 Roosevelt inaugurated for 3rd term, Henry A. Wallace inaugurated Vice President

22 Workers at Allis Chalmers plants go on strike

27 US and Britain begin conducting secret talks in Washington, DC

FEB 3 Federal Wage and Hour Law upheld in *US v. Darby Lumber Co.*

4 United Service Organization formed by six national non-profit organizations

24 OPM releases first industry-wide priority schedule

26 CIO calls strike at Bethlehem Steel plant

MAR 8 Death of writer Sherwood Anderson

11 Congress passes Lend-Lease Act

17 National Gallery of Art opens in Washington, DC

19 National Defense Mediation Board established

APR 9 US-Danish agreement pledges US defense of Greenland

The New York Times. LATE CITY EDITION

AMERICAN FORCES LAND IN FRENCH AFRICA;
BRITISH NAVAL, AIR UNITS ASSISTING THEM;
EFFECTIVE SECOND FRONT, ROOSEVELT SAYS

The North African and Italian Campaigns

American troops made their first major mark on the Allied war-effort in the North African campaign of 1942–1943. Here Erwin Rommel, Hitler's "Desert Fox," was fighting the British General Bernard Montgomery for control of Egypt and the Suez Canal, which would have been the gateway to India for the Axis powers. American tanks arrived in North Africa before Montgomery's famous victory at El Alamein in October 1942, and American troops, under General Dwight D. Eisenhower, played a crucial role in the sweeping offensive which led to the fall of Tunis on May 7, 1943, and the subsequent surrender of Hitler's armies in North Africa.

Right: A giant American carrier disgorges its troops on the North African coast.

Below: Black members of an engineer battalion in Algeria line up for noon mess during the North African campaign.

Once this threat to the Mediterranean had been eliminated, the Allies turned their attention to Italy. On July 10, 1943, Montgomery's Eighth Army and General George S. Patton's Seventh Army launched a massive amphibious attack on the island of Sicily, which fell on August 17. Then, on September 3 – the same day that the new government in Rome, having swept Mussolini into exile, signed an armistice with the Allies – the American Fifth Army under General Mark W. Clark spearheaded the invasion of the Italian mainland. German resistance was intense, and the Allied forces sustained high casualties as they fought their way ashore at Anzio and the Gulf of Salerno, and during their assault on the heavily fortified hilltop monastery of Monte Cassino. Not until June 1944 did they finally enter Rome.

U.S. troops go ashore at the beachhead in Sicily.

Troops of the 85th Division march through the Porta Maggiore, Rome, June 1944.

11 Office of Price Administration and Civilian Supply established by executive order

14 Wage increase of 10 cents per hour granted by steel industry to prevent strikes

16 OPA freezes steel prices

17 Yugoslavia surrenders to Germany

21-27 US, British and Dutch military officers meet in Singapore to formulate plan for strategic operations against Japanese attack on US

MAY 1 US Defense Savings Bonds and Stamps go on sale

15 Pres. Roosevelt denounces French collaboration with Germany, US government takes into protective custody French ships in American harbors

16 Wage increase of 10 cents per hour granted by General Motors to prevent strikes

20 German paratroops invade Crete

21 US merchant vessel *Robin Moor* sunk by German submarine

27 Pres. Roosevelt declares unlimited national emergency in radio broadcast from White House

JUN 9 North American Aviation Company seized by US troops acting on order of the President when strike interferes with production

12 Associate Justice Harlan Fiske Stone nominated Chief Justice of Supreme Court

14 German and Italian assets in US ordered frozen

16 German consulates in US ordered closed

22 German army invades Russia

24 Pres. Roosevelt promises aïd to Russia

25 Fair Employment Practices Committee established by executive order

28 Office of Scientific Research and Development established by executive order

JUL 7 US Marines take over from Britain in Iceland

20 Italian consulates in US ordered closed

25 Japanese assets in US ordered frozen

26 Pres. Roosevelt nationalizes armed forces of Philippines and places them under command of Gen. Douglas MacArthur

AUG 3 Gasoline curfew goes into effect in 17 eastern states

11 Pres. Roosevelt and PM Churchill sign Atlantic Charter

18 Selective Service Act Extension signed by the President

SEP 4 US destroyer *Greer* attacked off Iceland by German submarine

11 Pres. Roosevelt orders US Navy planes and ships to attack on sight Axis ships within US defensive waters

16 US Navy takes over protection of shipping as far as Iceland

20 Revenue Act of 1941 sharply increases taxes to raise defense funds

OCT 13 British RAF raid on Nuremberg, Germany

17 US destroyer *Kearny* attacked off Iceland by German submarine

17 Gen. Tojo appointed PM of Japan

27 Pres. Roosevelt, in Navy Day broadcast, states: 'America has been attacked. The shooting has started.'

27 United Mine Workers president John L. Lewis announces strike in 'captive' mines

NOV 3 US Ambassador to Japan Joseph Grew warns of imminent Japanese attack

17 Japanese begin negotiations with US State Department

20 Japanese propose that US lift trade restrictions and ignore Japan's activities in China and the Pacific

20 Pres. Roosevelt signs bill amending Neutrality Act of 1939

26 US rejects Japanese proposals and insists that Japan withdraw all forces from China and Indo-China

DEC 1 Japan rejects American proposal

3 Japanese consulates in US begin to burn secret documents

6 Pres. Roosevelt appeals to Emperor Hirohito to avoid war

7 Japanese attack US base at Pearl Harbor and US bases in the Philippines, Guam and Midway

7 Japanese envoys deliver reply rejecting American proposal of Nov 26

The War in the Pacific

Meanwhile, American troops had seen bitter action in the Pacific arena. In the wake of Pearl Harbor, the Japanese had established a massive military presence in the far-flung network of islands between Australia and the Chinese mainland, and they had forced General Douglas MacArthur to withdraw from the Philippines in December 1941, albeit with the prophetic words, "I shall return." On May 6, 1942, General Jonathan Wainwright's remaining army of American and Filipino troops on Corregidor was forced to accept at Japanese hands the greatest American military surrender since Appomattox.

The following day, however, the U.S. fleet repulsed a Japanese invasion force bound for Australia at the Battle of the Coral Sea, which marked the beginning of a new age of naval warfare, based on aircraft from carriers confronting each other at a great distance. In June, the Japanese and American navies clashed again, at the Battle of Midway, which also fell to the Allies.

The Battle of Midway was a watershed in the recovery of the Pacific. In August 1942 U.S. troops landed on Guadalcanal – a dense, malaria-ridden jungle of an island – and the battle for the islands began in earnest. It was a battle which would cost hundreds of thousands of lives before the Allies finally took the island of Okinawa, within striking distance of the Japanese mainland, in June 1945. Guadalcanal fell in February 1943, after six months of hellish fighting; Tarawa, at the southern tip of the Gilbert Islands, in November the same year; and Kwajalein, Guam, and Saipan during

Above: A new kind of warfare: U.S. planes bomb Japanese aircraft carriers at the Battle of Midway, June 1942.

Below: "I have returned:" General Douglas MacArthur wades ashore at Leyte in the Philippines, October 1944.

Above: The battle for the islands. The strain of jungle warfare takes its toll on a detachment of U.S. marines.

Below: Troops inspect damage to the giant deck of the U.S.S. Yorktown during the Battle of Midway.

7 Japan announces declaration of war

8 US declares war on Japan

10 Japanese forces invade Luzon in the Philippines

11 Germany and Italy declare war on US; US Congress declares war on Germany and Italy

15 3rd Supplemental Defense Appropriation Act authorizes $10 billion for open warfare

17 Adm. Chester Nimitz named commander of Pacific fleet

18 Pres. Roosevelt appoints special commission to investigate disaster at Pearl Harbor

19 Office of Censorship established by executive order

20 Draft Act requires men aged 18 to 65 to register, with liability for active military duty for all aged 20 to 45

20 Adm. Ernest J. King named commander in chief of US Navy

22 PM Churchill joins Pres. Roosevelt for war conference in Washington, DC

23 Wake Island, US territory in the Pacific, falls to Japanese

23 Industry-Labor Conference pledges no strikes or lockouts during the war

25 Hong Kong surrenders to Japanese

The Arts

★ Lillian Hellman's play *Watch on the Rhine*

★ Morris Graves' painting *Little Known Bird of the Inner Eye*

★ Orson Welles' film film *Citizen Kane*

1942

JAN 1 Declaration of UN signed by 26 nations

2 Manila falls to Japanese as US and Philippine forces withdraw to Bataan Peninsula

6 Pres. Roosevelt delivers State-of-the-Union message in which he calls for production of great numbers of planes, ships, tanks and guns

12 War Labor Board replaces National Defense - Mediation Board

14 Alien registration ordered by the President

15-28 Rio de Janeiro Conference: 21 American nations resolve to break relations with Axis

16 War Production Board replaces OPM

16 Death of actress Carole Lombard

24-27 In Battle of Macassar Strait, Japan suffers first great sea losses

26 US troops land in Northern Ireland

26 Commission investigating disaster at Pearl Harbor releases findings

28 Office of Civil Defense established to coordinate civilian tasks

30 Emergency Price Control Act goes into effect

31 US bombards Japanese naval bases in the Marshall and Gilbert Islands

FEB 6 US War Department announces Combined Chiefs of Staff, established by US and Britain

9 Daylight Savings Time begins

9 French liner *Normandie* burns and capsizes in New York Harbor

12 Death of painter Grant Wood

20 Pres. Roosevelt authorizes relocation of Pacific Coast Japanese-Americans

23 Oil refinery near Santa Barbara, Calif., shelled by Japanese submarine

27-MAR 1 In Battle of Java Sea, Allied squadron suffers heavy losses

MAR Over 100,000 Japanese-Americans are relocated from Pacific Coast to internment camps in inland locales

11 Gen. MacArthur leaves Philippines

17 Gen. MacArthur arrives in Australia to assume command of Allied forces in Southwest Pacific

29 Death of actor John Barrymore

APR 8 War Production Board halts all construction not essential to war effort

9 Bataan Peninsula falls to Japanese

10 Bataan Death March begins

18 US bombers raid Tokyo, Kobe, Nagoya and Yokohama in Japan

1944 as the American forces battled their way painfully towards Japan, meeting intense resistance at every point. On March 16, 1945, they took Iwo Jima after nearly a month of fighting, which cost 24,000 American lives, and planted the Stars and Stripes on the summit of Mount Suribachi in what became one of the symbolic moments of the war. By the time Allied troops landed on Okinawa, off the southern coast of Japan, the Japanese naval presence in the Pacific had been decimated. A few months earlier, Douglas MacArthur had fulfilled his promise by returning to Manila after a two-and-a-half year campaign to retake the Philippines, which had claimed almost half a million Japanese lives. The stage was now set for a final assault on Japan. In the meantime, though, events had been coming to a head in Europe too.

American and Filipino POWs on the notorious "Death March", Bataan, 1942.

18 War Manpower Commission established

28 'Dim-out' along Atlantic Coast goes into effect

MAY 4-8 In Battle of Coral Sea, Japanese fleet suffers heavy losses

5 Sugar rationing goes into effect

6 Japanese capture Corregidor in the Philippines

14 Women's Auxiliary Army Corps established by act of Congress

15 Gasoline rationing begins in 17 eastern states

18 Retail price ceilings go into effect

JUN 3-6 In Battle of Midway, Japan loses initiative in naval superiority

3-21 Japanese invade Attu and Kiska in the Aleutian Islands

13 Office of War Information established by the President

13-17 Eight German saboteurs land by submarine off coasts of Florida and Long Island, NY, but are captured

15-30 National scrap iron drive

17 First issue of *Yank,* Army newspaper, published

19 Pres. Roosevelt and PM Churchill begin conference in Washington, DC, to formulate plan for North Africa invasion

21 Oregon coast shelled by Japanese submarine

25 Maj. Gen. Dwight D. Eisenhower named commander of US forces in European theater

30 Civilian Conservation Corps terminated

JUL 4 USAF participates with British RAF in bombing raid on German targets on Continent

16 War Labor Board grants cost-of-living wage increase to certain steel workers

30 Women Appointed for Voluntary Emergency Service, women's branch of Naval Reserve, established by act of Congress

AUG 7 US troops invade Guadalcanal in first successful invasion of the Solomon Islands

12-15 US representative W. Averell Harriman and PM Churchill confer with Stalin on joint war effort

17 First US bombing raid in Europe

26 Wendell L. Willkie begins around-the-world tour

SEP 11 US signs rubber agreement with Mexico

OCT 1 First American jet airplane, XP-59, tested at Muroc Army Base, California

7 Pres. Roosevelt announces plan to establish UN Commission for Investigation of War Crimes

7 United Mine Workers withdraw from CIO

21 Revenue Act of 1942 increases taxes by $9 billion

26 In Battle of Santa Cruz: Japanese suffer heavy losses

NOV 3 Democrats maintain majority in House and Senate

7-8 Allies land in French North Africa

12-15 Naval Battle of Guadalcanal: US victory

13 Teenage Draft Act lowers age for conscription to 18 years

21 US-built Alcan International Highway, running from Canada to Alaska, officially opens

23 'Semper Paratus' – Always Ready Service, women's division of Coast Guard Reserve, established by act of Congress

28 Boston's Coconut Grove nightclub fire leaves 492 dead

28 Nationwide coffee rationing goes into effect

DEC 1 Nationwide gasoline rationing goes into effect

4 Works Progress Administration given 'honorable discharge' by Pres. Roosevelt

21 Supreme Court rules Nevada's six-week divorce notices valid

The Arts

★ William Faulker's story collection *Go Down, Moses*

★ John Steinbeck's novel *The Moon Is Down*

★ Thorton Wilder's play *The Skin of Our Teeth*

★ Humphrey Bogart and Ingrid Bergman in the film *Casablanca*

★ James Cagney in the film *Yankee Doodle Dandy*

★ Edward Hopper's painting *Nighthawks*

Operation Overlord

In the early hours of the morning of June 6, 1944, a massive amphibious force under General Eisenhower (now in command of all Allied forces in Europe) landed along a 40-mile stretch of the Normandy coast to set in motion "Operation Overlord," the Allied invasion of the European mainland. During the course of the following week, more than 300,000 troops were landed and began to battle their way through the devastated towns and countryside of Normandy and Brittany, driving the German army before them. Paris was liberated on August 25, soon to be followed by Brussels and Antwerp, and on September 12 General Hodges' First Army entered Germany itself.

Below: Bridge over the Seine in France

Inset: Much of Normandy was devastated during Operation Overlord, as Allied troops fought their way to Paris.

General Dwight D. Eisenhower in 1943.

D-Day issue of the New York Post, *1944.*

Allied landing craft approach the Normandy beaches.

JAN 14-24 Pres. Roosevelt, PM Churchill and French Gen. Charles de Gaulle meet at Casablanca; Eisenhower given command of North African theater

15 Japanese retreat from Guadalcanal

27 First US bombing raid on Germany

FEB 2 Germans begin retreat from Eastern Front

3 US War Department bans hard liquor from US Army establishments

7 Nationwide shoe rationing goes into effect

9 Pres. Roosevelt announces minimum 48-hour work week in war plants

9 US Marines recapture Guadalcanal

13 Women's Reserve of US Marine Corps established by act of Congress

25 Allies regain Kasserine Pass in Tunisia

MAR 1 Rationing of processed foods goes into effect

2-4 Battle of Bismarck Sea in the Pacific: US victory

APR 1 Rationing of meats, fats and cheeses goes into effect

8 Pres. Roosevelt freezes prices, wages and salaries by executive order

13 Jefferson Memorial in Washington, DC, dedicated

17 War Manpower Commission prohibits essential workers from leaving their jobs

MAY 1 Federal government seizes coal mines after striking workers refuse to obey War Labor Board order to return to work

11 US forces land on Attu in the Aleutian Islands

11-27 Pres. Roosevelt, PM Churchill and military planners meet at Trident Conference in Washington, DC

12 Axis campaign in North Africa ends

19 PM Churchill addresses US Congress

27 Office of War Mobilization established

JUN 9 Current Tax Payment Act, or 'Pay-As-You-Go Act,' goes into effect

14 In *West Virginia Board of Education v. Bernette*, Supreme Court rules invalid a state law requiring children to salute the flag under penalty of expulsion

20-22 Race riot in Detroit, Mich., leaves 34 dead, 500 injured

25 War Labor Dispute Bill enacted over Pres. Roosevelt's veto

JUL 10 Allies invade Sicily

16 Allies drop leaflets calling for surrender over Italy

19 Allies bomb Rome

25 Mussolini forced to resign; replaced by Marshal Badoglio

AUG 1 Race riot in Harlem, NY, leaves 5 dead and 410 injured

11-24 Pres. Roosevelt, PM Churchill and Canadian PM Mackenzie King meet in Quebec to discuss Pacific campaign

15 US and Canadian units recapture Kiska in the Aleutian Islands

16 US troops capture Messina, Sicily

17-21 USAF bombs Wewark air fields in New Guinea

28 US forces secure New Georgia in the Solomon Islands

SEP 3 Allied forces invade mainland Italy

8 Italy surrenders unconditionally to Allies

9 Allies land at Salerno, Italy

17 Allies capture Lae, New Guinea

21 House adopts Fulbright Concurrent Resolution, calling for US participation in international peace organization

OCT 13 Italy declares war on Germany

19-30 US, USSR and China collaborate on Moscow Declaration on postwar security and cooperation

NOV 1 US troops invade Bougainville in the Solomon Islands

3 Coal miners end six-month strike

5 Senate passes Connally Resolution, calling for US support for international peace organization

22 Pres. Roosevelt, PM Churchill and Chinese Gen. Chiang Kai-shek meet in Cairo to plan military strategy against Japan

With the Allied armies drawn up along the defensive Siegfried Line, the Germans mounted a spectacular counter-offensive through the Ardennes Forest, an assault only eliminated in January 1945 after the so-called "Battle of the Bulge." Then, on March 7, the First Army crossed the Rhine and drove on into the heart of Germany. German opposition crumbled as the massed Allied armies moved swiftly to meet the Soviet forces, advancing from the East, at Torgau in April. Russian troops entered the bombed-out shell of Berlin shortly afterwards, and Hitler, trapped in his bunker below the Chancellery, committed suicide before the city that was to have been the capital of his 1000-year Reich surrendered to the Allies on May 2. And five days later, Hitler's successor, Admiral Doenitz, delivered Germany's unconditional surrender to Eisenhower's headquarters in Rheims.

Below: U.S. troops at the Arc de Triomphe during the liberation of Paris.
Bottom: The 1st and 3rd U.S. Armies meet at Houffalize, Belgium, sealing off the Bulge battlefield.

U.S. POWs captured by German paratroopers at the Battle of the Bulge.

American infantrymen under fire on the advance to Houffalize.

23 US captures Makin in the Gilbert Islands

NOV 28-DEC 1 Pres. Roosevelt, PM Churchill and Stalin meet at Teheran to devise strategy for Allied invasion of Europe

DEC 15 Death of jazz musician Fats Waller

17 Chinese Exclusion Act repealed by Congress

24 Gen. Eisenhower named supreme commander of Allied Forces for invasion of Europe

27 Federal government seizes railroads threatened with shutdown by striking workers

The Arts

★ Betty Smith's novel *A Tree Grows in Brooklyn*
★ Martha Graham's dance *Death and Entrances*
★ Rodgers and Hammerstein's musical *Oklahoma*

1944

JAN 16 Gen. Eisenhower arrives in London to take up post of Supreme Commander, Allied Expeditionary Force

19 Federal government returns control of seized railroads to owners

22 War Refugee Board established by executive order of the President

31 US forces invade the Marshall Islands in the Pacific

FEB 3 US warships shell the Kurile Islands off northern Japan

20-27 USAF conducts series of massive raids on centers of German aircraft industry

MAR 4 US refuses to recognize government of Argentina when it fails to cooperate with Allies

6 First US bombing raid on Berlin

29 US Congress authorizes funds for UN Relief and Rehabilitation Agency

APR 3 In *Smith v. Allwright,* Supreme Court rules that the right to vote is not affected by color

4 Wendell L. Willkie defeated in Wisconsin primaries for Republican presidential nomination

17 Congress extends Lend-Lease

22 US forces invade New Guinea

26 US Army seizes Montgomery Ward plant for defying order of National Labor Relations Board

MAY 3 Meat rationing ends

8 First eye bank established by New York Hospital

18 Allies bomb Monte Cassino, Italy

20 US Communist Party votes to disband

23 Allies launch major offensive from Anzio beachhead

JUN 4 Fifth Army marches into Rome

6 D-Day: Allies invade Normandy

15 US Superfortresses bomb Yawatta on Kyushu Island

19-20 In Battle of Philippine Sea, Japanese are defeated

22 Pres. Roosevelt signs 'GI Bill of Rights'

26-28 Republican National Convention nominates Gov. Thomas E. Dewey of New York for President and Gov. John Bricker of Ohio for Vice President

JUL 6 French Gen. Charles de Gaulle arrives in Washington, DC for conference with Pres. Roosevelt

6 Ringling Brothers and Barnum and Bailey Circus tent fire leaves 168 dead and 250 injured

10 US Marines capture Saipan in the Pacific

18 Japanese PM Tojo resigns

19-21 Democratic National Convention nominates Roosevelt for 4th term and Sen. Harry S. Truman of Missouri for Vice President

20 German generals' attempt on Hitler's life

25 St Lô 'break-out' leads to collapse of German line in northwest France

AUG 8 Allies capture Brittany

9 US forces capture Guam

15 US Army invades southern France

21 Dumbarton Oaks conference opens at Wash., DC

25 Allied and French troops liberate Paris

The war against Germany was over; but it was a victory that came too late for President Roosevelt to celebrate. After a period of office longer than that of any other American president before or since, Roosevelt, whose health had long been deteriorating, collapsed and died at his home in Warm Springs, Georgia, on April 12. He had just finished drafting one of his famous "fireside chats," which had ended with the words "Let us move forward with strong and active faith." It was a fitting epitaph for one of the greatest statesmen of the 20th century.

Right: As Allied troops advance toward Berlin they encountered the full horror of the Nazi concentration camps. Here survivors of Dachau hail their liberators.

Below: Aerial view of Berlin, reduced to a shell by intensive Allied bombing.

New Yorkers celebrate the end of the war in Europe.

VE-Day revelry in Times Square, New York.

28 German forces in Toulon and Marseilles surrender to Allies

SEP 12 US troops enter Germany

11-16 Pres. Roosevelt and PM Churchill meet in Quebec

17-27 US and British forces conduct unsuccessful airborne invasion of Holland

OCT 20 US troops land in the Philippines

21 Allies capture Aachen, Germany

23-26 In Battle of Leyte Gulf, Japanese fleet suffers heavy losses in largest naval conflict of war

NOV 7 Roosevelt wins election for 4th term, Harry S. Truman elected Vice President

19 Pres. Roosevelt announces 6th War Loan Drive

DEC 15 Henry 'Hap' Arnold, Dwight D. Eisenhower, Douglas MacArthur and George C. Marshall given new rank, General of the Army

16 Germans begin Battle of the Bulge in the Ardennes

24 Band leader Glenn Miller reported missing

The Arts

★ John Hersey's novel *A Bell for Adano*

★ Tennessee Williams' play *The Glass Menagerie*

★ John Van Druten's play *I Remember Mama*

★ Jerome Robbins' ballet *Fancy Free*

1945

JAN 9 US 6th Army lands on Luzon in the Philippines

15 Nationwide dim-out ordered to conserve fuel

20 Roosevelt inaugurated for 4th term, Harry S. Truman inaugurated Vice President

FEB 4-11 Pres. Roosevelt, PM Churchill and Stalin meet at Yalta

4-24 US troops capture Manila

9 US Marines invade Iwo Jima in the Pacific

26 Midnight curfew ordered on entertainment establishments

MAR 7 US First Army crosses Rhine

16 Iwo Jima falls to US Marines

APR 1 US forces invade Okinawa

12 Pres. Roosevelt dies; succeeded by Harry Truman

16 Lend-Lease extended

18 War correspondent Ernie Pyle killed on Iwo Jima

23 US and Soviet forces meet in Germany

24 United Nations conference opens in San Francisco

28 Mussolini killed by partisans

30 Hitler dies in Berlin

MAY 7 Germany surrenders unconditionally

8 V-E Day marks end of European phase of war

8 Nationwide dim-out lifted

9 Midnight curfew on entertainment establishments lifted

JUN 5 US, Britain, France and USSR arrange division and occupation of Berlin

21 Japanese surrender on Okinawa

30 Office of Price Administration extended

JUL 1 NY State Commission Against Discrimination established

5 Gen. MacArthur declares Philippines liberated

16 First atomic bomb detonated near Alamogordo, New Mexico

17 Pres. Truman, PM Churchill and Stalin meet at Potsdam

26 Potsdam Declaration demands unconditional surrender of Japan

28 B-25 bomber flies into Empire State Building in NYC

AUG 6 US drops atomic bomb on Hiroshima

9 US drops atomic bomb on Nagasaki

14 Japanese unconditional surrender ends war

14 War Manpower Commission lifts all controls

14 Pétain sentenced to death for collaboration

15 V-J Day marks end of Pacific phase of war

17 Allies divide Korea at 38th parallel

"Prompt and utter destruction"

At their conference in Potsdam in July and August 1945, the Allied leaders, with President Harry S. Truman now speaking for the United States, issued a declaration in which they called on Japan to surrender, threatening her with "prompt and utter destruction" should she refuse. The agent of that destruction was a new weapon which had just been tested for the first time, with apocalyptic effect, at Los Alamos in the wastes of New Mexico. As the now terrifyingly familiar image of the mushroom cloud reared up over the desert, even the scientists who had been secretly working on the "Manhattan Project" for a number of years compared this overture to the nuclear age with the Biblical predictions of doomsday. Exactly three weeks later, on the morning of August 6,

Above: Unprecedented devastation: The ruins of Hiroshima after an American B-29 bomber dropped its single atom bomb on the city on August 6, 1945. An area of four square miles was completely leveled and tens of thousands of people were killed.

1945, the first atomic bomb was dropped on the Japanese city of Hiroshima. Three days after that, a second bomb fell on Nagasaki. Both cities were almost completely leveled by the blast. Nearly 100,000 people, the majority of them civilians, were killed immediately. Many thousands more died from the effects of radiation. On August 14 the Japanese Emperor Hirohito, for long regarded as an invincible god by his people, communicated Japan's surrender to the Allies. So – in a glimpse of Armageddon – the Second World War came to an end.

Below: The atom smasher in the Los Alamos laboratory. The "Manhattan Project" cost some $2 billion to bring to fruition.

18 Pres. Truman orders full restoration of civilian consumer production, collective bargaining and free markets

28 US forces land in Japan

29 Gen. MacArthur named Supreme Commander of Allied Powers in Japan

SEP 2 Japanese sign formal document of surrender aboard USS *Missouri* in Tokyo Bay

6 Pres. Truman recommends economic recovery plan to Congress

OCT 24 United Nations formally established

30 Shoe rationing ends

NOV 19 Gen. Dwight D. Eisenhower replaces Gen. George C. Marshall as Chief of US Army

20 Nuremberg war trial opens

21 175,000 United Auto Workers go on strike in General Motors plants

23 Meat and butter rationing ends

DEC 15 Pres. Truman appoints George C. Marshall Special Ambassador to China

20 Tire rationing ends

31 National Wage Stabilization Board replaces National War Labor Board

The Arts

★ Robert Frost's book *A Masque of Reason*

★ Sinclair Lewis' novel *Cass Timberlane*

★ Richard Wright's novel *Black Boy*

★ Rodgers and Hammerstein's musical *Carousel*

★ Joan Crawford in the film *Mildred Pierce*

1946

JAN 9 Western Electric telephone mechanics go on strike in 44 states

10 First General Assembly of UN meets in London

15 United Electrical, Radio and Machine Workers go on strike in 16 states

20 Central Intelligence Group established by executive order of the President

21 United Steelworkers Union closes down steel mills

24 Atomic Energy Commission established by UN

25 AFL votes to readmit United Mine Workers

FEB 15 ENIAC, electronic numerical integrator and computer, dedicated in Philadelphia

20 Employment Act of 1946 creates Council of Economic Advisors

MAR 13 United Auto Workers end 113-day walkout

APR 1 United Mine Workers go on strike

8 League of Nations Assembly meets for last time

MAY 14 Selective Service Act extended to Sept. 1

23 Railroad Trainmen and Locomotive Engineers Brotherhoods strike

30 United Mine Workers end strike

JUN 3 In *Morgan v. Commonwealth*, Supreme Court rules that buses must allow seating without regard to race on vehicles in interstate commerce

21 Frederick Moore Vinson named Chief Justice of Supreme Court

JUL 1 US begins atomic tests at Bikini in Marshall Islands

4 Pres. Truman proclaims Philippine independence

7 Mother Frances Xavier Cabrini becomes first US citizen to be canonized

15 Pres. Truman signs bill extending wartime price controls

27 Death of author Gertrude Stein in Paris

29 Paris Peace Conference begins

30 US joins UNESCO

AUG 1 Truman signs Fulbright Act, creating program for international educational exchange

1 Truman signs McMahan Act, creating Atomic Energy Commission

2 Congress passes Legislative Reorganization Act

SEP 20 Secy. of Commerce Henry A. Wallace resigns

Below: A glimpse of Armageddon: Mushroom cloud over Bikini Atoll, where the fifth atomic bomb was tested in 1946.

Below: The legacy of the second atomic bomb: Nagasaki lies in ruins, August 9, 1945.

Planning the post-war world: The Big Three meet at Yalta (February 1945) . . .

. . . and, with Truman now President, at Potsdam (July-August 1945).

The United Nations

Throughout the war, the Allied heads of government had met in a series of conferences to discuss the conduct and objectives of the struggle. By February 1945, when Churchill, Roosevelt and Stalin met at Yalta, victory seemed certain, and the three leaders set themselves the task of hammering out the shape of the post-war world. This crucial meeting, after which Roosevelt was widely criticized for making too many concessions to the Soviet Union, nonetheless laid the foundations for the division of Germany into four zones under the administration of Great Britain, France, the Soviet Union, and the United States. It obtained Stalin's agreement to hold free elections in Poland and other Eastern European countries, and established that the Soviets were prepared to support the proposed United Nations organization. The Allies had agreed on the need for such an organization as early as 1942, and details of the United Nations' structure and membership were further developed by the 50 nations which attended the Dumbarton Oaks conference near Washington in August 1944. The U.N. Charter was drawn up at the Conference of International Organization at San Francisco in April 1945 and was ratified by the Senate on July 28 the same year. It is indicative of the radical change, not only in the international climate, but also in American public opinion, that Roosevelt and Truman encountered none of the partisan resistance to the United Nations charter that had wrecked President Wilson's hopes for U.S. involvement in the precursor of the U.N., the League of Nations, barely a quarter of a century before.

The Truman Doctrine

The strains between the Allies which had been evident at Yalta tested the effectiveness of the U.N. machinery to the limit in the years immediately after the cessation of hostilities. The Potsdam conference had divided the war-ravaged territories of Europe between the great powers along lines which reflected the military position on the eve of victory. Soviet supremacy was recognized in Bulgaria, Romania, Hungary, Poland, and Yugoslavia, and by March 1946 Winston Churchill was speaking ominously of an "iron curtain" having descended across Europe "from Stettin in the Baltic to Trieste in the Adriatic." In February 1947, Great Britain appealed to the United States to support the struggle against Communist influence in Greece and Turkey, which her own resources were no longer equal to sustaining. This request – another sign, if any were needed, that the empires of the Old World were giving way to new empires of influence – led Truman to appeal to Congress for a massive program of economic and military aid to Greece and Turkey. In so doing, he formulated what was to become known as the Truman Doctrine. "I believe," he said, "that it must be the foreign policy of the United States to support free peoples who are resisting attempted subjugation by armed minorities or by outside pressures." The outside pressures he had in mind were clearly those of international Communism. The following month Bernard Baruch, in a speech in South Carolina, spoke the words which were to describe East-West relations for more than 30 years. "Let us not be deceived," he said, "We are in the midst of a Cold War."

Truman looks on as Stettinius signs the U.N. Charter in San Francisco.

OCT 16 Price controls on meat removed

23 UN meets in New York City

NOV 4 China and US sign friendship pact

5 Republicans regain control of Congress

9 Controls on most consumer goods removed

DEC 5 NYC chosen as permanent site for UN

7 Worst fire in US history sweeps Winecoff Hotel in Atlanta, Ga

31 Pres. Truman issues proclamation of formal cessation of World War II hostilities

The Arts

★ Robert Penn Warren's novel *All the King's Men*

★ Eudora Welty's novel *Delta Wedding*

★ Edmund Wilson's novel *Memoirs of Hecate County*

★ Arthur Miller's play *All My Sons*

★ Eugene O'Neill's play *The Iceman Cometh*

★ William Wyler's film *The Best Years of Our Lives*

1947

JAN 3 First session of 80th Congress covenes

8 George C. Marshall appointed Secretary of State

MAR 12 Pres. Truman proposes aid program for Greece and Turkey before Congress

21 Pres. Truman issues Executive Order 9835, establishing Loyalty Program for government employees and applicants for federal jobs

24 Congress proposes 22nd Amendment to limit president to two four-year terms

APR 7 Striking telephone workers achieve wage hikes

7 First annual Tony Awards presented for outstanding contributions to American theater

7 Death of Henry Ford

9 Tornado devastates Texas and Oklahoma

12 UN allows US trusteeship of Pacific Islands formerly under mandate to Japan

16-18 Ship explosion in Texas City leaves 377 dead

MAY 22 Pres. Truman signs Greek-Turkish Aid Bill

31 Pres. Truman allocates $350 million in relief for countries devastated by the war

JUN 5 George C. Marshall proposes 'Marshall Plan' for reconstruction of Europe in speech at Harvard

11 Sugar rationing ends

14 Peace treaties between US and Italy, Romania, Bulgaria and Hungary ratified by Senate

17 Pan-American Airways offers first around-the-world service

23 Congress passes Taft-Hartley Act over Pres. Truman's veto

JUL 7 Hoover Commission established to study organization of executive branch of Federal government

12 Marshall Plan conference begins in Paris

18 Congress passes Presidential Succession Act

25 National Security Act of 1947 establishes National Security Council, Central Intelligence Agency and National Military Establishment

AUG 15-SEPT 2 Inter-American Conference for Maintenance of Continental Peace and Security, Rio de Janeiro, produces Inter-American Treaty of Reciprocal Assistance

17 James V. Forrestal named first Secretary of Defense

17 US refers issue of Korean independence to UN

17-19 Hurricane devastates Florida, Mississippi and Louisiana

OCT 5 First televised presidential address

9 Pres. Truman supports UN proposal for autonomous Jewish and Arab state in Palestine

14 Bell X-1 research airplane achieves supersonic speed

18 House Un-American Activities Committee opens investigation into Communist influence in American film industry

25 Maine devastated by forest fire

29 President's Commission on Civil Rights releases findings

29 General Electric Company seeds cumulus clouds over forest fire at Concord, NH

Berlin schoolchildren cheer the arrival of an American plane during the airlift.

The Berlin Airlift

It was in this tense atmosphere of stand-off between the superpowers that the question of what should happen to Germany became a dangerous political flashpoint. When the Western powers began to make moves to create a separate West German Federal Republic in spring 1948, the immediate Soviet response was to begin a blockade of the divided city of Berlin, denying all access to the Western sectors. The situation was sensitive in the extreme. Truman recognized that any attempt to break the blockade by force could lead to open war, but at the same time, basic supplies had to be brought to the people. The solution was bold, imaginative, and extraordinarily successful. The Western powers began a massive airlift of essential foodstuffs and other supplies, which at its height was bringing in 7000 tons a day. It was a curious spectacle – squadron after squadron of planes delivering the wherewithal of life to a city on which, only three short years before, they had rained such death and destruction – but it broke the blockade without breaking the peace. The Soviet Union abandoned its strategy in May; but by then Stalin had proclaimed a separate German Democratic Republic in East Germany with its capital in Berlin.

European Recovery

At the end of the Second World War, much of Europe lay in ruins. Cities had been pounded into rubble, millions had died in the fighting or in the Nazis' extermination camps, and the economies of the major European powers were in tatters. The United States poured billions of dollars into Europe in the immediate aftermath of the hostilities, and in June 1947 Truman's Secretary of State, George C. Marshall, announced America's intention of drawing up a detailed plan of reconstruction with representatives of the European governments in order to put in motion a structured program of economic aid. The framework which emerged from these discussions – the European Recovery Plan (ERP), proposing the injection of some $17 billion into Europe over the following four years – was put before Congress in December 1947 and passed in April 1948, in the wake of the Communist seizure of power in Czechoslovakia the previous month. By the end of 1951, $12 billion had been spent in Europe under the ERP, which became popularly known as the Marshall Plan. In 30 years the United States had grown from an isolationist power, determined to avoid entanglements in the Old World, to the mainstay of European recovery and security. On April 4, 1949, that relationship was cemented once and for all with the signing in Washington of the North Atlantic Treaty. Fundamental to the consequent formation of the North Atlantic Treaty Organization (NATO) was the understanding that an attack on any one of the signatories would be interpreted as an attack on them all, and would be met by military force if necessary. Events had finally overtaken the principles laid down in George Washington's farewell address.

Eponymous architect of European Recovery: General George C. Marshall.

Demob happy: Homecoming soldiers pack the decks of the Queen Elizabeth *in New York harbor.*

NOV 25 Council of Foreign Ministers meets in London to discuss economy and government of Germany

19 Pres. Truman asks Congress for first installment of proposed $17 billion for four-year European Economic Recovery Program

DEC 19 Jackie Robinson signed by Brooklyn Dodgers

27 Record-breaking snowstorm strikes Northeast

29 Henry Wallace announces 3rd party candidacy for the presidency

The Arts

★ Laura Z. Hobsen's novel *Gentleman's Agreement*

★ Sinclair Lewis' novel *Kingsblood Royal*

★ Mickey Spillane's novel *I, the Jury*

★ Tennessee Williams' play *A Streetcar Named Desire*

1948

JAN 12 In *Sipeul v. Board of Regents of University of Oklahoma,* Supreme Court rules that no state can discriminate against law school applicant on basis of race

30 Death of aviator Orville Wright

FEB 2 Pres. Truman introduces civil rights package to Congress

7 Gen. Omar Bradley succeeds Gen. Dwight D. Eisenhower as US Army Chief

MAR 8 Supreme Court rules that religious training conducted in public schools is unconstitutional

15 Coal miners go on strike for better pensions

22 US announces land reform program for Korea

31 Congress passes 'Marshall Aid' bill

APR 3 Pres. Truman signs Foreign Assistance Act

30 OAS meets in Bogota, Colombia

MAY 14 US becomes first nation to recognize Israel

19 Mundt-Nixon Bill, requiring registration of - Communists in US, passes House

25 General Motors and United Auto Workers sign first sliding-scale contract

JUN 11 Vandenberg Resolution, allowing US to enter collective security pacts with non-Western Hemisphere nations, passes Senate

24 Selective Service Act requires men aged 18 to 25 years to register for military training

24 Republican National Convention nominates Gov. Thomas E. Dewey of New York for President and Gov. Earl Warren of California for Vice President

24 Soviets stop road and rail traffic to and from Berlin

25 Pres. Truman signs Displaced Persons Bill

JUL 15 Democratic National Convention nominates Truman for President and Sen. Alben W. Barkley of Kentucky for Vice President

17 State's Rights Democrats nominate Gov. Strom Thurmond of South Carolina for President

20 Twelve American Communist Party leaders indicted and charged with advocating overthrow of US government

22-25 Progressive Party nominates Henry A. Wallace for President

31 Idlewild International Airport in NYC dedicated by Pres. Truman

AUG 3 Former Communist Whittaker Chambers names Alger Hiss, ex-State Department official, as former Party member

14 US wins 33 gold medals at Olympics in London

SEP 9 North Korea establishes People's Republic; conflicts with US-backed administration in Seoul

NOV 2 Truman elected President in major political upset, Alben W. Barkley elected Vice President

DEC 15 Alger Hiss indicted by grand jury on two counts of perjury

The Arts

★ Norman Mailer's novel *The Naked and the Dead*

★ Jackson Pollock's painting *Composition No. 1*

★ The film *The Treasure of the Sierra Madre*

★ The film *Johnny Belinda*

★ Long-playing (LP) phonograph records introduced by Columbia Records

Truman and The Fair Deal

If the international situation absorbed much of the energies of Truman and his administration in the post-war years, they had plenty left for domestic affairs as well. The process of reassimilating millions of war veterans into society and of reconverting the American economy from its wartime pursuits to the demands of peace was handled far more effectively than had been the case after the First World War, but there were problems nonetheless. In particular, the demand explosion which followed the cessation of hostilities fueled a price inflation of some 34 per cent between 1945 and 1948. In this overheated economic atmosphere, President Truman, who had asked Congress for an expansion of the New Deal when he took office on Roosevelt's death, found himself embroiled during his first term of office in a number of battles over the thorny issues of price control and labor relations. However, his administration initiated some far-reaching pieces of legislation during these years, including the Employment Act of 1946, which for the first time enshrined in law the responsibility of the Government to maintain prosperity, and the National Security Act of 1947, which created a new and more effective administrative structure for the nation's defense and gave birth to both the National Security Council and the Central Intelligence Agency (CIA).

With the election of 1948, however, the Democratic Party split into warring factions after Truman was renominated on a strong civil rights platform. As a result, the President found himself standing not only against the Republican candidate, Thomas E. Dewey, but also against two other candidates from the Democratic camp. He mounted an energetic campaign, undertaking a 20,000-mile speaking tour of the country, but all the polls predicted a clear Republican victory. They were wrong. In one of the biggest electoral surprises of the century, Truman held on to the presidency with 303 electoral votes to Dewey's 189, though the popular vote was much closer. In his inaugural address he spoke of a "Fair Deal," which would extend Roosevelt's social security measures to what he saw as their natural conclusion and would continue the conservation and energy policies that had made the Tennessee Valley Authority the envy of the world. The 81st Congress, which convened in January 1949, began to convert this program into legislation, and also, in the Reorganization Act of 1949, gave the President authority to implement a far-reaching restructuring of the machinery of government itself.

But it would not be long before foreign affairs again came to dominate the domestic agenda. With the fall of China's American-backed Nationalist Government to the Communist régime of Mao Tse-Tung in 1949, the focus of the Cold War shifted suddenly to the Far East. And it was from a previously little-considered quarter of that region that, in the opening years of the next decade, the crisis came which would once more threaten the world's uneasy peace.

Joltin' Joe

Joe DiMaggio, the New York Yankees' record-breaking hitter and future husband of Marilyn Monroe.

Dashiell Hammett

Dashiell Hammett (left), author of *The Thin Man* and creator of the hard-boiled detective Sam Spade, set a new tone in crime fiction.

Joe Louis

The American boxing scene was dominated during the 1940s by Joe Louis (above), whose 11-year tenure of the world heavyweight title ended only with his retirement in 1949 at the age of 34.

First Sonic Boom

On October 14, 1947, Charles "Chuck" Yeager (above) became the first man ever to travel faster than the speed of sound when his specially designed Bell X-1 rocket plane, named *Glamorous Glennis* in honor of his wife, reached speeds in excess of 600 m.p.h. over the Californian desert.

Airlines

The U.S. airline network, which already covered some 50,000 miles in 1930, expanded very significantly during the 1940s, with airlines such as Pan Am advertising regular flights to many parts of the world.

1949

JAN 3 Supreme Court rules that states have right to ban closed shop

5 Pres. Truman delivers State-of-the-Union message to Congress in which he names his administration the 'Fair Deal'

7 Secretary of State Marshall resigns; succeeded by Dean Acheson

8 Fastest transcontinental flight made by USAF XB-47 jet bomber

14 Department of Justice files antitrust suit against ATT to separate it from Western Electric, Inc.

19 Congress raises salary of President to $100,000 per year plus tax-free expense allowance of $50,000

20 Truman inaugurated for first elective term, Alben W. Barkley inaugurated Vice President; Truman delivers address in which he describes 'Four Points' of major program to promote world peace

FEB 25 Flight altitude record set by WAC-Corporal guided missile

MAR 1 World heavyweight champion Joe Lewis retires

2 USAF Superfortress B-50 bomber completes first non-stop around-the-world flight

2 United Mine Workers president John L. Lewis orders two-week walkout of soft-coal workers

APR 4 US, Canada, Great Britain, France, Belgium, Norway, Denmark, Luxembourg, Iceland, Italy, Portugal and The Netherlands sign North Atlantic Treaty, forming NATO, in Washington, DC

20 Discovery of cortisone announced

MAY 12 Soviets lift Berlin blockade

20 Executive Council of American Federation of Labor rejects bid for reaffiliation proposed by United Mine Workers

31 Perjury trial of Alger Hiss opens in NYC

JUN 20 Pres. Truman signs Reorganization Act, allowing president to reorganize executive branch

27 In *Wolf v. Colorado*, Supreme Court rules that prosecutors may continue using evidence gained through illegal search and seizure

29 US withdraws last of its troops from Korea, leaving approximately 500 advisors

JUL 15 Pres. Truman signs Housing Act, providing for extended Federal aid for public housing

21 North Atlantic Treaty ratified by Senate

AUG 5 US stops aid to Nationalist China

10 Pres. Truman signs National Security Act of 1949, creating Deptartment of Defense and giving subcabinet status to secretaries of Army, Navy and Air Force

11 Gen. Omar Bradley becomes chairman of Joint Chiefs of Staff

25 First experimental color TV transmission

SEP 21 Pres. Truman signs Mutual Defense Assistance Act to provide military aid to US allies in NATO

OCT 1 US refuses to recognize Communist Chinese Government under Mao Tse-tung

14 Eleven leaders of US Communist Party, on trial for conspiracy to advocate violent overthrow of US Government, found guilty under Smith Act

24 Permanent UN headquarters in NYC dedicated

26 Fair Labor Standards Act amended to increase minimum wage to 75 cents per hour

OCT-NOV 11 Nationwide steel strike affects 500,000 workers

DEC 9 House Un-American Activities Committee chairman, J. Parnell Thomas, found guilty of payroll padding

26 Einstein's new general theory of relativity announced

The Arts

★ Arthur Miller's play *Death of a Salesman*

★ Rodgers and Hammerstein's musical *South Pacific*

★ Leonard Bernstein's composition *Symphony No. 2 for Piano and Orchestra*

Hope and Crosby

The comic partnership of Bob Hope and Bing Crosby found one of its most engaging vehicles in the series of so-called "road movies" made in the 1940s. In *Road to Zanzibar* (1941) (left) Hope and Crosby join up with their regular co-star Dorothy Lamour on safari in Africa.

Tennessee Williams

Another American playwright to come to prominence in the 1940s was Tennessee Williams (above), whose studies in familial and sexual tensions, *The Glass Menagerie* and *A Streetcar Named Desire*, were first performed in 1944 and 1947 respectively. The latter, centering around the experiences of Blanche DuBois when she visits the New Orleans slum in which her sister and brother-in-law live, won Williams a Pulitzer prize.

Here's Looking at You, Kid

One of the greatest films ever made, *Casablanca* became an overnight success when it was released in 1942. Directed by Michael Curtiz, it stars Humphrey Bogart as Rick Blaine, a cynical café owner who meets up with a former lover, Ilse Lund, played by Ingrid Bergman, in the town of the film's title during the Second World War. It features the song, "As Time Goes By" but *not* – or at least, not quite – the line "Play it again, Sam."

Yankee Doodle Dandy

The 1940s saw a resurgence of patriotic and romantic musical films, including Warner Brothers' immensely popular *Yankee Doodle Dandy*, directed by Michael Curtiz in 1942. Starring James Cagney as George M. Cohan, the song-and-dance man whose equally patriotic spectaculars during World War I did so much to set the tone of the American musical, the movie was nominated for eight Academy Awards. Cagney himself received an Oscar for his ebullient central performance.

Citizen Kane

Following his unforgettable radio performance in *The War of the Worlds*, Orson Welles transferred his attention, equally memorably, to the big screen in 1941, directing and starring in one of the all-time greats of cinema history, *Citizen Kane*. The film, made when the director was only 26, traces the public but nonetheless enigmatic life of a newspaper tycoon who "got everything he wanted, and then lost it." It remains Welles' masterpiece.

Alger Hiss

With the Cold War becoming a permanent fact of political life, the closing years of the decade witnessed an upsurge in anti-Communist activity in the United States under the auspices of the ever-suspicious House Committee to Investigate Un-American Activities (H.U.A.C.). Perhaps its most notorious case was that of Alger Hiss, a former State Department official, who was accused, in 1948, of passing secret documents to a member of the Communist Party in the 1930s. He denied the charge, but, when further evidence came to light, was indicted for perjury, the statute of limitation having expired on the espionage charge. After two trials he was found guilty and sentenced to five years in jail.

Frank Sinatra

The 34-year-old hearthrob, Frank Sinatra (right), who sang with the Harry James and Tommy Dorsey bands in the 1930s, starred in the immensely popular film *On the Town*, a musical about three sailors' 24-hour shore leave in New York, in 1949.

Glenn Miller

The bandleader Glenn Miller (left), famous for his *Moonlight Serenade* and *In the Mood* was lost presumed dead when his plane disappeared over the English Channel in 1944.

First Computers

The first ungainly steps were taken during the 1940s toward what would become an information revolution over the next four decades. In 1944 the International Business Machines Corporation (IBM) built its Mark I Calculator at Harvard, an enormous calculating machine which, for all its unreliability, pointed the way ahead for the development of smaller and more efficient computers, especially after the invention of the transistor in the late 1940s. Some idea of the scale of these early computers can be gained from the rear view of the Electronic Numerical Integrator and Calculator (ENIAC) (left), which was built at the University of Pennsylvania in 1946 and could perform 5000 calculations per second. The ENIAC computer, which was used primarily for military purposes, weighed in at some 30 tons.

Jitterbug

The new style of dancing which swept through America in the 1940s was less a specific set of movements than a fast and furious response to the latest in youth music, and became known as "jitterbugging." Right: Jitterbug dancers in Brooklyn, New York, in 1941.

Edward Hopper

This canvas by Edward Hopper (1882–1967), *Nighthawks*, painted in 1942, is typical of the artist's stark and haunting evocations of urban America. Late-night bars, motel rooms, deserted street scenes – all handled with strong contrasts of light and shade – constitute Hopper's characteristic landscape of loneliness and alienation.

THE EAST-WEST tensions that had surfaced in the immediate aftermath of the Second World War persisted throughout the 1950s. More than once, the jockeying of the superpowers for positions of international influence threatened to escalate regional conflicts into full-scale war. But somehow such strains on the fragile fabric of world peace as the Korean War, the French War in Indochina, the Suez Crisis, the Soviet invasion of Hungary, and the U.S. intervention in Lebanon, destructive of life and trust as they were, remained limited actions, rather than the catalyst for the "massive retaliation" of which John Foster Dulles spoke in his role as President Eisenhower's Secretary of State. Meanwhile, advances in military technology made the nature of that retaliation more terrible to contemplate than ever before. The arms race began in earnest during the decade with the development of the H bomb by both the Soviet Union and the United States, and by the end of the 1950s advances in Soviet rocket technology had fired the starting pistol for the space race too. If Dulles' vaunted "brinkmanship" succeeded in Europe, the Middle East, and the Far East, what lay beyond the brink was nonetheless so horrifying as to make many people question whether the risks were worth the gains.

By contrast with the vagaries of world affairs, the domestic front continued to see the steady advance of prosperity and, with the arrival in the White House of the much-loved war hero Dwight D. Eisenhower in 1952, a period of stable "middle of the road" politics. The paranoid and vindictive anti-Communist phenomenon of McCarthyism overreached itself by 1953, making room for slow but steady advances in the field of civil liberties as the Supreme Court blunted the more authoritarian edges of recent internal security legislation and overturned the judicial bases of racial segregation in the Southern states. At the same time, the Black civil rights movement was gathering new strength from the work and philosophy of a young Baptist minister from Alabama called Martin Luther King. The forces of prejudice and inertia were beginning to give way to the upsurge of egalitarianism that would characterize the 1960s.

The Korean War

The Berlin crisis of 1948–1949 had no sooner died down than the Far East erupted into conflict. Developments in Korea took everyone by surprise. The country had been surrendered to the Allies by Japan in 1945, and had been provisionally divided into two zones of influence along the line of the 38th parallel, the Northern area being occupied by Soviet and the Southern by U.S. forces. By 1949 this division had hardened with the creation of separate governments – a Communist régime in the North and a democratically-elected Republic in the South. U.S. troops withdrew from the Republic once the Government of President Syngman Rhee had been recognized by the United Nations, little suspecting that the 38th parallel was about to become the most

dangerous front of the Cold War.

On June 25, 1950, North Korea invaded the South in force, and within three days the Southern capital, Seoul, was in Communist hands. Ignoring a U.N. demand for them to withdraw, the North Korean troops pressed on southwards, and President Truman, without declaring war or receiving the official authorization of Congress, ordered General Douglas MacArthur, who was still stationed in Japan, to halt their advance. At the same time, the United Nations called on all its member governments to support South Korea. For a while, the U.S. troops barely hung on to the southern tip of the country, but with the arrival of U.N. reinforcements and a brilliant amphibious assault on Inchon in September, MacArthur, now Supreme Commander of the U.N. forces, was able to turn the tide. By October, he had retaken Seoul and was forging on to the 38th parallel, driving the North Koreans before him. But he didn't stop there. With U.N. backing, and despite an ominous threat by Communist China to send troops into North Korea if U.N. forces crossed the parallel, MacArthur pressed on northwards, taking the Northern capital, Pyongyang, on October 20 and continuing towards the Yalu River boundary between North Korea and Manchuria.

However, MacArthur had tragically underestimated the Chinese. He now found himself fighting what he described as "an entirely new war" as he stumbled into hundreds of thousands of Chinese troops, who had already crossed the border in secret. Mile by painful mile, the U.N. forces were driven back to the South, where they fortified themselves behind the 38th parallel. With the conflict threatening to escalate into an all-out superpower confrontation, a dangerous gulf now opened up between MacArthur and Truman. The President wanted to limit the war as far as possible to a defensive action. MacArthur, on the other hand, was all for launching a full-scale invasion of China, using nuclear arms if necessary, and as the weeks went by he became less and less restrained about saying so. When, in April 1951, a letter stating MacArthur's views was read out before Congress, Truman, with the complete support of his Joint Chiefs of Staff, promptly relieved him of his command. There was uproar in America. MacArthur returned home to a hero's welcome, and there were even calls for Truman to be impeached. Only when a Senate Armed Services Committee investigation found in Truman's favor did the furor die down. Peace talks began between the opposing forces, but it would take a change of President to bring the bloody "police action" in Korea to an end.

Enter "Ike"

That change occurred dramatically in the 1952 election. Having resisted nomination for the presidency in 1948, the Supreme Commander of NATO Forces in Europe, Dwight D. Eisenhower, now entered the ring, receiving the Republican nomination, with the young Californian senator Richard

A man for all seasons: Dwight D. Eisenhower – war hero and one of America's most popular presidents.

Milhous Nixon as his running mate. Eisenhower – or "Ike" as he was affectionately known – was enormously popular with the American people and conducted his campaign (the first in American history to make extensive use of the new medium of television) as a "Great Crusade for honest government at home and freedom throughout the world." When he promised to go to Korea and end the war himself if he were elected, his victory became a foregone conclusion. He received 33.8 million popular votes to the Democrat Adlai Stevenson's 26.5 million, and 442 electoral votes to Stevenson's 89. For the first time in more than 20 years, America had a Republican President.

Once in office, Eisenhower was quick to act on his pledge to end the Korean War. Peace talks were resumed – though not until the new Secretary of State, John Foster Dulles, had given a foretaste of his abrasive diplomatic style by threatening China with invasion if she didn't return to the negotiating table – and an armistice was finally signed on July 27, 1953, establishing a demilitarized zone around the 38th parallel, but otherwise leaving matters pretty much as they stood before the fighting began. Whether it was quite the "peace with honor" the American people had had in mind when they voted for their new President is open to question; but it put an end to a dangerously destabilizing conflict, which had claimed some 50,000 American and perhaps as many as two million North Korean and Chinese lives.

The "New Look"

The style of foreign policy embraced by Eisenhower and Dulles soon became known as the "New Look." As their approach to Korea had shown, it was a style characterized by a combination of tough talking and cautious diplomacy, backed up by a high level of personal contact with representatives of other governments. During the remainder of the decade this policy was to be severely tested, not only in the Far East, but also in the Middle East and Europe.

In the Far East, the French War against Chinese-backed Communist forces in Vietnam, which erupted almost as soon as the Korean War ended, led to a conference of the great powers in Geneva in 1954 and – in an ominous replay of recent history in Korea – the division of Vietnam along the 17th parallel. It also provided the spur for the creation of the South East Asia Treaty Organization (SEATO), a Far Eastern sister body to NATO, and to separate U.S. pacts with South Korea and the exiled Chinese Nationalist government of Chiang Kai-Shek,

entrenched on the island of Formosa (now Taiwan). The latter alliance was to raise the Far Eastern temperature yet again in 1958 when the Chinese began shelling the Nationalist-held islands around Formosa, and the U.S. Seventh Fleet was despatched to the area in a short-lived but provocative show of strength.

In the Middle East, America sent confusing signals to Colonel Nasser of Egypt by withdrawing an offer of funding for his grandiose Aswan Dam project and helped contribute to the political uncertainty that led to Nasser's seizure of the Suez Canal and Israel's subsequent invasion of the Sinai peninsula in 1956. The ensuing military action by Britain and France came to an abrupt and inglorious end when the United States refused to support it, but the whole affair did lasting damage to the Western Alliance and helped raise the Soviet Union's stock with Middle Eastern governments, as did America's military intervention in Lebanon after an Arab Nationalist rising in neighboring Iraq in 1958. For a time both episodes threatened to escalate into full-scale war.

The situation was no happier in Europe, where East-West tensions ran high after

A brief thaw in the Cold War? Vice President Richard M. Nixon meets Nikita Khrushchev at the Kremlin in 1959.

1950s

Korean War

President Eisenhower

McCarthyism

1950

JAN 2 Department of Commerce reports that since July 1945 foreign aid in form of grants and credits amounts to $25 billion

21 Paul Larsen named first chairman of Civilian Mobilization Office, intended to upgrade civil defense

24 Minimum wage of 75 cents per hour goes into effect

31 Development of hydrogen bomb by Atomic Energy Commission announced by Pres. Truman

FEB 9 Sen. Joseph McCarthy of Wisconsin charges State Department with harboring Communists

20 Sen. McCarthy reveals another list of suspected Communists, provoking Senate subcommittee investigation

20 In *US v. Rabinowitz*, Supreme Court rules that police have right to seize property without search warrant

MAR 7 Soviet consular official Valentin Gubitchev found guilty of conspiracy and attempted espionage against US

13 General Motors Corporation announces net earnings of $656,434,232, largest profit ever reported by US corporation

17 Discovery of californium, heaviest known element, announced by researchers at University of California, Berkeley

MAY 8 In *American Communications Association v. Douds*, Supreme Court rules that non-Communist statement required by Taft-Hartley Act does not violate Constitution

25 Brooklyn-Battery tunnel, longest tunnel in US, opens in NYC

JUN 5 Supreme Court bars segregation of Black students in two Southern universities

5 International Development Act, Point Four Program, signed by Pres. Truman

25 Korean War (1950-1953) begins when North Korean troops launch invasion across 38th parallel into South Korea; UN orders immediate ceasefire and withdrawal

26 Pres. Truman authorizes US Navy and Air Force to aid South Korean troops

27 UN Security Council adopts resolution calling for armed intervention in Korea

30 US troops sent to South Korea, US Navy ordered to blockade Korean coast

30 Selective Service Extension Act extends draft for one year

JUL 8 Gen. Douglas MacArthur named commander of UN troops in South Korea

20 Pres. Truman asks Congress to pass $10 billion rearmament program

West Germany was given full sovereignty and admitted to NATO in 1954 with a standing army of half a million men. Stalin's death in 1953, and the emergence of Nikita Khrushchev as Soviet leader, seemed to promise a period of friendlier relations, but the first ever superpower summit broke down without significant agreements in Geneva in 1955, and by the end of the decade Germany had again become the focus of a serious East-West crisis when Khrushchev suddenly demanded that Britain, France, and the U.S. withdraw from West Berlin within six months.

McCarthyism

American domestic affairs were relatively untroubled during the 1950s. There were, however, some disturbing undercurrents, one of the least edifying of which was the anti-Communist witchhunt conducted by Senator Joseph McCarthy of Wisconsin in the opening years of the decade. McCarthy, whose name has become a by-word for demagoguery, first caught the public eye during the feverish Red Scare that followed the conviction of the former State Department official Alger Hiss in 1950 on charges arising from espionage activity. The same year, Congress passed (over Truman's veto) the McCarran-Nixon Internal Security Act, which made it illegal to employ Communists in the defense industry, required Communist organizations to register a list of their members with the Attorney-General, and imposed political restrictions on immigration. McCarthy's claim to have a list of 205 members of the State Department who were card-carrying Communists was shown to be fraudulent, but his accusations became more and more extreme and wide-ranging as time went on, taking in not only writers, intellectuals, movie actors, and scientists, but also senior army officers, General Marshall, and even President Truman himself. By 1954 the spectacle had become more than most right-thinking Americans were prepared to tolerate, and, after being roundly censured by the Senate, McCarthy disappeared from public life as suddenly as he had emerged.

Civil Rights

Towards the end of 1953, President Eisenhower appointed Earl Warren to the post of Chief Justice of the United States. Warren had a conservative record, but under his leadership the Supreme Court embarked on a series of liberal decisions, which went some way towards limiting the erosion of personal liberties made possible by some of the internal security measures of the preceding years. More significantly still, in the famous case of Brown v. Board of Education of Topeka (1954), the so-called Warren Court gave a push to the cause of Black civil rights by deciding that racial segregation in schools constituted a violation of the Fourteenth Amendment. The decision killed the "separate but equal" principle upon which the segregationist Jim Crow laws of the Southern states had been erected by ruling

A state trooper ensures that a Black student gets to school unharassed.

that "separate educational facilities are inherently unequal," and in 1955 the Supreme Court instructed Federal district courts to introduce desegregation "with all deliberate speed."

Most of the border states complied fairly quickly. The Deep South, however, resisted fiercely. One of the ugliest confrontations took place at Little Rock, Arkansas, in September 1957, when the Federal district court decreed that nine Black students should be admitted to the previously segregated Central High School. The segregationist Governor of Arkansas, Orville Faubus, took every available step to prevent the students being enrolled at the school, including mobilizing the National Guard to bar the doors to them. Eisenhower, who had previously been equivocal about the court order, intervened to demand that the National Guard be withdrawn, only to see it replaced by a white mob which continued to keep the Black students out. In an extraordinary move, the President then removed the National Guard from Faubus' control and sent 1000 Army paratroopers to Little Rock

to escort the nine Blacks. Even so, there was still no mixed schooling in South Carolina, Georgia, Alabama, Mississippi, or Louisiana at the end of the decade.

Meanwhile, in Montgomery, Alabama, in 1955, the arrest of a Black woman, Rosa Parks, for refusing to give up her seat on a bus to a white woman led to a Black boycott of the city's buses. The leading figure in this campaign, which eventually led to the desegregation of Montgomery's bus services, was a 25-year-old Baptist minister by the name of Martin Luther King. Confirming as it did his belief that peaceful civil disobedience could win equality for Afro-Americans as it had won Independence for India, the Montgomery boycott was the beginning of a national struggle for King, which would lead to both honor and tragedy in the following decade.

"Dynamic Conservatism"

After the sometimes turbulent reformism of previous administrations, Eisenhower's presidency marked a return to what he liked to call "middle of the road" policies, or "dynamic conservatism." Partly dictated by the limits of Republican influence in Congress (Eisenhower's second election victory in

1956 was the first since 1848 in which the President's party had a majority in neither house of Congress), these policies extended the New Deal and the Fair Deal by catching an additional 10 million people in the social security net and raising minimum wages, while also reducing government involvement in business, conservation, and energy matters. For example, Eisenhower greatly reduced the funding of the Tennessee Valley Authority (which he regarded as an example of "creeping socialism"), gave the rights over offshore oilfields to the states rather than to Federal Government, and favored private enterprise in power production. In short, he dedicated himself to "finding things [the government] can stop doing rather than new things for it to do."

A Changing Nation

The 1950s were a time of great social change in America. Apart from a brief recession in 1957–1958, the decade saw a continuing growth in national prosperity, fueled by the post-war spending boom. The standard of living improved markedly for the average American citizen, with increased earnings and shorter working hours, and there was a massive expansion of educational opportunities for the young, especially at the higher levels. People found they had more free time, and, in response, a new leisure industry grew up to provide sporting and other facilities. The television set, a rarity in the 1940s, was well on the way to becoming universal in American homes by the end of the 1950s, with far-reaching implications for the way people would see themselves and the world around them and for the development of a new mass culture. The decade was also marked by a decrease in the population of some of the country's major cities, as people moved out into the rapidly growing suburbs, leaving the inner city areas to begin a process of decline the effects of which are still all too evident today. At the same time, big business continued to grow bigger, with giant corporations establishing structures of influence which transcended national boundaries. New industries sprang up to answer new needs, creating new employment opportunities in the process, and the first shot of a business revolution was fired when IBM put on the market the first electronic computing machine. Coolidge's dictum that "the business of America is business" had never been truer. By 1955 the United States, with just 6 per cent of the world's population, was producing no less than half of the world's goods.

At the same time, there were many who detected in the drift towards consumerism a loss of a national sense of direction in America, and who bewailed what they saw as an unquestioning acceptance of the status quo, even among the young. Such observers feared for the effects of materialism on American society and spoke of a "silent generation," content to subordinate its individuality to the demands of large conservative organizations. Whether or not they were right, it was only the lull before the storm. Before the following decade was out, the silent generation would have found its voice with a vengeance.

The TV decade: In 1947 there were 7000 U.S. sets, in 1960 54 million.

20 Senate Foreign Relations Committee publishes report that finds Sen. Joseph McCarthy's allegations of Communist presence in State Department without factual basis

AUG 4 US Army calls up 62,000 reservists

18 Special Committee to investigate crime in Interstate Commerce issues report that organized crime is taking over legitimate businesses

25 US Army seizes railroads by order of Pres. Truman to prevent scheduled strike

SEP 8 Defense Production Act authorizes wage and price controls

15 UN forces land at Inchon and press toward Seoul

21 Former Secretary of State George Marshall becomes Secretary of Defense

23 Internal Security Act, requiring registration of Communists and detention during national emergency and establishing Subversive Activities Control Board, passed over President's veto

26 UN troops recapture Seoul, South Korea

29 US-supported South Korean troops reach 38th parallel

OCT 7 UN forces invade North Korea

11 US crossing of 38th parallel provokes denouncement by Red Chinese

11 FCC authorizes Columbia Broadcasting System to begin color television broadcasts

20 UN troops capture Pyongyang, capital of North Korea

NOV 1 Two Puerto Rican nationalists attempt assassination of Pres. Truman at Blair House, Washington

7 Chinese Communist troops reported in action with North Korean forces by Gen. MacArthur

20 US troops reach Yalu River, on Manchurian border

29 UN forces retreat under heavy attack from Chinese Communist forces

DEC 5 UN troops abandon Pyongyang, North Korea

8 Pres. Truman announces ban on US shipment of goods to Communist China

16 Pres. Truman declares national emergency

19 North Atlantic Council names Dwight D. Eisenhower Supreme Commander of Western European Defense Forces

The Arts
★ Bette Davis in the film *All About Eve*
★ Billy Wilder's film *Sunset Boulevard*

1951

JAN 1 Congress allows the President to place freeze on prices

15 In *Feiner v. US* Supreme Court rules that a speaker displaying 'clear and present danger' of incitement to riot can be arrested

FEB 1 Communist China accused of aggression against Korea by UN

8 Nationwide rail service resumes after 12-day strike; workers granted pay rise

25-MAR 9 First Pan-American Games held in Buenos Aires, Argentina; US finishes second

26 Twenty-second Amendment limits presidential terms to two

MAR 14 Seoul, South Korea, recaptured by UN forces

24 Gen. Douglas MacArthur threatens China with bombing and naval bombardment

APR 4 Supreme Headquarters, Allied Powers (SHAPE) established in Paris by Gen. Dwight D. Eisenhower

5 Julius and Ethel Rosenberg convicted of passing top-secret information on nuclear weapons to USSR; both sentenced to death

11 Gen. MacArthur relieved of command in Far East by Pres. Truman

19 Gen. MacArthur speaks to joint session of Congress, urging military action against Communist China

28 OPS fixes beef prices

The Korean War

The Truman Doctrine in action, the undeclared war in Korea threatened to escalate into an all-out confrontation between the Eastern and Western blocs. American troops formed a significant part of the U.N. forces seeking to repel the North Korean invasion of the South which began in June 1950.

Left top: By the end of 1950 General MacArthur was reporting, ominously, that he found himself fighting "an entirely different war" in Korea from the swift "police action" he and Truman had expected. Crossing the 38th parallel and pressing northwards, MacArthur's men encountered a massive Chinese invasion force moving southwards to meet them. Here troops of the U.S. 24th Infantry Division retreat south before the Chinese advance, December 1950.

Left inset: The human face of war: a U.S. soldier shares his rations with a Korean child.

Right inset: President Truman and Douglas MacArthur greet one another at Wake Island in October 1950. Within months, warm handshakes were to give way to outright hostility, as the two men's views of the war diverged irreconcilably. In April 1951 MacArthur was dismissed from his command in Korea.

Left bottom: The reality behind *M.A.S.H..* Some 50,000 American soldiers and perhaps two million North Koreans and Chinese died in what has been called the 20th century's "forgotten war." Here a wounded U.S. soldier is evacuated to a field hospital by helicopter.

Below: Truman's dismissal of MacArthur was enormously unpopular with many people in the United States, even prompting calls for the President to be impeached. "Mac" on the other hand, was greeted as a hero when he returned home, as shown by this welcoming committee of young boys in a cold Chicago street in April 1951.

MAY 15 American Telephone and Telegraph announces that it is the first corporation to have more than one million stockholders

JUN 4 Supreme Court upholds Smith Act, concerning Communists in government

4 Supreme Court upholds state's right to require job applicants to sign non-Communist affadivits

14 UNIVAC, first electronic digital computer built for commercial purposes, dedicated and demonstrated in Philadelphia, Pa

19 Military draft extended to July 1, 1955; service lengthened to two years; age lowered to 18½

JUL 10 US participates in truce talks between UN and Chinese Communists at Kaesang

11-25 Flood covers more than one million acres of farmland in Kansas, Oklahoma, Missouri and Illinois; damage estimated at over $1 billion

AUG 1 Tariff concessions to Soviet-bloc nations cancelled by Pres. Truman

SEP 1 Tripartite Agreement by US, Australia and New Zealand provides for mutual defense

4 First transcontinental television broadcast reports President's opening address to Japanese Peace Treaty Conference

8 Japanese Peace Treaty signed by 49 nations in San Francisco, Calif; US permitted to maintain military forces in Japanese territory

OCT 10 Mutual Security Act authorizes $7 billion in aid to foreign countries

10 First transcontinental dial telephone service begins at Englewood, NJ

NOV 15 Nobel Prize in Chemistry awarded to Edwin McMillan and Glen Seaborg for their discovery of plutonium

DEC 20 First atomic-powered generator begins producing electricity at US Reactor Testing Station in Idaho

Also this year
★ Employment of women in industry reaches highest point in history

1952

JAN 8 US agrees not to launch atomic attack on Communist Europe without consent of Britain

24 UN negotiators announce that Korean truce talks have stalled

MAR 2 Supreme Court rules that persons termed subversives may be barred from teaching in public schools

18 Sen. William Benton of Connecticut attempts to discredit Sen. Joseph McCarthy's anti-Communist tactics

20 Japanese Peace Treaty ratified by Senate

26 Sen. McCarthy brings suit against Sen. Benton for libel, slander and conspiracy against him

APR 2 George F. Kennan becomes US Ambassador to Soviet Union

8 Federal takeover of steel mills in Youngstown, Ohio, ordered by the President to avert strike

MAY 8 Secretary of the Army Frank Pace announces development of atomic cannon

12 First woman ambassador to US, her Excellency Shrimati Vijaya Lakshmi, Pandit of India, received in Washington, DC

23 Railroad owners regain control of lines under US Army jurisdiction since August 27, 1950

26 US, Great Britain, France and West Germany sign peace treaty in Bonn

JUN 2 Presidential takeover of steel industry ruled unconstitutional by Supreme Court; mills returned to owners; strike resumed

14 First US atomic-powered submarine, *Nautilus*, dedicated by Pres. Truman in Groton, Conn.

27 McCarron Walter Act retains quota system for setting immigration levels

JUL 7 Republican National Convention nominates Dwight D. Eisenhower for President and Richard M. Nixon of California for Vice President

McCarthyism

America had known Red Scares before – most notably in the immediate aftermath of the First World War – but nothing had approached the ruthlessness and increasing lack of scruple of Senator Joseph McCarthy's crusade against Communism in the early 1950s.

Left: McCarthy, a junior senator from Wisconsin, exercised a power far beyond his apparent status between February 9, 1950, when he made his famous (and completely unsubstantiated) claim to have the names of 205 card-carrying members of the Communist Party who were active in the State Department, and 1954, when the increasingly inescapable demagoguery of his witchhunt led to his censure by the Senate.

Below: Television played a crucial part in revealing McCarthy's bullying methods during the Army-McCarthy hearings of spring 1954. McCarthy had accused senior Army personnel of being Communist infiltrators and the Army had, in return, accused McCarthy's close aide, Roy Cohn (seen behind McCarthy here during the hearings), of corruption.

Below inset: Hollywood was a particular target of McCarthy's attacks. Here the President of the Screen Actors Guild, Ronald Reagan, testifies before the House Un-American Activities Committee.

Opposite top: Supporters of McCarthy, here seen tabulating petition signatures, mounted a nationwide campaign to defeat the censure motion in 1954. Despite their efforts, the motion was passed by 67 votes to 22.

The traumas of the McCarthy years, which led to an exodus of many leading figures in the American arts and academic world, found their echo in one of the greatest of Arthur Miller's plays, *The Crucible*, which was first produced in 1953 (above). A disturbing evocation of the hysteria surrounding the Salem witch trials of 1692, the play's powerful implicit plea for tolerance had a clear contemporary application.

Meanwhile, in the world of motion pictures, Fred Zinnemann's classic western, *High Noon*, starring Gary Cooper (right) as a marshal standing firm against the forces of evil, carried its own suspenseful share of social commentary.

14 Price controls on nearly all fresh and processed vegetables and meats removed

21 Democratic National Convention nominates Adlai Stevenson for President and Sen. John Sparkman of Alabama for Vice President

24 Steel strike ends with agreement on wage and price increases

25 Puerto Rico becomes Commonwealth under US jurisdiction

SEP 23 Richard Nixon appears on television to defend himself against allegations of 'secret slush fund'

OCT 13 Rosenberg appeal of espionage conviction rejected by Supreme Court

23 Eight teachers dismissed by NYC Board of Education for alleged Communist activities

NOV 4 Dwight D. Eisenhower elected President, Richard M. Nixon elected Vice President

10 Supreme Court rules in favor of lower court decision banning segregation in interstate travel

16 US Atomic Energy Commission announces completion of hydrogen bomb testing at Eniwetok Atoll in the Marshall Islands

DEC 5 Pres.-elect Eisenhower visits Korea in hope of breaking stalemate in truce talks

Also this year

★ Unidentified flying objects reported across nation

The Arts

★ Ralph Ellison's novel *The Invisible Man*

★ Gene Kelly's film *Singin' in the Rain*

1953

JAN 2 Senate subcommittee reports that some of Sen. Joseph McCarthy's political activities had been 'motivated by self-interest'

20 Dwight D. Eisenhower inaugurated President, Richard M. Nixon inaugurated Vice President

21 Thirteen communist leaders convicted by federal jury in NYC of conspiring to overthrow US Government

FEB 2 Pres. Eisenhower states intention to lift US blockade of Taiwan

6 OPS lifts controls on wages and salaries

12 Price controls on eggs, poultry, tires and gasoline lifted

MAR 5 Death of Joseph Stalin

17 OPS ends controls on all prices

18 US protests Soviet Union's attack on US bomber in international waters

28 Death of athlete Jim Thorpe

APR 1 Department of Health, Education and Welfare established by Congress

24 Record taxes of $68.5 billion collected in 1952, according to Buereau of Internal Revenue

25 Record for filibustering set in Senate by Sen. Wayne Morse of Oregon, who held floor for 22 hours, 26 minutes

MAY 11 Tornadoes hit Waco and San Antonio , Tex., leaving 124 dead

25 First atomic artillery shell fired at US military testing grounds in Nevada

JUN 8 Tornado hits Ohio and Michigan, 139 dead

9 Tornado kills 86 in central Massachussetts

18 USAF plane crashes near Tokyo, killing 129; worst air incident to date

19 Convicted spies Julius and Ethel Rosenberg executed in electric chair; first Americans executed for treason during peacetime

JUL 27 Korean armistice signed at Panmunjom

29 US B-50 bomber shot down by Soviets off coast of Vladivostok, Siberia

AUG 7 Refugee Relief Act admits 214,000 foreign nationals to US

18 US, Great Britain and France invite Soviet Union to meet at Lugano, Switzerland, to discuss issues of world peace

SEP 26 US pledges military and economic aid to Spain in exchange for air and naval bases

ROCKING AROUND THE CLOCK

Fueled by the development of mass communications on an unprecedented scale, a new kind of popular music spread like wildfire among the youth of America in the 1950s. Soon to be called "rock 'n' roll," it sent moral shivers down the spines of the older generation with its driving beat, its sex-laden lyrics, and its apparent glorification of all that was uninhibited and rebellious.

The high priests of the new music were Bill Haley and his band, the Comets, whose song "Rock Around the Clock" leapt to the top of the charts in 1955 after it was used in the film *Blackboard Jungle*; Buddy Holly, composer and performer of such classics of the rock repertoire as "Peggy Sue" and "That'll Be the Day," whose early death in a 'plane crash in 1950 preserved his almost legendary status; and, above all, Elvis Presley, a former truck driver from Memphis, Tennessee, who arrived on the music scene in 1956 with the release of such rock standards as "Heartbreak Hotel" and "Blue Suede Shoes." The latter's highly sexually-charged performance on the Ed Sullivan TV show that year was watched by an estimated 54 million people, and made Presley's pelvis a national issue.

Left: The "King of Rock 'n' Roll," Elvis Presley, and (inset) his ecstatic audience.

Bill Haley, lead singer of the Comets.

The legendary Buddy Holly.

Eddie Cochran pays homage to Elvis.

Jerry Lee Lewis on his "music truck."

OCT 1 Pres. Eisenhower employs Taft-Hartley Law to prevent dockworkers' strike

5 Earl Warren sworn in as Chief Justice of Supreme Court

NOV 3 Soviet Union refuses to attend peace meeting unless it includes Communist China

DEC 4-8 Pres. Eisenhower meets with representatives of Great Britain and France in Bermuda to discuss exchange of atomic information

9 General Electric Corporation announces that it will dismiss all Communist employees

16 New airplane speed record set by USAF Maj. Charles E. Yeager, who flies Bell X-1A rocket-powered plane over 1600 mph

Also this year

★ Former Secretary of State George Marshall wins Nobel Peace Prize for work on Marshall Plan of economic aid to Europe

The Arts

★ James Baldwin's novel *Go Tell It on the Mountain*

★ Arthur Miller's play *The Crucible*

★ Science fiction and 3-D films thrill audiences

1954

JAN 12 Secretary of State John Foster Dulles announces United States commitment to policy of 'massive retaliation'

19 General Motors Company announces $1 billion expansion program

21 First US nuclear submarine, *Nautilus*, launched at Groton, Conn.

25-FEB 18 Berlin Conference of Big Four Foreign Ministers: US, Great Britain, France and USSR fail to reach agreement on reunification of Germany

FEB 2 Detonation of first US hydrogen bomb in 1952 at Eniwetok Atoll in the Pacific reported by Pres. Eisenhower

23 Polio vaccine administered to school children in Pittsburgh, Pa, by Dr Jonas E. Salk, developer of serum

MAR 1 Five congressmen shot on floor of House by Puerto Rican nationalists

1 OAS meets in Caracas, Venezuela, to discuss Communist threat in member countries

8 US and Japan sign mutual defense treaty

24 Hydrogen bomb test in the Marshall Islands on March 1 exceeds all estimates of its power according to statement made by Pres. Eisenhower

APR 2 International Longshoremen's Association ends strike in effect since March 3

7 Pres. Eisenhower supports continued use of foreign aid for France in Indochina

8 Construction of early warning radar announced by US and Canada

23-JUN 17 Army-McCarthy hearings

MAY 7 Dien Bien Phu in Northern Vietnam falls to Communist Vietnamese; US begins to prepare for limited military intervention

17 In *Brown v. Board of Education of Topeko*, Supreme Court finds that 'separate but equal' doctrine does not offer equal protection under laws providing public education

JUN 1 J. Robert Oppenheimer's request for reinstatement as consultant for Atomic Energy Commission denied

2 Sen. Joseph McCarthy charges that CIA has been infiltrated by Communists

15 US refuses further military aid to French in Southeast Asia

18 CIA-supported military force invades Guatemala from Honduras

20 UN Security Council calls for cessation of hostilities in Guatemala

29 CIO and US Steel Corporation sign two-year labor agreement that provides for wage increases and expanded welfare benefits

29 Arbenz-Guzman government in Guatemala overthrown by anti-Communist insurgents

James Dean

For all the critics' talk of a "silent generation," the 1950s witnessed the development, for the first time, of a recognizable "teenage market" – a market quickly supplied not only with clothes, music, and cigarettes, but also with tailor-made idols and role models. One of those whose carefully cultivated public image identified him most strongly with the sense of direction-less rebellion of this teen generation was the film star James Dean. His first star billing, in Elia Kazan's 1955 film *East of Eden*, established the role of the smolder-ing, rebellious adolescent which he immortalized later the same year in *Rebel Without a Cause* (above). However, by the time his next film, *Giant*, was released the following year, Dean was dead, killed when his sports car crashed after leaving the road outside Los Angeles. He was just 24.

THE MOST BEAUTIFUL THING ON WHEELS

DOLLAR FOR DOLLAR

you can't beat a

PONTIAC

THE OPEN ROAD IS A BRIGHT AND WONDERFUL INVITATION WHEN YOU'RE BEHIND THE WHEEL
OF A NEW PONTIAC–A BEAUTY, A SUPERB PERFORMER AND A GREAT VALUE!

Marlon Brando

Another of the teenage role models of the 1950s shot to fame in 1954 with his appearance in two films of urban violence and rebellion. In Laslo Benedek's controversial movie *The Wild One* Marlon Brando, one of the first actors identified with the new Method school, starred as the brooding leader of a gang of motor-cycle thugs who terrorize a small Amer-ican town (above). In the same year Brando also played a starring role in Elia Kazan's *On the Waterfront*, a powerfully atmospheric thriller which won a Best Picture award in 1955.

On the Road

With the spread of automobile ownership and a massive Federal program of expendi-ture on highway construction, the road began to establish itself as one of the central images of American popular culture. Left: 1950 Pontiac ad.

Polio Vaccine

A medical milestone was reached in 1953 with the development of the polio vaccine by Jonas E. Salk of the University of Pittsburgh (above). Independent tests confirmed Salk's results and the vaccine soon became widely available.

The Rosenbergs

The most sensational spy case of the Red Scare was that of Ethel and Julius Rosenberg (above), who were arrested on charges of having passed secret information about the atomic bomb program to the Soviet Union before 1947. They were found guilty of espionage in April 1951 and executed in 1953.

JUL 21 Geneva agreement signed by Big Four countries to end Indochina war

30 Resolution of censure against Sen. McCarthy for conduct unbecoming a senator introduced in Senate by Ralph E. Flanders, Republican of Vermont

AUG 2 Senate select committee organized to investigate charges of misconduct against Sen. McCarthy

11 Red Chinese indicate intentions to attack Taiwan

24 Communist Control Act strips Communist Party in America of privileges and immunities and subjects Party to penalties under Internal Security Act

30 Atomic Energy Bill permits private ownership of atomic reactors to produce electrical power and provides for sharing of information on atomic weaponry with European allies

SEP 3 Espionage and Sabotage Act authorizes death penalty for espionage and sabotage during peacetime

6 Groundbreaking ceremony for first atomic power plant, Duquesne Power Co., at Pittsburgh, Pa.

8 Australia, Great Britain, New Zealand, Pakistan, the Philippines, Thailand and US sign Southeast Asian Collective Defense Treaty, forming SEATO

27 Special Senate Committee calls for censure of Sen. McCarthy

OCT 13 USAF approves production of first supersonic bomber, B-58

30 US promises some $6.5 million to newly-elected Guatemalan President Carlos Castillo Armas

NOV 2 Democrats gain control of Congress

27 Alger Hiss leaves prison after serving 44 months

DEC 2 Sen. McCarthy condemned by Senate colleagues for conduct during Army-McCarthy hearings; ends anticommunist crusade

2 US and Taiwan sign mutual defense treaty

Also this year

★ Over 3000 persons considered to be security risks dismissed from federal employment

The Arts

★ George Cukor's film *A Star is Born*

★ Elia Kazan's film *On the Waterfront*

1955

JAN 1 US Foreign Operations Administration begins sending aid to Southeast Asia

14 Senate votes to continue investigation of communism

19 First televised presidential press conference

25 US and Republic of Panama sign treaty for cooperation over issues pertaining to Panama Canal

FEB 1 Southeast Asian Collective Defense Treaty ratified

MAR 1 Salaries of congressmen and federal judges increased by nearly 50 percent in bill passed by House

10 Pres. Eisenhower indicates willingness to resort to nuclear weapons in event of war

APR 1 Federal Republic of Germany receives sovereignty

MAY 15 Big Four ministers meet in Vienna to sign Austrian State Treaty, restoring borders to pre-1938 positions, prohibiting economic union with Germany and providing for withdrawal of occupation forces

23 General Assembly of Presbyterian Church announces that it will permit ordination of women ministers

31 Supreme Court declares that school desegregation will be under Federal District Court jurisdiction

JUN 22 US Navy patrol plane shot down by Soviet fighter planes over Bering Strait

JUL 18 Geneva summit conference attended by heads of state of US, Great Britain, France and USSR

18 Disneyland opens in Los Angeles

29 US announces plans to launch earth-orbiting satellites in 1957

AUG 2 Congress votes to build 45,000 public housing units by July 31, 1956

Disneyland

In July 1955 Walt Disney opened the massive theme park, Disneyland, on a 160-acre site near Los Angeles in California. The $17 million park with its fantasy castle and lifesize cartoon characters, would become one of the premier tourist attractions in the United States.

The Geneva Summit

The first ever "summit" conference was convened in July 1955 in Geneva, Switzerland, to discuss a whole range of East-West issues, including disarmament and German reunification. The U.S. delegation, headed by President Eisenhower himself, included Secretary of State John Foster Dulles (right), famous for his coinage "brinkmanship" and his doctrine of "massive retaliation."

The H-bomb

The nuclear arms race entered a new and more terrifying phase on March 1, 1954, with the testing of America's first true hydrogen bomb on Bikini Atoll in the Pacific. The new bomb had a destructive capacity some 500 times greater than the bomb which destroyed Hiroshima in 1945.

8 US meets with members of International Conference on the Peaceful Uses of Atomic Energy, in Geneva

12 Minimum wage increases to $1.00 an hour

SEP 24 Pres. Eisenhower hospitalized following heart attack

26 NY Stock Exchange reports heaviest single-day loss in history: $44 billion

30 Actor James Dean killed in car crash

OCT 6 United Airlines DC-4 crashes in Laramie, Wyo., killing 66; worst commercial airline disaster to date

18 Antiproton, new sub-atomic particle, discovered by nuclear physicists at University of California

NOV 25 Racial segregation on trains and buses crossing state lines banned by Interstate Commerce Commission

DEC 5 AFL-CIO formed; headed by George Meany

26 Five days of floods in California, Nevada and Oregon leave 74 dead

26 Reported traffic fatalities for Christmas holiday number record 609 lives

The Arts

★ Flannery O'Connor's book *A Good Man is Hard to Find, and Other Stories*

★ Cole Porter's play *Silk Stockings*

★ Tennessee Williams' play *Cat on a Hot Tin Roof*

★ George Abbott and Douglas Wallop's musical *Damn Yankees*

★ Fats Domino's song 'Ain't It a Shame'

★ Chuck Berry's song 'Maybelline'

★ Little Richard's song 'Tutti Frutti'

★ Bill Haley and His Comets song 'Rock Around the Clock'

★ James Dean in the film *Rebel Without A Cause*

★ Willem de Kooning, Jackson Pollock, Robert Motherwell and Adolph Gottlieb exhibited by MOMA

Marilyn

Marilyn Monroe appeared in a number of films in the 1950s (including the Billy Wilder classic *Some Like It Hot* in 1959), establishing herself not merely as the greatest in a long line of Hollywood sex symbols, but as a comic actress of real ability. The famous street scene in the 1955 film *The Seven Year Itch* (above) became something of an icon in its own right. The following year, in perhaps her most unlikely real-life role, she married the Pulitzer-prize-winning playwright Arthur Miller (left).

1956

JAN 9 Virginia passes amendment allowing state support for private schools

FEB 6 University of Alabama enrolls first Black student, Autherine Lucy; suspended after three days of violence

15 Federal court in New Orleans rules against all state laws supporting segregation

MAR 1 Autherine Lucy expelled from University of Alabama after the NAACP initiates legal suit

1 Pres. Eisenhower turns down request by Israel to purchase military arms from US

20 Major 156-day strike at Westinghouse Electric Corporation ends

27 Communist *Daily Worker* seized by IRS

APR 2-3 Tornadoes in Michigan, Wisconsin, Oklahoma, Kansas, Mississippi, Missouri, Arkansas and Tennessee leave over 45 people dead, thousands homeless and cause $15 million in property damage

5 Labor columnist Victor Riesel blinded by acid thrown in his face by attacker

8 Six marine recruits drown at Parris Island, SC, while on disciplinary march

19 Marriage of Hollywood actress Grace Kelly and Prince Rainier III of Monaco

MAY 2 Methodist Church calls for end to all segregation in church

4 Private atomic energy plants authorized by atomic energy commission

JUN 30 Worst commercial air disaster to date occurs when TWA Super-Constellation and United Airlines DC-7 collide over Grand Canyon, killing 128

JUL 19 US withdraws financial aid for Aswan Dam in Egypt due to country's association with Soviet Union

22 Panama Declaration confirms principles set by OAS guaranteeing use of Panama Canal

26 Egypt nationalizes Suez Canal

AUG 1 Salk polio vaccine becomes available to public

11 Death of painter Jackson Pollock, age 44, in auto accident at East Hampton, NY

A Future President

Ronald Reagan prepares himself for the perils of life at the top in one of his Hollywood roles from the 1950s.

First of the Big Jets

A new age in air transportation was launched with the introduction into regular commercial service of the giant Boeing 707 airliner by Pan Am in 1958. The new 707 could carry a total of 104 passengers in standard and 125 in tourist class and averaged a cruising speed of 575 miles per hour at 30,000 feet. Celebrating the sale of 45 707s to Pan Am three years earlier, the President of Boeing claimed that no major city of the free world would now be more than 12 hours away from the United States.

First U.S. Satellite

The United States finally succeeded in putting a satellite into space on February 1, 1958. Christened "Explorer" and weighing a mere 30lb, the satellite was launched atop a Jupiter-C rocket from the missile testing base at Cape Canaveral, Florida. It took 106 minutes to complete an orbit of the earth. The achievement followed the failure or postponement of previous American attempts to emulate the Soviet success in launching the first ever satellite, Sputnik I, in October 1957.

Billy Graham

The decade saw something of a religious revival in the U.S., one of the leading forces in which was the charismatic Baptist evangelist Billy Graham (left). Born in North Carolina in 1918, Graham launched a worldwide mission, backing up his oratory with some skilful media management.

Nautilus

The world's first nuclear-powered submarine was launched in 1954 at Groton, Connecticut. The sub, U.S.S. *Nautilus*, which weighed 2980 tons and cost some $5 million to build, undertook the first ever voyage under the ice cap of the North Pole in 1958 on her way to Portland in Great Britain.

Monkey in Space

Preparations for putting the first man in space continued with "Project Mercury" in 1959 in which a monkey called Sam (above) was launched into space to test the effects of acceleration forces and weightlessness. After a 13-minute trip Sam was parachuted back to earth and landed in the Atlantic, apparently suffering no ill effects.

GI Elvis

In 1958 Elvis Presley temporarily forsook the comfortable world of rock stardom when he was drafted into the U.S. Army. His conversion from singer to serviceman was followed with intense interest by the media, who photographed him getting his crew-cut as well as his swearing in, in Memphis on 24 March (left). Presley's experiences with the Army overseas later formed the basis of one of his most popular movies, *GI Blues*.

13 Democratic National Convention nominates Adlai Stevenson of Illinois for President and Sen. Estes Kefauver of Tennessee for Vice President

20 Republican National Convention nominates Dwight D. Eisenhower and Richard M. Nixon for second terms

SEP 7 Labor racketeer Johnny Dio and five others indicted by Federal Grand Jury for attack on labor columnist Victor Riesel

24 First transatlantic telephone cable runs 2250 miles from Scotland to Newfoundland

OCT 26 Seventy nations attend signing of Statute of the International Atomic Energy Agency

NOV 5 US achieves ceasefire in Sinai Peninsula after British-French-Israeli attack on Egypt

6 Eisenhower and Nixon win election for second terms

13 Supreme Court invalidates Montgomery, Ala., law providing for segregation in interstate bus travel

The Arts

★ Grace Metalious' novel *Peyton Place*

★ Eugene O'Neill's play *Long Day's Journey into Night*

★ Alan Jay Lerner and Frederick Loewe's musical *My Fair Lady*

★ Cecil B. DeMille's film *The Ten Commandments*

★ The film *Invasion of the Body Snatchers*

★ Elvis Presley's songs 'Heartbreak Hotel', 'Hound Dog' and 'Love Me Tender'

1957

JAN 5 Eisenhower Doctrine, offering protection to any Middle Eastern nation seeking aid against communist aggression, proposed before Congress

18 Three USAF jets, at speeds of over 500 mph, complete nonstop around-the-world flight

20 Dwight D. Eisenhower and Richard M. Nixon inaugurated for second terms in private ceremony

21 Public inaugural ceremonies carried as first nationally televised videotaped TV broadcast by NBC

FEB 8 US agrees to continue military support of Saudi Arabia in exchange for lease of Dhahran airfield

12 US Communist Party votes to remain independent of Soviet control

MAR 7 Eisenhower Doctrine approved by Congress

APR 1 US lifts ban on travel to Egypt, Israel, Jordan and Syria

29 First nuclear power reactor, at Fort Belvoir, Va, dedicated by Army Secretary

MAY 2 Death of Sen. Joseph McCarthy

6 Massachusetts Sen. John F. Kennedy wins Pulitzer Prize for *Profiles in Courage*

11 Pres. Eisenhower and South Vietnamese Pres. Ngo Dinh Diem meet in Washington, DC, and affirm committment to prevent spread of world communism

24 Rioters mob US Embassy in Taipei, Taiwan, after release of American soldier held on charge of killing Chinese national

JUN 2 Nikita Khrushchev suggests that world disarmament program begin with agreement between Soviets and US

27-28 Hurricane hits coast of Louisiana and Texas, leaving 531 dead or missing

AUG 13 Three US Embassy officials expelled from Syria on charges of plotting against government

29 Civil Rights Act of 1957 establishes Civil Rights Commission and provides penalties for violation of voting rights

29-30 New filibuster record set by South Carolina Sen. Strom Thurmond, arguing against Civil Rights Act for 24 hours, 27 minutes

30 In *Jencks v. US*, Supreme Court rules that defendant in Federal trial may only have access to FBI file material relating to testimony given in direct examination

SEP 4 Arkansas National Guard prevents Black students from entering Central High School in Little Rock

19 First underground atomic explosion set off at Nevada testing grounds

20 Arkansas Gov. Orval Faubus responds to Federal injunction and orders state militia out of Central High School in Little Rock

U.S. Marines in Lebanon

Holidaymakers on the beaches near the Lebanese capital, Beirut, helped American marines pull their equipment ashore from landing craft when President Eisenhower responded to the pro-Western Lebanese President Chamoun's request for American assistance in July 1958. The move, which involved sending a force of some 3500 troops to Lebanon, came against a background of anti-Government unrest in Beirut and only days after an armed Arab Nationalist uprising in neighboring Iraq had resulted in the murder of the Iraqi King Feisal and his Prime Minister. The arrival of the marines was condemned by the Soviet Union and its allies and for a time the situation threatened to escalate. Right: U.S. marines in full war kit rest near Beirut after their landing.

Revolution in Cuba

One of the most significant events in the shaping of modern American foreign policy occurred on January 1, 1959, when, after six years of revolutionary struggle, rebel guerrillas succeeded in toppling the beleaguered régime of the Cuban dictator Fulgencio Batista, who fled to the Dominican Republic. Amid general rejoicing at the fall of Batista, Dr. Manuel Urrutia was declared President of the new government and named as his Commander-in-Chief the rebel leader Dr. Fidel Castro (left), whose forces already controlled most of the east of the island. On January 8 Castro himself, together with 5000 of his troops, made a triumphant entry into the capital, Havana. The new régime was immediately recognized by the United States, though some doubts were expressed when the round-up of Batista officials was followed by swift trials and summary executions by firing squad. Those doubts deepened when Castro, who had disclaimed all presidential ambitions when his movement first took power, declared himself President in July.

Hawaii and Alaska

The final year of the decade saw the admission to the Union of the 49th and 50th states, thus, after more than 170 years, bringing the United States to its present complement. The admission of the two states, which both political parties had ostensibly favored since 1948, had long been delayed in Congress, but with the strategic importance of both territories, and particularly of Hawaii with its giant Pearl Harbor base, enhanced by the apparently endless continuation of the Cold War, and with Eisenhower himself lobbying strongly for admission, the time evidently seemed right to the 86th Congress which met in 1958. Alaska was accordingly admitted to statehood in January, and Hawaii in March 1959, the latter event being marked by this commemorative air mail stamp.

The Beat Generation

The most vibrant literary development of the 1950s was the rise of the Beat movement, a group of self-styled rebels against the hollow consumerist values of contemporary American society, who sought escape and enlightenment in a rootless bohemian lifestyle, not infrequently lubricated by drink and drugs. Their leader was Jack Kerouac (1922–1969) (left), whose semi-autobiographical novel *On the Road* (1957), became a sort of Beat bible. Also highly influenced by the Beatles were the poet Allen Ginsberg (1926–) (inset), whose collection *Howl and Other Poems* (1956) became the subject of an obscenity action, and his fellow poets Gregory Corso and Lawrence Ferlinghetti. The novelist William Burroughs (1914–) (below), whose controversial book *The Naked Lunch* appeared in 1959, also paid homage to the Beats in his work.

23 Rioting causes nine Black students to withdraw from Central High School

25 Pres. Eisenhower orders US Army troops to Little Rock to enforce desegregation

OCT 4 USSR launches first Earth satellite, *Sputnik*

NOV 1 World's largest suspension bridge, Mackinac Straits Bridge, between Michigan's upper and lower peninsulas, opened

25 Pres. Eisenhower suffers minor stroke

DEC 6 Teamsters' Union expelled from AFL-CIO due to alleged corruption

6 US Vanguard rocket explodes on launching pad at Cape Canaveral, Fla.

15 USAF test first Atlas Inter-continental Ballistic Missile

The Arts

★ James Agee's novel *A Death in the Family*

★ John Cheever's novel *The Wapshot Chronicle*

★ Jack Kerouac's novel *On the Road*

★ Arthur Laurents, Leonard Bernstein and Stephen Sondheim's musical *West Side Story*

★ Buddy Holly and the Crickets' song 'Peggy Sue'

★ Jerry Lee Lewis' song 'Whole Lotta Shakin' Goin' On'

1958

JAN 3 USAF announces formation of two squadrons of Strategic Air Command armed with intermediate range ballistic missiles

27 US and USSR sign pact to encourage exchanges in education, culture, sports and technology

31 First US satellite, *Explorer I*, launched at Cape Canaveral, Fla, by Army

FEB 7 Advance Research Projects Agency established by Defense Department to promote space exploration

MAR 17 *Vanguard I* satellite launched by US Navy

APR 1 Emergency Housing Act signed by the President

28 US begins atomic tests at Eniwetok Atoll in the Marshall Islands

MAY 12 US and Canada arrange North American Air Defense Command

13 Vice Pres. Nixon encounters hostile mobs in Caracas, Venezuela, during goodwill tour

14 US ships arms to Lebanon

JUN 8 US Army helicopter makes emergency landing in East Germany

29 Bomb explodes outside of Bethel Baptist Church, where minister is civil rights leader, Birmingham, Ala.

JUL 15 US Marines of 6th Fleet begin landing in Lebanon at request of government

19 International Red Cross arranges for release of American helicopter crew detained in East Germany

29 National Aeronautics and Space Administration established

AUG 5 US atomic submarine *Nautilus* makes world's first undersea crossing of North Pole

13 US withdraws 1700 Marines from Lebanon

25 Law granting pensions to former Presidents goes into effect

SEP 2 National Defense Education Act for government-backed student loans and support of education in sciences signed by the President

29 Supreme Court bars 'evasive schemes' on question of public school integration

30 Arkansas Gov. Orval Faubus closes four high schools in Little Rock to prevent desegregation

OCT 6 US atomic submarine *Seawolf* completes 60-day underwater voyage, setting world record

12 Synagogue bombed in Atlanta, Ga

12 US lunar exploration mission of *Pioneer* rocket fails

15 Eisenhower administration rejects Soviet proposal for permanent atomic test ban

31-DEC 19 US, Great Britain and USSR attend meeting to discuss suspension of nuclear testing

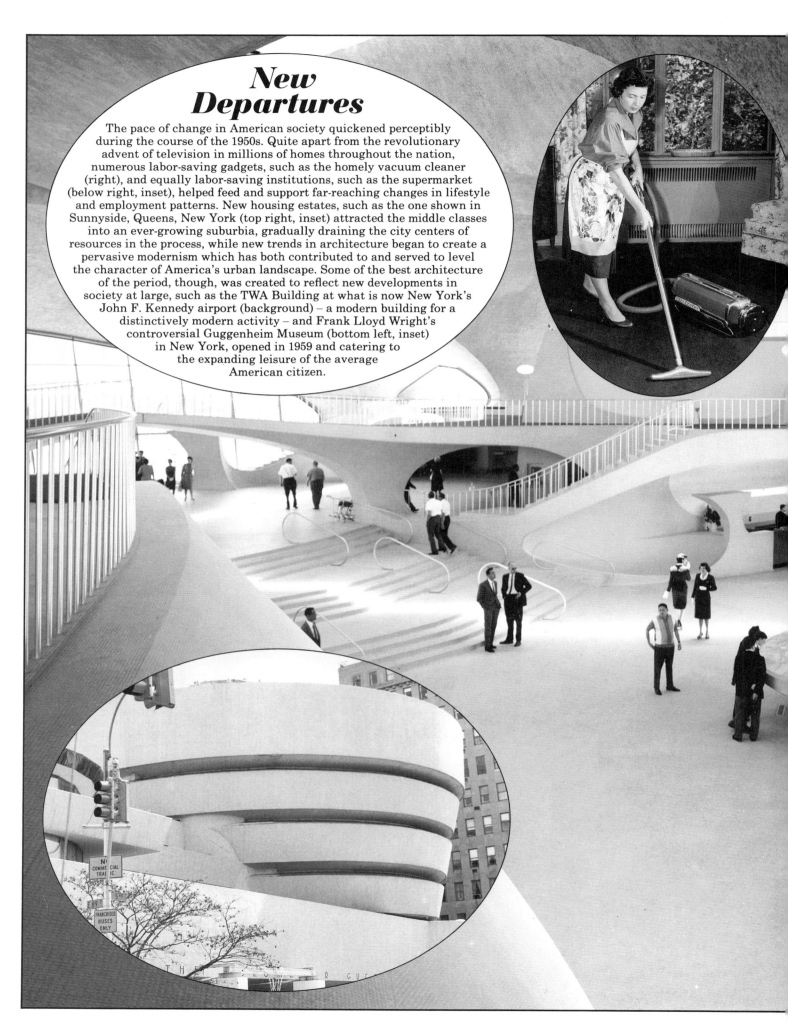

New Departures

The pace of change in American society quickened perceptibly during the course of the 1950s. Quite apart from the revolutionary advent of television in millions of homes throughout the nation, numerous labor-saving gadgets, such as the homely vacuum cleaner (right), and equally labor-saving institutions, such as the supermarket (below right, inset), helped feed and support far-reaching changes in lifestyle and employment patterns. New housing estates, such as the one shown in Sunnyside, Queens, New York (top right, inset) attracted the middle classes into an ever-growing suburbia, gradually draining the city centers of resources in the process, while new trends in architecture began to create a pervasive modernism which has both contributed to and served to level the character of America's urban landscape. Some of the best architecture of the period, though, was created to reflect new developments in society at large, such as the TWA Building at what is now New York's John F. Kennedy airport (background) – a modern building for a distinctively modern activity – and Frank Lloyd Wright's controversial Guggenheim Museum (bottom left, inset) in New York, opened in 1959 and catering to the expanding leisure of the average American citizen.

1959

JAN 3 Alaska enters Union as 49th state

8 US recognizes government of Fidel Castro in Cuba

FEB 10 Tornado devastates St Louis

MAR 5 US signs bilateral defense pacts with Iran, Pakistan and Turkey

18 Hawaii statehood bill signed by the President

APR 5 US Naval Research Laboratory reports three-fold increase in radioactivity over eastern US as result of atmospheric tests by Soviet Union during two-month period in 1958

7 Oklahoma ends 51 years of prohibition

15 Secretary of State John Foster Dulles resigns, suffering from cancer

25 St Lawrence Seaway, between US and Canada, opens

MAY 3 American Unitarian Association and Universalist Church of America merge

20 John Foster Dulles receives Medal of Freedom, highest US civilian award

20 American citizenship restored to 5000 Japanese-Americans who renounced it during World War II

22 Brig. Gen. Benjamin O. Davis Jr, USAF, becomes first Black American appointed to rank of Major General

24 Death of John Foster Dulles

28 Two monkeys launched into space by US Army from Cape Canaveral, Fla

JUN 8 Investigations of Communist activity conducted by Congress and states ruled constitutional by Supreme Court

9 US atomic submarine *George Washington*, capable of firing Polaris missile, launched at Groton, Conn.

11 D.H. Lawrence's *Lady Chatterley's Lover* banned from US mails by Postmaster General Arthur Summerfield

18 Arkansas law used by Gov. Orval Faubus to close Little Rock schools ruled unconstitutional by Supreme Court

JUL 9 Two American soldiers killed by Communist guerillas at Bienhoa, South Vietnam

15 United Steelworkers' strike affects 28 companies which produce 95 percent of country's steel

17 Death of jazz vocalist Billie Holiday

23 Vice Pres. Nixon arrives in Moscow, beginning two-week tour of USSR and Poland

AUG 4 Teamster president James R. Hoffo denounced for union abuses in special Senate committee report

7 NASA launches *Explorer IV* satellite from Cape Canaveral

12 About 250 segretationists demonstrate near Central High School in Little Rock to protest opening of integrated schools

21 Hawaii enters Union as 50th state

SEP 11 Secretary of Agriculture empowered to distribute surplus food, through food stamps, to impoverished Americans

14 Londrum-Griffin Act designed to curb racketeering and blackmail in labor organizations

15 Soviet Premier Nikita Khrushchev arrives in US on six-day visit

15 Civil Rights Commission extended for two years

OCT 9 Pres. Eisenhower invokes Taft-Hartley Act to break nationwide steel strike

NOV 10 *Triton* ,largest atomic submarine ever built, commissioned at Groton, Conn.

21 US and USSR sign agreement for two-year exchange program in science, culture and sports

DEC 16 Secretary of Defense Thomas S. Gates announces at NATO Council in Paris that US has nuclear superiority over USSR

The Arts

★ Truman Capote's novel *Breakfast at Tiffany's*

★ Philip Roth's collection *Goodbye, Columbus*

★ Lorraine H. Hansberry's play *A Raisin in the Sun*

★ Billy Wilder's film *Some Like It Hot*

★ Solomon R. Guggenheim Museum, designed by Frank Lloyd Wright, opens in NYC

MORE than any decade before it, the 1960s saw the pace of technological, social, and cultural change accelerate to the point where many of the older generation in America and elsewhere felt that the world in which they were living was becoming barely recognizable. After the comfortable conservatism of the Eisenhower régime, the administration of the dynamic young John F. Kennedy promised the American people the excitement of a "New Frontier" in domestic and international politics. The upsurge of hope which accompanied this new departure was to be cut cruelly short in Dallas, Texas, in November 1963, but even before Kennedy's untimely death it had become clear that the world was not easily to be moved from its accustomed paths. Confrontation with the Soviet Union over the new Castro régime in Cuba brought humanity closer to the brink of nuclear war than at any time before or since, and, despite a brief thaw in 1963, East-West relations remained locked in the sterile matrix of the Cold War.

In this atmosphere of unrelieved tension, foreign affairs dominated the American political agenda during the 1960s. In East Germany the Berlin Wall provided a potent symbol of the stand-off between East and West, and in Southeast Asia American involvement in the civil war in Vietnam, begun under Kennedy, became a festering wound under his successor, Lyndon B. Johnson. As more and more American forces were poured into this distant country with less and less sign of a victory on the horizon, the Vietnam War – the first to be fought under the "unblinking eye" of television – threatened to undo all the domestic achievements of Johnson's "Great Society." By the end of the decade, it had become the focus of widespread protest at home and abroad. The city streets and college campuses of America saw unprecedented scenes of unrest as students and others demonstrated against what they saw as the moral bankruptcy, not only of the Government's foreign policy, but of the whole American way of life. The election of the Republican Richard Nixon to the presidency in 1968, far from dissipating this unease, only moved it into a new and more bitter phase. To many the "national unity" of which Nixon spoke so eloquently during his campaign seemed fractured beyond repair.

Enter Kennedy

The 1960 presidential election campaign got underway against the background of escalating East-West tension. Hopes for a compromise solution to the Berlin crisis stalled amid recriminations after an American U-2 spy plane was shot down over the Soviet Union and a projected summit conference in Paris fell apart before talks could really begin. Events in the African Congo and in Cuba put further strains on relations between the superpowers, and the prospects for slowing the arms race took a nosedive after an East-West disarmament conference in Geneva broke up without agreement.

The two main presidential candidates presented the American people with a clear

"Ask not what your country can do for you ...": President John F. Kennedy – a new presidential style for a "new generation of Americans."

contrast. The Republican Richard Nixon, the sitting Vice President, was a highly-experienced politician, with a strong track record in foreign affairs and a high profile as acting President during Eisenhower's recent illnesses. A man who had worked his way to the top from humble beginnings in California, he was also associated with the anti-Communist crusade of the early 1950s, and had already acquired the unenviable nickname of "Tricky Dicky." The democratic candidate, the 43-year-old Massachusetts senator John Fitzgerald Kennedy, was relatively inexperienced, but exuded energy, charm, and charisma. The son of wealthy East Coast parents – his father was a former U.S. ambassador to London – he stood on a strong civil rights platform and promised to "get the country moving again" after what many saw as the directionlessness of the Eisenhower years. He was also the first Roman Catholic to stand for president since Alfred Smith in 1928.

The campaign featured the first ever live television debates between presidential candidates. Viewed by an estimated 70 million people, they bore witness to the extraordinary influence of the new medium and helped disperse the impression that Kennedy was too young and callow to hold the highest office in the land. In the final event, though, the election result was one of the narrowest in American history. Kennedy won 34,227,000 popular votes to Nixon's 34,108,000 – a margin of less than 0.2 per cent.

The New Frontier

At 43 Kennedy was one of the youngest Presidents ever to take office in the United States. His inaugural address in January 1961 made much of the fact that he represented "a new generation of Americans," and

committed his administration to exploring "a New Frontier" in American politics. In a much-quoted conclusion, the new President called on his fellow Americans to "ask not what your country can do for you – ask what you can do for your country." It was not long before commentators were speaking of a new style of presidency – vigorous, youthful, and forward-looking. But in practice the main measures of Kennedy's domestic program were bogged down in Congress during his lifetime, as the greater part of his energies became absorbed in overseas affairs. Here, too, the New Frontier was in many ways an extension of the old. The Cold War not only continued, but was soon to plunge the world into a crisis of unimaginable danger.

The Bay of Pigs

In 1959 the revolutionary leader Fidel Castro had toppled the dictatorial régime of Fulgencio Batista in the island of Cuba. At first, relations with the United States were good, but they deteriorated rapidly as Castro drew closer to the Soviet Union, raising the specter of a Communist beachhead just 90 miles off the American coast. Shortly after taking office, Kennedy discovered the existence of a CIA plan to invade Cuba from neighboring Guatemala, using a small army of American-trained Cuban exiles. The new President had severe doubts about the scheme, but he allowed it to proceed.

The result was one of the worst humiliations of his presidency. On April 17, 1961, a force of some 1400 men landed at the Bay of Pigs, only to be repulsed by a far stronger Cuban defense than they had expected. Instead of proving the trigger for a popular anti-Castro rising in Cuba, the invasion was a complete failure and within 72 hours had been roundly defeated. The whole incident took the wind out of the U.S. administration's sails and seriously damaged relations between America and the Soviet Union. Khrushchev and Kennedy met in Vienna the following year, but tensions remained high. In October 1962 they were almost to snap.

The Cuban Missile Crisis

In the fall of 1962, Kennedy received conclusive photographic proof that the Soviet Union was building offensive missile bases in Cuba. The new installations could have doubled the number of American cities and military bases threatened by Soviet nuclear attack, and swift action was imperative. Kennedy's military advisers urged him to launch an air strike against Cuba, but the President rejected this option in favor of a naval blockade – which he described as a "quarantine" – against the Soviet ships bringing military equipment to the island. At the same time, he threatened the Soviet Union with all-out retaliation should it attempt to break the blockade.

For six days the world held its breath as Khrushchev considered whether to accept the challenge thrown down by the Americans. Then, on October 28, he ordered the

Labels on image: LAUNCH PAD WITH ERECTOR — CHERRY PICKER — LAUNCH PAD WITH ERECTOR — MISSILE READY BLDGS — OXIDIZER VEHICLES — FUELING VEHICLES

1960s

Death of Kennedy

Martin Luther King

Space Race

1960

Reconnaissance photographs such as this one, released by the Pentagon in October 1962, awoke the U. S. Government to the threat to American security of the medium-range ballistic missile bases under construction in Cuba.

convoy to turn back and agreed to dismantle the missile bases. Kennedy showed considerable statesmanship in resisting the temptation to gloat at the Russians' climb-down, but his "brinkmanship" had taken the world as close to nuclear war as it had yet come.

The Cold War Continues

The Cuban missile crisis led to a brief thaw in East-West relations. A nuclear test ban treaty was signed in 1963 – a first move, in Kennedy's words, towards "getting the genie back in the bottle" – and a "hot line" was installed between the White House and the Kremlin. But for most of the 1960s the Cold War remained as frozen as ever. The Berlin Wall, built virtually overnight by the East German authorities in August 1961 to stem the flow of refugees to the West, came to symbolize the East-West confrontation for millions of people on both sides of the divide, and would continue to do so for almost 30 years. Both the Eastern and the Western blocs had their problems: independence movements in the Soviet Union's satellite states helped compound the difficulties caused for the Eastern alliance by the open split between the Soviet Union and China during the decade, while NATO unity was placed under great strain by the increasing disengagement of General De Gaulle's France. But with both America and the Soviet Union fueling the arms race with unprecedented levels of military expenditure throughout the decade, East-West relations remained a powderkeg waiting for a spark.

The Great Society

On November 22, 1963, the Kennedy era came to an abrupt end when the President was cut down by an assassin's bullet while driving through Dallas, Texas, on a speaking tour of the South to marshal support for his domestic reform programs. With the nation reeling from the shock of the tragedy, Vice President Lyndon B. Johnson was sworn in as 36th President of the U.S.A. on the plane that carried Kennedy's body back to Washington.

Johnson, a seasoned political operator, committed himself to continuing Kennedy's policies and received a resounding mandate to do so in the presidential election of 1964 when the voters rejected the perceived extremism of the conservative Republican candidate, Barry Goldwater of Arizona, in a Democratic landslide. Calling for the creation of the "Great Society," Johnson broke the Congressional logjam of Kennedy's New Frontier measures to push through the most far-reaching program of domestic legislation since Roosevelt's New Deal. New Acts increased Federal funding for education and housing developments and for conservation programs. The welfare system was extended with the implementation of Kennedy's cherished Medicare scheme, and the Economic Opportunity Act of 1964 marked the declaration of a national war against the root causes of poverty in the United States. Perhaps most significant of all, the new President threw his weight behind the strongest civil rights legislation since the days of Radical Reconstruction.

The Civil Rights Struggle

The cause of civil rights, particularly for America's Blacks, moved into a climactic phase during the 1960s. Protestors staged sit-ins and "freedom rides" to bring an end to segregation in transport and other public

JAN 3 Sen. John F. Kennedy announces candidacy for Democratic presidential nomination

4 Longest steel strike in nation's history ends

9 Vice Pres. Richard M. Nixon announces candidacy for Republican presidential nomination

19 US and Japan sign mutual defense treaty

25 Payola law proposed by Donald H. McGannon, chairman of NAB's TV code review board

FEB 1 Four Black students stage sit-in at lunch counter in Greensboro, NC, to protest 'whites only' serving policy

2 Twenty-third Amendment, banning poll tax requirement for Federal elections and allowing citizens of District of Columbia full voting privileges, opposed by Senate

MAR 15 Ten nations, including US, USSR, Britain and France attend Geneva disarmament conference

APR 1 First weather satellite, *Tiros 1*, orbited by US

14 Polaris missile fired from under water off San Clemente Island, Calif., for first time

MAY 1 Downing of U-2 Air Force reconnaissance plane over USSR

6 Civil Rights Act of 1960 signed by the President

7 US admits intelligence mission of downed U-2 Air Force plane

10 First undersea voyage around the world completed by nuclear submarine USS *Triton*

11 Pres. Eisenhower publically states that US has been conducting reconnaissance missions over Soviet territory for past four years

16 Paris summit conference canceled by Soviet Premier Khrushchev

19 Alan Freed, radio disc jockey, television personality and originator of term 'rock 'n' roll,' arrested on charges of commercial bribery, in payola scandal

JUN 2-13 Actors Equity strike closes Broadway theaters

4 US accuses Cuban government of undertaking campaign of slander

12 Pres. Eisenhower leaves on eight-day tour of Philippines, Taiwan, South Korea and Alaska

JUL 6 US cuts Cuban sugar imports by 95 percent due to poor relations

11 Democratic National Convention nominates Sen. John F. Kennedy of Massachusetts for President and Sen. Lyndon B. Johnson of Texas for Vice President

16 Pres. Eisenhower's trip to Japan canceled due to riots against mutual security treaty

27 Republican National Convention nominates Vice Pres. Richard M. Nixon for President and Henry Cabot Lodge of Massachusetts for Vice President

An age of protest: students clash with baton-wielding police on campus at San Francisco State College in January 1969.

facilities in the South, and the Student Nonviolent Coordinating Committee (SNCC) was born to orchestrate the campaign. In April and May of 1963, 100 years after emancipation, thoughtful Americans were shocked to see on their television screens the brutal police suppression of Black civil rights demonstrations led by Martin Luther King in Birmingham, Alabama, and there was widespread horror at the murder of civil rights workers, and even of Black children, in other incidents in the South. President Kennedy sent a strong civil rights bill to Congress, and he federalized the Alabama National Guard when George Wallace, the state's segregationist Governor, tried to prevent two Black students from taking up their places at the University of Alabama in Tuscaloosa. On August 28, 1963, the wave of Black protest crested in an enormous peaceful demonstration, when some 200,000 Black and white civil rights supporters marched to the Lincoln Memorial in Washington, where, in a powerful and moving address, Martin Luther King told them of his continuing dream of an equal and united America.

In 1964, despite an 83-day Southern filibuster in Congress, President Johnson pushed through the epoch-making Civil Rights Act, which created the Equal Employment Opportunity Commission and enacted wide-ranging prohibitions of discrimination on grounds of race or sex. The following year saw the passage of the Voting Rights Act, after thousands of protestors gathered in Selma, Alabama, to demonstrate against the virtual disenfranchisement of many Blacks by intimidation and local qualifications on the right to vote. The new Act, supported, like other planks of Johnson's civil rights program, by Earl Warren's Supreme Court, helped increase Black voter registration in Mississippi from just 6.75 per cent at the end of 1964 to almost 60 per cent by 1968, and worked similar changes elsewhere in the South.

But the decade also saw the fragmentation of the Black civil rights struggle into warring groups, especially after Martin Luther King, the arch proponent of peaceful struggle, was shot dead by a white extremist in Memphis, Tennessee, in April 1968. As race riots erupted in major cities right across the nation, such influential exponents of "Black power" as Stokely Carmichael and Eldridge Cleaver broke away from the SNCC to pursue the struggle by more militant means.

Vietnam

By 1965, however, the very real domestic achievements of the Johnson administration were already becoming obscured by the dark shadow of the war in Vietnam.

The sorry saga of U.S. involvement in the war which was to divide the nation had begun under President Kennedy. By the time of Kennedy's death there were already some 16,000 American military "advisers" in Vietnam, supporting the unpopular South Vietnamese Government against the ever-increasing attacks of the NLF, or Viet Cong, a South Vietnamese guerrilla army backed by the North Vietnamese Communist Government of Ho Chi Minh. President Johnson had fought the 1964 election on an anti-Vietnam-war platform but by the end of the year, which saw a controversial incident in which a U.S. ship was fired on by North Vietnamese vessels in the Gulf of Tonkin, he was already stepping up the U.S. presence in the South. Seeing the situation as a serious threat to the free world, Johnson reiterated Eisenhower's "domino theory" of Communist expansion in Southeast Asia, and in February 1965 ordered the bombing of targets in North Vietnam. In March he sent combat troops to the region for the first time.

Thus it was that the United States, the most powerful military force in the world, became embroiled in a conflict which would drag on without a conclusive victory for eight years. Like the British in the American Revolutionary War, the U.S. troops in Vietnam found it impossible to fight an effective conventional war against a dedicated guerrilla force in such inhospitable countryside. By the end of the decade, there were more than half a million U.S. troops in Vietnam. But despite the vastly superior numbers and equipment of the U.S. and South Vietnamese forces, despite the fact that by 1970 American planes had dropped on Vietnam more than half the entire tonnage of bombs dropped in the Second World War, and despite a campaign of chemical defoliation which laid waste to at least a million acres of land and decimated the region's agricultural economy, by 1968 the Viet Cong, who launched their massive Tet offensive against South Vietnamese towns in that year, were able to carry the war to the very threshold of the U.S. embassy in Saigon. By then, too, the war had become the focus of widespread protest at home, making it a key issue in the presidential election of 1968.

The Election of 1968

The 1960s saw an enormous upsurge in youth and student protest, as the so-called New Left reacted against what it saw as the authoritarian conservatism of the older generation and demanded a greater democratic say in the running of educational and other institutions. Increasingly, the protest came to coalesce around the issue of the Vietnam war, reaching a climax during the election campaign of 1968. In particular, the campaign of Eugene McCarthy for the Democratic nomination attracted large numbers of young people to its peace platform. There were ugly scenes outside the Democratic convention in Chicago when the party machine awarded the nomination to Hubert Humphrey, Johnson having declared that he would not seek renomination and Robert Kennedy, the other main contender, having been assassinated after winning the California primary. Crowds of young demonstrators clashed with police, many of whom reacted with great brutality despite the presence of television cameras. The presidential election campaign itself was scarcely less bitter. The political temperature was raised by the independent candidature of George Wallace, the man who had barred the door of the University of Alabama to Black students in 1963 and who now polled almost 10 million votes. The Republican candidate was Richard Nixon, who campaigned on a platform of law and order, an unspecified peace plan for Vietnam, and "national unity." On election day, the voters gave Nixon a slim popular majority.

A Giant Leap for Mankind

The 1960s were the decade of the space race. In 1961, the Soviet Union put the first man in space when Cosmonaut Yuri Gagarin orbited the earth once in Vostok 1. Five weeks later, President Kennedy inaugur-

ated the American Apollo program, dedicated to putting a man on the moon by the end of the decade. That ambition was finally achieved on July 20, 1969, when Neil Armstrong, watched by a television audience of some 600 million people (or one in five of the earth's population), stepped off the ladder of Apollo 11's lunar module in the Sea of Tranquillity with the words "That's one small step for a man, one giant leap for mankind." Ironically, the Cold War had been the cradle of one of the greatest scientific achievements in human history.

The Times They Are A'Changing

A revolution in fashion, music, the arts, and social attitudes swept America in the 1960s as the opening up of mass communications helped create and sustain a worldwide youth market. Mini-skirts, beads, and caftans became the hallmarks of a counterculture which expressed itself in such enclaves of the alternative lifestyle as the Haight-Ashbury area of San Francisco. The music of rock bands such as The Doors and The Rolling Stones came to symbolize their young audiences' rejection of parental values, while the "pop art" of Andy Warhol and his bizarre entourage drew a cult following for its parodies of images of mass-production. The contraceptive pill and the marijuana joint wrought far-reaching changes in the sexual and social mores of a generation, as thousands heeded the doctrine of such gurus of the drug culture as Timothy Leary to "tune in, turn on, and drop out." The massive Woodstock Festival in 1969 – proclaimed by many of its participants as the dawn of a new age – represented the high watermark of this alternative culture before it began to decline into the disillusionment and cynicism of the 1970s.

Andy Warhol's emblematic "Campbell's Soup."

SEP 9-12 Most destructive hurricane in US Weather Bureau history devastates Atlantic coast, killing 30

26 First of four televised debates between presidential candidates Kennedy and Nixon

NOV 8 John F. Kennedy elected President, Lyndon B. Johnson elected Vice President

30 Anti-integration riots in New Orleans; 200 arrested

The Arts

★ Harper Lee's novel *To Kill a Mockingbird*

★ Lillian Hellman's play *Toys in the Attic*

★ Tom Jones and Harvey Schmidt's musical *The Fantasticks*

★ Charles Strouse and Lee Adams' musical *Bye Bye Birdie*

1961

JAN 3 US breaks diplomatic relations with Cuba

17 Pres. Eisenhower, in farewell speech, warns of increasing power of 'military-industrial' complex

20 John F. Kennedy inaugurated President, Lyndon B. Johnson inaugurated Vice President

21 Robert F. Kennedy named Attorney General

25 Pres. Kennedy participates in first live televised press conference

FEB 22-23 Birth control as means of family limitation endorsed by National Council of Churches

23 Six-day airline strike ends

MAR 1 Peace Corps established by executive order of the President

13 Pres. Kennedy invites Latin American countries to join US in Alliance for Progress development project

26 Pres. Kennedy meets with British PM Harold Macmillan at Key West, Fla, to discuss problems in Laos

29 Twenty-third Amendment adopted

APR 17 CIA-trained Cuban exiles invade Cuba at Bay of Pigs and are defeated within 48 hours

MAY Navy Comdr Alan Bartlett Shepard Jr is first American in space, making suborbital flight of 300 miles aboard Project Mercury capsule *Freedom Seven*

25 Pres. Kennedy, in address to Congress, commits US to landing man on moon by end of decade

JUN 3-4 Pres. Kennedy meets with Soviet Premier Nikita Krushchev in Vienna

19 Supreme Court rules against use of illegal evidence in prosecuting state court cases

30 Death of inventor Lee De Forest

JUL 24 Eastern Airlines passenger jet en route to Tampa from Miami hijacked to Cuba by armed passenger

AUG 17 US and other members of Alliance for Progress meet in Punta del Este, Uruguay, and draw up charter of economic aid and developmental support

SEP 5 Hijacking bill makes air piracy federal offense

5 Agency for International Development established by Foreign Assistance Act of 1961

8 *Journal of American Medical Association* reports link between smoking and heart disease

15 US begins underground nuclear testing

15 Big Four ministers meet in Washington, DC, to discuss situation in Berlin

OCT 6 Pres. Kennedy advises American families to build or buy atomic fallout shelter

The Arts

★ Allen Ginsberg's *Kaddish and Other Poems*

★ Henry Miller's novel *Tropic of Cancer*

★ The musical *How to Succeed in Business Without Really Trying*

★ John Huston's film *The Misfits*

"We Shall Overcome"

The 1960s saw the Black struggle for civil rights in the United States develop from a campaign of peaceful civil disobedience in the Southern states into a nationwide crusade for equality which found its most important legislative expression in the Civil Rights Acts of 1964, 1965, and 1968.

Far left: Many Americans from all walks of life were shocked by the brutal police response to peaceful Black demonstrations against racial segregation in Birmingham, Alabama, in April 1963. Civil rights marchers were met with teargas, dogs, and water-cannon, triggering a chain-reaction of riots which engulfed the city's streets for several weeks. Here, three demon-strators link hands in an attempt to stand upright against high-pressure jets of water.

Center left: One of the first expressions of non-violent Black resistance to segregation of public facilities in the South was the campaign in which groups of Blacks staged "sit-ins" at the tables and counters of white-only restaurants. Integration of eating facilities was resisted in many parts of the South even after the 1964 Civil Rights Act made it compulsory. In this chilling picture, an Atlanta restaurant owner, gun in hand, forces Blacks testing the new legislation to leave his premises.

Bottom left: "Freedom Riders" – Black and white protestors who traveled on buses together in the South as a peaceful challenge to segregation of transport facilities – were also often met by violence. This bus was fire-bombed by white militants after it stopped for a tire-change in Anniston, Alabama, in May 1961.

Near left: In 1964 Martin Luther King spearheaded a campaign for Black voter registration in Alabama (where in the town of Selma, for example, only 335 out of about 14,000 Blacks were registered.) In March he led 25,000 people on a march from Selma to Montgomery. The picture shows the crowd in front of the state capitol as King addressed them.

Below: "I have a dream today ...": at one of the climactic moments of the Black civil rights struggle, King addresses a 200,000-strong crowd of civil rights supporters after their march on Washington, D. C., in August 1963.

319

"Ich bin ein Berliner"

The political map of Europe was changed literally overnight on August 13, 1961, when, at 2.30 a.m., the East German Government sealed the border between East and West Berlin and began the building of the wall that would divide the city for the next 28 years. The move abruptly stemmed the haemorrhage of refugees from the East since 1949, an exodus which numbered some 2.6 million people. The swift reinforcement of the wall, with its desolate no-man's land of barbed wire and watchtowers (below), made Berlin the focus, and in many ways the most potent symbol, of East-West confrontation during the Cold War era.

Tensions remained high, with East Germany regularly harassing Western air traffic over the city, and in June 1963, when President Kennedy visited West Berlin to make his famous "Ich bin ein Berliner" speech – with its ringing peroration "All free men, wherever they may live, are citizens of Berlin" – the East German authorities hung black drapes from the Brandenburg Gate (left) in order that he could not see, or be seen from, East Berlin.

West Side Story

George Chakiris (above) dances his way through the streets of New York to Leonard Bernstein's musical score in

Robert Wise and Jerome Robbins' cinematic retelling of the Romeo and Juliet story, *West Side Story*, released in 1961.

The U-2 Incident

The chances of progress at the 1960 superpower summit in Paris were torpedoed when, on May 1, an American U-2 aircraft piloted by Francis Gary Powers

(above) was shot down on a reconnaissance mission over the Soviet Union. Powers was convicted of spying after U.S. denials were shown to be untrue.

JAN 12 US Communist Party members denied US passports under new regulations

15 US tanks withdrawn from Berlin Wall

FEB 3 Trade ban with Cuba ordered by the President

20 Astronaut John Glenn is first American to orbit Earth, circling three times in Mercury space capsule

22 Robert Kennedy denounces Berlin Wall during meeting with West Berlin Mayor Willy Brandt

26 Segregation laws in interstate and intrastate transportation facilities ruled unconstitutional by Supreme Court

MAR 1 American Airlines Boeing 707 crashes at New York's Idlewild Airport, killing 95

13 Pres. Kennedy requests $4,878,500,000 for foreign aid in fiscal 1963

APR 10 US and Great Britain appeal to Soviet Union to agree to international test ban

19 *Skybolt*, first US airborne ballistic missile, launched from B-52 bomber at Cape Canaveral, Fla

25 US resumes atmospheric nuclear tests after three-year moratorium

MAY 6 First submarine-launched nuclear detonation exploded near Christmas Island

12 US sends naval and ground forces to Laos to support anti-Communist troops

JUN 25 In *Engel v. Vitale*, Supreme Court declares reading of prayers in New York public schools unconstitutional

JUL 6 Death of writer William Faulkner

10 Communications satellite *Telstar* placed in orbit

AUG 5 Death of film star Marilyn Monroe

17 FDA official Frances Kelsey cited by medical profession for stance against tranquilizer thalidomide

SEP 3 Death of poet E. E. Cummings

30 Black student James Meredith admitted to University of Mississippi against severe oppostion

OCT 10 Bill to safeguard public against harmful drugs signed by the President

22 Cuban missile crisis; Pres. Kennedy announces that US has photographic evidence of construction of Soviet missile bases in Cuba; demands removal of all missiles and dismantling of bases; requests UN Security Council and OAS support; and orders naval blockade around Cuba

28 Soviet Premier Krushchev announces that missiles and bases will be removed

NOV 6 Former Vice Pres. Nixon loses bid for election as governor of California

20 US announces intention to end naval blockade of Cuba

20 Executive order prohibiting racial discrimination in federally funded housing signed by the President

21 Pres. Kennedy and British PM Macmillan announce nuclear force within NATO

23 Cuba announces release of 1113 prisoners from 1961 Bay of Pigs invasion in return for $62 million worth of medical supplies, food and farming equipment

DEC 8 Costly 114-day newspaper strike in NYC begins

23 Strike by International Longshoremen's Association goes into effect along East Coast

Also this year

★ American James Watson is one of three recipients of Nobel Prize for Medicine and Physiology for discovering double helix structure of DNA

★ The 'twist' is born at The Peppermint Lounge nightclub in NYC

The Arts

★ Joseph Heller's novel *Catch-22*

★ Katherine Anne Porter's novel *Ship of Fools*

★ Edward Albee's play *Who's Afraid of Virginia Woolf?*

★ Leslie Bricusse and Anthony Newly's musical *Stop the World – I Want to Get Off*

★ Bette Davis and Joan Crawford in the film *Whatever Happened to Baby Jane*

Earthquake in Alaska

More than 100 people died when an earthquake struck Kodiak Island off the Alaskan coast in 1964. The tremor was followed by a tidal wave which engulfed fishing communities on the island (above).

Goodbye, Norma Jean

Marilyn Monroe, seen here in Andy Warhol's famous screen-print, was found dead at her Los Angeles home on August 5, 1962. The likely cause of death was given as suicide, but has been surrounded by mystery ever since.

Crime Inc.

America became a more violent country during the 1960s, with reported murders doubling between 1953 and 1968. Organized crime, too, flourished under Mafia bosses such as Sam Giancano (right).

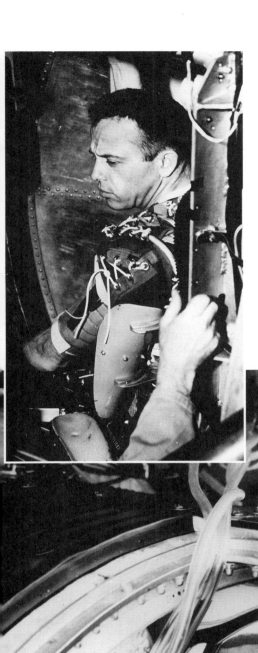

First Americans in Space

On April 12, 1961, the Soviet Union won the race to put the first man in space when cosmonaut Major Yuri Gagarin orbited the earth once in Vostok 1. President Kennedy immediately announced America's intention of putting a man on the moon by the end of the decade, and the U.S. space program moved rapidly into top gear.

Less than three weeks after his flight made Gagarin a household name throughout the world, Alan B. Shepard (left) became America's first man in space, making a sub-orbital flight from Cape Canaveral in Florida. It would be another nine months, however, before John H. Glenn (seen below in a flight simulator at Cape Canaveral) was able to claim the laurels as America's first man in orbit. Glenn made three orbits in his spacecraft Friendship 7, before returning to earth.

1963

JAN 29 Death of writer Robert Frost

MAR 19 US, Costa Rica, El Salvador, Guatemala, Honduras, Nicaragua and Panama sign agreement to act against Soviet aggression in Western Hemisphere

APR 5 J. Robert Oppenheimer receives Fermi Prize of US Atomic Energy Commission

9 Winston Churchill granted honorary US citizenship

10 Atomic submarine *Thresher* sinks in North Atlantic, killing 129

12 Rev. Martin Luther King, Jr, arrested in Birmingham, Ala., after participating in civil rights march

MAY 10 Atty Gen. Robert Kennedy orders halt to police action directed against civil rights demonstrators in Birmingham, Ala.

16 Astronaut Gordon Cooper launched into space flight of 22 orbits

JUN 8 American Heart Association begins anticigarette campaign

11 University of Alabama desegregated after Pres. Kennedy federalizes Alabama National Guard; two Black students enroll

12 Civil rights leader Medgar Evers assassinated by sniper in Jackson, Miss.

17 Supreme Court declares Bible reading in public schools unconstitutional

26 Pres. Kennedy welcomed by 2 million citizens of West Berlin

JUL 8 US bans virtually all financial transactions with Cuba

AUG 5 Comprehensive nuclear test ban treaty signed by US, Great Britain and USSR

28 Freedom march on Washington, DC, draws 200,000 participants

30 'Hotline,' emergency communications link between Washington, DC, and Moscow, goes into operation

SEP 15 Church bombing in Birmingham, Ala., leaves four young Black girls dead

24 Nuclear test ban treaty ratified by Senate

OCT 10 Nuclear test ban treaty takes effect

NOV 2 South Vietnamese Pres. Ngo Dinh Diem killed in coup

22 Pres. Kennedy assassinated in Dallas, Texas; Gov. John Connally wounded

22 Lyndon B. Johnson sworn in as President

24 Alleged assassin Lee Harvey Oswald shot and killed by nightclub owner Jack Ruby

DEC 17 Chamizal Treaty cedes small section of El Paso to Mexico

17 Pres. Johnson, in address to UN, calls for 'peaceful revolution' to eliminate hunger, disease and poverty

The Arts

★ Mary McCarthy's novel *The Group*

★ Elizabeth Taylor in the film *Cleopatra*

★ Peter, Paul and Mary's song 'Blowin' in the Wind'

★ The Beach Boys' song 'Surfin' USA'

★ Andy Warhol, Jasper Johns, Roy Lichtenstein and Robert Rauschenberg featured in first large-scale exhibition of pop art, at Guggenheim Museum, NYC

1964

JAN 8 Pres. Johnson delivers State-of-the-Union message on national 'war against poverty'

11 Surgeon General announces proof that cigarette smoking causes lung disease

23 Twenty-fourth Amendment ratified

28 USAF jet training plane shot down by Soviet plane over Erfurt, East Germany

FEB 25 Cassius Marcellus Clay (Mohammed Ali) defeats Sonny Liston in World Heavyweight Boxing Championship

MAR 16 Pres. Johnson requests $962 million for 'war on poverty'

Kennedy's Assassination

In one of the greatest political tragedies of the century, President John Fitzgerald Kennedy was gunned down in Dallas, Texas, on Friday, November 22, 1963. Three shots were fired from the sixth floor of a building near the junction of Elm Street and Houston Street as the presidential motorcade drove through the city's main business center (inset), and the President slumped forward, hit in the head and neck (below). With Mrs. Kennedy cradling her husband in her arms, the car sped to the Parkland Hospital, where Kennedy died half an hour later without regaining consciousness.

Within two hours, Vice President Lyndon B. Johnson had been sworn in at Dallas airfield on the plane carrying Kennedy's body back to Washington (near right). Also within hours, police arrested Lee Harvey Oswald, a 24-year-old former marine, and charged him with the murder, but two days later television viewers saw Oswald himself gunned down at point-blank range as he was being transferred to the county jail from the basement of Dallas police headquarters (opposite top). The gunman, a Dallas nightclub owner called Jack Ruby, was immediately arrested.

Kennedy's funeral was held in Washington on November 25 in the presence of the greatest gathering of heads of state in the history of America. Among the million mourners who paid their last respects to the late President was his three-year-old son, John Jr. (opposite bottom).

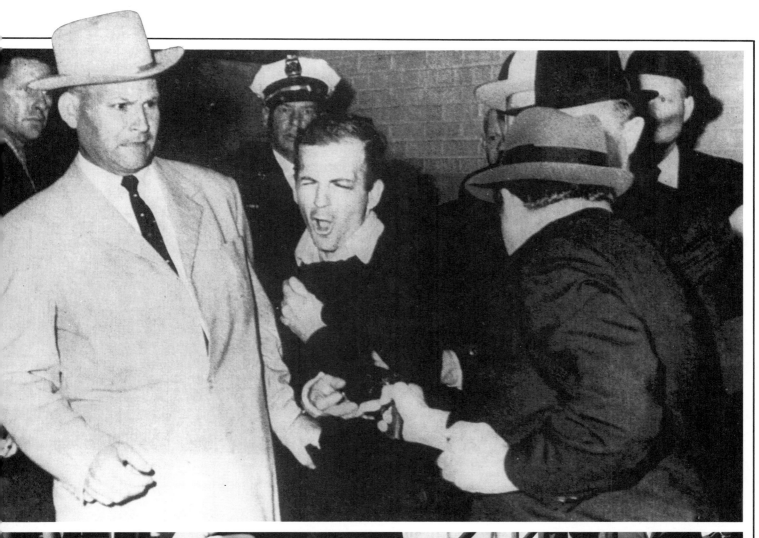

Created Equal?

Despite the significant advances made by the Civil Rights legislation of Johnson's presidency, America remained a deeply divided society in the 1960s. The problem of urban poverty remained a pressing one, with slums – such as those shown above, within sight of the Capitol in Washington itself – a familiar sight in many large towns as the flight of the better-off to the suburban fringe eroded the tax base of the inner cities and left them to decay. Inequalities persisted, too, between the expectations of the young and of their parents, and between the opportunities available to men and to women. Perhaps most intractable of all, racial divisions remained entrenched in the American way of life – not only between Blacks and whites, but among a wide variety of ethnic groups. For example, efforts continued in the 1950s to assimilate the ancient Indian tribes, causing bitterness which would erupt into Indian militancy in the 1970s.

Right: a Navajo grandmother spinning yarn in Arizona, one of some 100,000 Indians remaining on territory where their forebears had lived for at least 20,000 years.

Beatlemania, Stonesmania

Rhythm and blues music, from which the phenomenon of rock 'n' roll rose meteorically in the 1950s, had its roots deep in American, and especially in Black American, culture. In the early 1960s, though, it was mainly British bands who set the pace in popular music, and in 1964 the American public had the chance to see two of the greatest of them at first hand in the United States, as both the Beatles (top) and the Rolling Stones (above) staged American tours. The Beatles – John Lennon, Paul McCartney, George Harrison, and Ringo Starr – were greeted with particularly frenzied adulation by their teenage fans when they arrived in New York in February.

23 US attends UN conference on Trade and Development

25 Closing of schools to avoid desegregation ruled unconstitutional by Supreme Court

APR 5 Death of Gen. Douglas MacArthur

MAY 8 Pres. Johnson concludes two-day tour of Appalachia

19 Bugging of US embassy in Moscow announced by State Department

27 Major earthquake in Alaska kills 117 people and causes nearly $500 million in damage

JUN 22 Three civil rights workers, in Mississippi for voter registration drive, reported missing

22 Provisions of Internal Security Act of 1950 denying US passports to Communists ruled unconstitutional by Supreme Court

24 FTC announces that it will require health warnings on cigarette packages starting in 1965

JUL 2 Civil Rights Act of 1964 signed by the President

18 Race riot erupts in Harlem, NY

23 Senate passes antipoverty bill providing for $947 million in aid for measures to combat poverty

AUG 2-5 Two US destroyers patroling in Gulf of Tonkin off North Vietnam attacked by North Vietnamese P.T. boats; US forces sink two P.T. boats and bomb bases

4 Bodies of missing civil rights workers found in earth near Philadelphia, Miss.

7 Gulf of Tonkin Resolution gives President power to take necessary measures to defend US forces and prevent further aggression

24 Democratic National Convention nominates Lyndon B. Johnson for President and Hubert Humphrey of Minnesota for Vice President

28-30 Race riot erupts in Philadelphia

SEP 24 Warren Commission concludes that Lee Harvey Oswald acted alone in assassination of John F. Kennedy

OCT 14 Rev. Martin Luther King receives Nobel Peace Prize

20 Death of 31st President of US Herbert Hoover

29 Jewel robbery at Museum of Natural History, NYC

NOV 3 Lyndon B. Johnson elected President in landslide win, Hubert Humphrey elected Vice President

21 World's longest suspension bridge, Verrazano-Narrows Bridge in NY, opened

DEC 4 FBI arrests Mississippians on charges of conspiracy to abduct and kill three civil rights workers

The Arts

★ Carol Channing in the musical *Hello, Dolly!*
★ Zero Mostel in the musical *Fiddler on the Roof*
★ Stanley Kubrick's film *Dr Strangelove*
★ Supreme's song 'Where Did Our Love Go'
★ Beatles appear on Ed Sullivan Show

1965

JAN 4 In State-of-the-Union message, Pres. Johnson describes goals for 'Great Society'

4 Death of poet T.S. Eliot

20 Lyndon B. Johnson inaugurated for first elective term, Hubert Humphrey inaugurated Vice President

FEB 6 Vietcong guerrillas attack US military base in Pleiku, killing 8 and wounding 126

7 Pres. Johnson orders bombing of North Vietnamese bases

18 Defense Secretary Robert S. McNamara calls for nationwide network of bomb shelters

21 Malcolm X assassinated by rival black Muslims in NYC

MAR 7 State troopers attack 525 civil rights demonstrators in Selma, Ala., as they prepare to march to Montgomery to protest voting rights discrimination

8-9 US Marines land in South Vietnam to protect Air Force base at Danang

8 Supreme Court rules that person holding belief in supreme being may be exempted from military combat training and service

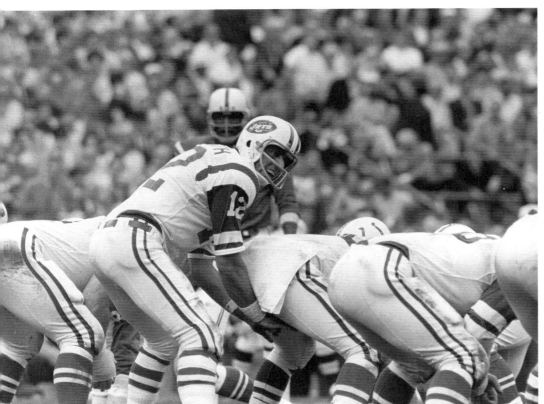

First Superbowl

A major new tournament was added to the sporting calendar in the 1960s with the advent of the Superbowl. Although intercollegiate football had been played on an amateur basis since 1869, it was only with the formation of the American Professional Football Association – later reorganized as the National Football League (N. F. L.) – in 1920 that organized professional games began in the United States. In the years after the Second World War, however, the popularity of professional football soared to win it a place second only to baseball as America's favorite spectator sport. In 1959 the American Football League was formed as a rival to the N. F. L., and it was following the agreement of the A. F. L. and the N. F. L. to merge in 1966 that the Superbowl was born as a play-off between the champions of the two leagues. The first Superbowl took place in 1967 between the Green Bay Packers and the Kansas City Chiefs, with victory going to the Packers. Below: Jim Taylor runs for the final Packers' touchdown in 1967. Left: The winning New York Jets in the 1969 Superbowl.

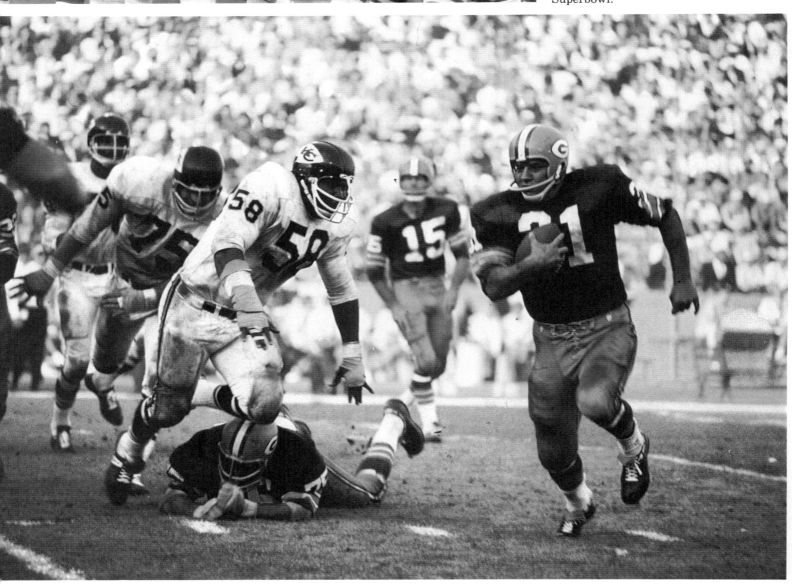

Billie Jean King

In 1968 Billie Jean King, the Californian tennis star whose talent and determination made her a leading light not only of the courts but also of the women's movement in America, won her third Wimbledon women's title in a row, equalling "Little Mo" Connolly's 1954 record for consecutive victories.

Sting Like a Bee

Heavyweight boxing was dominated during the 1960s by the towering figure of Cassius Clay (who changed his name to Mohammed Ali after joining the Black Moslem movement). Turning professional after winning an Olympic gold medal in 1960, Clay's light-footed, dancing style and precision delivery won him the world heavyweight title in February 1964, when he confounded the pundits by beating the legendary Sonny Liston in seven rounds. He repeated the feat the following year, seeing off Liston's challenge with a knock-out after less than two minutes. Clay's tenure of the championship was dogged by controversy – not least because of his aggressive taunting of opponents both inside and outside the ring – and in 1967 he was stripped of his title after refusing the Vietnam draft on religious grounds.

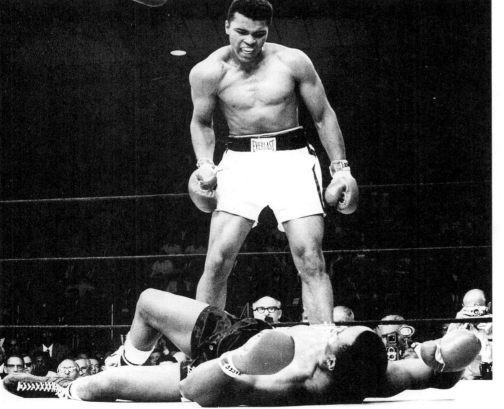

11 Unitarian minister James. J. Reeb of Boston dies in Selma, Ala., as result of attack

21 Civil rights march from Selma to Montgomery, Ala., begun by 3200 people led by Dr Martin Luther King, Jr, protected by over 2200 US troops; 25,000 gather in Montgomery

23 *Gemini 3*, first manned mission of Gemini project, launched from Cape Kennedy

25 Civil rights worker shot and killed in Alabama by KKK

APR 2 Pres. Johnson consents to increase military and economic aid to South Vietnam

6 NASA launches first commercial satellite, *Early Bird*

7 Pres. Johnson announces that US is willing to participate in 'unconditional' talks with Hanoi to end war

11 Series of 37 tornadoes hit Indiana, Iowa, Illinois, Wisconsin, Michigan and Ohio, killing 271 and injuring 5000

28 First contingent of Marines sent to Dominican Republic to protect US citizens during civil war

29 Commissioner of Education Francis Keppel announces that all public school districts are to desegregate their schools by autumn of 1967

MAY 9 Government announces total US fighting force of 42,200 men

17 First mass bombing raid in Vietnam War

JUN 26 Deployment of additional 21,000 US soldiers announced

JUL 14 UN Ambassador Adlai Stevenson dies; succeeded by Supreme Court Associate Justice Arthur Goldberg

26 Pres. Johnson announces decision to increase presence in Vietnam to 125,000 men

30 Medicare bill provides limited health care insurance for elderly and disabled

AUG 4 Pres. Johnson requests $1.7 billion for war effort

6 Voting Rights Act allows Federal Government to send registrars to supervise enrolment of voters in areas where literacy, knowledge and character tests have been suspended

11-16 Major race riot in Watts, Black section of Los Angeles, Calif. leaves 35 dead and hundreds injured

SEP 9 Department of Housing and Urban Development established

16 Three-week newspaper strike begins in NYC

OCT 1 Anti-pollution bill empowers Secretary of HEW to set emission standards on toxic pollutants in new diesel and gasoline powered automobiles

3 Immigration act abolishes quota system established on basis of national origin

15-16 Nationwide antiwar demonstrations followed by rallies and petitions supporting US policy

NOV 9-10 Northeast power blackout

15 Mandatory federal registration by members of Communist Party ruled unconstitutional by Supreme Court

DEC 4 *Gemini 7* launched from Cape Kennedy on 14-day, 206-orbit mission and rendezvous in space with *Gemini 6*

The Arts

★ Robert Wise's film *The Sound of Music*

1966

JAN 1-13 AFL-CIO's Transport Workers Union strike in NYC; results in 15 percent wage hike

12 In State-of-the-Union message, Pres. Johnson pledges to continue Great Society program and maintain commitment to South Vietnam

13 President announces resumption of US bombing raids over North Vietnam, after 37-day pause

FEB 8 Pres. Johnson concludes three-day conference with South Vietnam Premier Nguyen Cao Ky

MAR 2 US troop strength in Vietnam reaches 215,000

3 Cold War GI Bill of Rights grants special education, housing, health and job benefits to veterans who have spent at least 180 days in service since January 31, 1955

Vietnam

The war in Vietnam left deeper scars on the American psyche than any other conflict of the 20th century. What began as a battle to defend the South Vietnamese Government against domestic opposition groups backed by the North Vietnamese régime of Ho Chi Minh rapidly became a military nightmare in which the chief casualties were Vietnamese citizens on both sides of the border, and the citizens of neighboring Laos and Cambodia.

Right: Some 56,000 American troops were killed and another 300,000 wounded during the decade of fighting in Vietnam. Here, two U.S. marines carry a wounded colleague to safety.

Below: In February 1968 U.S. marines finally recaptured the ancient South Vietnamese imperial capital of Hue after a week of intense hand-to-hand fighting. Here a detachment of marines is pinned down by sniper fire behind a wall near the old citadel.

Inset: One of the most familiar images of the first war of the television age: helicopters played a crucial part in the conflict, ferrying troops and supplies into the hinterland of a densely forested country.

Opposite top: American military police arrest a Viet Cong guerrilla following a surprise attack on the U.S. embassy in the heart of the South Vietnamese capital, Saigon, in 1968.

Opposite below: Opposition to the war at home became increasingly vociferous as the decade went on. Anti-war posters parodied First and Second World War recruitment propaganda, and on April 9, 1969, 50,000 people marched against the war in New York.

VETERANS FOR PEACE IN VIETNAM

SUPPORT ANTI-WAR GIs

SINCE TALKS BEGAN 10 000 DEAD

I WANT OUT

The Tet Offensive

On January 30, 1968 – the Vietnamese lunar New Year, or Tet, holiday – the Communist forces in Vietnam began a major offensive against South Vietnamese towns and cities which would have a significant effect not only on the military situation on the ground, but also on public opinion in the United States itself. By their success in driving forward despite the full force of American military resistance, the Viet Cong guerrillas demonstrated to many, both in Vietnam and in the U.S., that the war was now rapidly becoming unwinnable for America.

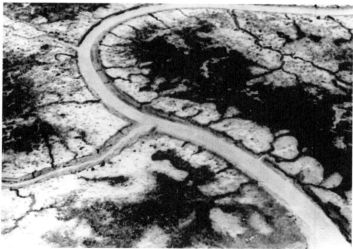

Defoliation

The dense forest cover in much of Vietnam afforded the Viet Cong a considerable strategic advantage, which the American military sought to reduce by a massive campaign of chemical defoliation, using powerful herbicides such as the notorious "Agent Orange." The resulting destruction – graphically shown in the contrast between these two photographs of mangrove forests near Saigon – laid waste to almost a million acres, turning Vietnam from a major rice exporter in 1967 to an importer in 1968, causing misery and starvation, and leaving a permanent scar on her countryside and her economy.

True Grit

The veteran Western star John Wayne (above) won an Oscar in 1969 – a full 30 years after his movie debut in *Stagecoach* – for his performance as a hard-drinking marshal in Henry Hathaway's film *True Grit*.

Exit L. B. J.

Looking tired and drawn, President Johnson (above), his social program and his popularity alike bogged down in the quagmire of Vietnam, announced to a shocked American television audience on March 31, 1968, that "I shall not seek and I will not accept the nomination of my party for a second term as your President."

16 *Gemini 8* makes first successful space docking; thruster rocket malfunction terminates flight

25-26 Antiwar demonstrations in San Francisco, Chicago, Boston, Philadelphia and Washington

APR 3 Death of Walt Disney

24 Five-month newspaper strike begins in NYC

27 ICC allows merger of Pennsylvania and New York Central Railroads; largest merger in US corporate history

MAY 15 Antiwar demonstration in Washington, DC, attended by 10,000

30 Unmanned *Surveyor I* makes US's first soft landing on moon

JUN 6 *Gemini 9* concludes mission after featuring largest spacewalk

JUL 8-AUG 19 Strike grounds planes of all major airlines

AUG 8 First successful artificial heart pump installed

NOV 3 Truth-in-Packaging bill requires accurate labeling of supermarket items

8 Republicans gain 3 seats in Senate and 47 in House

8 Edward Brooke of Massachusetts becomes first Black elected to Senate since Reconstruction

8 Ronald Reagan, former movie actor and former Democrat, elected Republican governor of California

The Arts

★ Sylvia Plath's collection of poems *Ariel*

★ Truman Capote's novel *In Cold Blood*

★ Angela Lansbury in the musical *Mame*

★ The Mamas and Papas' song 'California Dreaming'

1967

JAN 5 State Department announces 5008 Americans killed and 30,093 wounded in Vietnam since 1966; current troop strength is 380,000 soldiers

8-19 In Operation Cedar Falls, 16,000 US and 14,000 South Vietnamese soldiers participate in offensive against North Vietnamese positions 25 miles northwest of Saigon

10 Segregationist Lester Maddox becomes Governor of Georgia

16 First Black southern sheriff since Reconstruction, Lucius Amerson, sworn in at Tuskegee, Ala.

27 Space demilitarization treaty prohibiting orbiting of nuclear weapons and forbidding territorial claims on celestial bodies signed by US, USSR and 63 nations

27 Launch pad fire in *Apollo I* spacecraft during testing at Cape Kennedy, Fla, kills astronauts Virgil Gissam, Edward White and Roger Chafer

FEB 10 Twenty-fifth Amendment, providing for presidential succession, takes effect

MAR 1 Rep. Adam Clayton Powell of New York (accused of using government money for private purposes) denied seat in 90th Congress

7 Death of Alice B. Toklas

18 Tennessee's 'Monkey Law', prohibiting teaching of evolution theories, repealed

APR 12-14 Presidents of America Conference in Punta del Este, Uruguay, attended by 18 nations

15 Antiwar demonstration in NYC draws up to 400,000

17 Pro-Vietnam demonstration in NYC draws 70,000

MAY 19 First US air strike on central Hanoi, North Vietnam, launched

JUN 8 US communications ship *Liberty* attacked by Israeli torpedo boats and planes in international waters; Israel apologizes

12 In *Curtis Publishing Co. v. Butts*, Supreme Court rules that public personalities cannot receive payment in libel suits unless they can prove that misstatements were deliberate or made with reckless disregard for truth

12 State laws forbidding interracial marriages ruled unconstitutional by Supreme Court

30 General Agreement on Tariffs and Trade, negotiated by Kennedy administration, signed in Geneva by 53 nations; pledges 4.5 million tons of grain a year to developing countries

The End of the Dream

The leading voice of Black America was brutally silenced on the night of April 4, 1968, when Martin Luther King, the civil rights leader and Baptist minister, was gunned down in Memphis, Tennessee, by James Earl Ray, a white extremist. King, whose campaign for civil rights extended beyond the Black community to encompass all the dispossessed of America, was in Memphis to support a strike by the city's refuse collectors. He had walked out onto the balcony of his motel room for some air when shots were fired from a neighboring boarding house, bringing to an abrupt and tragic end the career which began with King's coordination of the Montgomery bus boycott in 1955.

Top: One of the hundreds of mourners who filed past King's coffin as he lay in state in Memphis. Middle: Members and friends of the King family at Martin Luther King's funeral at South View Cemetery, Atlanta. More than 150,000 people attended, including representatives of the U.S. Government.
Bottom: As news of King's death spread, serious rioting erupted in cities throughout the nation. Here, firemen battle to extinguish a blaze at a furniture store in the Black district of Harlem, New York.

A TRIBUTE TO
ROBERT FRANCIS KENNEDY
ONE DOLLAR

The Assassination—The Funeral • A Nation Mourns A Fallen Leader
The Hope and Dream of Youth • The Man and His Family
His Search for Knowledge and Understanding • The Statesman—
Servant of the People • His Greatness and Humility—An Appreciation

Robert Kennedy Assassinated

Barely two months after the death of Martin Luther King, America was shocked by another political assassination, when Senator Robert Kennedy (left) was gunned down after celebrating his success in the California primary elections for the Democratic presidential nomination. Kennedy, 42, the younger brother of the assassinated President and a former Attorney General, was shot in the head and shoulder by a Jordanian Arab, Sirhan Bishara Sirhan, who was immediately arrested. The shooting happened just after midnight at the Ambassador Hotel, Los Angeles, where the Senator had been making a victory speech to a packed meeting of his supporters. He was rushed to hospital where doctors fought to save him, but he died 24 hours later without regaining consciousness. Sirhan, a fanatical anti-Zionist, was protesting against Kennedy's support for Israel.

Chappaquiddick

In July 1969 Senator Edward Kennedy, brother of Robert and J. F. K., was given a suspended prison sentence for leaving the scene of an accident in which a woman passenger in his car was drowned. Mary Jo Kopechne died when the car, driven by the Senator, plunged over a bridge on Chappaquiddick Island, Massachusetts. Hours elapsed before Kennedy reported the accident, which was widely seen as marking the end of his own political ambitions.

JUL 16 AFL-CIO International Association of Machinists' strike affects 600,000 railroad employees

12-17 Race riot in Newark, NJ

23-30 Worst race riot in US history erupts in Detroit, Mich., following police raid on after-hours drinking club; 41 killed, 2000 injured, 5000 left homeless, some $200 million in property damage; federal troops summoned

26 H. Rap Brown, chairman of Student Nonviolent Coordinating Committee, arrested on charges of inciting riot following outbreak of racial violence in Cambridge, Md

29 Fire aboard USS *Forrestal* in Gulf of Tonkin kills 134 crewmen; worst naval accident in warzone since World War II

AUG 30 Thurgood Marshall becomes first Black justice of Supreme Court

SEP 10 *Surveyor 5* tests lunar soil

18 Secretary of Defense Robert McNamara, announces that US will develop 'thin' antiballistic missile system to shield US from possible nuclear attack from Red China

OCT 3 Death of folk singer Woody Guthrie

19 *Mariner 5* interplanetary space probe provides information about Venus

20 Seven Ku Klux Klan members convicted of conspiracy in 1964 murders of three civil rights workers in Mississippi

21-22 Antiwar demonstrations in Washington, DC, involve 35,000 protestors; 647 arrested

26 Order issued for cancellation of draft deferments of college students who violate draft laws or interfere with recruiting

31 Pres. Johnson reiterates US commitment to South Vietnam

NOV 14 Air Quality Act provides $428,300,000 to fight air pollution

20 National Commission on Product Safety established

DEC Nationwide 'Stop the Draft' movement organized by 40 antiwar groups; protestors arrested in Cincinnati, New Haven, Conn., Manchester, NH, and Madison, Wis.

5 More than 1000 antiwar protestors attempt to close down NYC induction center; 585 arrested, including Dr Benjamin Spock and poet Allen Ginsberg

14 Production of synthetic DNA announced by biochemists at Stanford University

Also this year
★ William Manchester's *The Death of a President* published
★ Marshall McLuhan and Quentin Fiore's *The Medium is the Message*

The Arts
★ The musical *Hair*
★ The Doors' song 'Light My Fire'

1968

JAN 22 Nuclear-armed SAC B-52 bomber crashes near Greenland, releasing radiation

23 Navy intelligence ship USS *Pueblo* seized in Sea of Japan by North Korean patrol boats for allegedly violating territorial limit

25 US aircraft carrier *Enterprise* sent to Sea of Japan in show of force

30-FEB 24 Tet offensive: massive assault by North Vietnamese forces throughout South Vietnam

FEB 8 Former Gov. of Alabama George C. Wallace announces candidacy for President as third-party candidate on law and order platform

MAR 12 Sen. Eugene McCarthy of Minnesota, campaigning on antiwar platform, wins 42 percent of vote in Democratic primary in New Hampshire

31 Pres. Johnson announces cessation of bombing north of 21st parallel in Vietnam and his decision not to run for reelection

APR 4 Civil Rights leader Martin Luther King, Jr, assassinated by sniper in Memphis, Tenn.

8 Operation Complete Victory offensive, involving 100,000 allied troops in Vietnam, begins

Black Militancy

Almost from its inception, the Black struggle for civil rights had been divided between those who supported non-violence and those who took a more militant line. In the late 1950s and 1960s the two strands developed in radically different directions, as anti-integrationist supporters of Black nationalism formed their own organizations in repudiation of Martin Luther King's policies of peaceful resistance. Notable among these groups was the "Lost Nation of Islam," also known as the Black Moslems, to which the controversial young activist Malcolm X (right) belonged until 1964, when he broke away to form the Organization of African-American Unity, only to be assassinated the following year. More militant still were the Black Panthers (below), under leaders like Eldridge Cleaver and Bobby Seale. In the mid-1960s even the Student Nonviolent Coordinating Committee fell into the hands of militant radicals such as Stokely Carmichael, who demanded that violence be met with violence.

Above: Black Panther poster.

8 Bureau of Narcotics and Dangerous Drugs established

23 Students for a Democratic Society lead seizure of five buildings at Columbia University in NYC to protest University's involvement in research connected with Vietnam war

24 Some 300 Black students occupy administration building at Boston University, demanding stronger emphasis on Black history in curriculum and increased financial aid for Blacks

MAY 10 Peace talks begin in Paris between US and North Vietnam

JUN 1 Death of Helen Keller

3 Pop artist Andy Warhol shot by Valerie Solanis

5 Sen. Robert F. Kennedy shot while campaigning in Los Angeles

6 Robert F. Kennedy dies; Jordanian immigrant Sirhan Sirhan is charged with murder

8 Ex-convict James Earl Ray arrested in London for murder of Martin Luther King, Jr.

14 Dr Benjamin Spock convicted of conspiracy to abet draft evasion

24 Resurrection City in Washington, DC, razed by police

JUL 1 Nuclear nonproliferation treaty signed by US, USSR and 59 other nations

AUG 7 Rioting erupts in Miami, Fla.

8 Republican National Convention nominates Richard M. Nixon for President and Gov. Spiro T. Agnew of Maryland for Vice President

10 Sen. George McGovern of South Dakota announces candidacy for Democratic presidential nomination

26 National Student Association reports that during first six months of the year there have been 221 major demonstrations at 101 colleges and universities

26-29 Democratic National Convention nominates Vice Pres. Hubert Humphrey for President and Sen. Edmund S. Muskie of Maine for Vice President

26-29 Antiwar protestors clash with police and national guardsmen outside Democratic National Convention in Chicago; protestors, bystanders and members of press beaten by police

OCT 31 End to US bombing of North Vietnam ordered by the President

NOV 6 Richard M. Nixon elected President, Spiro T. Agnew elected Vice President in one of closest elections in US history

6 Student strike begins at San Francisco State College

25 Death of author Upton Sinclair

DEC 20 Death of author John Steinbeck

21-77 *Apollo 8* orbits moon 10 times, yields spectacular photographs of Earth and moon

The Arts

★ Howard Sackler's play *The Great White Hope*

★ Roman Polanski's film *Rosemary's Baby*

★ Simon and Garfunkel's song 'Mrs Robinson'

Olympic Protest

American runners Tommie Smith and John Carlos (above) caused controversy at the 1968 Olympic Games in Mexico City when they raised gloved fists in a Black power salute and stared fixedly at the ground as the *Star Spangled Banner* was played. The protest – against the treatment of Black people in America – came as they were awarded gold and bronze medals respectively for their placings in the 200 metres. Both athletes were subsequently suspended from the games.

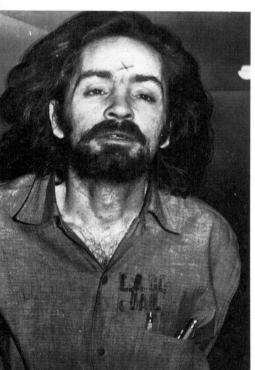

The Manson Murders

Charles Manson (left), the leader of a bizarre Californian commune known as "The Family," was arrested for the brutal murder of five people at the Hollywood mansion of the film director Roman Polanski on August 9, 1969. Among the victims was Polanski's wife, the actress Sharon Tate, who was pregnant at the time. At the subsequent trial, Manson and three others were given death sentences, later commuted to life imprisonment.

1969

JAN-MAR Torrential rains cause vast mud slides in southern California

JAN 20 Richard M. Nixon inaugurated President, Spiro T. Agnew inaugurated Vice President

MAR 10 James Earl Ray sentenced to 99 years in prison for murder of Dr Martin Luther King, Jr

14 Pres. Nixon requests funds to build ABM system to protect US offensive missile bases against Soviet or Chinese attack

APR 3 Combat deaths in Vietnam since 1961 reach 33,641

4 First artificial heart implant

7 Supreme Court rules unconstitutional laws that attempt to prohibit reading or viewing of obscene material in privacy of one's home

9 Group of 300 students, mainly SDS members, take over Harvard University's main administration building and evict eight deans

10 Some 400 state and local police clear Harvard administration building

Woodstock

During the weekend of August 15 to 17, 1969, an event occurred near White Lake, New York, which has acquired almost legendary status in the annals of the counterculture and became for many people an enduring symbol of both the hopes and the decadence of the youth movement in the 1960s.

The Woodstock Music Festival acquired a momentum of its own far beyond anything that the organizers had expected when they hired the 600 acres of Yasgur Farm for a rock and arts fair. Local people reacted with mixed emotions to what became a virtual pilgrimage of some 400,000 people to worship at the shrine of some of the decade's greatest rock stars (above and far right). Performers included Jefferson Airplane; Jimi Hendrix (below left), whose irreverent rendition of the *Star Spangled Banner* was one of the highlights of the weekend; and Janis Joplin (second from right), who has been described as one of the few white female singers with the power of a Black woman's voice. The festival was remarkably peaceful, although displays of nudity and drug-taking shocked members of the older generation (second from left). Staged to herald the new Age of Aquarius, Woodstock has since been seen by many as the crest of the wave which beached the hippies and "flower people" of the counterculture on the harsher sands of the 1970s. Both Hendrix and Joplin were to die of drug overdoses the following year.

Dr. Strangelove

Peter Sellers as the eponymous doctor in Kubrick's dark-toned anti-nuclear comedy, released in 1963.

Easy Riders

Peter Fonda and Dennis Hopper drop out and ride across America in Hopper's 1969 cult movie, *Easy Rider*.

Hair

The hugely successful rock musical, *Hair* (right), opened on Broadway in April 1968 under the direction of Tom O'Horgan.

2001

Another archetypal sixties experience, Stanley Kubrick's film *2001: A Space Odyssey* has been called "a trip without LSD."

Tune In ...

Born Robert Zimmerman in 1941, singer-songwriter Bob Dylan (above) became the predominant musical voice of the age of protest with songs such as *The Times They Are A'Changing, Like a Rolling Stone*, and *Blowing in the Wind*.

Turn On ...

Jim Morrison (above), the leather-clad lead singer of The Doors, combined anger and sexuality in such rock standards as *Light My Fire* and *Break On Through*.

And Drop Out

Experimentation was central to the alternative youth culture of the 1960s, with drugs such as marijuana and LSD fueling many a lyric and many a lifestyle.

23 Sirhan Sirhan sentenced to death for murder of Sen. Robert Kennedy

24 US B-52's drop nearly 3000 tons of bombs on area near Cambodian border northwest of Saigon

MAY 15 People's Park in Berkeley, Calif., attacked by police and National Guardsmen

18-26 Rehearsal for manned lunar landing performed by *Apollo 10*

20 US and South Vietnamese forces capture Hamburger Hill after ten-day bloody battle

JUN 6 Court testimony reveals that FBI had tapped phones of Martin Luther King, Jr

8 Pres. Nixon meets South Vietnam Pres. Nguyen Van Thieu on Midway to discuss Vietnam war; leads to troop reduction of 25,000 soldiers

JUL 16 *Apollo 11*, carrying Neil A. Armstrong, Edwin E. Aldrin, Jr, and Michael Collins, launched toward moon

18 Sen. Edward M. Kennedy involved in auto accident when car goes off bridge into waters off Chappaquiddick Island; passenger Mary Jo Kopechne drowns

20 *Eagle* is first manned vehicle to land on moon; Neil Armstrong is first man to walk on moon

27 Stonewall Uprising: over 400 police battle with over 2000 people protesting police raid on gay bar located on Christopher St in heart of Greenwich Village, NYC; incites nationwide Gay Liberation Movement

AUG 3 *Mariner 7* photographs Mars

9-10 Tate-LaBianca murders: actress Sharon Tate and 6 others slain by Manson 'family' in Los Angeles

15-17 Woodstock Music and Art Fair, Bethel, NY; 300,000 attend

17 Hurricane kills over 300 people and leaves 70,000 homeless in Mississippi, Louisiana and Alabama

SEP 16 US troop reduction of 35,000 from Vietnam announced

24 Trial of Chicago Eight begins; Tom Hayden, Abbie Hoffman, Jerry Rubin, Bobby Seale and others charged with conspiring to incite riots during 1968 Democratic convention

OCT 15 First Vietnam Moratorium Day observed by millions

27 Strike against General Electric Company begins

29 Supreme Court orders immediate desegregation of 33 Mississippi school districts

NOV 11 Pro-America demonstrations in support of US policy in Vietnam

14 Second Vietnam Moratorium Day begins with 'March Against Death' in Washington, DC

15 Largest antiwar rally in history of US occurs in Washington, DC, as 250,000 protest involvement in Vietnam War

17 First round of Strategic Arms Limitation Talks between US and USSR opens in Helsinki, Finland

19 *Apollo 12* makes second manned landing on moon

20 Some 78 American Indians seize Alcatraz Island in San Francisco bay and demand that it be turned over to Indian community

20 Use of pesticide DDT banned in residential areas

24 Nuclear Non-proliferation Treaty signed by US and USSR

24 Lt William L. Calley, Jr, charged with premeditated murder in massacre of some 102 South Vietnamese civilians at My Lai

25 Pres. Nixon orders all US germ warfare stockpiles destroyed

DEC 1 First draft lottery since World War II held in NYC

2 Boeing 747 makes first public flight

8 Raid on Black Panther headquarters in Los Angeles leads to four-hour shoot-out

30 Most far-reaching tax reform bill in US history signed by the President

The Arts

★ Kurt Vonnegut's novel *Slaughterhouse-Five*

★ Kenneth Tynan's musical *Oh! Calcutta!*

★ Dustin Hoffman and Jon Voight in the film *Midnight Cowboy*

★ Dennis Hopper's film *Easy Rider*

★ The Fifth Dimension's song 'Aquarius/Let the Sunshine In'

THE EAGLE HAS LANDED

"I believe this nation should commit itself to achieving the goal, before this decade is out, of landing a man on the moon and returning him safely to earth." So spoke President John Kennedy in the wake of the first orbital space flight by the Soviet cosmonaut Yuri Gagarin in April 1961, launching as he did so the most intense phase of the international space race. In July 1969, eight years and some $24 billion later, that goal was finally achieved.

Apollo 11's historic mission began at 9.32 a.m. on July 16 when the Saturn 5 rocket blasted off from the launch pad at Cape Kennedy in Florida (near right), entering the earth's orbit within 12 minutes. Three days and 240,000 miles later, the three astronauts – Flight Commander Neil A. Armstrong, Lieutenant Colonel Michael Collins, and Colonel Edwin "Buzz" Aldrin (from left to right below) – went into orbit around the moon, and at 1.47 p.m. on July 20, the lunar module, "Eagle," separated from the command module, "Columbia," and Armstrong and Aldrin began their descent to the lunar surface. At 4.17 p.m. the module's three landing probes touched down smoothly in the Sea of Tranquility – a mere four miles from the planned landing site – and as the message "The Eagle has landed" was relayed to earth, the Mission Operations Control Center at Houston, Texas, exploded into spontaneous celebrations (right).

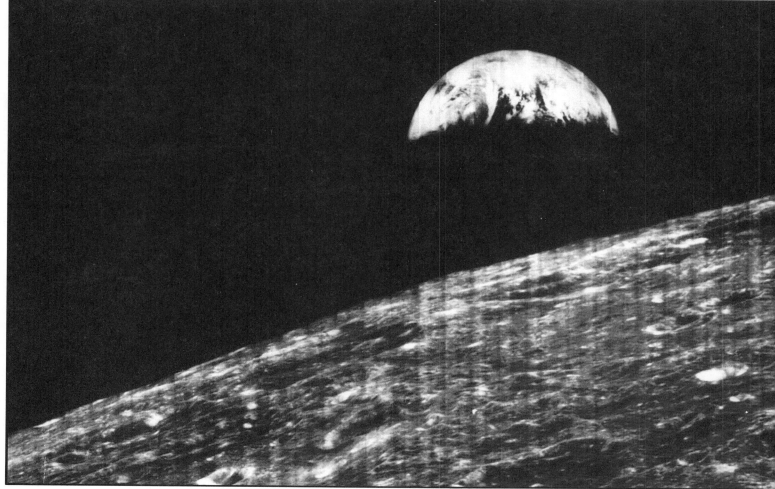

A Giant Leap

Just over six and a half hours after touchdown, and watched by a breathless television audience of some 600 million people on earth, Neil Armstrong emerged from the capsule and made his way slowly down the ladder to become the first human being to set foot on the moon, with the words "That's one small step for a man, one giant leap for mankind." Aldrin joined him shortly afterwards (far left) and together the two men set up a television camera to film themselves as they planted the Stars and Stripes, unveiled a plaque (inset below), collected samples from the lunar surface, and conducted various scientific experiments. During their eight and a half hour moonwalk (middle left), they received a congratulatory telephone call from President Nixon and demonstrated the effects of one-sixth gravity by jumping in their 16-layer moonsuits. Armstrong described the moon's surface as fine and powdery, and spoke of the "stark beauty" of its silent landscape (below).

"Eagle" rejoined the orbiting command module after 21 hours and 37 minutes on the moon. The return to earth went almost exactly according to schedule, and splashdown took place in the Pacific Ocean on July 24 (left).

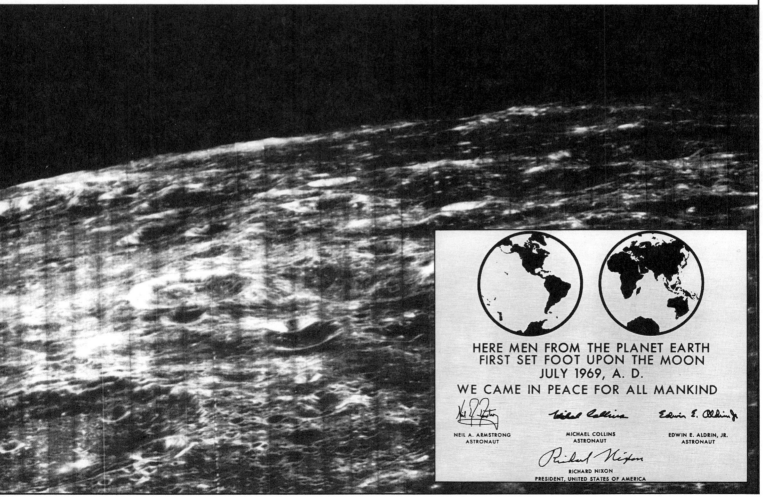

HERE MEN FROM THE PLANET EARTH
FIRST SET FOOT UPON THE MOON
JULY 1969, A. D.
WE CAME IN PEACE FOR ALL MANKIND

NEIL A. ARMSTRONG
ASTRONAUT

MICHAEL COLLINS
ASTRONAUT

EDWIN E. ALDRIN, JR.
ASTRONAUT

RICHARD NIXON
PRESIDENT, UNITED STATES OF AMERICA

THE 1970s were a decade of deep disillusionment in the United States. The war in Vietnam, which President Nixon had come to the White House promising to end, dragged on year after year, and, as the intensity of the conflict heightened, reports of the U.S.-backed invasions of Cambodia and Laos, and television pictures of the effects of American saturation bombing in North and South Vietnam, brought a new wave of protest throughout the nation. While American B52s in Indochina sought to bomb the North Vietnamese to the negotiating table, the security forces at home waged a campaign against alleged "subversion," which put in jeopardy the cherished political liberties of the First Amendment and shook many people's faith in the democratic nature of the American system.

Within months of the withdrawal of U.S. troops from Vietnam that faith was to be rocked to its foundations by the breaking of the Watergate scandal. The nation watched with horrified disbelief as evidence mounted of criminal activity at the highest levels of Government, and when Nixon resigned his office over the affair in 1974 the reputation of the presidency lay in tatters. President Ford's attempt to heal the damage by offering Nixon a free pardon served only to rub salt into the nation's wounds, while the presidency of Jimmy Carter, far from restoring public confidence in the country's institutions and its place in the world, left instead an impression of helplessness in the face of economic recession and the Iranian hostage crisis. The loss of national confidence in America's self-appointed role as the guardian of the free world was still further compounded in 1979 when the fragile flower of East-West détente was crushed by the Soviet invasion of Afghanistan. As the decade ended, there were many who looked to the 1980s with apprehension.

The War in Vietnam

During his election campaign in 1968, Richard Nixon had committed himself to finding a peaceful solution to the crisis in Indochina, but, despite the fact that peace talks had begun in Paris in 1969, the war continued with no settlement in sight. Nixon embraced a policy of "Vietnamization" – training and supplying the South Vietnamese army so that it could continue the war on its own – and began a phased withdrawal of U.S. troops, which would reduce the American military presence from its peak of 543,000 men in 1968 to just 39,000 in 1972. For a time there was a lull in protests at home, but when, in April 1970, Nixon ordered the invasion and bombing of Cambodia in a futile attempt to drive the North Vietnamese out of their border bases in that country, anti-war feeling erupted again with a vengeance. Four students were shot by police at Kent State University, Ohio, in the widespread demonstrations which followed, and in Vietnam itself the morale of U.S. troops was reported to be at an all-time low, with widespread desertions, insubordination, and drug abuse. The following year, Nixon ordered a similar incur-

The Establishment strikes back: One of the four student victims of the Kent State University shootings.

sion into Laos and launched a massive bombing campaign against targets in North and South Vietnam which left thousands of civilians dead. In 1972, he risked a substantial escalation of the conflict by mining harbors used by Soviet ships in the area, and even after Secretary of State Henry Kissinger announced during the election of that year that peace was at hand, U.S. B52s mounted the heaviest bombing campaign of the war in an attempt to batter the North Vietnamese into accepting America's terms.

"Peace with honor"

A ceasefire was finally signed in Paris on January 27, 1973. Nixon called it a "peace with honor," but when the last U.S. troops finally withdrew in the following March they left a region physically and economically ravaged by eight years of war, and a political vacuum which was all too soon to be filled by the very forces they had fought so long to resist. Saigon fell to North Vietnamese troops in 1975, precipitating the first wave of what would become a flood of South Vietnamese refugees, while in Cambodia the devastation wrought by U.S. bombing helped create the conditions for the ideological genocide of Pol Pot and the Khmer Rouge. In the United States itself, the Vietnam conflict left a bitter legacy of disillusion and resentment, quite apart from the physical and psychological damage inflicted on so many of those who had taken part. The most powerful nation on earth had been forced to recognize the limits of its influence on the world stage, even when that influence was backed by unprecedented military strength. Perhaps more disturbingly still, America had seen how authoritarian a

democratically elected executive could be in dealing with the widespread expression of popular dissent. The Vietnam experience led many people to question the values upon which American society had been based, and to wonder how well democracy was really functioning in the United States. In the wake of the 1972 election, that confidence would suffer another and perhaps still heavier blow as the full implications of the Watergate affair began to emerge.

The 1972 Election

From the moment he entered the White House in 1969, Nixon's advisers were planning his reelection in 1972. Members of the Cabinet often found it difficult to penetrate the screen of close associates – men like H. R. (Bob) Haldeman, John R. Ehrlichman, and the new Attorney-General, John Mitchell – with whom the President surrounded himself, and resented Nixon's tendency to tailor their domestic policy initiatives to the requirements of influential interest groups. In particular, Nixon's so-called "Southern strategy" – an attempt to wean away from George Wallace the Southern conservatives who had voted for him in large numbers at the 1968 election – led to some controversial stalling of civil rights programs and to a "law and order" policy which sometimes seemed to value order more highly than law. This strategy paid dividends in the 1972 election, when Nixon was returned to office with more than 60 per cent of the popular vote and the second largest majority of the electoral vote in American history. Nixon's campaign organization, the Committee to Reelect the President (soon to become notorious as CREEP), seemed to have done its job well.

Within months, however, that victory would turn to ashes. During the election campaign itself five burglars had been caught bugging phones and copying documents at the headquarters of the Democratic National Committee in the Watergate complex in Washington. Despite the Democratic candidate George McGovern's campaign attempts to implicate Nixon in what the President's press secretary dismissed as "a third-rate burglary," Attorney-General Mitchell denied that CREEP had been involved in any way. Two weeks later, however, he quietly resigned as the organization's head.

The Watergate Scandal

The five men arrested at the Watergate building, together with two men arrested afterwards, refused to testify at their trial, pleaded guilty, and received the maximum sentences available for their crimes. In response to a promise of clemency, however, one of the defendants, a known CREEP official, gave the trial judge, John J. Sirica, the first evidence of high level involvement in the break-in. A Senate investigating committee under Sam Ervin Jr. of North Carolina began to turn up indications that the burglary was in fact part of a fully-coordinated "dirty tricks" campaign during the 1972 election, which included illegal wiretapping, blackmail, and theft of personal documents.

Under the combined scrutiny of the committee and such tenacious press reporters as Carl Bernstein and Bob Woodward of the *Washington Post*, the revelations gathered momentum throughout 1973 and 1974, bringing the investigation closer to the White House with every turn. John W. Dean, the President's counsel, gave evidence of an elaborate cover-up at the highest levels to

America's first unelected President: Gerald Ford takes the oath of office, August 9, 1974.

prevent the full details of the Watergate story from coming out. He implicated the acting Director of the FBI, L. Patrick Gray, in this operation, and Gray was forced to resign. On April 30, 1973, two of the President's closest aides, Bob Haldeman and John Ehrlichman, also resigned, as did the new Attorney-General, Richard Kleindienst. Nixon went on television to protest his shock and innocence, promising a thorough investigation and assuring an increasingly skeptical public that there would be "no whitewash at the White House."

In July, the focus of the investigation shifted dramatically to the President himself. The Ervin Committee's televised hearings revealed, more or less by chance, that Nixon tape-recorded all his discussions at the White House, and Archibald Cox, the Watergate special prosecutor appointed by Nixon himself in response to pressure from the Senate, now demanded that the President hand over the relevant sections of his tapes to the committee. Nixon refused, offering edited transcripts instead, but Cox insisted. The President then told his Attorney-General, Eliot Richardson, to fire Cox. On Saturday, October 20, Richardson resigned rather than do this. Nixon then asked Richardson's deputy, William Ruckelshaus, to fire the special prosecutor, but he too refused and resigned the same evening. The third offical Nixon asked that evening, the Solicitor-General, Robert Bork, duly obliged, and Cox was dismissed.

This so-called "Saturday Night Massacre," combined with the resignation of the Vice President, Spiro Agnew, on corruption charges 10 days earlier, alienated many in Congress and elsewhere who had been prepared to give Nixon the benefit of the doubt, and talk of impeaching the President began in earnest. In April 1974 Nixon only added to his troubles by releasing a handful of tapes,

1970

FEB 4 Environmental cleanup program proposed by Pres. Nixon

18 Chicago Seven acquitted of conspiracy charges

26 Army announces that it will discontinue surveillance of civilian demonstrators and maintenance of files on civilians possibly involved in civil disturbances

MAR 18 Major nationwide postal workers' strike begins in NYC

APR 1 Cigarette advertising banned from television and radio

16 Second round of SALT talks opens in Vienna, Austria

17 *Apollo 13* lands safely after explosion ends mission

20 US troop reduction of 150,000 from Vietnam by end of year announced

22 Earth Day observed across country

29 Military invasion of Cambodia launched by 50,000 US and South Vietnamese troops

30 Military invasion of Cambodia announced by Pres. Nixon in televised address

MAY 4 Four students killed when National Guard troops fire at some 600 antiwar demonstrators at Kent State University in Ohio

5 Nuclear nonproliferation treaty goes into effect

8 Construction workers attack antiwar demonstrators at Wall Street, NYC

9 Antiwar rally in Washington, DC, draws 100,000

12 Harry Blackmum approved as associate justice of Supreme Court

14 Mississippi law enforcement officials kill 2 and injure 12 during violent demonstrations at Jackson State College

JUN 15 Conscientious objector status on moral grounds found constitutional by Supreme Court

18 Voting age lowered to 18

JUL 1 New York State abortion law leaves decision to woman during first 24 weeks of pregnancy

4 Honor America Day observed in Washington, DC

AUG 11 Jesuit priest Daniel J. Berrigan arrested by FBI for bombing-kidnapping conspiracy

12 US Post Office becomes independent government corporation

SEP 6 TWA airliner hijacked in Jordan by Palestinian terrorists

15 Over 340,000 members of UAW begin strike against General Motors

18 Death of rock guitarist Jimi Hendrix

22-28 Brush fires sweep across southern California

sections of which had been edited out. Then, when Cox's successor demanded that he hand over complete tape-recordings and Nixon again refused, the Supreme Court, despite its high number of Nixon appointees, ruled that he must comply. A few days later, on July 30, the Senate voted to impeach the President for obstruction of the course of justice and misuse of FBI, CIA, and Internal Revenue services for personal and partisan ends, and on August 9, knowing the extent to which the tapes would incriminate him, Richard Nixon became the first President in the history of the United States to resign his office.

The Ford Presidency

The new President, Gerald Ford, was the first to take office without having been elected by the American people, since he had been appointed to the vice presidency after the resignation of Spiro Agnew in 1973. Nonetheless, he was greeted with relief by a public shell-shocked by the revelations about the 1972 election and the subsequent cover-up. All hopes that Ford would be able to restore faith in the presidency were dashed, however, when, a month after taking office, he issued a free pardon to his predecessor, thus ensuring that the full details of Nixon's personal role in the corruption and criminality of the previous administration would never come to light. Meanwhile, evidence continued to emerge about illegal activity by the FBI and the CIA, both at home and abroad, under Nixon and his predecessors. In particular, indications that both organizations had been involved in widespread surveillance of American citizens with left-of-center views led many to question whether the Constitution of the United States could be relied on to prevent the kind of abuse of power more usually associated with totalitarian régimes.

Jimmy Carter

Public confidence in the democratic institutions of the American system was at a low ebb when Democrat Jimmy Carter, a previously little-known Southern businessman and Governor of Georgia, won a narrow victory in the presidential election of 1976. A man of transparent sincerity, Carter promised to restore honest and competent government to the nation after the traumas of the Nixon years, but the problems facing him were immense. Not only did he and his Cabinet fail to establish the kind of support in Congress that had enabled his Democratic predecessors to push through their domestic programs; he also suffered from an inability to deal effectively with the problems of rising inflation and unemployment which engulfed the Western economies following the increase in world energy prices after the Yom Kippur War of 1973.

In foreign affairs, too, Carter's successes were overshadowed by his more conspicuous failures. He won acclaim for his mediating role in the Egypt-Israeli conflict, an intervention which led to the signature of a peace treaty by the two countries'

leaders, Anwar el-Sadat and Menachem Begin, at the White House in March 1979, and he also helped carry forward the process of East-West détente which had been set in motion by Nixon's visits to China and the Soviet Union in 1973. Carter opened formal diplomatic relations with China in 1979, and in June of the same year met the Soviet leader Leonid Brezhnev in Vienna to sign the SALT II treaty, which set limits for the development of new strategic nuclear weapons and made provision for the reduction of existing stocks. But improvements in both superpower and Middle Eastern relations were put in jeopardy by violent events in the closing weeks of the decade. In November 1979 relations with the newly

formed Islamic revolutionary government of Ayatollah Khomeini in Iran plummeted after Iranian students, demanding the extradition of the deposed Shah from the United States, took 53 Americans hostage in the U.S. embassy in Teheran. The following month Soviet troops invaded Afghanistan. The shock waves from both developments were to be felt far into the 1980s.

Uncle Sam tries to regain the stature so badly shaken by the traumas of the early 1970s: The bicentenary of America's Independence in 1976 was an occasion for both pageantry and introspection.

Skylab

The American space station Skylab 4 (above) was launched into orbit on May 14, 1973. One of the solar shields was damaged shortly after lift-off, but was dramatically repaired in space when a mission manned by Charles Conrad, Joseph Kerwin, and Paul Weitz docked with Skylab some ten days later.

Apollo 13

Tragedy was narrowly averted in April 1970 when damage to Apollo 13 while it was orbiting the moon made it impossible for the spacecraft to return to earth under the power of its own engines. The world held its breath as the three astronauts – Jim Lovell, John Swigert, and Fred Haise (above) – piloted themselves back, near-miraculously, on the booster rockets of the lunar module in which they had planned to land on the moon.

OCT 4 Death of rock singer Janis Joplin

7 Nixon's five-point peace plan for Indochina rejected by North Vietnam

13 Black militant Angela Davis arrested in NYC on kidnapping, murder and conspiracy charges

NOV 2 Third round of SALT talks opens in Helsinki, Finland

12 Court-martial of Lt William L. Calley, Jr, begins

21 US raid on Sontay, North Vietnam, to free prisoners of war

DEC 2 Environmental Protection Agency activated

10 Threat of national rail strike

23 World Trade Center in NYC completed

31 National Air Quality Control Act tightens air pollution standards

Also this year

★ Masters and Johnson's *Human Sexual Inadequacy* published

★ Kate Millet's *Sexual Politics* published

★ Dr David Reuben's *Everything You Always Wanted to Know About Sex* published

The Arts

★ Saul Bellow's novel *Mr Sammler's Planet*

★ James Dickey's novel *Deliverance*

★ Paul Zindel's play *The Effect of Gamma Rays on Man-in-the-Moon Marigolds*

★ Anne Bancroft and Dustin Hoffman in the film *The Graduate*

★ The film *Catch-22*

1971

JAN 12 Rev. Philip F. Berrigan and five others indicted for conspiring to kidnap presidential advisor Henry Kissinger and bomb heating system of federal buildings in Washington, DC

12 Earth Act Group formed by Ralph Nadar

25 Supreme Court makes first decision on sex discrimination in hiring practices, ruling that businesses cannot deny employment to women with preschool children unless they apply same criteria to men

31 *Apollo 14* moon mission launched

FEB 8 South Vietnamese army aided by USAF launches attack on Laos

9 Earthquake in southern California kills 65 people and causes more than $500 million in damage

21 Tornadoes strike Louisiana, Mississippi and Tennessee, killing 93 and causing $10 million in damage

24 Supreme Court rules that illegally obtained evidence can be used to contradict defendant's voluntary testimony

MAR 1 Licensing of commercial whale hunters ordered halted

1 Capitol bombed by Weather Underground

15 Fourth round of SALT talks begins in Vienna, Austria

29 Lt William L. Calley, Jr, convicted of 1968 murder of 22 South Vietnamese civilians at My Lai

29 Charles Manson, Susan Atkins, Leslie Van Houten and Patricia Krenwinkel sentenced to death for 1969 Tate-La Bianca murders

APR 10-14 US table tennis team visits People's Republic of China

14 Twenty-one year trade embargo with People's Republic of China lifted

20 School busing as means of desegregation upheld by Supreme Court

23 Vietnam veterans return medals and military decorations in antiwar protest on steps of Capitol

24 Some 200,000 people attend antiwar demonstration in Washington, DC

MAY 1 Amtrak begins operation of intercity rail service

3 Mayday antiwar protest in Washington, DC

25 Supersonic transport program terminated

30 *Mariner 9* launched toward Mars

Vietnam: The Final Phase

The early years of the new decade saw a hardening of Nixon's and his military advisers' attitude toward the war in Vietnam. Determined to avoid further high American casualties, but equally determined to conclude a peace treaty on his own terms, Nixon pursued a policy of "Vietnamization," under which the burden of combat was progressively shifted toward South Vietnamese troops on the ground, with the U.S. providing military training and logistical support. This approach proved no more successful than direct American action had been in countering the Viet Cong, whose knowledge of the terrain and level of support in the villages of South Vietnam made it impossible to defeat them without inflicting massive casualties on the South Vietnamese civilian population. As the ineffectiveness of Vietnamization became increasingly apparent, Nixon decided this was a price he was prepared to pay. The early 1970s saw a vast escalation in American bombing, not only in the South but also in North Vietnam, Cambodia, and Laos. This rain of napalm and explosives (above) bludgeoned the North Vietnamese into a settlement in January 1973, but two years after the first American troops arrived home (right) North Vietnamese troops invaded the South in force. As they swept through the devastated countryside toward Saigon, Americans and Vietnamese alike began a panic evacuation from the major towns (opposite top). By the middle of 1975 South Vietnam was in Communist hands, and the aims for which America had fought for almost a decade had been entirely defeated.

Cambodia

Perhaps the most tragic casualty of the American intervention in Vietnam was the adjoining neutral nation of Cambodia. In 1970 Nixon launched an invasion of Cambodia, supported by heavy bombing, in an attempt to drive the North Vietnamese out of their bases inside the Cambodian border. In fact, it only forced them deeper into Cambodia itself, creating in the process a refugee problem of gigantic proportions as a million and more Cambodians fled to the cities from the border areas. The power vacuum which resulted from the ensuing economic chaos was filled in April 1975 by the hard-line Marxist régime of the Khmer Rouge, under its fanatical leader Pol Pot. In the years that followed, the Khmer Rouge turned Cambodia into a killing field (above), ruthlessly eliminating more than a quarter of their compatriots in their attempt to return the calender to Year Zero and the country to a laboring peasant economy.

JUN 11 Nineteen-month Indian occupation of Alcatraz Island off San Francisco ends

13 First installment of Pentagon Papers on Vietnam published in *New York Times*

28 State programs to underwrite nonreligious instruction in parochial schools ruled unconstitutional by Supreme Court

28 Dr Daniel Elsberg admits to delivering Pentagon Papers to *New York Times*

30 Twenty-sixth Amendment lowers voting age to 18

30 *New York Times* and *Washington Post* permitted to resume publication of Pentagon Papers on Vietnam

JUL 3 Death of rock singer Jim Morrison

6 Death of jazz singer and trumpeter Louis Armstrong

8 Fifth round of SALT talks in Helsinki, Finland

10-11 National Women's Political Caucus in Washington, DC, attended by over 200 women, seeks equal representation for women at all levels of political system

15 Future trip to China announced by Pres. Nixon

AUG 15 Ninety-day freeze on prices, wages and rents announced by the President

SEP 8 Kennedy Center opens in Washington, DC

9-13 Prison riot at Attica State Correctional Facility in New York results in deaths of 43 people

OCT 2 US calls for seating of People's Republic of China in UN

12 Future presidential trip to Moscow announced by Pres. Nixon

NOV 5 US announces sale of $136 million in feed grain to Soviets

12 US troop reduction of 45,000 from Vietnam announced

DEC 18 US devalues dollar by 8.57 percent to offset trade imbalance

26-30 Massive air bombardment of military installations in North Vietnam

1972

JAN 5 Space shuttle project approved by Pres. Nixon

13 Withdrawal of 70,000 American soldiers from Vietnam announced

25 Eight-point peace proposal to North Vietnamese and Vietcong made public

FEB 4 Sixth round of SALT talks begins in Vienna, Austria

5 Screening of passengers and luggage becomes mandatory on all domestic and foreign flights by US airlines

15 Atty Gen. John Mitchell resigns to become Chairman of Committee to Reelect the President

21-28 Pres. Nixon visits China

28 Murder trial of Black militant Angela Davis begins in San Jose, Calif.

MAR 17 Pres. Nixon proposes moratorium on busing

22 Equal Rights Amendment prohibiting discrimination on basis of sex passed by Senate and submitted to states

30 North Vietnamese troops launch massive attack against South Vietnam; US resumes bombing raids

APR 10 Treaty banning biological warfare signed by US and 120 other nations

MAY 2 Director of FBI J. Edgar Hoover dies

9 Mining of major North Vietnamese ports ordered by the President

15 Alabama Gov. George C. Wallace shot while campaigning in Maryland's Democratic primary

18 Gray Panthers, to combat discrimination against elderly, formed by Margaret Kuhn

22-30 First presidential visit to Moscow in history made by Pres. Nixon

26 US and USSR sign pact pledging nuclear freeze at current levels

JUN 8 Bill for federal aid to college and university students passed by Congress

12-17 Explo '72, youth fundamentalist conference at Cotton Bowl in Dallas, Tex., attended by 800,000

MASS PROTEST

Nixon's Vietnam policies, together with the Government's increasingly repressive approach to expressions of domestic dissent, raised the temperature of protest in the United States across a wide range of issues in the first half of the decade. The President, no doubt fearing that the country was on the verge of revolution, responded with unequivocal denunciation, hard-line police tactics, and widespread – and illegal – surveillance by the security forces, forcing many moderates to question the effectiveness of the democratic safeguards in the U.S. Constitution, and rendering the executive ever more remote from the apparent concerns of large sections of the population.

Right: The decade saw an upsurge in militancy by native American Indians, including, in 1975, the occupation of Wounded Knee by a group of Sioux, who were only evicted after two of their number had been killed by Federal agents. Here, a protestor gestures defiantly to the authorities after 500 Indians occupied the offices of the Bureau of Indian Affairs in Washington in November 1972, demanding recognition of Indian land rights.

Below: Opposition to the war became more and more vociferous after the invasion of Cambodia, with thousands of young Americans resisting the draft, many of them fleeing to Canada and Europe to escape the authorities. Here, a disabled Vietnam veteran joins anti-war protestors in a mass demonstration in Washington in April 1971.

Opposite: Environmental campaigners demonstrate against the level of pollution in New York City.

14 DDT ban announced by EPA

17 Five members of Committee to Reelect the President arrested at Democratic National Headquarters in Watergate complex for attempted burglary

19-29 Hurricane devastates Eastern Coast

29 State death penalties ruled unconstitutional, as cruel and unusual punishment, by Supreme Court

JUL 1 *Ms.* magazine launched, feminist leader Gloria Steinem editor

8 Nixon administration announces $750 million grain deal with Soviet Union

10-14 Democratic National Convention nominates George McGovern for President and Sen. Thomas F. Eagleton of Missouri for Vice President

11-SEP 1 Bobby Fischer wins world chess championship

AUG 1 Vice presidential nominee Thomas Eagleton announces withdrawal from race

3 Strategic arms treaty with Soviet Union ratified by Senate

12 Last US ground forces withdraw from Vietnam

21-23 Republican National Convention nominates Richard M. Nixon and Spiro T. Agnew for second terms

23 Some 1129 antiwar protestors arrested outside convention hall

26-SEP 11 At Summer Olympics, Munich, West Germany, US wins 33 gold medals; games suspended due to attack by Arab terrorists on Israeli team

SEP 14 Offensive weapons treaty with Soviet Union ratified by Senate

OCT 8 Sargent Shriver nominated Democratic vice presidential candidate

18 Water Pollution Control Act passed by Congress over President's veto

28 Consumer Product Safety Commission established

NOV 7 Richard M. Nixon and Spiro T. Agnew win election for second terms

13 International convention to control oceanic pollution signed by US and 90 other nations

22 Twenty-one year ban on travel to China lifted

DEC 7 *Apollo 17*, sixth and last lunar landing mission, launched

18 Full-scale bombing of North Vietnam resumed

29 *Life* magazine suspends publication after 36 years

31 EPA-ordered ban on DDT pesticide goes into effect

The Arts

★ Richard Bach's book *Jonathan Livingston Seagull*

★ Eudora Welty's novel *The Optimist's Daughter*

★ Neil Simon's play *The Sunshine Boys*

★ Ben Vereen in the musical *Pippin*

★ The film *The Exorcist*

1973

JAN 11 Pres. Nixon ends mandatory wage and price controls imposed in 1971

20 Richard M. Nixon and Spiro T. Agnew inaugurated for second terms

22 In *Roe v. Wade*, Supreme Court rules unconstitutional all state laws that prohibit voluntary abortions before third month of pregnancy

27 Vietnam peace agreement signed in Paris by Henry Kissinger, representatives of North and South Vietnam and Vietcong; requires cease-fire and withdrawal of US forces within sixty days

27 Draft ends

30 James W. McCord and G. Gordon Liddy convicted of breaking into and illegally wiretapping Democratic Party headquarters in 1972

FEB 7 Senate Select Committee on Presidential Campaign Activities established to investigate Watergate conspiracy

12 Dollar devalued 10 percent to improve foreign trade balance

28 Wounded Knee, S. Dak., occupied by militant members of American Indian Movement

MAR 25 Death of photographer Edward Steichen

Terrorism

The 1970s were the decade of international terrorism, with groups such as the Baader-Meinhof Gang in Germany, the I.R.A. in Ireland, and the various P.L.O. splinter movements establishing supply and training links across national boundaries. Bombings, hi-jacking of aircraft, and hostage-taking became common, with Americans and Israelis often being singled out by Palestinian terrorist groups. In September 1970, for example, Arab gunmen hi-jacked three British, Swiss, and American airliners and flew them to Dawson's Field, a desert airstrip near Amman in Jordan, where they held their 300 passengers hostage. After days of negotiation, the hostages were finally released in exchange for seven Arab detainees and the planes were blown up on the ground (below).

The difficulty of dealing effectively with this insidious new threat was tragically demonstrated the following year when Arab guerrillas struck again, this time at the Olympic Games in Munich (right). Just before dawn on September 5, eight hooded gunmen burst into the dormitory occupied by the Israeli athletics team, shot two people dead, and took nine others hostage, threatening to kill them unless 200 Arab guerrillas were released. The German authorities agreed to take the terrorists and their hostages to Fürstenfeldbruck military airfield where a Lufthansa airliner was waiting on the tarmac to fly them out of the country. There they were ambushed by German marksmen, but in the ensuing gun battle all nine hostages were killed by their captors.

The Chicago Seven

In February 1970, defendants at the so-called Chicago Seven trial – including Abbie Hoffman, Rennie Davis, and Jerry Rubin (from left to right above) – were cleared of conspiring to incite a riot during the 1968 Democratic Convention, but were given prison sentences for related offenses.

Patty Hearst

One of the most famous images of the 1970s was this CCTV picture of the newspaper heiress Patty Hearst, taken during an armed bank raid in San Francisco in April 1974. Hearst's whereabouts had been unknown since a revolutionary group had kidnapped her in February the same year.

APR 11 Mississippi River floods affect nine states

20 FBI director Patrick E. Gray resigns after admitting he destroyed Watergate evidence

30 Presidential Chief of Staff H.R. Haldeman, Presidential Counsel John Dean, and domestic affairs assistant John Erlichman resign, and Atty Gen. Richard Kleindienst submits resignation

30 Pres. Nixon makes public broadcast announcing resignations and denying involvement in break-in or knowledge of cover-up

MAY 3 Sears Tower in Chicago is world's tallest building

10 Former Cabinet members John Mitchell and Maurice Stans and financier Robert Vesco indicted in connection with illegal contribution of $200,000 to Pres. Nixon's reelection campaign

11 Charges against Daniel Ellsberg and Anthon J. Russo for theft and circulation of Pentagon Papers dismissed

14 *Skylab,* first US space station, launched into orbit

17 Senate Select Committee on Presidential Campaign Activities opens public hearings on Watergate affair

25 Archibald Cox sworn in as special Watergate prosecutor

JUN 13 Price freeze on retail goods announced by the President

16-25 USSR Party Secy Leonard Brezhnev visits US

21 Supreme Court declares that local community standards may be applied to suppression of pornography

24 Brezhnev addresses US in television broadcast

25 Former Presidential Counsel John Dean charges Pres. Nixon with authorizing payment of hush money to seven men accused of Watergate burglary

JUL 20 Pentagon officials admit that they gave Senate Armed Forces Committee false reports about 1969 and 1970 secret bombing raids into Cambodia

23 Senate panel subpoenas Watergate tapes

AUG 6 Vice Pres. Agnew reveals that he is currently under investigation by Justice Department for receiving kickbacks while serving as Baltimore County Executive and Governor of Maryland

14 Two Houston teenagers indicted for abuse and killings of 27 people over three-year period

14 Bombing raids into Cambodian territory halted

SEP 1 New York State enacts nation's toughest drug law

4 John Ehrlichman and G. Gordon Liddy indicted in connection with burglary of office of Daniel Ellsberg's psychiatrist in 1971

6 Former UMW president W. A. 'Tony' Boyle indicted on charges of ordering 1961 murders of labor dissident Joseph L. Yablonski and his wife and daughter

22 Henry Kissinger becomes Secretary of State

22 Dallas-Fort Worth Airport dedicated

28 Death of poet W. H. Auden

OCT 6 Yom Kippur War in Middle East begins

10 Vice Pres. Agnew resigns and pleads 'no contest' to a charge of tax evasion; receives fine and three years' probation

12 Rep. Gerald R. Ford, Republican of Michigan, nominated by Pres. Nixon for Vice President

15 Military aid to Israel announced by US

16 Maynard Jackson wins election in Atlanta, becoming first Black mayor of major southern city

16 Secy of State Kissinger and Le Duc Tho of North Vietnam receive Nobel Peace Prize; Tho declines

17 Oil embargo by 11 Middle Eastern states begins

20 Saturday Night Massacre: special Watergate prosecutor Archibald Cox fired; others resign

22 US and USSR sponsor UN resolution calling for cease-fire in Middle East

23 Eight impeachment resolutions introduced in House; Pres. Nixon agrees to release tapes

NOV 3 *Mariner 10* Mercury probe launched

7 War Powers Act, requiring congressional approval for commitment of US forces in combat abroad longer than 60 days, passed by Congress over President's veto

9 Six Watergate defendants sentenced

13 Executives of Gulf Oil and Ashland Oil companies plead guilty to illegal campaign contributions to Nixon reelection committee

16 Alaska Pipeline Bill signed by the President

Nixon Abroad

Nixon's achievements in the direction of East-West détente have been overshadowed by the Vietnam War and Watergate. In February 1972 he and Dr. Henry Kissinger flew to China for what were described as "serious and frank" talks with the Chinese leader Chairman Mao Tse-tung, aimed at normalizing relations between the two countries. During the week-long visit the President also attended a banquet for 700 people in the Great Hall of the People in Peking and visited the Great Wall with his wife (top).

Three months later Nixon was in the Soviet Union, meeting the Soviet leader Leonid Brezhnev to sign the SALT Treaty – which limited the development of nuclear weapons systems in both countries – and heralding what he called "a new age in the relationship between our two great and powerful nations" (above).

21 Watergate tape reveals 18-minute gap

27 Pres. Nixon's personal secretary Rosemary Woods claims to have caused five minutes of erasure of tape

DEC 6 Gerald R. Ford sworn in as Vice President

11 Most-favored-nation status denied USSR due to emigration restrictions

15 American Psychiatric Association asserts that homosexuality is not a mental illness

The Arts

★ Thomas Pynchon's novel *Gravity's Rainbow*

★ Lanford Wilson's play *Hot L Baltimore*

★ Hugh Wheeler and Stephen Sondheim's musical *A Little Night Music*

★ Stevie Wonder's record album *Inner Visions*

1974

JAN 4 Pres. Nixon refuses to surrender tapes and documents subpoenaed by Senate Watergate Committee

15 Expert states that 18-minute gap in critical White House tape was caused by deliberate erasure

30 In State of the Union address, Pres. Nixon states that he will not resign

FEB 4 Patricia Hearst, granddaughter of William Randolph Hearst, is kidnapped from her Berkeley, Calif., apartment by Symbionese Liberation Army

8 *Skylab 3*, last of NASA projects to test humans' ability to live and work in space, returns to Earth

12 SLA demands that Randolph Hearst begins program of food distribution to the poor

MAR 18 Arab oil embargo against US lifted

APR 3 Pres. Nixon announces he will pay $465,000 in back taxes

3-4 Tornadoes strike from Georgia north to Canada, killing 350

15 Patricia Hearst participates in bank robbery

MAY 2 Former Vice Pres. Spiro T. Agnew disbarred in Maryland

17 SLA shootout in Los Angeles

JUN 12 Pres. Nixon begins week-long tour of Middle East

27 Pres. Nixon visits Soviet Union for five days of summit talks

JUL 18 Independent legal services corporation established by Congress to provide legal aid to the poor

24 Supreme Court orders Pres. Nixon to turn over tapes subpoenaed by Special Prosecutor Leon Jaworski

29 First women Episcopal priests ordained in Philadelphia

30 Two articles of impeachment voted against Pres. Nixon by House Judiciary Committee

AUG 5 Pres. Nixon releases tape transcripts revealing that he has impeded Watergate investigation

8 Pres. Nixon announces his resignation in televised address

9 Gerald R. Ford sworn in as President

20 Nelson A. Rockefeller, former Governor of New York, nominated for Vice President by Pres. Ford

SEP 4 Diplomatic relations with East Germany established by US

7 CIA covert operations against Chile's Marxist government disclosed

8 Pres. Nixon pardoned by Pres. Ford for any crimes he may have committed or participated in while in office

12 Violent protests erupt at South Boston High School on first day of court-ordered busing

16 Conditional pardon for draft evaders and military deserters announced by the President

17 Senate Foreign Relations Committee orders investigation into alleged CIA overthrow of Chilean Pres. Salvador Allende Gossens

OCT 8 Franklin National Bank of New York declared insolved; biggest bank failure in US history

10 Commodity Futures Trading Commission established

15 Campaign reform law provides public funding for presidential primary and elections and sets limits on spending for presidential and congressional campaigns

Busing

Tempers flared in the early 1970s over the question of the racial desegregation of schools, which had been ordered by a Supreme Court decision in 1969, and in particular over the contentious issue of "busing" – i.e. transporting Black pupils into areas with predominantly white schools and vice versa. The Government appeared to vacillate between enforcement of desegregation and appeasement of segregationist Southern interests, with Nixon seeming to throw his weight behind the anti-busing lobby.
Above: Police move in to break up racial disturbances in Boston during the busing dispute. Below: Parents in Brooklyn, New York, make clear their opposition to enforced busing.

Watergate

Throughout the latter part of 1973 and the first half of 1974, the American people watched with horror and disbelief as evidence mounted of the scale of the Nixon administration's involvement in corruption and malpractice during the 1972 election campaign and in the cover-up operations which followed the break-in at the Watergate Building.

Opposite bottom: Where it all began: The headquarters of the Democratic National Committee in the Watergate Complex in Washington, D.C.

Near right: "Tricky Dicky": By May 1973 some newspapers, such as the one in which this cartoon appeared, were already casting serious doubt on the President's denials of involvement in what was fast becoming the scandal of the decade.

Opposite top: Carl Bernstein (left) and Robert Woodward, whose dogged researches into the story behind the Watergate break-in and the activities of the Committee to Reelect the President did much to keep the story

in the public eye and to ferret out the whole disturbing truth. Their paper, the *Washington Post*, was awarded a Pulitzer Prize for their work.

Below right: A secret serviceman arrives at the U.S. District Court in Washington with a metal suitcase containing White House tapes for delivery to U.S. District Judge John Sirica. Convenient gaps in the tapes released by the White House still further discredited the President in the eyes of the American public.

Below left: "No whitewash at the White House ..." Nixon appeared on television on a number of occasions during the Watergate affair to protest his ignorance and innocence of what had been happening in his name. His disavowals fell on increasingly skeptical ears, and, with impeachment staring him in the face, his last appearance before the TV cameras was to deliver his resignation address.

Opposite middle: All the President's men: Nixon's fall was swiftly followed by the conviction on conspiracy charges of some of his closest White House aides.

NOV 5 Democrats increase majorities in both houses of Congress

5 Ella Grasso of Connecticut becomes first elected woman governor

21 Freedom of Information Act passed by Congress over Pres. Ford's veto

23-24 Pres. Ford and Secy Leonard Brezhnev meet in Vladivostok and sign tentative agreement limiting offensive weapons

DEC 19 Nelson A. Rockefeller sworn in as Vice President

21 *New York Times* reports illegal domestic activities of CIA during Vietnam War years

Also this year
★ Victor Marchetti and John D. Marks' *The CIA and the Cult of Intelligence* published

★ Carl Bernstein and Robert Woodward's *All the President's Men* published

1975

JAN 1 John Erlichman, H. R. Haldeman, Robert C. Mardian and John Mitchell convicted of obstructing Watergate investigation

5 Commission on CIA domestic activities appointed by the President to investigate allegations of illegal domestic activity

FEB 14 Northern Marianas become US commonwealth

MAR 17-20 Doctors strike in NYC

APR 4 US transport plane crashes shortly after takeoff from Saigon, South Vietnam, killing 200 refugees

30 US completes evacuation of South Vietnam as Saigon surrenders to Communists

MAY 14 Military operation to recover US merchant ship *Mayaguez*, seized by Khmer Rouge of Cambodia, ordered by the President

JUN 4 Discovery of 620 million year-old marine worms reported by paleontologists in North Carolina

10 Domestic CIA activities violating agency's charter disclosed by Rockefeller Commission

14 Allegations of FBI burglaries and break-ins confirmed by agency director Clarence B. Kelley

JUL 8 Pres. Ford announces candidacy for Republican presidential nomination

15 Apollo-Soyuz space mission begins

28 Voting Rights Act of 1965 extended for seven years

31 Former Teamsters president James R. Hoffa reported missing

AUG 1 Charter of Conference on Security and Cooperation in Europe signed by US and 34 other nations

SEP 5 Assassination attempt against Pres. Ford by Lynette A. 'Squeaky' Fromme

18 Patricia Hearst captured by police in San Francisco

22 Assassination attempt against Pres. Ford by Sara Jane Moore

28 Admission of women to US military academies authorized by Congress

NOV 10 Parents of Karen Anne Quinlan, comatose for seven months, lose bid in NJ Superior Court to have life-support system turned off

20 Bipartisan Senate investigating committee charges CIA and FBI with illegal surveillance of US citizens and with plotting to assassinate foreign leaders

DEC 4 CIA cleared of allegations of direct participation in 1973 overthrow of Chilean government

5 Pres. Ford concludes five-day tour of Far East

6 Creation of first artificial animal gene reported by Harvard scientists

The Arts
★ E. L. Doctorow's novel *Ragtime*

★ The musical *A Chorus Line*

★ Robert Altman's film *Nashville*

★ Jack Nicholson in the film *One Flew Over the Cuckoo's Nest*

★ Steven Spielberg's film *Jaws*

| *H. R. Haldeman* | *John Mitchell* | *John Ehrlichman* | *Robert Mardian* |

The Middle East

American foreign policy in the closing years of the decade was dominated by developments in the Middle East, where the instability that had made the region a political powderkeg for so many years was dangerously heightened by events in Afghanistan and Iran. The revolution in Afghanistan, and the subsequent Soviet invasion in support of the new pro-Communist Government there in 1979, added a new source of East-West tension to the political map; while in Iran, in the same year, the flight of the U.S.-backed Shah and the return of the Ayatollah Khomeini from exile led to a sharp deterioration in relations between the Iranian and U.S. Governments as Iran demanded the return of the Shah from the United States to face trial (inset). The taking hostage of the staff of the U.S. embassy in Tehran in support of this demand caused outrage at home (right) and provided President Carter with one of his most intractable diplomatic problems.

Meanwhile, the tensions between Israel and her Arab neighbors, which had led to military confrontations throughout the 1960s and 1970s (below), were eased somewhat by Carter's notable success in mediating between Israel's premier Menachem Begin and Egypt's President Anwar el-Sadat. The signing of a peace treaty by the two leaders in Washington in March 1979 was a diplomatic triumph for the U.S. President (far right) and led to a Nobel Peace Prize for Begin and Sadat.

1976

JAN 30 Supreme Court rules that federally imposed limits on campaign spending violate First Amendment

FEB 12 Production of Red Dye No. 2 banned

17 Reform of US intelligence organizations announced by Pres. Ford

25 ER America begins operations in Washington, DC

MAR 26 Supreme Court upholds ruling allowing states to outlaw homosexual acts

26 Four-year US-Turkish military pact signed

APR 5 Death of reclusive billionaire Howard Hughes

21 Production of convertible by US auto industry halted

22 West Point cheating scandal reported

22 Barbara Walters becomes first anchorwoman of network television news program

MAY 24 Concorde supersonic jet service between US and Europe inaugurated

28 Nuclear test pact signed by US and USSR

JUN 16 UN Ambassador to Lebanon Francis E. Melroy, Jr, and aide assassinated

JUL 2 Supreme Court upholds death penalty

4 Bicentennial celebration

14-15 Democratic National Convention nominates Jimmy Carter for President and Sen. Walter F. Mondale of Minnesota for Vice President

19 Republican National Convention nominates Gerald Ford for President and Sen Robert J. Dole of Kansas for Vice President

20 *Viking 1* lands on Mars

20 Last US forces in Thailand withdrawn

27 Some 160 Americans evacuated from Beirut, Lebanon

27-AUG 31 Legionnaires' disease claims lives of 29 people

SEP 1 Rep. Wayne L. Hays of Ohio resigns in shadow of investigation of sexual liaison with former employee, Elizabeth Ray

10-12 TWA 727 hijacked to Paris by Croatian terrorists

18 Some 50,000 people attend 'God Bless America' rally sponsored by Sun-myung Moon's Unification Church in Washington, DC

OCT 20 Koreagate investigation announced by Justice Department

NOV 2 James Earl Carter elected President, Walter F. Mondale elected Vice President

18 Death of artist Man Ray

DEC 15 Major oil spill near Nantucket, Mass.

20 Death of Mayor Richard Daley of Chicago

The Arts

★ Philip Glass and Robert Wilson's opera *Einstein on the Beach*

★ Ntozake Shange's play *For Colored Girls Who Have Considered Suicide/When the Rainbow is Enuf*

★ Robert De Niro in the film *Taxi Driver*

★ Peter Finch and Faye Dunaway in the film *Network*

1977

JAN 1 First woman Episcopal priest in US, Jacqueline Means, ordained

17 Mark Gary Gilmore becomes first prisoner to be executed in 10 years

19 Tokyo Rose pardoned by Pres. Carter

20 Jimmy Carter inaugurated President, Walter F. Mondale inaugurated Vice President

21 Pres. Carter grants unconditional pardon to almost all Vietnam War draft evaders

28-29 Blizzard paralyzes East and Midwest

MAR 18 US travel restrictions to Cuba, Cambodia, Vietnam and North Korea lifted

APR 28 Christopher J. Boyce convicted of supplying data on satellites and CIA codes to Soviet Union

"Say Hey"

1973 saw the retirement from professional baseball of the great Black all-rounder Willie Howard Mays Junior (known to an affectionate public as "Say Hey" Willie Mays). One of the great outfielders of the game, Mays (above) was also a brilliant hitter and base-stealer, winning the National League's home-run title in 1955, 1962, 1964, and 1965. Born in Fairfield, Alabama, in 1931, he began his professional career at the age of 17, playing for the Black Barons in the Negro National League, but in 1951 he hit the big time with his first appearance for the New York Giants, whom he led out of the doldrums to win the world championship three years later. Mays, who won the most valuable player award in 1954 and 1965, spent the last two years of his career with the New York Mets.

Basketball

That other quintessentially American sport, basketball, continued to be big business in the 1970s, attracting audiences of millions of people. Among the most popular sides were the Boston Celtics and the Original Celtics of New York City, but few teams caught the public imagination as completely as the Harlem Globetrotters (right). Touring independently of the major leagues, the Globetrotters held spectators spellbound throughout the world with their combination of skill, theatricality, and sheer physical stature.

Cults

Concern about the power of religious and quasi-religious cults in the United States was heightened in the late 1970s by allegations of brainwashing against the Reverent Sun-myung Moon (seen above officiating at a mass wedding in Seoul) and his Unification Church – popularly known as the Moonies – and by the horrific mass-suicide of followers of the Reverend Jim Jones, more than 900 of whom were found dead after drinking cyanide at the People's Temple, Jonestown, in Guyana in November 1978 (top).

30-MAY 2 Some 2000 members of Clamshell Alliance occupy construction site of nuclear reactor in Seabrook, NH, some 1400 protestors arrested

MAY 3 US and Vietnam begin talks in Paris to normalize relations

10 Death of actress Joan Crawford

28 Fire at Beverly Hills Supper Club in Southgate, Ky, kills 164 people

JUN 6 Development of neutron bomb by US reported in *Washington Post*

20 Medicaid funding for abortions ruled not obligatory by Supreme Court

29 Robert Hall, nation's largest retail clothing chain, closes

JUL 1 Water rationing instituted in Los Angeles, Calif., during severe drought

13 Blackout occurs in NYC and parts of Westchester County after electrical storm

19 Flooding in Johnstown, Pa, kills 76 and causes $200 million in property damage

28 Trans-Alaska pipeline goes into operation

AUG 4 Department of Energy established

10 David Berkowitz arrested in Son of Sam murder case

12 Space shuttle *Enterprise* completes first test flight

16 Death of singer Elvis Presley

SEP 7 Panama Canal treaties, transferring control of Canal Zone and Canal to Panama by year 2000 signed

NOV 13 Final installment of *L'il Abner* comic strip, created by Al Capp

18-21 First National Women's Conference draws 1442 delegates to Houston, Tex., to call for passage of ERA and elimination of institutional discrimination

The Arts

★ David Mamet's play *American Buffalo*

★ George Lucas' film *Star Wars*

★ Steven Spielberg's film *Close Encounters of the Third Kind*

1978

JAN 25-26 Blizzard strikes Midwest, killing about 100 people

FEB 5-7 Blizzard in New England kills 60 people

8 Egyptian Pres. Anwar el-Sadat begins six-day visit to US

MAR 15 More than 1000 striking farmers hold rally in Washington, DC, and release 73 goats at steps of Capitol to protest proposed farm legislation

16 Panama Canal treaty ratified by Senate

25 Longest coal miners' strike in nation's history ends after 110 days

APR 6 Retirement age bill gives most workers option of retiring at age 70

18 Second Panama Canal treaty ratified by Senate

MAY 20 *Pioneer Venus 1* launched toward Venus

JUN 6 Proposition 13, California constitutional amendment to reduce property taxes, approved by 65 percent of California voters

15 Tellico Dam project in Tennessee halted to protect snail darter protected by Endangered Species Act of 1973

28 In *Bakke v. University of California*, Supreme Court declares strict racial quotas illegal

JUL 6-10 US scientific delegation visits People's Republic of China to promote scientific and technological exchanges

15 American Indian Movement leads 2700-mile march from Alcatraz Island, Calif., to Capitol steps in Washington, DC, to protest legislation depriving Indians of land rights

AUG 9 NYC newspaper strike, lasting 88 days, begins

SEP 12 Middle East Peace Conference at Camp David attended by Pres. Carter, Egyptian Pres. Anwar el-Sadat and Israeli PM Menachem Begin

Three Mile Island

America's worst nuclear accident happened at a power station on Three Mile Island in Harrisburg, Pennsylvania, in 1979. Radioactivity was released into the atmosphere and the adjacent River Susquehanna when the uranium core of one of the pressurized water reactors overheated in the early hours of March 28. Thousands of people left their homes in the surrounding area as radiation inside the reactor building reached levels of 75 times higher than those required to kill a human being. A subsequent inquiry criticized the National Regulatory Commission for its handling of the crisis.

Top: The four cooling towers of the Three Mile Island nuclear power plant, during the shutdown. Above: More than 65,000 people converged on Washington in the aftermath of the disaster, shouting "No more Harrisburgs" and demanding a reduction in U.S. reliance on nuclear energy. Right: Almost a year after the disaster, these technicians, checking for radioactivity, became the first people to enter the airlock leading to the damaged reactor at Three Mile Island.

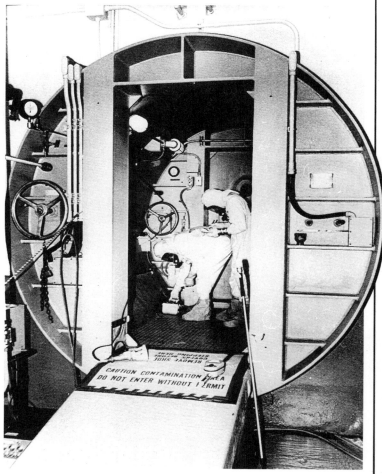

Watergate Revisited

National trauma becomes entertainment: Dustin Hoffman as Carl Bernstein and Robert Redford as Bob Woodward in Alan J. Pakula's suspenseful 1976 film of the events following the Watergate break-in, *All the President's Men*.

The Godfather

Marlon Brando adds padding to the Method as he passes the succession to Al Pacino in Francis Ford Coppola's violent 1972 blockbuster of the New York Mafia, *The Godfather*.

Henry Kissinger

One of the great influences on U.S. foreign policy, as National Security Advisor and Secretary of State to Presidents Nixon and Ford, Henry Kissinger was awarded the Nobel Peace Prize in 1973.

OCT 6 Deadline for ratification of ERA extended to June 1982

6 Hannah H. Gray becomes first woman university president in US, at University of Chicago

20 Worst week in Wall Street history ends

NOV 9 Death of artist Norman Rockwell

18 Rep. Leo Ryan of California and others murdered near Jonestown, Guyana, by members of American religious sect, People's Temple; leads to mass suicide of 911 cult members

27 Mayor George Moscone and city supervisor Harvey Milk of San Francisco shot to death in City Hall by former supervisor Dan White

DEC 16 Cleveland, Ohio, becomes first American city to default since depression

The Arts

★ John Irving's novel *The World According to Garp*

★ The musical *Ain't Misbehavin'*

★ The film *Saturday Night Fever*

1979

JAN 1 US opens diplomatic relations with China and severs relations with Taiwan

12 Midwest blizzard kills 100

FEB 1 Newspaper heiress Patricia Hearst released from jail

5 Protesting farmers drive tractors, trucks and campers into Washington, DC, and cause massive traffic jam

8 Severing of military ties with Nicaragua announced

14 US ambassador to Afghanistan kidnapped and killed in Kabul

MAR 26 Egyptian-Israeli peace treaty signed in Washington, DC

28 Major nuclear accident occurs at Three Mile Island, near Harrisburg, Pa

MAY 25 DC-10 crashes after takeoff from Chicago's O'Hare Airport, killing 273 people

29 Death of actress Mary Pickford

JUN 7 MX missile system approved by Pres. Carter

13 Sioux nation granted $17.5 million in land claim suit involving area of Black Hills, S. Dak.

18 SALT 2 signed in Vienna, Austria, by Pres. Carter and Soviet Pres. Leonid Brezhnev

JUL 11 *Skylab* breaks up upon reentering Earth's atmosphere over Indian Ocean and Australia

SEP 23 Nuclear weapons protest draws 200,000 to NYC

OCT 17 Department of Education established

NOV 3 Shootout in Greensboro, NC, between KKK members and participants in anti-Klan rally leaves five demonstrators dead and eight wounded

4 US embassy in Iran seized by Iranian revolutionaries, taking 53 American hostages

13 Ronald W. Reagan, former president of Screen Actors Guild and former Governor of California, announces candidacy for Republican presidential nomination

15 George Meany retires as head of AFL-CIO

21 US embassy in Islamabad, Pakistan, besieged

DEC 2 US embassy in Tripoli, Libya, attacked by mob

3 Eleven youths trampled to death at rock concert in Cincinnati, Ohio

21 Senate approves federal bailout for Chrysler Corporation

The Arts

★ Norman Mailer's novel *The Executioner's Song*

★ Bernard Pomerance's play *The Elephant Man*

★ Mark Medoff's play *Children of a Lesser God*

IN THE perspective of history, the 1980s may come to be seen as a pivotal decade, not only in the story of the United States, but in the whole relationship between the Eastern and Western power blocs. In America the presidency of Ronald Reagan, for all its controversies, was seen by many as the beginning of a long delayed healing process after the traumas of Vietnam and Watergate. In the wider world, the advent of Mikhail Gorbachev in the Soviet Union finally brought to an end the sterile conservatism of the Brezhnev years and launched a new era of openness and reconstruction in both domestic and international affairs. East-West relations, plunged back into the deadlock of the Cold War by the Soviet invasion of Afghanistan in 1979, became warmer than at any time since the end of the Second World War as the leaders of the two superpowers cast aside the rhetoric of confrontation in favor of handshakes and fireside chats at summits in Geneva, Reykjavik, Washington, Moscow, and Malta. Far-reaching arms agreements led to a reduction of both the American and the Soviet military presence in Europe, while the perceived threat of nuclear war, under which international relations had been conducted for more than a generation, seemed for the first time to recede into the middle distance.

Perhaps most momentous of all were the events of the closing months of the decade. The world watched in astonishment as, one after another, the entrenched Communist régimes of the Eastern European satellite states unraveled in the face of unprecedented popular protest until, in November 1989, that most potent symbol of the Cold War, the Berlin Wall itself, was finally torn down amid emotional scenes of reconciliation and reunion. What years of diplomacy and saber-rattling had failed to achieve seemed suddenly within grasp as a result of the spontaneous concerted action of ordinary people. A democratic revolution seemed poised to sweep through the heartland of the Warsaw Pact. After years of tension and mutual distrust, a new age seemed about to begin.

The Hostage Crisis

All American eyes were trained on Iran as 1980 began. Despite a flurry of diplomatic activity, the 53 American hostages were still held in the U.S. embassy in Teheran, and on April 7 President Carter broke off diplomatic relations with the régime of Ayatollah Khomeini and imposed economic sanctions on Iran. Then, on April 24, he launched a daring raid to release the hostages by force.

The operation was a catastrophe. The task force of anti-terrorist commandos was forced to land in a remote desert area in Eastern Iran when three of their helicopters developed faults. Deciding to abandon the rescue attempt, they refueled for take-off, but in the process one of the helicopters collided with a transport plane, killing eight people. The rest of the team flew out, leaving the desert sands littered with the burnt-out remains of their planes and the bodies of their colleagues. In Iran, reaction to the failure of the raid was jubilant, with crowds chanting and cheering in the streets. In a display of medieval barbarity, the remains of the dead men were put on show and mutilated at a press conference in Teheran. The whole fiasco was a heavy blow to American pride and to Jimmy Carter's already fragile reputation.

Enter Reagan

The election of 1980 marked the end of Jimmy Carter's presidential career. His Republican opponent, the 68-year-old former movie actor and Governor of California, Ronald Reagan, was a charismatic right-winger who made much of the need to restore America's tarnished reputation in the world. With Carter personally identified with the humiliation of the hostage crisis – polling day marked the beginning of the hostages' second year in captivity – and with the economy locked in an apparently endless spiral of inflation and unemployment, Reagan began to gain ground in the closing days of the campaign. The result, when the votes were counted, was an even

Jimmy Carter watches from the wings as President Reagan is sworn in.

1980s

"Star Wars?" Reagan's Strategic Defense Initiative (SDI) and equivalent Soviet research threatened an arms race in space.

more resounding victory for him than had been expected. With 43.9 million popular votes to Carter's 35.5 million, Reagan won 489 electoral votes to Carter's 49. Even in the South, only Carter's state of Georgia remained loyal to the sitting President.

On January 21, 1981, the day after the new President's inauguration, the 52 remaining hostages disembarked onto the tarmac of Rhein-Main Air Base in West Germany. They were greeted by ex-President Carter, to whose unremitting diplomatic efforts they owed their release, but it was Ronald Reagan who gained the glory. Two months later, the nation rallied still more wholeheartedly to his side when Reagan showed remarkable courage and sang-froid in the face of a bizarre assassination attempt in Washington. Economic problems persisted, but Reagan's personal popularity seemed set to survive them.

The International Scene

Despite the impact of Reagan's economic policies, which combined to reduce Government expenditure on social welfare services with a massive increase in defense spending and led to a budget deficit of record proportions in the 1980s, domestic affairs were largely overshadowed by epoch-making events on the world stage during his two terms of office – events which were to accelerate to a dizzying pace during the first year of George Bush's administration. From the outset, Ronald Reagan adopted the rhetoric of the Cold War, labeling the Soviet Union "the Evil Empire" and intervening both

covertly and openly in Central America to counter the perceived threat of Marxism in America's "backyard." At the same time, he launched what many saw as a new and very highly dangerous phase in the arms race with the Strategic Defense Initiative, popularly (if chillingly) known as "Star Wars." In the Middle East the Iran-Iraq war provided a permanent bloody backdrop to the regional tensions inherent in the Arab-Israeli conflict, with both confrontations threatening to escalate into wider clashes under the spur of international terrorism. With Reagan's reelection by a landslide in 1984, and with the dead hand of Brezhnev still guiding the Soviet Union under his successors, Andropov and Chernenko, the world seemed destined for a further prolonged period of international tension.

"A fresh start"

On March 10, 1985, however, the ailing Soviet leader, Konstantin Chernenko, died, to be succeeded as General-Secretary of the Communist Party by the 54-year-old Mikhail Gorbachev. The youngest member of Chernenko's Politburo, Gorbachev brought with him an astonishingly fresh approach to the domestic and international problems of the Soviet Union, not least in admitting that they existed. *Perestroika* – reconstruction – and *glasnost* – openness – became the watchwords of a far-reaching crusade for economic revitalization and for freedom from the ideological and bureaucratic shackles of the Brezhnev era.

The effects of Gorbachev's succession on East-West relations were not slow in making themselves felt. On November 20, 1985, Reagan and Gorbachev met for the first time in Geneva for the first U.S.-Soviet summit since President Carter met Leonid Brezhnev

1980

JAN 4 Pres. Carter announces measures to protest Soviet invasion of Afghanistan

24 Pres. Carter announces US willingness to sell weapons to China

25 Labor statistics reveal that 1979 inflation rate was highest in 33 years

29 Escape of six Americans from Iran with aid of Canadian embassy personnel revealed

FEB 3 Details of Abscam FBI investigation into corruption of public officials released

2-3 Prison riot at Santa Fe, NM, state prison leaves 33 inmates dead, and 89 injured

MAR 15 Pinobscat Indian tribe in Maine accepts $81.5 million settlement for land taken from it in violation of Indian Non-Intercourse Act of 1790

17 Refugee Act of 1980 broadens definition of term 'refugee' to include people from any part of world

13 Ford Motor Company acquitted of reckless homicide in Ford Pinto case

31 Bank deregulation bill raises interest rate ceiling for small depositors, permits interest on checking accounts and raises limit on federally insured accounts

APR 2 Crude Oil Windfall Profits Tax Act signed by Pres. Carter

7 US severs diplomatic relations with Iran

11 Equal Opportunity Commission issues regulations prohibiting sexual harassment of women by superiors in government or business

24 US hostage military rescue mission in Iran ends as three helicopters fail and one crashes

24 Rep. John Anderson, Republican of Illinois, announces independent candidacy for President

26 Secretary of State Cyrus Vance resigns, succeeded by Sen. Edmund Muskie of Maine

29 Washington for Jesus rally draws 200,000 evangelical Christians

MAY 5 Exxon named as largest US corporation by *Fortune* magazine

9 Freighter *Summit Venture* rams Sunshine Skyway Bridge over Tampa Bay, Fla, killing some 35 people

17-19 Race riots in Miami Fla, leave 18 dead, and 400 injured

18 Eruption of Mt St Helens in south western Washington State kills some 26 people

JUN 16 Supreme Court rules that laboratory organisms can be patented

in Vienna in 1979. The three-day meeting produced no striking new initiatives, but was widely seen as reducing international tensions. The world's television cameras captured a remarkable degree of personal rapport between the two leaders, who spent two hours in private talks, accompanied only by their interpreters, in the Fleur d'Eau villa on the shores of Lake Geneva – a conversation which immediately entered the folklore of East-West meetings as "the fireside chat." While crucial differences between the two countries remained – not least over the "Star Wars" program and such regional conflicts as the Sandinista-Contra war in Nicaragua – both leaders pledged their administrations to work for peace and the reduction of nuclear arsenals. President Reagan encapsulated the new mood of co-operation when he spoke of "a fresh start" in East-West relations.

East Meets West

Geneva was the first of a series of summit conferences which punctuated the 1980s, keeping the lines of communication open between the United States and the Soviet Union and also serving to sustain mutual confidence in the face of such potentially destabilizing incidents as the Palestinian terrorist attack on the *Achille Lauro* (in which a disabled American citizen was murdered in October 1985) and the U.S. airstrike against Colonel Gadaffi's Libya in April 1986. In October 1986 the two leaders met again, this time at Reykjavik in Iceland, for what was described as a mini-summit. Here, too, there were private talks and, despite a complete news blackout, rumors of a major new agreement on arms control. President Reagan's firm commitment to the Strategic Defense Initiative once again proved a serious sticking-point, and the Reykjavik meeting broke up without the significant progress that had been hoped for, but in December 1987 Gorbachev flew to Washington for another summit meeting at which the finishing touches were put to the agreement which had proved so elusive at Reykjavik. On December 8, Reagan and Gorbachev signed the INF treaty, the first agreement ever to eliminate an entire category of offensive nuclear weapons. Further agreements on arms control, human rights, and regional issues were concluded on the American President's return visit to Moscow in 1988, and a major bone of contention between the superpowers was removed in 1989, shortly after George Bush's inauguration as the 41st President of the United States, when Soviet troops finally withdrew from Afghanistan. (In one of the most telling symbols of the change in the atmosphere between the superpowers during this extraordinary decade, American Vietnam veterans flew to the U.S.S.R. to counsel Soviet veterans of Afghanistan and help them come to terms with their parallel experience of the horrors of war.) President Bush picked up the threads of personal contact by meeting the Soviet leader in Malta in 1989 at a summit the storminess of which was confined to the weather.

The Future

Toward the end of 1989 the focus of international attention shifted to a series of extraordinary events in Eastern Europe, the full implications of which have yet to become clear. In 1963 President Kennedy had stood at the Brandenburg Gate in Berlin, overlooking the newly-erected wall between the Eastern and Western sectors of the city, and delivered his famous "Ich bin ein Berliner" speech. To jubilant cheers from the crowd, he had said "All free men, wherever they may live, are citizens of Berlin." In November 1989, in an emotional climax to the tide of reform which had loosened the once unshakeable hold on power of the Communist parties in Poland, Hungary, Czechoslovakia, Bulgaria, and East Germany, and would go on to topple the Stalinist régime of Nicolai Ceausescu in Romania, the first official breach was made in the Berlin Wall. For the first time in 30 years, citizens of East Germany were able to walk freely into the West while border guards, who would have shot them dead for the attempt only weeks before, stood by chatting and smiling. To many in the West who watched this remarkable peaceful revolution, events seemed finally to have caught up with Kennedy's words. The post-War political map of Europe, in the formation of which the United States had played so prominent a part, was being redrawn before the eyes of the world. The "new breeze" of freedom, of which President Bush had spoken in his inaugural address in January 1989, seemed to have become a gale, sweep-

Fireside chat: Ronald Reagan and Mikhail Gorbachev meet in Washington.

ing through the hollow structures of the Eastern bloc, and bringing democracy, or the hope of democracy, in its wake.

Where these momentous events will lead, and what part the United States will have to play in them and in the world which emerges from them, remains to be seen. For all the pace of change in recent years, international tensions remain, as do stockpiles of nuclear weapons large enough to destroy mankind many times over. The nuclear disaster at Chernobyl, and recent revelations about the scale of the damage we have already inflicted on the environment, have brought home to the world with unprecedented clarity the need for global solutions to the problems which face us as we approach the threshold of the 21st century. As two world wars have shown, and countless smaller conflicts have reminded us, peace and democracy are fragile plants, continually in need of sustenance. But today, for the first time in many years, there does seem genuine cause for hope that the movements emerging from the glacial landscape of the Cold War – movements nurtured by the same ideals on which America herself was founded more than two centuries ago – will indeed prove "a new birth of freedom," and that, in Lincoln's timeless words at Gettysburg, the future will bring still stronger sureties "that government of the people, by the people, for the people, shall not perish from the earth."

Iran

After the catastrophic failure of Carter's attempt to rescue the U.S. hostages in Iran by force at the beginning of 1980 (top), relations between the United States and the ever more firmly consolidated Islamic revolutionary régime of the Ayatollah Khomeini remained dangerously strained throughout the decade. The hostages were released in 1981 after intense diplomatic activity in the closing months of 1980, but by then war had broken out between Iran and neighboring Iraq, creating a new and enduring source of international tension in the already troubled Middle East.

20 Deregulation of trucking industry

23-AUG 15 Heatwave and drought devastates the South, Southwest and mid-Mississipi River Valley

27 New law requires draft registration by men aged 19 and 20

JUL 14-17 Republican National Convention nominates Ronald Reagan for President and George Bush of Texas for Vice President

AUG 11-14 Democratic National Convention nominates Jimmy Carter and Walter F. Mondale for second terms

SEP 19 Fuel explosion at *Titan 2* missile site near Damascus, Ark., forces evacuation of 1400 people

OCT 2 Rep. Michael Joseph Myers, Democrat of Pennsylvania, expelled from House after Abscam conviction

28 Carter-Reagan television debate

NOV 4 Ronald Wilson Reagan elected President, George Bush elected Vice President

21 Fire at MGM Grand Hotel in Las Vegas, Nev., kills 84

21 'Who Shot J.R?' episode of TV show *Dallas* breaks viewing record

22 Death of actress Mae West

DEC 8 John Lennon shot and killed in NYC

The Arts

★ John Kennedy Toole's novel *A Confederacy of Dunces*

★ Martin Scorsese's film *Raging Bull*

1981

JAN 7 Record trading on NY Stock Exchange

20 Ronald Reagan inaugurated President, George Bush inaugurated Vice President

20 Iranian hostage crisis ends as 52 Americans are released

FEB 17 Chrysler Corporation reports largest loss in US business history

18 Pres. Reagan calls for $41 billion in cuts in Carter budget

23 Federal court rules that educational institutions receiving federal funds need not provide equal athletic programs for men and women

MAR 2 Reagan administration announces intention to send 20 more advisors and $25 million in military equipment to support Duarte junta in El Salvador

13 World's largest diamond, Star of Peace, sold for $20 million

23 Supreme Court rules state can pass legislation prohibiting teenage abortions without parental consent

30 Pres. Reagan shot by John W. Hinckley outside Washington Hilton Ballroom

APR 12-14 Space shuttle *Columbia* makes maiden voyage

21 Major Saudi arms sale announced

24 Fifteen-month grain embargo on USSR lifted

30 Sen. Harrison Williams of New Jersey convicted of bribery in connection with Abscam investigation; all seven congressional members accused found guilty

JUN 6 Nationwide competition to design Vietnam War Memorial won by Yale undergraduate Maya Yang Lin

8 Supreme Court rules that women can sue for equal pay even if their work is not identical with male employees'

12-AUG 9 Longest major league baseball strike in sports history

18 Hoof and mouth disease vaccine produced by genetic engineering announced

21 Wayne Williams arrested and charged with two murders in Atlanta, Ga; believed to have committed 28 over past two years

JUL 17 Two aerial walkways collapse at Hyatt Regency Hotel in Kansas City, Mo., killing 113 and injuring 190

AUG Nationwide air traffic controllers' strike started by 13,000 members of PATCO

4 E.I. du Pont Nemours, largest chemical company in US, purchases Conoco, ninth largest oil company

Miami Riots

In the summer of 1980 a wave of serious race rioting swept the city of Miami, causing deaths and extensive damage (above), after four policemen were acquitted of murdering a Black businessman.

Mount St. Helens Eruption

One of the greatest natural disasters to hit the United States in modern times occurred in Washington State on May 18, 1980, when Mount St. Helens erupted, hurling vast quantities of smoke, ash, and debris into the air (left) and triggering a chain reaction of flooding and mudslides in the region. The volcano, 45 miles northeast of Portland, had been monitored by seismologists since becoming active in March, and residents had been evacuated from most areas. However, the force of the eruption was greater than had been expected, and a number of deaths occurred. Hundreds of square miles were devastated by the blast.

First Woman Supreme Court Justice

In July 1981 President Reagan nominated the first woman ever to sit as a justice of the Supreme Court, Sandra Day O'Connor (right). She was sworn in by Chief Justice Warren Burger in September.

"I forgot to duck"

Just ten weeks after his inauguration in 1981, Ronald Reagan became the victim of a bizarre assassination attempt. As the President was leaving a hotel in Washington, D.C., where he had been addressing a trade union convention, six shots rang out and he fell to the ground, his security men closing ranks around him. Reagan was rushed to George Washington University Hospital where he underwent a two-hour operation to remove a bullet from his left lung. His assailant, John Warnock Hinckley, the 25-year-old son of an oil executive, was immediately arrested. He had apparently planned the shooting in order to impress the film actress Jodie Foster, whom he had never met but with whom he was obsessed.

Death of John Lennon

In another tragic reminder of the violence endemic in American society in the 1980s, the musician, writer, and peace campaigner, John Lennon, was shot dead outside the Dakota Building where he lived in New York City on December 8, 1980. The murderer, Mark Chapman, approached the 40-year-old former Beatle as he was walking home from a recording session and fired a number of times at point blank range. The Dakota Building became the focus of many tributes over the weeks following Lennon's death (above).

4 Pres. Reagan's income tax reduction plan passed by Congress with slight modification

10 Production of neutron bomb authorized by Pres. Reagan

19 Two Libyan jets shot down by US Navy fighters about 60 miles from Libyan coast after they open fire on US jets

25 *Voyager 2* mission reveals thousands of rings around Saturn

SEP 21 Sandra Day O'Connor becomes first woman member of Supreme Court

OCT 2 Pres. Reagan presents five-point defense program, including construction of 100 B-1 bombers and 100 MX missiles

8 Ban on commercial reprocessing of nuclear fuel lifted by Pres. Reagan

28 Saudi arms sale approved by Senate

NOV 14 Space shuttle *Columbia* completes second mission, becoming first reusable spacecraft to complete second flight

DEC 4 Domestic intelligence operations by CIA and other agencies authorized for first time in executive order issued by Pres. Reagan

18 Constitutionality of religious services in campus buildings by student organizations at public colleges and universities upheld by Supreme Court

28 Reprisals against USSR for its role in imposition of martial law in Poland and crack-down on Solidarity movement announced by Pres. Reagan

The Arts

★ Russell Hoban's novel *Riddley Walker*

1982

JAN One of worst winters in US history

5 Federal judge in Arkansas overturns state law requiring teaching of creationism in public schools

8 AT & T agrees to divest itself of 22 Bell Telephone operating systems

9-17 Record low temperatures in the South, Midwest and Plains states cause 261 deaths

13 Air Florida Boeing 737 crashes into bridge over Potomac River, killing 78 people

26 In his State of the Union message, Pres. Reagan states intention to transfer many social welfare programs to state and local control

FEB 6 Pres. Reagan's proposed budget for fiscal 1982 includes projected deficit of $91.5 billion

27 Wayne Williams convicted for killing 2 of 28 young people found murdered in and around Atlanta, Ga

MAR 10 Economic sanctions against Libya as protest against its involvement in international terrorist organizations, announced by Pres. Reagan

11 Marathon Oil Company agrees to merge with US Steel in $6 billion deal

MAY 1 World's Fair opens in Knoxville, Tenn.

21 First British troops land in Falklands; US supports action

JUN 6 Israeli army invades southern Lebanon

12 Some 500,000 people participate in nuclear arms control demonstration in NYC

15 Supreme Court rules that children of illegal aliens are entitled to public education, in decision against Texas law

21 John W. Hinckley, Jr, found not guilty by reason of insanity in 1981 shooting of Pres. Reagan and three others

24 Supreme Court rules that President cannot be sued for damages for actions taken while in office

30 Equal Rights Amendment defeated, falling 3 states short of 38 required for ratification

JUL 9 Pan American jetliner crashes after takeoff from New Orleans International Airport in Louisiana, killing 154

16 Rev. Sun-myung Moon, leader of Unification Church, sentenced to 18 months in prison and fined $25,000 for tax fraud and conspiracy to obstruct justice

19 Census Bureau reports 7.4 percent increase in poverty since 1980

Beirut

The 1980s were the decade in which the Lebanese capital, Beirut, was reduced to anarchy as opposing factions fought for supremacy on its streets. The international peacekeeping force in the city was subjected to continual harassment by militia groups, two of the worst incidents occurring on April 18, 1983, when 60 people were killed in a suicide attack on the U.S. embassy (left), and on October 23, 1983, when more than 300 U.S. and French soldiers were killed in simultaneous bombings at their Beirut headquarters. All U.S. troops were withdrawn in 1984.

Shuttle Diplomacy

Secretary of State Alexander Haig (above) played a crucial mediating role in the conflict between Britain and Argentina over the Falkland Islands in 1982. Britain sent a naval task force to recover the islands after they were invaded by Argentinian troops in April.

KAL 007

All 269 passengers and crew of a South Korean airliner were lost presumed dead after Soviet fighter aircraft shot it down over the militarily sensitive territory of Sakhalin on the night of August 31, 1983. The Boeing 747, which was on a flight from New York to Seoul, had veered off course into Soviet airspace after leaving Alaska. Amid widespread international condemnation of the shooting, the Soviet Union claimed that the plane had been on a spying mission and had failed to respond to warnings. Left: Relatives of passengers on KAL flight 007 react to the tragic news at Kimpo International Airport.

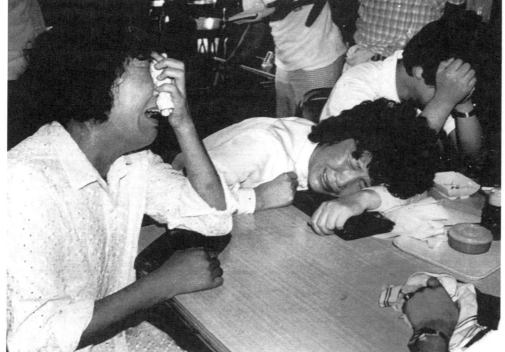

IBM PC

Another step was taken towards the universal availability of cheap information technology in 1983 when the IBM organization launched its long-awaited new personal computer. The IBM PCjr (above), which was soon to become a familiar sight in homes and offices throughout the Western world, offered a number of advanced features, including enhanced graphics, sound capabilities, and the capacity to communicate with other computers via an optional modem.

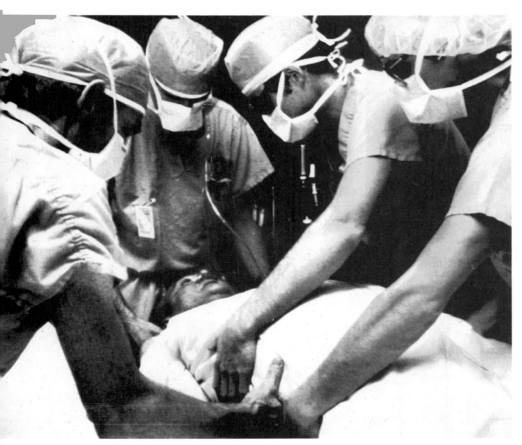

First Artificial Heart

Medical history was made on December 2, 1982, when Dr. Barney B. Clark, a 61-year-old former dentist from Seattle, Washington, became the first human being ever to be given a permanent artificial heart. The life-saving operation, which took more than seven and a half hours, was performed at the University of Utah Medical Center in Salt Lake City by a team of surgeons headed by Dr. William DeVries. Dr. Clark died in March 1983, though his artificial heart remained operative. Above: Surgeons prepare Dr. Clark for the operation.

28 San Francisco becomes first US city to ban sale and possession of handguns

AUG 5 House rejects resolution that would freeze US and Soviet arsenals at present levels

19 Congress passes bill authorizing tax increase of $93.8 billion

20 About 800 US Marines land in Beirut, Lebanon, as part of multinational force to oversee withdrawal of PLO

26 Manville Corporation, nation's largest producer of asbestos, files for bankruptcy

SEP 8 Pres. Reagan announces that he will not block bill proposed by North Carolina Sen. Jesse Helms to allow prayer in public schools

8 American Lutheran Church, Association of Evangelical Lutheran Churches and Lutheran Church in America merge

12 ICC approves merger of Union Pacific, Missouri Pacific and Western Pacific railraods

15 *Today* national newspaper begins publication

29-OCT 1 Cyanide-laced Tylenol capsules kill seven people in Chicago area

OCT 26 Reagan administration shows record budget deficit of over $110 billion for fiscal 1982

NOV NFL ends 57-day strike

23 Labor Department report indicates 6 percent rise in cost of living over 12-month period

DEC 2 Barney B. Clark, 61, receives first successful artificial heart transplant at University of Utah Medical Center

2-9 Storms and floods in Midwest force evacuation of 35,000

23 Bill increasing federal gasoline tax by five cents per gallon to fund highway and bridge repairs, approved by Congress

The Arts

★ Alice Walker's novel *The Color Purple*

★ Harvey Fierstein's play *Torch Song Trilogy*

★ Arthur Kopit and Maury Yeston's musical *Nine*

★ Steven Spielberg's film *E.T.: The Extraterrestrial*

1983

FEB 22 Discovery of large amounts of carcinogenic chemical dioxin in soil around Times Beach, Mo., leads to federal government offer to buy homes and businesses

MAR 9 Ann McGill Burford resigns as head of EPA as result of charges of favoritism to industry

23 Barney Clark, first recipient of artificial heart, dies 112 days after transplant

30 First California condor chick born in captivity hatched at San Diego Zoo

APR 4 Death of actress Gloria Swanson

4-9 Space shuttle *Challenger* makes maiden voyage into orbit

18 US embassy in Beirut, Lebanon, almost totally destroyed by car-bomb explosion

20 Supreme Court rules that construction of nuclear power plants can be barred by states for economic reasons

30 Death of choreographer George Balanchine

MAY 24 MX missile research and development funds totaling $625 million authorized by Congress

JUN 24-28 Sally K. Ride becomes first US woman astronaut in space as member of crew of space shuttle *Challenger* in its second flight

25 Washington Public Power Supply System defaults; largest governmental unit to fail in US history

28 Proposed abortion amendment allowing legislation to curb or ban abortions rejected by Senate

AUG 21 Milwaukee youths, ages 17 to 22, accomplish break-ins of some 60 computers nationwide

27 Some 250,000 people participate in march on Washington, DC, commemorating 1963 civil rights march led by Rev. Martin Luther King, Jr

Invasion of Grenada

In October 1983 United States forces invaded the small Caribbean island of Grenada after a military coup toppled the moderate faction of the ruling New Jewel movement there. The coup was headed by the Marxist military commander Hudson Austin and led to the arrest and execution of the country's Prime Minister, Maurice Bishop. President Reagan described the régime of the new Revolutionary Military Council as "a threat to the security of the United States," claiming that a new airport being built with Cuban assistance on the island was a military facility. The U.S. marines met stronger resistance than had been expected and it was not until November that they were able to leave the island's government in the hands of a pan-Caribbean force, pending new elections.

Nicaragua

Following the overthrow of the Nicaraguan dictator General Anastasio Somoza by the left-wing National Liberation Sandinista Front in 1979, the U.S. Government pursued a policy of destabilization against the new régime, which was seen, particularly by the Reagan administration, as a potential Communist beachhead in Central America. The United States supplied arms and support to the anti-Sandinista Contra rebels, who conducted a guerrilla war of ambush and sabotage throughout the decade in an attempt to secure the overthrow of the Nicaraguan President, Daniel Ortega. However, President Reagan's attempt to increase funding for the Contras met with Congressional opposition, the House of Representatives voting to reduce the appropriation and seeking control over expenditure. Right: Contra rebel leaders orienteering in Southern Nicaragua in 1984.

The *Achille Lauro* Affair

Public opinion in America was outraged in October 1985 by the murder of an elderly and disabled U.S. citizen during the hijacking of a cruise liner by Palestinian terrorists in the Mediterranean. The incident occurred after the Italian ship *Achille Lauro* was stormed by four Palestinians, who held its passengers and crew hostage for almost 48 hours, demanding the release of Arab prisoners in Israel. After tense negotiations between Egypt and the P.L.O., the hi-jackers were given safe passage out of Egypt, only to be intercepted by American planes and forced to land in Italy, where they were arrested. Left: Passengers show their relief on arrival in Port Said harbor.

TWA Hi-jack

In June 1985, a Boeing 747 flight from Athens to Rome was hi-jacked by two Lebanese Shi'ite Moslems, who killed a U.S. passenger and held others hostage for more than two weeks. Above: A terrorist gestures defiance from the plane.

Born in the USA

1984–1985 saw the American rock star Bruce Springsteen (above) playing to massive audiences in America and Europe on his *Born in the USA* tour. The newly-released album's patriotic title belied its disillusioned view of American life.

30-SEP 5 Lt Col. Guion S. Bluford, USAF, is first Black astronaut in space

SEP 5 Sanctions against USSR, in response to downing of South Korean airliner, announced by Pres. Reagan

20 Multinational Force in Lebanon Resolution authorizes US Marines to remain in Lebanon for another 18 months

OCT 9 Secretary of the Interior James Watt resigns after receiving criticism for bigoted remark

23 US Marine headquarters in Beirut, Lebanon, destroyed by explosive-laden truck; 241 die

25 US forces launch invasion of Grenada after bloody coup by pro-Cuban Marxists

NOV 2 Federal holiday honoring Martin Luther King designated for observance on third Monday of January

11 First US cruise missiles arrive in Great Britain

DEC 4 US warplanes attack Syrian positions near Beirut, Lebanon, in retaliation for Syrian attack on US planes

22 FTC approves joint US-Japanese auto venture by General Motors and Toyota of Japan

28 US announces withdrawal from UNESCO due to political bias and financial mismanagement

The Arts

★ John Chase's novel *During the Reign of the Queen of Persia*

★ Michael Jackson's record album *Thriller*

★ Francis Ford Coppola's films *The Outsiders* and *Rumble Fish*

1984

JAN 8 Texaco, Inc., third largest US oil company, agrees to take over Getty Oil Company in $10 billion deal

10 Restoration of full diplomatic relations with Vatican after period of 117 years announced in Washington, DC

29 Pres. Reagan announces candidacy for reelection

FEB 3 First case of surrogate conception announced by team of California physicians

29 Last US Marines withdrawn from Lebanon

MAR 5 Supreme Court rules that city can make Nativity scene part of official Christmas display without violating constitutional separation of religion and state

29 Series of tornadoes kills some 67 people in Carolinas

APR 22 Death of photographer Ansel Adams

23 Identification of AIDS virus announced by federal researchers

26-MAY 1 Pres. Reagan makes trip to China

26 Death of jazz pianist and band leader 'Count' Basie

MAY 7 Establishment of Agent Orange victims' fund announced by manufacturers

8 USSR withdraws from 1984 Olympics

30 Development of chicken pox vaccine announced

JUN 4 Successful cloning of DNA from extinct animal reported by scientists at University of California

14 Southern Baptist Convention passes resolution opposing ordination of women

15 Gulf Corporation agrees to takeover by Standard Oil Company of California for $13.4 billion

30 Death of playwright Lillian Hellman

JUL 16-19 Democratic National Convention nominates Walter F. Mondale of Minnesota for President and Rep. Geraldine Ferraro of New York for Vice President

17 Pres. Reagan signs bill giving states until October 1, 1986 to raise legal drinking age to 21 or face 5 percent cut in federal highway funds

18 Deficit Reduction Act of 1984 raises taxes by about $50 billion and cuts spending by $13 billion through 1987

AUG 20-23 Republican National Convention nominates Ronald Reagan and George Bush for second terms

25 Death of author Truman Capote

30-SEP 5 Space shuttle *Discovery*, third of four US space shuttles makes maiden flight

The *Challenger* Disaster

Tragedy struck the U.S. space program on January 28, 1986, when the space shuttle *Challenger* exploded shortly after take-off from Cape Canaveral in Florida, killing all seven astronauts on board. The tragedy happened just 74 seconds into the shuttle's tenth mission and within full sight of the crowds gathered at the launch pad. Media attention focused on the fate of Christa McAuliffe, a high school teacher from New Hampshire, who had won a contest to be the first ordinary citizen in space. The accident – the first in which U.S. astronauts had died since 1967 – was traced to a faulty seal in one of the twin solid-fuel rocket boosters and led to staff changes at the top of N.A.S.A..

Below: The crew of *Challenger* leave their quarters for the launch pad. From front to back: Francis Scobee, Judy Resnik, Ron McNair, Michael Smith, Christa McAuliffe, Ellison Onizuka, and Greg Jarvis.

Right: The space shuttle *Challenger* takes off on its fateful mission. The solid-fuel rocket booster on the right of the picture was the cause of the disaster.

Opposite top: Well-wishers, relatives of the crew, and Space Center personnel watch in horrified disbelief as the shuttle explodes ten miles above the ground.

Opposite bottom: Workmen at Cape Canaveral lower debris from the *Challenger* into an unused missile silo for storage.

SEP 20 US Embassy in Beirut bombed, killing 23

OCT 1 Secretary of Labor Raymond J. Donovan indicted on charges of participating in a multimillion dollar scheme to defraud NYC Transit Authority

7 First Reagan-Mondale televised debate

11 Dr Kathryn D. Sullivan becomes first US woman astronaut to walk in space

11 Bush-Ferraro televised debate

16 Baboon heart transplanted to 15-day-old baby girl at Lorna Linda University Medical Center in California

NOV 6 Ronald Reagan and George Bush win election for second terms

DEC 11-12 Discovery of 7000-year-old human skulls reported by Florida archeologists

20 Development of megabit memory chip announced by Bell Laboratories

The Arts

★ William Kennedy's novel *Ironweed*

★ The film *Indiana Jones and the Temple of Doom*

1985

JAN 18 US withdraws from World Court proceedings initiated by Nicaragua, which charges US with conducting secret war by aiding rebel contra forces

20 Ronald Reagan inaugurated President; George Bush, inaugurated Vice President

20-21 Record cold spell strikes US

24-27 *Discovery* makes first secret military space shuttle flight

MAR 4 EPA orders ban on leaded gasoline

18 American Broadcasting Company bought by Capital Cities Communications in first sale of major network

27 Supreme Court rules that police cannot shoot fleeing criminal suspects who are unarmed and not considered dangerous

28 Death of artist Marc Chagall

APR 8 Union Carbide Corporation sued by government of India for deaths and injuries caused by plant disaster at Bhopal

MAY 12 First woman conservative rabbi, Amy Eilberg, ordained at Jewish Theological Seminary in NYC

21 Patricia Frustaci gives birth to seven children in California; largest multiple birth on record

JUN 4 Supreme Court invalidates Atlanta law permitting one minute of prayer or silent meditation in public schools

14 TWA jetliner hijacked in Athens, Greece by two Shiite Muslim terrorists

JUL 1 Supreme Court rules that public school teachers cannot enter parochial school classrooms to provide instruction

19 Christa McAuliffe, 36, highschool teacher and mother of two from Concorde, NH, selected from 11,000 applicants to become first teacher to fly aboard space shuttle

23 US and China sign nuclear energy accord in Washington, DC

AUG 2 Delter Airlines L-1011 crashes at Dallas-Fort Worth Airport, killing 133

2 Montgomery Ward and Company announces discontinuation of its catalog, first mail order catalog in US

11 Cloud of toxic gas released from Union Carbide plant in Institute, W. Va, injuring 135 people

23 TVA shut down its last nuclear power plant, Sequoyah facility at Daisy, Tenn., due to doubts about safety

30 First secret delivery of TOW anti-tank missiles to Iran

SEP 1 Wreck of *Titanic* found by US-French exploratory team

9 Mild sanctions against South Africa announced by Pres. Reagan

11 Pete Rose of Cincinnati Reds sets new major league baseball record of 4192 career hits

14 Second secret arms delivery to Iran

Live Aid

Madonna (left) was one of the stars of the largest ever fund-raising concert, Live Aid, for the victims of the Ethiopian famine in July 1985.

Falling Prophets

In 1988 the fundamentalist preacher Jimmy Swaggart (right) joined fellow evangelist Jim Bakker in disgrace after being photographed visiting a prostitute.

Cory

In an extraordinary upsurge of popular support, Mrs. Corazon Aquino (here seen speaking during her energetic election campaign) swept to power in the Philippines in February 1986. Mrs. Aquino, the widow of the assassinated opposition leader Benigno Aquino, was inaugurated President when large sections of the population refused to accept President Ferdinand Marcos' claims to have won the election. Amid widespread accusations of electoral fraud, Marcos and his wife Imelda, who had ruled the Philippines since 1965, were forced to step down and flee the country after the U.S. withdrew its support for them. Aquino dubbed the spontaneous mass expression of popular dissent – similar to that which Eastern Europe would see later – "people power."

The Bombing of Libya

In April 1986, U.S. aircraft, flying from bases in Britain, launched bombing raids against targets in the Libyan cities of Tripoli and Benghazi, apparently in response to alleged involvement by the Libyan leader, Colonel Gadaffi, in the bombing of a Berlin nightclub in which American soldiers were killed and injured. There was widespread international criticism of the raid.

Black Monday

The long bull market in stocks and shares came to an abrupt end on Monday, October 19, 1987, when the New York Stock Exchange registered a staggering one-day fall in values – twice that of the Wall Street Crash of 1929. More than 600 million shares changed hands as investors scrambled to sell, triggering similar falls on exchanges in London and Tokyo. Some observers blamed computer "program trading" for the severity of the collapse.

14 Rev. Benjamen Weir, one of American hostages in Lebanon, released and back in US

26-27 Hurricane strikes North Carolina and New York metropolitan area, forcing evacuation of 28,000 coastal residents

OCT 7-10 Italian liner *Achille Lauro* hijacked in Mediterranean by four members of Palestinian Liberation Front; one American killed

NOV 4 Democrats regain control of Senate

20-21 Pres. Reagan and Communist Party Secretary of USSR, Mikhail Gorbachev, conduct summit meeting in Geneva, Switzerland

26 Random House acquires rights to Ronald Reagan's biography for $3 million

DEC 4 National Security Advisor Robert McFarlane resigns

10 Highest award for damages in US history upheld by Texas state judge; Pennzoil Company awarded $11.1 billion in suit against Texaco, Inc. for interfering in Pennzoil's agreement to acquire Getty Oil Company

11 Gramm-Rudman bill to eliminate federal deficit by 1991 passed by Congress

12 Arrow Airlines charter jet crashes in Gander, Newfoundland, killing 248 US Army soldiers and crew of 8

27 Terrorists attack Rome airport in Italy and Vienna airport in Austria, killing 18 and wounding 110, including 5 US citizens

30 Nine men and one woman belonging to white supremacist gang, the Order, convicted in Seattle on racketeering charges connected to conspiracy to start racist revolution

The Arts

★ Carolyn Chute's novel *The Beans of Egypt Maine*
★ Don DeLillo's novel *White Noise*
★ Garrison Keillor's book *Lake Wobegon Days*
★ John Huston's film *Prizzi's Honor*

1986

JAN 7 Pres. Reagan orders economic sanctions against Libya in retaliation for alleged Libyan involvement in terrorist attacks

24 *Voyager 2* makes new discoveries on mission to planet Uranus

28 Space shuttle *Challenger* explodes 74 seconds after liftoff at Cape Canaveral, Fla, killing all seven astronauts aboard, including schoolteacher Christa McAuliffe

FEB 14-20 Torrential rains in far West leave 33,000 homeless

19 UN treaty outlawing genocide ratified by Senate

MAR 6 Death of artist Georgia O'Keeffe

7 US orders cut in Soviet UN staff in NYC

11 Rev. Charles E. Curran, liberal theologian at Catholic University of America in Washington, DC, ordered by Vatican to retract his views on birth control and other sexual issues

20 Contra aid bill providing $300 million for Nicaraguan rebel forces rejected by Congress

24 US and Libya clash in Gulf of Sidra when Libyan forces fire at US fleet on maneuvers

25 Total of $20 million in military aid to Honduras approved by Congress

27 Volcanic eruption on Augustine Island, southwest of Anchorage

APR 2 Terrorist bombing aboard TWA jet flying from Rome to Athens kills four Americans

5 Terrorist bombing in West Berlin discotheque kills US soldier and wounds 60 Americans

14 US air strike against Libya launched in retaliation for terrorist acts

16 First surrogate birth of test tube baby announced at Mount Sinai Hospital in Cleveland, Ohio

22 Department of Agriculture approves first genetically altered virus to be released into environment

27 BBDO International, Doyle Dane Bernbach Group and Needham Harper Worldwide merge to form largest ad agency

Irangate

In 1987 a scandal which many in the media and elsewhere compared to Watergate rocked the Reagan administration. Hearings began in May into the so-called Iran-Contra affair, in which profits from the sale of arms to Iran were diverted to support the Contra rebels fighting against the Sandinista government in Nicaragua, circumventing a Congressional ban on aid to the Contras and flying in the face of President Reagan's foreign policy statements in respect of trade with Iran. In July the key figures in the case, Lieutenant-Colonel Oliver North (left), his secretary Fawn Hall (right), and the President's former National Security Adviser, Admiral John Poindexter (below), appeared before Committees of the House of Representatives to answer questions about their part in the affair. Despite much speculation, neither Reagan himself nor the C.I.A. chief William Casey, who died in May, were called.

The public hearings, which were televised, became a media event, with Oliver North in particular acquiring the status of a national hero for his uncompromisingly patriotic and unapologetic stance (bottom right). Admiral Poindexter, who was widely expected to implicate the President directly in the scandal, in fact claimed he had withheld information from Reagan in order to provide "deniability" if the affair ever came to light. (Reagan, giving evidence to a later hearing after he had left the White House, claimed to remember virtually nothing of the affair.) Poindexter was given a prison sentence in 1990, and one of North's convictions was overturned on appeal the same year.

27 Video pirate interrupts Home Box Office broadcast

28 General Motors named as largest US corporation by *Fortune* magazine

29 Some 800,000 books lost in fire at Los Angeles Central Library

MAY 5 Supreme Court rules that opponents of capital punishment may be barred from juries in capital cases

13 Justice Department commission on pornography concludes that such material is potentially harmful

19 New gun control law weakening 1968 federal gun control law signed by Pres. Reagan

25 Hands Across America; some 6 million people link hands in 4150-mile chain from NYC to Long Beach, Calif., to raise money for hungry and homeless in US

30 Genetically eningeered tobacco planted on Wisconsin farm

JUN 5 Ronald W. Pelton, former National Security Agency employee, convicted of espionage

13 Death of 'King of Swing' Benny Goodman

17 Conservative Associate Justice William H. Rehnquist named to succeed Warren E. Burger as Chief Justice of Supreme Court

17 Conservative Antonin Scale named to Supreme Court

19 Richard W. Miller becomes first FBI agent to be convicted of espionage, for passing information to USSR

19 Two people in Seattlė, Wash., poisoned with cyanide contained in Extra Strength Excederin

27 International Court of Justice declares US actions against Nicaragua a violation of national law

30 Supreme Court rules that homosexual relations are not protected by Constitution

JUL 3-6 Liberty Weekend celebration for restoration of Statue of Liberty

OCT Tax Reform Act of 1986 signed by the President

NOV 3 Lebanese magazine *Al Shira* reports former National Security Advisor Robert McFarlane carried out secret mission to Tehran involving transfer of military spare parts

12 Admission by Pres. Reagan of covert arms sales to Iran

20 Attorney General Edwin Meese initiates internal review of Iran-Contra affair on order of the President

25 Edwin Meese announces that between $10 million and $30 million from arms sales to Iran have been diverted to Swiss bank accounts for use of Nicaraguan antigovernment Contras by Israelis or Iranians directed by Marine Lt Col. Oliver North, NSC official, with knowledge of Adml Poindexter and former Assistant to the President for National Security Affairs, Robert McFarlane

25 National Security Advisor Adml John Poindexter resigns

25 NSC official, Lt Col. Oliver North dismissed

DEC 1 Lt Col. North refuses to testify before Senate intelligence committee, citing constitutional right under amendment against self-incrimination

2 Frank Carlucci succeeds Adml John Poindexter as National Security Advisor

3 Adml Poindexter refuses to testify before Senate committee

19 Federal court appoints independent counsel Lawrence E. Walsh to investigate possible criminal violation of federal laws by Reagan administration

1987

JAN 6 Democratic Rep. James Wright of Texas succeeds Thomas P. 'Tip' O'Neill as Speaker of the House

13 Eight men convicted of being figures in organized crime commission sentenced by federal grand jury

15 US and USSR resume arms talks in Geneva

FEB 2 Independent counsel appointed to investigate lobbying activities of former presidential aide Lyn Nofziger on behalf of Wedtech Corp.

2 CIA director William Casey resigns

4 Death of pianist Liberace

9 Former National Security Advisor Robert McFarlane attempts suicide

Earthquake in San Francisco

Disaster struck San Francisco on October 17, 1989 when an earthquake, registering 6.9 on the Richter scale, devastated the Bay area of the city. The tremor caused more than 80 deaths, although early reports put the figure much higher. Most of the casualties occurred when the top deck of the double-decker Nimitz freeway fell onto rush-hour traffic travelling on the lower deck (above). The earthquake, which resulted from long-expected activity along the San Andreas Fault, was the worst to hit San Francisco since 1906.

Hurricane Hugo

Between September 17 and 23, 1989, the Northeast Caribbean and the Southeast United States were ravaged by the fiercest storm for a decade. Hurricane Hugo swept out of the Atlantic, devastating parts of Guadeloupe, Montserrat and the Virgin Islands before hitting Puerto Rico and the coast of mainland America near Charleston, South Carolina. Winds of up to 140 m.p.h. left many dead and homeless, causing flooding and widespread damage (left).

Yellowstone Inferno

A series of disastrous forest fires swept through Yellowstone Park in September 1988, following a long dry summer. The blazes, which raged out of control for several days, devastated almost 100,000 acres of the country's oldest national park before burning themselves out. Here, firefighters mop up some of the damage near Mammoth Hot Springs in the aftermath of the fires.

Drought

In 1988 the United States suffered its driest spring since the Dust Bowl years. Many agricultural regions were designated disaster areas as some 30 states were struck by the severest drought since 1934. The Midwest and the South were worst affected, as pasture lands became arid plains, waterways dried up, and dust storms scoured off more than 13 million acres of topsoil. Commodity prices soared as grain stocks fell, and financial support was planned for stricken farmers.

10 Surgeon General C. Everett Coop recommends television messages to combat AIDS

14 Economic sanctions against Poland lifted

22 Death of artist Andy Warhol

26 Report of Tower Commission emphasizes role of White House Chief of Staff Donald Regan in mismanaging Iran-Contra affair

27 Donald Regan resigns; replaced by Howard Baker

MAR 2-3 FBI director William Webster nominated for CIA director

4 Pres. Reagan addresses nation on Iran-Contra affair

5 Joint congressional hearings on Iran-Contra affair

6 Death of former CIA director William Casey

8 Democratic presidential candidate Gary Hart withdraws from race following reports concerning association with model and actress Donna Rice, 29

11 Wedtech investigation extended to include Attorney General Edwin Meese

19 Rev. Jim Bakker, Assemblies of God television evangelist and PTL head, resigns ministry in sex scandal

31 Custody of one-year-old 'Baby M' awarded to biologic father William Stern; biologic mother Mary Beth Whitehead, who acted as surrogate mother, stripped of all parental rights

APR 17 US imposes 100 percent tariff on certain Japanese computers, television sets and power tools

17 US frigate *Stark* hit by Iraqi missiles in Persian Gulf

21-22 Senate and House committees vote to grant Adml Poindexter limited immunity in exchange for testimony

22 Supreme Court rules that use of death penalty by state is constitutional even if statistics show that it is applied in manner which discriminates on racial basis

JUN 3 Democratic Rep. Mario Biaggi of New York indicted in Wedtech affair

JUL 1 Controversial justice Robert H. Bork nominated for Supreme Court

7 Oliver North gives public testimony on Iran-Contra affair

28 Alan Greenspan succeeds Paul Volcker as chairman of Federal Reserve Board

AUG 3 Iran-Contra hearings end after 250 hours of testimony from 28 witnesses in over 11 weeks

SEP 21 US seizes Iranian ship planting mines in international waters in Persian Gulf

23 Death of choreographer Bob Fosse

OCT 19 Stock Market collapses

19 Bernard Goetz fined $5000 and sentenced to 6 months in prison for carrying unlicensed concealed weapon

19 Four US destroyers bombard two Iranian oil installations in Persian Gulf

22 US announces curtailment of high technology items to China as protest against its sale of Silkworm missile to Iran

23 Senate rejects Bork nomination

26 US bans Iranian imports

31 Death of scholar Joseph Campbell

NOV 18 Iran-Contra report is critical of Pres. Reagan and administration

21 Some 1000 Cubans in federal detention center in Oakdale, La, riot in response to repatriation agreement

DEC 8 US and USSR sign INF treaty to reduce size of nuclear arsenals in Washington, DC

15 Gary Hart resumes campaign for Democratic presidential candidate

16 Michael Deaver convicted on three counts of perjury

The Arts

★ T. C. Boyle's novel *World's End*

★ Toni Morrison's novel *Beloved*

★ Tom Wolfe's novel *The Bonfire of the Vanities*

AIDS

The 1980s saw the emergence of a virtually unknown disease, which some scientists predicted would become the most serious threat ever to the survival of the human race. Governments across the world responded to calls from the medical profession for urgent action to contain the rapid spread of AIDS (Acquired Immune Deficiency Syndrome), a disease which attacks the immune system, thus leaving its victims no resistance to infection. In particular, experts urged a campaign to raise public awareness of the disease, which is transmitted through infected blood and other bodily fluids, in an attempt to prevent it spreading from the high-risk groups – homosexual men and intravenous drug users – to the wider community. In 1988 it was estimated that some five million people could be infected with the HIV virus worldwide, of whom 150,000 had already developed the full-blown disease. The largest number of cases were reported in the United States – though the highest incidence of the disease is believed to be in Africa – and in a controversial response to the crisis a presidential commission on AIDS approved confidential reporting by doctors on the names of infected individuals, and proposed that state officials should notify those individuals' sexual partners. With scientists apparently little nearer to finding a cure, and with AIDS acting as a catalyst for widespread discrimination against sufferers and homosexuals in the West, San Francisco became the scene of angry demonstrations by the largest ever gathering of AIDS sufferers when the Sixth International Conference on AIDS was held there in 1990. The scale of the problem was graphically illustrated by the city's mayor: in his opening speech he declared that three times as many San Franciscans died of AIDS in the 1980s as had died in the two world wars, Korea, and Vietnam combined.

Below: AIDS sufferers lead a demonstration of 300,000 at the 13th annual Gay Freedom Day Parade in San Francisco, June 26, 1988.

Top right: Screening blood for evidence of the HIV virus.

Bottom right: U.S. Department of Health Undersecretary Don Newman launches the Government's first AIDS awareness campaign in Washington, September 30, 1987.

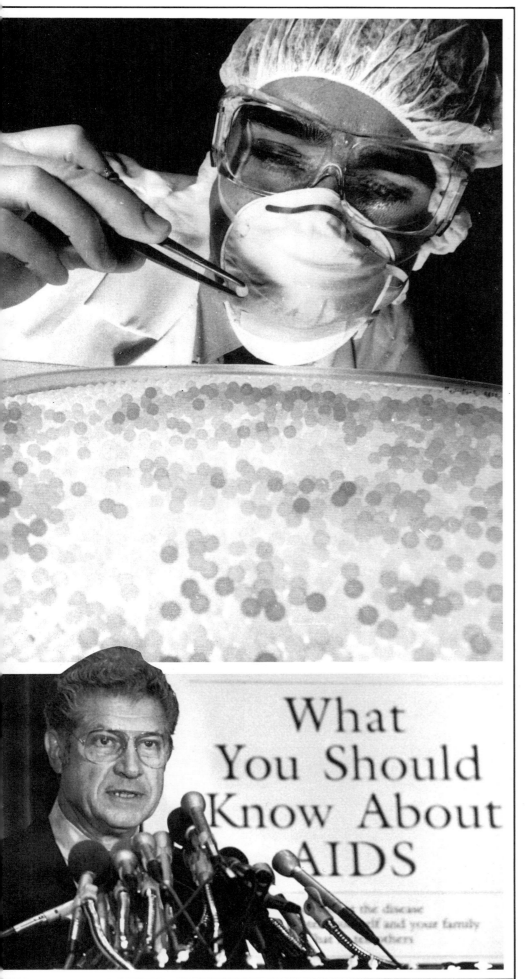

What
You Should
Know About
AIDS

JAN 2 US and Canada sign free trade pack

14 US announces withdrawal of 72 F-16 jet fighters from Spain

FEB 5 US indicts Panamanian Gen. Manuel Noriega on charges of taking millions of dollars in bribes from violent drug traffickers

18 Anthony M. Kennedy, Pres Reagan's third choice, becomes an associate justice of Supreme Court

24 Supreme Court overturns lower court award of $200,000 to Rev. Jerry Falwell for emotional distress caused by *Hustler* magazine parody

MAR 2 NATO allies meet in Belgium to discuss future arms control policies in relation to USSR

13 Lt Col Oliver North indicted by federal jury on charges of conspiracy to defraud government

29 Six top officials of Department of Justice resign over Meese investigation

APR 17 Death of sculptor Louise Nevelson

18 US and Iran clash in Persian Gulf

20 Senate votes in favor of giving $20,000 and official apology to each Japanese-American interned by government orders during World War II

MAY 28 Pres. Reagan and Mikhail Gorbachev meet in Moscow

JUN 10 Death of writer Louis Dearborn L'Amour

JUL 3 US missile cruiser *Vincennes* accidentally shoots down Iranian airbus, killing 290 people

5 Attorney General Edwin Meese resigns

18 Meese cleared of criminal allegations due to insufficent evidence

18-21 Democratic National Convention nominates Gov. Michael Dukakis of Massachusetts for President and Sen. Lloyd Benston of Texas for Vice President

AUG 15-18 Republican National Convention nominates Vice President George Bush for President and Sen. J. Danforth Quayle of Indiana for Vice President

25 West Germany identifies Clyde L. Conrad, former US Army sergeant, as key figure in 14-year-old European espionage ring

SEP 27 Welfare reform bill passed by Congress

29 Space shuttle *Discovery* successfully launched from Cape Canaveral, Fla; first US attempt at manned spaceflight since 1986 *Challenger* disaster

OCT 11 Bank of Credit and Commerce International S.A. charged with money laundering for cocaine traffickers

12 US officials announce that Sunstrand Corp. agrees to plead guilty on charges of fraud against Department of Defense for overcharging on military contracts

14 Genocide treaty approved by Senate

15 US promises aid increase to Philippines for use of military bases

17 US announces $3.5 billion loan to Mexico

21 US government indicts Ferdinand Marcos, former president of Philippines, his wife, Imelda, and eight associates

22 Comprehensive drug bill aimed at reducing supply and consumption of illegal drugs passed by Congress

NOV 1 George Bush elected President, J. Danforth Quayle elected Vice President

19 Insider Trading and Securities Fraud Enforcement Act signed by the President

22 US unveils B-2 Stealth bomber

DEC 14 Secretary of State George Shultz announces US intention to hold talks with PLO

22 Bomb aboard Pan Am Boeing 747, flying from London to NYC, over Lockerbie, Scotland, kills 270

The Arts

★ Raymond Carver's story collection *Where I'm Calling From*

★ Thomas Flanagan's novel *The Tenants of Time*

★ Tracy Chapman's record album *Tracy Chapman*

★ Martin Scorsese's film *The Last Temptation of Christ*

★ The film *Who Framed Roger Rabbit?*

The Lockerbie Disaster

On December 22, 1988, 270 people were killed when Pan Am flight 103 crashed onto the small town of Lockerbie in southern Scotland. The accident happened at 7.19 p.m. as the Boeing 747 was on its way from Frankfurt to New York. After a bomb exploded on board at 31,000 feet, the aircraft plunged to earth and crashed across a major road before ploughing into the town, sending a fireball 300 feet into the air and leaving a crater 50 feet deep and 30 yards long. Many of those who died were Americans returning to the U.S. for Christmas.

Crack

The spread of drug abuse in the U.S. became a major political issue in the late 1980s. Particular attention was focused on a virtual epidemic of "crack" – a highly-addictive smokeable cocaine derivative – which brought misery and violence to the streets of America's major cities.
Left: A crack raid in Washington.

Batman

The hugely successful film *Batman*, starring Jack Nicholson as the Joker, brought the comic strip hero to the big screen in 1989.

Michael Jackson

The reclusive American rock star, Michael Jackson (above), whose album *Thriller* was one of the bestselling records of the 1980s, staged a spectacularly successful world tour in 1988.

"Old Pineapple Face"

Manuel Noriega (below) was finally ousted from power in Panama in December when U.S. troops invaded, ostensibly in response to threats against American citizens there. The operation, which was intended to be swift and decisive, dragged on for days, with troops loyal to Noriega counterattacking and the President himself going to ground in the Vatican Embassy.

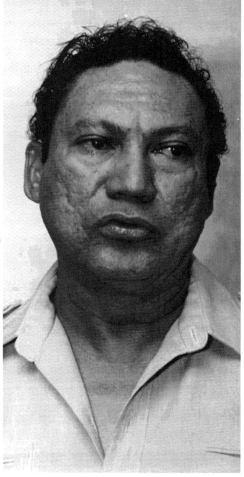

JAN 4 Two US F-14 jets shoot down two Libyan MIG-23 fighters off Libyan coast

20 George Bush inaugurated President, J. Danforth Quayle inaugurated Vice President

FEB 7 US criticizes Israel for treatment of Palestinians living in occupied West Bank and Gaza Strip

12-17 Secretary of State James Baker conducts tour of capital cities of 14 European member countries of NATO to discuss modernization of tactical nuclear missiles

21 Trial of Marine Lt. Col. Oliver North opens

24-27 Pres. Bush attends funeral of Emperor Hirohito of Japan and visits China and South Korea

MAR 3 Robert McFarlane, former National Security Advisor to Pres. Reagan, sentenced for withholding information from Congress

9 Senate rejects nomination of John Tower to post of Defense Secretary; first instance of Senate refusal to confirm Cabinet appointment in 30 years

13 California state Assembly votes to outlaw 40 types of automatic weapons

14 Bush administration imposes temporary ban on importation of semi-automatic weapons

17 Richard Cheney named Defense Secretary

18 First conviction in Pentagon procurement case

24 Oil tanker *Exxon Valdez* grounded on Alaskan coast, releases some 11 million gallons of crude oil into Alaskan waters; worst oil spill in US history

APR 7 Michael R. Milken, former head of high risk, high-yield 'junk-bond' department at Drexel Burnham Lambert, Inc., pleads not guilty to 98 counts of fraud in most extensive securities investigation in US history

11 Northrop Corporation, one of nation's largest defense contractors, indicted for falsifying tests on nuclear armed cruise missile components and supplying equipment known to be below government standards

17 House announces decision to bring charges against Speaker of the House Jim Wright for 69 alleged instances of improper financial conduct

MAY 4 Lt Col. Oliver North convicted of obstructing Congress, unlawfully destroying government documents and accepting illegal gratuity; acquitted on nine other counts

4 Unmanned space probe *Magellan* launched aboard space shuttle *Atlantis* on 15-month exploration of Venus

16 US-Japanese development of FSX advanced fighter plane approved by Senate

31 Speaker of the House Jim Wright resigns in shadow of allegations of financial impropriety

JUN Supreme Court rulings on discrimination and affirmative action detract from civil rights gains

4 Thomas S. Foley elected Speaker of the House

21 Supreme Court invalidates federal and state laws which make burning of US flag criminal offense

26 Supreme Court rules that states are entitled to execute murderers as young as 16 years old and those who are mentally retarded

JUL 3 In *Webster v. Reproductive Health Services,* Supreme Court rules that individual states can restrict availability of abortions

AUG 9 Bill for relief of savings and loan institutions signed by the President

SEP 3-4 Labor Day weekend rioting in Virginia Beach instigated by students attending Greekfest

5 Pres. Bush announces $7.9 million National Drug Control Strategy

OCT 5 Bill outlawing desecration of US flag, providing for up to 1 year in prison and $1000 fine for violators, approved by Senate

12 House approves flag legislation

17 Earthquake strikes San Francisco, killing some 100 people

23 Explosions at Phillips Petroleum Co. plant in Pasedena, Tex, leaves 2 dead, 22 missing and 124 injured

24 Television evangelist Jim Bakker sentenced to 45 years in prison and fined $500,000 for 24 counts of fraud and conspiracy

The *Exxon Valdez*

The worst ever pollution disaster to occur in American waters took place in March 1989 when a giant oil tanker ran aground off the coast of Alaska. The 937-foot *Exxon Valdez* was holed on a reef in Prince William Sound, 25 miles from the port of Valdez, and a massive slick of some 10 million gallons of crude oil, covering 1600 square miles of water, was washed ashore along 100 miles of coastline in one of the richest wildlife sanctuaries in North America. While the authorities struggled to contain the slick with floating booms and detergent, irreparable damage was done to the local fauna, including thousands of seals, otters, and migratory seabirds.

Right: The *Exxon Baton Rouge*, the smaller ship in the photograph, lies alongside the crippled *Exxon Valdez* in a vast slick of oil as she attempts to unload her remaining cargoes of crude.

Below: The clean-up begins: workmen spray the oil-covered rocks on Smith Island in Prince William Sound.

Inset: One of the disaster's many helpless victims.

Two other manmade disasters helped raise environmental issues to the top of the political agenda in the 1980s. In 1984, 2000 people died and 180,000 were treated in hospital after poisonous gas escaped from a pesticide factory in Bhopal in the Indian state of Madhya Pradesh. A cloud of highly toxic methyl isocyanate from the Union Carbide plant drifted over the surrounding shanty town, causing its victims instant respiratory difficulties, foaming at the mouth, and unconsciousness. Some 200,000 survivors fled the town.

1986 saw the world's worst ever nuclear accident, when a fire at the Chernobyl nuclear power station in the Ukraine contaminated much of Europe with radioactive fall-out. Meltdown was avoided by sealing the damaged reactor with concrete (above), but restrictions were imposed on animal foodstuffs in many countries as tests showed levels of radioactivity well above normal in grazing animals such as sheep, cows, and reindeer. There was widespread criticism of the Soviet Union's secrecy and slow response to the disaster.

The Great Thaw

1989 witnessed changes in the political map of Europe more far-reaching than any since that map was first drawn in the aftermath of the Second World War. Spontaneous upsurges of popular dissent engulfed country after country in Eastern Europe, rocking to their very foundations the entrenched Communist régimes of the Soviet bloc. Despite the ominous shadow of the Tiananmen Square massacre in Beijing (in which more than 1000 people may have died when the Chinese authorities cracked down violently on demonstrations in support of greater democracy (top left)) vast crowds appeared on the streets of the Eastern European capitals to demand democratic reform, and one by one the governments of the Warsaw Pact – Poland, Hungary, Czechoslovakia, Bulgaria, East Germany – staggered and fell under the apparently unstoppable tide of their citizens' peaceful mass protest. In November, television viewers throughout the world witnessed emotional scenes in Berlin as the Berlin Wall – for so long the most potent symbol of East-West confrontation – was finally breached and tens of thousands of East German citizens crossed into the West (top right) to be reunited with friends and relatives from whom they had been separated since the closing of the border in 1961. Finally, in Romania, the hard-line Stalinist régime of Nicolai Ceausescu, which met the first wave of street protests in Timisoara and Bucharest with an extreme show of violence in which thousands may have been killed, was swept from power by a coalition of the army and pro-democracy factions (bottom right) and summarily executed by firing squad.

As Germany moved with breakneck speed towards reunification, and as N.A.T.O., in its London declaration of July 1990, officially recognized that the Warsaw Pact no longer represented a military threat to the West, the Soviet leader Mikhail Gorbachev – in many ways the fountainhead of all the changes in Eastern Europe – began, despite continuing warm relations with President George Bush (bottom left) and the British and West German Governments, to look increasingly beleaguered at home. The Cold War might be over, but as the 1990s began, many were questioning whether Gorbachev, the prime mover in the great thaw of the 1980s, would survive the pace of political change in the Soviet Union itself.

The 1990s

What the 1990s will bring for the United States, both domestically and internationally, is more than ever in doubt as the 1990s begin. Domestically, the accumulated social problems of the 1980s remain high on the political agenda for most ordinary Americans. The related crises of drug addiction, homelessness, and rising crime rates continue to cast a shadow over the everyday lives of many people in the major cities – crises compounded by enduring racial tensions, as witnessed most recently in the Marion Barry case in Washington and the so-called "jogger rape" case in New York City. "Taking back the streets" has proved a rallying cry for many law-abiding US citizens.

At the same time, the country appears poised on the brink of economic recession, with Federal attempts to contain its massive budget and trade deficits threatened by Congressional deadlock and by the financial implications of the crisis in the Persian Gulf. While the commercial effects on the United States of the political and economic changes in Europe have yet to become clear, the military situation in the Gulf has thrown into doubt the "peace dividend" until recently hoped for from the relaxation of East–West tension. Whatever its outcome, the Middle Eastern crisis has already demonstrated not only the strengths of the emerging new world order, but also the fact that threats to its stability are by no means limited to the relationship between the traditional superpowers and their respective allies.

Dick Tracy

In one of his most highly-publicized roles, Warren Beatty (above) co-starred with Madonna and a host of other well-disguised celebrities as the eponymous detective in the movie *Dick Tracy*.

Whither NATO?

Determining the post-Cold War military role of NATO, declared a primarily political organization in July 1990, will be one of the main diplomatic tasks of the 1990s. Above: NATO maneuvers in Norway.

Hostages

In April 1990, American hostages Robert Polhill and Frank Reed were released from captivity in Lebanon after Syrian and Iranian mediation. Reed (above), a 57-year old educationist, had been held, blindfolded 24 hours a day, for 3½ years after being kidnapped by the Organization of Islamic Dawn.

The Flag

A demonstrator sets fire to the Stars and Stripes on the Capitol steps to test a new Federal law against desecration of the US flag.

JAN 1 500,000 gallons of heating oil spill into New York Harbor after pipeline is hit by Exxon-owned vessel

3 Panamanian Gen. Manuel Noriega surrenders to US military

22 US-Soviet strategic arms reduction talks resume in Geneva

18 Longest and most expensive criminal trial in US history ends when Raymond Buckey and his mother Peggy McMartin Buckey, both of Los Angeles, Calif., are acquitted of 52 counts of child abuse

18 Marion Barry, Mayor of Washington, DC, arrested for cocaine possession

22 Worst computer breakdown in history of US telephone system

24 Retired Air Force general Richard V. Secord sentenced for his role as one of the principle participants in Iran-Contra scandal

FEB Death of artist Keith Haring

13 US and Soviet Union announce intention to reduce number of troops stationed in Central Europe

16-17 Former US President Ronald Reagan attends Los Angeles court in order to answer questions concerning his role in Iran-Contra scandal

20 Flag Protection Act declared unconstitutional by federal court

20 Drexel Burnham Lambert, Inc., files for bankruptcy; largest in Wall Street history

MAR 9 US Pacific territory of Guam passes highly restrictive anti-abortion law; enforcement suspended

22 Idaho passes anti-abortion law; vetoed by Governor

APR 7 Former National Security Adviser John M. Poindexter found guilty on all five felony counts arising from his role in Iran-Contra affair

22 US lecturer Robert Polhill, kidnapped by Islamic Jihad in Beirut in 1987, freed in West Beirut

30 US director of Lebanese International College, Frank Reed, kidnapped by Islamic Jihad in Beirut in 1986, released into Syrian custody in West Beirut

MAY 22 Bill passed outlawing discrimination against mentally and physically disabled; promises more employment opportunities and increased access to public facilities

31-JUN 3 Pres. Bush and Soviet Pres. Mikhail Gorbachev hold summit meeting in Washington, DC, and sign set of accords normalizing commercial relations between US and USSR for first time in 50 years

JUN US-Soviet summit in Washington, DC

JUN Savings and Loan institutions go bankrupt

AUG 2 Iraq invades Kuwait

5 US sends over 200 marines into besieged capital Monrovia, Liberia, to protect and evacuate US citizens and secure US installations during civil war

6 UN Security Council votes to impose total economic blockade on Iraq in retaliation for invasion of Kuwait

7 US announces that it will send several thousand troops and some combat aircraft to Saudi Arabia as part of multi-national defense force to confront imminent threat of Iraqi invasion

8 Iraq annexes Kuwait

8 US troops land at Dharan, Saudi Arabia

9 Iraq closes its borders to foreigners attempting to leave Iraq and Kuwait

10 Emergency Arab summit meeting in Cairo fails to reach solution to Gulf crisis

12 US announces that it will impose blockade on Iraq and occupied Kuwait

20 Iraq confirms that a number of Westerners have been rounded up and moved to military bases and other potential targets

24 Embassies in Kuwait refusing to obey Iraqi demands to close are surrounded by troops

SEP 4 US Navy impounds Iraqi ships

6 Iraqi troops shoot and wound US civilian

18 Pentagon announces US military base closures and cuts in 10 countries around the world

The Gulf Crisis

The cause of world peace suffered a serious setback with the invasion of Kuwait by Iraq in the late summer of 1990. Troops loyal to the Iraqi President, Saddam Hussein (top left), crossed the Kuwaiti border in force on August 2, driving the ruling al-Sabah family into exile, and shortly afterwards Saddam Hussein announced the annexation of Kuwait. An unprecedented coalition of United Nations member states imposed sweeping economic sanctions against Iraq, and the U.S. President, George Bush (top right), began a massive military build-up in the Gulf area as the spearhead of a multi-national force to defend against further Iraqi aggression and to enforce withdrawal. Thousands of Westerners and other foreign nationals initially held hostage in Kuwait and Iraq as a "human shield" against U.N. attack had begun to be released by the end of the year, but with the number of U.S. and other forces in the region increasing by the day (above, equipped for chemical warfare), and with Iraq seeking to link withdrawal from Kuwait with Israeli withdrawal from the occupied territories, a diplomatic solution to the crisis seemed as elusive as ever by the end of November, when a U.N. Resolution authorized the use of force if Iraq had not withdrawn from Kuwait by January 15, 1991.

SEP 26 US announces planned withdrawal of 40,000 troops from W Europe over next 12 months

30 Eleventh-hour draft budget agreement for fiscal 1991 averts imposition of Gramm-Rudman-Hollings law on deficit reduction

OCT 3 Germany officially reunifies

6 Space shuttle *Discovery* launches *Ulysses* probe at Cape Canaveral

7 Following failure to agree deficit reduction package, some government services, including the Statue of Liberty and the White House, closed to the public

14 Composer and musician Leonard Bernstein dies

26 Marion Barry, Mayor of Washington D.C., handed six-month prison sentence and $5000 fine for cocaine possession

28 Budget reduction package agreed by both Senate and House of Representatives; Congress adjourns

NOV 2 Ivana Trump files for divorce from tycoon Donald Trump

6 Democrats make gains in Congress in mid-term elections; voters in California reject 'Big Green' package of proposed environmental legislation

9 Bush announces massive increase in US troops in the Gulf to more than 400,000

18 Iraq announces release of all foreign hostages

19-21 CSCE summit in Paris formally ends Cold War

21 Michael Milken, the 'junk bond king,' sentenced to 10 years in prison for financial malpractice

22 Bush visits troops in Saudi Arabia

29 UN Security Council Resolution 678 authorizes use of 'all necessary means' to ensure Iraq's withdrawal from Kuwait and sets deadline of Jan 15, 1991

30 Bush offers talks to Iraq

DEC 2 Composer Aaron Copland dies

12 Bush agrees to send food aid to the Soviet Union

20 Soviet Foreign Minister Edward Shevardnadze resigns

1991

JAN 9 Secretary of State James Baker meets Iraqi Foreign Minister Tariq Aziz in Geneva in last-ditch attempt to avoid war

15 UN deadline passes without Iraqi withdrawal from Kuwait

16 War in Gulf begins with Allied bombardment of targets in Iraq and Kuwait

FEB 18 Tariq Aziz flies to Moscow for peace talks with President Gorbachev

22 Iraq and Soviet Union agree 8-point peace plan but this is unacceptable to Allies. President Bush issues ultimatum for withdrawal from Kuwait

24 Land war begins

26 Saddam Hussein orders his troops to withdraw

27 Kuwait City recaptured by Allied forces

28 Ceasefire in the Gulf announced

Air War

Less than 24 hours after the U.N. deadline of January 15 passed without seeing an Iraqi withdrawal from Kuwait, Allied forces launched massive air attacks on targets in Iraq and Kuwait. The Iraqi response to this first phase of the so-called "air war" was remarkably muted, although Saddam Hussein swiftly carried out his threat to retaliate against Israel in the event of attack by the U.N. forces by firing a number of Scud missiles at the Israeli cities of Tel Aviv and Haifa. Among the array of high-tech weaponry deployed for the first time during the war were Patriot missiles, an anti-aircraft system which proved effective in countering incoming Scud missiles, and a number of Patriot launchers such as the one shown here were stationed in Israel. By the end of January, Allied commanders were able to claim air supremacy in the Gulf.

Stormin' Norman

As Commander-in-Chief of the Allied forces in the Gulf, U.S. General Norman Schwarzkopf was the man responsible for converting Operation Desert Shield, the defense of Saudi Arabia from Iraqi attack, into Operation Desert Storm, the U.N. military campaign to liberate Kuwait.

Ecological disaster

The war also brought environmental catastrophe. A massive oil-slick formed, caused by Iraqi forces pumping oil into the sea to hamper any amphibious assault, and retreating troops set light to nearly 800 oil wells, leaving thick black smoke in the skies over Kuwait.

Land War

In a last ditch attempt to avoid a bloody battle on the ground Iraqi Foreign Minister Tariq Aziz flew to Moscow on February 18 for peace talks initiated by President Gorbachev. An 8-point peace plan was proposed but this was deemed unacceptable by the Allies who continued to demand an immediate and unconditional withdrawal from Kuwait and issued a new deadline. Iraqi troops made no move to withdraw and hours later Allied forces advanced into Kuwait where they met little resistance. Within a matter of days thousands of Iraqi soldiers had surrendered and Kuwait City had been liberated. A ceasefire was announced on February 28 and Allied and Iraqi military met to discuss plans for peace.

Index

Figures in italics refer to captions

Acadia (now Nova Scotia) 34
Achille Lauro (cruise liner) 368, *374*
Adams, John 46, 47, 50, 53, *57*, *60*, 80, 104
and Declaration of Independence 48, *54*
as President 60, 69, 70, 73, 90
and XYZ affair 70
Adams, John Quincy 60, *90*, 118, *121*
and Armistad case 96, *100*
and Missouri question 82
and Monroe Doctrine 88
as President 88, 90
Adams, Samuel 44, 45-6, 48
Afghanistan,
Soviet invasion 346, 348, 360, 366
Soviet withdrawal 368
African Methodist Episcopal Church 40
"Agent Orange" *332*
Agnew, Spiro 347, 348
Agricultural Adjustment Act 248
Aguinaldo, Emilio 175, *182*
AIDS *384-5*
Aix-la-Chapelle, Treaty of (1748) 35
Alabama 82, 86, 128, 296, 316
civil rights *319*
Alamo, the 93, 94, *94*, 105, *108*
Alaska 10, 105, *145*, 186, 188, 372, 388
admitted to the Union 310, *310*
earthquake *322*
Albany, New York 34
Albany Congress 36
Albany Plan of Union (1754) 36, 60
Alcott, Bronson 106
Alden, John 23, *24*
Aldrin, Edwin "Buzz" *342*, *345*
Algonquin Indians *11*, 35
Ali, Mohammed *329*
Alien and Sedition Acts 69
Alleghenies 37
Allen, Ethan 48, *54*
Alton, Illinois *124*
American Anti-Slavery Society 96
American Birth Control League *220*
American Civil War 52, 70, 102, 112, 113, 114, 118, 120, 123, 128-40, 146, 160, 161, 162, 172, *211*, *246*
American Federation of Labor 186
American Football League *328*
American Independence Bicentenary *348*
American Professional Football Association (A.F.L.) *328*
American Tobacco Company 188
Amherst, Jeffrey 37, 42
Amistad (slave-ship) 96
Andropov, Yuri 367
Anglo-American War (1812-14) 80-83, 84, 88
Annapolis, Maryland 46
Anne, Queen 33, 34, *34*, 35
Anniston, Alabama *319*
Anthony, Susan B. *143*, *220*
anti-slavery movement 40, 96, 119, 124
Antietam Creek *132*, 133, *133*
Anzio, Allied invasion 271
Apache Indians 148, *168*
Apollo 13 *349*
Apollo space program 317, *342*
Appalachians 32, 35, 41, 42, 47, 56, 66, 72
Appomattox Court House, Virginia 108, 138, 139, 141, *272*
Aquino, Benigno 378
Aquino, Corazon *378*
Arapahoe Indians 148
Argentina, and Falklands War 372
Arizona 11, 14, *168*, 186, 202, *326*
Arkansas 128
Armstrong, Louis "Satchmo" 224, *230*, *232*
Armstrong, Neil 317, *342*, *345*
Army of the Potomac 129, 130, *132*, 133, 134
Arthur, Chester A. 160, 161
Articles of Confederation 57, 59, 62
Astaire, Fred *254*
Astor Place Opera House, New York *114*
Atlanta, Georgia 134, 136, *137*, *167*
Atlantic and Great Western railroad *127*
Atlantic Charter 264
Attucks, Crispus 45
Augusta, U.S.S. 264
Austin, Stephen Fuller 94, *94*
Ayllon, Vasquez de 15
Aztecs 11, 13

Baader-Meinhof Gang 354
Babcock, Orville E. 146
Badger, George E. *105*
Bahamas 10, 13, *13*
Bakker, Jim *378*
Baltimore 32, 37, *40*, *148*
siege of 81, *81*
Baltimore, George Calvert, Lord 28
Baltimore and Ohio railroad company *127*
Bank of the United States, Philadelphia *71*, 82, 92, *99*
Barbary pirates 77
Barnum, Phineas T. *101*
Barré, Isaac 44
Barrow, Clyde *256*
Bartholdi, Frederic Auguste *170*
Baruch, Bernard 202, *206*, 268, 285
baseball *218*, *328*, 362
basketball *362*
Bastille, taking of *64*
Bataan, "Death March" *275*
Batista, Fulgencio 310, 314
Batman (film) *387*
Bay of Pigs 314
Bazares, Guido de las 15
Bear Flag *114*
Beat movement *311*
Beatles *327*, 371
Beatty, Warren *392*
Dick Tracy (film) *392*
Beaumont, Texas *196*
Beauregard, P.G.T. 129
Bedloe's Island, New York *170*
Beef Trust 188
Begin, Menachem 348, *360*
Beirut, Lebanon 310, *310*
U.S. embassy attacked *372*
Belize 91
Belknap, William W. 146
Bell, Alexander Graham *154*, *155*
Benedek, Laslo, *Wild One* (film) *304*
Benghazi, bombed by U.S. *379*
Benson, Thomas *112*
Bergman, Ingrid *290*
Bering Sea, fishing dispute 174
Bering Strait 10
Berkeley, John, Lord 28
Berlin, Irving,
Alexander's Ragtime Band 217
"Cheek to Cheek" *254*
Top Hat (film) *254*
Berlin Airlift 286, *286*
Berlin Wall 315, *320*, 366, 368, 390
Bernstein, Carl 347, *358*, *365*
Bernstein, Leonard, *West Side Story 321*
Bhopal disaster *389*
Big Foot, Chief *176*
Big Horn, Rocky Mountains 34
Bikini Atoll *283*, *306*
Bill of Rights (1689) 29
Bill of Rights Amendments 59, 62
Billy the Kid (William H. Bonney) *158*
Birmingham, Alabama 316, *319*
Black Barons 362
Black Hawk, Chief *97*
Black Hills, South Dakota 148, *152*
Black Monday (Stock Exchange crash) *379*
Black Panthers *336*
"Black Sox" scandal *218*
Blackboard Jungle (film) *303*
Blacks,
in American Civil War 139, *139*
civil rights 147-8, 172, 173, *174*, 186, 213, 294, 296, *296*, 315-16, *319*, 334, *336*
colonial 38, 40
emancipation 140, *140*, *141*, 142, 146, *174*, 186
franchise *152*, 173, 186
and jazz *230*, *232*
in North African campaign *270*
position in American society 74, 160, 161, 173, *326*
poverty *240*
see also slavery
Blaine, James G. 160, 161, 173
Boeing 707 (airliner) *308*
Bogart, Humphrey *290*
Bolivar, Simon *91*
Bolivia 91
Bonney, William H. (Billy the Kid) *158*
Book of Mormon 107
Boone, Daniel 56, *66*
Booth, John Wilkes 139, *139*
Bork, Robert 347
Boscawen, Edward 37
Boston, Massachusetts 33, 37, 47, 48, 56
busing dispute *357*
and Stamp Act 44
Boston Celtics 362
Boston Massacre 45-6, *45*
Boston Tea Party 46-7, *46*
Bow, Clara *226*
Bowie, Jim 93
Braddock, Edward 36, 37
Bradford, William 23, 24-5
Bradstreet, John 37
Brady, Mathew *136*
Bragg, General 134
Brandenburg Gate, Berlin *320*, 368
Brando, Marlon *304*
The Godfather 365
Brandywine Creek, Battle of 51
Bray, Dr Thomas 30
Breed's Hill, Battle of 48
Brendan the Navigator, St 10
Brewster, William 24
Brezhnev, Leonid 348, *356*, 366, 367
Britain 41-8, 92, 200, 202, 249, *263*, 295, 296, 390
Alaskan border dispute 188
and American Civil War 146
and Atlantic Charter 264
and *Caroline* incident 93, *100*, 104
cotton trade 129
Expeditionary Force *265*
Falklands War 372
fishing dispute 172, 174
and Louisiana Purchase 72-3
and Monroe Doctrine 88, 105
naval rivalry 223
and Revolutionary War 50, 51, 56, 317
war with France 68, 69, 74, 80
war with U.S. (1812-14) 80-83
British East India Company 46
British Empire 31, 41, 43, 44, 50
Brook Farm, Massachusetts 106
Brooklyn Bridge *166*
Brooklyn Heights *99*
Brooks, Louise *226*
Brooks, Preston 119
Brown v. Board of Education of Topeka (1954) 296
Brown, John 119, *120*
Brown University 39
Browne, Carl 172
Brunswick, N. Carolina 48
Bryan, William Jennings 172, *172*, 200, 202, *243*
Buchanan, James 128
Buell, D. C. 131
Buena Vista, Battle of 105, 106, 108
Buffalo, New York *148*, 186, *193*
"Bulge, Battle of the" 278, *278*, *279*
Bull Run Creek 129, *129*, 130, 133
Bunker Hill, Battle of 48, *52*
Bureau of Indian Affairs 352
Burger, Warren *370*
Burgoyne, John 51
Burke, Edmund 44
Burnside, A. E. 133
Burr, Aaron 73, *73*
Burroughs, Edgar Rice *216*
Tarzan of the Apes 216
Burroughs, William *311*
Naked Lunch 311
Bush, George 367, 368, *390*, *393*
busing *357*
Byrnes, James F. 268

Cabot, John 18
Cabot, Sebastian 18
"Calamity" Jane (Martha Jane Cannary) *183*
Calhoun, John C. 88, 92-3, 104, 118, *121*
California 18, 104, 105, 108, 112, 118, 188, 249, *252*
admitted to the Union *118*
Chinese community *163*
declared a republic *114*
election of 1968 317, 335
gold rush 106, *114*, *116-17*, 120
Manson murders 337
railroad *126*
California Railroad Company *169*
Calloway, Cab *261*
Cambodia 330, 346, 350, *351*, 352
Cambridge, Massachusetts 27
Camden, Battle of 56
Camden, Charles, Lord 42
Canada 248, 352
and *Caroline* incident *100*
French colony 16, 19, 32-5, *32*, 37, 48
invasion of 80, 81, 84
Niagara Falls Bridge *180*
and Treaty of Ghent 82
and Van Buren 92
Canning, George 80
Cape Breton 34, 35
Cape Canaveral, Florida *308*, *323*, *376*
Cape Cod 23
Cape Cod Bay 23
Cape Horn 117
Cape Kennedy, Florida *342*
Capitol, Washington, D. C. *144*, *326*
Capone, Al *225*, *234*
Caribbean 14, 32, 51, 56, 76, 382
Carlos, John *337*
Carmichael, Stokely 316, 336
Carnegie, Andrew 146, 148, *154*, 188
Carnegie Homestead Steel Works 172, *173*
Caroline incident 93, *100*, 104
"carpetbaggers" 142, *142*
Carranza, Venustiano 201, *214*
Carter, Jimmy 346, *360*, *366*
and Egypt-Israeli conflict 348, 360
Iran hostage crisis 360, 366, 367, *369*
SALT II treaty 348
Carteret, Sir George 28
Carthage, Illinois 107
Cartier, Jacques 16, *16*
Cascade Mountains 10
Casey, William 380
Castro, Fidel 310, *310*, 314
Cather, Willa *238*
Catt, Carrie Chapman *220*
Cavendish, Thomas 18
Cayuga Indians 36
Ceausescu, Nicolai 368, 390
Centennial Exposition (1876) 154
Central America 367
Central Intelligence Agency (CIA) 288, 314, 348, 380
Central Pacific railroad *127*, *144*
Chakiris, George *321*
Challenger (space shuttle) *376-7*
Chamberlain, Clarence *236*
Chamoun, Camille 310
Champlain, Lake 33, 36, 81
Champlain, Samuel 16
Chancellorsville, Battle of 134, *134*
Chaplin, Charlie *211*
Gold Rush 224, *228*
The Kid 224, *228*
Chapman, Mark 371
Chappaquiddick Island, Massachusetts *335*
Chapultepec *108*
Charles I, King 22, 26, 28
Charles II, King 28, *29*
charleston (dance) *233*
Charleston, S. Carolina 37, 46, 56, *124*, 128, *128*, 382
Charlestown 47
Charlestown Peninsula *52*
Charlotonia project 42
Chattanooga, Battle of 134, *135*, 136
Chateau Louis, Quebec 33
Chernenko, Konstantin 367
Chernobyl, nuclear accident 368, *389*
Cherokee Indians 80, *92*, 96
Cherokee Strip, Oklahoma *168*
Chesapeake, U.S.S. 74
Chesapeake Bay 15, 19, 32, 56, 132
Cheyenne Indians 148
Chiang Kai-Shek 295
Chicago 90, 107, *148*, *188*, *210*, 247, *256*, 317
Fire *149*
gangsters *225*
Haymarket Riot *169*
jazz 224, *230*
Life Insurance Building *198*
Robie House *210*
World Columbian Exposition *177*, *198*
Chicago Seven *355*
Chicago White Sox *218*
Chickawa Indians 96
Child Labor Act (1916) *212*
Chile 18, 172, 173
Chilton, Mary *24*
China 249, 266, 288, 295, 315
and Korean War 294, 299
Nixon visits 348, *356*
U.S. "dollar diplomacy" 200
U.S. Open Door policy 188, *192*
Chirico, Giorgio de *241*
Choctaw Indians 96
Christian Science *153*
Church of Latter-day Saints 107, *111*
Churchill, Winston *265*
and Atlantic Charter 264
"iron curtain" speech 264, 285
at Potsdam conference *284*
at Yalta conference *284*, 285
Cincinnati, Ohio 107
Cincinnati Reds *218*
City Point, Virginia *136*
Civil Rights Act (1875) 147
Civil Rights Acts *319*
Clark, Dr Barney B. *373*
Clark, Mark W. 271
Clark, William 72, 73, *78*, 79, *79*
Clay, Henry *99*, *115*, 118, 121
and "American System" 104, 107
and Tariff Act 93, 115
and "War Hawks" 80, 84, 88, 99
Cleaver, Eldridge 316, 336
Clemenceau, Georges 203, *209*
Clemens, Samuel Langhorne *see* Twain, Mark
Cleveland, Grover *167*
achievements 161, 167
election campaign 160-61
and Hawaiian uprising 174, *177*
and labor relations 172, 188
and Pan-American Conference 173
Cleveland, Ohio 90, 107, 187, 246
Clinton, George 68, 73
Clinton, Sir Henry 48, 51, 56
Cobb, Ty *218*
Coca-Cola *167*
Cochran, Eddie *303*
Cody, "Buffalo" Bill *176*
Cohn, Roy 300, *300*
Cold Harbor 134
Cold War 264, 285, 288, *292*, 294, *295*, 310, 314, 315, 317, *320*, 366, 367, 368, 390
Colden, Lieut. Governor 44
Colfax, Schuyler 147
College of New Jersey (later Princeton University) 39
Collins, Michael *342*
Colombia 186
Panamanian Revolution 188, 200
Colorado 148, *157*, 249
Colt, Samuel *100*
Colt Revolver *100*
Columbia, S. Carolina 136
Columbia University 39
Columbus, Christopher 10-14, *10*, *13*, 16, *177*
Columbus, New Mexico *214*
Comanche Indians 148
Comets (rock 'n' roll group) *303*
Committee of Correspondence 46
Compromise of 1850 99, 118, 124
Concord, Massachusetts 47, 48, 50
Confederate States of America 128-31, 133, 134, 136, 138, 139, 140, 146, 172
Congress, formation of 59
Connecticut 27, 34, 47, 57
1662 charter 29
Connolly, "Little Mo" *329*
Conrad, Charles *349*
Constitution 81, 92
forging of 56, 58-9, 60, 62, 69
presented to Washington *62*
and slavery 65
Constitution, U.S.S. "Old Ironsides" 81, *85*
Continental Congresses
First 47
Second 48, 50
Contras, Nicaragua 368, *374*, 380
Coogan, Jackie *228*
Coolidge, Calvin 222-3, *223*, 297
Cooper, Gary *301*
Cooper, James Fenimore *114*
Last of the Mohicans 91
Leatherstocking Tales 91, *114*
Pioneers 91
Copland, Aaron *259*
Billy the Kid 259
Coppola, Francis Ford, *The Godfather* (film) *365*
Coral Sea, Battle of the 272
Corinth, Mississippi 131
Corliss steam engine *154*
Cornwallis, Charles, Lord 48, *52*, 56
Coronada, Francisco Vasquez de 14, 15
Corregidor, U.S. surrender 272
Corso, Gregory *311*
Cortes, Hernando 13, 15, 17
Courgues, Dominique de 17
cowboys 146, 148, *157*, *158*
Cox, Archibald 347, 348

Coxey, Jacob 172
"crack" 386
Crazy Horse 159
Credit Mobilier scandal 146
Creek Indians 82, 86, 96
Creek War 86
Creel, George 202
"Creole Jazz Band" 230, 232
Crockett, Davy 93, 94
Crosby, Bing 290
Crow Indians 148
Crown Point 36, 37, 48
Cruze, James, Covered Wagon (film) 226
Cuba 21, 37, 186
   Bay of Pigs 314
   revolution (1959) 310, 314
   and Spanish-American war 172, 174-5, 182, 186
Cuban missile crisis 314-15, 315
cults 363
Cumberland Landing, Virginia 132
Currency Act (1764) 43
Curtiss Field, Long Island 236
Curtiz, Michael, Casablanca (film) 290
Custer, George 148, 159
Czolgosz, Leon 187

D-Day 276
Dachau, concentration camp 280
Dakota 152, 157
Dakota Building, New York City 371
Dakota Oglala Indians 159
Dakota Sioux Indians 176
Dale, Governor 20
Dale Creek Bridge 180
Dali, Salvador 241
Dallas, Texas 314, 315, 324
Darrow, Clarence 243
Dartmouth, William Legge, Earl of 47
Dartmouth College 39
Daugherty, Harry M. 222
Davis, Jefferson 97, 105, 108, 128, 128, 129, 136, 138
Davis, Rennie 355
Dawes, William (Billy), Jr 47
Dawson City 180
Dawson's Field, U.S. hostages held 354
De Mille, Cecil B.
   King of Kings 226
   Ten Commandments 224, 226
De Soto, Hernando 14, 14
Deadwood, S. Dakota 157, 158
Dean, James 304
   Giant 304
   Rebel Without a Cause 304
Dean, John W. 347
Debs, Eugene 206
Decatur, Stephen 77
Declaration of Independence 48, 49, 50, 50, 54 56, 57, 59, 69, 74, 92, 175
Declaratory Act (1766) 44
Delaware 28, 30, 128
Democrats 88, 104, 147, 160, 161, 172, 186, 200, 220, 247, 288, 314, 315, 317, 347, 348, 355, 358
Dempsey, Jack 216
Deseret (Mormon state) 111
Desirade, W. Indies 37
Detroit 81
DeVries, Dr William 373
Dewey, George 175
Dewey, Thomas E. 288
Dickinson, Emily 176
Dickinson, John 44-5, 47, 48
Dietrich, Marlene 254
Dillinger, John 256
DiMaggio, Joe 288
Dingley Tariff Act (1987) 189
Dinwiddie, Robert 36
Discovery (ship) 19
Disney, Walt 306
   Fantasia 291
   Steamboat Willie 224, 228
Disneyland, California 306
District of Columbia 118
Dixon, Jeremiah 39
Doenitz, Karl 278
Dominican Republic 72, 188, 200, 201, 223, 310
Doors, The (rock group) 317, 341
Dorchester Heights 48
Dorsey, Tommy 292
Dos Passos, John 238
Douglas, Stephen A. 118, 120
Douglass, Frederick 141
Drake, Sir Francis 18

Drane and Alexander (vaudeville duo) 216
Dreiser, Theodore 239
   American Tragedy 239
   Sister Carrie 239
drought (1988) 383
Dulles, John Foster 294, 295, 306
Dumbarton Oaks conference 285
Duryea Brothers 179
Dust Bowl 246, 249, 252, 383
Dutch East India Company 28
Dutch Reformed Church 39, 40
Dylan, Bob 341
   Blowing in the Wind 341
   Like a Rolling Stone 341
   Times They Are A'Changing 341

"Eagle" (lunar module) 342, 345
Earhart, Amelia 236
Eastman, George 163
Eaton, John H. 92
Eaton, Mrs 92
Economic Opportunity Act (1964) 315
Eddy, Mary Baker 153
   Science and Health with Key to the Scriptures 153
Edison, Thomas Alva 155, 178, 195
Edwards, Jonathan 40
Ehrlichman, John 346, 359
Eiffel, Gustave 170
Einstein, Izzy 234
Eisenhower, Dwight D. 276, 294
   and Black civil rights 296
   "domino theory" 316
   and "dynamic conservatism" 296-7, 314
   elected president 294
   ends Korean War 294-5
   at Geneva summit 306
   and Hawaii 310
   and Lebanon 310
   in North African campaign 270, 270
   in Operation Overlord 276
   receives German surrender 278
Eliot, T.S. 238, 239
   Waste Land 238, 239
Elizabeth I, Queen 18
Elk Hills, California 222
Ellington, Edward Kennedy "Duke" 224, 261
Ellis Island, New York 184
Emancipation Proclamation 139
Embargo Act (1807) 74
Emergency Banking Act 247
Emergency Relief Appropriation Act (1935) 248
Emerson, Ralph Waldo 106, 107, 114, 119
   Representative Men 120
Empire State Building 198
Employment Act (1946) 288
Enforcement Acts (1870/71) 147
England,
   colonial wars 32-7
   and colonization 17-18, 23-32
   see also Britain
ENIAC computer 293
Eric the Red 10
Erie, Lake 11, 35, 81, 90
Erie, Pennsylvania 268
Erie Canal 90, 99
Erie Railroad Company 172
Ervin, Sam, Jr 347
Esch-Cummins Transportation Act 222
Espionage Act (1917) 202
Evans, Hiram Wesley 242
"Explorer" satellite 308
Exxon Baton Rouge (ship) 388
Exxon Valdez (oil tanker) 388

Fairbanks, Douglas 211, 224, 226
   Don Q Son of Zorro 226
   Thief of Baghdad 226
Falkland Islands, U.S. shuttle diplomacy 372
Fall, Albert B. 222
Fallen Timbers, Battle of 69
Farmers' Alliance 172
"Farmers' Revolt" 172
Farragut, David 131, 134
Faubus, Orville 296
Faulkner, William 238, 239
   As I Lay Dying 224
   Sartoris 239
   Soldier's Tale 239
   Sound and the Fury 224, 239
Federal Bureau of Investigation (FBI) 256, 348
Federal Convention (1787) 59, 60, 69

Federal Emergency Relief Act 248
Federal Government
   and Constitution 62, 65
   formation of 59
Federal Reserve Act (1913) 200
Federal Trade Commission Act 200
Federalists 68, 69, 72, 73, 81, 104
Feisal, King 310
Ferdinand, King of Spain 13
Ferlinghetti, Lawrence 311
First Amendment 69, 346
Fisk, "Jubilee Jim" 151
Fitzgerald, F. Scott 238
   Beautiful and Damned 224
   Great Gatsby 222, 224, 238
   This Side of Paradise 224
Fitzgerald, Scottie 238
Fitzgerald, Zelda 238
Fleury, André-Hercule de 34
Florida 14-19, 42, 56, 82, 88, 92, 128, 175
"Flyer" (plane) 192
Flying Cloud (clipper) 120
Fonda, Peter 340
Food and Drug Act 196
football 328
Foraker Act (1900) 186
Forbes, Charles R. 222
Ford, Gerald 346, 347, 348
Ford, Henry 179, 194, 223, 269
Ford, John, Stagecoach (film) 254
Ford Motor Company 194, 224
Formosa (later Taiwan) 195
Forrest, Edwin 114
Fort Apache 41
Fort Caroline 16
Fort Clatsop 73, 79
Fort Donelson 130, 131
Fort Duquesne 36, 37
Fort Frontenac 37
Fort Henry 130, 131
Fort Hudson 134
Fort Mims 86
Fort Necessity 36
Fort Niagara 36, 37, 41
Fort Oswego 36, 37
Fort Pitt 37
Fort Sumter 128, 128, 129
Fort William Henry 36
Foster, Jodie 371
Founding Fathers 60
Fox Indians 97
France 68, 69, 74, 80, 202, 249, 263, 295, 296
   colonial wars 32-7, 41
   colonization 15-17, 31
   and Louisiana Purchase 108
   and Moroccan crisis 188-9
   and Revolutionary War 48, 51
   and Statue of Liberty 170
   and XYZ affair 69, 70
Francis I, King of France 15, 16
Franklin, Benjamin 37-8, 39, 42, 60
   and Albany Plan 36
   and boycotts 46
   and Declaration of Independence 48, 54
   and Federal Convention 59
   scientific interests 60
   and Treaty of Paris 56
Fredrick Hall, New York 58, 59
Fredericksburg, Battle of 133, 133, 134
Frelinghuysen, Theodorus 40
Frémont, John C. 105, 112, 114
French and Indian War (1754-63) 35-7, 36
French Revolution 64, 68
Friendship 7 spacecraft 323
Frobisher, Martin 18
Frontenac, Louis, Comte de 33, 33
Frost, Robert 239
   New Hampshire 239
Fugitive Slave Act 124

Gable, Clark 254
Gadaffi, Colonel 368, 379
Gadsden, Christopher 47
Gagarin, Yuri 317, 323, 342
Gage, Thomas 47, 48
Galena, Illinois 130
Gama, Vasco de 13, 14
Garay, Francis de 15
Garfield, James A. 160, 160
Garrison, William Lloyd 96
Garvey, Marcus 240
Gaspee, The (ship) 46
Gates, Horatio 56, 58
Gaulle, Charles de 315
Gehrig, Lou 218
General Electric 178, 268

Geneva disarmament conference (1960) 314
Geneva summit conferences
   1955: 295, 296, 306
   1985: 367-8
George, Lake 36
George III, King 37, 42, 44, 46, 48, 52, 56, 57, 84, 104
George Washington University Hospital 371
Georgia 30, 44, 47, 56, 82, 128, 136, 242, 296, 367
"Georgia Jazz Band" 230
Germany 32, 33, 120, 202-3, 204, 206, 209, 249, 263, 285, 296, 314, 354
   attacks Venezuela 188
   Berin Airlift 286
   Blitzkrieg 264
   invaded by U.S. 276, 278
   Kennedy visits 320
   mercenaries from Hesse 48
   Moroccan crisis 188-9
   reunification 390
Geronimo 168
Gerry, Elbridge 70
Gershwin, George 233
   Lady Be Good (musical) 224, 233
   Rhapsody in Blue 224, 233
Gettysburg, Battle of 134, 135, 368
Ghent, Treaty of 81, 82
Giancano, Sam 322
Gilbert, Sir Humphrey 18
Gilbert Islands 272
Ginsberg, Allen 311
   Howl and other Poems 311
Glamorous Glennis (rocket plane) 289
Glasgow, Ellen 238
Glenn, John. H. 323
Godspeed (ship) 19
gold rush 104, 106, 114, 116-17, 120, 152, 157, 163, 180
Golden Hind, The (ship) 18
Goldwater, Barry 315
Goliad, Texas 93
Gompers, Samuel 186
Gorbachev, Mikhail 366, 368
   and Bush 390
   and Reagan 367-8
Graham, Billy 308
Graham, Martha 233
Grand Canyon 15
"Grange, the" 143
Granger movement 172
Grant, Ulysses S. 130
   in American Civil War 130-32, 134, 136, 136, 138, 138
   in Mexican War 105, 108, 128
   as President 142, 146, 146, 147, 153, 154, 160, 172, 222
Grasse, Admiral de 56
Gray, L. Patrick 347
Great Awakening 40
Great Depression 222, 224, 244, 246, 246, 247, 249, 250-1, 254, 256, 262
Great Exhibition, London (1851) 122
Great Lakes 32, 34, 56, 82, 90, 120
Great Plains 79, 107, 111, 117, 118, 146, 148, 151, 157, 158
Great Salt Lake 107, 111
Great Seal of the United States of America 64
Great Strike (1877) 148, 148
Green Bay Packers 328
Green Mountain Boys 54
Greenbriar Company 35
Greene, Nathanael 56
Grenada 37, 42
Grenville, George 42, 44
Griffith, David Wark 211
   Birth of a Nation 211
Groton, Connecticut 309
Guadalcanal, Battle of 272
Guadaloupe 37, 382
Guadalupe Hidalgo, Treaty of 105-6
Guam 175, 266, 272
Guatemala 11, 314
Guggenheim Museum 312
Guerriere, HMS 85
Guiteau, Charles 160, 160
Gulf crisis, the 393, 394
Guyman, Oklahoma 252

H-bomb 306
Haig, Alexander 372
Hair (musical) 340
Haise, Fred 349
Haiti 13, 72
   American occupation 200, 201, 215
Haldeman, H. R. (Bob) 346, 359
Haley, Bill 303
Halifax, Nova Scotia 48

Hall, Fawn 380
Halley's Comet (1910 appearance) 212
Hamilton, Alexander,
   death 73
   and Federal Convention 59
   and French Revolution 69
   and Jefferson 72
   and Newburgh Conspiracy 58
   as Secretary of Treasury 68, 68, 71, 82
Hammett, Dashiell 288
   Thin Man 288
Hampton Roads, battle of the ironclads 131
Handy, W. C. 217
Hanna, Marcus Alonzo 172, 186
Harding, Warren 222, 222, 223
Hardy, Oliver 228
Harlem 334
   Cotton Club 261
Harlem Globetrotters 362
Harper's Ferry raid 119, 120
Harriman, Edward H. 188
Harrisburg, Pennsylvania (nuclear accident) 364
Harroun, Ray 201
Harrison, Benjamin 160, 161, 172, 174, 177
Harrison, George 327
Harrison, William H. 107
   and Battle of the Thames 84
   and Battle of Tippecanoe 80, 84, 86
   election of (1840) 104, 160
Hartford, Connecticut 27, 81, 81, 258
Harvard University 29, 38, 293
Hathaway, Henry, True Grit (film) 333
Hauptmann, Bruno 257
Havana 37, 174
   Castro enters 310
Hawaii 172, 186
   admitted to the Union 310, 310
   annexation 174, 177
Hawaiian Islands 266
Hawke, Edward 37
Hawkins, Sir John 18, 21
Hawthorne, Nathaniel 101, 106, 114
   Blithedale Romance 101, 106
   House of the Seven Gables 101, 120
   Scarlet Letter 101, 120
Hay, John 175
Hayes, Rutherford B. 146, 147, 148, 159, 160, 161
Hayne, Robert Young 92
Hearst, Patty 355
Hearst, William Randolph 181
Hemingway, Ernest 238, 260
   Farewell to Arms 224
   Sun Also Rises 224
   To Have and Have Not 260
Henderson, Richard 42
Hendrix, Jimi 338
Henry, Patrick 47, 48
Henry VIII, King 17
Hickock, "Wild Bill" 157
Hill, James J. 188
Hillsborough, Wills Hill, Viscount 44
Hinckley, John Warnock 371
Hindenburg (airship) 258
Hirohito, Emperor 282
Hiroshima, bombed 264, 282, 282, 306
Hispaniola, Haiti 13
Hiss, Alger 292, 296
Hitler, Adolf 246, 249, 259, 263, 264, 270, 278
Ho Chi Minh 316, 330
Hodges, Courtney 276
Hoffman, Abbie 355
Hoffman, Dustin 365
Holliday, Billie 261
   Strange Fruit (song) 261
Holly, Buddy 303
Holmes, Oliver Wendell 114
   Autocrat of the Breakfast Table 120
Hong Kong, attacked by Japan 266
Honolulu, revolution 174
Hooker, "Fighting Joe" 134
Hooker, Rev. Thomas 27
Hoover, Herbert 222, 223, 247
   acceptance speech 223
   and Great Depression 250-51
   and "Hoovervilles" 246, 251
   and Wall Street Crash 224
Hoover, J. Edgar 256
Hope, Bob 290
Hopewell, New Jersey 257
Hopi Indians 11
Hopkins, Harry L. 248, 248, 249

396

Hopkins, Stephen 47
Hopkinson, Francis 54
Hopper, Dennis 230
  Easy Rider (film) 340
Hopper, Edward 293
  Nighthawks 293
Horseshoe Bend, Battle of 82, 86
"Hot Five" 232
Houdini, Harry (Ernst Weiss) 197
House Committee to Investigate Un-
  American Activities (H.U.A.C.)
  292, 300
House of Representatives, creation
  of 59, 62
Houston, Sam 93, 94, 94, 104
Houston, Texas 94
  Mission Operations Control
  Center 342
Howe, Sir William 48, 52
Howells, William Dean 161
Hubertusburg, Treaty of 37
Hudson, Henry 18, 18, 28
Hudson Bay, fur trading 34
Hudson highlands 194
Hue, S. Vietnam 330
Huerta, Victoriano 201
Hughes, Howard 258
Humphrey, Hubert 317
Hunt, Richard Morris 198
Hurricane Hugo 382
Hussein, Saddam 393, 394
Hutchinson, Ann 27
Hutchinson, Thomas 44, 45
Hutchinson, William 36

Idaho 151
Ide, William 114
Illinois 42, 82, 97, 172
Incas 11, 13
Independence, Missouri 96
Independence Day 50, 54, 216
Indian Territory 96, 168
Indiana 82
Indianapolis 500 211
Indians 27, 29, 35, 39
  alliance with British 69, 80, 80
  attacks on settlers 66, 80
  in colonial wars 34-7
  contacts with explorers 73, 78, 79
  driven westward 88, 96
  first contact with Europeans 11-
    16, 12, 17, 18
  militancy 326, 352
  and Pilgrim Fathers 24-5, 25
  and Pontiac's Conspiracy 41
  and Proclamation of 1763 42
  in Virginia 19-23
  in war of 1812 81, 82, 84
  way of life destroyed 148, 158, 159,
    168, 176, 186
Indochina 294, 346
INF Treaty 368
International Business Machines
  Corporation (IBM) 293, 297
  launches PC 373
Interstate Commerce Act (1887) 161,
  188
Intolerable Acts 47
Iowa 249
I.R.A. 354
Iran,
  hostage crisis 346, 348, 360, 366,
    369
  U.S. sale of arms to 380
  war with Iraq 367, 369
Irangate 380–81
Iraq 393, 394
Ireland 17, 29, 33, 112, 120
  explorers 10
  immigrants 30, 112, 120
  I.R.A. 354
Iroquois Indians 11, 28, 36
Irving, Washington 114
Isabella, Queen of Spain 13
Iwo Jima, capture of 274, 274

Jackson, Andrew 93, 104, 106, 118,
  119, 160, 189
  and Battle of Horseshoe Bend 86
  defense of New Orleans 81, 82, 84
  and Indian resettlement 96, 97
  and the "Negro question" 124
  and Nullification Crisis 92-3, 96
  as President 88, 92
Jackson, Michael 387
  Thriller 387
Jackson, Michigan 119
Jackson, "Shoeless" Joe 218
Jackson, Thomas "Stonewall" 129,
  129, 132, 133, 134
Jamaica 31
James, Harry 292

James, Henry 181
  Awkward Age 181
  Spoils of Poynton 181
  Tragic Muse 181
  Turn of the Screw 181
  What Maisie Knew 181
James, Jesse 157
James I, King 19, 21, 26
James II, King 26, 29, 33
Jamestown, Virginia 19-23, 19, 22,
  26, 29
Japan 188, 249, 266
  attack on Pearl Harbor 264, 266,
    266
  naval rivalry 223
  Pacific war 272, 274
  U.S. trade with 120, 122
Jarvis, Greg 376
Jay, John 60, 69
Jay Cooke and Company 150
jazz 217, 222, 224, 230, 232, 233, 261
Jeffers, Robinson 238
  Tamar and Other Poems 238
Jefferson, Thomas 59, 60, 74, 88, 92,
  104, 188, 198
  admires French Revolutionaries
    69
  and Blacks 74
  and Burr plan 73, 74
  and Central Bank proposal 68
  drafts Declaration of
    Independence 48, 50, 54
  inaugural address 72
  and Indian resettlement 96, 97
  interests 74
  and Lewis-Clark expedition 79
  and Louisiana Purchase 72, 104,
    108
  and Napoleon 76
  as President 72
  on slavery 82
  trade embargo 74, 76, 80
Jefferson Airplane 338
Jefferson Memorial, Washington 74
Jenkins, Robert 34
Jenkins' Ear, War of 34-5
Jenny, William 198
Jim Crow laws 296
Jitterbug 293
John F. Kennedy airport 312
Johnson, Andrew 141, 141, 142, 142,
  145
Johnson, Hugh S. 248
Johnson, Lyndon B. 33
  and Civil Rights Act 316, 326
  and the "Great Society" 315
  sworn in as President 324
  and Vietnam 314, 316, 333
Johnson, Tom L. 187
Johnson, Sir William 36, 37, 42
Johnston, Joseph 131
Johnstown, Pennsylvania (flood) 167
Jolson, Al 232
  Jazz Singer (film) 224, 232
Jones, Jim 363
Jones, Samuel M. 187
Jonestown, Guyana (mass-suicide
  at) 363
Joplin, Janis 338
Joplin, Scott 217
  The Entertainer 217
  Maple Leaf Rag 217

KAL 007, Korean airliner 372
Kanagawa, Shogun of 122
Kansas 105, 118
  agrarian depression 172
  Dust Bowl 249
  Slave battle 119, 119
Kansas City Chiefs 328
Kansas-Nebraska Act 118, 119
Kazan, Elia,
  East of Eden (film) 304
  On the Waterfront (film) 304
Kearny, Stephen 105
Keaton, Buster,
  Go West 224, 228
  The Navigator 228
Kellogg-Briand Pact 222, 223
Kennedy, Edward 335
Kennedy, John F. 314, 335
  and Apollo space program 317,
    323, 342
  assassination 315, 324
  civil rights bill 316
  and Cuban missile crisis 314-15
  and "New Frontier" 314
  visits West Berlin 320, 368
Kennedy, Robert 317, 335
Kent State University, Ohio 346, 346
Kentucky 42, 56, 66, 128
Kerouac, Jack 311

On the Road 311
Kerwin, Joseph 349
Key, Francis Scott 81
Khmer Rouge 346, 351
Khomeini, Ayatollah 348, 360, 366,
  369
Khrushchev, Nikita 295, 296, 314-15
Kimpo International Airport 372
King, Billie Jean 329
King, Martin Luther 294, 296, 316,
  319, 334, 335, 336
"King Cotton" 70, 82, 88
King George's War (1744-48) 35
King William's War (1690) 33
King's College (later Columbia
  University) 39
King's Mountain, Battle of 56
Kiowa Indians 148
Kissinger, Henry 346, 356, 365
Kitty Hawk, N. Carolina 192
Kleindienst, Richard 347
Klondike Gold Rush 152, 180
Knights of Labor 169
Knox, Henry 59
Kodiak Island, Alaska 322
Kopechne, Mary Jo 335
Korea 188
  occupied by U.S. forces 294, 299
Korean War 294-5, 298-9, 384
Ku Klux Klan 142, 147, 147, 242
Ku Klux Klan Act (1875) 147
Kubrick, Stanley,
  2001: A Space Odyssey (film) 340
  Dr Strangelove (film) 340
Kuwait 393, 394
Kwajalein 272

Labrador 42
LaFollette, Robert M. 187
Lakehurst, New Jersey 258
Lamour, Dorothy 290
Land Ordinance (1785) 56
Lansing, Robert 202
Laos 330, 346, 350
Latin America 88, 202
Laudonnière, René de 16
Laurel, Stan 228
Lawrence, Kansas (sacking of) 119
Lead, Dakota 157
League of Nations 200, 202, 203, 209,
  223, 249, 264, 285
Leary, Timothy 317
Lebanon, U.S. intervention 294, 295,
  310, 310, 372
Lee, Henry 69
Lee, Mary Ann 107
Lee, Richard Henry 47, 48
Lee, Robert E. 128
  in American Civil War 128, 132,
    132, 133, 133, 134, 135, 138, 138
  in Mexican War 105, 108, 130
Leigh, Vivien 254
Lend-Lease Act 264
L'Enfant, Major Pierre Charles 70
Lenin, V. I. 215
Lennon, John 327
  assassinated 371
Levine, Charles A. 236
Lewis, Jerry Lee 303
Lewis, Meriwether 72, 73, 78, 79, 79
Lewis, Sinclair 238
  Main Street 224
Lexington, Massachusetts 47, 48, 52
Leyte, Philippines 272
Liberal Republicans ("Mugwumps")
  160
Liberty Bonds 206, 268
Libya, U.S. air-strike 368, 379
Liliuokalani, Queen of Hawaii 174,
  177
Lincoln, Abraham 128, 130, 142
  in American Civil War 130, 132,
    134, 136, 138
  assassination 139, 139, 141, 141
  elected President 128
  election campaign 118, 120
  Gettysburg address 368
  in Illinois militia 97
  Preliminary Emancipation
    Proclamation 133
Lincoln Memorial, Washington 316
Lindbergh, Charles 224, 236, 257
Lippmann, Walter 222
Liston, Sonny 329
Little Big Horn 148, 159
Little Rock, Arkansas 296
Live Aid 378
Livingston, Robert R. 48
Lloyd, Harold, Safety Last 228
Lloyd George, David 203, 209
Lockerbie Disaster 386
Lodge, Henry Cabot 203

Loewy, Raymond 241
London Company 19, 21, 22, 23, 26
Long Island 28
Longfellow, Henry Wadsworth 106,
  114
  The Courtship of Miles Standish
    120
  The Song of Hiawatha 114, 120, 121
Los Alamos, New Mexico 282, 282
Los Angeles,
  Ambassador Hotel 335
  Angelus Temple 240
  unemployment 209
Louis, Joe 288
Louis XIV, King of France 32, 33, 34
Louis XVI, King of France 68
Louisbourg, Cape Breton 34, 36, 37
Louisiana 35, 37, 72, 72, 82, 128, 256,
  296
Louisiana Purchase 72-3, 79, 104,
  108, 118, 145
Love, Nat ("Deadwood Dick") 158
Lovell, Jim 349
Lowell, James Russell 106, 120
Loyal Company 35
Loyalists 48
Lusitania, sinking of 202, 202
Lyman, Phineas 42

MacArthur, Douglas 272, 272, 274,
  294, 299, 299
McAuliffe, Christa 376
McCarran-Nixon Internal Security
  Act 296
McCarthy, Eugene 317
McCarthy, Joseph 296, 300, 301
McCarthyism 294, 296, 300-301
McCartney, Paul 327
McClellan, George B. 130, 130, 132,
  132, 133
McCormick reaper 120
Macdonough, Thomas 82
McGovern, George 347
Mackenzie, William L. 100
McKinley, William 172, 174, 175,
  186, 187, 193
McKinley Tariff Act (1890) 172
McNair, Roy 376
McPherson, Aimee Semple 240
Macready, William Charles 114
Madero, Francisco 201
Madison, James 59, 60
  and central bank proposal 68
  and Federal Convention 60
  as President 72, 74, 80-82, 84
Madonna 378
Mafia 322, 365
Magellan, Ferdinand 13, 14
Magellan, Strait of 18
Maine 15, 27, 28, 33, 82, 249
Maine, U.S.S. 174
Malay Peninsula, attacked by Japan
  266
Malcolm X 336
Malta, summit meeting 366, 368
Mammoth Hot Springs, Yellowstone
  National Park 383
Manchuria, invaded by Japan 188,
  266
Mandan Indians 79
"Manhattan Project" 282, 282
Manhattan Island 28, 28
Manila, Philippines 37
  occupied by U.S. 175
  in World War II 266, 274
Manson, Charles 337
Mant, Thomas 42
Mao Tse-Tung 288, 356
Marcos, Ferdinand 378
Marcos, Friar 14
Marcos, Imelda 378
Mardian, Robert 359
Marie Galante 37
Marshall, George C. 286, 286, 296
Marshall, James W., starts gold rush
  117
Marshall, Chief Justice John 70, 73,
  73
Marshall Plan 286
Martha's Vineyard 28
Marx Brothers, Duck Soup 254
Mary II, Queen 29, 33
Marye's Heights 133
Maryland 28, 32, 34, 44, 57, 59, 128,
  133, 141
  border dispute 39
Mason, Charles 39
Mason-Dixon Line 39-40
Massachusetts 33, 34, 44-7, 58, 77, 82
  founding of 23, 24, 26, 27
Massachusetts Bay Colony 25, 26, 27
Massachusetts Bay Company 26, 26

Massachusetts Charter (1691) 47
Massasoyt (Indian chief) 24
Massillon, Ohio, unemployment in
  172
Mathewson, Christy 218
Maya people 11, 13
Mayflower (ship) 23, 24, 24, 25
Mayflower Compact 23, 25
Mays, Willie Howard, Jr 362
Meade, George 134, 135
Meat Inspection Act 196
Melville, Herman 86, 106
  Moby-Dick 86, 120
Memphis, Tennessee 131, 309, 316,
  334
Mendoza, Antonio de 14
Menéndez de Aviles, Pedro 16
Menlo Park, New Jersey 155
Merchant Marine Act 222
Meronocomoco (Indian settlement)
  20
Metropolitan Museum of Art, New
  York 162
Mexican War 104-6, 106, 107, 108-9,
  111, 112, 114, 118
Mexico 202, 223
  and the Alamo 93, 94
  Aztecs 11
  and Burr plan 73
  Revolution 200, 201, 214
  Spanish conquest 13-14, 15
  and Van Buren 92
  War with U.S. 104-6, 106, 107, 108-
    9, 111, 112, 114, 118
Mexico, Gulf of 82, 102
Mexico City 15, 105, 108, 130
  Olympic Games 337
Miami Riots 370
Michigan 42
Middle East 360-61, 367, 369
Midway 266
  Battle of 272, 273
Mifflin, Thomas 47
Millay, Edna St Vincent 238
  Few Figs From Thistles 238
Miller, Arthur 307
  The Crucible 301
Miller, Glenn 292
  In the Mood 292
  Moonlight Serenade 292
Miller, Thomas W. 222
Minnesota, Dust Bowl 249
"minutemen" 47, 47
Miquelon Island 37
Mississippi 82, 128, 142, 296, 316
Mississippi steamboats 102-3
Missouri 82, 88, 96, 97, 119, 123, 128,
  158, 249
Missouri Compromise 93, 96, 99, 104,
  106, 118, 119, 123, 161
Missouri Debate (1819-20) 96
Mitchell, John (Attorney-General)
  346, 347, 359
Mitchell, John (mine-workers'
  leader) 183
Mitchell, Margaret, Gone with the
  Wind 254
Mobile, Alabama 82
Mohawk Indians 36
Molasses Act (1733) 31, 43
Monitor, U.S.S. 131
Monroe, James 82, 88, 174, 222
Monroe, Marilyn 288, 307, 322
Monroe Doctrine 88, 91, 105, 174, 188
Montana 79, 151
  Dust Bowl 249
Montcalm de Saint-Véran, Louis
  Joseph, marquis de 36, 37
Monte Cassino, assult on 271
Montgomery, Alabama 296, 319, 334
Montgomery, Bernard 270, 271
Monticello 74, 198
Montpelier, Vermont 213
Montreal 16, 33, 34, 37
Montserrat 382
Moody, Lady Deborah 27-8
Moody, Helen Wills 243
Moon, Sun-myung 363
Moonies 362
Moore, James 48
Moore's Creek Bridge 48
Moran, George Bugs 225
More, Sir Thomas, Utopia 18
Morgan, John Pierpont 148, 178,
  188, 193
Morgues, Jacques le Moyne de 16
Mormons 107, 111
Moroccan crisis 188-9
Morris, Gouverneur 59, 60
Morris, Robert 58
Morrison, Jim 341
  Break on Through 341

Light My Fire 341
Morse, Samuel F. B. *113*
Morton, Jelly Roll *217*, 224, *230*
Black Bottom Stomp 230
Dead Man Blues 230
Morton, Levi P. *170*
Moscow, Summit meeting 366
Mott, Lucretia *143*
Munich, Olympic Games (1971) *354*
Muscle Shoals, Alabama 222
Mussolini, Benito 249, *263*, 271

Nagasaki, bombed *283*
Nantucket 28
Napoleon Bonaparte 69, *76*, 81
empounds American cargoes 74, 80
and Louisiana Purchase 72, 104
Narraganset Bay 27
Narraganset Indians 25, 27, *28*
N.A.S.A. 376
Nashville, Tennessee 131
Nasser, Gamal Abdel 295
Nast, Thomas *146*, *147*, *153*
National American Woman Suffrage Association (NASWA) *220*
National Football League (N.F.L.) *328*
National Industrial Recovery Act 248, 249
National Labor Relations Act (1935) 249
National Recovery Administration (NRA) 248
National Republicans 104
National Security Act (1947) 288
National Security Council 288
National Woman Suffrage Association (NWSA) *143*
Nautilus, U.S.S. (submarine) *309*
Nauvoo, Illinois 107, *111*
Navajo Indians *326*
Navigation Acts 31
Navratilova, Martina *243*
Nebraska 14, 118, *151*, 249
Neutrality Act (1937) 249
Nevada *157*
New Amsterdam (later New York) 28, *28*
"New Deal" 82, 246-90, 268, 288, 297, 315
New England 28, 33, 34, 38, 40, 73, 74, 81, 82
Dominion of 29
founding of 23-7, *24*
New England Company 26
New France 32
New Hampshire 27, 59
New Harmony, Indiana 107
New Haven, Connecticut 38
New Jersey 26, 28, 29, 34, 38, 200, *262*
New Mexico 11, 14, 104, 105, 106, 108, 118, *158*, 186, 202, 249
New Netherlands 23, 28
New Orleans 32, 37, 56, 69, 72, *150*
in American Civil War 131
jazz 224, *230*, *232*
New Orleans, Battle of 81, 82, *84*
New York (colony) 15, 26, 28, *28*, 29, 33, 34, 36, 37, 41, 44, 46, 47
New York Central Railroad Co. *127*
New York City 28, *38*, 50, 56, 60, *62*, *64*, 81, 90, 146, *182*, 186, *195*, *206*, *209*, *210*, *211*, *236*, *258*, *287*, *293*, *312*, *327*, *330*, 362
Brooklyn *357*
Central Park *251*
Clay presidential campaign *115*
corruption 146, *146*
electricity *178*
expansion *99*, 107
financial center 223
Grand Central Station *149*
jazz *230*, *232*,
Lower East Side *165*, *179*
Mafia 365
pollution *352*
Prohibition *234*
skyscrapers *198*
Stock Exchange *150*, *193*, 224, *244*, 246, *379*
theater riots *114*
Times Square *242*, *281*
Union Square *162*
Wall Street *145*, 148, *151*, 244
in World War I *204*
New York Giants 362
New York Jets *328*
New York Mets 362
New York World Fair (1853) *122*
New York World Fair (plane) *258*
New York Yankees *288*
Newburgh Conspiracy 58
Newfoundland 10, 18, 42
Newman, Don *384*
Newport, Christopher 19, *19*, 20
Newtown, Massachusetts 27
Niagara Falls 93, 100
Niagara Falls Bridge *180*
Niblo, Fred, *Ben Hur* (film) *226*
Nicaragua 200, 201, 223
Sandanista-Contra war 368, *374*, 380
Nicholas, II, Tsar, deposed 202
Nicholson, Francis 34
Nicholson, Jack 387
Nina (ship) 13
Nixon, Richard Milhous 294, *295*
anti-Communist 314
busing dispute 357
elected President 317, 346
and Vietnam 346, 350, 351, 352, 356
visits China and Soviet Union *356*
Watergate scandal 347-8, 356, *358*
Non-Intercourse Act 80
Noriega, Manuel *387*
Norris, George W. 222
North, Frederick, Lord 46, 56
North, Oliver *380*
North Anna 134
North Atlantic Treaty 286
North Atlantic Treaty Organization (NATO) 264, 286, 294, 295, 296, 315, 390
North Carolina 15, 28, 38, 56, 128, 136
North Dakota 79, 186, 249
Northern Pacific Railroad Co. 172
Northern Securities Company 188
Northwest Ordinance (1787) 56
Nova Scotia 10, 34, 56
Novarro, Ramon *226*
Nullification Controversy 92-3, *99*

O'Banion Gang *225*
O'Connor, Sandra Day *370*
Oglethorpe, James Edward 30
Ohio 42, 69, *242*
Ohio Company 35
Ohio Company of Associates 66
O'Horgan, Tom *340*
Okinawa, capture of 272, 274
Oklahoma 96, *168*, 186, *242*
Dust Bowl 249, *252*
Oklahoma Land Rush *168*
Oklahoma, U.S.S. *266*
Old State House, Philadelphia 59, 62, *62*
Oliver, King 224, *230*
Olney, Richard 174
Olympic Games,
Mexico City (1968) *337*
Munich (1972) *354*
Omaha 172
Onandaga Indians 36
Oneida Indians 36
O'Neill, Eugene *238*
Beyond the Horizon 224
Desire Under the Elms 224
Emperor Jones 224
Strange Interlude 224
Onizuka, Ellison *376*
Ontario, Lake 11, 36, 37
Orders in Council 80, 81
Oregon 79, 82, 104, 105, 147, *168*, 187, *242*
Oregon Trail 96
Organization of African-American Unity 336
Original Celtics 362
"Original Dixieland Band" *230*
Orlando, Vittorio 203, *209*
Ortega, Daniel 374
Oswald, Lee Harvey *324*
Otis, James 44, 46
Overlord Operation 276, *276*
Owen, Robert 107
Owens, Jesse *259*

Pacino, Al 365
Paine, Thomas *55*
Common Sense 45, 48, *55*
Pakenham, Sir Edward 82
Pakula, Alan J., *All the President's Men* (film) *365*
Pan Am *289*, *308*, *386*
Pan-American Exposition (1901) 186, *187*, *193*
Pan-American Union 173
Panama, Isthmus of 18, 117, 188
Panama, U.S. invasion 387
Panama Canal 188, *189*
Paramount, *Beyond the Rocks* (film) *226*
Paris, Treaties of
1763: 37
1783: 56, 60, *64*
1899: 175, 186
Parker, Bonnie *256*
Parker, Dorothy *238*, *239*
Enough Rope 239
Sunset Gun 239
Parker, Sir Peter 48
Parks, Rosa 296
Patton, George S. 271
Pawtucket Indians 24
Pearl Harbor 264, 266, *266*, *272*, 310
Pedro, Dom, Emperor of Brazil *154*
Pelican, The (ship) 18
Pemberton, J. S. *167*
Pendleton Act (1883) 160
Peninsula Campaigns 132, *132*
Penn, William 28-9, *29*, 37
Penn family 28
Pennsylvania 31, 32, 34, 38, 41, 57 134
border dispute 39
founding of 28-9, *29*
Pennsylvania Dutch 38
Pennsylvania railroad company *127*
Pensacola 82
Pentagon *315*
People's Temple, Jonestown *363*
Pepperell, William *36*
Perry, Oliver 81
Pershing, John J. 214
Peru 11, 13, 18
Petersburg 132, 138
besieged 134, *135*
Philadelphia 37, 38, 40, 46, 47, 50, *50*, 51, 59
Centennial Exposition *154*, *170*
German settlers 30, 38
Philadelphia and Reading railroad company 172
Philip II, King of Spain 16, 18
Philippines 200
and Cory Aquino *378*
in Spanish-American War 175, *182*, 186
in World War II 266, 272, *272*, 274
Phillip, David Graham, *Treason of the Senate* 187
Phips, Sir William 33, *33*
Picawillany (Indian village) 35
Pickford, Mary *211*
Pilgrims/Separatists 23-6
Pinckney, C. C. 70
Pinkerton Agency *173*
Pinta (ship) 13
Pitcairn, Major 47
Pitt, William, the Elder 37, 44
Pittsburgh 36, 37, 66, *148*
Plattsburg 82
Plessy v. Ferguson (1896) 173
P.L.O. 354, 374
Plymouth, Massachusetts 23, 25, 26
Plymouth Company 26
Plymouth Rock 23, *24*, 25
Pocahontas, Princess 20, *20*, *21*, *76*
Poe, Edgar Allan *112*, 120
Poindexter, John *380*
Pol Pot 346, 351
Polanski, Roman 337
Polk, James K. 104, 105, 106, 108, *108*, *114*
Polo, Marco 12
Ponce de Léon, Juan 14
Pontiac (Indian chief) 41-2, *41*
Pontiac automobile *304*
Pontiac's Conspiracy 41
Pony Express *113*
Pope, John 133
Populist party 172, *172*
Port-au-Prince, Haiti *215*
Port Royal (later Annapolis) 33, 34, 35
Portsmouth, New Hampshire 188
Portugal 13-16
colonial wars 33, 34
Potsdam conference 282, *284*, 285
Pottawatomie Creek 119
Pound, Ezra *238*, *239*
Cantos 238
Powers, Francis Gary *321*
Powhatan, Chief 20, *20*, *76*
Prescott, Samuel 47
President, creation of office 59, 62
Presley, Elvis *303*, *309*
GI Blues (film) *309*
Preston, Captain 45, 46
Prevost, Sir George 81-2
Prince William Sound *388*
Princeton, U.S.S. 104, *105*
Princeton University 38-9
Proclamation Line 42
Proclamation of 1763 42
Prohibition 222, *225*, *234*
"Project Mercury" *309*
Promontory Point, Utah *127*, *144*
Providence, Rhode Island 27, 39
Puccini, Giacomo,
Girl of the Golden West 195
Madam Butterfly 195
Puerto Rico 175, 186
Pullman Palace Car Company 172
Puritans 23, 25, 26-7, 29, 40, 45
Pyongyang, N. Korea 294

Quakers 28, 29, 34, 40
Quartering Acts 43, 47
Quasi-war (1798-1800) 69
Quebec 16, 32, *32*, 33, 34, 42, 47, 56
capture of (1759) 37
Quebec Act 47
Queen Elizabeth (liner) *287*
Quincy, Josiah 46

ragtime *217*
Rainey, Ma *230*
Raleigh, Sir Walter 18, 19, 21
Randolph, Edmund 59
Randolph, Peyton 47
Rankin, Jeanette *220*
Rariton, New Jersey 40
Ray, James Earl 334
Ray, Man *241*
Reagan, Ronald *300*, *307*, *366*, *368*, 370
assassination attempt *371*
elected President 366-7
and "the Evil Empire" 367
and Gorbachev 367-8
Iran-Contra affair 380
and Nicaragua 374
Rebecca (ship) 34
"Red Hot Peppers" *230*
Redcoats 44, 45, 48, *48*, 52, 56, 81, 82, 84
Redford, Robert *365*
Reed, Frank *392*
Reed, Thomas B. 160, 161
Remington, Frederick *158*
Reorganization Act (1949) 288
Republican Party (formed 1854) 88, 112, 118, 119, *122*, 142, 147, 160, 161, 172, 186, 189, 200, 203, 222, 288, 294, 296, 314, 315, 317
Republicans 68, 73
Resnik, Judy *376*
Revenue Act (1764) 43
Revere, Paul 47, *47*
Revolutionary War (1775-83) 28, 39, 47, 48, *48*, 50-51, *51*, *52*, 56, 57, 60, 68, 80, 90, 317
Reykjavik, summit meeting 366, 368
Rhee, Syngman 294
Rhode Island 34, 46, 77
founding of 27
Rhode Island College (later Brown University) 39
Ribault, Jean 16, 17, *17*
Richardson, Eliot 347
Richmond, Virginia 128, 129, 132, 134, 136, *136*, *137*, 138, *140*
Riis, Jacob, *How the Other Half Lives 165*
Rio Grande 105, 106
Roanoke Island 18, 19
Robbins, Jerome *321*
Robinson, Bill *261*
rock 'n' roll *303*, *327*
Rockefeller, John D. 146, 148, *153*
Rocky Mountains 10, 34, 79, 96, *112*
Rogers, Ginger *254*
Rolfe, John 21, *21*, 23
Rolling Stones 317, *327*
Rome, U.S. troops enter *271*
Rommel, Erwin 270
Roosevelt, Franklin Delano *247*
death 280, 288
declares war 266
and Lend-Lease Act 264
New Deal 246-7, 248, 249, 268, 315
at Yalta conference *284*, 285
Roosevelt, Theodore *186*, 196, 247
conservation 188, 248
and Moroccan crisis 188-9
progressivism 186, 187, 200
and Russo-Japanese War 188
in Spanish-American war 175, *175*
trust-busting 188
Rosenberg, Ethel and Julius *305*
Ross, Harold *241*
Ross, Robert 81, 84
Royal African Company 22
Royal Navy 18, 28, 74
Rubin, Jerry *355*
Ruby, Jack *325*
Ruckelshaus, William 347
Russia,
and Alaska *145*
Revolution 202, *215*
war with Japan 188
see also Soviet Union
Russo-Japanese War (1904-1905) 188
Rutgers University 39
Ruth, Babe *218*
Rutledge family 47
Ryswick, Treaty of 33

Sacramento Valley 106, *117*
el-Sadat, Anwar 348, *360*
Saddam Hussein, *393*
Saigon,
"Agent Orange" *332*
fall of 346, 350
U.S. embassy attacked 317, *330*
St Augustine, Florida 16, 17, *17*, 18
St Dominque 72
St Helens, Mount (eruption) *370*
St John's, Newfoundland 18
St Kitt's 34
St Louis *72*, 79
Whiskey Ring 146
St Lucia 37
St Pierre island 37
St Valentine's Day Massacre *225*
St Vincent 37
Saipan 272
Sakhalin, Soviet Union 372
Salem, Massachusetts 27, *27*, *301*
Salerno, Gulf of 271
Salisbury, Robert Cecil, Lord 174
Salk, Jonas E. *305*
SALT Treaty *356*
SALT II Treaty 348
Salt Lake City *111*, 373
Salvador, Bahamas 10
Samoset 24
Sampson, William 175
San Antonio, Texas 93
San Francisco *118*, *148*, *169*, 355
AIDS sufferers *384*
Chinese community *163*, *197*
earthquakes *190*, *382*
Golden Gate Bridge *260*
Haight-Ashbury area 317
Stock Exchange *150*
San Francisco State College *316*
San Juan Hill, Cuba *175*
San Lorenzo el Real, Treaty of 69
San Salvador *13*
Sandanista Front, Nicaragua 368, 374, 380
Sandys, Sir Edwin 21, 22, 23
Sanger, Margaret *220*
Santa Anna, Antonio Lòpez de 93, 94, 104, 105, 108, *108*
Santa Fe 105
Santa Maria (ship) 13
Santagnel, Luis de 13
Santiago, Cuba 175
Saratoga 51, 56
Sargent, John Singer *163*
Madame X 163
Satourioua (Indian chief) 16
Saturn 5 rocket *342*
Sauk Indians 97
Savannah, Georgia *30*, 51, 136
Schuyler, Peter 33, 34
Scobee, Francis *376*
Scopes, John *243*
Scotland 17, 19
immigrants 30
Scott, Dred 119, *123*
Scott, Winfield 105, *108*
Scottsboro Case *257*
Seale, Bobby 336
Sears, Isaac 44
Sedition Act (1918) 202
Selective Service Act (1940) 264
Sellers, Peter *340*
Selma, Alabama 316, *319*
Selznick, David, *Gone with the Wind* (film) *254*
Senate, creation of 59, 62
Seneca Falls *143*, *220*
Seneca Indians 36
Seoul, S. Korea 294, 372
Seven Years War 37, 41, 42, 44, 47
Seward, William 139, *145*
Shah of Iran 348
Shakers 107
Sharpsburg, Battle of *132*, 133, *133*
Shaw, Anna Howard *220*
Shaw, Chief Justice 107
Shawnee Indians 80
Shays, Daniel 58
Shays' Rebellion 58-9, *58*

Shenandoah Valley 37, 129, 132
Shepard, Alan B. 323
Sherman, Roger 48, 59
Sherman, William Tecumseh 134, 136, 136, 137, 140
Sherman Anti-Trust Act 164, 172, 188
Shiloh, Battle of 131
Shreve, Lamb and Harmon 198
Sicily, U.S. invasion 271
Sikorsky, Igor 258
Simmons, William J. 242
Sinatra, Frank 292
 On the Town (film) 292
Sinclair, Upton,
 The Jungle 187, 188, 196
Singer, Isaac 122
Sioux Indians 11, 148, 152, 159
Sirhan, Sirhan Bishara 335
Sirica, John J. 347, 358
Sitting Bull, Chief 159, 176
Skylab 4 space station 349
skyscrapers 198
Slater, Samuel 77
slavery 18, 26, 30, 32, 34, 38, 65, 92, 104, 124-5
 abolition 140, 141, 142, 147, 186
 and American Civil War 120, 133, 140
 on cotton plantations 70, 88
 established in U.S. 22, 29
 John Brown's revolt 119
 and Missouri Debate 82, 93, 96, 106, 118
 Nat Turner's revolt 97
 North-South divide 40, 118, 123
 see also Blacks
Smith, Alfred 314
Smith, Bessie 232
Smith, John 20, 20, 21, 76
Smith, Joseph 107, 111
Smith, Michael 376
Smith, Moe 234
Smith, Tommie 337
Smith Island, Prince William Sound 388
Social Security Act (1935) 249
Society of Friends 28
Somoza, Anastasio 374
Sonoma, California 114
Sons of Liberty 44, 46
Sousa, John Phillip 183
South America 11, 13, 14, 15, 17, 88, 91
South Carolina 28, 30, 36, 38, 44, 48, 51, 56, 92, 93, 136, 296
 secedes from Union 128, 128
South Dakota 249
South East Asia Treaty Organization (SEATO) 295
South Pass, Oregon Trail 159
South View Cemetery, Atlanta 334
Southampton, Virginia 96, 97
Southern Creek Indians 80
Soviet Union 278, 294, 295, 305, 310
 arms race 367
 and Berlin Airlift 286
 Chernobyl disaster 389
 and Cold War 264, 285, 315
 and Cuba 314
 and Gorbachev 368, 390
 invasion of Afghanistan 346, 348, 366
 Nixon visits 348, 356
 shoots down S. Korean airliner 372
 space race 317, 323, 342
 Sputnik I 308
 U-2 incident 321
 see also Russia
Spain 21, 31, 48, 88
 and Burr plan 73
 colonial wars 33, 34, 37
 conquest of New World 13-18
 and Florida 56, 82
 and Louisiana Purchase 72-3
 and Mexico 94
 and Mississippi River 69
 and Spanish-American War 172, 174-5, 182, 186
 Spanish Civil War 249
Spanish Succession, War of the 33-4
Speedwell (ship) 23
Spindletop well, Texas 196
Spirit of St Louis (plane) 236
Spotsylvania Court House 134
Springfield, Massachusetts 59, 179
Springsteen, Bruce 375
 Born in the USA 375
Sputnik I satellite 308
Squanto 24-5
Stalin, Joseph 286

death 296
 at Potsdam conference 284
 at Yalta conference 284, 285
Stamp Act (1765) 43, 43, 44
Standard Oil Company, Ohio 148, 153, 164, 187, 188
Standard Oil Trust 153
Standish, Miles 24
Stanton, Edwin M. 142
Stanton, Elizabeth Cady 143, 220
"Star-Spangled Banner, The" (Key) 81, 337, 338
"Star Wars" program 367, 367, 368
Starr, Ringo 327
Stars and Stripes 54, 105, 112, 114, 184, 214, 274, 274, 345
Statue of Liberty 181, 184
Steffens, Lincoln, Shame of the Cities articles 187
Stein, Gertrude 259
Steinbeck, John 260
 East of Eden 304
Sternberg, Josef von, Blue Angel (film) 254
Stettinius, Edward 285
Stevens, Thaddeus 142
Stevenson, Adlai 294
Stimson, Henry L. 223
Sting, The (film) 127
Stoddart, Amos 72
Stokowski, Leopold 291
Stowe, Harriet Beecher 123
 Uncle Tom's Cabin 120, 123
Strategic Defense Initiative (SDI) 367, 367, 368
strikes 161, 172, 188
 Great Strike (1877) 148, 148
 Haymarket Riot 169
Stuart, John 42
Stuyvesant, Peter 28
Suez Crisis 294, 295
Sugar Act (1764) 42, 43
Sullivan, Ed 303
Sullivan, Louis 198, 210
Sumner, Charles 142
Sun Valley, Idaho 260
Sunnyside (home of Washington Irving) 114
Sunnyside housing estate 312
Superbowl 328
Superman comic 262
Supreme Court, creation of 59, 62
Suribachi, Mount 274, 274
Susan Constant (ship) 19
Sutter's Mill 117
Swaggart, Jimmy 378
Swanson, Gloria 226
Swigert, John 349

Taft, William Howard 189, 189, 200
Taiwan 295
Talleyrand-Périgord, Charles de,
 and Louisiana Purchase 72
 and XYZ affair 70
Tammany 146
Tampa Bay, Florida 14
Taney, Chief Justice 119, 123
Tarawa, capture of 274
Tarbell, Ida M., History of the Standard Oil Company 187
Tariff Act (1832) 92, 93, 115
"Tariff of Abominations" 88, 92
Tate, Sharon 337
Taylor, Jim 328
Taylor, Zachary 105, 106, 108
Tea Act (1773) 46
Teapot Dome, Wyoming 222
Tecumseh, Chief 80, 81, 84, 104
Teheran, U.S. embassy 348, 360, 366
Temperance movement 115, 220
Tennessee 42, 56, 66, 128, 220, 257
Tennessee, U.S.S. 266
Tennessee Valley Authority (TVA) 248, 288, 292
Tenskwatawa (the Prophet) 80, 86
Teotihuacan 13
terrorism 354
Tet offensive 317, 332
Teton Sioux Indians 11
Texas 14, 15, 92, 120, 128, 142, 158, 202, 248, 249
 and the Alamo 93, 94
 annexation question 104-6, 108, 115
 Panhandle 252
 and slavery 96, 104
Thames, Battle of the 80, 81, 84
Thanksgiving 12, 25, 25
Thirteen Colonies of America 50, 51, 52
Thomas, George 136
Thomson, J. Edgar 148

Thomson-Houston Electric 178
Thoreau, Henry David 106
 Walden 120
Thorpe, Jim 218
Three Mile Island (nuclear accident) 364
Tiananmen Square massacre 390
Ticonderoga 36, 37, 48, 54
Tilden, Samuel J. 147
Tippecanoe, Battle of 80, 84, 86, 104
Titanic 212
Tobago 37
Tobago 37
Toklas, Alice B. 259
Tokyo, Commodore Perry's expedition 122
Toledo, Ohio 187, 216, 246
Tonkin, Gulf of 316
Topeka, Kansas 194
Tordesillas, treaty of 13, 15
Townshend, Charles 44, 44
Townshend Acts 44-5, 46
Trade Acts 31
Transylvania project 42
Trenton, New Jersey 50
Trinity Church, New York 145
Tripoli, bombed by U.S. 379
Tripolitan War 77
Trotsky, Lev 215
Truman, Harry 264, 285, 299
 and Berlin Airlift 286
 and the Fair Deal 288
 and Korean War 294, 299
 and McCarthyism 296
 at Potsdam conference 282, 284, 285
Truman Doctrine 285, 299
Tryon, William 46
Tubman, Harriet 118, 124
Turner, Frederick J. 180
Turner, Nat 96, 97
Tuscaloosa, Alabama 316
Tuscarora Indians 36
Tuskegee Institute, Alabama 196
TWA Building, New York 312
TWA hi-jack 375
Twain, Mark 102, 160, 161, 161, 212
 Huckleberry Finn 161
 Life on the Mississippi 102
 Man that Corrupted Hadleyburg 161
 Mysterious Stranger 161
Tweed, William Marcy 146, 146
Tyler, John 100, 104, 105, 161

U-2 spy plane 314, 321
U20 submarine 202
U.N. Charter 285, 285
Underground Railway (slave liberators) 118, 124
Underwood-Simmons Tariff Act (1913) 200
Unification Church 362
Union Carbide 389
Union Pacific railroad 127, 144, 146, 158, 172
United Artists 211
United Mine-Workers of America 183, 188
United Nations 264, 285, 294, 394
United Negro Improvement Association (UNIA) 240
University of Alabama 316, 317
University of Pennsylvania 39, 391
University of Pittsburgh 305
University of Utah Medical Center 373
University of Virginia 74
Upper Creek Indians 82, 86
Upshur, Abel P. 104, 105
U'Ren, William S. 187
Urrutia, Manuel 310
U.S. Steel Corporation 188, 193
Utah 107, 118
Ute Indians 148
Utrecht, Treaty of (1713) 34

Valdez, Alaska 388
Valentino, Rudolf 224, 226
 The Sheik 226
Van Buren, Martin 96
 and Caroline incident 93, 100
 and Eaton affair 92
 election of (1840) 104
Vandalia/Walpole Company 42
Vanderbilt family 165
vaudeville 216
Venezuela 174, 188
Veracruz, Mexico 18, 105, 201, 214
Vermont 48, 81, 249
Vernon, Edward 34-5
Verrazano, Giovanni da 15-16

Versailles, Treaty of 203, 209, 222, 223, 249, 263
Vespucci, Amerigo 13
Vetch, Samuel 33-4
Vicksburg, Mississippi 131, 134
Vidor, King, Big Parade (film) 226
Viet Cong 316, 317, 330, 332, 350
Vietnam,
 French war in 295
 U.S. involvement 314, 316-17, 329, 330, 332, 346, 350-51, 352, 356, 366, 384
Villa, Francisco "Pancho" 201, 201, 214
Vinland 10
Virgin Islands 382
Virginia 18, 19, 26, 28, 30, 34, 36, 40, 47, 56, 59, 84, 128, 139, 142
 In American Civil War 134
 secedes from Union 128
 tobacco trade 21, 22, 23
Virginia Company of London 19, 23
Volstead Act 222, 234
Voting Rights Act (1965) 316

Wainwright, Jonathan 272
Wall Street Crash 222, 224, 244, 246, 246, 250, 379
Wallace, George 316, 317, 346
Walpole, Sir Robert 34
Walpole family 42
War Hawks 80, 81, 84
War of Independence 29, 41, 44
 see also Revolutionary War
Warhol, Andy 317, 322
 Campbell's Soup 317
Warm Springs, Georgia 280
Warren, Earl 296, 316
Warren, Joseph 46
Warsaw Pact 366, 390
Washington, Booker T. 186, 196
 Up From Slavery 196
Washington, D. C. 159, 160, 203, 367, 371, 384, 386
 in American Civil War 128, 129, 130, 132, 133, 134, 141
 attacked by British (1814) 81, 85
 the Capitol 144, 326
 Lincoln's death 139
 planned as capital 70
 and Prohibition 234
 protest marches 172, 220, 246, 319, 352, 364
 slums 326
 summit meeting 366, 368
 Watergate Complex 358
Washington, George 34, 47, 64, 134, 286
 and Anglo-French war (1790s) 69, 74
 and Central Bank plans 71
 in colonial wars 36, 37
 Constitution presented to 63
 first administration 56, 59, 68, 74, 82
 inauguration 58, 68
 people's affection for 60, 69
 in Revolutionary War 48, 50, 60
Washington State 370
Watergate Building 358
Watergate scandal 346, 347-8, 356, 358-9, 365, 366, 380
Watertown, New York 213
Wayne, "Mad Anthony" 69
Wayne, John 254, 333
 Stagecoach 333
 True Grit 333
Webster, Daniel 92, 99, 104, 118, 121
Weitz, Paul 349
Weld, Theodore D. 96
Welles, Orson 262, 291
 Citizen Kane (film) 291
 War of the Worlds (broadcast) 262, 291
Wells, H. G., War of the Worlds 262
West Indies 31, 32, 34, 38, 69
 British 42, 43
West Roxbury, Massachusetts 106
West Virginia 128, 129
West Virginia, U.S.S. 266
Western Electric 241
Western Union Telegraph Company 178
Westernland, S.S. 184
Westinghouse, George 178
Wetzler, Joseph 178
Weyler, Valeriano 174
Wharton, Edith 238
 House of Mirth 197
Wharton, Thomas 42

Wheeler, Joe 175
Wheelock, Eleazar 39
Whigs 104, 119
Whiskey Rebellion (1794) 68
White, John 12
White House,
 attacked by British (1814) 81
 completed 80
 Jackson's inauguration 88
White Lake, New York 338
Whitefield, George 40
Whitman, Walt 106, 121
 Leaves of Grass 120, 121
Whitney, Eli 70, 82
Wilder, Billy,
 Seven Year Itch (film) 307
 Some Like it Hot (film) 307
Wilhelm II, Kaiser 188, 189
Willard, Jess 216
William and Mary University 38
William of Orange 29, 33
Williams, Roger 27, 28
Williams, Tennessee 290
 Glass Menagerie 290
 Streetcar Named Desire 290
Williams v. Mississippi (1898) 173
Williamsburg, Virginia 37, 39
Willow Run, Detroit 269
Wilmington, N. Carolina 48
Wilmot, David 118
Wilson, Woodrow 106, 200, 215, 223
 the Fourteen Points 203, 264
 and League of Nations 264, 285
 and Mexican Civil War 200-202, 214
 and Treaty of Versailles 203, 209, 222
 and Volstead Act 234
 and women's suffrage 220
 in World War I 202, 206
Winthrop, John 26
Wisconsin 42, 187, 252
Wise, Robert 321
Wolfe, James 37, 37
Wolfe, Thomas, Look Homeward, Angel 224
women's rights movement 115, 143, 152, 220
women's votes 143, 152, 220, 222
Woodhull, Victoria 152
Woodstock Music Festival 317, 338
Woodward, Robert 347, 358, 365
Woolworth, F. W. 213
Works Progress Administration (WPA) 248-9, 248
World War I,
 aftermath 209, 222, 300
 home front 206
 U.S. mobilization 200, 202, 204
World War II,
 entry of U.S. 266
 invasion of Europe 276, 276, 277, 278, 278, 279, 280, 280
 invasion of Italy 271, 271
 Japan attacked 274, 274, 275
 Japan surrenders 282
 Lend-Lease 264
 mobilization 268, 268, 269
 North African campaign 270, 270
 Pacific war 272, 272, 273,
Wounded Knee,
 Battle of 176
 occupied by Sioux 352
Wray, Fay 254
Wren, Sir Christopher 37
Wright, Frank Lloyd 210, 312
Wright, Orville 192
Wright, Wilbur 192
Writ of Assistance 44
Wyeth, Nathaniel J. 96
Wyoming 143, 148, 151, 152, 249

XYZ affair 69, 70

Yale University 38
Yasgur Farm, Woodstock 338
Yeager, Charles "Chuck" 289
Yellowstone National Park 151
 forest fires 383
Yom Kippur War 348
York, Duke of 28, 29
 see also James II, King
Yorktown 52, 56
Yorktown, U.S.S. 273
Yorktown Peninsula 132
Young, Brigham 107, 111

Ziegfeld Follies 195
Zimmermann, Alfred 202
Zinnemann, Fred, High Noon (film) 301

Zuni Indians 11, 14

Picture acknowledgements

The publishers would like to thank all those who have supplied photographs for use in this book and apologize to any whose contribution may have been inadvertently omitted from these acknowledgements. We are particularly grateful to Ben Hopkins at the Hulton Picture Company, Peter Newark, Pat Redfern at Topham, Julie Quiery at Popperfoto and Jane Fisher at Associated Press.

(Abbreviations: A. P. = Associated Press, P.A. = Press Association)

Aquarius, Hastings, England 339bl. Associated Press, London 300c; 346; 347; 350t; 350b; 351b; 354t; 355t; 358br; 359t; 370bl; 372t; 376r; 377; 378tr; 380t; 380b; 381b; 381t; 382t; 382b; 384; 385b; 386b; 388t; 389b; 390t; 390b; 391t; 391b. Bridgeman Art Library, London 54b; 60br; 74-5b; 101b; 115b; 122t; 124cr; 126tc; 130b; 136b; 158-9; 164br; 262b; 268t; 317 (Copyright The Estate and Foundation of Andy Warhol, 1990 courtesy ARS, N.Y.). Anne S. K. Brown Military Collection, N.Y. 134-5. Culver Pictures, N.Y. 156-7. Design Museum, London 242tr. Dover Pictorial Archive Series, N.Y. *Dictionary of American Portraits* 82/contents; 83b; 143t; 189b; 193c; 197c; 200; 222; 223t; 223b. Mary Evans Picture Library, London 10; 14; 17t; 17b; 18; 20; 26; 28t; 29; 32; 33l; 43; 50; 53t; 53c; 60c; 60t; 62-3; 66l; 68t; 76b; 94b; 100b; 100t; 112l; 112t; 113b; 114b; 115t; 118; 120b; 121t; 123c; 124cl; 127tr; 126-7; 128bl; 129b; 154t; 155t; 162t; 165t; 166t; 178t; 178b; 179b; 193t; 194t; 195b; 224. James Flores/ NFL Photos, Los Angeles 328b. John Frost Newspapers, New Barnet, Hertfordshire, England 49; 128br; 138t; 149t; 202; 244t; 358t. Granger Collection, N.Y. 31; 42; 70tl; 71tl; 77c; 91b; 105; 128tl; 135c; 167tl; 172; 176br; 177t; 182tr. Ronald Grant Archive, London 226t; 227b; 228tl; 254tr; 255t; 255c; 304tl; 304tr; 321t; 333t; 340tr; 340bl; 365b; 387t. Robert Harding Library, London 64b; 65t; 76t; 98b; 103b; 182tl; 326t. Hulton-Bettman Archive, London/N.Y. 2-3; 8; 16; 17t; 19; 22; 24t; 27; 36t; 36b; 40b; 44; 45; 51; 52-3; 54b; 60-1; 63t; 64t; 72; 79l; 79r; 81t; 83t; 84-5; 85t; 87b; 91t; 92; 96t; 96-7; 100c; 102-3; 108b; 109; 110t; 110-11; 111b; 117b; 119; 122bl; 122c; 122br; 124b; 125; 126-7; 126tl; 131t; 131b; 132t; 132b; 133t; 134t; 136tl; 137t; 137b; 138b; 140t; 142t; 144t; 144b; 145b; 148; 150c; 150b; 151br; 152b; 155b; 155c; 156tc; 15^tr; 162b; 163tl; 164t; 165b; 167tr; 167b; 168tl; 168b; 169b; 169c; 170t; 171; 173; 174; 176bl; 177b; 179t; 180t; 180c; 180b; 181b; 182b; 183t; 183bl; 183br; 184t; 184c; 184b; 185t; 185b; 188; 189t; 190; 191t; 191cr; 191b; 192t; 193b; 194c; 194b; 195t; 195c; 196t; 196bl; 197t; 197b; 198r; 199l; 199r; 203; 204t; 204b; 205t; 206b; 207t; 207c; 207b; 208; 209b; 210t; 210b; 212tr; 213t; 213b; 214t; 214br; 215t; 216t; 216bl; 217b; 218t; 219tl; 220tl; 220tr; 220bl; 220-1b; 221t; 225b; 226b; 231t; 232l; 233tl; 233tr; 233b; 234b; 235t; 235c; 235b; 236t; 236; 237t; 237b; 238l; 238r; 239bl; 239c; 239tr; 239br; 240t; 240bl; 240br; 242t; 242b; 243tl; 243b; 243r; 244b; 245tl; 248t; 250t; 250cl; 250-1; 251b; 252t; 252br/contents; 252-3; 253t; 256bl; 256bc; 256br; 257b; 258br; 259tr; 260tr; 260br; 261tl; 261b; 262tr; 263b; 268b; 269t; 269b; 270tl; 270tr; 270b; 271t; 271b; 272b; 273t; 280t; 280b; 281t; 281b; 282-3t; 282b; 283bl; 284t; 284b; 286t; 287; 288t; 288br; 288bl; 289b; 290tr; 291b; 292t; 293tl; 294/contents; 297; 299; 300b; 305t; 306bl; 307bl; 308t; 308bl; 309c (U.S. Dept. of Defense); 310c; 311t; 311b; 312t; 313t; 313b; 315; 318tl; 318c; 318-9tr; 318b; 318br; 320t; 321b; 322br; 323b; 324b; 324c; 324t; 325b; 326t; 328t; 331bl; 332t; 333b; 345t; 348; 351t; 352t; 352b; 353 (Peter Gould); 356t; 357t; 360t (Lea Hawley/Consolidated News Pictures); 360-1b; 361c; 362b; 363t; 364t; 364bl; 370t (Phil Sheffield/Tampa Tribune); 365br. 370br; 371b; 374t; 374c; 378tl;

388b; Katz Pictures, London 394tl (Roger Hutchings); 394c (Steve Bent); 394b (Steve Bent). Kobal Collection, London 229; 232b; 290tl; 291t. Andre Laubier, Bath, England 276-7b; 277b; 278t. London Features International, London 302; 303tl; 303bl; 303br. Los Angeles Times 388br. Magnum Photos Ltd, London 341br. Mander and Mitchenson Theatre Collection, Beckenham, Kent, England 239tl; 301c. Ingres' Violin 1924, Man Ray © ADAGP, Paris and DACS, London 1990 241br. Mansell Collection, London 33r; 55t; 95t; 102b; 112tr, 116b, 215b. Missouri Historical Society 78r. National Baseball Library, N.Y. 219b. Peter Newark's Western Americana 11; 12; 13; 15; 21; 23; 24b; 28b; 35; 37; 38; 40b; 41; 46; 47; 48; 52b; 52t; 54c; 56; 57; 58t; 58b; 60cl; 60bl; 62bl; 65b; 65c; 68b; 70tr; 70-1b; 73l; 73r; 75c; 77t; 77b; 78l; 78-9; 80b; 80t; 81b; 84b; 85b; 86-7; 89b; 90b; 93/contents; 94t; 96-7b; 97tr; 97t; 98t; 98c; 99l; 99r; 101t; 102c; 104; 106; 107; 108c; 108t; 111; 112bl; 112br; 113t; 114t; 116tl; 116tc; 117t; 118; 120t/contents; 121bl; 121br; 123t; 123b; 124t; 128tr; 129t; 130tl; 130tr; 136t; 139c; 140b; 141t; 142b; 143b; 145t; 146r; 147; 149b; 151t; 151bl; 153t; 153bl; 153br; 154bl; 154br; 156tl; 158tl; 160; 163tr; 163b; 164bl; 166b; 168tr; 170b; 171tl; 175; 179c; 187; 190bl; 191cl; 196br; 198l; 201; 206t; 209b; 212t; 212tl; 212b; 217tl; 217tr; 218bl; 218bc; 218br; 225t; 230t; 230b; 231b; 232t; 234t; 246; 248b; 256t; 257t; 258bl; 259tl; 261t; 262bl; 266; 267t; 272t; 274b; 276tl; 276tr; 279t; 283br; 289b; 293tr; 298b; 298cr; 298cl; 304b; 307br; 312b; 314; 330c; 331br; 335t; 336tr. The New Yorker Magazine Inc, cover drawing by Rea Irvin 1925, 1953 241bl. Octopus Publishing Group Ltd, London 30 (N.Y. Public Library); 34 (National Portrait Gallery); 39 (N.Y. Public Library); 61b (Library of Congress); 61t (Roger Viollet); 86b (Public Archives, Canada); 89t (Library of Congress); 95b (Peter Newark); 114c (Library of Congress); 116 (Denver Library); 129c (Library of Congress); 132t (Library of Congress); 133b (U.S. Signal Corps.); 135t/contents (U.S. Signal Corps); 139t (Library of Congress); 139b (Library of Congress); 141b (Library of Congress); 146l/contents (Culver); 158tl (Arizona Historical Society); 159t (Smithsonian); 176t (Minnesota Historical Society); 181t (Library of Congress); 186; 192b (Science Museum); 211b; 214bl (Peter Newark); 227t (Paramount); 228; 241 (Vogue); 254tl; 254b; 255b (National Film Archive); 263t (A.P.); 290b; 292br; 293b (Art Institute of Chicago); 301b (National Film Archive); 307t; 309b; 312-13 (T.W.A.); 322bl; 323 (NASA); 326b; 340tl; 341t; 343 (NASA); 344-5b (NASA); 345br (NASA); 344tl/contents (NASA); 349t (NASA); 349b (A.P.); 368. Pictorial Press, London 341bl. Popperfoto, London 245tl; 245b; 257c; 265tl; 306br; 310t; 316, 320b; 325t; 327t; 327b; 329t; 329b; 330b; 330t; 331t; 332bl; 332br; 335b; 340br; 342bl; 354b; 359c; 362t; 371t; 372b; 372cr; 373b; 376bl; 378b; 383t; 383b; 387bl; 387br. Redferns, London 338br. Rex Features, London 375b. Syndication International, London 25; 66-7b; (Library of Congress); 66-7t (Library of Congress); 90t (Library of Congress); 99b (Chase Manhattan Bank); 152t (Library of Congress); 386t. Topham, Edenbridge, Kent, England 75t; 161; 205b; 216br; 247; 252bl; 258t; 259b; 260l; 264b (A.P.); 265tr; 265b; 267b; (A.P.); 273b; 274t; 275t; 275b; 277t; 278b; 279b; 282bl; 289t; 295; 296; 298t; 300t; 301t; 302; 303tr; 305b (A.P.); 308br; 309t; 310b (A.P.); 311c (A.P.); 318b; 318tr; 322t; 328-9t; 334t (A.P.); 334b (A.P.); 334br; 334c (A.P.); 336b (A.P.); 336tl (A.P.); 337t (A.P.); 337b; 339bc; 342r; 344tr; 346; 355t (A.P.); 355b; 356b-7b; 358bl; 359b (A.P.); 361t; 363b (A.P.); 364br; 366; 367; 369; 373t; 374b; 375t; 379t; 379b; 392t (Touchstone); 392c; 392bl; 392br; (A.P.); 393tl (A.P.); 393b (A.P.); 393tr (P.A.); 394tr (A.P.).